THE

GOSPELS:

WITH

MORAL REFLECTIONS ON EACH VERSE.

By PASQUIER QUESNEL.

WITH

An Introductory Essay,

BY THE REV. DANIEL WILSON, D.D.
VICAR OF ISLINGTON: NOW BISHOP OF CALCUTTA.

REVISED BY THE REV. HENRY A. BOARDMAN, D.D.

IN TWO VOLUMES.—VOL. II.

PHILADELPHIA:
PARRY & McMILLAN,
SUCCESSORS TO A. HART. LATE CAREY & HART.
1855.

STEREOTYPED BY L. JOHNSON AND CO.
PHILADELPHIA.

Printed by T. K. & P. G. Collins.

THE

GOSPEL OF JESUS CHRIST,

ACCORDING TO

LUKE.

CHAPTER VII.

SECT. I.—THE CENTURION.

1. Now when he had ended all his sayings in the audience of the people, he entered into Capernaum.

A good pastor, of whom Christ is the model, proceeds continually from instruction to action, and from action to instruction. Words speak only to the understanding, works speak to the heart.

2. And a certain centurion's servant, who was dear unto him, was sick, and ready to die.

In sickness and necessity masters ought to act like fathers toward their servants. That which heathens can do upon mere human motives of compassion, honour, interest, or friendship, a Christian master ought to perform upon Christian motives, having respect to Christ in the person of his servant. Death may perhaps in a very little time make the master and the servant equal; and God may place the servant above the master. We must by charity anticipate this equality; and honour beforehand this superiority by the spirit of humility.

3. And when he heard of Jesus, he sent unto him the elders of the Jews, beseeching him that he would come and heal his servant.

It is a good presage, and a favourable omen that a man will obtain the favour which he asks, when he does not think himself worthy to obtain it by himself. He has already obtained something better than what he desires, in having received sufficient light to know himself, and humility not to think of himself more highly than he ought to think.

4. And when they came to Jesus, they besought him instantly, saying, That he was worthy for whom he should do this: 5. For he loveth our nation, and he hath built us a synagogue.

The centurion is praised by men upon the account only of his external works, which interest caused them chiefly to consider. Christ reserves to himself the commending of his heart, and the discovering to us the riches of it.

6. Then Jesus went with them. And when he was now not far from the house, the centurion sent friends to him, saying unto him, Lord, trouble not thyself; for I am not worthy that thou shouldest enter under my roof:

It is unprofitable for a man to receive the sacramental representation of Christ, if he does not receive him into his heart as the centurion did. Let us, after his example, endeavour earnestly to attract him into ours by a prayer full of faith, humility, simplicity, and confidence. It is this which draws Christ into the house of this pious Gentile, while he seems to go thither as following the Jews, and only upon their recommendation. Thus it very often happens, that the blessing which God sheds upon a family, a parish, a community, or a church, is occasioned by some devout soul whose heart is known only to God, though men may attribute it all to others.

7. Wherefore neither thought I myself worthy to come unto thee: but say in a word, and my servant shall be healed.

We can no way render ourselves worthy of Jesus Christ and his grace, but by acknowledging ourselves unworthy of them. The just idea which the centurion has of the almighty power of God, and of Christ, in healing bodies by the sole motion of his will, is the pattern of that which we ought to frame concerning the almighty power of his grace, in healing souls of concupiscence. He does what he pleases with the heart, as well as with the body; being equally the creator of both. It is Christ himself who, in the cure of the paralytic, teaches us to judge thus of the one by the other.

8. For I also am a man set under authority, having under me soldiers,

and I say unto one, Go, and he goeth; and to another, Come, and he cometh; and to my servant, Do this, and he doeth *it*.

The pride of the synagogue, which attributed all to the merit and virtue of the works of the law, is figured by the Jews, the friends of the centurion: the faith of the church, which ascribes all to the pure mercy of God, and to the almighty operation of his will upon ours, is represented by the faith of the centurion, who is the first-fruits of the Gentiles. He shall rise up in judgment at the last day against those who, after the experience of so many ages, and the instructions of so many saints and doctors, dare yet dispute with God his omnipotent power over the heart of man.

9. When Jesus heard these things, he marvelled at him, and turned him about, and said unto the people that followed him, I say unto you, I have not found so great faith, no, not in Israel.

Christ praises the virtue of men boldly and plainly, because he praises his own gifts in them, and gives them the grace not to grow vain upon them. The preference of the Gentiles before the Jews is here lightly intimated by Christ, as founded upon the too mean idea which the Jews had of his grace. Our blessed Lord's sincerity is equal, both when he praises and when he blames: but he blames the Jews when they are present, and praises the centurion only in his absence; because he does not praise him for his own sake, but for the benefit and advantage of others.

10. And they that were sent, returning to the house, found the servant whole that had been sick.

This cure is the reward and effect of faith, prayer, and humility: the goodness of God toward men being so great, that he is pleased that the very virtues and graces which he confers upon them should be counted unto them instead of merit. It is God himself who, by the gifts of his mercy, disposes and prepares the sinner for his cure; and nothing can contribute to the reception of his grace but what is the effect of his grace itself.

SECT. II.—THE WIDOW OF NAIN.

11. ¶ And it came to pass the day after, that he went into a city called
Nain; and many of his disciples went with him, and much people. 12.
Now when he came nigh to the gate of the city, behold, there was a
dead man carried out, the only son of his mother, and she was a widow:
and much people of the city was with her.

This dead man of Nain is the emblem of a sinner dead in sin. Happy the sinner when mercy comes to meet him, at least before he is buried in his evil habits, and has filled up the measure of his sins; after which he is, as it were, buried in oblivion before God! Let us admire this meeting of Christ and the sinner, of life and death,—a meeting accidental in appearance, but appointed in the eternal order of the divine predestination. The church, whom Christ at his ascension left a widow, bewails the spiritual death of every one of her children as that of an only son; since the whole body may be considered as comprised in some manner under every one of its members. It is almost the whole employment of this widow to follow sinners, and in this life to lament their death, until they have all either found Jesus Christ, or, by being buried, have lost all hopes of finding him. Let us bear her company, by joining our tears and prayers to hers in behalf of sinners.

13. And when the Lord saw her, he had compassion on her, and said unto her, Weep not.

Christ is moved only by the tears of his church; that is, by the repentance which is performed in her bosom by his Spirit. He hearkens only to her charity, which is continually intent on the salvation of her children, whom she every day brings forth anew to life. He regards only her prayers for the conversion of those sinners for whom she prays, while they do not pray at all for themselves. Happy is that person who is in the bosom of this mother, and for whom she prays continually! Happy will this mother, at present disconsolate, be, when her Lord going forth to meet her, and she him, he shall say to her, "Weep not,"—because there will then be no longer any occasion to weep, after the sanctification of all the elect. Nothing comforts her in her widowhood but the conversion of sinners, and the hopes of seeing all tears one day wiped from her eyes.

14. And he came and touched the bier: and they that bare *him* stood still. And he said, Young man, I say unto thee, Arise.

It is a very great mercy that God does not abandon us under the death of sin, but vouchsafes to come to meet us. Whenever he strikes a sinner's body with some disease, his senses with some objects, and his ears with some words, which, by the means of his grace, prove instrumental to his conversion, he may then be said to touch the living coffin of a dead soul. Men are not sensible that these strokes proceed from a hand of grace and mercy while they are yet under the death of sin; and they very frequently never reflect upon them, even when they are risen again. What acknowledgment is not due to God from a young man who is carried out by his passions to the grave of a sinful habit, wherein he would be buried forever; but grace stops them betimes, raises him again, and gives him a new life!

15. And he that was dead sat up, and began to speak. And he delivered him to his mother.

He whom God teaches effectually, (1.) Rises or sits up, by forsaking his sins; (2.) Begins to speak, in confessing them; (3.) Puts himself into the hands of his mother, in submitting himself to the power and discipline of the church, resigning himself up to the conduct of her ministers, and living by her spirit. When Christ delivers us into the hands of our mother he does not thereby leave us, because she herself is in the hands of her Lord. Since the sinner is restored to the church, it is plain that he had been torn from her, that he was no longer a living member of this body of Christ, and that he was joined to it only by a dead faith. Happy the sinner who is restored to it forever, to live to all eternity in this immortal body of the only Son of God!

16. And there came a fear on all: and they glorified God, saying, That a great prophet is risen up among us; and, That God hath visited his people.

The conversion of sinners is an undoubted proof of the incarnation of the Son of God, which is the great visit he has made to his people. Were but the eyes of our faith quick and clear-sighted, what effects would not those wonderful conversions produce in us, which are frequently the subject of the world's raillery? So great is the blindness under which it lies, that a sinner is often frightened at such conversions, and is really afraid lest the grace and mercy of God should come and snatch him away from his pleasures and the other objects of his passions. We glorify thee, O Lord, for all thy mercies toward sinners, and we desire and implore them for ourselves. The common people readily acknowledge that miracles are the necessary proof of an extraordinary mission in the church; and learned men, puffed up with pride, refuse to acknowlege the necessity thereof, and choose rather to deliver themselves up to seducers.

17. And this rumour of him went forth throughout all Judea, and throughout all the region round about.

God changes offence or scandal into edification by the conversion of sinners. Even an outward change of life is a thing scarce ever heard of out of the true church. She alone has this privilege, because she only has the Holy Ghost, who alone can change the heart. Let us inviolably adhere to this house of mercy.

SECT. III.—JOHN'S DISCIPLES SENT TO CHRIST.—THE PRAISES OF JOHN.

18. And the disciples of John shewed him all these things.

John's humility and charity, by a holy kind of address, turn that to the advantage of his Master which, perhaps, the emulation of these disciples caused them to look upon with an evil eye. He who is ambitious of having the pre-eminence, knows how to set his own advantages in the best light, and to expose the infirmities of others. John takes the time when Christ appears with the greatest lustre, and he himself is under the lowest state of humiliation, to undeceive his disciples. Curiosity, perhaps, as well as jealousy, causes these disciples to talk of the news of what passes in the world: John takes from hence an occasion to instruct them. It is thus that we may make a good use of worldly news, when we are either in such circumstances that we cannot well be acquainted with it, or have not virtue enough to live without it.

19. ¶ And John calling *unto him* two of his disciples sent *them* to Jesus, saying, Art thou he that should come? or look we for another?

He who is only to conduct souls to Christ ought to send all his disciples to Him, and not retain them in attendance upon himself. That man does enough for the souls under his care who puts them in the way of addressing themselves to God and Christ as they ought, and of being attentive to his word and inspirations, to the voice of faith and to his miracles, and to the instructions, mysteries, and conduct of his life. John shows us that all the science taught in his school consisted only in disposing men to expect the deliverer. Lord, we expect and look for no other; but we expect thee in another state and condition. They expected thee as the Author of faith and righteousness; but we expect thee as He who is to be the Finisher and Crown thereof.

20. When the men were come unto him, they said, John the Baptist hath sent us unto thee, saying, Art thou he that should come? or look we for another?

How commendable is this simplicity and fidelity of these disciples, in doing and saying nothing but what was prescribed to them! It is by the way of the obedience of faith that we must go to Christ, that we must speak to him, hear him, and contemplate his wonders. They ask but one thing, because that comprehends all. It is sufficient to be once assured that it is Christ who speaks to us, that it is our Redeemer who promises us his grace, and draws us after him.

21. And in that same hour he cured many of *their* infirmities and plagues, and of evil spirits; and unto many *that were* blind he gave sight.

The language of a Christian is, to do the works of a sick man healed, and of a slave set at liberty; as that of Jesus Christ is, to perform those of a sovereign physician, and of an almighty deliverer. Lord, we know thee by this language. It is thou who must cure our infirmities and diseases, and close the wounds of our hearts. It is thou who comest to deliver us from our darkness and blindness, and from all the remains of the evil spirit's dominion within us. Perform thy work in us, O Jesus; for nothing can hinder thee from accomplishing thy will, and working our salvation.

22. Then Jesus answering said unto them, Go your way, and tell John what things ye have seen and heard; how that the blind see, the lame walk, the lepers are cleansed, the deaf hear, the dead are raised, to the poor the gospel is preached.

The mission of Jesus Christ is extraordinary, and therefore he proves it by his miracles. He works them upon the soul as well as the body, (1.) Enlightening the understanding. (2.) Rectifying the will. (3.) Blotting out sins. (4.) Making himself heard by the ears of the heart. (5.) Converting even the most hardened sinners, and restoring to them the life of the soul. And, (6.) Teaching his ways to the humble. We must be of the number of these poor, if we desire to have any part in the riches of faith and of the true knowledge of the gospel. Grant us, Lord, this poverty of spirit, which gives a sight to the treasure of the divine truths. Disperse the false glimmerings of human wisdom, to make way for the light of thy Holy Spirit!

23. And blessed is *he*, whosoever shall not be offended in me.

How corrupt is man, since he takes occasion of scandal or offence from the best things, and even from Christ himself! The sinner would willingly have such a Saviour as should comply with human passions; and would fain go to God by ways conformable to those of the world: he finds the directly contrary in Christ and his gospel, and this is what offends and keeps him at a distance from them. Religion is contrived after such a manner that every thing therein tends to make God known to the children of faith, to edify them, and unite them to Jesus Christ; and, at the same time, to offend, discourage, and keep off the wise and the lovers of the world, and to hide the truth, and even God himself, from such as have no other eyes but those of flesh and human reason. A God concealed and hid in the flesh, in infancy, humiliations, sufferings, etc.,—this is what exercises and nourishes the faith, and inflames the charity of the former, but increases the infidelity, and disgusts the pride of the latter.

24. ¶ And when the messengers of John were departed, he began to speak unto the people concerning John, What went ye out into the wilderness for to see? A reed shaken with the wind?

The humility of John renders him unmovable. Whoever has not this virtue, is a reed shaken with the wind.

25. But what went ye out for to see? A man clothed in soft raiment? Behold, they which are gorgeously apparelled, and live delicately, are in kings' courts.

The world is the seat of excess, sensual delights, and impenitence, and of all things which are opposite to Christianity. Happy is he who lives at a distance from it! It is not absolutely impossible to be saved therein, because with God all things are possible; but it is extremely dangerous and very toilsome to have the work of our salvation to do in a place where every thing is contrary thereto. Solitude and the court are set in opposition the one to the other by Jesus Christ. In the former piety and repentance take refuge, to be secure from the wickedness of this world; to the latter resort luxury and pleasure, in order to reign there without control.

26. But what went ye out for to see? A prophet? Yea, I say unto you, and much more than a prophet. 27. This is *he* of whom it is written, Behold, I send my messenger* before thy face, which shall prepare thy way before thee. [* *Fr.* Angel.]

It is a very great sight, and most worthy of the holy curiosity of a Christian, to see a religious man disengaged from all earthly things, and devoted entirely to God and Christ. In this short description which Christ here gives of John, he draws the character of a holy pastor and of a perfect director of souls. (1.) He must, like a prophet, be illuminated of God, replenished with his word, and instructed in his ways, and in the methods of his conduct. (2.) He must be more than a prophet, and have somewhat more than light and knowledge in his mind. He ought to have so lively a faith, as not to see Jesus Christ only at a distance, but, as it were, even to touch him, to breathe nothing but him, to be an image of him in his whole life, and, like John, to represent him in all his actions. (3.) He must have all the qualities which the Scripture requires in a pastor, insomuch that it may seem to have spoken of him. (4.) He must be sent by a lawful call and mission. (5.) He must be as it were an angel, having no interest on earth but that of the church, stooping even down to the earth by his humility and zeal in the service of souls, and ascending up to heaven by his prayers and his love of heavenly things. (6.) He ought to have no other business than to prepare the way for Jesus Christ in souls, and to count all things else as nothing. (7.) He must learn, even from his function itself, that souls are to be conducted to Christ by degrees, and that this is not the business of a moment; that he is to instruct them by the word, to cleanse them by repentance, and to keep them in the way, before he admits them to the enjoyment of Christ in the communion, which is only for those who are well prepared.

28. For I say unto you, Among those who are born of women there is not a greater prophet than John the Baptist: but he that is least in the kingdom of God is greater than he.

There is a very great difference between the saints of this life and those of the other: a greater still between such as have only gifts profitable to others, namely, gifts of prophecy, of preaching, or of directing souls; and those who are united to God by his love, in whom his grace reigns, and who are rich in Christian virtues. True greatness consists in God's living and reigning in us, and in our being obedient to his will, and our relying upon his Spirit. That which proceeds from external gifts, and such as do not sanctify of themselves, is dangerous, and to desire them is pride and presumption.

29. And all the people that heard *him,* and the publicans, justified God, being baptized with the baptism of John.

How happy is a man when he knows how to value as he ought the grace of repentance, and to improve the time of mercy! It is by repentance that the designs of God are accomplished, and that he is most glorified; because nothing more fully displays his goodness in giving up his own interests, his wisdom in bringing good out of sin itself, which is the greatest evil, and his almighty power in changing the heart at his pleasure, and causing men to love and embrace that which is most contrary to his inclinations. It is by the works of a true conversion, and not by bare words, that men express a sincere acknowledgment for the gift of repentance.

30. But the Pharisees and lawyers rejected the counsel of God against themselves, being not baptized of him.

The illiterate people and great sinners profit more by the word of God, than the doctors of the law and the great pretenders to devotion. Men frequently, through a false greatness of soul and a wicked elevation of mind, despise small things, and thereby deprive themselves of great ones which are annexed to them; as the grace of receiving Christ was to the reception of John's baptism, which was designed to prepare them for the other. Religion is full of these dependencies and connections between the least and the greatest things. The humble submit to them and are saved; the proud reject them and are lost. God can easily make himself amends in the way of justice, and repair whatever loss his glory has sustained, by the refusal of his mercy; but nothing can repair that person's loss who rejects repentance.

SECT. IV.—JESUS CHRIST AND JOHN REJECTED BY THE JEWS.

31. ¶ And the Lord said, Whereunto then shall I liken the men of this generation? and to what are they like? 32. They are like unto children sitting in the marketplace, and calling one to another, and saying, We have piped unto you, and ye have not danced; we have mourned to you, and ye have not wept. 33. For John the Baptist came neither eating bread nor drinking wine; and ye say, He hath a devil.

The more God displays his goodness in opening to men several ways which lead to himself, the more he discovers the depth of those wounds which sin has made in their hearts. Charity alone can heal them: and these external means, by their being ineffectual, show plainly the necessity there is of a remedy which may reach the heart, and work powerfully therein. Obstinacy, and the spirit of contradiction, are the effect of envy and covetousness. Both Jesus Christ and John were calumniated; and who then will complain of being so? Let us not pretend to satisfy the world, since they could not do it. The outward austerity of John is the pattern of a retired life.

34. The Son of man is come eating and drinking; and ye say, Behold a gluttonous man, and a winebibber, a friend of publicans and sinners!

The life of Jesus Christ, common in appearance, is an emblem of that of priests. Though we consult the fancy of the world never so much, unless we approve of its conduct, it will never approve of ours. The part we have to take is to follow, without any human respect whatever, that course of life which God requires of us, and to perform the duties of our state and calling, without being at all solicitous concerning the judgment of men. It is the property of a Pharisee to take offence at a physician's visiting the sick, or a pastor's seeking sinners in order to lead them to Christ: but there are measures to be observed to avoid danger, and to give our neighbour no just occasion of offence. A clergyman, who either industriously hunts after plentiful tables, or frequents them too often, cannot fail of giving it.

35. But wisdom is justified of all her children.

The different ways of holy men justify the wisdom of God. It is neither austerity of life, nor liberty in the use of all things, nor poverty, nor abundance, which really distinguish the children of God from those of the world, but charity and concupiscence. The former leads to God by all manner of ways; the latter never finds him in any, because it corrupts all by its malignity.

SECT. V.—THE WOMAN ANOINTING THE FEET OF JESUS.

36. ¶ And one of the Pharisees desired him that he would eat with him. And he went into the Pharisee's house, and sat down to meat.
37. And, behold, a woman in the city, which was a sinner, when she knew that *Jesus* sat at meat in the Pharisee's house, brought an alabaster box of ointment,

We see in this woman the emblem of a true conversion. Grace attracts the most desperate sinners, for the encouragement of such souls as are most abandoned to sin, and to teach them not to despair of salvation. The first grace is, to know that there is a Saviour who waits for our repentance, and came for the sake of sinners. The second is, to seek him; which is done by prayer and by the desires, which are, as it were, the feet and wings of the heart. The third is, not to delay seeking him one moment. The fourth, to find him by faith. The fifth, to speak to God and Christ at first, no other way but by the motions of the heart. And the sixth, to have an inward shame and confusion, which may make us despise all that to which we may be exposed in the sight of men.

38. And stood at his feet behind *him* weeping, and began to wash his feet with tears, and wipe *them* with the hairs of her head, and kissed his feet, and anointed *them* with the ointment.

The seventh grace is, to learn of this patient that the feet of Christ are the happy portion of a truly converted sinner. The eighth, not to be ashamed, in any place or on any occasion, to have recourse to the mercy of God, and to weep for our sins. The ninth is, to be convinced, that as we have spared nothing in the commission of sin, so we ought to spare nothing in making satisfaction to God. The tenth is, to be moved with compassion toward the poor, who are the feet of Christ, and to let them partake of the good things we have received from God. To kiss Christ's feet, is to serve and relieve the poor with respect and love, and with such a faith as causes us to discover and honour Jesus Christ in them. The eleventh grace is, to submit ourselves to his ministers, who are likewise his feet in another sense, because they bring peace and the grace of reconciliation to true penitents. The twelfth and last grace is, to make that useful and serviceable to charity which before served only to concupiscence.

39. Now when the Pharisee which had bidden him saw *it*, he spake within himself, saying, This man, if he were a prophet, would have known who and what manner of woman *this is* that toucheth him; for she is a sinner.

It is one sign of pride to despise sinners, and to be unable to endure the goodness of God toward those whom he draws to himself. The proud person is at the same time cruel and unmerciful toward sinners, and irreligious toward God: he accuses him of not knowing sinners; and it is he himself who knows not his God, and removes still farther from him. I know thee, O Jesus, by thy love to sinners. Thou knowest them better than they know themselves. It is thou who drawest them to thyself, who inspirest them with confidence to approach thee, and who givest them a faith full of love, whereby they touch thee, and are reconciled to thee.

40. And Jesus answering said unto him, Simon, I have somewhat to say unto thee. And he saith, Master, say on.

How lovely is this gentleness of Christ! How fine a pattern is it to imitate, when we would reclaim or instruct any one. Courteousness is so far from being contrary to holiness, that it is an effect of it. We do not become barbarians in becoming Christians. We must learn to reconcile fidelity, in the performance of our duty, with that civility and obliging carriage which we owe our neighbour. We cannot possibly better requite hospitality, nor acknowledge our obligation to our neighbour in a better manner, than by giving him the wholesome advice whereof he stands in need, and assisting him in the attainment of salvation.

41. There was a certain creditor which had two debtors: the one owed five hundred pence, and the other fifty. 42. And when they had nothing to pay, he frankly forgave them both. Tell me therefore, which of them will love him most.

Miserable is he who loves not God, after having received from him many benefits, and the pardon of many sins! How much more does a Jew owe to God, who has wrought so many wonders for him, than a heathen, who has received nothing but the gifts of nature? But how much more, without comparison, does a Christian owe than a Jew, an orthodox person than a heretic, and a man particularly called to the service of God, than one abandoned to the torrent of the world? We always owe a vast debt to God, whether he shows his mercy either in pardoning our sins or in preventing them.

43. Simon answered and said, I suppose that *he*, to whom he forgave most. And he said unto him, Thou hast rightly judged.

The greatness of God's mercy toward us is the measure of our love toward him; but what possible return can we make for a mercy which is infinite, with a heart so small and narrow as our own? Our ignorance of what God has forgiven us, either in pardoning or preventing, and the knowledge we have of the corruption of our heart, are sufficient to convince us that we are those to whom he has forgiven most. There are two graces which are necessary above all others to a penitent: the first, to have a sight and sense of what he owes to God; the second, to judge rightly of it. Grant us, Lord, a third, in enlarging our hearts by a most grateful love, and such as may be, in some measure, worthy of thy mercies.

44. And he turned to the woman, and said unto Simon, Seest thou this woman? I entered into thine house, thou gavest me no water for my feet: but she hath washed my feet with tears, and wiped *them* with the hairs of her head.

Let us be so far from making within ourselves proud comparisons, in order to exalt ourselves above great sinners, as rather to make such as may serve to humble us, by comparing our own infidelities with the good which we see in others. God alone knows the worth of a soul in his own sight, and at what rate it ought to be valued. Men lose all by vanity, they regain all by humility; and even the very sins of penitents may be of use to this purpose, by the grace of Christ. It is at his feet that this miracle is wrought; it is there that we must submit and humble whatever seems best and loftiest in ourselves.

45. Thou gavest me no kiss: but this woman, since the time I came in, hath not ceased to kiss my feet.

A penitent should never cease to kiss the feet of Christ by a lively faith, and to make some return for his charity, by loving him in the poor, and in the lowest members of his mystical body.

46. My head with oil thou didst not anoint: but this woman hath anointed my feet with ointment.

God speaks in behalf of that person who silently suffers the envy and contradiction of the world, which are one part of mortification. A deficiency in works is a certain proof of a defect in love. Let us pour on Jesus the oil of works of mercy in serving his members, if we desire his mercy to be poured upon ourselves. Spiritual works of mercy, in order to the salvation of the soul, which is the main business, penetrate like oil, and reach the heart; those which relate to the body are like a perfume or fragrant ointment, which diffuses its sweet odour in the church by edification and good example.

47. Wherefore I say unto thee, Her sins, which are many, are forgiven; for she loved much: but to whom little is forgiven, *the same* loveth little.

There is no saving mercy where there is no love of God; but great is the mercy where men love much. Nothing more inflames the heart of a penitent toward God, than the consideration of those sins from which he has washed him in the blood of his Son, and of those from which he has preserved him in changing his heart by his grace. He who thinks that less love is due from him, because he has sinned less, little understands the nature of sin, or of that mercy which preserves us from it, or the wickedness of which, without that mercy, man is capable by reason of his corruption.

48. And he said unto her, Thy sins are forgiven.

Happy that person to whom God speaks these words, so as to reach the bottom of his heart; for God at the same time performs what he says! These dispositions, Lord, are not less thy work, than the forgiveness of sin itself. Do thou therefore work them in our hearts. Do thou thyself dispose and prepare us for this by thy other gifts.

49. And they that sat at meat with him began to say within themselves, Who is this that forgiveth sins also?

It is Christ in the church, and she by him, who absolves, as well as baptizes. He who believes the latter, ought likewise to believe the former; since it is the same person who has declared both. Let us often exercise our faith upon this comfortable truth. Let us take care not to say within ourselves that which heretics speak aloud. Though men sit with Christ at the table of the church, they may, notwithstanding, sometimes have suggestions of infidelity: they must resist them by faith.

50. And he said to the woman, Thy faith hath saved thee; go in peace.

Faith produces righteousness, and righteousness gives peace. Faith is never alone in a heart; and it is very lively there when it causes a man to seek Christ, to adhere to him, and humble himself at his feet, drawing from his eyes tears of repentance, and disposing him to give all to God, and to his neighbour for God's sake. How solid and substantial is peace, when it is the fruit of such a repentance! A good pastor ought to nourish this peace in those who are once thoroughly converted. Confidence is always good when it is regulated by faith.

CHAPTER VIII.

SECT. I.—THE PARABLE OF THE SOWER.

1. AND it came to pass afterward, that he went throughout every city and village, preaching and shewing the glad tidings of the kingdom of God: and the twelve *were* with him,

The zeal, vigilance, and charity of Christ are the pattern of a bishop in the visitation of his diocese, accompanied with his evangelical labourers, and teaching his people in person. If he cannot exactly imitate so great a simplicity, poverty, and toil, yet he ought at least to come as near them as possible, and to cut off all excess, pomp, and ostentation, and to spare others all superfluous and needless expense. Let us take great care to avoid, as much as possible, worldly equipage and retinue, while we are labouring to advance the kingdom of God: to do otherwise is to establish that which we would destroy, and to destroy that which we would establish.

2. And certain women, which had been healed of evil spirits and infirmities, Mary called Magdalene, out of whom went seven devils,
3. And Joanna the wife of Chuza, Herod's steward, and Susanna, and many others, which ministered unto him of their substance.

Jesus receives these assistances and ministrations, (1.) To honour poverty, by subjecting himself thereto. (2.) To humble himself, in receiving from his creatures. (3.) That he may depend upon the providence of his Father. (4.) To make way for the gratitude and charity of those he had healed. And, (5.) That he may not be burdensome to those to whom he goes to preach. It has, in all ages, been the proper lot of pious ladies to labour in establishing the kingdom of God, by the exercise of charity toward the ministers of Christ and toward the poor. These women carry about with them living proofs of the mission and charity of Christ, having been miraculously healed by him. In this travelling church he gives us a representation of his church on earth, wherein the ministry of the truth and that of charity ought to be inseparable.

4. ¶ And when much people were gathered together, and were come to him out of every city, he spake by a parable:

Men run to Christ as to a new spectacle; and he makes use of their curiosity to draw to him his elect. He chooses out a little good ground, made such by his grace, from amid a large quantity full of stones and thorns, exposed to birds who prey upon it, and to men who trample it under their feet. A good pastor ought to be such as Christ. He must sow the word in all places, to the end it may fall upon some in which it will spring up, and bear eternal fruit.

5. A sower went out to sow his seed: and as he sowed, some fell by the way side; and it was trodden down, and the fowls of the air devoured it.

See here what a heart is which either despises or neglects the word of God, and thereby renders ineffectual all the light, desires, and inclinations to good which he has sown in it. This is one of the most common faults of the world, wherein the love of earthly things is, as it were, the feet which treads down the seed; and the love of glory as the fowls which devour it. In vain do men flatter themselves, as if they were not of the world, if they love it, and seek its conversation; this is to be by the way side, though not to be in it. Whoever loves the world, will never retain the word of God in his heart.

6. And some fell upon a rock; and as soon as it was sprung up, it withered away, because it lacked moisture.

What man, when he considers his own hardness and insensibility, has not reason to fear that he has a heart of stone as to the things of God? The tears of repentance are that wholesome moisture which nourishes the love of God's word and of the truth, and which keeps the heart from growing hard, and the seed sprung up from withering away.. Lord, my heart is in thy sight like land where there is no water: let the rain of thy grace descend upon it, and cause this fountain of the tears of true repentance to spring up therein!

7. And some fell among thorns; and the thorns sprang up with it, and choked it.

How can the love of evangelical truths possibly subsist in a heart full of the thorns of worldly lusts? Fear lest thy own is such. How oft are we deceived in this matter, when we see the love of God's word, good desires, and even good works, subsist for some time together with vanity, ambition, luxury, and other lusts, and even grow up together with them! Sooner or later the thorns will choke the seed, if they be not plucked up in time.

8. And other fell on good ground, and sprang up, and bare fruit a hundred-fold. And when he had said these things, he cried, He that hath ears to hear, let him hear.

The fruit shows plainly whether we belong to the good ground. But let us tremble, when we see so little which is good, in comparison of the rest. All that which bears fruit does not preserve it to maturity. The wind of temptation blows down abundance of it; the worm of pride and of riches devours a great quantity; and the rottenness of unclean pleasures destroys as much. How little good grain, O Lord, is carried into thy celestial granaries! Vouchsafe to cause me to become part of thy wheat.

9. And his disciples asked him, saying, What might this parable be?
10. And he said, Unto you it is given to know the mysteries of the kingdom of God: but to others in parables; that seeing they might not see, and hearing they might not understand.

The understanding of the Scriptures and mysteries is not given to all. It must be humbly begged of Him who is the Author and sovereign Dispenser thereof. No man has any reason to complain of God, who is the master of the secrets of his own kingdom; but those to whom he communicates them have abundant reason to adore and acknowledge in themselves the mercy which they never deserved. Hear and study the Scriptures: in them all religion is to be found, all the conduct of God, all the mysteries of Christ, and whatever passes in the formation and government of his church. They are an adorable mixture of clearness and obscurity, which enlightens and humbles the children of God, and blinds and hardens those of this world: but the light proceeds from God, and the blindness from the creature.

SECT. II.—THE EXPLICATION OF THE PARABLE.

11. Now the parable is this: The seed is the word of God. 12. Those by the way side are they that hear; then cometh the devil, and taketh away the word out of their hearts, lest they should believe and be saved.

The power of the devil over the hearts of the children of the world is greater than it is imagined, and is not sufficiently dreaded. The number, diversity, and incumbrance of the affairs of the world; the continual motion and hurry in which worldly men are; that chain of employments which to appearance are neither good nor bad, and of new designs which succeed one another; and that circle of pleasures, amusements, and vanities,—these are the things wherein that art and policy consists which the devil uses, in order to render the word, good thoughts, and good desires fruitless, and to take away God's seed out of their hearts and minds.

13. They on the rock *are they*, which, when they hear, receive the word with joy; and these have no root, which for a while believe, and in time of temptation fall away.

Temptation makes it evidently appear whether we are really the servants of God. When the root of charity is wanting, the word of God can do but little in the heart, and that little is not lasting. Good inclinations and piety frequently continue, on no other account but only because nothing opposes them, and because the darling passion of the heart is not contradicted; but all disappears when once we are threatened with the loss of that which we love more than God, without being sensible of it. Let us take great care not to defer, till the time of temptation and trial, the necessary work of subduing and rooting out of our hearts whatever may hinder the truths of salvation from entering in and fixing there. They grow hard by evil habits: we must labour to weaken and conquer these, if we desire the seed should take root in those, and remain secure in times of storm and tempest.

14. And that which fell among thorns are they, which, when they have heard, go forth, and are choked with cares and riches and pleasures of *this* life, and bring no fruit to perfection.

Riches and pleasures are the thorns of life: they choke

all good desires whatever which are in the heart. There are three sorts of persons in whom Christian truths become unfruitful, through engagements which succeed either a good education, or a regular way of life, or retirement:—(1.) A young person of quality, who goes forth from under the care of a father, a mother, a prudent tutor, or a Christian preceptor, and enters into the world, into offices of state, into designs of establishing himself, etc., which makes him forget all. (2.) A man who quits a private life, to give himself up entirely to trade, to business, and to the desire of riches. (3.) One who passes from the holy repose of retirement to a soft, idle, and effeminate life, and seeks nothing but his own ease. Let every man examine and judge himself.

15. But that on the good ground are they, which in an honest and good heart, having heard the word, keep *it*, and bring forth fruit with patience.

To receive the seed of the word, to keep it in the heart, and to bring forth fruit, are three different gifts of God, which we must beg of him; but the chief gift of all is the good and perfect heart. The good heart which is fit to love, receive, retain, and practise the law and word of God, is that which has not these three bad qualities above mentioned, and in which charity is stronger than concupiscence. There are three kinds of patience which are necessary for the elect, in order to bring forth fruit worthy of heaven: the patience or perseverence of prayer, necessary to keep and preserve the seed in expectation of God's proper time and season; the patience of Christian perseverance, in bringing forth fruit to the end without being tired; and the patience of resistance and suffering in trials and persecutions, either internal from evil habits, or external from the hands of men. What, then, must we always pray, always labour, and always contend? This is the portion of the elect, the fruit of the divine word in their heart, and the continual exercise of their patience.

SECT. III.—THE CANDLE UPON A CANDLESTICK.—WHOEVER HATH, SHALL HAVE MORE.—CHRIST'S MOTHER AND BRETHREN.

16. ¶ No man, when he hath lighted a candle, covereth it with a vessel, or putteth *it* under a bed; but setteth *it* on a candlestick, that they which enter in may see the light.

It is a matter not merely of counsel, but of duty and obligation, that we should not possess graces, light, and talents to no purpose. It is still a greater piece of infidelity to hold the truth in captivity to unrighteousness, and to the love of temporal conveniences. It is not sufficient to salvation for a man to believe in his heart the truth of the gospel, he must make profession of it, and not be ashamed to give testimony thereto. Neither is it sufficient for him even to have been justified by faith and charity, but he must perform the works of them, and edify the church and those who desire to enter into it.

17. For nothing is secret, that shall not be made manifest; neither *any thing* hid, that shall not be known and come abroad.

Well and good men may disguise their irregular intentions to themselves and others: they will one day appear manifest to the eyes of the whole universe. We hide ourselves from men for the short moment of this life; we thereby avoid little troubles and inconveniences, and enjoy some small conveniences and advantages from the favour of the great, which passes away like a shadow: but when this shadow is vanished, then the light of the great day, which will make every thing manifest—truth, which will judge every thing, and justice, which will punish every thing and forever—shall make unrighteousness evidently known, and overwhelm the cowardly and hypocritical.

18. Take heed therefore how ye hear: for whosoever hath, to him shall be given; and whosoever hath not, from him shall be taken even that which he seemeth to have.

Whoever improves the grace he has received, receives abundantly more. What person is there, who, either opening the gospel, or receiving from the mouth of pastors and preachers the seed and light of God's word, seriously reflects and considers how he ought to read or hear it; what use he is obliged to make of it; what account will be demanded of every truth; what reward God has decreed to the faithful use of it; and what punishment both to the abuse and to the making no use at all thereof? A man has properly nothing at all, when he has neither the knowledge of the Scriptures nor the gifts which should be instrumental thereto, in such a manner as is profitable to salvation. Very often, even in this life, all is taken away as a punishment of infidelity, ingratitude, and the abuse of God's gifts; and the light is turned into darkness.

19. ¶ Then came to him *his* mother and his brethren, and could not come at him for the press. 20. And it was told him *by certain* which said, Thy mother and thy brethren stand without, desiring to see thee.

He who has an ardent love for Christ cannot be long absent from him. Whatever private conversations the blessed Virgin might have with her Son, this earnest desire to hear from his mouth the word of God, and to see him exercise the public functions of his ministry, was very commendable. To go to hear those whom God fills with his Holy Spirit, that they may preach his truths worthily, is a respect and honour which we owe to his mission, his word, his goodness, and his designs. If ever curiosity were holy and allowable, it was this of desiring to hear the word made man, speak to men with all the knowledge and power of God. Had we but a lively faith, we should find the same advantage in his word.

21. And he answered and said unto them, My mother and my brethren are these which hear the word of God, and do it.

An ecclesiastical person, a Christian, ought to forget everybody, and even his relations, when the service of God is in question. Faith and charity are the things which unite us closely to him, by causing us to adhere to his word and truth. Christ does not despise his mother, but only shows us upon what account she is to be esteemed; namely, on the account of her constant attention to divine truth, of her faithfulness in making all the use of it which was required of her, and of that union of grace and love which she had with his sacred humanity, not so much because she had given it him, as because the Son of God had made it his own by causing it to subsist in his divine person. Let us learn of her to love Christ in such a way as is worthy of him, and never to apply ourselves to holy things but after a holy manner.

SECT. IV.—THE TEMPEST APPEASED.

22. ¶ Now it came to pass on a certain day, that he went into a ship
with his disciples: and he said unto them, Let us go over unto the other
side of the lake. And they launched forth. 23. But as they sailed, he
fell asleep: and there came down a storm of wind on the lake; and they
were filled *with water*, and were in jeopardy.

The present life is but, as it were, a passage from one shore to another—from time to eternity. The world is the lake over which we must pass, the storm of wind is temptation, and the water with which the bark is filled is that corruption which slides insensibly into the heart by the senses. Christ is asleep in respect of us when he suffers us to be tempted, when negligence causes our faith and vigilance to slumber, and the fervency of prayer begins to abate. If we do not see what the dangers of this life are, because they are not always sensible, let us but open the eyes of our faith, and we shall behold them with horror. Christ seems not to watch over us in the time of temptation, and as if he permitted all to the devil; but he sees and governs all things with a sovereign knowledge and wisdom.

24. And they came to him, and awoke him, saying, Master, Master, we perish. Then he arose, and rebuked the wind and the raging of the water: and they ceased, and there was a calm.

Let us but awake Christ by prayer when the storm arises, and the calm will be immediately restored to our heart. Let us make prayer familiar to us; for without his grace we are in danger of perishing every moment. When we have Jesus Christ at the bottom of our heart, we have reason to hope that temptations will be no more than trials, and that they will only serve to awaken our faith, to render us more watchful in prayer, and to make the almighty power of his grace manifest in us. The illustrious manner in which it shows itself in this miracle, is an emblem of that which grace performs in gaining the victory over temptations. It is to prayer that God joins these wonderful effects.

25. And he said unto them, Where is your faith? And they being afraid wondered, saying one to another, What manner of man is this! for he commandeth even the winds and water, and they obey him.

In temptation our faith is frequently asleep, and we imagine it is Christ who is so. Vouchsafe, O Jesus, often to repeat this wholesome reproof at the bottom of my heart; but do it in such a manner as may fill me with a holy dread, and an admiration of faith, at the sight of thy conduct toward thy elect and toward thy church. He who has made her triumph over so many persecutors, is always with her to defend her. Even creatures the most insensible are subject to him. The greater proportion and dependency there is between the sovereign and the created reason, between the unchangeable and all-powerful will, and the weak and changeable will of man, the more ought we to believe that God can act upon this as sovereign Lord, and as God, without doing violence to its nature or injuring its liberty, but, on the contrary, healing and perfecting both, by the communication of his supreme reason and his divine liberty.

SECT. V.—THE LEGION OF DEVILS CAST OUT.—THE SWINE DROWNED.

26. ¶ And they arrived at the country of the Gadarenes, which is over against Galilee. 27. And when he went forth to land, there met him out of the city a certain man, which had devils long time, and ware no clothes, neither abode in *any* house, but in the tombs.

A soul possessed with the sin of uncleanness is, without comparison, a more horrid spectacle than this to the eyes of faith. The effects of this possession are these:—1st, It renders the heart a slave to sin and the devil in a more servile, shameful, grievous, and insuperable manner. 2d, It strips a man of all the divine gifts, and of all modesty. 3d, It causes him to wander and run about after the creatures, and to fly from his own heart, which is his house, and the proper place of his retirement. 4th, It changes this house, which ought to be holy, and to be the temple of the Holy Ghost, into a noisome sepulchre, full of infection. My God, suffer not this change! Lord, preserve those from corruption who make but one body with thyself! O Holy Spirit, defend thy temple from this profanation!

28. When he saw Jesus, he cried out, and fell down before him, and with a loud voice said, What have I to do with thee, Jesus, *thou* Son of God most high? I beseech thee, torment me not.

The 5th effect of the sin of uncleanness in one possessed with it, is, that it causes him to look upon Christ, who is purity itself, as a mortal enemy. The 6th effect is, that it renders all converse and intercourse with Christ insupportable to him, and inclines him to make, if possible, even that of religion subservient to his brutal passion. What union is there not between the head and the members, and what conformity ought there not to be answerable to this union? But what separation, what disparity does not the sin of impurity cause? The 7th effect of the passion of an unchaste person is, that it causes him both to fear lest God should come and disturb the bad peace of his conscience with some remorse, and audaciously to accuse him of injustice, when he would take him off from his impure life. Lord, were I ever to be so miserable, hearken not to the complaints or desires of my corrupt heart, but to the voice of thy own mercy. Torment me, and shake the bed of my criminal repose, until thou hast thoroughly awakened me!

29. (For he had commanded the unclean spirit to come out of the man. For oftentimes it had caught him: and he was kept bound with chains and in fetters; and he brake the bands, and was driven of the devil into the wilderness.)

The 8th effect of the sin of impurity is, that it makes the unchaste person afraid lest God should convert him too soon. The 9th, that it causes him to violate all laws, to despise all admonitions, and to harden himself against all manner of threatenings. The 10th effect of this vice is, that it is the source of all sorts of temptations. The sinner is free only as to evil, without the grace of his Redeemer and Deliverer. This alone renders him free to do good, by breaking the chains which he has made of his own will. A sinner who flies from the presence of his God, and from his own heart, who is free from righteousness, and a slave to sin and the devil, whither is he not driven? The region of heresy and sin is a most frightful wilderness, without water, without shelter, and without any path whereby to return out of it. We must inevitably perish therein, O Jesus, unless thou thyself vouchsafest to come and seek us, and to lead us back into the ways of thy truth and righteousness!

30. And Jesus asked him, saying, What is thy name? And he said, Legion: because many devils were entered into him.

The 11th effect of this sin is, that it is always accompanied with many others. An unchaste person is fastened to sin by all the powers of his soul, and all the senses of his body. How many devils have we not to fear! The devil of wicked thoughts, in the mind; that of filthy representations, in the fancy; that of unchaste desires, in the heart; that of curiosity, in the ears; that of impudence, in the countenance; of wandering glances, in the eyes; and a whole legion upon the tongue, etc. O Jesus, who can deliver me from these furious enemies of my salvation, if I am abandoned by thee!

31. And they besought him that he would not command them to go out into the deep.

The 12th effect of the passion of the unclean person is, that it causes him to frame a thousand different desires and unjust prayers, and even to wish that God himself was not just, that so his irregularities might go unpunished. The devil is permitted to be in the air and upon the earth, on purpose to exercise the elect, and to reap his harvest of the wicked, until the time of Christ's coming to reap his at the last judgment. He dreads hell, not so much because it is the place of his punishment, as because he can find none to tempt there,—all there being his own already. The devil is afraid of hell; and yet there are men who either fear it not at all, or, at most, only like the devils, with a servile and slavish fear. If these persons never attain to a filial fear, what can they expect but the portion of devils?

32. And there was there a herd of many swine feeding on the mountain: and they besought him that he would suffer them to enter into them. And he suffered them.

The 13th effect of impurity in a heart possessed therewith is, that it causes it continually to seek new objects to satisfy its passion, and to abandon itself to every thing which is most detestable therein. This forced humiliation and suppliant condition of the devil show us plainly that he is but a slave, and can do nothing by himself. How great is the infidelity of those who dread his power! How foolish and sacrilegious is their confidence, who consult him, who trust to his promises, and expect from him that assistance and wealth which he is not able to give them! He is only then to be feared, when a man does not fear sin. He is the hope of none but the desperate.

33. Then went the devils out of the man, and entered into the swine: and the herd ran violently down a steep place into the lake, and were choked.

The 14th effect of impurity is, that the unchaste person meets with his punishment even in the gratification of his desires, and perishes miserably with the accomplices of his passion. There is not a more dreadful sign of the wrath of God, than when he abandons the sinner to his lusts, and permits him to find means of satisfying them. His satisfaction lasts but for a moment. The devils who enter into the swine are an emblem of those persons who seek all their happiness in sensual pleasures, and shorten their days by those very pleasures which plunge them the sooner into eternal misery.

34. When they that fed *them* saw what was done, they fled, and went and told *it* in the city and in the country. 35. Then they went out to see what was done; and came to Jesus, and found the man, out of whom the devils were departed, sitting at the feet of Jesus, clothed, and in his right mind: and they were afraid. 36. They also which saw *it* told them by what means he that was possessed of the devils was healed.

The 15th effect of this vice is, that it takes away all good sense and reason, stupefies a man, and makes him become, as it were, a brute. The 16th and last effect is, that nothing but a miracle can recover him from this sinful habit. If Christ has not wrought one upon thee by a mercy of deliverance and cure, he has done it at least by a mercy of prevention; and even that prevention could not be effected, but by delivering and curing the will. A person possessed is a spectacle of horror to men, and his deliverance a subject of admiration; and the unchaste person, of whom the other is only a figure, is often esteemed, caressed, and envied under his miserable possession; and on the contrary despised, avoided, and ridiculed by the world, as soon as ever God has delivered him. O judgment of the world! O corruption of man's heart!

37. ¶ Then the whole multitude of the country of the Gadarenes round about besought him to depart from them; for they were taken with great fear: and he went up into the ship, and returned back again.

The knowledge of Jesus Christ, and the love of salvation, cannot long subsist together with the love of pleasures, and with an affection for temporal possessions and the ease of this present life. Little does he know the value of a Saviour or of salvation, who chooses rather to be rich without Christ, than to be poor with him. The carnal man willingly renounces him, in order to enjoy that which he loves. Men will not understand that it is a happiness to be deprived of the objects of their desires, and delivered from the occasions of sin. In vain does God work miracle upon miracle to disengage us from them; there must be one wrought upon the heart itself to break its chains. Blind and senseless wretches, to be afraid of their Deliverer, even after he had delivered them from a legion of devils in the person of their countryman! Terrible is the judgment upon sinners, when God hears their prayers, as he does this of the devil. Vouchsafe to continue with me, O Lord, and hearken not to the irregular desires of my heart.

38. Now the man, out of whom the devils were departed, besought him that he might be with him: but Jesus sent him away, saying,

He who has passed his life in uncleanness ought not to think of following Christ in the company of the apostles, that is, in the priesthood. It is a sort of irregular and mistaken devotion, for a man to be made a priest upon no other view but that of withdrawing himself from vice and disorder, and of avoiding the occasions of sin. Bishops and priests ought to be penitents, (1.) As being subject to the sins and infirmities of the righteous. (2.) In order to prevent sins of another nature, and to suppress the principle and cause of them which they carry within themselves. (3.) On the account of the sins of their people and of the whole church, after the example of Christ. But the state of priesthood and episcopacy is [properly] a state of holiness, and not [merely] of penance.

39. Return to thine own house, and shew how great things God hath done unto thee. And he went his way, and published throughout the whole city how great things Jesus had done unto him.

He who is cured of the vice of uncleanness ought—(1.) To live retired, either in his own house, or elsewhere, according to his state and ability, that he may there seriously consider the great things God hath done unto him and the mysteries which Christ has accomplished for all sinners, and reflect with gratitude on the graces he received in order to his own conversion. (2.) He ought to offer up continual thanksgivings to God. (3.) To make amends for the scandal he has given. And, (4.) To publish the mercy of God, when he comes abroad into the world. We ought not to make the least difficulty of acknowledging our own misery, when the glory of God is concerned, and of publishing his mercy, when the edification of our neighbour depends upon it.

40. And it came to pass, that, when Jesus was returned, the people *gladly* received him; for they were all waiting for him.

Jesus Christ brings joy and gladness to a heart which has long expected and waited for him. The vicissitudes of devotion and coldness in a soul cause it to set a greater value upon the assistance of grace. God sometimes suffers men to desire and expect him a long time, that he may find their hearts better disposed and prepared to receive him. It is a great matter to know how to expect God as we ought, and to wait his proper time without remissness and growing cold.

SECT. VI.—THE DAUGHTER OF JAIRUS RAISED.—THE BLOODY ISSUE HEALED.

41. ¶ And, behold, there came a man named Jairus, and he was a ruler of the synagogue; and he fell down at Jesus's feet, and besought him that he would come into his house: 42. For he had one only daughter, about twelve years of age, and she lay a dying.

Whenever we perceive our souls begin to grow weak in piety, to faint in the performance of our duty, or to be ready to fall through the violence of any temptation, our only way is, to humble ourselves, to have recourse to Christ, and to invite and beseech him, by an humble and fervent prayer, that he would vouchsafe to come by his grace into the house of our heart. The generality of persons either hazard or neglect the salvation of their souls, as if each of them had several, and might venture one. We have each of us but one only soul: we must love it exclusively of all things else, and fear its loss as that which is irrecoverable; we must be greatly concerned for it under all occasions of sin, which is its death; and often in its behalf fall down at Jesus's feet, who is its only physician.

—But as he went the people thronged him. 43. ¶ And a woman having an issue of blood twelve years, which had spent all her living upon physicians, neither could be healed of any,

Remission of sins is granted only while we are in the way, that is, during the time of this life. Concupiscence is a shameful, inveterate, and continual disease, which proceeds from original sin, and is incurable, and not to be healed by any but Jesus Christ. The law, philosophy, confidence in our own strength, and the presumption of free-will, do but inflame and increase it. Happy are we, notwithstanding, if, after having experienced the insufficiency of human, natural, and external remedies, we are truly humbled, and fully convinced, that thy grace, O Jesus, is the only remedy for the disease of the soul and the sickness of concupiscence!

44. Came behind *him*, and touched the border of his garment; and immediately her issue of blood stanched.

In order to be cured, we must (1.) Approach Christ by a belief of his power and goodness, and of the necessity of his healing grace. (2.) We must think ourselves unworthy to appear in his presence, and to be looked upon by him. (3.) We must cast ourselves at his feet, and there pour out our heart in prayer. (4.) We must adore his sacred humanity, as the source of our own sanctification. (5.) We must unite ourselves to him by partaking of his mysteries, the spirit and virtue of which are to purify our souls, humbly desiring him to apply them to us. (6.) We must take care to honour his divine word, to render it familiar to us, and to put it in practice.

45. And Jesus said, Who touched me? When all denied, Peter and they that were with him said, Master, the multitude throng thee and press *thee*, and sayest thou, Who touched me?

Abundance of Christians, as it were, press upon Jesus Christ, in hearing his word, receiving the sacrament, and performing the outward part of religion; but few touch him by a lively faith, by a true Christian life, by the prayer of charity, and by the meditation, love, and imitation of his mysteries. Those numerous assemblies and multitudes of people who fill the churches and make the crowd at sermons, and yet cease not to go on in their usual course, in following the world and their own passions, throng and press Christ, but do not touch him.

46. And Jesus said, Somebody hath touched me; for I perceive that virtue is gone out of me.

There is not so much as one good thought or inclination but what proceeds from Christ, and is an emanation from that fulness of grace and truth which is in him. God and Christ know in themselves the good which we do, because it is God who produces it in us by Jesus Christ: God by Christ, by his merits, by his Spirit, by his sacred humanity, as the instrument of the Divinity in all the works of sanctification, and in whatever has any relation thereto, particularly miracles. What virtue would there not stream forth from this fire of love to inflame our heart, when we possess it by the holy eucharist, had we but the heart of this poor woman—an humble heart, more to be desired, by far, than the most precious thing in the world!

47. And when the women saw that she was not hid, she came trembling, and falling down before him, she declared unto him before all the people for what cause she had touched him, and how she was healed immediately.

Humility, simplicity, acknowledgment, and confusion, when we reflect upon the gifts we have received of God, are the faithful guardians of grace, which we ought to imitate in this poor woman. It is a sign that this grace has penetrated very deep into the heart, when we begin to be ashamed and confounded at the sight of our own unworthiness. How far is this disposition, both from the insensibility of those who receive the blessings of God without being in the least affected with them, and from the ingratitude of those who look upon them as a debt!

48. And he said unto her, Daughter, be of good comfort: thy faith hath made thee whole; go in peace.

There is no inward peace, but only by the cure of our lusts; no cure but by the grace of Christ; and no grace but by faith, which is the first of all. Christ frequently praises faith, not with design to oppose it to good works, but to show that it is the fountain of them, and to take the Jews off from their confidence in the works of the law and in their own righteousness. Do thou, O Jesus, give, preserve, increase, perfect, and consummate in us this principle of true righteousness and of every good work! thou who art the Author and Finisher of faith!

49. ¶ While he yet spake, there cometh one from the ruler of the synagogue's *house*, saying to him, Thy daughter is dead; trouble not the Master.

It is usual for faith to find itself tempted and weakened by flesh and blood, when it is at the very point of receiving that which it desires. Those whom the devil cannot ruin by a confidence in themselves, he endeavours with all his might to ruin by taking from them their confidence in God and Christ. In losing this confidence they lose the very soul of prayer; and in losing that, they lose all. Let us on no account be afraid to importune God with the earnestness of prayer: it is this importunity which he requires; in this consists the perseverance of prayer, to which every thing is promised.

50. But when Jesus heard *it*, he answered him, saying, Fear not: believe only, and she shall be made whole.

The word of God nourishes and strengthens faith, and faith supports prayer under all occasions of discouragement: but this threefold knot is tied only by the grace of him who gives it to whom he pleases. God would have us prepare ourselves for the reception of his mercy by confidence and faith; but even this faith and confidence, and all preparation for his mercy, are no other than so many gifts of this very mercy itself. No human impotency, no natural impossibility whatever, ought to discourage us; because it is neither from man nor from nature that our salvation is to come, but from the almighty will of God.

51. And when he came into the house, he suffered no man to go in, save Peter, and James, and John, and the father and the mother of the maiden.

A man ought to have abundance of discretion, to know when to discover and when to conceal the works of God.

52. And all wept, and bewailed her: but he said, Weep not; she is not dead, but sleepeth.

How little faith do we generally show in affliction, and on the death of our relations! We weep and bewail them, most commonly, either out of ceremony or interest: whereas we ought either to weep through faith, in casting our eyes upon sin, which is the cause of death; or to rejoice through faith in considering that the dead are delivered from sin, and from concupiscence, the source of it. Death, considered as an accident of nature, suggests only sentiments which savour of the corruption of nature; but, considered in the order settled and appointed by God, it is a necessary penance, the completion of the Christian sacrifice, the passage to a better life, the deliverance of a prisoner, the recalling of an exile, and the end of all the miseries of a sinner.

53. And they laughed him to scorn, knowing that she was dead.

The faith of true Christians, who look upon death only as a sleep, and expect the life of the world to come as their happiness, appears a folly to the eyes of the world. It is in this respect that the death of a Christian is a mystery of faith, as well as that of Jesus Christ. We behold one thing in it, and we believe another; a humbling and abasing death, which is the seed, and, as it were, the sacrament of a blessed life. The folly and delusion of the world will likewise appear in their turn, when it shall be evidently seen that so many deaths which seemed glorious to its eyes, were only the seed and the beginning of an eternal death.

54. And he put them all out, and took her by the hand, and called, saying, Maid, arise.

Christ touches with his grace a soul dead in sin, and raises it by his power. Thou hast wrought this miracle, O Lord, more than once upon my heart: but I believe, I hope, I expect another to be wrought upon my body, when thou shalt reanimate dust and ashes by thy almighty voice, and command the dead to rise and appear before thee. Grant, O Jesus, that I may continually live in this hope, and let it be the constant rule of my conduct and behaviour!

55. And her spirit came again, and she arose straightway: and he commanded to give her meat.

When the soul is truly risen again, it may be fed with the holy eucharist, and not before. This is the bread of the living, and not of the dead; and if the dead eat it, it only makes them die the more. When once we shall be raised with that resurrection which will be performed in an instant, we shall then eat in the kingdom of God that bread which is the life thereof, and shall be forever satisfied with that food of our souls which is God himself, as being eternal truth.

56. And her parents were astonished: but he charged them that they should tell no man what was done.

By this example, Christ plainly teaches how necessary humility is to those whose labours are directed to the salvation of souls. The more extraordinary the conversions are, the more care they who have been instrumental in them by their ministry ought to take not to ascribe to themselves the honour of them. Christ, who is the truth, has no fear upon his own, but only upon man's, account, who is nothing but vanity; and who is apt so much the more criminally to attribute to himself the works of God, as they are more divine. Let not this poison, Lord, insinuate itself into my heart!

CHAPTER IX.

SECT. I.—THE MISSION AND POWER OF THE APOSTLES.

1. Then he called his twelve disciples together, and gave them power and authority over all devils, and to cure diseases.

The call to the ministry, and the application to the exercise of it, are two different graces: we must depend upon

Christ for both. A man is often unsuccessful in the functions of the ministry, not for want of a call, but because he chooses and undertakes such a particular function of his own head, and upon other considerations than that of God's glory. The power of absolving is one thing; the gift of moving and converting sinners, by casting out the devil of vice and curing the diseases of the soul, is another.

2. And he sent them to preach the kingdom of God, and to heal the sick.

A man ought not to labour in the church till he has received (1.) A call; (2.) Power; (3.) Mission; and (4.) Instruction. Our blessed Lord, when he sends his apostles, gives them at the same time means to prove their mission, and by outward miracles to oblige men to look upon them as the ministers of God: it is this which distinguishes them from false apostles, to whom the devil gives a mission without miracles. Christ here gives them the power to work only such miracles as should be beneficial to mankind; to teach them not to act in the spirit of Elias, or in that of the old law, but in the spirit of the Saviour, and of his law, consisting wholly of gentleness and love. He does not give them the power to make rich, but to restore health, which is a blessing more natural, innocent, and common to all than riches.

3. And he said unto them, Take nothing for *your* journey, neither staves, nor scrip, neither bread, neither money; neither have two coats apiece.

The mission and poverty of the apostles is the pattern of that of missionaries. Those who preach up the love of eternal possessions, and an indifference to all perishing enjoyments, ought to do it by their life and conversation. Men will never be able to establish the kingdom of God in the hearts of people, so long as they do not appear fully persuaded themselves of those truths which they preach. And how can they appear to be so, if they plainly contradict them in their practice and behaviour? In order to persuade others to be unconcerned for superfluities, a man must not himself appear too much concerned even about necessaries.

4. And whatsoever house ye enter into, there abide, and thence depart.

A minister ought to be very careful not to wander from

house to house upon human motives. If he have the spirit of evangelical poverty, he will think himself well everywhere. The love of the conveniences of life is a great hinderance to the work of God in a missionary or a minister of the gospel; because the poor, who cannot accommodate him with them, are those with whom there is most to be done in the business of salvation; and the rich, who enjoy them, are more likely to inspire into a minister an affection for them, than he is to wean those from them.

5. And whosoever will not receive you, when ye go out of that city, shake off the very dust from your feet for a testimony against them.

How extremely dangerous is it not to receive the blessing which offers and presents itself to us! Though we do not dishonour the ministers of the truth in the very manner here set down, yet we do it, perhaps, in several others which are criminal. Is it nothing, think we, to decry them by calumnies, to cause them to be driven away and persecuted out of envy, to represent their doctrine as false and corrupt, to render them useless in any manner whatever, and to hinder the fruit of the divine word in their mouth? Alas, who can express what damage is hereby done to the church, and what crimes a man thus renders himself either directly guilty of, or in some measure accountable for!

6. And they departed, and went through the towns, preaching the gospel, and healing every where.

They who would imitate Christ, must seek rather to instruct the poor than the rich, and join, as much as they are able, bodily relief with spiritual instruction. O wonderful goodness of our blessed Saviour, to be the Saviour of bodies as well as of souls! Hereby he makes it evident that he came to reform the whole man, corrupted by sin in the outward man as well as in the inward. If ever such miracles were wrought by any others besides Christ and his servants, let his religion and doctrine be taken for a mere human invention; but let it be owned by all for the true religion, if it be a thing unheard of, that men should cure, not only some particular person by choice, but all manner of sick persons without distinction.

7. ¶ Now Herod the tetrarch heard of all that was done by him: and he was perplexed, because that it was said of some, that John was risen from the dead;

Ambition and a bad conscience are endless causes of perplexities and disquiets. There is a very great difference between knowing all that was done by Christ, and knowing it after a saving manner. Herod was extremely well informed of all, because he needed only eyes and ears to be so; but he was not in the least changed or altered thereby, because no man knoweth the Son to any benefit or advantage, but only he to whom the Father has been pleased to reveal him. Thou hast vouchsafed, O my God, to reveal to me this Son, in whom is my salvation and eternal life; but cease not, I beseech thee, to reveal him to my heart, lest it should know him only unprofitably.

8. And of some, that Elias had appeared; and of others, that one of the old prophets was risen again. 9. And Herod said, John have I beheaded; but who is this, of whom I hear such things? And he desired to see him.

Let us admire how fruitful in false notions of religion the mind of man is when it is not enlightened of God. Natural curiosity, with respect to men of God, produces nothing of itself toward salvation. It is instrumental thereto when God designs it for that purpose, as in Zaccheus; it is prejudicial when men have not grace to make a good use of it, as in the case of Herod. The death of John, in which Herod's veneration for him terminated, the design of this tyrant upon the life of Christ, and the scorn he made of him at the time of his passion, are the works which make it evidently appear from what principle this desire to see Christ proceeded. What an example is this for the great!

SECT. II.—THE RETURN AND RETIREMENT OF THE APOSTLES.—THE MIRACLE OF THE FIVE LOAVES.

10. ¶ And the apostles, when they were returned, told him all that they had done. And he took them, and went aside privately into a desert place belonging to the city called Bethsaida.

Ministers, after the evangelical labours, ought, (1.) To give an account thereof to the prelates. (2.) To recollect themselves in retirement with Christ. (3.) To interrupt sometimes the course of their instructions, on purpose to make them the more desired. See here the pattern of a bishop, intent on forming under his eyes the subordinate pastors, and who is wont to retreat with them from time to time in that retirement, to reform whatever they may find amiss in themselves, by prayer, by paternal instructions, by private conferences, and by examining the maxims which they follow, the conduct which they observe, and the faults to which they are subject in the administration of the sacraments, in preaching, in catechetical lectures, etc.

11. And the people, when they knew *it*, followed him: and he received them, and spake unto them of the kingdom of God, and healed them that had need of healing.

Observe here four effects of the goodness of Christ: (1.) He receives those well who seek him. (2.) He instructs them. (3.) He heals them. (4.) He feeds them. This is the pattern of the four chief duties of a good pastor. He is happy, when his charity has so far gained the hearts of his sheep that they themselves seek him who should seek them. More happy still, if he instructs them with so much care and blessing that he sees the fruit thereof in the cure of their souls. But most happy of all, if he has nothing more to do than only to feed them in the desert of this life, till they come to be satisfied in their own country.

12. And when the day began to wear away, then came the twelve, and said unto him, Send the multitude away, that they may go into the towns and country round about, and lodge, and get victuals; for we are here in a desert place.

God would have men sensible of human weakness, before he exercises his divine power. We can want nothing when we have Jesus Christ; much less, if we have forsaken all to seek him in retirement. It is a counsel merely human, to advise a man to leave the safety and sweetness of solitude on purpose to seek in the world a subsistence, which is never wanting but to those who are themselves wanting in fidelity to their state and condition, in trust to the providence of God, and in affection toward Jesus Christ. There is no barren desert for the creature, when faith in the Creator is lively and fruitful.

13. But he said unto them, Give ye them to eat. And they said, We have no more but five loaves and two fishes; except we should go and buy meat for all this people.

The pastors ought themselves to feed their sheep: Christ, who commands them to do it, helps their insufficiency. God does not command things impossible; those which appear so being impossible only to human weakness. But his commandment admonishes us, both to do whatever is in our power, and to beg of him whatever is not; and then he himself comes to our assistance, on purpose to make us able to perform it. We offer up an excellent prayer, when we join a grateful acknowledgment of the benefits we have received already to an humble confession of our own inability to do that which God requires of us more. Command, Lord, but, at the same time, give that which thou dost command.

14. For they were about five thousand men. And he said to his disciples, Make them sit down by fifties in a company. 15. And they did so, and made them all sit down. 16. Then he took the five loaves and the two fishes, and looking up to heaven, he blessed them, and brake, and gave to the disciples to set before the multitude.

See here the duties of a true bishop, who would feed his people with the word of God: (1.) He ought to exhort them to hear it with an humble and sedate reverence, perfectly free and disengaged from all secular cares. (2.) He must first take this food, and fill himself therewith. (3.) He ought frequently to lift his heart up to God. (4.) To draw down the divine blessing upon his people by his prayers and good works. (5.) He must break the loaves, by giving such instructions as are suited to the capacity of all. (6.) He must do that by the hands of holy priests which he cannot do by himself. (7.) He must perform every thing with order and discipline in the distribution of this bread of the soul, and religiously observe the division of parishes, of which we may here behold a slight draught. (8.) He must give that to the subordinate pastors which they are to give to the people; that is, he must fill them with solid instructions and the knowledge of salvation, furnish them with means of attaining it, and put into their hands the doctrine which has been transmitted down from Christ by those of the apostles.

17. And they did eat, and were all filled: and there was taken up of fragments that remained to them twelve baskets.

The word of God is extremely nourishing, and not to be exhausted or consumed. The more one is filled therewith, the more plentifully does it abound to him who reads it. That pastor who, upon an unforeseen necessity of preaching God's word, commits himself to him, and, in speaking out of the abundance of his heart, trusts entirely to his promise, finds sufficient both to fill his people, and plentifully to feed himself. Even the fragments, which remain after the feast of God's word, are precious; a man ought to gather them up for himself by meditation, after he has fed others by preaching.

SECT. III.—PETER'S CONFESSION.—THE CROSS TO BE BORNE.—WE MUST LOSE ALL IN ORDER TO BE SAVED.

18. ¶ And it came to pass, as he was alone praying, his disciples were with him; and he asked them, saying, Whom say the people that I am?

Christ asks his disciples concerning their faith, after prayer, and in the privacy of retirement, on purpose to teach bishops, not to instruct nor examine into the faith of inferior pastors in the presence of the people; and to do it with abundance of prudence, and after having begged of God the Spirit of wisdom. He asks for his apostles that very faith whereof he demands of them an account, and shows Peter that the revelation made by the Father was the fruit of the prayer of the Son. (Matt. xvi. 17.) We must pray before we catechize, after the example of this adorable Head of catechists; and much more prayer is still necessary, in order to form the ministers of the church.

19. They answering said, John the Baptist; but some *say*, Elias; and others *say*, that one of the old prophets is risen again.

There is nothing but what is either uncertain or false, when the spirit of man undertakes to speak of God. Christ gave occasion to his disciples to mention the several errors of the world in relation to his person, that they might be the more fully convinced that their faith did not proceed from themselves. This is the use which we ourselves ought to make of those mistakes and false conjectures of the mind of man which fill the world. Every thing ought thus to be instrumental to the increase of our gratitude, our love, and our faith, that we may be of the number of those to whom all things work together for good.

20. He said unto them, But whom say ye that I am? Peter answering said, The Christ of God.

There is nothing but what is true and certain, when the Spirit of God speaks by his ministers. The faith of the pastors ought to be more enlightened than that of the people. Christ applies himself to establish and confirm in his apostles the belief of his incarnation as the foundation of all religion. It is all contained in brief under this great expression, "The Christ of God;" that is to say, a man anointed and consecrated by his personal union with the eternal Son of God, to be the High Priest of the Christian religion, the true Worshipper of God, the Saviour and Mediator of men, and the Head, who, pouring out of the fulness of his Spirit and grace upon sinners, makes them Christians, and forms them into his mystical body, to which he gives his own name, and of which he raises up a living and eternal temple to God his Father.

21. And he straitly charged them, and commanded *them* to tell no man that thing; 22. Saying, The Son of man must suffer many things, and be rejected of the elders and chief priests and scribes, and be slain, and be raised the third day.

There is a time to speak, and a time to be silent, concerning the divine mysteries. Man is both unworthy and incapable of hearing them, before Christ has, by his sufferings and death, merited for him the grace requisite thereto. We have here a symbol of the faith, or a short creed, taught by Christ himself, which comprehends all under the three great mysteries of his incarnation, his passion and death, and his resurrection. How profitable, how pleasant is it, to make this the continual object of our faith, adoration, love, imitation, meditation, and hope!

23. ¶ And he said to *them* all, If any *man* will come after me, let him deny himself, and take up his cross daily, and follow me.

What is meant by the connection of this verse with the

former, if not that the mysteries of the Head must be accomplished likewise in the members; and to those who have by the baptism of the Spirit been made partakers of the divine nature in Christ, are one day to partake of his resurrection; but not unless they have partaken of his sufferings and death. To suffer and to die the death of the gospel, is to resist in ourselves the spirit and inclinations of Adam, continually to crucify the flesh with its affections and lusts, to imitate the sufferings of Christ by mortification, and to die to our own passions, in order to follow the motions of his Spirit. Take particular notice of these words, "to them all," and "daily:" no person then is excused, no day excepted. Of what, therefore, do those think, to what do they aspire, who make every day a day of pleasure, luxury, and diversion? Who has a right to shake off the yoke of the cross, but only he who designs to have a right to nothing but hell?

24. For whosoever will save his life shall lose it: but whosoever will lose his life for my sake, the same shall save it.

He who loves himself with respect to his life only, hates himself as to eternity. See here that which makes all the vast difference which there is between the life of true Christians and that of worldly persons. Both would willingly be saved and live happy: but the former purchase, through the merits of Christ, the blessed life of eternity, by the cross and the mortifications of this momentary life; the latter purchase a mere shadow of transitory felicity, by an eternal cross and death, and a punishment without end. Teach me, Lord, to save my life by losing it, and to be every day extremely careful not to lose it even in seeking to save it. For it is thou, O Saviour of the world, who art the great master and teacher of this important and only necessary lesson!

25. For what is a man advantaged, if he gain the whole world, and lose himself, or be cast away?

Nothing can compensate the loss sustained by him who loses his soul. Let us then rather suffer the loss of all things, than that of our salvation. Let us but weigh the gain and the loss which there is in following or not following the rules of the gospel, and we shall soon be convinced that it is no better than madness to be in the least doubt or suspense what to do. By doing the first, we lose at the most nothing but what we must necessarily lose in a few years, or perhaps months, and what a philosopher or a reasonable man judges unworthy of his fondness and affection. By not doing it, we lose every thing to all eternity!

26. For whosoever shall be ashamed of me and of my words, of him shall the son of man be ashamed, when he shall come in his own glory, and *in his* Father's, and of the holy angels.

Whosoever is ashamed of the truth while it is humbled and oppressed in this world, shall be humbled and confounded before truth itself, glorious and triumphant, in heaven. It is a holy kind of boldness, not to be ashamed of the humiliations of Christ, or of any thing in his ways which seems a debasement to the eyes of the world. It is very just that he, who in time has preferred himself before God, should in eternity be abandoned to his own choice. Whoever has not thought God worthy of him, is by no means worthy of God. The testimony which God requires of us, renders him neither more rich nor more happy; but upon his, our eternal happiness entirely depends. Though the being faithful to him may cost us our lives, what do we lose which we do not receive in him again an hundred-fold?

SECT. IV.—THE TRANSFIGURATION.

27. But I tell you of a truth, there be some standing here, which shall not taste of death, till they see the kingdom of God.

That which Christ does here with respect to his apostles, he frequently does with respect to his elect, by a certain confidence and presage of the glory he prepares for them imprinted on the bottom of their hearts. We see this kingdom established in the world by grace now almost seventeen ages; and yet untractable and obstinate minds can hardly be persuaded of the truth of it. I know, O Lord, that I cannot behold the consummation and glory of it without dying; give me, therefore, that desire and earnest longing which I ought to have for that happy moment which is to transport me into that eternal kingdom!

28. ¶ And it came to pass about an eight days after these sayings, he took Peter and John and James, and went up into a mountain to pray.

In order to a perfect knowledge of the mysteries of Christ, and the secrets of his kingdom, he must raise us above ourselves. This is a privilege granted to very few. In order fully to learn Christ, it is necessary to pray much; and in order to pray as we ought, we must have him with us, and raise ourselves with and by him from the earth toward the holy mountain. It belongs to him to conduct us to God his Father. Take and separate my heart, O Jesus, from this tumult and confusion of human things; lift it up, unite it to, and fix it on thyself, and on thy Father, by a true Christian prayer.

29. And as he prayed, the fashion of his countenance was altered, and his raiment *was* white *and* glistering.

It is in prayer that God discovers himself to men; it is by this that the inward part of man is altered, and, as it were, transfigured. A soul nourished with prayer appears even outwardly white and glistering, through recollection, modesty, mortification of the senses, simplicity, silence, candour of behaviour, and innocency of manners.

30. And, behold, there talked with him two men, which were Moses and Elias:

The law and the prophets breathe nothing but Jesus Christ; and it is prayer which is the key of the Scriptures, which lets us into the spirit of the law, which gives us an insight into the prophecies, and therein discovers the mysteries of Christ. There are three things which we must have continually before our eyes when we read the Scriptures of the Old Testament: namely, Jesus Christ, who is therein typified and foretold; the law of charity, to which that of Moses tends; and the economy of the church and the sanctification of the elect, which are represented in the prophets, and prefigured even in all the histories of the Old Testament, and in all the events which are related there.

31. Who appeared in glory, and spake of his decease which he should accomplish at Jerusalem.

Christ appears but one moment in his glory, and even then

speaks of his sufferings and death. Let us learn of him never to lose sight of that moment which is to separate us from this world. In the midst of joy, and even of spiritual prosperity, we ought to remember that we must purchase the joys of the heavenly Jerusalem by the sacrifice of ourselves. Christ's decease, or departure out of the world, comprehends two things: his death, which, being suffered in obedience, opens heaven, as that of Moses, happening by the express command of God, was almost immediately followed by the people's entrance into the land of promise; and his ascension, which was prefigured by the taking up of Elias into heaven.

32. But Peter and they that were with him were heavy with sleep: and when they were awake, they saw his glory, and the two men that stood with him.

The sight of Christ's glory, and the presence of Moses and Elias, are a representation of that lively faith concerning heavenly things, and of that knowledge of the Scriptures which Christ gave to his apostles and to apostolical men to qualify them for the work of the gospel. The sleep and waking of the disciples are an emblem of the sleep of death, and of our being awaked at the resurrection, which will open our eyes to the beauties of eternity, and unfold to us all the mysteries and truths of the law and the prophets. O desirable moment, when, being waked, as it were, out of a profound sleep, all the beauty of this world will appear to us only as a dream, and the light of eternity shall clearly show us Jesus Christ and his whole church glorified in God!

33. And it came to pass, as they departed from him, Peter said unto Jesus, Master, it is good for us to be here: and let us make three tabernacles; one for thee, and one for Moses, and one for Elias: not knowing what he said.

They know not the nature of the Christian religion, who would fain enjoy rest and glory before labour and suffering. The rest and satisfaction which prayer and meditation afford, is very sweet and pleasant to one who has a relish of truth, and a mind open to the mysteries of the Scriptures, so as to discover in them Christ and his church. This is, as it were, a third heaven, which a man must leave, in order to form

Christ and his church in hearts by the ministry of the word, when he is called thereto by God.

34. While he thus spake, there came a cloud, and overshadowed them: and they feared as they entered into the cloud.

God frequently permits a cloud to overshadow the light which has illuminated a man in prayer, and fear to succeed the consolation which he has tasted therein. He thereby teaches souls to rely on nothing here below, and entirely to depend upon him from one moment to another. Christ enters into the cloud when he leaves us under the obscurity of faith, by withdrawing from us that light and sensible comfort which we sometimes experience in our devotions. The secret is, to believe, and to put our whole trust and confidence in God.

35. And there came a voice out of the cloud, saying, This is my beloved Son: hear him.

See here a representation of the perfect adoption of the children of God. Christ is substituted in the place of Moses, to give us not only the law, but the spirit and truth of it. Whom will we hear, if we refuse to hear Jesus Christ? He speaks to us in so many divers manners, by his life, by his death, and by all his mysteries; by his gospel, by his church, and by his servants; by his benefits, by his chastisements, and by his inspirations. Shall we be deaf to so many different voices?

36 And when the voice was past, Jesus was found alone. And they kept *it* close, and told no man in those days any of those things which they had seen.

Jesus alone is to us instead of the law, the sacrifices, and the prophets. Our true happiness consists in looking upon him alone as our law and pattern; in following him alone as our Moses in the desert of this world; and in desiring his Spirit alone instead of that of Elias. Since truth is not properly ours, but God's, we must be so faithful as not to speak of divine truths but only so far as the Spirit moves us thereto, either by himself or by those who have a right to open our mouths. It is always the safest way not to divulge or publish extraordinary favours and graces: they are a treasure which ought to be carefully hid, for fear lest vanity should rob us of it.

SECT. V.—THE LUNATIC.—THE PASSION FORETOLD.

37. ¶ And it came to pass, that on the next day, when they were come down from the hill, much people met him.

After the sweetness of retirement and the repose of prayer, a man must return to his employment and resume his labour. God shows the ministers of the gospel the fruit of retirement and prayer, in the eagerness of the people, who came either to hear the word or to seek a cure. It is a very great comfort to a pastor, when those whom he ought to seek in all places, come on purpose to meet him, and in some measure anticipate his pastoral care.

38. And, behold, a man of the company cried out, saying, Master, I beseech thee, look upon my son; for he is mine only child.

He who begs one look of mercy, begs every thing. God has already looked upon that person, who, knowing the absolute necessity of this look, desires and implores it. To beg it with a loud cry, is to beg it with a great faith and an ardent prayer. There are but few among the crowd whose faith cries out after this manner. That which it ought above all things to believe is, that Christ is Lord of the heart, and can with one single look change and cure it. Our soul, our heart is, as it were, our only child. He who thinks seriously of this, must conclude that he has no other business in the world besides the salvation of this only child, the loss of which is irreparable.

39. And, lo, a spirit taketh him, and he suddenly crieth out; and it teareth him that he foameth again, and bruising him, hardly departeth from him.

How dreadful is that man's condition whom sin has possessed from his youth! The devil is absolute master of his heart, renders his tongue a world of iniquity, causes him by continued relapses to cleave more and more to the earth, and kindles every day new passions which shake and torment him. The intervals are very rare and short in a habitual sinner: a lively and ardent passion is always seeking to satisfy itself, and by so doing renders itself more incurable. Vouchsafe, O Lord, to grant eyes to sinners, that they may perceive the total subversion of their hearts, and all the disorder and confusion which sin has caused therein.

40. And I besought thy disciples to cast him out; and they could not.

God often suffers sinners to struggle a long time against their evil habits, on purpose to make them sensible of the nature of sin. The first endeavours of a sinner, represented to us by the prayer of this man, are not altogether fruitless, though they may seem to be so, since they increase his desire of deliverance, and convince him that Christ alone is the Saviour.

41. And Jesus answering said, O faithless and perverse generation, how long shall I be with you, and suffer you? Bring thy son hither.

Want of faith is an obstacle to abundance of graces. It is with great justice that Christ blames it, and that not without some indignation, after all which he had done to establish faith and confidence in his sovereign power. This reproach and emotion are not an effect of impatience, but a transport of zeal, which makes his long patience to be more particularly observed. It hereby evidently appears, that he did not seek his own satisfaction, when he continued so long with this faithless and perverse people. Who, after this, will suffer himself to be guided by his aversions or inclinations?

42. And as he was yet a coming, the devil threw him down, and tare *him*. And Jesus rebuked the unclean spirit, and healed the child, and delivered him again to his father.

When a soul is willing to be converted, the devil makes his last efforts; but Christ renders them ineffectual by his grace. Whatever he permits the devil to do against his elect, is only for the glory of his own grace, and to the confusion of the tempter. It is by his almighty power that he casts the devil out of the body and the soul, and puts his Spirit into possession of the heart of man. He need only exert one single act of his will, in order to make all things obey him; and no created will can hinder that which the Omnipotent will would have me do, by causing me to will it.

43. ¶ And they were all amazed at the mighty power of God. But while they wondered every one at all things which Jesus did, he said unto his disciples, 44. Let these sayings sink down into your ears:*

for the Son of man shall be delivered into the hands of men. [*Fr. Hearts.]

It is not enough to admire the effects of the mighty power of God; we must also apply ourselves to consider the sufferings of Christ, which are far more inconceivable to human understanding. Happy the child of the cross, who carries a livelier impression thereof in the bottom of his heart than in his memory! It is a thing extremely rare and uncommon, for us to endeavour to alter the minds of those who are intent on admiring us, by setting before their eyes whatever is most humbling, and tends to create the meanest opinion of us. The example which Christ gives us of this, is not very grateful to the children of Adam. To see a God suffer in the flesh, is something much more wonderful than to see him cast out devils by his Spirit. He delivers men from the power of the devil; and he suffers himself to be delivered into the hands of men: his power gives way to his love.

45. But they understood not this saying, and it was hid from them, that they perceived it not: and they feared to ask him of that saying.

How much above the understanding of man are the designs of God concerning the death of his Son! We must show more fidelity and humility in adoring them, than curiosity in desiring to pry into them. The carnal man does not willingly consider objects which exact of him great duties, and such as are grievous to nature. He who fears that he shall find in the passion of Christ an obligation to suffer, and to crucify the flesh with him, does not love to employ his thoughts on that mystery. Lord, deliver me from this carnal fear; and make me love to ask thee, and to inquire concerning this subject, by meditating upon thy Scriptures, and invoking thy Spirit by prayer.

SECT. VI.—HE WHO THINKS HIMSELF THE LEAST, IS THE GREATEST.—HE WHO IS NOT AGAINST CHRIST, IS FOR HIM.

46. ¶ Then there arose a reasoning among them, which of them should be greatest.

What blindness is it in the members of a head intent on nothing but humbling himself, to think of nothing but exalting themselves! Self-love must needs be strangely delighted with the thoughts of greatness, since men are not exempt from them in the very school of humility. Christ takes off his disciples from the consideration of his power, to fix their minds upon that of his humiliations; and they leave this profitable subject to think of their own greatness, and how to raise themselves above others. Lord, deliver me not up to this irregular inclination.

47. And Jesus, perceiving the thought of their heart, took a child, and set him by him.

Christian childhood obliges us to be humble, meek, and sincere. Man, in innocence, had God alone for his pattern, being created in his image: man, in a state of sin, is reduced to frame himself by a child, and to study him as his pattern, having by sin rendered himself like the very beasts themselves. Since, then, we ought to imitate a child, it is thy divine childhood, O Jesus, on which I will fix my eyes, not only as the pattern which I am to consider, but as the object which I ought to adore and love, which is to sanctify me, and in which I may certainly find the grace to imitate thee in that state and condition.

48. And said unto them, Whosoever shall receive this child in my name receiveth me; and whosoever shall receive me, receiveth him that sent me: for he that is least among you all, the same shall be great.

It is counted as nothing in this world to despise or treat those ill whom Christ represents under this figure; because God but seldom punishes or rewards in this life. They who have faith depend upon his word, and rest assured of his faithfulness. God is in Christ, and Christ in his members, who conform themselves to his inclinations with the docility of a child: he takes a particular care of them, and accepts in them all the good which is done to them. True greatness consists in humility; but it is a spiritual greatness, which carnal men do not understand,

49. ¶ And John answered and said, Master, we saw one casting out devils in thy name; and we forbade him, because he followeth not with us.

Holy persons in this life are not always free from a zeal without knowledge, nor from emulation in their conduct. Every one ought carefully to examine himself upon this point.

The name of Jesus Christ is powerful and terrible to the devil, even in the mouth of one who is a stranger to him. From the time when Christ first condescended to make use of such to work miracles as do not follow him, he condemns the jealousy and envy of his disciples. Religious societies, as well as private persons, have great reason to preserve themselves from this spirit, which makes them either faintly commend, or openly condemn, the good which is done by other societies. They are not settled in the church for their own glory, but for that of their Master.

50. And Jesus said unto him, Forbid *him* not: for he that is not against us is for us.

It is the part of true charity to love and to justify that which is good, in what place or person soever it is found. There is no neutrality for the heart in the kingdom of God: it must be either for Christ or for his enemy. It is not so as to the outward profession: a man may openly favour the church, and yet neither have anything of the spirit of it, nor belong at all to God.

SECT. VII.—JAMES AND JOHN ARE FOR CALLING DOWN FIRE FROM HEAVEN.

51. ¶ And it came to pass, when the time was come that he should be received up, he steadfastly set his face to go to Jerusalem,

That man knows himself but little who does not fortify himself, by faith and prayer, against temptation and the fear of sufferings, when he foresees them. The apprehension of death ought not in the least to discourage those who know that it is the way which leads to the heavenly Jerusalem. Let thy strength and steadfastness, O Jesus, fortify our weakness, and raise our drooping spirits at the prospect of that day which takes a true Christian out of this life, only to reunite him to thee, O life eternal, whom the Father has vouchsafed to give us.

52. And sent messengers before his face: and they went, and entered into a village of the Samaritans, to make ready for him. 53. And they did not receive him, because his face was as though he would go to Jerusalem.

Men have but little inclination to expose themselves to repulses, when they foresee them as our blessed Saviour did. He exposes both himself and his disciples to them, because he would accustom them thereto by his own example. Piety often renders us odious or disagreeable to those who have deserted it. Such conjectures are proper to acquaint us thoroughly with ourselves, and to satisfy us whether we really seek God, and desire to please none but him. When we have once taken the road to heaven, we have but little credit any longer in the world. Nothing can give us a greater assurance that we are in the way of salvation, than to see ourselves despised and rejected of those who will not think of any other life. God frequently separates us from such persons by means of some repulses and disgusts, without which we should have continued always fond of them.

54. And when his disciples James and John saw *this*, they said, Lord, wilt thou that we command fire to come down from heaven, and consume them, even as Elias did?

It often happens, that the ministers of the church, under pretence of zeal for her interests, offend against Christian meekness. The church knows no such thing as revenge, and her ministers ought not to know it either. Their wrath should be incensed against sin, not against the sinner. The fire of heaven is one day to come down to purify the world by destruction: at present, it comes down only to sanctify it by edification. We must consult God, and address ourselves to Christ, in order to know our duty, and to learn to moderate our zeal.

55. But he turned, and rebuked them, and said, Ye know not what manner of spirit ye are of.

The growing cold on the account of ill usage, and, much more, sharpness and bitterness of mind, are not according to the Spirit of Christ. The disciples of a God who dies for his enemies, ought to think of nothing but laying down their lives for those very persons who do them harm: so far must they be from revenging themselves on those who only refuse to do them good. God permits the inclinations of concupiscence to appear sometimes in the holiest persons, on purpose that they may acknowledge that charity is a gift of God; and that all the world may plainly see, that there is no person whatever in whom nature is not corrupted.

56. For the Son of man is not come to destroy men's lives, but to save *them*. And they went to another village.

The spirit of the new law is a spirit of meekness and charity. The ministers of the church ought always to remember, that they are the disciples of him who came only to do good, and that their ministry is a ministry of salvation. Nothing is more distant from his Spirit, than for a man to make use of authority, force, or violence, to enter upon a benefice, or to settle himself in a city, only under pretence of doing good there: Christ having not thought fit to oblige even a single village to receive him in his necessity, and having blamed his apostles upon somewhat of the like nature.

SECT. VIII.—THE MAN WHO WOULD HAVE FOLLOWED CHRIST. —WE MUST NOT LOOK BACK.

57. ¶ And it came to pass, that, as they went in the way, a certain *man* said unto him, Lord, I will follow the whithersoever thou goest.

Human presumption undertakes and embraces every thing with eagerness, and thinks nothing too difficult. Christian humility has for its foundation the acknowledgment of a man's own inability as to every thing which is good, a belief of the necessity of grace in order to perform it, a conviction of his own unworthiness to receive this assistance, and a firm hope in the free mercy of God, and in the grace of Jesus Christ.

58. And Jesus said unto him, Foxes have holes, and birds of the air *have* nests; but the Son of man hath not where to lay *his* head.

Abundance of persons seem to seek Jesus Christ, who only, under his name, seek ease, honour, self-satisfaction, the conveniences of life, etc. If they find that which they seek, it will be only to their greater condemnation. The poverty of Christ, is the patrimony of those who make profession of following him in the way of perfection. All his true children ought to love, honour, and imitate it, in some measure at least, and to have their hearts prepared for it. They are unworthy to serve him, who seek other things in his service. O Jesus, Saviour of men, how few are there who honour thy poverty, in bearing it with thy Spirit; not to reckon those who fly from it, and have it in abhorrence! Cause us, Lord, by the power of thy grace, to love this virtue.

59. And he said unto another, Follow me. But he said, Lord, suffer me first to go and bury my father.

Fondness for relations is an obstacle to salvation. Christ rejects the person who desired to follow him, and draws him who was for delaying it; to teach us that his will and grace ought to fix our call, and not our own choice and appointment. Self-love never wants pious pretences to excuse itself, with some decency, from doing the will of God. Happy that person whom God does not abandon to the resistance and opposition which he makes to the grace of his call!

60. Jesus said unto him, let the dead bury their dead; but go thou and preach the kingdom of God.

The ministers of the church cannot be too often told that they should leave the world to the people of the world. When the heart is sincere, and nothing hinders from entering into the way which Christ shows us, but only the fear of being wanting in some pious offices, he soon makes us surmount this obstacle. When God accompanies his external word and commandment with the unction of his Spirit, and the internal power of his grace, it works in the heart that obedience which it requires. It is as dangerous not to preach the kingdom of God when a man is called to that office, as it is to intrude himself into it of his own accord. It is not complying with the designs of God either way.

61. And another also said, Lord, I will follow thee; but let me first go bid them farewell, which are at home at my house.

Self-love always finds something to lay hold of, in order to maintain itself in its liberty. The devil thinks he has gained enough, in making a man defer the good which he cannot altogether prevent. We run a very great risk in not doing the works of God at the very time when he requires them to be done. The devil desires only a little time; and a voluntary delay involves us frequently in difficulties which are involuntary, and out of which we shall perhaps never be able to extricate ourselves. God certainly well deserves to be obeyed without the least delay. That which we object to the execution of his designs, is sometimes the very thing from which he would chiefly disengage and set us loose.

62. And Jesus said unto him, No man, having put his hand to the plough, and looking back, is fit for the kingdom of God.

How dangerous a return is it for a man to seek the world again, after he has once quitted it! If to have still a fondness and affection for things in themselves indifferent be to look back, how criminal is the pursuit of worldly desires in those who are consecrated to God! Pastors who still retain some claims and pretensions to the world, cannot be faithful ministers. A man is a slave to the world from the time that he stands in need of it. He who thinks it necessary to cultivate its favour, is not far from betraying the interests of God and the church.

CHAPTER X.

SECT. I.—THE MISSION AND INSTRUCTION OF THE SEVENTY DISCIPLES.—THE IMPENITENT CITIES.

1. After these things the Lord appointed other seventy also, and sent them two and two before his face, into every city and place, whither he himself would come.

Christ sends his disciples two and two, to teach them to labour in the church in the spirit of concord and charity. The office of priest is to prepare men to receive Jesus Christ. He who prepares the will of sinners himself, by turning it as he pleases with an almighty facility, has no need of the ministry of his servants; but his design is, to join the members of his body one to another by a mutual dependence, and to give to his church a form of government suited to its present state upon earth.

2. Therefore said he unto them, The harvest truly *is* great, but the labourers *are* few: pray ye therefore the Lord of the harvest, that he would send forth labourers into his harvest.

A man must not of his own accord run to the harvest; but he must pray the Lord of the harvest, that he would send forth labourers, and must be himself disposed to labour. This person complains of negligent pastors and scandalous ministers, who might perhaps have turned away this judgment from the church, had he but prayed as he ought. When we see any of that profession corrupt and disorderly, let us descend into ourselves, and attribute it to our own sins and negligence. The church is obedient to this command of our blessed Lord when it prescribes fasts and prayers. Let us join with her, and with her offer up our fasts, our prayers, and our groans.

3. Go your ways: behold, I send you forth as lambs among wolves.

Lambs among wolves are the disciples of Christ amid the people of the world, in order to convert them, more by labour, patience, good example, meekness, and charity, than by the word itself. It belongs to thee, O Lamb without blemish, who didst deliver thyself up to wolves, and who changest at thy pleasure wolves into lambs,—it belongs to thee to guard both the pastors and lambs of thy flock from those wolves who assault them, either openly or in sheep's clothing.

4. Carry neither purse, nor scrip, nor shoes; and salute no man by the way.

Christ puts the trust and confidence of his ministers to all imaginable trials, that they may learn once for all to depend entirely upon God in whatever relates to their ministry, and to rely on none but him. In order to be a true evangelical minister, a man must be fond of nothing, not even of life itself; he must be always ready to expose it to wolves, and to neglect, when God requires it, the ordinary means of preserving it, but never taken up with the care of making friends on purpose to procure them.

5. And into whatsoever house ye enter, first say, Peace *be* to this house.

Christian peace is the greatest good which we can wish to our neighbour. This is the wealth which the truly poor in Christ's account distribute in all places. Those who enter into houses, and creep into families, only to make divisions and to profit thereby, are very unworthy of so sacred a ministry. No house is to be excluded from this blessing, not even that of an enemy.

6. And if the son of peace be there, your peace shall rest upon it: if not, it shall turn to you again.

God would have the word of peace delivered to all, though all be not children of peace and of the promise. It belongs not to men to make this distinction; it is hid in God from all eternity, and shall be entirely made manifest at the end of the world. An evangelical labourer turns every thing to advantage, as well the hardness and impenitence of some as the fidelity and obedience of others.

7. And in the same house remain, eating and drinking such things as they give: for the labourer is worthy of his hire. Go not from house to house.

To maintain the ministers of the church is according to divine and natural right; but they themselves are not to make use of it, but only with edification, and in the spirit of poverty. That man who uses the credit which the gospel gives him in order to procure good entertainment, well deserves to have no other reward. He always finds sufficient who seeks no more than the necessaries of life: it is only sensuality which is never satisfied. A labourer in the gospel must expect at the hands of men no other recompense but a comfortable subsistence: that which he expects from God is neither sensible nor temporal.

8. And into whatsoever city ye enter, and they receive you, eat such things as are set before you:

An evangelical labourer, to satisfy the necessities of life, may make use of all such things as are set before him, and are not forbidden, provided it be done without either eagerness or affection. If a missionary, a pastor or a preacher, do not show a great indifferency toward every thing which relates to bodily wants, he will never be able much to advance the work of God. He ought to imitate his Master, who preached up the contempt of these things by contemning them himself.

9. And heal the sick that are therein, and say unto them, The kingdom of God is come nigh unto you.

The shepherd and Bishop of souls takes great care to recommend the joining, as much as possible, temporal relief with spiritual. He never sent his disciples to do the least hurt to men, but always to do them good. The conquerors of the earth destroy all with fire and sword, to render themselves masters of the kingdoms of others; the Son of God sends his ministers, with no other intent but freely to offer his kingdom to all men, and to oblige them to accept it by all sorts of benefits. This kingdom is come nigh unto us: we have but one step to make. Let us only pass from the love of ourselves to the love of God, and his kingdom is our own.

10. But into whatsoever city ye enter, and they receive you not, go your ways out into the streets of the same, and say, 11. Even the very dust of your city, which cleaveth on us, we do wipe off against you: notwithstanding, be ye sure of this, that the kingdom of God is come nigh unto you.

Miserable is that person who receives not the truth nor the wholesome admonitions which are given him. To be deprived of the word of God, and of the assistance of his ministers, is a punishment which is so much the greater, as it is less sensible to sinners. Let us fear and tremble, lest the truth, which is preached to us as a means of salvation, should, through the hardness of our hearts, become a testimony against us.

12. But I say unto you, that it shall be more tolerable in that day for Sodom, than for that city.

Since the rejecting of the truth and the maxims of the gospel is more severely punished than the greatest crimes, let us take great care that we do not shut our heart against some of them. Christ being the only refuge of sinners, whoever rejects him, and refuses to have him for his Saviour, what other refuge can he promise himself? The men of Sodom made an attempt only against angels; the Jews against Jesus Christ whilst he was passible and mortal; but wicked Christians do this against him in his glorious and immortal state: how much more rigorously, therefore, will the divine justice be executed against Christians, who abuse Jesus Christ and his blood, and despise his graces?

13. Woe unto thee, Chorazin! woe unto thee, Bethsaida! for if the mighty works had been done in Tyre and Sidon, which have been done in you, they had a great while ago repented, sitting in sackcloth and ashes.

It is an adorable abyss of the divine judgments, that the

gospel should be preached to those who were to reject it, and not to those who would certainly have repented. Where is the merit upon which heretics pretend that God regulates the distribution of his favours and graces? Let us acknowledge that he distributes them according to a method full of wisdom and power, in the causes and reasons whereof we are altogether ignorant.

14. But it shall be more tolerable for Tyre and Sidon at the judgment, than for you.

The impenitency of the Jews is punished in proportion to the favours which they received; the same conduct will be used toward private persons. The knowledge of God's law is a blessing for which we ought to return him the greatest thanks; and yet, if we make not a good use of this blessing, it becomes the occasion of a more dreadful vengeance. The more light and knowledge we have received, the more ought we to fear and to humble ourselves; because, without a grace of heart and will, our will, left to itself, will certainly abuse this knowledge.

15. And thou, Capernaum, which art exalted to heaven, shalt be thrust down to hell.

The higher sinners are exalted in this world, the lower shall they be thrust down and humbled in hell. A state of great elevation is a very dangerous one; because the falls from thence are seldom very light. That is a very blind joy which proceeds from seeing ourselves, our relations, or our friends advanced to higher stations or great power. The fear of falling from them, which arises from an irregular love of grandeur and advancement itself, is the fear of reprobates; but the fear of keeping them to the day of our death, even though God should call upon us to forsake them, and of falling from thence into an eternal abyss of misery, is the fear of a Christian, who loves his salvation above every thing, and sees the danger of being lost in a state wherein there is so much opposition to the humility of the gospel.

16. He that heareth you heareth me; and he that despiseth you despiseth me; and he that despiseth me despiseth him that sent me.

How extremely dangerous is it not to hear those who

speak to us on the part of God, and not to obey the pastors who conduct us in his name! It is one and the same truth, which is in the Father by his essence, in the Son by his eternal generation, in the apostles by divine, and in the bishops by apostolical tradition. So long as this trust is kept inviolable, in hearing these, we hear the Father and the Son. The pastoral authority which, as well as the truth, has God himself for its fountain, is communicated to the Son by the mission of his Father, that is, by his incarnation; to the apostles by the mission of the Son; and to the bishops by succession: an authority always venerable.

SECT. II.—THE RETURN OF THE DISCIPLES.—NAMES WRITTEN IN HEAVEN.—MYSTERIES HID FROM THE WISE.

17. ¶ And the seventy returned again with joy, saying, Lord, even the devils are subject unto us through thy name.

It is a thing very extraordinary, for men not to take too much complacency in the success of those works which God performs by their hands. The apostles themselves are not proof against it. Every state of superiority is dangerous for those who have from Adam inherited a desire to distinguish themselves from others, and to bear rule. One is ready enough to own that all success is the gift of God; but the delight and complacency one is apt to take in having this gift preferable to others, and the joy of being taken notice of by men on this account, are deplorable effects of self-love.

18. And he said unto them, I beheld Satan as lightning fall from heaven.

What dreadful fall is this! but how common is it in the church! How many angels, on the account of their ministry, of the purity of their life, and of the eminency of their grace, fall from heaven by their infidelity? and we tremble not! God knows how to make us find sufficient cause of humiliation in those very things from which we take occasion to be puffed up. If grace is not in a state of security in heaven in an angel, who will not tremble upon earth, since he carries this treasure in so weak a vessel?

19. Behold, I give unto you power to tread on serpents and scorpions,

and over all the power of the enemy; and nothing shall by any means hurt you.

The benedictions, etc. of the church are founded upon this declaration of the Son of God, which is, as it were, her title. The prayers of the church are a sort of public archives, in which her titles and powers are kept; and the abuse which may be made of them cannot do them any prejudice. The want of piety and the negligence of ministers, and the want of faith in Christians, hinder the effects of this power. It is the shame of some of the sons and daughters of the church, that they choose rather to put their trust in superstitious and ineffectual means, than to have recourse with faith to that power which Christ here gave unto her.

20. Notwithstanding, in this rejoice not, that the spirits are subject unto you; but rather rejoice, because your names are written in heaven.

Let us not rejoice in the great and extraordinary gifts of God, but only in his mercy toward us. That which may be in common both to good and bad, and which was given to Judas as well as to the other apostles, is not a proper subject of our joy. It is but a small matter for us to deliver the bodies of others from the power of the evil spirit, if he remain master of our heart by means of our passions. When the love of God is written in our hearts by his Spirit, and in our hands by good works, we ought then to have this confidence, that our names are written in heaven as heirs of eternal life.

21. ¶ In that hour Jesus rejoiced in spirit, and said, I thank thee, O Father, Lord of heaven and earth, that thou hast hid these things from the wise and prudent, and hast revealed them unto babes: even so, Father; for so it seemed good in thy sight.

Let us follow the inclinations of Christ's heart; let us make that our joy which is his. Let us rejoice with him at the contemplation of the designs of his Father in relation to mankind. Let us adore what he adores: these mysteries hidden from the wise and prudent; this conduct which is so adorable, and adored by Christ himself. Nothing is worthy of our joy any more than of his, but that only which makes known to us the destruction of the kingdom of the devil, and the advancement of the kingdom of God in his church. It was the consolation of our blessed Saviour, amid his afflictions, and upon the prospect of his sufferings and death, to converse with his Father upon the subject of his designs toward his elect; for whom are all things, and who are the fruit of his sacrifice. Every thing relating to this subject is worthy of the joy, adoration, acknowledgment, and contemplation of the Son of God, particularly the magnificence of his gracious designs, the election of those in whom he intends to accomplish them, and the means he employs to that end, though to the eyes of men they seem but weakness, meanness, and folly. Nothing is more worthy of the majesty of God, than to raise a mere nothing up to himself, and to do it by the abasement of the Creator, and the humiliation of the creature after his example.

22. All things are delivered to me of my Father: and no man knoweth who the Son is, but the Father; and who the Father is, but the Son, and *he* to whom the Son will reveal *him.*

Observe here, power, knowledge, and love, (for in God to will is to love:) the three principles which produced the church, and every thing which contributes to the framing of it, namely, authority, truth, and charity. They are, as it were, divided in God by his personal properties, reunited in Christ by the incarnation, and communicated to the church. The Son alone, from all eternity, receives the authority of the Father by a generation, the principle whereof is the truth subsisting, and productive of the consubstantial love of the Father and the Son, which is the Holy Ghost. All things are delivered to Christ by his incarnation and temporal mission; for God was in Christ reconciling the world to himself, and communicated himself, and wrought by Jesus Christ, according to these three properties, which the Christian religion represents, adores, and imitates. Every thing therefore ought to pay homage thereto. Every hierarchical action in the pastors ought to be an act of authority, truth, and charity. Every Christian action in the faithful, an act of homage and obedience to the authority, truth, and love of God, and such as has nothing in it contrary to them. Every thing is performed in the church in the way of paternal and pastoral authority; in the way of knowledge revealed, of truth taught, and of the word preached by a particular mission; and in the way of love inspired, of grace freely dispensed, and of ministries distributed according to the will and call of the divine Spirit, and received with submission, adoration, and gratitude toward the adorable Trinity and the personal properties thereof.

23. ¶ And he turned him unto *his* disciples, and said privately, Blessed *are* the eyes which see the things that ye see:

Blessed is that person who, with Christian eyes, with the eyes of faith, sees that which the Jews saw only with carnal eyes—namely, the Mediator and way of our salvation, the victim of our reconciliation, the author and finisher of our faith, and the principle of all grace, of all perfect love, and of every good thing in us. Take from me, O Lord, those eyes which, seeing, see not. Give me the eyes of the heart, which, in seeing, love, obey, and imitate thee, and are continually fixed upon thee, as the eyes of servants look unto the hand of their masters.

24. For I tell you, that many prophets and kings have desired to see those things which ye see, and have not seen *them;* and to hear those things which ye hear, and have not heard *them.*

What have we done for God to deserve this preference? He prevented all our desires, by giving himself to us (before ever we could so much as think of him) in giving us his Son, of whom the prophets, kings, and patriarchs saw nothing but the types and shadows. O beneficial gift to every one who makes use of it to promote his own salvation, by taking him for the rule of his life, imitating him as his pattern, having recourse to him by humble and persevering prayer, and depending upon him in all things! But a very fatal gift to every one who makes no use at all of it! If it were a happiness to see Jesus Christ in the infirmity and humility of his flesh, what a happiness must it be to see him in his glory, to possess him in eternity, to live his life, to be transported with his joy, inebriated, as it were, with his pleasures, and blessed with his very felicity!

SECT. III.—THE LOVE OF GOD AND OF OUR NEIGHBOUR.

25. ¶ And, behold, a certain lawyer stood up, and tempted him, saying, Master, what shall I do to inherit eternal life?

How many times have we, like this lawyer, tempted God

in prayer! We often beg of him to instruct us in his will, as if we really intended to do it, while, at the same time, we neglect to do that which we know of it already. There are but too many who place the best part of their devotion in asking questions, and hearing a spiritual guide or director, concerning those things which they sufficiently understand; and who waste both his time and their own in such discourses as are of little or no advantage at all. The gospel would save them abundance of this trouble, if they would but therein sincerely consult the truth itself, and practise that which they know.

26. He said unto him, What is written in the law? how readest thou?

Jesus Christ himself refers us to the law of God, though he was truth in itself, and could give such holy instructions. In vain do we seek after other lights and ways besides those which we find there. It is the Spirit of God which dictated the law, and made it the rule of our life; it is injurious to him for us either not to study it, or to prefer the thoughts of men before it. The first question which will be put to a Christian at the tribunal of God will be to this effect,—"What is written in the law? What have you read in the gospel? What use have you made thereof?" What answer can that person return, who has not so much as read it, though he has had sufficient ability and opportunity to do it?

27. And he answering said, Thou shalt love the Lord thy God with all thy heart, and with all thy soul, and with all thy strength, and with all thy mind; and thy neighbour as thyself.

Our heart and our time ought not to be divided in the love of God. Whatever is in man, and belongs to him, ought to be referred ultimately thereto. We must love our neighbour as we love ourselves, when we love God and ourselves only for God's sake. Christ does not command the love of our neighbour till after he has commanded and explained the love of God, without which the rule which he gives would be false. If the love of God be not the prevailing principle and motive, in the use we make of our mind, our will, our senses, talents, health, strength, etc., we are deficient in the observation of this precept.

28. And he said unto him, Thou hast answered right: this do, and thou shalt live.

Do this in me, O Lord, and then I shall do it; cause me to live, and I shall live: for without thee I can do nothing, (John xv. 5;) and it belongs to thee to make me perfect in every good work, doing in me thyself that which cannot be well-pleasing in thy Father's sight but through thee alone, (Heb. xiii. 21.) To live without charity is not properly living; and charity itself does not live long without good works. True piety does not consist in knowledge, but in practice; and that knowledge of which we make no use, will serve only to our condemnation.

29. But he, willing to justify himself, said unto Jesus, And who is my neighbour?

The more a sinner endeavours to justify himself before God, the more he condemns himself. A man must be very vainly puffed up with learning, not to know who is his neighbour; for he who knows not this, knows nothing of charity. My God, how much is learning to be dreaded, when charity does not render it useful, edifying, holy, religious, mindful of Christ, who is our chief neighbour, of the church as his spouse, and of our brethren as his members!

SECT. IV.—THE PARABLE OF THE SAMARITAN.

30. And Jesus answering said, A certain *man* went down from Jerusalem to Jericho, and fell among thieves, which stripped him of his raiment, and wounded *him*, and departed, leaving *him* half dead.

This man, fallen among thieves, is an emblem of the deplorable condition of a sinner, who having withdrawn himself from being under the hand of God, and from his dependence on him, is fallen into that of the devil, has lost the state of original innocency, and is banished from the heavenly Jerusalem, sinking gradually every day into the lowest abyss of misery, being stripped of righteousness, grace, immortality, and of all the gifts of God, covered with the wounds of sin and concupiscence, full of ignorance and infirmity, unable to do any good, capable of all evil, and having no longer any thing left but only hope in Jesus Christ and in his grace, which keeps him from being altogether dead, and past recovery, as the rebellious angels are.

31. And by chance there came down a certain priest that way; and when he saw him, he passed by on the other side.

Neither Moses nor Aaron, neither the priests nor the saints of the natural law, neither the patriarchs nor the prophets, were able to repair lost man. They saw and felt the wounds of sin, but could not heal them; and they passed their whole life without seeing the salvation of the world, except only in hope. No, my Saviour, there is no man like myself who can give me the least relief: thou alone, O God-man, art my only refuge.

32. And likewise a Levite, when he was at the place, came and looked *on him*, and passed by on the other side.

Let us observe and acknowledge in this Levite the inability of the law, and of the ancient sacrifices, to expiate the guilt, or to heal the wound of sin. The law makes it known by forbidding it; and by this very means is an occasion of exciting and increasing it, so far is it from weakening it or stopping its course. The whole time of the law passed away, without making any thing but transgressors of the law of all those in whom the grace of Christ did not act beforehand and by way of anticipation.

33. But a certain Samaritan, as he journeyed, came where he was; and when he saw him, he had compassion *on him*.

Jesus Christ, the true Samaritan, a stranger to us before the incarnation, separate from sinners, and journeying, as it were, among us by becoming man, vouchsafed to look upon sinful man, grovelling on the earth, and wounded in every part. O Saviour and Guardian of my soul, cease not to cast thy eyes upon it, to observe its wounds, and to have compassion on its miseries!

34. And went to *him*, and bound up his wounds, pouring in oil and wine, and set him on his own beast, and brought him to an inn, and took care of him.

The Son of God unites to and takes upon himself the sinner and his sins, in order to cure them; pours into his wounded heart his healing, smooth, strong, and delicious grace; binds up his wounds with the bands of his commandments, and brings him into his church. No merit or desert of ours drew down upon us the assistance of our blessed Saviour, to whom we were strangers, and even enemies, when he undertook to save us. Teach us, Lord, to do good indifferently to everybody, and to do it gently and efficaciously, without sparing any thing which may be serviceable either to the body or the soul.

35. And on the morrow when he departed, he took out two pence, and gave *them* to the host, and said unto him, Take care of him: and whatsoever thou spendest more, when I come again, I will repay thee. 36.
Which now of these three, thinkest thou, was neighbour unto him that fell among the thieves?

Happy is that man whom God brings off from the highway where he was wounded, and places in the inn—namely, in the church on earth, where we remain as travellers and strangers till we are perfectly cured. It is in this house of unity that God has left the two pence of truth and charity, to be employed by his ministers toward the salvation of souls until his return. The church is the house of salvation. The labours of faithful ministers will certainly be rewarded by Christ, provided they have laboured by his appointment, for his sake, and by his Spirit. It is till the time of his coming again, that is, till the last judgment, that this reward is reserved.

37. And he said, He that shewed mercy on him. Then said Jesus unto him, Go, and do thou likewise.

Our neighbour is he who stands in need of our assistance, let him be what he will. Blood, interest, friendship, inclination, or vain generosity, are but private and selfish motives: the common ties of nature, and those of grace, are the things which ought to give us a common satisfaction or concern for the happiness or misery of other men. Mercy is a natural debt, not a service which is arbitrary and left to our own discretion. The being miserable is sufficient to give a man a right to the mercy of his neighbour.

SECT. V.—MARTHA AND MARY.—THE ONE THING NECESSARY.

38. ¶ Now it came to pass, as they went, that he entered into a certain village: and a certain woman named Martha received him into her house. 39. And she had a sister called Mary, which also sat at Jesus's
feet, and heard his word.

Martha is the emblem of an active life, busied about things

relating to our neighbour, through the necessity of charity; and Mary her sister is that of a contemplative life, which is intent only on God, through the love of truth.. These two kinds of life ought to be united, like two sisters, in a Christian. It is the lot and portion of a son or daughter of the church to hear Jesus Christ in prayer, and in reading his word, with silence, humility, peace of mind, assiduity, disengagement from all business, and with a holy eagerness of desire. Happy portion this, for persons to pass their life at Jesus' feet, when God does not call them to any other employment!

40. But Martha was cumbered about much serving, and came to him, and said, Lord, dost thou not care that my sister hath left me to serve alone? bid her therefore that she help me.

Happy is the house wherein Martha calls Mary to her assistance, and where prayer and love of retirement sanctify labour and external occupations! It would be a very great misfortune and disorder indeed, if Mary should envy Martha; if one should prefer the noise and hurry of business before the quietness of silence and solitude, of prayer and attendance upon God. It is a very considerable grace for a man to be sensible of the weight and danger of outward employments, and upon this consideration to complain of them before God, without envying the grace of another. Though our labour have God, Christ, and the church for its end, yet it is apt to distract and dry up the heart, and to cause murmuring, when it is not undertaken in the spirit of mortification and submission to the will of God. Martha does well in calling Mary to her assistance: prayer ought to support labour. It is common for ministers who are truly the servants of God to complain of the difficulty of recollecting themselves, and that they find their minds subject to distractions in prayer.

41. And Jesus answered and said unto her, Martha, Martha, thou art careful and troubled about many things:

The more active our temper is, the more watchful ought we to be over ourselves, even in the employments of charity, lest we be troubled and distracted thereby. We must avoid hurry and eagerness in acting: this generally proceeds from that great desire which men have of success, which is always seeking to satisfy itself, to avoid blame, and to acquire praise by satisfying others. That activity which the Spirit of God inspires is quiet and peaceable, because it submits itself to God, and desires nothing but his will. Trouble proceeds from hence, that we would willingly do more, or in another manner, than we are able, and that we would fain distinguish ourselves.

42. But one thing is needful; and Mary hath chosen that good part, which shall not be taken away from her.

The one thing needful is to live for God. That which regards only the life of the body and the present world is not absolutely necessary, since it is, on the contrary, necessary for us to wean ourselves from them both, and sometimes even to sacrifice the former. Nothing is necessary but what is either eternal, or leads to eternity. Martha's employment is good; but that of Mary is better, because she begins here below that which she is to do in heaven. Deliver us, O Lord, from those necessities which proceed only from concupiscence, and likewise from every thing which stifles the spirit of prayer, withdraws us from the presence of God, and hinders us from following that which alone is truly necessary.

CHAPTER XI.

SECT. I.—THE LORD'S PRAYER.

1. And it came to pass, that, as he was praying in a certain place, when he ceased, one of his disciples said unto him, Lord, teach us to pray, as John also taught his disciples.

By this example we may understand how profitable and edifying public prayer is in the church, or in common in families. God often affixes great blessings to a good example; this is a debt which is owing from masters of families, and from all superiors, to those who are under their care or have any dependence upon them. Pastors are obliged, in relation to prayer, to give not only example, but also instruction, in imitation of Jesus Christ and John. One single person, being moved and edified by this good example of our Lord, conceives a love for prayer, desires to know how to pray, is sensible that of himself he is not capable of doing it, addresses himself to Christ, obtains from him this divine pattern, procures this treasure for the rest of the disciples and for the whole church, and becomes the occasion of the infinite good which this prayer has produced, and will produce therein, to the end of the world. A person must needs have prayed very much himself, to be able to teach others to pray. It belongs properly to none but the God-man to teach how God would be prayed to by man.

2. And he said unto them, When ye pray, say, Our Father which art in heaven, Hallowed be thy name.

The Lord's Prayer is an abridgment of religion, and contains the object and duties thereof. The order of our petitions shows the order of our desires, and the order of our desires that of our love, in which the true worship of God does consist. God, who is Father of the eternal truth, and, together with his Son, the principle from whence the Holy Ghost proceeds, will be served by children, not by slaves, will be worshipped in spirit and in truth, and sought after for the sake of himself, and for the sanctification of his name. The first motive, then, of our actions, and the first desire of our heart, is the glory of God in this world by the reign of grace and the sanctification of souls.

— Thy kingdom come.

The second motive of our actions and desire of our heart is, the coming of the kingdom of God by his glory, which will be the perfection of the divine adoption, the fulness of the knowledge of God and Christ, the consummation of holiness and charity, the perfect establishment of the kingdom of God by the union of all the elect to their Head, and by completing the whole mystical body in God to all eternity.

— Thy will be done, as in heaven, so in earth. 3. Give us day by day our daily bread.

The third motive of our actions and desire of our heart ought to be, that of our own sanctification and of the assistance of God. Grace is the bread of a Christian, as glory is his patrimony; and he ought to esteem, desire, and pray for grace, in the same proportion that he desires the glory to which it leads. The bread of the body and of the soul is whatever is necessary to the nourishment of both. A poor traveller begs his bread every day, and eats only to strengthen himself for his journey. Let us also, like travellers, beg ours, and let us hasten toward the country where we shall be filled with the bread of God without having any occasion to ask for it.

4. And forgive us our sins; for we also forgive every one that is indebted to us.

The fourth motive of our actions and desire of our heart is, that of the forgiveness of our sins and of the mercy of God. It is not sufficient for a traveller to have his provisions ready, and to be plentifully fed; he must remove all impediments which may either stop or retard his journey; he must pay his debts, finish all his suits at law, and agree with all his adversaries. It is easy for a good Christian to do all this. Charity alone does it for him, if he has but that in his heart; and if he has it not, let him not cease to seek and beg it of Him who never fails to give it to every one who asks it as he ought.

— And lead us not into temptation; but deliver us from evil.

The fifth and last motive of our actions and desire of our heart is, that of perseverance in the love of God above all things. Let us always remember that we travel in a country where every place is full of enemies and of great dangers. A traveller is generally afraid of those who may rob him of his money. How comes it to pass, then, that a Christian is under so little apprehension of losing grace, which is his whole treasure and subsistence? This alone renders him unworthy to preserve and keep it. So far as we esteem and know the value of it, so far are we careful to watch and pray, lest it should be taken away from us by temptation. To pray not to be led into temptation, is to pray for the gift of perseverance. And how careful ought we to be in endeavouring to obtain a gift upon which our eternal happiness depends, and which we deserve so much the less to receive the more we are persuaded that we do deserve it, and the less solicitous we are to obtain it! Lord, I expect it from thy pure mercy alone. I do not ask not to be tempted at all, but that I may meet with the temptations only of thy elect, which serve to increase their love toward thee, and cause them to cleave unto thee with the greater steadfastness.

SECT. II.—THREE LOAVES BORROWED.—ASK, SEEK, KNOCK.

5. And he said unto them, Which of you shall have a friend, and shall go unto him at midnight, and say unto him, Friend, lend me three loaves;

How great is the advantage and privilege of a Christian, who prays, not to a friend, but to a Father, and a Father who does not wait for our soliciting him, but presses us himself to ask him; who has no difficult moments or unseasonable hours, but whom we find ready at all times, not barely to lend, but even to give, and that not only more than we deserve, but more than we ask or could presume to ask. The bread of the mind is truth; the bread of the heart is to do the will of God; the bread of the whole man is Jesus Christ and his grace: give us, Lord, these three, and never cease to give them.

6. For a friend of mine in his journey is come to me, and I have nothing to set before him:

The friend whom we ought to love most is our soul: it is in a journey from the very time that it is united to the body, and comes into the world; and it finds here nothing but poverty, indigence, and infirmity. It is to thee, O my God, that I have recourse in behalf of my soul; for I have nothing to set before it. Thou hast been pleased to give it the life of faith: vouchsafe likewise to nourish it with hope, and to strengthen and support it by charity.

7. And he from within shall answer and say, Trouble me not: the door is now shut, and my children are with me in bed: I cannot rise and give thee.

The importunity and violence which we use toward God in prayer, are very grateful to him; or rather, we never properly offer any violence at all to him, but when we force him to refuse us by rendering ourselves unworthy to receive his gifts. The door of his mercy is always open during this life. He, from within his house, which is heaven, hears those who pray on earth. The supreme rest and happiness which he enjoys in himself with his saints, does not make him insensible to our pains and miseries; and he need not quit the least part of that happiness in order to assist and relieve us. Rise, Lord, and behold the weariness, hunger, and wants of this poor traveller.

8. I say unto you, Though he will not rise and give him, because he is his friend, yet because of his importunity he will rise and give him as many as he needeth.

Perseverance in prayer obtains every thing. The odd conduct and irregular behaviour of worldly people serve for the instruction of the righteous, to whom charity makes every thing useful and advantageous. Man is hard-hearted even to his friends, when it must cost him something to assist them; because most commonly it is only either his own satisfaction, or his interest, which he loves in them. God does good to all, because he is goodness itself, because he communicates his good things without diminishing them, because he works in all things without being wearied, and because he loves without the least interest.

9. And I say unto you, Ask, and it shall be given you; seek, and ye shall find; knock, and it shall be opened unto you.

A man, in order to offer up a good prayer, must ask with the humility of a beggar, he must seek with the carefulness of a good servant, and he must knock with the confidence of a friend. It is either through pride, hard-heartedness, or want of power, that men suffer themselves to be importuned by others, and make them wait for their gifts so long: God does it out of kindness, wisdom, and love, and in order to the more plentiful effusion of his gifts and mercies, since he himself engages to form in us the piety, perseverance, and other dispositions of prayer, and to proportion thereto the magnificence of his gifts and the abundance of his graces.

10. For every one that asketh receiveth; and he that seeketh findeth; and to him that knocketh it shall be opened.

It is by charity that we must ask, seek, and knock; it is by this that we obtain every thing; it is by this that we make a good and persevering use of any gift already received. When we do not receive that which we ask, let us always believe either that we do not ask it as we ought, or that it is good for us not to receive it. We must receive refusals from God as gifts with adoration and thanksgiving, because it is really a great gift for us not to receive that which he foresees we would abuse, and the abuse of which would incense his wrath against us.

11. If a son shall ask bread of any of you that is a father, will he give him a stone? or if *he ask* a fish, will he for a fish give him a serpent?

Let us never fear that God will give us a stone instead of bread; but let us fear lest we ourselves should change the bread of God into a stone, by the hardness of our own heart. Whoever receives the sacrament without profit, and eats and drinks the representative body and blood of Christ without being nourished by them, he changes the bread of heaven into a stone. Judas received them into his mouth, and the serpent entered into his heart, because he received them with the heart of a serpent.

12. Or if he shall ask an egg, will he offer him a scorpion?

What ought we not then to expect from so good a Father as God is in relation to us? And how can his gifts possibly do us any hurt, so long as we take care to keep our heart sound and good? The Scripture may be compared to an egg, which we must open in order to discover the truths of religion therein contained, and on which a good heart feeds, taking it with the salt of wisdom and discretion. Heretics and libertines find therein that which poisons them, because they have the heart of a scorpion.

13. If ye then, being evil, know how to give good gifts unto your children; how much more shall *your* heavenly Father give the Holy* Spirit to them that ask him? [**Fr.* Good.]

It is the goodness of God which is the fountain of all his gifts. The good Spirit is the Spirit of love, which God urges us to ask of him. This is the only gift which in itself is worthy of God, and of those to whom he has already vouchsafed to give his Son. There is nothing which we ought to ask more frequently and earnestly than this; and yet there is nothing which is by the generality of persons asked more seldom and with greater indifference. It is a shame to Christians that their vows, devotions, etc. have almost all of them no other end but health, the gaining of a suit at law, or some other temporal advantage. We are very ready to ask for good success in our affairs; but we seldom ask for that good Spirit which makes even the worst affairs beneficial and advantageous to us, through the good which it causes us to make of them.

SECT. III.—THE DUMB DEVIL.—THE BLASPHEMY OF THE JEWS.—A DIVIDED KINGDOM.

14. ¶ And he was casting out a devil, and it was dumb. And it came to pass, when the devil was gone out, the dumb spake, and the people wondered.

The devil shuts up the mouth of those whom he hinders from praising God, from praying to him, from confessing their sins, from bearing witness to truth and innocence, or from giving admonition, instruction, and comfort to those who need them, and to whom they are due. The mouth is generally shut with respect to all these duties, only because the heart is shut toward God, and open to temporal interests, and to human fears and motives. Lord, it belongs to thy Spirit to cast out this dumb devil. Thou hast the key of David; and if thou dost but vouchsafe to open the heart and the mouth, no man is able to shut them.

15. But some of them said, He casteth out devils through Beelzebub the chief of the devils.

That which proceeds from the Spirit of God, is every day ascribed to the evil spirit by the rash judgments of men. Two spirits so contrary to each other have likewise ways as directly contrary. The Spirit of God inclines men to excuse even bad actions as much as possible, by the uprightness of the intention; the evil spirit endeavours to decry the very best, condemning either the intention or the means. We ought to be forced by the plainest evidence to condemn our neighbour; and we often condemn him contrary to all evidence.

16. And others, tempting *him*, sought of him a sign from heaven.

Infidelity has never sufficient arguments for conviction. Faith, though wise and discreet, having likewise humility and sincerity, is satisfied with such as God is pleased to use. To one who has a sincere faith, it is enough that God has once declared himself. He who is not content with this, wants faith, not proofs. Lord, I do not ask of thee new signs or miracles: thou art thyself the greatest of all. Faith is that which is necessary for me,—this is the thing which I ask of thee.

17. But he, knowing their thoughts, said unto them, Every kingdom divided against itself is brought to desolation; and a house *divided* against a house falleth.

How much ought we to love unity, without which nothing can subsist, since it is one of the properties and marks of God's works, and above all of his church! Every communion which separates itself from this church is no other than a house divided against itself, which will certainly fall. The church alone, founded upon a rock, is preserved in the midst, and against all the assaults, of schismatical churches or of false religions, which all conspire its destruction.

18. If Satan also be divided against himself, how shall his kingdom stand? because ye say that I cast out devils through Beelzebub.

There can be no concord between Christ and Belial. It is a foolish and senseless calumny, to endeavour to make it believed that a man is an enemy of the church, when he is wholly intent on establishing truth of doctrine and holiness of manners therein, and on casting out of it the devils of error and sin. We must therefore, following the example of Christ, not cease to serve the church in the midst of all the calumnies and oppositions of false brethren.

19. And if I by Beelzebub cast out devils, by whom do your sons cast *them* out? therefore shall they be your judges.

The corruption of the heart is the cause of the corruption of the understanding and judgment. Passion makes men frequently condemn that in some which they approve in others. As nothing is so common as these personal errors and heresies, so nothing is more criminal than to employ these means to render those whom we do not love odious to the world.

20. But if I with the finger of God cast out devils, no doubt the kingdom of God is come upon you.

Wherever the reign of the devil and of self-love ceases,

there God and charity must needs reign. We cannot be assured that God reigns in a soul, but only when the devils which possessed it, that is, its lusts and evil habits, are cast out, not by other devils or lusts, but by the love of righteousness and the hatred of sin; which is done by the finger of God—namely, by his Holy Spirit.

SECT. IV.—THE STRONG MAN ARMED.—THE DEVIL RE-ENTERING.

21. When a strong man armed keepeth his palace, his goods are in peace:

The world and the sinner are the habitation of the devil, until Christ take possession of them by his incarnation and grace. We are all born under the dominion of this strong person armed; and have all been his house and his possession, by being born slaves to sin. Would to God we had never been so by our own will, and that we had not given ourselves to him more than once! We cannot have too frequent occasions of humbling ourselves on this account; and all the truths which have any relation to this matter, put us in mind of doing it.

22. But when a stronger than he shall come upon him, and overcome him, he taketh from him all his armour wherein he trusted, and divideth his spoils.

Blessed be thou, O my God, for that thou hast not left this enemy in possession of my heart, but hast been pleased to re-enter upon thy rights, and to reinstate thyself therein, by overcoming in me concupiscence by a stronger charity. Without concupiscence, the devil has no power: that is the thing wherein he places his whole strength and confidence. Christ takes from him all his armour whenever he roots out of the heart the love of pleasures, the desire of riches, and the pride of life.

23. He that is not with me is against me; and he that gathereth not with me scattereth.

Indifference is a crime in a pastor and minister of the church, who is a man of God, obliged by his profession to have the interests of Christ and of his spouse at heart. In vain does he flatter himself that he does no evil, if so be that he do no good. He disperses the flock of God, if he is not diligent in seeking and bringing home the sheep which are gone astray, in securing those which are in the fold, and in feeding, strengthening, and curing them. That person scatters who does not gather with Jesus Christ, in the unity of his body, in his Spirit, and by his grace.

24. When the unclean spirit is gone out of a man, he walketh through dry places, seeking rest; and finding none, he saith, I will return unto my house whence I came out.

The rage of the devil against those who are returned to God, is greater than we can imagine. We have but little knowledge of this enemy of our salvation, if we suffer ourselves to grow careless after having been delivered from his yoke. No person has greater reason to be afraid of his assaults and snares than one who has vanquished him, if the victory either puff him up or render him less vigilant. A converted sinner is a place which the devil has lost, the weak sides and avenues whereof he perfectly knows, and in which he very often keeps a correspondence.

25. And when he cometh, he findeth *it* swept and garnished.

Nothing is more likely to recall the devil into a reconciled sinner, than for him either not to confirm and secure his reconciliation by good works, or to have only the outward part of them, or to take great complacency and satisfaction in them as in his own proper righteousness. Such a soul seems to be swept and garnished on purpose to invite the devil back again.

26. Then goeth he, and taketh *to him* seven other spirits more wicked than himself; and they enter in, and dwell there: and the last *state* of that man is worse than the first.

How dangerous are relapses! If the Jews, delivered from their bondage in Egypt, and become the people of God by the covenant of the law, fell into a state much worse than their first, by the abuse of that covenant and by rejecting Jesus Christ,—alas! what is the last state of a Christian, who falls from the divine adoption by losing the grace of his baptism, by trampling under foot the blood of Christ, and obliging his Holy Spirit to withdraw from him, and give place to the evil spirit!

SECT. V.—THE BLESSEDNESS OF THE MOTHER OF CHRIST.—THE QUEEN OF THE SOUTH.—THE NINEVITES.

27. ¶ And it came to pass, as he spake these things, a certain woman of the company lifted up her voice, and said unto him, Blessed *is* the womb that bare thee, and the paps which thou hast sucked.

The holy Virgin is not blessed in having borne Christ, on any other account, but only because he, being much more the holiest of saints, made her worthy to be his mother by sanctifying her. The virtue of children is the glory of those who gave them birth and good education.

28. But he said, Yea, rather, blessed *are* they that hear the word of God, and keep it.

Christ does not blame the praise here given to his mother, but he completes and perfects it, by intimating that her blessedness proceeded from having borne the Son of God in her heart, even before she bare him in her womb; and from her having been nourished herself with the milk of the word and will of his Father, even before she nourished his Son with her own milk. Let us imitate Jesus Christ, who always prefers those who belong to him according to the Spirit before those who belong to him according to the flesh. Blessed is that person who hears the word and keeps it!

29. ¶ And when the people were gathered thick together, he began to say, This is an evil generation: they seek a sign; and there shall no sign be given it, but the sign of Jonas the prophet.

Nothing shows more clearly the hardness and corruption of these hearts, than their asking a new miracle—counting, it seems, all those as nothing which they had seen before. Their incredulity with respect to that which he promised, and which he gave them in his resurrection, ought fully to convince man that the most extraordinary are capable only of hardening the heart the more, unless God change it by an inward miracle of his grace, and render it attentive to the voice of external miracles. My God, this is the miracle which I ask of thee:—grant that I may not have the heart of a Jew, in relation either to all those which thou hast wrought for me, or to all those which I have every day before the eyes of my flesh and of my faith!

30. For as Jonas was a sign unto the Ninevites, so shall also the Son of man be to this generation.

The resurrection of Christ was the last of his miracles for the Jews, and filled up the measure of their impenitence. It was the first for the Gentiles—the signal that they should be called to repentance, and the cause and pattern of their conversion, prefigured by that of the heathen Ninevites. Let thy resurrection, O Jesus, be truly to me, both the end of my falling and the beginning of a new life. The mysteries of Christ, which to those who have faith are sources of grace, become to proud and incredulous hearts occasions of their falling and being hardened in sin.

31. The queen of the south shall rise up in the judgment with the men of this generation, and condemn them: for she came from the utmost parts of the earth to hear the wisdom of Solomon; and, behold, a greater than Solomon *is* here.

Unbelieving Christians will be condemned even by infidels. What pains do people take to satisfy their curiosity, and perhaps only to see a man? Would they do as much in order to their own salvation, and to know Jesus Christ? This example will confound those Christians at the day of judgment who have not vouchsafed to open the New Testament, that they might hear the incarnate Wisdom speaking therein, and learn from his mouth the words of eternal life. We have no occasion to cross the seas, or to go far to hear him: we need only hearken to the church everywhere, which is the mouth of the true Solomon. How great is the comfort when, at the foot of the gospel, our faith tells us, "Behold, a greater than Solomon is here!" This is He who possesses and gives true wisdom.

32. The men of Nineveh shall rise up in the judgment with this generation, and shall condemn it: for they repented at the preaching of Jonas; and, behold, a greater than Jonas *is* here.

Graces not received as they ought, and the abuse of the divine benefits, harden the heart. What a repentance was this, at the preaching of a person unknown, of a different nation and religion, and working no miracles, and this only to avoid temporal evils! Where is that of the generality of Christians, though instructed by the Son of God himself, and by which they are to deliver themselves from an eternity of torments, and to gain heaven? Let us not wait till the last day, either of the world or of our life, ere we make this comparison, and understand what we owe to Christ and to our own souls.

SECT. VI.—THE CANDLE ON A CANDLESTICK.—THE SINGLE EYE.

33. No man, when he hath lighted a candle, putteth *it* in a secret place, neither under a bushel, but on a candlestick, that they which come in may see the light.

The truths of the gospel are not to be concealed, nor held captive in unrighteousness; but the people are to be instructed in them. The Scripture, and particularly the gospel, is our candle. It is the Spirit of God which has lighted and placed it on the candlestick of the church, that the light of it might be seen by all the faithful. To forbid Christians the reading of the Scripture, is to forbid the use of light to the children of light, and to make them suffer a sort of excommunication. Thou, O Lord, wast pleased to invite everybody to hear thee, and didst expressly forbid thy apostles to hinder little ones from coming to thee: do not permit me, then, to be hindered from hearing thee in thy gospel, which is to me instead of thy visible presence; nor suffer this candle to be put under a bushel or in a secret place.

34. The light of the body is the eye: therefore when thine eye is single, thy whole body also is full of light; but when *thine eye* is evil, thy body also *is* full of darkness.

The single eye is an upright, pure, and Christian intention. It is a great misfortune for a Christian, and much more for a clergyman, to have either false lights and prejudices in his mind, or corrupt passions and intentions: all his designs, his judgments, and the whole conduct of his life are generally infected thereby. This was that which made the Jews judge so ill of Christ, and reject him; and it is this which makes Christians judge so ill of their brethren, and set themselves against them without any foundation.

35. Take heed therefore that the light which is in thee be not darkness.

An irregular intention corrupts the whole action; a false

light causes a man to fall into abundance of faults. It is one of the most dangerous, for us to be unwilling to examine, according to Christ's direction, whether that by which we are led be not rather darkness than light. It is an inexhaustible spring of rash judgments, divisions, and sins, for men to adhere inflexibly to their own prepossessions, and to resolve no more to hear nor receive any instruction than if they were infallible.

36. If thy whole body therefore *be* full of light, having no part dark, the whole shall be full of light, as when the bright shining of a candle doth give the light.

When a man's heart and inclinations tend to God, and he walks toward him, following a sure guide, such as is the gospel or the church, he has peace in his heart, and walks as in a way of light. Every thing which moves the heart must be very right and pure; the least irregular aim, the least dark intention, is capable of spreading great darkness over the whole conduct and behaviour.

SECT. VII.—THE OUTSIDE OF THE CUP.—NEGLECT OF CHARITY.

37. ¶ And as he spake, a certain Pharisee besought him to dine with him: and he went in, and sat down to meat.

It is necessary to converse familiarly with sinners, in order to gain them to God; but it must be done with prudence and circumspection. A minister of God ought not to eat at the table of others either often or of his own accord. He may sometimes yield to importunity, and to considerations of usefulness, decency, or charity; but never to his own inclination, or to the desire of good cheer.

38. And when the Pharisee saw *it*, he marvelled that he had not first washed before dinner.

This Pharisee, by immediately showing his Pharisaism, discovers the reason which brought the Son of God to his house: it was more to instruct than to be entertained. It is easy to pass from the practice of some external action to a fondness for it; from fondness to superstition; from superstition to a condemnation of those who do not practise it; from a condemnation to a contempt of them; and from a contempt to an open schism and separation.

39. And the Lord said unto him, Now do ye Pharisees make clean the outside of the cup and the platter; but your inward part is full of ravening and wickedness.

Christ here teaches his ministers not to be parasites, who purchase their good meals at the expense of truth. He does not speak the language of one who has sold his liberty, or who is lavish of his commendations out of interest. Who can say that he is entirely free from this Pharisaical hypocrisy? Where is that person to be found, who, by the inward purity of the motions of his heart, takes as much care not to offend the eyes of God, as he does not to displease men by his outward behaviour?

40. *Ye* fools, did not he that made that which is without make that which is within also?

This apparent severity of expression is often useful and even necessary to awaken the sinner, and to give him a more lively sense of his faults. There are no sinners whatever, who think themselves wiser, or more applaud their own actions, than hypocrites do; and it is for this very reason that our blessed Lord exposes the folly of their conduct. Nothing is more foolish than to pretend to be devout by a grave and serious appearance; to endeavour to please men who cannot possibly make us happy; and not to be at all solicitous to please God, upon whom our happiness depends; to bestow all our care on the outside, not considering that it is in mind and heart that we are made after the image of God, and that, without giving him these, it is not possible to please him.

41. But rather give alms of such things as you have; and, behold, all things are clean unto you.

He who has pity on the poor shall be saved, provided he have likewise pity on his own soul, in rendering himself acceptable to God. Hypocrisy and avarice, when joined together, are almost incurable. In beginning to oppose covetousness by giving alms, we weaken hypocrisy; because the latter is oftentimes only an effect of the former, and because God shows mercy to those who themselves show it to others.

SECT. VIII.—WOES PRONOUNCED AGAINST THE PHARISEES, SCRIBES, AND LAWYERS.

42. But woe unto you, Pharisees! for ye tithe mint and rue, and all manner of herbs, and pass over judgment and the love of God: these ought ye to have done, and not to leave the other undone.

Observe here the several marks and characters of the devotion of the Pharisees, and of all those who act by their spirit: First, They are very exact in trifles, in order to gain reputation and credit; but they destroy the commandment concerning the love of God, to flatter the desires of the world, of whose favour they are extremely fond. It ought to be the chief care of a pastor, to establish religion in the heart by the love of God, which worships him in spirit and in truth, and by the love of our neighbour, which includes in it judgment or justice. External performances are but the outside of these things.

43. Woe unto you, Pharisees! for ye love the uppermost seats in the synagogues, and greetings in the markets.

The second character of the imitators of the Pharisees is, that they seek to be the first or chief in the church, to teach and preach in the chief pulpits, and to be honoured by the people. Pride does not consist in being the first or chiefest, but in loving the esteem and distinction which attend upon the first place, and seeking the advantages which accompany it. It is a misfortune to be exposed to them, because it is very rare not to be corrupted by them.

44. Woe unto you, scribes and Pharisees, hypocrites! for ye are as graves which appear not, and the men that walk over *them* are not aware *of them.*

The third mark or character of these imitators is, that they hide their corrupt maxims under an external piety and a false charity. It is a dreadful judgment on hypocrites, when God suffers them to conceal their corruption according to their heart's desire: their being exposed to public shame would be a step toward their conversion. It is the same in proportion with respect to the lesser instances of hypocrisy and feigned humiliations, from which few are altogether exempt.

45. ¶ Then answered one of the lawyers, and said unto him, Master, thus saying thou reproachest us also.

The fourth character of hypocrites is, that they think themselves incapable of committing faults, that they cannot bear being reproved for them, and that they are no further concerned at the disgrace of others than as it falls upon themselves. We see two very contrary affections in the proud. The fear of being despised, persuades them that they are taxed whenever we reprove the faults of others; and the esteem they have of themselves, makes them believe that our discourse is never directed to them, when we exhort to the practice of virtue.

46. And he said, Woe unto you also, *ye* lawyers! for ye lade men with burdens grievous to be borne, and ye yourselves touch not the burdens with one of your fingers.

The fifth mark or character of the imitators of the Pharisees is, that they observe no part of that themselves to which they oblige others; and that they indiscreetly load them with the burden of many unprofitable performances, without concerning themselves whether their heart is devoted to God. True charity is compassionate, willing to take upon itself the burden of others, and far from laying upon them one which is too grievous to be borne: whereas hypocrites aim at nothing but gaining to themselves honour from the austerities which they impose upon others, without consulting their strength.

47. Woe unto you! for ye build the sepulchres of the prophets, and your fathers killed them.

The sixth character of hypocrites is, that they spare nothing to persuade the world that they honour those who have laid down their lives for the truth, and that they condemn their persecutors, though they themselves persecute the truth and those who preach it. Those persons who inherit the vices of their fathers, can never sincerely condemn their crimes.

48. Truly ye bear witness that ye allow the deeds of your fathers: for they indeed killed them, and ye build their sepulchres.

Seventhly, Hypocrites imitate the wicked who are gone before them. Cruel as their fathers, they are continually hatching mischievous designs in their hearts against the servants of God living in their own age, and, at the same time, make a show of honouring the saints of ages past.

49. Therefore also said the wisdom of God, I will send them prophets and apostles, and *some* of them they shall slay and persecute:

In the eighth place, they make no scruple to destroy or ruin those who contradict them no otherwise than by opposing their passions in teaching them the truth. The wisdom of God must needs draw abundance of glory from the fidelity of a minister who gives up his life rather than renounce the truth or be wanting to his ministry; since, in order to make way for it, he permits so great a crime, even foreseeing it.

50. That the blood of all the prophets, which was shed from the foundation of the world, may be required of this generation.

The ninth mark or character of hypocrites is, that they draw down the curse of God upon a whole people, by engaging them in their passions. The blood of the prophets, that is, the injustice and violence done to the ministers of the Lord, is that which generally fills up the measure of iniquity, and brings down utter desolation upon states and kingdoms. Other sins are punished in private persons: God revenges these as injuries done to himself, after a most dreadful manner, and by the ruin and desolation of whole nations.

51. From the blood of Abel unto the blood of Zacharias, which perished between the altar and the temple: verily I say unto you, It shall be required of this generation.

The tenth character of hypocrites is, that they flatter themselves with the hopes of impunity; but the justice of God will certainly punish them, all in general, and every one in particular. Abel is counted among the prophets, because he prefigured or foreshowed Jesus Christ by his innocence and death, as Cain did Judas and the Jewish people, by his treachery, envy, and fratricide. Extraordinary crimes, which put an end to the patience of God, are punished with a general punishment; because the corruption and impenitence are then become general, the people join in the sins of their leaders, and they seem to have heaped up and surpassed all the wickedness of preceding ages.

52. Woe unto you, lawyers! for ye have taken away the key of knowledge: ye entered not in yourselves, and them that were entering in ye hindered.

The eleventh mark or character of hypocrites is, that they

imagine themselves alone in possession of knowledge, though they be ignorant, and endeavour to keep others in ignorance as much as possible. It is a wretched and damnable artifice of those who would tyrannize over the consciences of men, to introduce and continue ignorance in the church. They who are resolved not to follow the light, are far from endeavouring to disperse the darkness, by the favour of which they securely reign.

53. And as he said these things unto them, the scribes and the Pharisees began to urge *him* vehemently, and to provoke him to speak of many things: 54. Laying wait for him, and seeking to catch something out of his mouth, that they might accuse him.

The twelfth and last character of the imitators of the Pharisees is, that they place all their strength in confidence, craft, and deceit; whereas sincerity, humility, and trust in God are the whole strength of the righteous. It is the common way of heretics and false teachers to be provoked by the advice which is given them, and at the imputations with which they are justly charged, to clear no one point, to answer by new questions, and to seek to surprise their adversaries, or to catch something out of their mouth that they may accuse them. Thy wisdom and light, O Lord, can disperse all their artifice and darkness. Cast the bright beams of this light on those who are to defend themselves against these subtle and deceitful men. Raise and animate their heart, that they may not be wanting to the cause of truth; guide their tongues, that they may not be deficient in prudence, nor expose the truth by any indiscretions or unseasonable transports of zeal.

CHAPTER XII.

SECT. I.—THE LEAVEN OF THE PHARISEES.—WE MUST FEAR GOD ONLY, TRUST IN HIM, AND CONFESS HIM.

1. In the mean time, when there gathered together an innumerable multitude of people, insomuch that they trode one upon another, he began to say unto his disciples first of all, Beware ye of the leaven of the Pharisees, which is hypocrisy.

Great and habitual hypocrites, and whose hypocrisy tends to seduce the minds of men by error, or to corrupt their manners by sin, ought not to be concealed. But to qualify a man to tax others with this vice, he must either know the bottom of the heart, as Jesus did, or there must be such full proof and evidence of the thing, that he may be certain of it. Some particular persons among the Pharisees might be exempt from this crime; and yet this did not hinder Christ from bringing a general charge against the whole body; because private good ought to give way to public.

2. For there is nothing covered, that shall not be revealed; neither hid, that shall not be known.

In vain, when we are about to commit a sin, do we shun the sight of men, since we cannot possibly avoid that of our Judge. The darkness of the night, and the light of the day, to him are both alike. Sooner or later the hypocrite will be known for what he is; and he is often discovered even in this life. It is just that those who have not the least esteem and value for the life to come, should not even in this be secure of enjoying always the short pleasure of a vain reputation.

3. Therefore, whatsoever ye have spoken in darkness shall be heard in the light; and that which ye have spoken in the ear in closets shall be proclaimed upon the housetops.

The more a sinner endeavours to hide himself here, with the greater shame and confusion shall he be covered hereafter in the sight of all the world. That which constitutes the peace and satisfaction of a good man is, that he does nothing in secret of which he need be ashamed at the day of judgment; and that he shuns the eyes of men on no other account but only that he may not receive from them his reward. Let us often reflect upon this truth, that our Judge is our Witness, and that the thickest darkness is so far from covering us from his sight, that it becomes bright and clear, so as to show us plainly to him with all our most secret lusts and desires. It is not enough for a minister of the truths of the gospel not to corrupt them in secret, but he must produce them to open daylight, and preach them in the face of the whole world.

4. And I say unto you, my friends, Be not afraid of them that kill the body, and after that have no more that they can do.

We ought to fear, not the death of the body, since it must

die, but that of the soul, which was created to live eternally. Christ is not of the number of those friends who are altogether for sparing those they love the trouble of present evils, and for lulling them asleep as to those of eternity, for fear of disturbing and grieving their minds. True friendship consists in exciting our friends to do their duty, and saving their souls at the expense of all things. A man has but one life to lose, and one soul to save; and it is madness to sacrifice the salvation of the soul to the preservation of the life of the body, instead of sacrificing the latter to the salvation of the former.

5. But I will not forewarn you whom ye shall fear: Fear him, which after he hath killed, hath power to cast into hell; yea, I say unto you, Fear him.

What darkness must have overspread the mind of man, what corruption must there be in his heart, since it was requisite that God should take upon him our flesh, to teach us that he alone ought to be feared! It is our fondness for the present life and the conveniences thereof which makes us fear men, and is the cause that we cannot prevail with ourselves to fear none but God. He alone is able to disengage the heart from these things who is Lord of it at present, and who shall hereafter be its life and eternal felicity. Teach us, Lord, this necessary lesson. Grant that I may love nothing which it is in the power of men to give or take away, to the end that thou mayest be the sole object of my fear as well as of my love.

6. Are not five sparrows sold for two farthings, and not one of them is forgotten before God?

The providence of God is the comfort of the righteous. The little faith we have as to the care, vigilance, and concern of God, in every thing which relates to us, is the source of all human disquiets and fears. His wisdom cannot be surprised, his power cannot be forced, his love cannot forget itself: this ought to make us easy and satisfied, yet so as not to neglect human means. Man distrusts God, and fears that he is forgotten by him, because he judges of God by himself, is very apt to forget him, and to be unfaithful to him.

7. But even the very hairs of your head are all numbered. Fear not therefore: ye are of more value than many sparrows.

Some men admire the providence of God over the smallest creatures, who yet, upon occasion, are uneasy and solicitous, as if they believed none with respect to themselves. God watches over every thing, without debasing himself; he acts in every thing, without growing weary; and he is sufficient for every thing, without multiplying himself: and this because he need only will, and because whatever good he designs his creatures, he wills it by his power and his love. He alone knows our value, because he alone knows how much he loves us, and because he is himself the price of our love. Since God is mindful of man with so much goodness, how can man be so unmindful of God?

8. Also I say unto you, Whosoever shall confess me before men, him shall the Son of man also confess before the angels of God:

Christ will treat us at the day of judgment as we have treated him in the time of our life. Happy is that person who confesses him in his heart, with his mouth, and by his works! We should esteem it an honour to declare for Christ if it cost us none of our worldly pretensions, as if he was not capable of making us amends for whatever we can lose for his sake, and as if it were not sufficient to be owned by him as joint-heirs, and called to possess his inheritance together with him.

9. But he that denieth me before men shall be denied before the angels of God.

What despair must be the portion of that soul which Jesus Christ denies and renounces! To whom can it belong but to the devil, whom it chose for its master when it refused to acknowledge Christ for its Lord and its God? Every age has its proper manner of confessing or denying Christ, as every age has its proper way of persecuting those who do confess him. The disposition whereby we are ready to give up our life and our blood is requisite at all times; and when a man has it, he sits very loose from every thing else. The less we lose at present, the more culpable are we if we are unwilling, when occasion requires, to relinquish it for the sake of Christ.

10. And whosoever shall speak a word against the Son of man, it shall be forgiven him: but unto him that blasphemeth against the Holy Ghost it shall not be forgiven.

To what remedy can the sinner have recourse, if he reject the Holy Ghost, who alone calls him to repentance, and gives him the grace and the will to perform it. He who through fear renounces Christ, is not far from speaking against him; but to renounce the faith through infidelity, and to call every thing which the Spirit of God has done by Christ and his apostles a mere illusion,—this is a blasphemy out of which men seldom or never recover, because the root of faith is plucked up, and every principle of life extinguished.

11. And when they bring you unto the synagogues, and *unto* magistrates, and powers, take ye no thought how or what thing ye shall answer, or what ye shall say:

Who would not despair of being able to stand against so many sorts of temptations, if Christ did not assure us that it is neither by our own understanding nor strength that we are to resist them? It is the chief foundation of our hope, not to place our trust and confidence in ourselves, but to be thoroughly sensible of our own ignorance and weakness.

12. For the Holy Ghost shall teach you in the same hour what ye ought to say.

The knowledge of our own inability would serve only to make us despair, if Christ had not promised that his Spirit should supply all our defects, and do all in us. This Spirit is that perfect Master, who enlightens the understanding, inflames the heart, and forms the very words in our mouth. O Holy Spirit! thou art my only hope: be not wanting to me in my need, and at the hour of temptation. Instruct me in the manner peculiar to thyself, by causing me to know, love, and perform my duty.

SECT. II.—WE MUST BEWARE OF COVETOUSNESS.—THE WORDLY RICH.—THE RICH TOWARD GOD.

13. And one of the company said unto him, Master, speak to my brother, that he divide the inheritance with me.

The possessions of this world are only occasions of division, trouble, and scandal: the certain way for a man to enjoy peace, is not to set his heart upon them. The strictest and closest ties are not proof against interest and the desire of riches. Would to God that Christians, after the example of this person, instead of going to law, would refer their interests to the determination of understanding and charitable arbitrators! This is the fruit of a good sermon; and a pastor ought to preach in such a manner as to gain the confidence of the faithful to that degree, that they may believe they put their interests into the hands of Christ in putting them into his.

14. And he said unto him, Man, who made me a judge or a divider over you?

A person consecrated to God ought not to concern himself with temporal affairs, any further than charity and the order of discipline engage him therein, without prejudice to more essential duties. Our blessed Lord could have decided this difference in a moment; but the example of a perfect disengagement from worldly things, was more necessary for the ministers of the church than that of a charity applying itself to temporal concerns. A common father [or pastor] ought not to run the risk of losing that confidence which is necessary with respect to the affairs of salvation, by concerning himself with the temporal interest of one of the parties without the consent of the other.

15. And he said unto them, Take heed, and beware of covetousness: for a man's life consisteth not in the abundance of the things which he possesseth.

It is not for the ministers of the church to meddle with the partition of estates, or with the differences in families; but they ought to teach the faithful the rules of Christian piety, and the means of avoiding all injustice. This vice still proceeds from covetousness, and therefore this is the thing which must be rooted up. A man's life does not consist in superfluities, but in necessaries: the safest way is to keep to these. A man is really covetous, not only in taking away the goods of others, but likewise in preserving and securing his own with too much affection and concern.

16. And he spake a parable unto them, saying, The ground of a certain rich man brought forth plentifully: 17. And he thought within

himself, saying, What shall I do, because I have no room where to bestow my fruits?

Peace is to be found in evangelical poverty or in Christian mediocrity: there is nothing but vexation in riches, though ever so well acquired. Great wealth is but a great incumbrance, when a man has not learned to wean his affections from it. How can such things be called goods, of which even the abundance vexes and disturbs the mind, which cannot be preserved without great pains and cost, and which, through the fear of losing them, become the torment of him who possesses them? There are no true goods, O my God, but only those which thou designest for thy elect—namely, the good things of heaven, which increase by desires, which are laid up only in the heart, which enlarge it, which, by multiplying, make room for themselves therein, and which secure and preserve themselves; because to love them always is sufficient of itself to keep us from ever losing them.

18. And he said, This will I do: I will pull down my barns, and build greater; and there will I bestow all my fruits and my goods.

The rich are full of designs concerning this life till the very time of their death, without thinking of eternity. Vain and foolish employment of the children of this world, to pass their life in removing, heaping, and raising up earth to afford a momentary spectacle to the eyes of their flesh, or a transient amusement to the desires of their heart! Senseless wretch! to call those things which were liable to perish in a moment all his goods, and thereby to renounce the good things of eternity, and God himself, the only sovereign and infinite Good! How comes it to pass that this rich man does not apprehend that, in bestowing [from love to Christ] this superfluity which perplexes him in the hands of the poor, he may, without any further charge, securely lay up a treasure for eternity?

19. And I will say to my soul, Soul, thou hast much goods laid up for many years; take thine ease, eat, drink, *and* be merry.

The rich are often surprised by death in the midst of their delights. The most common fruit of wealth is a soft and voluptuous life. Labour, fasting, and the godly sorrow of repentance are the portion of the elect in this life; that of the reprobate is idleness, sensuality, and pleasure. There are few who speak as this rich man did; but the world is full of rich persons who live like him. It is a great misfortune for the generality of the rich that they are not poor, and that they have such great possessions as to live in pride, idleness, and luxury; but who is sensible of this? Moderate poverty is a great talent in order to salvation, but it is one which nobody desires. How many rich men, like this here before us, have only just time to look upon their riches, and then die, without any enjoyment of those on earth, and without the least hopes of those in heaven!

20. But God said unto him, *Thou* fool, this night thy soul shall be required of thee: then whose shall those things be, which thou hast provided?

A strange but very common blindness this, for men to heap up immense riches, and to build palaces for a moment of life which remains, and not to think at all of eternity, which follows this moment! God does not pronounce this sentence upon each rich man in particular, but he speaks here to all. Nothing is more inculcated in the Scriptures than the folly of the rich and the vanity of riches; but no person applies it to himself. Those whose wisdom, conduct, and address the world so highly extols, for having raised a great fortune for their children, and in a little time—those very persons God calls by no other name than that of fools.

21. So *is* he that layeth up treasure for himself, and is not rich toward God.

Nothing but a curse attends those riches, the use of which is not directed toward God and salvation. It is the property of the covetous man to lay up treasure, not for his own occasions, nor for those of others, but merely for himself, in order to make riches his delight, his happiness, and his god, instead of making them the riches of his God, by laying them out according to his law and will, transmitting them to heaven by the hands of the poor, and employing them to his glory and to the salvation of souls.

SECT. III.—WE MUST NOT BE SOLICITOUS ABOUT FOOD AND RAIMENT.—WE MUST SEEK GOD ALONE.

22. ¶ And he said unto his disciples, Therefore I say unto you, Take no thought for your life, what ye shall eat; neither for the body, what ye shall put on. 23. The life is more than meat, and the body *is more* than raiment.

It is very easy to pass from solicitousness to covetousness; therefore, to avoid the latter, we must secure ourselves from the former. Who is He who formed our body; who composed it of so many different parts, and joined those parts together in so just a proportion; who causes them to receive spirits and life by means of so many different vessels; who preserves the temperature of the humours, so necessary to its health and conservation, and keeps off so many inward and outward accidents, and so many dangers which are capable of destroying it? Is he not the same God? And can we, then, fear that he will suffer us to want that little which is necessary to feed and clothe this body? That person who, with faith and gratitude, often reflects upon what he has already received from God, is far from distrusting his providence for the time to come.

24. Consider the ravens: for they neither sow nor reap; which neither have storehouse nor barn; and God feedeth them: how much more are ye better than the fowls?

The sight and consideration of the world is a continual lesson for a rational creature; and faith finds something everywhere to increase and strengthen itself, from the conduct which God observes therein. The care which he takes of the most useless, voracious, and destitute animals, from the time of their birth, upbraids men with their uneasiness and distrust. Man knows but too well his own excellence, and how to set himself off when he would gain the confidence of others. But he forgets what he is when he should put his confidence in God.

25. And which of you with taking thought can add to his stature one cubit?

An anxious concern about the future gives man abundance of trouble, and is of no manner of use to him: confidence in

God is always useful and beneficial, and yet he cannot persuade himself to trust in him. He can add nothing to the work of God: it is God alone who formed him, who causes him to grow up to his full stature and perfection, and preserves him by the ordinary means which he has appointed. If these fail us, he supplies the want of them by extraordinary ways, which are equally in his hands with the other, unless our distrust render us unworthy of them.

26. If ye then be not able to do that thing which is least, why take ye thought for the rest?

True confidence must needs be a thing extremely rare and very necessary, since Christ recommends it to us with so much earnestness. Let the experience of our own inability as to those things which are least, oblige us at last to resign ourselves up entirely to God on all extraordinary occasions, and to acknowledge that it is through his blessing alone that our most ordinary cares and endeavours succeed.

27. Consider the lilies how they grow: they toil not, they spin not; and yet I say unto you, that Solomon in all his glory was not arrayed like one of these.

Let us learn of Christ to make a good and holy use of the works of God, and to contemplate in them his greatness, majesty, paternal providence, perfections, and conduct. Man, who is nothing but weakness, affects to distinguish and set himself off by great things; God can make his greatness admired in the least, and cause his providence to shine forth in the meanest of his creatures.

28. If then God so clothe the grass, which is to-day in the field, and to-morrow is cast into the oven; how much more *will he clothe* you, O ye of little faith?

Here is a matter of humiliation for the great: the gayety of their clothes does not come near the beauty of a flower or herb of the field. Here is matter of consolation and confidence for the poor: they have a great treasure if they have a great faith. If nothing was ever wanting to man, he would always have great reason indeed to praise God, and to give him thanks for his bounty and liberality; but he would have no occasion to exercise his faith and trust. To be sensible of benefits is a human virtue; but it is a divine virtue to depend upon an invisible God as if he were visible, and with confidence to expect every thing from him, without any other security but his word.

29. And seek not ye what ye shall eat, or what ye shall drink, neither be ye of doubtful mind.

Christ does not forbid the labour of the body, but the uneasiness and distrust of the mind. Men seek human supports; but a Christian, who is somewhat more than a man, ought to rest only upon a divine foundation, which is the goodness and promise of God. The mind which has faith for its support, is not doubtful and wavering: he who has it not, is like a building in the air, and without foundation.

30. For all these things do the nations of the world seek after: and your Father knoweth that ye have need of these things.

Distrust is the property of infidels, and trust or confidence the virtue of the children of God. For men to rely upon their own industry, care, and labour, is to resemble the heathens; it is peculiar to those who have God for their Father, to trust to his love and tenderness, without giving themselves up to negligence or sloth.

31. ¶ But rather seek ye the kingdom of God; and all these things shall be added unto you.

Is it not evident, that the generality of men do the direct contrary to that which God requires of them, seeking all other things first; and frequently them alone; and yet expect the kingdom of God should be added unto them? Do not these words of Christ seem likewise to be misplaced, who here obliges us to seek that which depends least upon our search, and to expect to receive that which depends most upon own labour? The reason of this is, because sloth is more usual, and more to be feared, in the business of salvation, and uneasiness more common with respect to temporal concerns.

SECT. IV.—THE LITTLE FLOCK.—OUR TREASURE AND OUR HEART MUST BE IN HEAVEN.

32. Fear not, little flock; for it is your Father's good pleasure to give you the kingdom.

It is the small number which is saved; and therefore we

ought to fear to be of that great number of the reprobate. The goodness of God toward his elect is all their security. Who would not have despaired, if Christ had only said, "Seek ye the kingdom of God," etc., and had not here added, that this kingdom is the gift of God—of God as a Father, which, by consequence, includes the gift of divine adoption, a free gift, depending upon the good pleasure of his will, and proceeding from his paternal love; and a gift of an unchangeable kingdom to all those who are to compose this little flock in heaven? Give us, Lord, that which thou commandest. Cause and enable us to seek, find, and preserve that righteousness which alone leads to this kingdom, and gives a right thereto.

33. Sell that ye have, and give alms; provide yourselves bags which wax not old, a treasure in the heavens that faileth not, where no thief approacheth, neither moth corrupteth.

God freely gives his kingdom, and yet it must be purchased. The poor are those who sell it, and receive the price. This price is just what we are able to give: it costs little, if we have but little; much, if we have much. But we must give all, either by actually parting with every thing, if God, by calling us to perfection, require it of us; or at least by disengaging our heart from every thing, if God vouchsafe to be satisfied therewith. We can give nothing but what we have received; and we receive even the grace to give it, and the hundred-fold of that which is given by us. The treasure we give is liable to perish four ways—to be worn out, wasted, stolen, and corrupted; and we receive it again, a treasure which is eternal, which faileth not, and which cannot possibly be either lost or corrupted. It is the hand of the poor which works this miracle.

34. For where your treasure is, there will your heart be also.

Happy is that person who has nothing on earth which detains and fixes his heart there. Every one lays up his treasure on earth, if he take not great care; and this earthly treasure is whatever he loves contrary to the will of God, and and in which he seeks his own satisfaction. One person, his gold, silver, furniture; his estate, grandeur, glory; his business, diversions, pleasure, etc. Another, his learning, books, reputation, ease; his friends, their esteem, applause, and company, the sweetness of their conversation, etc. And it is thou alone, O my God, whom we ought to seek in all these things, who shouldst be to us even all things, and the only treasure of our heart.

SECT. V.—THE WATCHFUL, FAITHFUL, AND WISE SERVANT.

34. Let your loins be girded about, and **your* lights burning; [**Fr.* Have lighted lamps in your hands.]

Christ here proposes to us several means of securing our salvation:—First. According to the custom of servants, soldiers, and travellers, who used to gird up their upper garment, a Christian ought to be always ready to do the will of God, as a vigilant and faithful servant; to fight as a soldier of Christ, against sin and the enemies of his salvation; and to remove to another country, as a stranger and pilgrim upon earth. Second. He must have in his hand the lamp of faith, always lighted by reading and meditating upon God's word, always burning with the love of God and of his neighbour, and always filled with the oil of good works.

36. And ye yourselves like unto men that wait for their lord, when he will return from the wedding; that, when he cometh and knocketh, they may open unto him immediately.

Third. A Christian must live in expectation of his Lord, who will return from the wedding, when (the number of those espoused souls whom God designs to take eternally to himself being complete) he shall come to judge the world, and to consummate the happiness of the elect by the resurrection of their bodies, or when he comes to take the righteous out of this present world. He who expects his master is always in that state wherein he desires to be found. Fourth. A Christian must not look upon death with concern and anxiety, but with submission, love, joy, and, if possible, with the earnestness and impatience of a good servant, who waits for his master's return after a long absence, who opens to him immediately, and goes out to meet him.

37. Blessed *are* those servants, whom the lord when he cometh shall find watching: verily I say unto you, that he shall gird himself, and make them to sit down to meat, and will come forth and serve them.

Fifth. The Christian, in order to secure his salvation, must live in Christian watchfulness, intent upon his duty, not suffering his heart to be overcharged with the cares of this world, with the love of life, or with carnal pleasures, never losing sight of the last moment, or of that eternity which follows it, and continually observing all the motions of his own heart. Happy that person who, living only to and for God in this world, shall in the other sit down at God's table, and there live in and upon God himself to all eternity!

38. And if he shall come in the second watch, or come in the third watch, and find *them* so, blessed are those servants.

Sixth. The Christian must look upon every hour as that which may possibly be his last. The generality of mankind place their happiness in things which cause their eternal misery. The only true happiness of this life is to secure a happy eternity; and this is done by Christian vigilance.

39. And this know, that if the goodman of the house had known what hour the thief would come, he would have watched, and not have suffered his house to be broken through.

Seventh. A Christian must at all times suspect and mistrust the artifices and snares of the devil. With what care do people watch, that they may not lose their money, their furniture, and other perishing things! It seems as if the soul were the only thing not worth the pains of being watched and guarded!

40. Be ye therefore ready also: for the Son of man cometh at an hour when ye think not.

Eighth. The Christian must take care to keep his conscience clear, and always ready to appear before the Son of God. He who would be always ready, ought always to be under some penitential exercise, and to cleave to nothing which may hinder him from going to God, and doing that which is pleasing in his sight. Are not so many sudden and unexpected deaths sufficient to convince us of the folly of depending upon life, and assuring ourselves of one single moment, though Christ had not given us any warning against it?

41. ¶ Then Peter said unto him, Lord, speakest thou this parable unto us, or even to all?

Ninth. Every one ought to persuade himself that the truths

of the gospel are addressed to him in particular. The ministers of the Lord are often those who apply those truths least to themselves which they preach to others, and are likewise soonest surprised by death. No state, no condition, no age, is excused from watching: because death is the punishment of all, and it is nature which is condemned thereto. There is no safer way we can take, than to count ourselves in the number of those who are to be surprised: the only reason why so many fall into this misfortune is, because they flatter themselves that they shall not.

42. And the Lord said, Who then is that faithful and wise steward, whom *his* lord shall make ruler over his household, to give *them their* portion of meat in due season?

The tenth and last means to secure our salvation is, to be faithful in performing the duties of our state in the time of our life, if we would be found at that of death employed in the work which God has committed to our care. Observe here two main qualities in a pastor. The first is fidelity, in not appropriating to himself the gifts of God, as time, talents, etc. The second is prudence, in employing them to the profit of his household, which is the church. Whoever remembers that he is only a steward, is far from desiring to command and dispose of every thing as master. God will be served in his own way, not in ours. A man must, not only in order to his admittance into the ministry, depend upon and be directed by him, as the Master of the family, but also as to the quality, measure, and time of the food which he is to give, both to all in general, and to every one in particular. It is a great part of pastoral prudence to give the proper portion, and to do it in due season.

43. Blessed *is* that servant, whom his lord when he cometh shall find so doing.

Miserable then is he whom death surprises either doing evil or doing nothing, or doing that which God does not require of him! A pastor's life is a life of labour, and of a labour which must be continued to his very last breath. If he be not found intent upon his work when his Lord cometh, how can he have any right to the blessedness belonging to the faithful and wise servant? He must never quit his station, either through discouragement, or idleness, or indifference.

44. Of a truth I say unto you, that he will make him ruler over all that he hath.

The labour is great, but the reward is without measure. We should be able to comprehend it, could we comprehend all the riches of God—that is, God himself. To see the idleness of so many pastors and ministers of the church, can any one think that they really believe this promise, confirmed with a kind of oath by truth itself?

SECT. VI.—THE VIOLENT AND UNFAITHFUL SERVANT.

45. But and if that servant say in his heart, My lord delayeth his coming; and shall begin to beat the menservants and maidens, and to eat and drink, and to be drunken;

One cause of our forgetfulness as to our duty, and of our contempt of God's law, is, that we are apt to flatter ourselves with the hopes of a long life, and to look upon death as at a great distance. The two common vices of wicked pastors, from which a great many more proceed, are—(1.) Their ruling with a spirit of imperiousness, with severity and violence. (2.) Their enjoying, in ease and idleness, the conveniences and pleasures of life, and the temporal advantages of their dignity. My God! whither are not sinners led by a forgetfulness of death and of thy judgments? Suffer us not, we beseech thee, to fall into it.

46. The lord of that servant will come in a day when he looketh not for *him*, and at an hour when he is not aware, and will cut him in sunder, and will appoint him his portion with the unbelievers.

The punishment of an unfaithful minister, as well as of every wicked Christian, is—(1.) An untimely, sudden, or unexpected death. (2.) An eternal separation from God. (3.) An everlasting torment with the devils and the reprobate. Death has nothing in it which is either dreadful or of fatal consequence to him who lives in continual expectation of it. But under what despair must he necessarily fall whom it surprises in the midst of pleasures, in a course of sin, and a total forgetfulness of God! Let us say to ourselves every day, and if possible every hour, that the Lord is at the door, and that the moment which will decide our eternal state is at hand.

47. And that servant, which knew his lord's will, and prepared not *himself*, neither did according to his will, shall be beaten with many *stripes*.

How much is knowledge to be dreaded, when our charity and works are not answerable thereto! To be ignorant of our Lord's will and our own duty, is a sin which deserves punishment, or is rather itself a punishment of sin; but not to do according to his will when we do know it, is a criminal contempt of the law of God. This knowledge comes from thee alone, O Lord, and likewise the use which I ought to make of it. Grant that I may apply myself hereto, not out of a fear of punishment, but from a sincere love of thee!

48. But he that knew not, and did commit things worthy of stripes, shall be beaten with few *stripes*.

The ignorance of our duty toward God as our Creator and Lord, may sometimes extenuate our sin in transgressing his law; but it can never entirely exempt us from guilt. Lord, it belongs to thee to disperse the darkness of our ignorance, as it does to heal the corruption of our sinful inclinations and desires.

—For unto whomsoever much is given, of him shall be much required; and to whom men have committed much, of him they will ask the more.

The more graces a man has received, the more reason has he to fear, and the greater obligation to labour for God. An enlightened pastor trembles under the weight of the talents he has received for the benefit of souls, as well as under the weight of the souls he is to serve by those talents. Every thing is given by God as upon account: we must therefore make it appear, how it has been laid out, and be answerable for all which is charged to us. God will allow the servant whatever he has disbursed for his Master's glory; but how can the servant return those gifts which he has parted with to vanity, and consumed upon his lusts and passions? How can he recover those souls which have been lost through his negligence?

SECT. VII.—FIRE SENT ON THE EARTH.—DIVISION.—THE TIME OF THE MESSIAS NOT KNOWN.—WE MUST AGREE WITH OUR ADVERSARY.

49. ¶ I am come to send fire on the earth; and what will I, if it be already kindled?

The fervour of charity, a zeal for the salvation of souls, a love of mortification, and the heat of persecution, adversity, and affliction, are so many sorts of fire which consume the filth of a sinner, and complete the sacrifice of a Christian and of a minister of the gospel. O Jesus, cast, I beseech thee, one spark of thy heavenly fire into my heart! Let thy love be kindled therein, and consecrate it to thy will: the fire of that divine love, I mean, sent by Christ on the earth on purpose to consume all sin, and consecrate man to his God.

50. But I have a baptism to be baptized with; and how am I straitened till it be accomplished!

Christ had his passion continually present to his mind. His love for the cross condemns the tenderness and delicacy of Christians, and much more that of pastors. The earnest desire by which he is straitened is, to bring forth his church by his pains, to wash her in his blood, to give her life by his own death, and to establish the kingdom and glory of his Father by the sacrifice of himself. This disposition of the High Priest of good things to come, in not regarding his life, so he can but promote the glory of God and the salvation of sinners,—how suitable is it to his holiness, how fit to be engraved on the heart of every pastor!

51. Suppose ye that I am come to give peace on earth? I tell you, Nay; but rather division:

God came indeed to bring division on earth, but such a division as separates us from the creature only to unite us to the Creator; and makes us hate the spirit of the world in order to follow that of God. For peace with God and peace with the world are altogether inconsistent. There are but too many ministers of the church, as well as private Christians, who seem to believe that Christ came with no other design but to introduce a carnal peace and a sensual repose. We can scarce think otherwise, when we see them entirely taken up in settling themselves therein, and making even religion and Christ himself subservient to that purpose. What! shall we be unwilling to do any thing which may set us at variance with the world, and make us break with it? How opposite is this to the design and spirit of Jesus Christ!

52. For from henceforth there shall be five in one house divided, three against two, and two against three. 53. The father shall be divided against the son, and the son against the father; the mother against the daughter, and the daughter against the mother; the mother in law against her daughter in law, and the daughter in law against her mother in law.

There is no union, how close and natural soever it be, which we must not resolve to break, rather than separate ourselves from unity itself, when faith and the interests of God are in question. A small temporal interest often occasions a misunderstanding in families the most united; but a miracle of grace is necessary to produce a separation upon the motives of piety and religion. Send, Lord, this salutary division, the work of the Spirit of unity alone, among those who are separated from thee, only because they are too closely united one with another!

54. ¶ And he said also to the people, When ye see a cloud rise out of the west, straightway ye say, There cometh a shower; and so it is. 55. And when *ye see* the south wind blow, ye say, There will be heat; and it cometh to pass.

The mind of man has but little insight into the things of God, because it applies itself but little to them, and is diverted from them by his passions; but in those of nature, and of the present life, it is very discerning, because his curiosity, interest, and other passions give a relish to the study of these things, and make them grateful to his understanding or senses. It is toward the setting sun, that is, toward Christ dying, that we must turn ourselves, to the end that the shower of blood which wet his cross may produce a shower of tears to wash our heart. It is to his heart, all inflamed with charity, that we must address ourselves, in order to have our own inflamed with this divine fire.

56. *Ye* hypocrites, ye can discern the face of the sky and of the earth; but how is it that ye do not discern this time?

The true knowledge of a Christian penitent consists in being able to discern the time of repentance and mercy, which incessantly glides away and will never return. The infallible marks of the time of salvation, which are prophecies and miracles, will condemn all incredulous persons, who are apt enough to be full of confidence in unprofitable and uncertain sciences. The ignorance of hypocrites is either pretended or judicial. To them every thing is obscure in mysteries, and uncertain in religion, either because they reject the light, which they will not follow, or because they are delivered up to their own darkness, as the punishment of their pride and hypocrisy. How fatal is this state, and how much to be dreaded!

57. Yea, and why even of yourselves judge ye not what is right?

Righteousness and truth seldom find admittance into the minds of men, unless some interest open their eyes, or grace work this miracle. When there is any danger of losing some temporal good, nothing escapes their penetration and prudence; but they shut their eyes against all light, when they are obliged to sacrifice either some temporal good, or some passion, to the only true and eternal good. Very often a little reflection upon ourselves, and upon our ordinary conduct, would enable us to judge what we ought to do in order to our salvation; but even this reflection, which we think need cost nothing, is only to be obtained by the gift of God.

58. ¶ When thou goest with thine adversary to the magistrate, *as thou art* in the way, give diligence that thou mayest be delivered from him; lest he hate thee to the judge, and the judge deliver thee to the officer, and the officer cast thee into prison.

We must not delay to appease and quiet the remorses of our conscience; but the only way to do it as we ought, is to avoid, or to make some amends for the evil with which it upbraids us, in preventing the justice of God by a speedy repentance. There is not so much as one moment to be lost, since we cannot be certain of one moment. Men improve their time with consummate skill and prudence, when the interests of this mortal life are concerned; but they squander it away in a foolish and desperate manner, when their everlasting salvation lies at stake. Thou, O Lord, givest us these moments, on which eternity depends: give us likewise, we beseech thee, the grace to employ them in such a manner as eternity deserves!

59. I tell thee, thou shalt not depart thence, till thou hast paid the very last mite.

Observe here the dreadful severity of the judgments of God. Wise and prudent is he who prevents it by repentance, and by a faithful performance of all the good which his conscience dictates and grace inspires. When we are once out of the way of repentance and mercy, what can we expect but the rigour of an inflexible justice? Where there is no longer charity, there is no longer any return to God. When there is no more time, there is no more hope for eternity.

CHAPTER XIII.

SECT. I.—THE NECESSITY OF REPENTANCE.—THE BARREN FIG TREE.

1. There were present at that season some that told him of the Galileans, whose blood Pilate had mingled with their sacrifices. 2. And Jesus answering said unto them, Suppose ye that these Galileans were sinners above all the Galileans, because they suffered such things?

Jesus restrains the rashness of human judgments. No man is punished without being a sinner; but they are not the greatest sinners who are punished most in this life. It is only in the other that God punishes with the view chiefly of inflicting punishment; and that his justice proportions the punishment to the sin. Here the punishment proceeds, either from his mercy, which would fain save the sinner; or from his holiness, which purifies the saints; or from his providence, which establishes the belief of his justice; or from his wisdom, which by means of fear puts a stop to sin.

3. I tell you, Nay: but, except ye repent, ye shall all likewise perish.

Impunity hardens and stupefies the sinner, through his abuse of the patience of God; but it is this very patience which induces the elect to love repentance and mortification, well knowing that sin must be punished either in this world or in the next, either by the justice of God, or by the voluntary affliction of the sinner. To repent is not a matter of counsel, but of absolute necessity. He who defers doing it, hazards no less than eternity. Let us not imitate the Jews, who were in effect massacred and sacrificed in the temple to the justice of God, for not having profited by the admonitions of the Son of God, so as to be converted before the destruction of Jerusalem.

4. Or those eighteen, upon whom the tower in Siloam fell, and slew them, think ye that they were sinners above all men that dwelt in Jerusalem?

Open sins are not always the greatest, nor the punishments which are visible to the eyes of men such as are most to be feared. Christ here gives us to understand, that all human events or natural accidents happen only according to God's appointment; and that he makes every thing subservient to his designs and judgments. Would to God we were so faithful as to observe the hand of God, and to have recourse to him in every thing which happens to us by means of the creatures! Whether we suffer by the injustice of men, (ver. 1,) or by unforeseen accidents, (ver. 4,) Christ here informs us that it still proceeds from the justice of God, who makes use of both to chastise us, either as a judge or as a father.

5. I tell you, Nay: but, except ye repent, ye shall all likewise perish.

Why does Christ repeat this truth so frequently and forcibly, but only because there are fewer true penitents than we imagine, and because men are not sufficiently convinced of the necessity of repentance? There is no medium: either repentance or damnation. It is a small thing to perish in the ruins of a city as the Jews did, or in the ruins of the world as at the last day, if a man has taken timely care to secure his soul by repentance: but how great must be the despair when the first death is followed by the second! Let us seriously reflect on this.

6. ¶ He spake also this parable; A certain *man* had a fig tree planted in his vineyard; and he came and sought fruit thereon, and found none.

This barren fig tree is faith without works. It is not enough for a man to be grafted on Jesus Christ by baptism, as all Christians are; to be planted in the true church, as the orthodox; to be associated to the priesthood of Christ, as the clergy; or to be incorporated into some society for the propagation of religion: the life must be answerable to the holiness of the baptism, church, priesthood, and religion. Let us seek for fruit ourselves in our lives, before Jesus Christ come to do it. Lord, how canst thou possibly find any, if thou thyself dost not first produce it in our hearts by thy grace?

7. Then said he unto the dresser of his vineyard, Behold, these three years I come seeking fruit on this fig tree, and find none: cut it down; why cumbereth it the ground?

How many years does God wait for the fruit of his mysteries and graces, and we yield him nothing but ineffectual promises and barren resolutions! Public chastisements, calamities, and diseases are so many admonitions from God in order to our conversion, and threaten us with his wrath and indignation. They are the voice of God; and when we are deaf thereto, it is he whom we refuse to hear. Life is conferred upon us, to no other end but that we should serve God, perform repentance, and work out our own salvation. He who does no part of this, well deserves to have it immediately cut off and taken from him.

8. And he answering said unto him, Lord, let it alone this year also, till I shall dig about it, and dung *it:* 9. And if it bear fruit, *well:* and if not, *then* after that thou shalt cut it down.

The patience of God with respect to sinners is one of the most surprising things imaginable, when we consider what God and what the sinner is; and yet who is there who frequently think of this, adores it, renders thanks for it, and co-operates with it? They are the prayers and labours of holy pastors, which suspend the wrath of God and attract his mercy. A soul subsists sometimes only by the sighs and penitential exercises of him to whose care God has committed it; and a community, a church, and a whole people, by nothing but the tears, charity, good works, and fidelity of a small number of God's servants, who faithfully perform their duty. Let us fear that the building is near its fall, when God removes the pillars of it. The patience of God is great, and of long continuance; but it is wearied out at last, when it has no effect upon sinners.

SEÇT. II.—THE WOMAN BOWED TOGETHER.—THE SABBATH-DAY.

10. ¶ And he was teaching in one of the synagogues on the sabbath.
11. And, behold, there was a woman which had a spirit of infirmity eighteen years, and was bowed together, and could in no wise lift up *herself*.

Christ confirms his word and mission by a miracle, joins works to instruction, and shows, by the cure of the body, what he came to perform on the soul. Into what condition does a long habit of sin put a soul which is possessed thereby? What will become of it, O Lord, unless thou vouchsafest, by thy almighty grace, to deliver it from this voluntary bondage, to rectify its will and inclinations, which are become altogether earthly, and to raise and lift it up toward thyself?

12. And when Jesus saw her, he called *her to him*, and said unto her, Woman, thou art loosed from thine infirmity.
13. And he laid *his* hands on her:

It is this preventing eye of the mercy of God which seeks the sinner in the depth of his misery; it is his inward word which calls him; his sovereign will which draws and heals him; and his beneficent hand which confirms and strengthens him, heaps his blessings upon him, and leads and conducts him in the way of salvation.

—And immediately she was made straight, and glorified God.

God alone can reform and correct his own work, both in nature and in grace. We must resign ourselves up entirely to him. He whose will is omnipotence itself, has no occasion either for time or means to accomplish his works. Lord, thou canst perform, now thou art in heaven, whatever thou didst upon earth: thou canst effect in the heart whatever thou didst then on the body. Rectify in me, I beseech thee, every thing which is not conformable to the rule of thy holy will. The gratitude and acknowledgment of the creature is a new benefit of the Creator; and the glory which we render him for his gifts is still a fresh obligation and engagement to glorify him again.

14. And the ruler of the synagogue answered with indignation, because that Jesus had healed on the sabbath day, and said unto the people, There

are six days in which men ought to work: in them therefore come and be healed, and not on the sabbath day.

Religion often serves to cover envy and avarice: we cannot be too much upon our guard against this sort of imposture. Ye great pretenders to zeal for the sanctification of the Sabbath, blind judges of the works of God, unjust accusers of his elect, and ignorant interpreters of his law, learn not to confound the servile works of men with the works of God, mercenary employments with acts of charity, and common labour with necessary assistance and relief. The one are forbidden by the law to be exercised on the sabbath day; the other are the completion of the law, the sanctification of the Sabbath, and that very rest which God commands to be observed, which consists in resting in him by holiness and charity.

15. The Lord then answered him, and said, *Thou* hypocrite, doth not each one of you on the sabbath loose his ox or *his* ass from the stall, and lead *him* away to watering?

Necessity and charity are laws which are superior to all others. Men are always ready, either out of interest or envy, to condemn every thing in those whom they do not love. When the essence of religion is made to consist in ceremonies and external usages, every seeming violation of them passes for irreligion and profaneness. This is, in the judgment of Christ himself, the vice of hypocrites, as well as to have two different measures, and to object, as a crime in others, that which they practice every day themselves.

16. And ought not this woman, being a daughter of Abraham, whom Satan hath bound, lo, these eighteen years, be loosed from this bond on the sabbath day.

Nothing is more proper for the Lord's day than the work of the Lord, which is to destroy the works of Satan. What grievous bonds are those of the devil, which confine the body in this sad condition! But how much more grievous and fatal are the bonds of sin, which detain souls as slaves under his tyranny, chained down to earthly pleasures and desires, and unable to lift their hearts up toward God, or to desire the things of heaven! It is the office of a good pastor to spend his life in labouring to deliver them, and thereby conduct them to the eternal sabbath.

17. And when he had said these things, all his adversaries were ashamed: and all the people rejoiced for all the glorious things that were done by him.

Men cannot long resist the truth, but it does not convert all those whom it confounds. The passions blind the understanding, and harden the heart against it: that of the common people opens itself thereto without difficulty, because not corrupted either by envy or interest. It is always time to show by our joy, and other religious dispositions, how much we are concerned in the mysteries, works, and glory of Christ. We ought, in reading them, to be transported with joy in our heart, if we have any love toward Jesus Christ.

SECT. III.—THE GRAIN OF MUSTARD SEED.—THE LEAVEN IN THE DOUGH.

18. ¶ Then said he, Unto what is the kingdom of God like? and whereunto shall I resemble it?

The good disposition of these people, which comes originally from Christ himself, engages him to instruct them in the truths of salvation, and concerning the kingdom of God. He has more regard to the good and honest heart, which he gives to the simple, than to the bad disposition of conceited scholars, which proceeds from themselves. It frequently happens that some pious souls which are ready to embrace whatever is good, which are faithful to God and earnestly desirous of his word, prevail with him not to remove out of a country a faithful minister.

19. It is like a grain of mustard seed, which a man took, and cast into his garden; and it grew, and waxed a great tree; and the fowls of the air lodged in the branches of it.

The imperceptible growth of grace and of the church is much to be admired; but neither the beauty nor the perfection of the church is to be seen in this life. Here every thing relating to her appears little, because she is as yet in a state of humiliation; her light being obscure, her charity imperfect, and her children not yet become fowls of heaven. When will it be, O my God, that thy spouse will arrive at her perfect age; that this tree will attain to the greatness, extent, and height which thou hast designed it; and that we, being perfectly disengaged from the earth, shall lodge in the branches of it, to contemplate thee to all eternity?

20. And again he said, Whereunto shall I liken the kingdom of God.

A good pastor is never weary of instructing his flock, no more than a tender nurse is of giving suck to her infant. There always remains abundance to be said concerning the kingdom of God, because there are no words nor comparisons which can express the beauty and riches thereof.

21. It is like leaven, which a woman took and hid in three measures of meal, till the whole was leavened.

Grace penetrates the soul, raises and transforms it, and changes the whole man into one entirely new, the darkness of his understanding into the light of God, the depraved love of his heart into a holy love, and the corruption of his senses into a regular and religious use. How then will it be when God shall penetrate all our faculties with the light of his glory, and with the virtue of his divine essence, and be himself entirely in us! Let his kingdom, which thou, O my God, hast promised us, come; and let it be speedily established in our hearts!

22. And he went through the cities and villages, teaching, and journeying toward Jerusalem.

A pastor who instructs his people with care, who visits his flock in the country, and is continually intent on his duty,—such a pastor advances very fast toward the heavenly Jerusalem. What fidelity, what courage ought not these toils and labours of the Prince of pastors in seeking his sheep, to inspire into the pastors of the church! Form, O Lord, by thy Spirit, unwearied imitators of thy zeal!

SECT. IV.—FEW SAVED.—THE STRAIT GATE.—THE PRETENDERS TO RIGHTEOUSNESS REJECTED.

23. ¶ Then said one unto him, Lord, are there few that be saved? And he said unto them,

Men are more inclined to ask curious questions than to desire necessary instructions. Let us learn of Christ to speak with great discretion concerning hidden mysteries and such truths as are of no general use. The truths which relate to practice, and which are instrumental in setting us forward in the way of salvation, are those which ought to employ our minds.

24. Strive to enter in at the strait gate: for many, I say unto you, will seek to enter in, and shall not be able.

Christ here gives an implicit answer to the preceding question; for as there are few who strive to enter in at the strait gate, so there are few who are saved. Men may make devotion as easy as they please, they may widen the gate of heaven, and flatter themselves and others that their salvation is continually in their hands: the direct contrary is true, since truth itself assures us so. There is nothing which is more an object of faith than that which the Author of faith here teaches us—namely, that salvation is neither for the slothful and idle, who will not strive, nor for such as will not enter in at the strait gate, nor yet for those who presume to the very last, either upon their own strength or upon the grace of God. God has his proper seasons, which we must by no means let slip. There will certainly come a time when, by a just judgment, we shall not be able to do any thing, though we would ever so fain, because we would not do it when we might.

25. When once the Master of the house is risen up, and hath shut to the door, and ye begin to stand without, and to knock at the door, saying, Lord, Lord, open unto us; and he shall answer and say unto you, I know you not whence ye are.

A false righteousness, and a repentance which comes too late, are equally rejected. No sinner ought, at any time, to believe that there is no more mercy for him, since God commands him to hope to the end; but he ought likewise to believe, since Christ himself declares so, that, unless he be converted now immediately, there may come a time (and who can tell how soon?) when he shall seek to enter in, and shall not be able; when he shall knock at the door, and it shall not be opened to him; when he shall pray, and shall not be heard! Dreadful truths these! but such as are absolutely necessary to be known. To endeavour to conceal them is to affect to be wiser than wisdom herself, who has revealed them to us.

26. Then shall ye begin to say, We have eaten and drunk in thy presence, and thou hast taught in our streets.

The being familiarly acquainted with Christ himself in the flesh, is no manner of use in order to salvation, without works. What will it signify to the incredulous Jews, to have seen our blessed Saviour and his miracles, and to have heard his word from his own mouth, but only that they will undergo a severer punishment on that account? Those Christians who are distinguished from infidels and impious persons by nothing but the external use of the word and sacraments, will not be owned as Christians by Him who will judge of Christianity by the life and by the works. God is not satisfied at the time of death with those communions only of ceremony, nor with those shows of piety which are not accompanied with a truly converted and Christian heart.

27. But he shall say, I tell you, I know you not whence ye are; depart from me, all *ye* workers of iniquity.

It is very just that those who would not acknowledge Christ for their Master and Pattern, by obeying and imitating him during their life, should be altogether unknown to him at death and judgment. Not to be owned by Jesus Christ, is sufficient to our condemnation. Whoever does not belong to him, can belong only to the devil. This external separation of the creature from its God is a dreadful punishment; but the sinner separated himself first from God by a will which, by means of his death, becomes eternal. He who does not tremble at this word "Depart," nor endeavour to lead a life which may show him to be a Christian, has either no faith at all, or only so much as will be to his condemnation.

28. There shall be weeping and gnashing of teeth, when ye shall see Abraham, Isaac, and Jacob, and all the prophets, in the kingdom of God, and you yourselves thrust out.

The tears of penitents flow for a moment, and produce an eternal happiness: those of the damned are eternal, and eternally fruitless and ineffectual. The joy and happiness of the elect will be the despair and punishment of the reprobate; because, in hell, envy will reign and be at its utmost height, as charity will be perfect in heaven. If we would not have the glory of the saints become the object of our envy then, let us earnestly endeavour, by imitating their fidelity now, to become the partners and companions of their felicity. The Jews, who were instructed by Jesus Christ himself, seemed to have great advantages above Abraham and the prophets; but a lively faith supplied all defects, and the sight of Christ himself could not supply the defect of that alone.

29. And they shall come from the east, and *from* the west, and from the north, and *from* the south, and shall sit down in the kingdom of God.

Let us be transported with joy, because the kingdom of God is established in the remotest countries; but let us, by our fidelity, take care that our grace be not transferred thither. We must co-operate by our prayers, desires, cares, and acts of charity, to enlarge the bounds of this kingdom, if we cannot do it by our labours and ministry. We secure ourselves a place in this kingdom, when we contribute to the entrance and admission of others into it.

30. And, behold, there are last which shall be first, and there are first which shall be last.

What amazing changes are these! an exaltation of a moment is succeeded by an eternal humiliation in the damned; and a transient humiliation is crowned with everlasting glory in the elect. That the primacy or first place in power, glory, riches, learning, etc., with which men are so intoxicated in this world as to sacrifice every thing thereto, should vanish away and be the cause of their abasement, is not so very strange and surprising. But that which ought to humble the greatest saints, and to make them tremble, is, that even the primacy in religion, piety, and the sublimest virtues, undergoes sometimes the same fate.

SECT. V.—HEROD CALLED A FOX.—THE PASSION FORETOLD.—JERUSALEM A MURDERING CITY.

31. ¶ The same day there came certain of the Pharisees, saying unto him, Get thee out, and depart hence; for Herod will kill thee.

There is no stratagem or artifice whatever, of which the devil does not make use by his ministers to obstruct the work of God, to cause his servants to quit their station, and to cool their zeal. Power in the former, and love of life or ease in the latter, are the things which he most commonly employs to that purpose. The only shield which is proof against every thing, is to fear and love nothing but that which is eternal.

32. And he said unto them, Go ye, and tell that fox, Behold I cast out devils, and I do cures to-day and to-morrow, and the third *day* I shall be perfected.

Let us imitate the steadfastness and constancy of Christ, in performing our duty in spite of all the opposition of the world. When God has intrusted us with any work, we must labour without intermission, and finish it without any apprehensions from men. A minister of God has need of knowledge, to discover the wiles of the serpent; of fidelity, to discharge all the duties of his ministry; and of courage, to despise death,—for which reason he must pray and humble himself very much. A true pastor ought to labour toward the salvation of souls, in casting out the devil of concupiscence, and procuring them the health of charity; and to be as diligent in doing this as if he had but three days to live. Happy that pastor who, like Jesus Christ, lives only to fight against the devil, and to do good to men, and looks upon death as a desirable sacrifice!

33. Nevertheless I must walk to-day, and to-morrow, and the *day* following: for it cannot be that a prophet perish out of Jerusalem.

Our life belongs to God; and that of his ministers is more especially in his hands, because it is bound up with his designs concerning his church. The threats of men are nothing, so long as God permits them to do nothing. Christ assigns the time and place of his death, as having them more in his own power than those who were to inflict it on him. The victim was not to be sacrificed far from the temple; the truth was to be accomplished near its types and figures; and Jerusalem to fill up the measure of her sins, in crucifying the Saviour of the world.

34. O Jerusalem, Jerusalem, which killest the prophets, and stonest them that are sent unto thee; how often would I have gathered thy children together, as a hen *doth gather* her brood under *her* wings, and ye would not!

How great is the goodness of God! how great the obdurateness of the sinner! Jerusalem, which killed the prophets, is an emblem representing to us the world, in whose power it is to use the servants of God despitefully, and to persecute the ministers of his word. Whoever does this, makes a part of that criminal city. This Jerusalem would not have her children gathered together; but, notwithstanding this, our blessed Saviour gathers under his wings all those of her children whom he has chosen to salvation. In the mother, he shows how far a depraved will can go in resisting the Holy Spirit; in the children, he shows the power which his grace has over the will, in subjecting it freely to itself. Make us hear, O Jesus, this voice of thy love, and we shall then come unto thee. Place us under the shadow of thy wings, and we shall be in safety.

35. Behold, your house is left unto you desolate: and verily I say unto you, Ye shall not see me, until *the time* come when ye shall say, Blessed *is* he that cometh in the name of the Lord.

The soul, abandoned by the light of truth, no longer knows God with a saving knowledge. What a frightful desert is a heart, when God withdraws and leaves it! What darkness overspreads it, when the eternal Light shines no longer therein! Let us take great care that our repeated acts of infidelity do not invariably lead us, like the Jews, into that dismal state. God was at last wearied with their disobedience and infidelity, after having afforded them so many opportunities of conversion, and sent them so many preachers of repentance. If he should likewise grow weary of our frequent relapses and revolts, as he did of theirs, what would become of us?

CHAPTER XIV.

SECT. I.—THE DROPSICAL PERSON HEALED ON THE SABBATH DAY.

1. AND it came to pass, as he went into the house of one of the chief Pharisees to eat bread on the sabbath day, that they watched him.

Christ goes not into public company, except when there is some good to be done. The world takes notice of every thing in ecclesiastical persons, and in the great: this obliges them to a particular care in all their actions. How corrupt is the heart of man! This Pharisee, instead of opening his heart to the light and grace offered him in this visit of our blessed Saviour, opens it only to malice and malicious suspicions. How should we be able of ourselves to profit by the afflictions which God sends us, since, without the assistance of his grace, we abuse even the most engaging instances of his favour!

2. And, behold, there was a certain man before him which had the dropsy.

It is sufficient sometimes that our miseries be only exposed to the eyes of mercy. Mercy is of a preventing nature, and, without staying for our solicitation, is disposed to do us good. The pride of man's heart, which this dropsical person represents, stood in great need of such a charitable physician as Jesus Christ.

3. And Jesus answering spake unto the lawyers and Pharisees, saying, Is it lawful to heal on the sabbath day?

How great must the corruption be, where one is obliged to propose it as a question, Whether it be lawful to do good? It is not out of ignorance, but charity, that Christ asks this question, on purpose to give these men an occasion of reflecting upon their own thoughts, and by their answer to engage them in such as are good. The captious and malicious questions of deceitful and pharisaical hearts, are very contrary to this discreet and charitable disposition.

4. And they held their peace. And he took *him*, and healed him, and let him go;

There is, in wicked persons, a silence proceeding from pride, malice, impotence, dissimulation, and craft; but it cannot hide their hearts from Him who sees the inmost recesses of it. One ought to have no manner of regard to them, when an opportunity of doing good works presents itself. Let this hand, which gives such sovereign relief, be extended over my heart, O Jesus, and heal its spiritual dropsy, the swelling of its pride, the fulness of its corruption, and its greediness and thirst after earthly things.

5. And answered them, saying, Which of you shall have an ass or an ox fallen into a pit, and will not straightway pull him out on the sabbath day? 6. And they could not answer him again to these things.

The meekness and goodness of our blessed Saviour shows itself on all occasions. He instructs, without insulting; he sees the disorder and confusion of these proud spirits, without exposing it; and he reduces them to silence, without desiring to triumph over them. One cannot too often occasion men to reflect upon the depravity of their heart, so manifest in their being unwilling to allow charity to do that for the glory of God and the salvation of their neighbour, which a small temporal interest causes them to do without the least hesitation.

SECT. II.—THE LOWEST PLACE IS TO BE CHOSEN.—THE POOR ARE TO BE INVITED.

7. ¶ And he put forth a parable to those which were bidden, when he marked how they chose out the chief rooms; saying unto them,

Corrupt nature inclines us always to prefer ourselves to others, and to appropriate to ourselves the best of every thing. Pride, which is the principle from whence this eternal preference proceeds, is the dropsy which Christ would cure in these guests. When quality, custom, or laws have regulated and settled places in public assemblies, a man may then take them, but he must not love them. When nothing of this nature is settled, the law of humility and the love of order are the only judges of what is proper.

8. When thou art bidden of any *man* to a wedding, sit not down in the highest room; lest a more honourable man than thou be bidden of him;

To take the highest place when it is not our due, is a piece of vanity which is plain and visible; obstinately to refuse it, is another instance of the same vice, though it be more private and concealed. Humility takes as much care to avoid the ostentation of an affected refusal as the open seeking a superior place. This parable does immediately relate to the outward behaviour; but the thing signified thereby is inward humility, which prefers itself to none, and is not at all ambitious of the first place in the esteem of others.

9. And he that bade thee and him come and say to thee, Give this man place; and thou begin with shame to take the lowest room.

Shame generally attends the proud person. It is neither the fear of being humbled, nor the desire of being exalted by men, which ought to divert us from seeking the chief places; but the knowledge of our own vileness, the love of order, the spirit of mortification, a hatred of pride, a true sense of humility, and a desire to conform ourselves to the example of Christ, and to obey his gospel. It is one thing to hate the punishment of the proud, and another to act by their spirit: the latter is always bad, the former not.

10. But when thou art bidden, go and sit down in the lowest room; that when he that bade thee cometh, he may say unto thee, Friend, go up higher: then shalt thou have worship in the presence of them that sit at meat with thee.

That which, in the parable, is no other than a vice, is a virtue in that which is signified by it. Human glory is altogether unworthy of a Christian's love: the glory which comes from God is that alone which is worthy of his ambition. The only means to attain to this glory is humility; but humility expects it only from the pure bounty of God, desires it only for his glory, and receives it only by abasing itself, and, as it were, losing itself in him. Lord, humble my heart, and cause it to love that place which belongs to it, that it may not become unworthy of that which thou hast merited for it.

11. For whosoever exalteth himself shall be abased; and he that humbleth himself shall be exalted.

This is the unchangeable conduct of God in respect of the humble and the proud. The carnal man will not comprehend it; because he prefers the vain and momentary glory which is offered him by the world, before the substantial and eternal glory which God has promised him. It does by no means belong to man to exalt himself, since of himself he has nothing which is good, since he knows not whether he shall always retain the good he has, and since nothing is more deceitful than the judgment which he forms concerning himself. Let us wait with patience one moment: the day of eternity will discover to us both our own heart and that of others.

12. ¶ Then said he also to him that bade him, When thou makest a

dinner or a supper, call not thy friends, nor thy brethren, neither thy kinsmen, nor *thy* rich neighbours; lest they also bid thee again, and a recompense be made thee.

Our charity must be perfectly disinterested, if we desire to be recompensed by him who has not the least interest in loving us. To make sometimes entertainments and presents, in order to keep up a good understanding and Christian friendship, is to serve the purposes of charity; and God will place them to account, if charity be likewise the soul and principle of them. They are entirely lost as to heaven, if we have only earthly views of interest, pleasure, vanity, ambition, or human friendship. There are very few who regulate these expenses by Christian motives; as if it were not necessary to be Christians, even in the most common actions of civil life.

13. But when thou makest a feast, call the poor, the maimed, the lame, the blind:

A man finds his friends, his brethren, his kinsmen, and his neighbours in these poor people, since he finds in them Jesus Christ, who is all things to those who are entirely his. He who consecrates to these miserable wretches his estate, his cares, his labours, his services, and his life, may perhaps be counted a fool; but how much true wisdom lies concealed under this seeming folly! This is a mystery of faith: we must believe in it something very different from what we see.

14. And thou shalt be blessed; for they cannot recompense thee: for thou shalt be recompensed at the resurrection of the just.

Happy that person who receives not from men the recompense of his charity! God himself will be his recompense. We should think ourselves happy in being able to purchase the friendship of some great prince, the heir of a rich crown, by lending him in his wants, and when he is in no condition to repay us. The poor are so many distressed princes: the kingdom of heaven is theirs; and therefore to lend them in their necessities, is to make our own fortune. What do we not venture upon a deceitful hope, upon an uncertain futurity? Here every thing is sure, every thing is certain, since the gospel is answerable for it, since Christ himself is security for the poor, and since, whatever we lend to them is lent to him in their persons.

SECT. III.—THE PARABLE OF THE GUESTS WHO EXCUSED THEMSELVES.

15. ¶ And when one of them that sat at meat with him heard these things, he said unto him, Blessed *is* he that shall eat bread in the kingdom of God.

He who thinks with faith on the treasures and delights of heaven, is not able to contain his joy. Jesus speaks to all present concerning the eternal reward; and only one single person seems to open his heart, and to feed upon it. The bread of the kingdom of God is God himself: it is with him, as being eternal truth, that those shall be fed and satisfied who have fed Jesus Christ in his members. It is by the infusion, communication, and intimate union of the sovereign good with the soul, that those shall be eternally nourished who have given part of their perishing goods to the poor. Blessed is he who opens his heart and his purse to them!

16. Then said he unto him, A certain man made a great supper, and bade many:

How highly is the honour of eating at a king's table esteemed in the world? But that God should invite a sinner to the delights of his glory, and to the participation of his joy—what transcendent goodness and mercy is this! Men invite others to their table, because they have occasion for them to be subservient to their pleasure, their interest, or to some other designs, which plainly show their wants: God alone, happy in himself, communicates his good things out of pure bounty and an abundant fulness.

17. And sent his servant at supper time to say to them that were bidden, Come; for all things are now ready.

God sends his own Son, clothed in the form of a servant, to invite and conduct us to the heavenly supper. The time of walking by faith, in order to go to this supper, is chiefly since the incarnation, death, and resurrection of our blessed Saviour. All things are ready, because he has done all things necessary to our salvation, has merited all things for us, is himself the banquet, and is gone to prepare the place for us which we are to have. Let us therefore go to this divine banquet with all the fervency of our faith.

18. And they all with one *consent* begin to make excuse. The first said unto him, I have bought a piece of ground, and I must needs go and see it: I pray thee have me excused.

Diverse obstacles to salvation are here denoted: First, idleness, pleasure, and the pride of riches. Can we possibly look upon wealth as a real good, if it be a hinderance of our salvation? And is it not certainly so, when the heart is entirely fixed upon it, taken up with it, makes it its treasure, and is possessed thereby; insomuch that it loses all relish of heavenly enjoyments, and can find no time to use any endeavours to render itself in any measure worthy of them? Men make a necessity of that which proceeds from nothing but their passions, as if the only true necessity did not consist in opposing their passions, and sacrificing them to their eternal happiness.

19. And another said, I have bought five yoke of oxen, and I go to prove them: I pray thee have me excused.

The second obstacle to salvation here mentioned, contains under it the curiosity of the mind and senses, labour, employment, and business. What are the generality of men, who are entirely taken up with these things, but mere beasts, bearing a most heavy yoke, slaves to those whom they serve, always stooping toward the earth, seeing nothing but that, and wholly employed in moving and turning it up? How innocent soever any employment may be in itself, it ceases to be so when it hinders us from thinking on God, when it fills up our whole life, busies our whole mind, and causes us to forget that we were made for heaven, and that the means of attaining thereto is our only necessary affair. Too much leisure and too much business are both equally dangerous with respect to salvation.

20. And another said, I have married a wife, and therefore I cannot come.

The third obstacle to salvation here mentioned comprehends the lust of the flesh, too great a fondness toward our family, pleasures, disorders, excesses, etc. The sacred bond of marriage, which ought to be a help toward salvation, is but too often the utter ruin of it. If a woman, given to Adam in a state of innocence by the hand of God himself, was, notwithstanding, the cause of his fall, by means of a fondness and compliance contrary to his duty, who has not reason to be afraid lest he should meet with a snare in marriage through the bad disposition of his own heart. These ties of flesh and blood are the most difficult to be broken. The persons mentioned before, excuse themselves civilly: this man bluntly declares he cannot come. Some damn themselves in a rude and brutal, others in a civil and well-bred, manner.

21. So that servant came, and showed his Lord these things. Then the master of the house being angry said to his servant, Go out quickly into the streets and lanes of the city, and bring in hither the poor, and the maimed, and the halt, and the blind.

The contempt of God's word provokes his justice. We must acknowledge ourselves to be poor, incapable of doing any good, blind, and sinners, if we desire to partake of the divine mercy. It is a great misfortune, but very difficultly owned as such, for a man to have any thing in this life on which he may set his affections, and wherein he may place a kind of felicity. It is, on the contrary, a great happiness, and as difficult to be comprehended, for a man to have nothing in this world which may make him love it. We are always ready to go to the heavenly banquet, when we are thoroughly sensible of the poverty, misery, and dangers of this life. It is much easier to make poverty than riches a means of salvation. A rich man, who would be saved, must wean and disengage his heart from his wealth: a poor man, the more he loves his poverty, the fitter is he for heaven, and the greater right has he thereto.

22. And the servant said, Lord, it is done as thou hast commanded, and yet there is room.

Every place shows that the kingdom of heaven is for the poor. The gospel is very seldom preached, or instruction given to them, without some fruit. It is proper to them to be of a teachable and open disposition, and fit to receive the impression of the truths of salvation: whereas the minds of the rich, who are proud and conceited, are generally unteachable, shut up, and hardened against the word of God and against his ministers. The places in heaven are numbered, and yet there is always room for those who will work out their salvation. The bosom of God is the place where this heavenly banquet is prepared; it is there that we are to be filled with his good things. How can either room or provisions ever be wanting there, since we are to be in God, and to feed upon him!

23. And the lord said unto the servant, Go out into the highways and hedges, and compel *them* to come in, that my house may be filled.

Observe here the mercy, freeness, and efficacy of the divine vocation! From what errors, what forgetfulness of God, does he not recover those sinners, to whom he has determined to make known his truth, and to open his celestial mansions? He seeks those who fly from him, overcomes those who resist him, and causes those who hate to love him. Void of all understanding is he who despairs either of his goodness or his power, in what abyss of sin and misery soever he finds himself. There is no empty space in the house of God: none of the elect, who are the fulness of the body of Christ, shall be wanting to it; all his designs concerning them will certainly be accomplished. Vouchsafe, Lord, to draw our rebellious hearts toward thyself; exercise, we beseech thee, that sort of violence upon us which does not force and necessitate our wills, but sets them perfectly at liberty, and heals them.

24. For I say unto you, That none of those men which were bidden shall taste of my supper.

He who loves the world, and the things which are in the world, will be excluded from the heavenly supper, unless he disengage his affections from them before the appointed hour. This is a dreadful sentence, but such as is executed every day and every moment. There are four sorts of grace vouchsafed to sinners, and denoted here by these four terms: Sinners bade or invited, ver. 16; called, ver. 17; brought, ver. 21; compelled, ver. 23. The grace of invitation and of outward call is not sufficient; none ever enter who are not either brought and led by the gentle and powerful hand of grace, or even compelled by an extraordinary conduct of God, which breaks their chains, and tears them from their passions. It is an unsearchable judgment of God, that he should only invite and call those who were nearest, and whose hearts were not set upon any evil thing, leaving them to their own inclinations and desires, and that he should cause others to be brought in, and, as it were, compelled, who seem to have been less fit, at a greater distance, and in no manner of expectation of such a favour. My God, thou art the sovereign Master of our destiny; it belongs solely to thee to dispose of it as thou pleasest!

SECT. IV.—RELATIONS ARE TO BE HATED.—THE CROSS MUST BE BORNE.—A TOWER TO BE BUILT.—A KING TO BE FOUGHT WITH.—SALT HAVING NO SAVOUR.

25. ¶ And there went great multitudes with him: and he turned, and said unto them, 26. If any *man* come to me, and hate not his father, and mother, and wife, and children, and brethren, and sisters, yea, and his own life also, he cannot be my disciple.

It is a law that we should hate our kindred, and whatever is derived from Adam, whenever they divert us from following Christ; but then this hatred does not consist in wishing them any ill, but in consenting to lose them rather than lose the supreme good. Are there many in this disposition, to abandon their life and that which is most dear to them, rather than to forsake God in disobeying his law? Are we in this disposition ourselves—we who so often prefer a mere trifle before him? He builds without a foundation who pretends to be the servant of God without loving him, or to love him as he ought, without preferring him above all things whatsoever.

27. And whosoever doth not bear his cross, and come after me, cannot be my disciple.

How can we presume to call ourselves Christians, when we live in ease and pleasure instead of bearing our cross; when we follow the world, which is the enemy of Christ, and conform ourselves to its manners, instead of following our Head, and practising his gospel? No man can be saved who is not the disciple of Christ; and no man is his disciple unless, being convinced of the truth of his doctrine, he loves his precepts, applies himself to the observation of them, makes them the rule of his life and behaviour, and glories in having him for his Master, and in imitating his example. If this be so, how few Christians are there—how few true disciples of Christ!

28. For which of you, intending to build a tower, sitteth not down first, and counteth the cost, whether he have *sufficient* to finish *it?*

To build the tower of our salvation will cost us very dear; nay, we must lay out all we have on this work—at least we must be ready to do it in the disposition of our heart. We are but little concerned about this matter when we take no time to consider of it, to examine the state we intend to embrace, to weigh the obligations thereof, and, above all, those of Christianity, which is our first calling. Retirement, repose, prayer, and meditation upon the fundamental truths of piety, are necessary in order thoroughly to understand the holiness of the Christian religion, and our own obligations and duties. Men would fain be Christians at too cheap a rate, and for this reason they are none at all; and they entertain that foolish desire only because they have never seriously thought of this matter.

29. Lest haply, after he hath laid the foundation, and is not able to finish *it*, all that behold *it* begin to mock him, 30. Saying, This man began to build, and was not able to finish.

Those who have either renounced the true religion, or not performed the duties of it, will be exposed to a public shame and a universal confusion at the day of judgment. They run the risk of making apostates rather than Christians, who baptize adult persons before they have well instructed them in the faith and duties of Christianity. Without doing this, they do not properly list soldiers into the service of Christ, but only prepare deserters from it. From whence do the frequent relapses of sinners proceed, if it be not from our not allowing them time to become true penitents, and by prayer and retirement to settle and confirm themselves in the knowledge and love of true piety and religion?

31. Or what king, going to make war against another king, sitteth not down first, and consulteth whether he be able with ten thousand to meet him that cometh against him with twenty thousand? 32. Or else, while the other is yet a great way off, he sendeth an ambassage, and desireth conditions of peace.

This comparison intimates to us that the life of a Christian is a state of continual war; that there is no virtue without fighting; and that we must be always ready and prepared. The devil, the world, and our own passions are the enemies against whom we are to fight, but of whom we must never desire any conditions of peace. Our consultation is prayer; our counsel is Jesus Christ; Christian virtues are our army; and the all-powerful grace of our blessed Saviour is our strength.

33. So likewise, whosoever he be of you that forsaketh not all that he hath, he cannot be my disciple.

To forsake all, in order to follow Christ, is a counsel of perfection, and an apostolical virtue. To renounce all, in order to be Christ's disciple, is a precept necessary to salvation. We renounce all when we do not set our heart and affections upon any thing here below; when we are ready to forsake every thing at the command of God; when we make use of it, like travellers, only as provision for our journey toward our own country, and are far from looking upon it as a blessing fit to detain us, and to take possession of our heart. This is a disposition as necessary to make a good Christian, as money is to build a tower, or an army to fight a battle.

34. ¶ Salt *is* good: but if the salt have lost his savour, wherewith shall
it be seasoned? 35. It is neither fit for the land, nor yet for the dung-
hill; *but* men cast it out. He that hath ears to hear, let him hear.

A lukewarm or a corrupt Christian is more insupportable to the eyes of God than a heathen. To what purpose is an indiscreet zeal of making proselytes, either by baptism, or repentance, or the priesthood, without observing the proper rules for trying the spirits, whether they are of God, but only to render them worthy of a greater condemnation? There is nothing more corrupt than a wicked Christian, a false penitent, or a priest without vocation and piety. Of how great importance is it, that bishops, missionaries, etc. should value more the having a small number of good Christians, true penitents, and holy priests, than a great number of such as are fit for nothing but to dishonour the church and to people hell!

CHAPTER XV.

SECT. I.—THE SHEEP AND THE PIECE OF SILVER FOUND.—JOY IN HEAVEN OVER ONE PENITENT.

1. THEN drew near unto him all the publicans and sinners for to hear him.

Christ draws sinners to him, and does not treat them as persons unworthy to hear his word. To hear it with pleasure, is one of the first marks of conversion. To what end did our blessed Saviour come into the world, if it were not that the sick might seek their Physician, that the blind might draw near to the light, the ignorant to truth, and the miserable to mercy? To draw near to Christ by faith, prayer, love, and meditation upon his word, is almost every thing which is to be done in this life.

2. And the Pharisees and scribes murmured, saying, This man receiveth sinners, and eateth with them.

Pride corrupts the best principles. We ought to avoid sinners on some occasions, either through fear of being corrupted, or in obedience to the church, which would put them to shame, in order to their spiritual good. But we must not avoid them either out of contempt or ill-nature, or to the prejudice of the duties either of Christian charity or the pastoral care. Envy and ignorance in the ways of God, make men find an occasion of scandal or offence in the most edifying charity. An envenomed heart puts a bad construction upon the very best actions of its neighbour.

3. ¶ And he spake this parable unto them, saying, 4. What man of you, having a hundred sheep, if he lose one of them, doth not leave the ninety and nine in the wilderness, and go after that which is lost, until he find it?

Several duties of a good pastor toward a soul which is gone astray are here denoted. The first is, to have, in some measure, a greater regard and concern for it, than for those which are safe in the fold. The second is, to seek it with care and perseverance. As a mother never shows herself more a mother than when she has lost her child; so a pastor cannot better show the bowels of his charity, than by his zeal and tenderness for sinners. A hireling may perhaps be a little diligent in seeking and bringing back a sinner; but none but a pastor and a father seeks until he find him.

5. And when he hath found *it*, he layeth *it* on his shoulders, rejoicing.

The third duty of a pastor is, to support the infirmities of souls with a discreet mildness, regulated by the divine law; to be sensible of their wounds through a compassion which laments them; and to bear their sins as his own by an humble and fervent repentance. The fourth duty of a pastor is, joyfully to undergo the labour which is necessary to bring souls back to their duty. Nothing is burdensome to charity; nothing is difficult or troublesome to him who loves souls for the sake of God, and considers how great things Christ has done for them. A woman becomes a mother, only by bringing forth; and she cannot bring forth without pain. This is an emblem of a true pastor.

6. And when he cometh home, he calleth together *his* friends and neighbours, saying unto them, Rejoice with me; for I have found my sheep which was lost.

The fifth duty of a pastor is, to manifest by his joy his charity for sinners, and his value for souls. A soul is a kingdom. As many as we can bring back to God are so many kingdoms reconquered: and nothing equals the joy of a conqueror. We must ultimately refer this joy to Christ, since the victory and conquest proceed from him. The sixth duty of a pastor is, to excite others to return thanks and praise to God for the graces which souls have received by his ministry. It belongs properly to the church to praise God for the conversion of sinners; because it is to form her body that he delivers them from the power of the devil; and because he hears only the voice of his spouse, and of those who pray in and with her, and in her house.

7. I say unto you, that likewise joy shall be in heaven over one sinner that repenteth, more than over ninety and nine just persons, which need no repentance.

It is reasonable there should be joy in heaven over a repenting sinner, since it is for heaven, and by the assistance of heaven, that this miracle is wrought on earth. The church triumphant, and the church militant, are but one heart and soul; and the same spirit which prays for the increase and accomplishment of God's kingdom, in the saints of heaven and in those of earth, rejoices also in them both, to see that it is forming, and that the kingdom of the devil declines, by the loss of those members which are torn from him.

8. ¶ Either what woman having ten pieces of silver, if she lose one piece, doth not light a candle, and sweep the house, and seek diligently till she find *it?*

There are three common sources of sin in the church, and in particular sinners: (1.) Want of knowledge, ignorance of duty, and weakness of faith. (2.) Public disorders, and corruption of manners in the house of God. (3.) The negligence of pastors. There are, on the contrary, three sources likewise of reformation in the church, and of the conversion of sinners. The first is, "To light the candle"—that is, to illuminate and revive faith by the means of good books, and, above all, by inspiring the soul with the love of God's word according to that of the royal prophet, "Thy word is a lamp unto my feet, and a light unto my path;" and by propagating the knowledge of the mysteries of religion, and of the duties of Christianity. The second is, to purge the church from the pernicious maxims of corrupt morality, and from public disorders. The third is, to give to particular churches enlightened and zealous pastors, and such as may labour with an indefatigable care in the conversion and sanctification of souls.

9. And when she hath found *it,* she calleth *her* friends and *her* neighbours together, saying, Rejoice with me; for I have found the piece which I had lost.

The piece of silver had not been found, if it had not been sought. The sheep had never returned to the fold, if it had not been brought back. How then should the sinner ever surrender himself into the hands of God—how should the heretic ever return to the church, unless God himself vouchsafe to seek him, unless a good pastor take the pains to carry this sheep, which had strength enough to go astray, but cannot take one step toward a return! It is thy grace, O Jesus, which gives this occasion of joy to thy church; it is also to thy glory that she ultimately refers it all!

10. Likewise, I say unto you, there is joy in the presence of the angels of God over one sinner that repenteth.

The conversion of sinners is the joy of angels as well as of men. The more a man is a friend of God, the more sensible is he of every thing which relates to his interests. He who is unconcerned about them, has reason to mistrust the state and condition of his own heart. It is a torment to the devil, by reason of his envy, to behold the holiness of the just, and the conversion of sinners: the charity of the angels causes them to take part therein, by their assistance, their joy, and their thanksgiving. Wo to those priests who, being angels by their ministry, become no better than devils through their envy and jealousy; or who, instead of rejoicing, are troubled at the good which does not pass through their hands!

SECT. II.—THE PRODIGAL SON.

11. ¶ And he said, A certain man had two sons: 12. And the younger of them said to *his* father, Father, give me the portion of goods that falleth *to me*. And he divided unto them *his* living.

The prodigal son is an emblem of a sinner. How dangerous is it for us to desire to be at our own disposal, to live in a state of independency, and to be governed only by ourselves! It is the greatest mark of the wrath of God, for him to hearken to this proud inclination of our corrupt heart, and to leave us to ourselves. What is the will of man, light and inconstant as it is, if it be not ruled and governed by the unchangeable and supreme will of the Creator! It withdrew itself from his guidance and direction even when it was sound, and, by so doing, impaired and ruined its health; and therefore, now that it is blind, sick, and fainting, how extremely does it want the support of his divine hand!

13. And not many days after the younger son gathered all together, and took his journey into a far country, and there wasted his substance with riotous living.

Man cannot be guided long by himself without finding, by fatal experience, that he is under the direction of a very blind and deceitful guide. The misery of a sinner has its degrees, and he generally arrives step by step at the highest pitch of it. The first degree of his misery is, that he loses sight of God, and removes at a distance from him? There is an infinite distance between the love of God and the love of ourselves; and yet we pass in a moment from the one to the other! The second degree of the sinner's misery is, that the love of God no longer reigning in his heart, carnal love and desire must necessarily reign therein, and corrupt all his actions. The third degree is, that he loses all the spiritual riches of his soul. Self-love is a very bad guardian, and a great waster of the divine gifts. He only who bestows them on us can secure them; and we endeavour to lose them if we pretend to keep them without him.

14. And when he had spent all, there arose a mighty famine in that land; and he began to be in want.

The fourth degree of a sinner's misery is, that, having forsaken God, and lost his grace and his love, he can find nothing elsewhere but poverty, misery, and want. It is just that he who thought he could be happy without God, should find, at a distance from him, nothing but affliction, necessity, and oppression. How empty is that soul which no longer enjoys the bread of truth! What a famine is there in that heart which is no longer nourished with charity!

15. And he went and joined himself to a citizen of that country; and he sent him into his fields to feed swine.

The fifth degree of the sinner's misery is, that he renders himself a slave to the devil. The farther a man removes from the supreme and sovereign Good, the more likewise does darkness overspread his understanding, the more heavy does the yoke of concupiscence sit upon his will, and the more absolutely does the will surrender itself up into the hands of the only master whom he deserves to meet with, who would not continue in the service of Jesus Christ. We are never sensible of this misery until God makes us feel it. The sixth degree of it is, that the sinner finds by experience the hardship and rigour of his slavery. There is no master so cruel as the devil; no yoke so heavy as that of sin; and no slavery so mean and vile, as for a man to be a slave to his own carnal, shameful, and brutish passions.

16. And he would fain have filled his belly with the husks that the swine did eat: and no man gave unto him.

The seventh degree of the sinner's misery is, that, having deprived himself of every thing which he could lawfully and innocently possess, he, in his hunger, feeds upon a thousand criminal desires of worldly pleasures and riches, wherein he imagines he shall find something to satisfy his lusts. Miserable is he, in not obtaining that which he desires; and yet more miserable would he be, if he did obtain it! The pleasures of the world are the pleasures of swine, always stooping toward the earth, always wallowing in filth and mire.

17. And when he came to himself, he said, How many hired servants of my father's have bread enough and to spare, and I perish with hunger!

Let us observe here the several degrees of a sinner's conversion. The first is, that he knows his misery, and the corruption of his own heart: but how should he ever know this, if the light which he deserted first did not first return toward him, and come to seek him in the abyss of his darkness? We cannot "come to ourselves," unless God return to us; as we are far from ourselves, when we are far from God. It is the utmost misery, when God permits the sinner to be lulled asleep in the criminal pleasure of sin, without being awakened by any affliction; or when a continual and undisturbed prosperity make him lose the very remembrance of the true and substantial felicity. It is a beginning of happiness, for a man thoroughly to comprehend the misery of sin, and to envy the happiness of those who serve God.

18. I will arise and go to my father, and will say unto him, Father, I have sinned against heaven, and before thee,

The second degree of the sinner's conversion is, that he resolves to forsake sin, and the occasion thereof. A man cannot forsake them both too soon, though it were only through an imperfect motive of interest, and more from a sense of the grievous consequences of sin than from a hatred of sin itself. Grace purifies all in the sequel. The third degree of conversion is, when a sinner turns toward God, looks upon him as his Father, entertains a desire to return to him, takes a resolution of doing it, and is convinced that he must not delay it one moment, because he cannot too soon cease to be miserable, or, without the greatest folly, by a delay run the hazard of being so eternally. The fourth degree of the conversion of a sinner is, his making a confession of his sin, and beginning that confession by a name of love, "my Father;" because the love of God is the foundation of true repentance. The chief motive to the hatred of sin is, because it is contrary to the goodness of God, and because he, who is the best of all fathers, is offended thereby.

19. And am no more worthy to be called thy son: make me as one of thy hired servants.

The fifth degree of a sinner's conversion is, his humbling himself, as being altogether unworthy of the grace and mercy of God. It is love and the Spirit of adoption which give us a right to call God our Father: we lose this right, when we lose that love, and when that Spirit is withdrawn from us. The acknowledgment of our own unworthiness is an acceptance of the humiliation which is due to a sinner. We love it when we love God; because it is the appointment of his justice, which is God himself.

20. And he arose, and came to his father. But when he was yet a great way off, his father saw him, and had compassion, and ran, and fell on his neck, and kissed him.

In the sixth place, a true penitent, how earnest soever he may be to be reconciled to God, does not leave his state of life to go to desire reconciliation, until after he has settled and confirmed himself in the dispositions above mentioned. In the seventh place, God with his grace anticipates the penitent in all the steps he takes in order to return to him. He is careful to receive him with a fatherly tenderness, since it is his goodness which causes him to return. He pours into the heart of true penitents so much comfort and delight, and caresses them in such a manner, as inspires them with a holy confidence of the pardon of their sins and of reconciliation, denoted, as here, by the holy kiss. A pastor to whom a penitent comes as a father, ought to have the heart and deportment of one, and imitate him whose place he holds.

21. And the son said unto him, Father, I have sinned against heaven, and in thy sight, and am no more worthy to be called thy son.

The eighth degree of a sinner's conversion is, his openly owning his sin and bearing the shame of his ingratitude. The particular marks of God's favour and goodness toward a true penitent, never cause him to lay aside the resolution he has taken of humbling himself. He is faithful to his promises, and it is even an effect of the goodness of God that he is so. How unworthy soever he may acknowledge himself to be called a child of God, yet he cannot forbear calling him Father: it is a contest between confidence and humility; the former restores what the latter takes away.

22. But the father said to his servants, Bring forth the best robe, and put *it* on him; and put a ring on his hand, and shoes on *his* feet:

In the ninth place, the more a penitent humbles himself, and the more unworthy he thinks himself of every thing, the higher does God raise him, and heap upon him the greater benefits. He treats him as his son,—so far is he from depriving him of the name, and giving him time to take that of a servant. In the tenth place, to the grace of reconciliation God adds abundance of other graces, with which he covers the nakedness of a converted sinner, clothing him with Jesus Christ, his righteousness, his merits, his virtues, etc. In the eleventh, he seals this new covenant with a lively impression of his Spirit, which is the seal of adoption, a pledge of the inheritance in heaven, and an earnest of the eternal promises. In the twelfth place, he gives him such graces and assistances as enable him to walk in the way of his commandments and in the practice of good works, to secure himself from serpents and to tread upon scorpions, which are the devil and his temptations.

23. And bring hither the fatted calf, and kill *it;* and let us eat, and be merry:

The thirteenth degree of the conversion of a sinner is, that, being reconciled, he has a right to be present at the Christian sacrifice; and, in the fourteenth place, to be fed with the flesh of Christ, which is the seal of reconciliation on the part of the church. My God, what joy must necessarily arise in a soul which has recovered Christ, which feeds upon him, which receives in him the fruit and grace of his mysteries, and which tastes anew this heavenly gift! Come, sinners, taste and see how sweet the Lord is. Blessed is he who hopes in him!

24. For this my son was dead, and is alive again; he was lost, and is found. And they began to be merry.

The fifteenth degree of a sinner's conversion is, that, for the time to come, he leads the life of a person newly found and raised from the dead. He must not live, either to the world, which caused him to lose himself; or to sin, which give him death; or to himself, who could neither find nor raise himself again: but he must live to Him who was made man on purpose to seek him, who died to raise him to life, and who vouchsafes to become his food, his passover, and his banquet. Let his life, therefore, be one continued act of thanksgiving.

25. Now his elder son was in the field: and as he came and drew nigh to the house, he heard music and dancing.

The sixteenth effect of the conversion of a sinner is, the joy of the church, which shows itself more on this occasion than for the fidelity of a just person; because it is a double triumph, to see the devil's power diminished, and the number of the servants of God increased. This is to imitate God, who infuses more sensible comforts into the heart of a new convert than into that of one who has always served him. This is not the proper place for the reward of souls, but only for the gaining them over to religion. The conduct of God toward the strong is severe and rigorous: he suffers them to toil and labour, far from the comforts of their Father's house, and exposed to heat and cold. But they shall be abundantly rewarded by the possession of the inheritance.

26. And he called one of the servants, and asked what these things meant. 27. And he said unto him, Thy brother is come; and thy father hath killed the fatted calf, because he hath received him safe and sound.

God comforts his church by the return of souls which were thought to be lost. He does not convert them all at once, that he may from time to time renew her gratitude and acknowledgment, that he may give her comfort under the losses which she sustains, and that he may encourage the weak by the sight of what his grace continually performs in souls. We ought to be sensible of his designs, and to have the same dispositions with the church.

28. And he was angry, and would not go in: therefore came his father out, and entreated him.

The seventeenth and last degree of the conversion of true penitents is, their enjoying such graces as are capable of raising envy in the minds of the just, or of the imperfect, or of those who are but little instructed in the ways of God. The most righteous persons are not exempt from these temptations. God is the sole master of his own gifts; and he dispenses them always with the greatest wisdom: it belongs to us to adore his conduct and designs. He is not less ready to support the righteous in their troubles, and to cure their imperfections, than to assist the weak in their beginnings; but he applies himself to each in such a manner as is most agreeable to their state and condition.

29. And he answering said to *his* father, Lo, these many years do I serve thee, neither transgressed I at any time thy commandment; and yet thou never gavest me a kid, that I might make merry with my friends:

Those who have laboured much and for a long time in the church, ought carefully to secure themselves against one temptation—namely, the imagining that God is in their debt. There is danger in employing our thoughts too much upon the good we do, in reckoning up the years of our service, in desiring to be rewarded in this life, and to enjoy the conveniencies and pleasures of it. Let us leave this matter to God, and not pretend to account with him.

30. But as soon as this thy son was come, which hath devoured thy living with harlots, thou hast killed for him the fatted calf

Condescension toward the weak is subject to be censured and blamed. The readiness with which God goes to meet them, is above the thoughts and imaginations of men. We ought to have more compassion toward sinners than indignation at their sins, and to speak of them neither with severity nor with contempt. We must avoid making comparisons of this nature: it is the grace of God which distinguishes us; it is humility which preserves his gifts.

31. And he said unto him, Son, thou art ever with me, and all that I have is thine.

The righteous, being united to God, have a right to the heavenly inheritance by his grace. He who thoroughly comprehends how great the favour of the divine adoption is, and that which Christian hope encourages a child of God to expect in the world to come, looks upon every thing as else than nothing. Those are for selling beforehand part of the eternal inheritance, who desire temporal rewards or satisfactions. That person will never envy the happiness of those who enjoy them, who thoroughly understands these two sentences: that God is ever with him as his Father, and that God is his as his patrimony and inheritance. This is what God speaks to his children, as often as faith speaks it to them in meditation and prayer. Whoever, in the like temptations, has recourse to these two truths, will certainly receive from them abundance of strength and consolation.

32. It was meet that we should make merry, and be glad: for this thy brother was dead, and is alive again; and was lost, and is found.

These words are repeated by the father of the family. Of so great importance is it to make it evident that a sinner is dead in the eyes of faith, because God whom he forsakes is the life of his soul, as his soul is the life of his body. A Christian's sin is a brother's death; and in proportion to our concern for this, is our joy at his resurrection. Let us have a brotherly heart toward our brethren; since God has that of a father toward his children, and seems to be afflicted at their loss, and to rejoice at their being found again, as if they were necessary to his happiness.

CHAPTER XVI.

SECT. I.—THE PARABLE OF THE UNJUST STEWARD.

1. And he said also unto his disciples, There was a certain rich man, which had a steward; and the same was accused unto him that he had wasted his goods.

We are all the stewards of God, sent into the world to employ, to our own salvation, the riches and talents which God has put into our hands, and which are by no means our own. He alone is truly rich, and no man has any thing but what he has received from Him as a sum trusted with him, and for which he must pay interest. What will become of him who has been so far from improving it to his master's advantage, that he has wasted even the principal? The only reason why we are so apt to do this is, because we do not frequently enough reflect upon the moment when we shall be accused and judged. Not to use it according to the design and intention of God, is no other than to waste it.

2. And he called him, and said unto him, How is it that I hear this of thee? give an account of thy stewardship; for thou mayest be no longer steward.

There are three things at the death of a reprobate which are very terrible:—(1.) His being obliged to appear with a guilty conscience before holiness itself. (2.) His having an exact account to give of his whole life, and of whatever he has received. (3.) His seeing himself deprived of all forever. The most holy persons in the world will be accused, examined, and judged concerning the use they have made of their natural talents, and of supernatural gifts, which both belong to God; concerning the employment of their understanding, time, and wealth; and concerning the use which they either have or have not made of Jesus Christ, of his graces and mysteries, and of the sacraments and all the helps of religion. Let us therefore make use of all these talents as persons who must give a strict account of them.

3. Then the steward said within himself, What shall I do? for my

lord taketh away from me the stewardship: I cannot dig; to beg I am ashamed.

What remains to a soul which has lost God and his grace, but only sin and the consequences thereof, a proud poverty, and a slothful indigence; that is, a universal inability as to labour, prayer, and every good work conducting to salvation? He is exceeding rich in the sight of God who knows perfectly how to pray to him, all true riches being obtained by prayer. It is a double poverty to want every thing, and to be able to ask nothing.

4. I am resolved what to do, that, when I am put out of the stewardship, they may receive me into their houses.

Few persons are seriously concerned who shall receive their soul after death, and supply its wants; but the generality of men are very earnest in seeking a retreat for this miserable body which must rot. There is nothing which they are unwilling to do, no industry which they will not employ, to secure themselves from temporal poverty; that of the soul is the only poverty of which they are insensible, and the only reason why they are so, is because they are ignorant of the nature and consequences of it. Make me sensible of my poverty, O my God, my sovereign good, the possession of whom alone gives the true riches, and the loss of whom is the only real poverty!

5. So he called every one his lord's debtors *unto him*, and said unto the first, How much owest thou my lord? 6. And he said, An hundred measures of oil. And he said unto him, Take thy bill, and sit down quickly, and write fifty.

When we know not how to pray ourselves, we must engage the prayers of the poor, who will speak to God in our behalf. The last refuge of a sinner is alms, which is the art of turning our master's goods innocently to our advantage, and making to ourselves friends of his. Heaven belongs to the [pious] poor in a peculiar manner; it is their patrimony and inheritance. Alms are likewise instrumental to the salvation of the poor themselves: for we thereby hinder them from falling into murmuring, impatience, despair, etc., and give them occasion to praise God, to adore his providence, and to put their confidence therein.

7. Then said he to another, And how much owest thou? And he said, An hundred measures of wheat. And he said unto him, Take thy bill, and write fourscore.

A Christian ought to serve his neighbour out of a pure and disinterested charity, and to give alms for the sake of Christ alone. Alms spiritual or temporal, though defective, imperfect, and done for our own interest, are notwithstanding beneficial to the imperfect and to great sinners; because they engage the poor and pious souls to solicit the mercy of God for them.

8. And the lord commended the unjust steward, because he had done wisely: for the children of this world are in their generation wiser than the children of light.

The children of this world are wiser in the management of affairs which are of no moment at all, than Christians are in that which alone is necessary. The use which the former make of their reason, to carry on their worldly designs, will condemn the little use which the latter make of their faith in the business of salvation. It is by this faith that these are children of light; and it is by leaving it useless and unemployed, that they fall back into darkness. True wisdom consists in knowing how to make every thing instrumental to our salvation. We never want means to save ourselves, when we earnestly will and desire it. Faith finds remedies and assistance in the greatest poverty, because it can make a treasure of poverty itself

9. And I say unto you, Make to yourselves friends of the mammon of unrighteousness: that when ye fail, they may receive you into everlasting habitations.

The great secret in the holy policy of rich sinners, is to make to themselves friends in heaven by giving alms. This is the only way to sanctify riches, which are almost always either the fruit or the seed of unrighteousness and injustice, and which, by this means, become the fruit of charity and the seed of glory. Whenever we squander them away in foolish and criminal expenses, we make enemies of them, who will accuse us at the tribunal of God. But we make them friends, advocates, and protectors against the great day, when [from love to Christ] we distribute them among the poor. It is our part to entreat, and, as it were, court the poor; so far should we be from treating them roughly and with contempt, and from disheartening and tiring them out by our delays and mortifying usage.

SECT. II—THE BEING FAITHFUL IN THAT WHICH IS LEAST. —GOD AND MAMMON.

10. He that is faithful in that which is least is faithful also in much: and he that is unjust in the least is unjust also in much.

That which is little is little; but to be always faithful, even in the least things, is somewhat which is very great. It is dangerous voluntarily to commit the least faults, because they may possibly have very great and fatal consequences. Avarice, and the ill use of earthly riches, is an abuse of things of the smallest value; but the love of the world, which is the principle from whence this abuse proceeds, is the source of the greatest evils. A man does not indeed become perfect by alms alone, but it may be the beginning of the highest perfection.

11. If therefore ye have not been faithful in the unrighteous mammon, who will commit to your trust the true *riches?*

Such riches as may be acquired by criminal methods, possessed by the most wicked persons, and are extremely valued by the world, cannot possibly be the true riches. Charity in this world, and glory in the other, are the only riches which we cannot abuse; but earthly riches are almost always abused, without an extraordinary grace. Those things which serve to arm injustice, which are the object of the most violent desire, and the cause and occasion of almost all the evils upon earth,—how can such things possibly render a man happy? Lord, either deliver or defend us from the malignity of this sort of riches, which may ruin, but cannot save us!

12. And if ye have not been faithful in that which is another man's, who shall give you that which is your own?

Earthly riches are false goods, and foreign to a Christian. His own proper and true wealth is not of this world, any more than himself. The good things of this world are only lent and trusted in our hands for use, and not for enjoyment. As we ourselves, are really nothing but what we are in Christ

Jesus, so we have no stock nor inheritance but in him. All the rest is foreign to us. We are made Christians in order to enjoy heaven and eternity; and therefore heavenly and eternal treasures are those alone which are properly our own. Let us weigh, in the balance of faith, the three qualities which our blessed Saviour gives them—"great," ver. 10, "true," ver. 11, "our own," ver. 12, whereas those he ascribes to earthly riches are, that they are little, contemptible, false, and foreign.

13. ¶ No servant can serve two masters: for either he will hate the one, and love the other; or else he will hold to the one, and despise the other. Ye cannot serve God and mammon.

Strange is the blindness of the covetous wretch, to set mammon in the place of his God! If we must choose one of these two masters, is there any room to deliberate upon the choice? It is a real slavery to love riches, to employ all our time and care about them, and to surrender our heart to them. If we have any faith in the word of Christ, let us believe what he here tells us so plainly,—that we cannot possibly reconcile the love of God with the love of money; that God cannot bear a rival in the heart of his creature; and that we do not love God at all, if we love any thing together with him which we do not love for his sake.

SECT. III.—GOD ABHORS THAT WHICH APPEARS GREAT.—HEAVEN TAKEN BY VIOLENCE.—MARRIAGE.

14. And the Pharisees also, who were covetous, heard all these things: and they derided him

Truth, when it opposes the love of worldly things, is generally treated with contempt and derision by worldly-minded men. A preacher who strikes at the darling passions, is very unwillingly heard. God will, in his turn, deride and laugh at those who now deride him and laugh at his word. It has the least influence upon covetous persons of all others, because this passion, rendering the heart altogether earthly, extinguishes therein all faith, which has no other object but heavenly and invisible things.

15. And he said unto them, Ye are they which justify yourselves be-

fore men; but God knoweth your hearts: for that which is highly esteemed among men is an abomination in the sight of God.

How many things do we admire which are an abomination in the sight of God! How different is his judgment from that of the world! And yet it is this latter which men generally applaud, and dare not declare for the former. Of what advantage is it to hypocrites to attract on themselves praises which are as false as their righteousness? It is the heart which shall be judged by Him who sees the secrets of it: it is by the heart that we must please Him. The judgment of men will change, when that of God shall be manifested to their eyes; and it is already made manifest by the gospel to all those who have evangelical eyes.

16. The law and the prophets *were* until John: since that time the kingdom of God is preached, and every man presseth into it.

It is now no longer a time for men to place their glory and religion in a worship wholly figurative, in prophetic ceremonies, and in empty promises, since the kingdom typified, foretold, and promised, is established upon earth. It is not, therefore, a legal, external, and carnal righteousness, peculiar only to the Jews, which we must now offer to God, but a Christian, internal, and spiritual righteousness, which consists in charity common to all nations, which alone is worthy of God and his kingdom, which alone is capable of taking it by a holy and generous violence; an internal worship, which does not exclude the external, but supports, animates, sanctifies, and renders it acceptable to God.

17. And it is easier for heaven and earth to pass, than one tittle of the law to fail.

The immutability of the divine word, in relation either to happiness or misery, yields as much comfort to the righteous as it gives despair to the wicked. Every thing is accomplished and perfected by the coming of the kingdom of God; the shadows by the light, the figures by the truth, the prophecies by the event, the promises by the effects, the imperfection of the Jewish dispensation by the evangelical perfection, fear by charity, and the law by grace. Without this grace, O Lord, what should I be as long as I live, but only a

Jew, intent on the shadow and fashion of this world, which passes away, and oppressed under the insupportable yoke of the law?

18. Whosoever putteth away his wife, and marrieth another, committeth adultery: and whosoever marrieth her that is put away from *her* husband, committeth adultery.

The indissolubility of marriage is of divine right. The good which the law did not presume to hope for, is become the common law of Christians; the evil which it was forced to tolerate, is intolerable in the church. Men may deceive her by surprise, and impose upon her by false pretences, but they cannot make her approve that which Christ condemns, or condemn that which he approves.

SECT. IV.—THE PARABLE OF THE RICH MAN AND LAZARUS.

19. ¶ There was a certain rich man, which was clothed in purple and fine linen, and fared sumptuously every day:

It is then certainly true, that for a man to be rich, to be clothed magnificently, to fare sumptuously, and to take no care of the poor, is sufficient to his damnation; because it is sufficient to hinder him from leading a Christian life. How can we possibly reconcile a life of repentance, mortification, and the cross, with a soft, sensual, and voluptuous life; the humility and poverty of Christ, with the pride and superfluity of riches; and the love of this present life, of ease, and of the world, with a constant opposition to our passions, with the care of our salvation, and the desire of eternal happiness? A life which is most abhorred by men, on the account of such gross crimes as are plain and visible to the eyes, is, in the sight of God, more supportable sometimes, and less dangerous, than a life which, though entirely heathenish, is covered with an external innocency, and with worldly civility and good breeding.

20. And there was a certain beggar named Lazarus, which was laid at his gate, full of sores,

Poverty, the neglect and desertion of men, afflictions and diseases, are a condition which is very hard and grievous to nature; but how advantageous is it with regard to heaven, how much is it to be preferred before that of a wicked rich man, when God enables us to bear it humbly and patiently by his grace? How many wounds in the soul do these sores of the body heal, when the hand of the sovereign Physician applies them as a remedy to the diseases of the heart?

21. And desiring to be fed with the crumbs which fell from the rich man's table: moreover the dogs came and licked his sores.

This representation of the hard-heartedness of a rich man, and of the patience of a holy beggar, contains in it an important lesson, which deserves well to be studied both by rich and poor. This rich man cannot plead that he is oppressed with the multitude of the poor, for this beggar is alone; or that he is at a distance from him, for he is at his very gate; or that his misery is unknown to him, for it is exposed to his eyes: neither can he say that he might work, for his weakness forces him to lie on the ground; or that he was troublesome, for he speaks not one word; or that he wanted a great deal, since he would have been contented only with crumbs: nor, lastly, can he pretend either that his servants took care of him, since not one of them relieves him; or that nobody put him in mind of this object, since his very dogs do it by their example, easing this poor wretch as much as they are able. We cannot, without indignation, read in the gospel this instance of hard-heartedness; but do we not, almost every day, behold in the world instances of the like nature without being affected by them? We there frequently see rich men, who are less sensible than beasts of the misery of the poor, who look upon them as no better than beasts, and have even less care and concern for them than they have for these.

22. And it came to pass, that the beggar died, and was carried by the angels into Abraham's bosom: the rich man also died, and was buried;

The [pious] poor have three advantages: (1.) That they do not set their hearts so much upon this life. (2.) That they are sooner delivered from it, by reason of the miseries of the body. (3.) That they find a new, blessed, and immortal life in the bosom of God, which is the mansion of his children. On the contrary, the rich, who live wickedly, are exposed to a threefold misfortune: (1.) That they make themselves chains, which bind them more strongly, and for a longer time, to the love of a life which serves only to multiply their sins. (2.) That they leave it with regret. (3.) That they fall from one death into another. What joy must it be to a man, at the end of a miserable but short life, to find the bosom of God open to receive him, in order to his being eternally happy there! But how great the despair when, at the conclusion of a life which pleasures and the fear of death make appear even shorter than it is, a man finds the abyss of hell open to swallow him up, and confine him there to all eternity! Can we sufficiently reflect upon the difference of these two states?

23. And in hell he lifted up his eyes, being in torments, and seeth Abraham afar off, and Lazarus in his bosom.

Hell is to the damned not only a prison and a place of death, but likewise a place of torments, which make them feel that there is a God. His justice forces them to open and lift up their eyes toward him, which they had always kept shut against his law, or turned down toward the earth. That small glimmering of light which is left them, whereby they perceive the happiness of the elect, serves only to augment their rage and despair. Lord, open now the eyes of the rich, that they may see the deceitfulness of their riches, and lift up their eyes toward the treasures which are invisible.

24. And he cried and said, Father Abraham, have mercy on me, and send Lazarus, that he may dip the tip of his finger in water, and cool my tongue; for I am tormented in this flame.

After death there is no longer any time for fatherly kindness and mercy: it is in vain to cry out and call upon it in hell. In vain would any one there implore the assistance of the poor whom he has despised: they are deaf and insensible to the entreaties of those who have been deaf to their groans, and unmoved by their tears. It is very just that he, who has refused to give the crumbs which fell from his table to a poor wretch who desired them, should eternally desire a drop of water, and not receive it. "Blessed is he who considereth the poor and needy: the Lord will deliver him in the time of trouble," Ps. xli. 1.

25. But Abraham said, Son, remember that thou in thy lifetime receivedst thy good things, and likewise Lazarus evil things: but now he is comforted, and thou art tormented.

The quality of being the [professed] children of God, which wicked Christians received in baptism, shall be remembered even in hell—but it will be to their greater damnation. This word "son," which is a word of tenderness, is here used to show us that God does not punish out of any transport of anger or passion, but out of a calm and sedate love of his own justice. Riches are the good things of reprobates, because they love them passionately, and place all their happiness in them; and because God either seldom permits his elect to enjoy them, or weans their affections from them. It is then a very miserable state and condition, for a man to have every thing according to his desire in this world, and quietly to enjoy the pleasures and satisfactions of life; since there needs no more to expose him to an eternal misery. The cross of Christ is the portion of Christians: he who bears it not, has no part in him. Let those tremble with fear who are unwilling to suffer any thing, and abhor the very name of mortification and the cross. Happy is that person who makes it his comfort and consolation during the short moment of this present life!

26. And beside all this, between us and you there is a great gulf fixed: so that they which would pass from hence to you cannot; neither can they pass to us, that *would come* from thence.

How great is the gulf and separation between the saints in heaven and the damned in hell! and yet we do not reflect upon it. There is no communication between heaven and hell; no more society between the righteous and the wicked; no more mixture of the elect with the reprobate, as in the church on earth. As eternal happiness consists in the perfect communion of God and his elect, of Christ and his members; so eternal damnation consists in being excommunicated by a general and irrevocable excommunication, deprived forever of God, of Christ, and of their Spirit, and condemned to the society of devils and their torments to all eternity. The latter have not the least hope of ever leaving that place of punishment, nor the former any fear of falling from their blessed state.

27. Then he said, I pray thee therefore, father, that thou wouldest send him to my father's house: 28. For I have five brethren; that he may testify unto them, lest they also come into this place of torment.

The false and selfish compassion of the damned who suffer for others, being an irregular affection, can serve only to increase their sufferings. No prayers nor desires are heard in hell; because there is no charity to form them. A rich man, who, by leaving his relations an example of a soft and voluptuous life, and likewise riches to enable them to imitate his example, leaves them two means of damning themselves, is punished in hell for so doing; and it is this punishment which the rich man before us would willingly avoid. One part of damnation consists in being exposed to the reproaches of those whom we have loved in a wrong manner, and thereby made companions in our misery. A rich man, in the torments of hell, will wish that he could, by means of the poor themselves, make satisfaction for the thefts of which he has been guilty, with regard to them, by his criminal expenses and hard-heartedness; but it will be then too late.

29. Abraham saith unto him, They have Moses and the prophets; let them hear them.

We have Moses and the prophets as well as they; and we have, moreover, Christ and the apostles, the gospel and the apostolical writings, and yet we neglect them. It is a very great instance of negligence for a man not to inform himself of his duty, by reading the word of God while he has opportunity to do it; and it is to expose himself to this reproach, when there is no longer any time to receive the least advantage from it. What is it to hear the word of God as we ought, but to read it with faith, respect, and obedience; to make it the rule of our opinions, our conduct, and our life; and to have recourse to it in all our doubts, afflictions, and infirmities, as our only light, consolation, and strength?

30. And he said, Nay, father Abraham; but if one went unto them from the dead, they will repent.

That man is under a great delusion who waits for somewhat extraordinary to convert him, and engage him to set about the work of his salvation. The wicked foolishly flatter themselves that proofs are wanting to their faith; whereas faith is the only thing which is wanting in the midst of the most plain and evident proofs. The Son of God, who came down from heaven to preach repentance to us, and who returned from hell [or the place of departed spirits] to confirm his preaching, has not been able to persuade us to repent: and yet we imagine, that we should perform this duty if either an angel come from heaven, or a dead man from the grave, to declare to us the absolute necessity thereof.

31. And he said unto him, If they hear not Moses and the prophets, neither will they be persuaded, though one rose from the dead.

He who gives no credit to the Scripture, gives none to miracles, since it is filled with those of Christ and his apostles. Passion has no other design, but to gain time, and to get rid of those proofs which press too hard upon and incommode it, under pretence of desiring better; and when such are produced, they serve only to provoke and harden it the more. Christ did raise another Lazarus, and the Jews would fain have sent him back to the grave, and from that very time resolved upon the death of Christ himself. This Saviour rose from the dead, and it was this very resurrection which hardened that perfidious people, and served to fill up the measure of their sins. In vain does the sun of truth shine upon him who is blinded by passion. Let this but cease, and every thing will appear plain. Faith is satisfied with such proofs as God vouchsafes to afford it; incredulity never has enough.

CHAPTER XVII.

SECT. I.—OFFENCE OR SCANDAL.—FORGIVENESS OF INJURIES.—INCREASE OF FAITH.

1. THEN said he unto the disciples, It is impossible but that offences will come: but woe *unto him*, through whom they come!

God, to whom nothing is impossible, could prevent all offences or scandals; but he chooses rather to reduce them by his wisdom within the order of his providence, and to make them instrumental to the sanctification of the elect, to the manifestation of his justice, and to his other designs. Whatever good God brings out of evil, can by no means excuse the sinner; because he has no manner of share in that good. A public sin does not always escape a public punishment; because the honour of God's justice is often, as it were, engaged to inflict it.

2. It were better for him that a millstone were hanged about his neck, and he cast into the sea, than that he should offend one of these little ones.

Miserable is that person who, being already oppressed with the burden of his own sins, draws upon himself the guilt of other men's, by being to them an occasion of offence. It is a terrible judgment upon this sort of sinners, that God does not by an early death prevent the first causes of offence or scandal which they give to souls. Who is there who thoroughly comprehends how great a sin it is to cause one single soul to lose its innocency, by being thereto an occasion of sin? This is sufficient to draw upon any person the curse of God. But how much more, when the scandal or offence becomes the source of an infinity of others, and causes the loss of a world of souls; as an heresiarch, or an impious person does, who keeps, as it were, a school of libertinism, who justifies and authorizes sin, etc.

3. ¶ Take heed to yourselves: If thy brother trespass against thee, rebuke him; and if he repent, forgive him.

It is not sufficient for the charity of a true Christian not to give any occasion of sin to others: it must likewise assist them in reforming their lives, and even forgive the trespasses committed against it. Let us seriously consider these words of our blessed Lord; for it is not without reason that he admonishes us to take heed to ourselves on these occasions. Instead of mildly rebuking our brother, we are apt to brood upon our displeasure at the bottom of our heart, where enmity, bitterness, disgust, contempt, and aversion are nourished by a thousand disadvantageous thoughts and malicious reflections, and take deep root therein. All that is gained by rebuking him in a harsh manner, is only to inflame the wound which he has given himself, to render it incurable, and frequently to make us want his pardon who before wanted ours.

4. And if he trespass against thee seven times in a day, and seven times in a day turn again to thee, saying, I repent; thou shalt forgive him.

Charity and true mercy have no bounds. It is the greatest folly imaginable, to refuse mercy to others, so long as we stand in need of the mercy of God toward ourselves; and who does not stand in need of it every moment, even to the hour of his death? As the kindness and gentleness of God toward us is the rule and pattern of that which we owe to others, so our rigour and severity toward others is, as it were, the rule and pattern of that which God will exercise toward us. There is nothing more dangerous to such as have need of an infinite mercy, than to set bounds and limits to their own.

5. And the apostles said unto the Lord, Increase our faith.

How necessary is this prayer continually throughout the whole course of our life; and especially when we are to forgive injuries, and to sacrifice to charity the deceitful sweetness of revenge! Faith decays every moment, unless it be supported by prayer. Prayer owes its birth to faith; but faith owes its increase to prayer; and both are a gift of God in every degree. Lord, thou alone canst infuse, preserve, increase, and perfect thy gifts in us, and make them helpful and subservient one to another.

6. And the Lord said, If ye had faith as a grain of mustard seed, ye might say unto this sycamine tree, Be thou plucked up by the root, and be thou planted in the sea; and it should obey you.

Faith is a thing which appears mean and contemptible to the eyes of the carnal man; and yet there is nothing more strong and powerful. Lord, I do not ask this gift of thee, either to pluck up trees by the root, or to remove mountains, but to root out of my heart self-love and concupiscence,—that accursed tree which bears nothing but corrupt fruit, and to sink it in the sea of thy blood. Command, O Lord, and thou shalt be immediately obeyed.

SECT. II.—WE ARE UNPROFITABLE SERVANTS.

7. But which of you, having a servant ploughing or feeding cattle, will say unto him by-and-by, when he is come from the field, Go and sit down to meat?

The church is the field and the flock of the Lord: his ministers are not masters or owners thereof, but labourers and shepherds; and consequently their life is a life of labour, care, and vigilance. This is their portion or task during the day of this life; this is their duty, were there no manner of reward to be expected, since every creature was made to serve his Creator. Let us not expect here below either rest, or reward, or comforts, or caresses from our Master: let us mind nothing but to do his will, to carry on the work in his field, and to feed his sheep: this is the way to be accounted worthy both of his table and his inheritance in heaven.

8. And will not rather say unto him, Make ready wherewith I may sup, and gird thyself, and serve me, till I have eaten and drunken; and afterward thou shalt eat and drink?

One labour continually succeeds another; but it is not sufficient barely to work, unless we do it for God. We then make ready wherewith our Master may sup, when we ultimately refer to him all the glory of our works,—a repast to which he alone has a right. Christ is likewise served, fed, and nourished by us, when we gain over souls to him, which being his fulness, augment and fill his body, and bring it to its perfect age and stature. Happy that person who, through his service and fidelity, is deemed worthy to be admitted to the heavenly banquet, and to have God himself for his food and nourishment there!

9. Doth he thank that servant because he did the things that were commanded him? I trow not.

We are more God's, than a slave is his master's. We do no more than what we ought, when we even spend ourselves in his service, since we have received every thing only from and for him. It is the glory of the creature, to be employed in the works of the Creator; and it is still a new obligation, to receive from him the qualifications which enable us to labour therein. Let us not boast of any thing, since no manner of good proceeds from our own stock, not even so much as a good thought or a good desire. Our stock is our nothing; and all our pretensions are built entirely upon the goodness and liberality of our Master.

10. So likewise ye, when ye shall have done all those things which are commanded you, say, We are unprofitable servants: we have done that which was our duty to do.

There is not a more unprofitable servant in the world, than one who can do nothing unless his master work with him, and work more than he; who can bring him no profit by his labour; and cannot do any thing as he ought, and in a manner which is pleasing and acceptable to him. Such is man left to himself; such is he, who, acting by the spirit of bondage to the law, performs only the external part thereof; and who is not moved and acted by the Spirit of the adoption of children, which causes them to perform the commandment upon a principle of love. My God, I acknowledge with joy, that I owe every thing to thy mercy, and that all thy rewards are acts of pure grace; because all our deserts are thy gifts, and it is thou who workest in us all our good works.

SECT. III.—THE TEN LEPERS.—THANKSGIVING.

11. ¶ And it came to pass, as he went to Jerusalem, that he passed through the midst of Samaria and Galilee. 12. And as he entered into a certain village, there met him ten men that were lepers, which stood afar off:

The leprosy of sin renders us unworthy to approach and draw near to God. There is no deadly sin whatever but carries in it excommunication in respect of God, since it deprives us of God himself. That man who is sensible of his own unworthiness to draw near to God, is then actually drawing near to him. This sense of our unworthiness is the thing by which our repentance must begin. We know nothing of the nature either of sin, or of true repentance, when we would fain be reinstated immediately in the possession of those advantages which we have lost by sin, and are unwilling to bear the shame and confusion of being separated from them.

13. And they lifted up *their* voices, and said, Jesus, Master, have mercy on us.

Prayer must be strong and earnest, when the disease is

great and inveterate. The gift of prayer, in the beginning of conversion, is a great gift; and it is preserved by prayer itself. The farther we see ourselves from God, the higher must we lift up our voices. All that we have to ask in this condition is the mercy of God; and it is of and through Jesus Christ that we must ask it. The double leprosy of ignorance and concupiscence requires a double mercy: a Master to disperse the darkness of the understanding by his light; and a Jesus or Saviour to deliver the heart from its slavery by the infusion of his love. Have mercy on us, O Jesus, our Master and our Saviour!

14. And when he saw *them*, he said unto them, Go shew yourselves unto the priests. And it came to pass, that, as they went, they were cleansed.

Respect, love, and submission toward the church, are here intimated and recommended to us in the conduct of the Son of God. So speedy a cure is the reward of so ready an obedience. God would have us submit, before all things, to the ordinary means of salvation. We ought as much as possible to prevent calumnies, as Jesus Christ here does, by submitting exactly to the laws.

15. And one of them, when he saw that he was healed, turned back, and with a loud voice glorified God,

Acknowledgment for favours and blessings received is so much the more acceptable to God, because it is so rare. A heart which is very grateful cannot defer testifying its gratitude one moment. The world is full of persons who lift up their voice in the church to pray for benefits and favours, and who continue dumb when they have once received them. The design of God in conferring them upon us is to be glorified for them.

16. And fell down on *his* face at his feet, giving him thanks: and he was a Samaritan.

What acknowledgment and gratitude, then, do those owe to God whom he has so often cured of an infinite number of sins! This is a thing of which we are the least sensible, while we very carefully preserve the remembrance of a temporal blessing, of the cure of any bodily distemper, etc.

True gratitude is always accompanied with humility; and this humility is so much the greater in proportion to the greatness of the evil, and to the sense a man had of his unworthiness to be delivered from it. Let, then, a recovered sinner be always prostrate in mind and heart at the feet of his Deliverer.

17. And Jesus answering said, Were there not ten cleansed? but where *are* the nine? 18. There are not found that returned to give glory to God, save this stranger.

Those who are of the household of faith, are oftentimes more subject to ingratitude than strangers, because they are less sensible of their own unworthiness. It is a great blessing for a man to have always been within the pale of the church, or in the way of piety; but the faults he has committed in that state are the greater, and the pardon received for them the more valuable. To render to God the glory of his mercies is to deserve [or to invoke] new; to be forgetful of them is to dry up the fountain from whence they flow.

19. And he said unto him, Arise, go thy way: thy faith hath made thee whole.

The lower a penitent prostrates himself at the feet of Christ by a thankful humility and a humble thankfulness, the higher he lifts him up, and the more he encourages him to walk in his ways. Christ praises the faith of man, to the end that man may praise the grace of God, which is the principle from which it proceeds, and frequently beg this principle of him. It is faith which gives birth to the life of grace in sinners: it is faith likewise which increases and perfects it in the righteous.

SECT. IV.—THE KINGDOM OF GOD WITHIN US.—THE COMING OF CHRIST.—THE DAYS OF NOAH AND OF LOT.

20. ¶ And when he was demanded of the Pharisees, when the kingdom of God should come, he answered them and said, The kingdom of God cometh not with observation:

The kingdom of God does not consist in the pomp or splendour of the world: it is in vain to seek it therein. Every one would willingly find it without waiting and preparing himself for it; but every one runs the risk of never finding it, who does not live in a constant expectation of it, and in a continual disposition to receive it. Carnal men, big with the conceits of a carnal kingdom, the power, riches, and greatness of which have a visible appearance, are far from perceiving and owning the kingdom of God, which is established only upon the ruins of that love which they have toward false happiness. The kingdom of grace is visible to none but those who have invisible eyes, and to whom invisible things are all in all.

21. Neither shall they say, Lo here! or, lo there! for, behold, the kingdom of God is within you.

It is in the heart of man that the kingdom of God and of his grace is established by obedience and love; and this kingdom was made visible and manifest only by miracles, by the subjection of the devil to the power of Christ, and by the obedience of those who forsook all to follow him in his state of poverty. It is very just that we should not find it, if we will not know it by those marks which he has given us of it in his word. A heart which is humble, meek, charitable, and disengaged from earthly things, will always find it, because they are these very virtues which make the kingdom which it seeks.

22. And he said unto the disciples, The days will come, when ye shall desire to see one of the days of the Son of man, and ye shall not see *it*.

We must make good use of the times of grace, peace, indulgence, and light, to prepare ourselves against those of destitution, trouble, temptation, suffering, and darkness. The apostles profited but little by the visible presence and sensible graces of Christ; and had not the Holy Ghost taught them all things anew, and brought all things to their remembrance, what would have become of them in the times of false Christs and of persecutors? Let us fear these times, in which Christ seems to be withdrawn; and let us establish and strengthen ourselves in his doctrine and love, that we may not have the misfortune to be surprised in our weakness.

23. And they shall say to you, See here; or, see there: go not after *them*, nor follow *them*.

It is not to the bare name of Christ, but to his doctrine and precepts, that we must adhere, since there are false

Christs and false gospels. Let us not follow him whom men point out to us, but him whom God points out in the Scriptures, and authorizes by miracles. There are false churches as well as false Christs; and the true spouse is known by the same marks with the true Bridegroom.

24. For as the lightning, that lighteneth out of the one *part* under heaven, shineth unto the other *part* under heaven; so shall also the Son of man be in his day.

The brightness and quickness with which Christ was made known in the world by the preaching of the gospel, may very justly be compared to lightning. As it is one and the same lightning which shineth from the one part under heaven to the other, so it is the same faith, the same Christ, and the same Christian society; and this universality is one of the properties of the true faith, the true Christ, and the true church. That which is now done successively by faith, will be done in an instant, when the Son of man shall visibly appear to all mankind, in order to judge the world. Now is the day of men: it will be then the day of the Lord.

25. But first must he suffer many things, and be rejected of this generation.

Suffering and the cross of Christ are the only means chosen by God to form his church, and to fit and prepare her to appear with Christ at the great day. None of his members are excused from walking in this way: they must suffer, and be hated of the world, before they can partake of his glory. And a man may justly be said to be hated and rejected of the world, when he follows those maxims which it hates and rejects, and exposes himself to persecution on that account.

26. And as it was in the days of Noah, so shall it be also in the days of the Son of man.

The hour of death and that of judgment are uncertain. That which happened in former ages, is a figure of what will happen in the last times. The use which a Christian ought to make of the Scriptures of the Old Testament, according to the institution of God and the advice of Christ, is therein to study his own duties, and to contemplate Christ and his church. The old world, surprised by the deluge, after a course of preaching and impenitency for a hundred years together, is an emblem of that which happens to the generality of men at the time of death, and of that which will happen at the last day to the whole world.

27. They did eat, they drank, they married wives, they were given in marriage, until the day that Noah entered into the ark; and the flood came, and destroyed them all.

The life of men in the days of Noah represents to us, in a lively manner, the sottishness and strange stupidity of wordly men, who are entirely taken up with this present life, and regard not in the least the threats of the divine wrath. It looks as if this life were given to men to no other end, but only that they might acquire such a share of the good things thereof, as will enable them to pass it at their ease, in the midst of all sorts of conveniences, in abundance, and with splendour; and that they might endeavour to perpetuate their name and family by advantageous matches. For is not this the thing which takes up the whole care and concern of those whom the world styles people of fashion, and that which generally makes them unhappy reprobates?

28. Likewise also as it was in the days of Lot; they did eat, they drank, they bought, they sold, they planted, they builded;

To see the life of the generality of mankind, would one not be apt to imagine that they were made only to establish themselves upon earth, to eat and drink, and to perform the business of the natural or civil life; and that the world to come did not at all relate to them? They will open their eyes at the time of death; but God grant it may not be to as little purpose as men opened theirs in the days of Noah and Lot! These two dreadful histories are read with the same indifference with which the Roman history is read; and yet they are types and prophecies of the miserable end of the sinners who read them, if not prevented by a timely repentance.

29. But the same day that Lot went out of Sodom it rained fire and brimstone from heaven, and destroyed *them* all.

What can these words and this figure mean, but only that the greatest part of mankind are surprised by death, while some are thinking only of their pleasures, others of their fortune? Let us learn of Lot to despise and forsake every thing, if there be occasion, rather than continue exposed to the wrath of God. Let us lose no time in deliberating: the danger is always great and imminent when a man is not sure of one moment, and eternity lies at stake. One moment's delay had exposed Lot to inevitable destruction by the fire and brimstone of Sodom: we have infinitely more to fear.

30. Even thus shall it be in the day when the Son of man is revealed.

A sudden and universal deluge, and a rain of fire and brimstone, are only types and shadows of the last desolation. "Even thus shall it be in the day," etc., are not words spoken at random: they are words of faith, which assure us that the world shall be surprised, that the wrath of God shall pour down upon sinners like a rain, and swallow them up like a deluge, and that a very small number shall escape his justice. A false notion which men frame to themselves of a mercy without rule or means, encourages the greatest part of the world in the neglect of their salvation. Let us judge of the divine justice by these two examples, since it is to this end that our blessed Lord proposes them to us.

31. In that day, he which shall be upon the housetop, and his stuff in the house, let him not come down to take it away: and he that is in the field, let him likewise not return back.

Let us leave that to perish which must perish: let us save our immortal part. There is nothing, among all the good things of the world, which deserves that we should hazard our life for it, much less our soul. Life is short, death is at the gate, the hour is uncertain; and at that hour, whatever we love and value in the world will be taken away from us: what folly is it, then, to set our affections upon any thing here below! Let us not be solicitous to change that state and condition wherein God has thought fit to place us; but let us therein, with patience, wait for that state which will never change.

32. Remember Lot's wife.

When we have once quitted the world, we must not think any more of it; nor return to our former inclinations when God has weaned us from them. A man is sometimes so great an enemy to his own good, that he regrets the loss of wicked company, and of those opportunities of ruining himself, from which he has been delivered through the mercy of God. This is a piece of ingratitude which he cannot bear, and which he punishes very severely. We must, even with joy, relinquish our friends and relations, our wealth and temporal advantages, and raze them out of our memory, whenever they become obstacles to our salvation. We love them with a criminal fondness when we leave them with grief and anxiety.

33. Whosoever shall seek to save his life, shall lose it; and whosoever shall lose his life, shall preserve it.

Happy is the loss when a man loses himself, full of sins and corrupt inclinations, and subject to death, in order to find himself again innocent, full of charity, immortal and glorious! The love alone of this short and perishing life can make us resolve to lose all in order to save it; but we must resolve to lose even this life itself, for the sake of one infinitely better and eternal. Had we but faith, should we not be willing to do more for the life of the soul than for that of the body? But that which we do now is the direct contrary.

34. I tell you, in that night there shall be two *men* in one bed; the one shall be taken, and the other shall be left.

Men save and lose their souls in all places and in all states and conditions. First. In the state which belongs to those who live retired from the noise of the world, or are most closely united together. It is an advantage to be united to holy persons, either by friendship or relation; but if we desire to improve this advantage as we ought, and to be saved with them, we must imitate their example. God can easily discern in all places, and distinguish those who are his. It is in the night of tribulation, persecution, extreme calamity, and death, that this distinction is made. Let us prepare ourselves for it while it is day.

35. Two *women* shall be grinding together; the one shall be taken, and the other left. 36. Two *men* shall be in the field; the one shall be taken, and the other left.

The second state is of such as labour for the necessaries of life, or in troublesome and tumultuous employments, the noise and hurry whereof hinder them from hearing the voice of God and the warnings of approaching calamity. The third state is of those who, being neither in business nor in retirement, lead a free and easy life at their own discretion. God has his elect, and the devil his slaves, who are the reprobate, in all places and in all conditions of life: it is therefore necessary in all for men to labour and watch, that they may be of the number of those who belong to God, and that they may avoid the snares of the devil.

37. And they answered and said unto him, Where, Lord? And he said unto them, Wheresoever the body *is*, thither will the eagles be gathered together.

The elect are the eagles: Christ is their prey and nourishment for eternal life. Happy he who is of the number of these spiritual eagles, who soar toward heaven to seek Jesus Christ there, the eternal Truth, and to fasten unchangeably upon him; and not of the number of the ravens, who seek only to gorge themselves with the things on earth! These eagles and ravens are here below mixed together in the church, which is the body of Christ, diffused throughout the world, and composed of all nations; but in heaven none but eagles will be gathered together, and reunited in this immortal body, of which Christ is the head, the strength, the food, the joy, and the eternal felicity.

CHAPTER XVIII.

SECT. I.—THE PARABLE OF THE IMPORTUNATE WIDOW AND UNJUST JUDGE.—THE ELECT HEARD.

1. And he spake a parable unto them *to this end*, that men ought always to pray, and not to faint;

Prayer is a duty properly belonging to such as are poor and needy; and sighing is the portion of the miserable. They must be continual in this life, because we are continually oppressed with wants and miseries. The tempter is never weary in assaulting us: let us never grow weary in resisting him with the arms of prayer. To pray always, and to speak but little, is one of the paradoxes of the gospel: this duty requires little of the tongue, much of the heart. A man may be justly said always to pray, when he has God always present to his mind, and always desires him; whether he do it standing or kneeling, in rest or labour, in grief or joy.

2. Saying, There was in a city a judge, which feared not God, neither regarded man:

If perseverance in prayer triumph over the most obstinate wickedness of an unjust judge, can we have the least apprehension that our prayers will not prevail with God, who is goodness itself? He must needs be very desirous to grant, who so readily inspries men with the confidence to ask. No hard-heartedness whatever is more inflexible than that of an unjust judge; and yet a poor widow overcomes it by her perseverance. What then must necessarily be the success, when the Spirit of God prays to him in his saints?

3. And there was a widow in that city; and she came unto him, saying, Avenge me of mine adversary.

The portion of Christian widows consists in affliction and the cross, in constancy and perseverance in prayer. It is from such a widow that we must learn to pray well, because she is an emblem of the church, and of every soul which has no hope but in God. A widow who is desolate and oppressed, without relations, friends, substance, and support,—what other refuge can she have but humble prayer, assiduous supplication, and importunate perseverance? Such is my soul in thy sight, O my God! and even more desolate, since it has not even the power to pray unto thee, unless thou vouchsafest to bestow it on me as a gift and an alms.

4. And he would not for a while: but afterward he said within himself, Though I fear not God, nor regard man; 5. Yet because this widow troubleth me, I will avenge her, lest by her continual coming she weary me.

How many actions which appear good, have neither the love of God, nor that of our neighbour, but only self-love, for their motive and principle! What other reward can we expect for such, except that which is due to self-love? God, by his infinite love and wisdom, makes these actions subservient to his designs concerning his elect, and to the comfort and consolation of the oppressed. Whenever he pleases, he causes justice to be done by the most unjust judge, whose heart is in his hand, as well as that of the most upright. It is in him, therefore, that we must put our trust and confidence, but without neglecting human means. But we are apt too frequently to ascribe all the glory of the success to these means, and to forget Him who alone made them useful and effectual.

6. And the Lord said, Hear what the unjust judge saith.

We may, after the example of our Lord, make a good use even of the worst examples. Every thing serves to display the justice and goodness of God, by way either of conformity or opposition, either as lines which form the resemblance thereof, or as shadows which heighten the lustre and liveliness of the colours. Faith has the art of changing poison into a safe remedy, and the most venomous herbs into wholesome food.

7. And shall not God avenge his own elect, which cry day and night unto him, though he bear long with them?

To sigh and pray is the portion of the elect in this life. God hears them sooner or later, in one manner or another; either delivering them at present, or making their afflictions and oppressions instrumental to the good of the church, and to the increase of their glory and happiness in the world to come. Those who have no notion of any other happiness or misery but in this life, have likewise no notion of any deliverance but the present; but those who count them as nothing, triumph, by the power of hope, over the very triumphs of the wicked. To pray as one of the elect, it is necessary, (1.) That our prayer be like a cry, by its strength, fervency, and elevation toward God. (2.) That it be persevering and continual. Neither the night, nor sleep, interrupts the prayer of the elect, because their heart watches by the dispositions in which sleep seizes them; and because even their body, while under it, still preserves mortification and humility, which speak to God in silence, and are always heard.

8. I tell you that he will avenge them speedily. Nevertheless, when the Son of man cometh, shall he find faith on the earth?

The delusion under which the rich, and those who place their happiness in this world, lie, consists in this: That they reckon upon a long life, and do not consider that even the longest is but a shadow which passes away. A double error this, from which faith secures the elect, by convincing them, on the word of Christ, that not only life, but even all ages put together, are but a short time. All manner of good accompanies a lively faith; when this is wanting, every thing else is so. Vouchsafe, Lord, to give me such a faith as thou wouldst find in me at thy coming; and grant that it may be in me the source of a true confidence and a persevering prayer.

SECT. II.—THE PARABLE OF THE PHARISEE AND THE PUBLICAN.—CHRISTIAN CHILDHOOD.

9. And he spake this parable unto certain which trusted in themselves that they were righteous, and despised others:

There are two infallible marks by which the true devotion may be discerned from the false. The first is, when a man relies only upon the mercy of God and the grace of Christ, being fully persuaded that, without this grace, he has in himself nothing but an inclination to evil, and an utter inability to do good. The second is, when he concerns himself wholly about his own sins and miseries, and when the more he beholds in others the more he fears in himself. We never despise others, but when we do not know ourselves. Nothing is more contrary to humility, and by consequence to true piety, than despising our neighbour.

10. Two men went up into the temple to pray; the one a Pharisee, and the other a publican.

To judge of these two men by their profession, who would not have chose to have the heart of the Pharisee, rather than that of the publican? But God judges quite otherwise in this case. Let us learn not to judge of others at all, since in order to judge well it is necessary to know the heart. A man may be corrupted in a holy state or profession; he may be sanctified in one which is very common and ordinary. It is the heart, and not the habit, which renders us the servants of God.

11. The Pharisee stood and prayed thus with himself, God, I thank thee, that I am not as other men *are*, extortioners, unjust, adulterers, or even as this publican.

This prayer, so full of ostentation, pride, presumption, and vain confidence in his own merits, is very agreeable to the character of a Pharisee. Let us take great care that we have not the spirit and heart of such a person, either in whole or in part. In prayer, nothing is better than thanksgiving, provided it be very humble and Christian, and not to boast of the advantages we possess, but to pay homage for them to him from whom we have received them. He who knows that piety does not consist only in abstaining from gross sins, and performing the external part of some virtues, never thanks God for what he has received, without humbling himself for his pride, which may corrupt the divine gifts in him, and trembling with fear lest he have nothing but the shadow and outward appearance of virtue. When a man compares himself with such as are notoriously wicked, he may think himself a saint; but he will always find himself criminal when he compares himself with the saints.

12. I fast twice in the week, I give tithes of all that I possess.

Exemption from gross faults, and the external performance of good works, are a source of pride and complacency in those who have not laid a foundation of humility. Bodily mortification and liberality in alms are apt to puff men up, and do sometimes cause more hurt and prejudice to a soul, than it would receive either from luxury or avarice. A fault which truly humbles, is more useful and profitable than a virtue which puffs up with pride; because a false virtue is a veil which hides our vices from us. It is a very miserable condition in which we are here below, where we have as much to do to secure ourselves from the sight which the devil gives us of our own goodness, as from the evil which he earnestly endeavours to put into our hearts.

13. And the publican, standing afar off, would not lift up so much as *his* eyes unto heaven, but smote upon his breast, saying, God be merciful to me a sinner.

My God, how different are the motions of grace from those of corrupt nature! Grace changes the sinner's pride into a salutary confusion, inspires him with a holy indignation against himself, and inclines him to make a sincere confession of his sins, and to offer up humble, fervent, and continual prayer. That which a true penitent thinks himself to be in the sight of God, the same he is willing to appear in the sight of men—namely, the last of all. He is thoroughly sensible how much sin has degraded him; and he lays claim to nothing but a right to perform penance, and to humble himself. He approaches God by standing afar off, out of respect and reverence; he attracts his eyes, by not presuming to lift up so much as his own unto heaven; by not sparing himself, he, in some measure, deserves that God should spare him; and, by acknowledging his own misery, he obtains mercy.

14. I tell you, this man went down to his house justified *rather* than the other: for every one that exalteth himself shall be abased; and he that humbleth himself shall be exalted.

Pride destroys all good works in the sight of God: humility covers all manner of sins, and is to a sinner instead of all virtues. The proud prayer of a pretender to righteousness is so far from blotting out sin, that it is itself turned into sin. Humiliation is the way to glory, because it is the mark of a sincere conversion: pride is the distinguishing character of an impenitent heart. Lord, form in me such a heart as thou wilt crown; give me that humility which thou wilt exalt!

15. And they brought unto him also infants, that he would touch them: but when *his* disciples saw *it*, they rebuked them.

It is not sufficient to pray either with the importunity and perseverance of a poor widow who sues for justice, or with the humility and dejection of the publican; we must do it likewise with the simplicity, and often with the silence, of an infant. A man must not pretend to play the orator in his addresses to God: he is not to be persuaded by human arguments, or to be gained by eloquence. Nothing is more persuasive with him than a plain and simple faith; nothing more eloquent than an humble silence. The imperfection of charity and knowledge in this present life, exposes the humble and the little ones to suffer frequent repulses even from good men; but they have nothing of this nature to fear when they present themselves before God, who rejects none but those who are great in their own eyes.

16. But Jesus called them *unto him,* and said, Suffer little children to come unto me, and forbid them not: for of such is the kingdom of God.

The perseverance of the prayer of the righteous is victorious over temptation; the humility of the prayer of penitents obtains mercy; but the simplicity of the saints renders them worthy of a kind of familiarity with God, to have a particular and intimate union with him, to be capable of being always in his presence, to be his favourites, and to enter even at present, as it were, into the possession of his kingdom. The prayer of the just, and that of the penitent, are for all those who are in this life; but the most sublime prayer, the prayer of intimate union, familiarity, and contemplation, is only for those among the saints whom God particularly calls thereto. To be ambitious of exalting ourselves to this honour is not the property of children, who suffer themselves to be led and carried thereto, but it is the property of presumptuous persons, who are full of their own strength and merit. How desirable are simplicity, innocence, and humility of heart, since they obtain so free an access to Jesus Christ, and give a right to the kingdom of heaven!

17. Verily I say unto you, Whosoever shall not receive the kingdom of God as a little child shall in no wise enter therein.

It is necessary, beyond expression, to bring along with us the simplicity and docility of a child, when we set ourselves to read or meditate upon the truths of the gospel, which is the treasure of Christian prayer. It is properly and principally in this duty of prayer that God offers his kingdom to us, by causing us therein to see the laws of it, and by discovering to us the paths of salvation, and the ways of perfection. The proud, the great, and the wits of the age generally reject this kingdom, while children receive it; because, wherever either reason or the love of earthly things prevails, men are not in a disposition to receive the kingdom of God, which is the kingdom of faith, and contains only such good things as are invisible.

SECT. III.—THE RICH MAN FOLLOWS NOT CHRIST.—THE DANGER OF RICHES.

18. And a certain ruler asked him, saying, Good Master, what shall I do to inherit eternal life?

The thoughts of eternal life are very rare in a young man of quality. Happy is he to whom God vouchsafes to give them! Men ought, after the example of this person, to be fully persuaded that they cannot be saved without doing something; that the first step is, to get themselves instructed in the way to heaven; and that, in order to do this, they must seek after an understanding master and a virtuous guide. Few give themselves the trouble to take these necessary steps, because there are very few who think seriously how they may be saved. If faith be necessary even to a poor man's believing another life, how much more is it so to a great and rich person, who has nothing which gives him any distaste toward this, and who wants nothing which can contribute to the gratification of his senses!

19. And Jesus said unto him, Why callest thou me good? none *is* good, save one, *that is*, God.

It is not sufficient to have a guide to show us the way; we must likewise have strength to walk therein, and none but God can give it us. This whole strength consists in the goodness of the heart; and no heart can be good but by partaking of the supreme goodness. A good director of the conscience ought to take care, after the example of Christ the good Master, to instruct those concerning the necessity of God's grace, who, through the heat of good desires, are apt to believe that they have need of nothing but only to learn what they ought to do. God alone is good, and the fountain of all goodness: every man is corrupt, and stands in need of a restorer to cause him both to will and to do that which is good.

20. Thou knowest the commandments, Do not commit adultery, Do not kill, Do not steal, Do not bear false witness, Honour thy father and thy mother.

Christ seems to forget the interests of God, that he may recommend those of our neighbour. But it sufficiently showed our duty toward God, to say that he is God, alone supremely good, and consequently alone worthy to be supremely loved and adored. Our neighbour belongs to God; and whatever he possesses is an effusion and participation of the being and goodness of God. We therefore offend him whenever we make any attempt upon the wife, life, goods, or reputation of our neighbour. It is an impiety for a man not to honour his father and mother, because it is no other than to dishonour the power, authority, and goodness of God, of which they are the channels, the instruments, and the emblems. God is the principle or first cause of our being, life, and of all the other natural gifts which we enjoy; but it is by and in our parents that he is so, and it is in them that he would receive from us the homage due for all those things.

21. And he said, All these have I kept from my youth up.

Such a one thinks he has done all, who has not yet begun. A man never keeps the law of God as he ought, but only when he keeps it upon a principle of love toward God himself, and through a faithful adherence to his will; and this is a matter concerning which it is very dangerous to flatter ourselves. It is not the work of the hands which we must consider, but the disposition of the heart; and who knows that?

22. Now when Jesus heard these things, he said unto him, Yet lackest thou one thing: sell all that thou hast, and distribute unto the poor, and thou shalt have treasure in heaven: and come, follow me.

Two things are necessary to salvation:—(1.) To observe the general law which is common to all. (2.) To be faithful in performing that which God requires of every one in particular. To distribute all to the poor, in order to follow Christ in his state of poverty, is only a counsel of perfection. But if God require it, it is a precept of necessity, to obey which we must always be in readiness and disposition; nothing being more necessary than to obey God, and to prefer his will before all things. Christ cannot own those for his disciples who are fond of perishing treasures. They are a weight too heavy for a man, who carries it in his heart, to be able to follow Christ. To leave our wealth to rich relations, is to discharge ourselves indeed of it, but it is not to give it to God. It is to the poor that we must intrust it, if we desire to have treasure in heaven.

23. And when he heard this, he was very sorrowful: for he was very rich.

We are not fully sensible of the fondness which we have for earthly things, any other way than by the difficulty which we find in parting with them, and by the grief and sorrow which we undergo in losing them. It is a certain sign that virtue is not solid and substantial, when it sinks under the first trial. There are abundance of persons who lack but one thing, and who are detained in the way by one single affection which they cannot surmount. We have great reason to fear lest that which at the beginning was only an obstacle to perfection, should in the end prove an obstacle to salvation.

24. And when Jesus saw that he was very sorrowful, he said, How hardly shall they that have riches enter into the kingdom of God!

Where there is abundance of riches, there is generally abundance of worldly love; and worldly love cannot enter into the kingdom of charity. If we will not, as to this truth, refer ourselves to the judgment of Him who is himself the way to heaven and the door of salvation, we are resolved blindly to cast ourselves headlong into destruction. If salvation be so marvellously difficult to such as have great riches, even lawfully acquired, what must it be to those who love and pursue them with eagerness and passion, who heap them up by all sorts of methods, and whose hearts are entirely taken up and possessed by them!

25. For it is easier for a camel to go through a needle's eye, than for a rich man to enter into the kingdom of God!

Who would believe this truth, if the Son of God himself did not deliver it? It is very hard and difficult to those who put their trust in earthly treasures; but this difficulty proceeds from their heart, not from the truth. To forbid men the love of riches, what is it but to take away toys from children, a sword from a madman, and from worldly desires that which feeds and nourishes them? A rich man is not properly one who only possesses great wealth, but one who is possessed thereby; not one who distributes it among the poor, as being only a steward, but one who makes it the instrument of his passions, and places his supreme good and happiness therein.

26. And they that heard *it* said, Who then can be saved?

There are but few who are at all terrified by this truth, because the generality of the rich stop their ears that they may not hear it. Since the number of the poor is, without comparison, always greater than that of the rich, why should these men say, "Who then can be saved?" Is it not because there are very few who do not desire and love riches, and who are not rich at least in heart?

27. And he said, The things which are impossible with men are possible with God.

The salvation of a rich man is a double miracle, and a thing which is more rare and uncommon than we imagine. Lest despair should throw us into sloth and idleness, Christ promises, that the things which, by reason of our own weakness, are impossible to us, shall become possible by the power of God. If it be impossible for a rich man to sit loose to his riches, it is so only because he continues wilfully under his weakness, and will not have recourse to Him who admonishes him, by his commandment, to do that which he is able, and to beg that which he is not, and who confers his grace upon men in order to make them able.

28. Then Peter said, Lo, we have left all, and followed thee.

A man may be rich without riches: he may leave all, without having ever possessed any thing. It is by the heart that we cleave to earthly possessions; it is by renouncing them in our heart that we disengage ourselves from them. We leave them, when we cease to desire them, and shut our hearts against all worldly hopes; because we possess them more by desire, hope, and love, than by possession itself. We do not properly leave or forsake any thing, but only when we do it by the Spirit, and for the sake of Christ, and in order to follow him by imitating his example; because otherwise, whatever our hands let go, is retained by the desire of our hearts.

29. And he said unto them, Verily I say unto you, There is no man that hath left house, or parents, or brethren, or wife, or children, for the

kingdom of God's sake, 30. Who shall not receive manifold more in this present time, and in the world to come life everlasting.

God finds means to recompense, even in this life, Christian virtue, which engages a man to forsake all, either to preserve his fidelity to the faith and the truth, or to follow Christ in the way of perfection. How rich in the sight of God is the apostolical poverty of a minister of Christ, who renounces all hopes of any thing in this world, that he may dedicate himself to the salvation of souls, and serve Jesus Christ in a state of poverty! It is the work of God alone to cause a man, under an extreme poverty, and a total destitution of all things, to find satisfaction, joy, consolation, and true peace, while the rich of the world find nothing in their false treasures but an inexhaustible source of fears, troubles, vexations, disquiets, and frequently of all sorts of miseries. Nothing affords greater matter of comfort to a person deprived of every thing for the sake of God, than to see his paternal care exert itself on every occasion, and prevent all his wants, at the same time concealing itself under human means. That which a man finds again in Christian charity, which is, as it were, the stock of Providence, is something very different from that which he would find in his own. It becomes a hundred-fold increased by the blessing which God sheds upon it—but who knows the value thereof?

SECT. IV.—THE PASSION FORETOLD, BUT NOT UNDERSTOOD.

31. ¶ Then he took *unto him* the twelve, and said unto them, Behold, we go up to Jerusalem, and all things that are written by the prophets concerning the Son of man shall be accomplished.

We do not know, as Christ did, the time of our sacrifice, but we know very well that we are continually advancing toward that moment; that possibly it is at no great distance; and that it is much more necessary for us than it was for him to think seriously of it, and to prepare ourselves for it. Christ thinks with pleasure on the accomplishment of his Father's orders concerning him, how rigorous soever they are; and we, for our parts, either think with trouble and anxiety concerning death, which will happen at the time and in the manner appointed by God, or else use our utmost endeavours not to think of it at all.

32. For he shall be delivered unto the Gentiles, and shall be mocked, and spitefully entreated, and spitted on:

The treachery, humiliations, pains, and ignominies which preceded the death of Christ, admonish us to prepare ourselves for our own by mortification and humility. Nothing but a forgetfulness of this sacrifice can induce a man to give himself up to pleasures, at a time when he is upon the very point of appearance before his Judge. And who can pretend to say that he is not?

33. And they shall scourge *him*, and put him to death; and the third day he shall rise again.

Nothing is so capable of giving us comfort, and fortifying our weakness against the fear of painful diseases and the dread of death, as the remembrance of the sufferings, death, and resurrection of Jesus Christ. His sufferings sweeten and sanctify ours; his death changes the punishment of a criminal into a sacrifice of atonement; and his resurrection is the pattern and principle of a new and eternal life, for all those who die in the spirit of mortification, and with submission to the justice of God.

34. And they understood none of these things: and this saying was hid from them, neither knew they the things which were spoken.

The mind of man is naturally shut against the knowledge of the cross, of sufferings, and of death; and especially of those of a God. As criminal as man is, and how worthy soever he is of death, yet nothing but daily experience can force him to believe that he must die; how then, without faith, should he ever believe this of Him who is innocence itself! Open, Lord, our understandings to these truths which are so necessary; and cause our hearts to submit themselves thereto with an humble love.

SECT. V.—THE BLIND MAN HEALED.

35. ¶ And it came to pass, that as he was come nigh unto Jericho, a certain blind man sat by the way side begging:

Let us take care to contemplate ourselves in this emblem of the blindness, ignorance, misery, and poverty into which man is cast by sin, with respect to heavenly things. What is the sight of corporeal things, of which the blind are deprived, but only a source of temptations, snares, and sins? But not to know ourselves to be blind as to the things of salvation, and to want those eyes which alone can discern the truth, O God, what blindness is this! and yet scarce any one is sensible of it, and very few desire to be cured.

36. And hearing the multitude pass by, he asked what it meant.

The cure of a sinner is sometimes linked to, and depends upon, a first motion which seems natural, upon curiosity or mere chance; and yet it is really no other than a gift of God, who intends to heal him. Whenever we earnestly desire to be cured of any bodily disease, we are mindful of every thing, we neglect nothing, and we ask advice of people upon the very least probability of finding what we seek. Why then, O my God, should we be so stupid and sluggish with respect to those things which may contribute to the cure of our souls?

37. And they told him, that Jesus of Nazareth passeth by.

Happy news for this poor blind man! but more happy still for the sinner, that the Author of light and the sovereign Physician is to be found and met with in his way. Jesus passes in this life for the sake of sinners, because they themselves pass away, and must therefore make use of time while they have it. The opportunities of salvation are continually passing away: it is the greatest folly imaginable to let them slip by our delays; and we are far from doing it when the cure of our bodies is the thing in question.

38. And he cried, saying, Jesus, *thou* Son of David, have mercy on me.

There is no occasion to move this blind man to cry out—the love of sight is a sufficient motive. He who does not pray desires nothing; a strong desire either causes a man to pray much, or is itself fervent prayer. We may judge of our heart by our prayer, without any fear of deceiving ourselves. We are certainly insensible of our spiritual diseases, when we do not find ourselves inclined and moved to pray; and we are blind to our miseries, when we do not seek at all to obtain mercy.

39. And they which went before rebuked him, that he should hold his peace: but he cried so much the more, *Thou* Son of David, have mercy on me.

Happy is that person whom nothing can hinder from crying out incessantly after his Deliverer! We sometimes condemn persons for praying too long or too often, not perceiving that it is God who constrains them thus to pray, by opening and fixing their eyes upon their own wants and failings, and upon the blessings which they wait for, and by giving them a lively sense of their misery, and an ardent thirst after righteousness.

40. And Jesus stood, and commanded him to be brought unto him: and when he was come near, he asked him,

The prayer of faith renders Christ attentive to our miseries. It is the fruit of perseverance and earnestness in prayer, to engage at length the goodness of God to cast his eyes upon us. When we are once got above the censures of the world, and resolve in good earnest to labour after conversion, God declares himself in favour of us, and causes us to come near unto him. Let the sinner be then transported with joy, for his recovery draws nigh.

41. Saying, What wilt thou that I shall do unto thee? And he said, Lord, that I may receive my sight.

We cannot too often pray for the bright and active light of faith. Men prefer the light of the day, an advantage common to them with flies, before all earthly riches, no part of which is desired by this blind man; and yet the generality prefer even these perishing riches to the light of faith, and to that infinite source of light which is promised us in heaven. How corrupt is reason! How blind a judge is sense! How little does carnal man know how to choose his own happiness!

42. And Jesus said unto him, Receive thy sight: thy faith hath saved thee.

I have eyes and see not, neither am I worthy to see; but vouchsafe, O Lord, only to say to my soul, "Receive thy sight!" and it will presently perceive that thou art its God, that thou alone art worthy to be served, and that all other things are but vanity and vexation of spirit. God, by the sole motion of his will, enlightens and heals the soul as well as the body; he commands, and is immediately obeyed. Faith is properly ours, because we believe by an act of our will; and yet it is the gift of God, because it is he who worketh in us both the will to believe and the act of believing itself. He first gives us faith to pray, and then grants all the rest to prayer.

43. And immediately he received his sight, and followed him, glorifying God: and all the people, when they saw *it*, gave praise unto God.

Love follows faith. The mind, enlightened of God, carries the heart toward him. Happy is that blind person to whom God gives not only eyes to know him, but likewise feet to follow, a tongue to praise, and a heart to love him! To follow Christ is to imitate him, and to lead such a life as is answerable to what he has done to enlighten our minds. The glory which we ought to render him consists not in words, but in works. A true conversion, which no way contradicts itself, but is followed by an edifying life, makes known the power and majesty of God in a more eminent manner than the greatest external miracles.

CHAPTER XIX.

SECT. I.—ZACCHEUS.

1. And *Jesus* entered and passed through Jericho. 2. And, behold, *there was* a man named Zaccheus, which was the chief among the publicans, and he was rich.

Jesus shows the truth of his word by plain and visible effects: in the rich man, abandoned to the love of his wealth, (chap. xviii.) how difficult the salvation of the rich is; in Zaccheus, how easy it is by the assistance of God's grace. Men have double chains to break when they are rich, and are likewise in a post wherein they grow every day richer, as when they have the management of the public treasure. The public good, perhaps, requires that a man should continue in his place; but if his eternal salvation require that he should leave it, is there the least room for deliberation? Another person besides thee may take upon him the care of the public revenues; but none but thou thyself can save thy own soul.

3. And he sought to see Jesus* who he was; and could not for the press, because he was little of stature. [**Fr.* to know him.]

A desire to know spiritual and invisible riches, is an extraordinary grace in a person who abounds in earthly. The first seed of salvation for such a man is, to desire to know his Saviour; but none but he who sowed the seed in his heart can make it bring forth fruit therein. There are two impediments which hinder the conversion of such a person,—the crowd of the world and its affairs, and the littleness of the heart of man for the things of salvation. It is absolutely necessary to leave this crowd, and to be lifted up by grace, in order to endeavour earnestly to know and follow Jesus Christ. Those great men, considered in their public offices, civil or military, are yet often, in respect of the business of salvation, even less than children.

4. And he ran before, and climbed up into a sycamore tree to see him; for he was to pass that *way.*

It is a great gift, and very necessary in order to a true conversion, for a man to have a holy eagerness to raise himself above earthly things, that he may see and know Christ, and to surmount all the obstacles which proceed from the world and from corrupt nature. One need only be really willing to think seriously of salvation, and to set about this work, and all outward obstacles will appear as nothing. They are almost all surmounted, when once we are got above the judgments and discourses of men, which generally stop those who are exposed to them. Had Zaccheus considered worldly honour, his rank, his office, and his wealth, he would never have taken this method, which exposed him to the laughter of the people; but then he would not have seen Christ, and perhaps had never been saved. Men are sometimes lost by refusing to take some certain steps upon which God has made their salvation to depend.

5. And when Jesus came to the place, he looked up, and saw him, and said unto him, Zaccheus, make haste, and come down; for to-day I must abide at thy house.

Make haste and descend, O sinner, into thy original nothing; for it is in thy heart that Christ intends to abide, by means of the communion, or by his other favours; and it is by humility that the heart is prepared to receive him. God gives men a desire to know him; and he goes even beyond this desire, by giving himself to be possessed by them. His designs concerning souls begin first to appear by the call to conversion. This is the effect of the notice taken of them by his mercy, by which he determined to make his abode in those souls. He chooses of his own accord, and without any invitation, because his love precedes all merit, and because he shows grace and favour to whom he pleases, and does it with an absolute authority.

6. And he made haste, and came down, and received him joyfully.

So ready and sincere an obedience makes it evident that Christ spoke to the heart of Zaccheus, and had already taken possession of it. His joy shows plainly, that he knew the good which he possessed, that he was far from thinking himself worthy of it, and that he was not at all solicitous what judgment the scribes and Pharisees would pass upon this matter. The sincerity of our desires is known by our works. In receiving the poor, or giving them sufficient to procure themselves lodging, we imitate the example of Zaccheus, and receive Jesus Christ himself: but then we must, like him, do this joyfully, and with love.

7. And when they saw *it*, they all murmured, saying, That he was gone to be guest with a man that is a sinner.

The ways of God's mercy toward sinners are hid from carnal men, as well as his designs in the incarnation of his Son. Alas! who can say that there does not happen to himself somewhat like that which we here see in these blind persons, who blame our blessed Saviour for that very thing which ought to render him the more amiable; who undertake to judge of the heart, which is altogether unknown to them; and who do not in the least perceive the change of that of Zaccheus in his humility, obedience, and his whole behaviour? It is thy work alone, O Jesus, to search into sinners, even to the very bottom of their hearts; and without this remedy, what would become of them?

8. And Zaccheus stood, and said unto the Lord, Behold, Lord, the

half of my goods I give to the poor; and if I have taken any thing from any man by false accusation, I restore *him* fourfold.

True conversion shows itself by the change of life. We cannot possibly secure our salvation, without making satisfaction to men by an exact restitution, rather exceeding than deficient; and without making satisfaction likewise to God, as far as we are able, by alms proportioned, in some measure, to our substance and our sins. A true penitent regards not the censures of the world, and vindicates himself only by his works. He leaves his justification to Him who knows his heart, and has no other thought but to condemn himself. The judgment which, of his own accord, this penitent passes against himself, will condemn those hard and impenitent hearts who reject all the remedies which are offered them, and who will do nothing to make the least atonement for their crimes.

9. And Jesus said unto him, This day is salvation come to this house, forasmuch as he also is a son of Abraham.

Men sometimes despise a poor sinner, and at the same time he is an elect of God, a child of promise, an Israelite indeed, and an heir of the blessings promised in a figure to Abraham. Those whom God has chosen from all eternity to salvation, cannot fail of receiving grace. Grant, Lord, that a lively faith, and a life of faith, may make us true children of Abraham, and give us a right to expect his inheritance!

10. For the Son of man is come to seek and to save that which was lost.

These are comfortable words for sinners. How much soever they are gone astray, let them not despair, since no less a person than God is come to seek them. What progress soever the righteous have made, let them not imagine that they have no longer any occasion of being sought. They have still their wanderings as well as sinners; and always carry in their own hearts an evil principle which leads them out of the way. Lord, seek in me that which is gone astray; save that which is lost; and preserve that which thou hast already found!

SECT. II.—THE PARABLE OF THE TEN POUNDS.

11. And as they heard these things, he added and spake a parable, because he was nigh to Jerusalem, and because they thought that the kingdom of God should immediately appear.

These words, so full of comfort and consolation, give none at all to these worldly souls, in whom they only raise a desire and expectation of a present deliverance and a temporal kingdom. Men frequently render the most sacred truths altogether fruitless and ineffectual as to themselves; because their hearts being filled with the things of this world, can neither relish nor comprehend those of the other. The kingdom of God is indeed about to appear immediately; but it is the kingdom of a God crucified, and reigning upon the cross, in order to reign by the cross in our hearts.

12. He said therefore, A certain nobleman went into a far country to receive for himself* a kingdom, and to return. [**Fr.* Take possession of.]

Christ is truly a person of great birth, being born the Son of God from all eternity, and the son of David according to the flesh. He concealed the greatness of his first birth, and regarded not that of the second, to confound the vanity of men, and to teach them humility. The glory of which he is gone to take possession, is a country far remote from the low condition of man: it is the life of heaven, which differs vastly from that of earth: it is a state of power and immortality, which bears no resemblance with this state of weakness. Let us comfort ourselves: he will certainly return to conduct us thither.

13. And he called his ten servants, and delivered them ten pounds, and said unto them, Occupy till I come.

The belief of the return and second coming of Christ, and the uncertainty under which he has left us as to the time of his coming, ought to awaken us from our slumber. We have but very little faith, if we are not continually preparing ourselves against his return, by making a good use of the gifts of God. There is no person whatever, who has not some of these gifts to improve. The common sort of Christians have the knowledge of God and Christ, the call to the true church, instructions, and many other graces: beside these gifts, the ministers of the church ought to improve whatever they have received for the salvation of others. How few of them are there who take care to employ their talent, and to employ it well! They either lose it by vanity, or let it lie useless through sloth.

14. But his citizens hated him, and sent a message after him saying, We will not have this *man* to reign over us.

This is no more than a mere shadow of the rebellion of a sinner against his God. Whoever will not have Jesus Christ to reign over him, cannot possibly avoid being a slave to sin under the dominion of the devil. None but a fool or a madman would speak as these citizens do: and yet we say the very same thing by our works, when we do not live according to the law of Christ. Whoever blindly follows the maxims of the world, which is an enemy to Christ, declares plainly enough, by so doing, that he disclaims the authority and government of Christ. Preserve in me, O Lord, the will which thou hast vouchsafed to give me, never to have any other king over my heart beside thyself!

15. And it came to pass, that when he was returned, having received the kingdom, then he commanded these servants to be called unto him, to whom he had given the money, that he might know how much every man had gained by trading.

How great will the sinner's despair be, when he must give an account of the employment of his time, and of the use of his understanding, will, and senses, of all his substance, of all the graces he has received, and even of the blood of Jesus Christ! The account which pastors must give, will be, without comparison, much more dreadful. Souls are the treasure of Christ: it is in these he desires to grow rich. A pastor who neglects them, and does not employ his ministry and authority, his time and talents, his industry and labours, to gain them for God, alas! what answer will he be able to make to him who has intrusted them to his care? Lord, open the eyes, and touch the heart of those unfaithful servants, who do nothing in thy church but scandalize and ruin souls.

16. Then came the first, saying, Lord, thy pound hath gained ten pounds.

How great will be the consolation of the just man, whose

conscience shall give testimony of his fidelity at the hour of death! What joy will a good pastor experience, who has preserved and increased the flock of Christ, and sacrificed himself to gain over souls to him! Such a one appears with the greater confidence, because he ascribes nothing to himself, but attributes all to grace. It is the Lord's gift, and not the servant's industry, which produces this gain and advantage; and it is even a part of this gain, to render to God all the glory of his gifts.

17. And he said unto him, Well, thou good servant: because thou hast been faithful in a very little, have thou authority over ten cities.

God praises and rewards his own gifts, in praising and rewarding the goodness and faithfulness of his servants. The only true and advantageous praise is that which God will give at the last day: let us be very careful not to anticipate that time, by desiring the praise of men, which is so deceitful, false, and dangerous. The gifts which God bestows on men in this life, are not to be compared with those of the world to come. Our virtues are in themselves but a small and inconsiderable matter; and God, in rewarding them, has more regard to his own mercy, than to their worth and value.

18. And the second came, saying, Lord, thy pound hath gained five pounds. 19. And he said likewise to him, Be thou also over five cities.

Fidelity has several degrees, as talents are different, and not one shall lose its reward from Him whose justice and goodness are equally infinite. Fidelity is the thing which God requires: it is this which makes the good servant; it is this which makes all his merit in the sight of God. The honour, riches, power, and authority of a temporal government, are but a faint shadow and resemblance of that which he shall receive at the hands of God, who has faithfully managed andim proved the wealth of his sovereign Master. It is to this advancement and greatness, that all Christian ambition ought to tend.

20. And another came, saying, Lord, behold, *here is* thy pound, which I have kept laid up in a napkin:

This negligent and slothful servant ought to make all pastors and clergymen tremble, who imagine that they lead an innocent life if they do but avoid the grosser sins, and only lead an easy and quiet life in idleness and indolence. In a priest it is a great evil not to do any good. Not to use the gifts of God is to abuse them. He loses them who does not make them serviceable to the good of the church. Rest is a crime in one who is called to a laborious life; and we cannot live to ourselves alone, when we belong to the church.

21. For I feared thee, because thou art an austere man: thou takest up that thou layedst not down, and reapest that thou didst not sow.

It is a strange blindness for a man to imagine that he can justify himself by accusing God of injustice! Self-love, which conducts itself in the affairs relating to heaven by views only of interest, and by a servile fear, will never make any other than mean-spirited and slothful ministers, and such as are unconcerned for the glory of God. Love never frames to itself any idea of God which is unworthy of his goodness and mercy; and it is always ready to hope in him and to labour for him. Servile fear represents God to itself no otherwise than as a hard, austere, imperious, and unjust Master; and this it does to palliate its own idleness, to have some pretence to murmur against him, and to screen itself from his justice.

22. And he saith unto him, Out of thine own mouth will I judge thee, *thou* wicked servant. Thou knewest that I was an austere man, taking up that I laid not down, and reaping that I did not sow: 23. Wherefore then gavest thou not my money into the bank, that at my coming I might have required mine own with usury?

The sinner, accused by his own conscience, and confounded by his own wickedness, will be able, at death and judgment, to find no excuse but such as will serve only to increase his condemnation. Self-love forms to itself a God according to its own fancy and the humour of its different passions: sometimes such a one as is mild and indulgent without rule or measure; at other times, one who is excessively rigorous and severe. It is only by the word and dispensations of God that we can frame a true notion of his justice and his mercy. A false notion of his mercy encourages abundance of bad Christians in the neglect of their salvation, and a forgetfulness of their duty: a false notion of his justice and severity, in respect of those punishments which he will inflict for the faults committed in the direction of souls, increases idleness and sloth in a great number of ministers. It is therefore of the utmost importance imaginable for a man to know God well, and not to judge of him any otherwise than according to the representation which he has been pleased to give of himself in the Scriptures.

24. And he said unto them that stood by, Take from him the pound, and give *it* to him that hath ten pounds.

He who has not charity, which alone causes men to make a good use of God's other gifts, shall be deprived even of these. The righteous are gainers by the loss of the wicked: the grace which one person neglects to use is frequently transferred to another. The grace of being zealous for the salvation of souls, of relieving the poor, and of promoting and advancing the works of God, is sometimes neglected by those who are peculiarly obliged thereto by their ministry; and is given to inferior ministers, to voluntary labourers, to laymen, and to devout women.

25. (And they said unto him, Lord, he hath ten pounds.)

Nothing appears more surprising to carnal men, than to see the holiest persons growing daily richer, and still acquiring new virtues. It is our duty, without the least envy, to admire the goodness of God in heaping his mercies upon them, and causing them to make a continual progress in fidelity. It is his glory to show that a soul, to which nothing seems to be wanting, is visibly raising itself to higher degrees of perfection, by proceeding from the observation of the ten commandments to an exact practice of the evangelical counsels. The one is the recompense of the other. Let us not admire this after a supine and fruitless manner.

26. For I say unto you, That unto every one which hath shall be given; and from him that hath not, even that he hath shall be taken away from him.

The righteous person, being exactly faithful, increases continually in charity: the wicked becomes continually poorer and more unworthy, by the increase of his sensual affection. Faith is nourished by good works, and grows stronger by the good which it causes a man to do; it grows weak and decays, from time to time, in those who live not by faith, and who do not perform the works thereof. Grace, piety, the love of God, and a zeal for his glory, increase in a pastor or a priest in proportion to his labours for the good of the church, and the salvation of souls: every thing diminishes, and is at last entirely lost, in those who appear the most pious, when they neglect their ministry and do not labour at all in the work of God.

27. But those mine enemies, which would not that I should reign over them, bring hither, and slay *them* before me.

Those who will not go to Jesus Christ in order to receive life, shall one day be brought before him to receive the sentence of eternal death. That which is separated in the parable is joined in the truth signified thereby: a man being always an enemy of Christ when he is a wicked servant, and a slothful, idle, and unfaithful minister. To be deprived of all the gifts of God, of all sorts of good things, and to lose the beatific life—that is, the sight and love of God in which it consists,—this is a double death which will never have an end; and will be the eternal portion of all those who would not that Christ should reign here below in their hearts by charity, but have refused to yield obedience to his will, and to perform the duties belonging to their state.

SECT. III.—CHRIST'S ENTRY INTO JERUSALEM.

28. ¶ And when he had thus spoken, he went before, ascending up to Jerusalem.

Christ, our head and pattern, goes before us toward the cross and to the sacrifice: can we refuse to follow him? It is the comfort and consolation of his faithful ministers, who, in performing their duty, expose themselves to all kinds of danger to see Jesus Christ at their head, and to fight and suffer under his conduct, after his example, and by his grace. Men are very willing to follow him to Jerusalem, there to celebrate the passover with him; but very rarely do they follow him so as to be willing to be together with him the Sacrifice of the passover. Whoever is associated to the priesthood of Christ, ought to love all the functions thereof; of which it is one of the principal for a man to sacrifice himself for the advantage of Christ's church, and for all the designs of God his Father.

29. And it came to pass, when he was come nigh to Bethphage and Bethany, at the mount called *the mount* of Olives, he sent two of his disciples, 30. Saying, Go ye into the village over against *you;* in the which at your entering ye shall find a colt tied, whereon yet never man sat: loose him, and bring *him hither.*

The office of priests and preachers is, to go to seek those who have not yet borne the yoke of the gospel, to assist them in breaking the bands of sin, and to lead and conduct them to Jesus Christ. In order to this, it is necessary for them to be sent by him: mission being the source of all ecclesiastical authority, and the door by which they must enter into all the sacred functions. God is pleased to represent his greatest designs to us by the meanest and lowest things; as the conversion of the nations, the framing of his church, and the sanctification of souls bound and held captive by sin, are represented by what passes here. The work of God is a work of humility: this virtue ought likewise to be the distinguishing character of the workmen.

31. And if any man ask you, Why do ye loose *him?* thus shall ye say unto him, Because the Lord hath need of him.

How different are the needs of God from those of men! The creature has need of the Creator, the sinner of mercy, and the sick person of the sovereign Physician, through indigence, misery, and weakness. God has need of the poor, the miserable, and the sick, only to make his riches, goodness, and omnipotence the more evident and illustrious. Vouchsafe, Lord, to count it thy glory to make them shine forth in me!

32. And they that were sent went their way, and found even as he had said unto them. 33. And as they were loosing the colt, the owners thereof said unto them, Why loose ye the colt? 34. And they said, The Lord hath need of him.

The designs of God must be accomplished, and they are all contained in the mystery of Christ entire, including both the head and the members. His church is necessary to him, because she is his spouse, his fulness, and his body; and this body is composed of all nations, which, through ignorance of the true God, were become like beasts, without reason or understanding. The easiness which these disciples find in bringing away the colt, denotes that easiness wherewith the almighty power of God would bring all people into the church by the preaching of the apostles, and that docility which grace inspires into the most savage and untractable hearts. Remember, Lord, that my heart is of the number of those over which all power has been given unto thee.

35. And they brought him to Jesus: and they cast their garments upon the colt, and they set Jesus thereon.

That which God requires of us by these circumstances wherein Christ appears to the eyes of our faith, is to carry this Saviour in our hearts and bodies; to be humble, teachable, and obedient to his word; to suffer ourselves to be guided by his Spirit; by no means to contradict the holiness of his precepts; to go forward with peace and meekness in his ways, bearing the yoke of our duty; and to be always disposed to follow the will of Him whom we carry within ourselves. It is not through want of power, but through mystery, that Christ chooses to be assisted by his apostles. He hereby teaches us that it is the part of his ministers to prepare souls for him, to be workers together with him toward their sanctification, and to serve him by their ministry, in engaging them to bear the yoke of the gospel.

36. And as he went, they spread their clothes in the way.

It is an instance of generosity well becoming a Christian, to make every thing subservient to the triumph and reign of Christ in the church. We must, if it be necessary, strip ourselves of all, that he may reign and triumph in our hearts. We here see the power of Christ over the hearts of men in this sudden and general agreement of all the people, who, without the least unwillingness, spread their clothes in the way, to honour Jesus Christ. But what shall we think, when we see millions of martyrs pour out their blood, and lay down their lives for the glory of his name, and Christians without number renounce all things, and trample under foot honours and riches, in order to follow him!

37. And when he was come nigh, even now at the descent of the mount of Olives, the whole multitude of the disciples began to rejoice

and praise God with a loud voice, for all the mighty works that they had seen;

A man is not truly a disciple of Christ when he is unconcerned for his glory. The progress of the gospel in the remotest countries, the triumph of Christ over hearts the most barbarous, and the conversion of the most unknown people, ought to transport us with joy if we love the kingdom of God. If the mighty works which God has wrought publicly for the salvation of the world and the establishment of the church, require a public joy, every one ought in proportion to praise and bless God for that which he has done in his heart, and for all the particular mercies which have contributed to his salvation.

38. Saying, Blessed *be* the King that cometh in the name of the Lord: peace in heaven, and glory in the highest.

What joy does not a true Christian feel, when he has reason to think that he is drawing nigh to the heavenly Jerusalem in following Christ, and that the perfect kingdom of God is about to appear! How much greater will be the joy of the blessed in that great day of the complete triumph of Christ and his elect! Let us go forth to meet him by our desires; and let us with the saints say, "Blessed be the King who cometh in the name of the Lord!" The remembrance of the mysteries of Christ will be an eternal subject of praise and benediction in heaven. It is there that peace will forever flourish, and that we shall fully taste the fruit of glory: here we have nothing but the seed and the bud thereof.

39. And some of the Pharisees from among the multitude said unto him, Master, rebuke thy disciples.

The praise of God is troublesome to the ears of the world; and envy cannot hear the good which is spoken of others. The proud, like the Pharisees, will not have Christ to reign over them, and cannot bear our insisting upon the kingdom of his grace. Of what should the disciples of truth speak more willingly than of this amiable kingdom, which is the principle of their righteousness here on earth, and the foundation of the hope, peace, and glory of heaven?

40. And he answered and said unto them, I tell you that, if these should hold their peace, the stones would immediately cry out.

God makes every thing in nature pay him honour as he

pleases, and can give even to stones a tongue whenever he thinks fit. In vain does the world oppose his designs, and strive to suppress his glory when he intends to make it manifest. God does not leave it always in the power of carnal men to depress his servants; whenever he thinks fit to honour them, he very easily finds means to do it. He forms, as often as he pleases, devout worshippers and zealous defenders of his glory, even out of persons who were before as hard and insensible as the very stones.

SECT. IV.—CHRIST WEEPS OVER JERUSALEM, AND DRIVES THE BUYERS AND SELLERS OUT OF THE TEMPLE.

41. ¶ And when he was come near, he beheld the city, and wept over it,

Such are the grief, the compassion, and the tears of Christ over a soul which ruins itself by its own wickedness. Tears very different from those of men, who weep through weakness, passion, interest, or hypocrisy. These of Christ are holy and sanctifying tears—tears of religion and zeal for the glory of God, and which make part of his sacrifice; they are tears of compassion and charity toward sinners, and of instruction and consolation to penitents. Teach us, O Jesus, to weep as Christians and penitents, not on account of such good things as perish, of which our sensual affection is deprived, nor on the account of such evils as pass away with time, but through a hatred of sin, the only real evil, and for the loss of thy grace and love, the only things which are truly good. Teach priests to weep, as such, over the afflictions of the church, for the blindness of sinners, and from a sense of the interests of God.

42. Saying, If thou hadst known, even thou, at least in this thy day, the things *which belong* unto thy peace! but now they are hid from thine eyes.

It is a matter of great importance to know the time and ways of salvation, which slip away from us whenever we neglect them. The greatest misfortune does not consist in a man's being a sinner, but in not knowing either his sin or the remedy thereof, and in rejecting the saving hand of Him who would heal him by repentance. The time of performing this is but a day, and this is the day of the sinner; whoever lets this opportunity pass without improving it, will see what the days of vengeance, the great days of the Lord, are. Herein lies the great blindness of the sinner, in that he prefers the false peace which he finds in sin, in his passions, and in the delights and pleasures of the present life, before the true and substantial peace of repentance and the cross. My God, how many are there from whose eyes all these mysteries of salvation are hid, and to whom the truths of repentance and mortification are incomprehensible! Let us make a good use of the light of faith, lest it should be taken away from us.

43. For the days shall come upon thee, that thine enemies shall cast a trench about thee, and compass thee round, and keep thee in on every side,

Whoever will not come within the order of God's mercy, must inevitably fall within the order of his justice. Those Christians who reject and crucify Christ by their sins will, without doubt, be punished more severely than the Jews. Our blessed Saviour speaks here only of the temporal punishment which was to be inflicted upon the Jews, to the end that all may understand that this is but a figure and shadow of that which the divine justice prepares for sinners in the other life. My God, who can conceive the deplorable state and condition of a soul delivered up to the devil, and treated like a rebellious city, which is abandoned to the plunder of the enemy after a long and dreadful siege! We cannot possibly escape the justice of God, when once the proper time to appease it is past. Let us therefore make haste to do it.

44. And shall lay thee even with the ground, and thy children within thee; and they shall not leave in thee one stone upon another; because thou knewest not the time of thy visitation.

It is extremely dangerous to neglect the time of the Lord's visitation, his grace, his word, and his chastisements. If God, by such external punishments as these, take vengeance on the Jews for their contempt of Christ's external visitation, by his incarnation, preaching, miracles, and mysteries, what ought not an unfaithful soul to fear which he has visited internally, and made his habitation, palace, and royal city, by his grace and sacraments, and by the application of the fruits of all his mysteries? Graces and virtues are, as it were, the stones with which God builds himself a house and a city in our heart. There is no longer any thing of all this in hell; no more good thoughts or desires, which are, as it were, the children of our hearts, where they are conceived and formed by grace. Lord, let the serious consideration of so great a desolation as this excite in me a salutary dread of losing thee, and cause me to profit by all the visitations of thy grace and mercy.

45. And he went into the temple, and began to cast them out that sold therein, and them that bought;

Avarice, merchandise, simony, and a mercenary spirit in the church,—these are all insupportable to Jesus Christ. The zeal for the sanctity of the church and the sanctification of souls, with which he ought to be inflamed who enters into the ecclesiastical state and ministry, is here signified unto us by the zeal of Christ upon his entrance into the Jewish temple. This is one of the plainest marks of a true call, because the very end of this ministry is to labour in advancing the sanctification of God's name, and the salvation of souls. This is the only merchandise which is permitted them, and for which they ought to give all that they have.

46. Saying unto them, It is written, My house is the house of prayer; but ye have made it a den of thieves.

A man is no better than a thief in the church when he does not therein honour God, nor serve souls, by performing the acts of religion in spirit and in truth. He who performs them only with his lips, carelessly and negligently, robs God of that glory which he does not pay him, deprives souls of that assistance which they should receive from thence, and everybody of that edification and good example which he owes them. Prayer is good in all places; but there is a particular blessing which attends it when offered to God in the house of prayer, the house of God himself. God is present everywhere: but Jesus Christ the High Priest, by whom our prayers are to be offered up to God, and the sacrifice through the merits of which we must offer them, is present here below, more peculiarly in the eucharist, which is the throne of his mercy, where the miserable have access to God.

47. And he taught daily in the temple.

The zeal of priests ought not only to be employed in reproving sinners and inveighing against disorders; it ought likewise to excite them to instruct the people in the truth, and inform them concerning their duties. The fidelity of a minister of the church consists in not being weary with doing this, after the example of Christ, who did it daily. Can a pastor, when he considers this, seek for rest here below? The church is not only a house of prayer, but also a house of instruction: it is there that we must learn to adore and serve God. The Catholic church, of which our churches are an emblem, is not only the house of charity, which prays therein; and of the Holy Spirit, who there maketh intercession in the saints with groanings which cannot be uttered; but it is likewise the house of truth, which teaches there by pastors lawfully sent.

— But the chief priests and the scribes and the chief of the people sought to destroy him,

The reward which Christ received in this world, for teaching the people daily, and seeking the glory of his Father, was to endure for his sake the contradiction of sinners, and to be continually exposed to the wicked designs of his enemies. Can we pretend to claim any other here below? The conclusion of the day is the time when the workmen receive their wages: till then, labour and difficulties are their portion.

48. And could not find what they might do: for all the people were very attentive to hear him.

The fidelity and diligence of Christ in the exercise of his ministry, even when the chief priests and the scribes sought to destroy him, is rewarded by the affection which the people have for his word. God, one way or another, preserves and protects his faithful ministers against their enemies, and gives them great comfort and encouragement by opening the people's hearts to their instructions. A true pastor thinks nothing troublesome and grievous, when he finds himself useful in advancing the work of God. The proficiency of souls is his whole delight.

CHAPTER XX.

SECT. I.—BY WHAT AUTHORITY?—THE BAPTISM OF JOHN, FROM WHENCE?

1. AND it came to pass, *that* on one of those days, as he taught the people in the temple, and preached the gospel, the chief priests and the scribes came upon *him* with the elders, 2. And spake unto him, saying, Tell us, by what authority doest thou these things? or who is he that gave thee this authority?

Envy and hatred have no manner of regard either to the holiness of the place, or to the goodness of the work, or to truth itself, when the taking away the credit of a person who gives umbrage is the thing in question. They leave no stone unturned to oppress him, but employ the sacred ministry, the holy Scripture, and the secular authority to this purpose. The wicked, when they cannot excuse their crimes, do what they can to ruin the authority of the pastors who reprove them for them. The question these men put to our blessed Saviour would have been just, had he not anticipated and rendered it unnecessary by such evident proofs of his extraordinary mission. We have always a right to ask this question, where no true miracles appear to warrant such a mission.

3. And he answered and said unto them, I will also ask you one thing; and answer me: 4. The baptism of John, was it from heaven, or of men?

Christ does neither evade the question nor despise authority, by forcing these envious persons either to discover the malice of their hearts or to return an answer to their own demand, by owning the authority of John, who had borne witness to his divine mission. This conduct of the Son of God can by no means serve to justify the refusal of heretics as to the proof of their mission: since they never wrought any miracles, as Jesus Christ did; since they were never foretold by the prophets, as he was; since they have no John for a witness; since they reject the authority of the church which asks them this question—a thing which Christ did not do; and since they do not put their answer upon a just and equitable condition, as he did.

5. And they reasoned with themselves, saying, If we shall say, From heaven; he will say, Why then believed ye him not?

A minister of the church is in the most miserable disposition which can possibly be imagined, when he will neither acknowledge nor publish the truth, but only so far as it is serviceable to his designs, and suppresses it without scruple when he finds his own condemnation therein. In vain do men endeavour to hide and conceal their craft and malice within themselves: God, who sees all things, can neither be ignorant of it, nor let it go unpunished.

6. But and if we say, Of men; all the people will stone us: for they be persuaded that John was a prophet.

He who forbears speaking against the truth only through fear of men, has betrayed and dishonoured it already in his heart, and is judged at the invisible tribunal of God. These enemies of the truth did not deserve the honour of giving their testimony to one who had been a martyr for it. The common people were fully persuaded that John was a prophet, because he had led the life and died the death of the prophets: but to the eyes of the learned, blinded with envy and wickedness, all this appears as nothing.

7. And they answered, that they could not tell whence *it was.*

A wicked person values not a lie, when he thinks it useful to his designs. Truth can easily find the way to reduce haughty and conceited scholars to a necessity of owning their ignorance. These men undertake to judge of the mission of Christ, and yet are forced to own that they cannot tell whence that of John was. Men fall from one error and disorder into another when they are resolved, at any rate, to persecute the truth: to be given up to lying is a punishment proportioned to this crime.

8. And Jesus said unto them, Neither tell I you by what authority I do these things.

It is suitable to the prudence of Christ's ministers, and to the dignity of his word, not to expose it to the malice of the wicked. God, who discovers himself to the simple, hides his light from the crafty, and confounds the false prudence of the world. Christ does not tell these men from whence his authority came; but his miracles tell them very plainly. They who did not believe these, would not have believed him upon his bare word. The silence of the truth is one of the most terrible punishments of the divine justice in this world.

SECT. II.—THE PARABLE OF THE VINEYARD AND HUSBANDMEN.—THE CORNER-STONE REJECTED.

9. Then began he to speak to the people this parable; A certain man planted a vineyard, and let it forth to husbandmen, and went into a far country for a long time.

A pastor ought to look upon his church as a vineyard planted by the hand of Christ, of which he is only the husbandman, hired to cultivate it with care, and to render all the fruit thereof to his Master. Christ, who is absent from his vineyard as to his visible presence, is continually present there by his protection, by his Spirit, and by his invisible presence in the eucharist. Faithful pastors live as having him for a constant witness of their conduct, and labour as under his inspection. He is at a distance only to those who have no faith. The good pastor watches and labours as expecting his Master every moment, and believing him to be at the very door. The hireling is negligent and slothful, because his faith as to the coming of the Supreme Pastor is extinguished and dead, and because the moment of this present life seems to him a long time.

10. And at the season he sent a servant to the husbandmen, that they should give him of the fruit of the vineyard: but the husbandmen beat him, and sent *him* away empty.

Christ demands the use of his graces, and the fruit of his mysteries and his blood, of those to whom he has intrusted the dispensation of them, by calling them to the sacred ministry. It is a most dreadful state to be found at death under a total incapacity of answering this demand. As it is always a proper season to work in the Lord's vineyard, so it is always a proper season to require the fruit thereof. He requires both the one and the other of his ministers by his inspirations. They do despite to his Spirit who reject them, and who live in idleness or luxury, appropriating to themselves all the advantages of the ministry, without doing any thing in the church for the glory of God or the salvation of souls.

11. And again he sent another servant: and they beat him also, and entreated *him* shamefully, and sent *him* away empty.

The holy Scripture may be looked upon as a second servant, which calls upon and urges the ministers of the Lord to labour in gaining souls and consecrating them to him. It is but too true that the word of God is abused and shamefully treated by those to whom God has sent it in order to their salvation, and to that of his church. We too often see mercenary and faithless pastors read it without any respect, make it subservient to their vanity and ambition, despise its admonitions, and treat it as a profane and dangerous book.

12. And again he sent a third: and they wounded him also, and cast *him* out.

A wicked pastor involves himself continually more and more in sin, and is provoked by all those admonitions to do his duty which are given him either by God himself, or by men animated with his Spirit, or by the example of such a conduct as is truly pastoral. These seldom fail of being persecuted by those who look upon their life as a condemnation of their own. Pastors who walk disorderly cannot bear with any patience the most charitable admonitions; and men seldom admonish them of their duty without suffering for it.

13. Then said the lord of the vineyard, What shall I do? I will send my beloved son: it may be they will reverence *him* when they see him:
14. But when the husbandmen saw him, they reasoned among themselves, saying, This is the heir: come, let us kill him, that the inheritance may be ours.

Whoever proposes to himself to satisfy his worldly desires in the priesthood or pastoral office, will make no difficulty of sacrificing Christ and his whole religion to them. When covetousness, ambition, or the love of pleasures has once taken possession of the heart of a priest, he is but little concerned that abundance of souls perish, and that Christ is crucified afresh, provided he can but gratify his passion. They may justly be said to kill Jesus Christ in souls, who, by their negligence, are instrumental in causing them to lose the life of faith and grace. They kill him in the poor, who let such die with hunger or misery, while they waste their patrimony in luxury and excess.

15. So they cast him out of the vineyard, and killed *him*. What therefore shall the lord of the vineyard do unto them?

Jesus Christ, excommunicated by the Jews and put to death without the gate of Jerusalem, to bear the curse denounced against the sinner, teaches pastors to expose themselves to every thing, rather than to be wanting to the truth, to the salvation of souls, and to Jesus Christ himself. There are some occasions on which they ought to be ready, as Paul and as Jesus Christ were, to be anathematized by unjust excommunications, which are never ratified in heaven, that they may continue internally united to Christ and the church in performing their duty. They who, to satisfy their passion and hatred, are for casting out of the church those who are resolved not to forsake it, are in reality for casting Christ out of his vineyard, and out of Jerusalem, in order to crucify him.

16. He shall come and destroy these husbandmen, and shall give the vineyard to others. And when they heard *it*, they said, God forbid.

Men may resolve, if they think fit, not to hear the denunciation of those punishments which are due to mercenary, idle, unjust, and turbulent pastors, such as are guilty of robbing the poor: the misery which attends them will thereby become the more dreadful. The Judge, the Lord of the vineyard, shall come; and who will be able to abide his presence? He will destroy all prevaricating and unfaithful ministers; and what refuge can be found when God undertakes to destroy the sinner? He will give the vineyard to others; and what despair must be their portion who have no more communion with the church, no part in Christ, and no longer any God but an avenger, eternally intent on punishing sin!

17. And he beheld them, and said, What is this then that is written, The stone which the builders rejected, the same is become the head of the corner?

Christ himself, the foundation, cement, and ornament of his church, was rejected by those who flattered themselves with being the builders thereof. What therefore must not those of his ministers expect who are resolved to walk in his steps? He shows the scribes their ignorance in not knowing the Messias by the Scriptures, of which they imagined they had the key. He who judges of the holiness and virtue of the ministers of Christ in this life, by the ill usage which they here receive from the world, beholds them only with the eyes of Jews and Pharisees. Their lot and portion here below is to be treated as the Prince of pastors was: it is in heaven that they will enter into his power and glory.

18. Whosoever shall fall upon that stone shall be broken; but on whomsoever it shall fall, it will grind him to powder.

The punishment of sinners is terrible even in this world; but it is without remedy in the other. The Jews rejected, despised, and put Christ to shame only in the time designed for his humiliations and the ignominy of his cross; and yet their punishment was beyond example: what then will that of Christians be, who, as far as in them lies, crucify him afresh, and put him to an open shame in the very time appointed for his reign, and in his state of glory and power? They who persecute good men in this world, are only instruments of good to them; and are themselves broken to pieces, like a glass which falls upon the hardest stone. But how dreadful will their punishment be, when he, who comes to avenge his elect, shall appear with them, and employ all his majesty to confound, and all his power to punish these miserable wretches!

SECT. III.—GOD AND CESAR.

19. ¶ And the chief priests and the scribes the same hour sought to lay hands on him; and they feared the people: for they perceived that he had spoken this parable against them.

A soul is in a very desperate condition indeed, when the most wholesome admonitions, and the denunciations of the greatest miseries, do but provoke and carry it to greater excesses. My God, what is the heart of man when left to himself! The fear of God and of his eternal justice makes not the least impression upon him; and the fear of men and of temporal evil restrains and governs him. Fear restrains only the hand; but the heart is abandoned to sin so long as it is not guided and directed by the love of righteousness.

20. And they watched *him*, and sent forth spies, which should feign themselves just men, that they might take hold of his words, that so they might deliver him unto the power and authority of the governor.

The mask of piety is often serviceable to the wicked in the execution of the worst designs. To be exposed to the artifices of hypocrisy is a very uneasy and difficult condition for good men, wherein they have great occasion for Christian prudence. Charity forbids us to judge of our neighbour's heart; and prudence requires us not to trust to outward appearances. Prudence ought to guide charity, to prevent its being imposed upon; and candour ought to accompany prudence, that it may not be too suspicious: but it is thy light, O Jesus, which must enlighten both; it is thy Spirit which must make them act; and prayer is the thing which attracts and draws down both these.

21. And they asked him, saying, Master, we know that thou sayest and teachest rightly, neither acceptest thou the person *of any*, but teachest the way of God truly:

We ought always to suspect the praises which are given by men devoted to the world. The wicked person is so corrupted, that he seldom speaks truth but with an intent to deceive; but truth is so powerful, that it makes use even of his tongue to condemn him. The knowledge which a minister of the truth has of his duties, renders his sin the greater when he either betrays it out of respect of persons, or corrupts it by falsehood and lies. Let us consider neither the design of those who deliver the truth, nor the ill use they make thereof, but the truth itself, and the account which God will require us to give of it. It is a light carried by a wicked wretch, which, notwithstanding, shows us the way, and discovers to us the precipices. The power of God shines forth more illustriously, and his wisdom is the more to be admired, when he makes even the enemies of truth instrumental in publishing and promoting it.

22. Is it lawful for us to give tribute unto Cesar, or no?

None but an impious person makes any question concerning his duty toward his sovereign. He who will not bear the yoke of God, bears that of his prince with great regret, and thinks of nothing but how to shake it off. He who serves

God, serves his king; and it is one part of religion to honour God in the most lively image of his greatness and sovereign power. How can any one call in question the rights of this second majesty, without offending the first and eternal Majesty, in whose word they are plainly declared; or pretend to dispute an obedience which ought never to be contested?

23. But he perceived their craftiness,* and said unto them, Why tempt ye me?" [* *Fr.* Malice.]

No veil can hide from the eyes of God that which passes in the most secret corner of man's heart. Of what advantage is it to the sinner to deceive the eyes of men for a moment, by concealing his wickedness from them under the deceitful appearance of piety and virtue? He who is to judge all things sees them all, and will, by the light of the great day, expose every thing to open view which is now so carefully disguised and concealed from the sight of men. Christ discovers the hidden malice of his enemies, who designed to surprise him; but he discovers likewise, at the same time, the goodness, gentleness, and patience of his own heart, in reproving with such soft words so black an instance of hypocrisy and malice.

24. Shew me a penny. Whose image and superscription hath it? They answered and said, Cesar's.

The prince's name and image, and the right of giving money its current value, are marks of sovereign authority over his subjects: how then, O Jesus, can I ever dispute thine over my heart, and over all that I am; how can I do this, who bear thy name and image, and who have no worth or value, but that only which thou art pleased to give us! Thou, Lord, canst increase my value, canst render me worthy of that sacred name thou causest me to bear, and canst renew thy image in me,—and all this I hope for from thy grace.

25. And he said unto them, Render therefore unto Cesar the things which be Cesar's, and unto God the things which be God's.

We see here one of the principal titles which kings have to obedience and subsidies by divine right. It is one part of the law of God and of Christian piety to be subject to them in every thing which belongs to their jurisdiction. We must never separate these two sentences which Christ has joined with so much wisdom, that so we may never do any thing contrary to the rights of God in obeying princes, and never violate the rights of princes under pretence of doing service to God. The more zealous princes are in "rendering to God the things which be God's," and in obliging others to do the same, the more faithful will God cause their people to be in rendering to princes the things which are theirs.

26. And they could not take hold of his words before the people: and they marvelled at his answer, and held their peace.

God guides and directs that person's tongue whose heart is devoted to him. One of the most proper ways to preserve peace without doing any prejudice to the truth, to take away from its enemies all pretences of doing it without provoking them, to change their artifices into admiration, and to put them to silence without the expense of many words, is carefully to weigh every word which we are about to speak, when we lie under any obligation to speak at all. It is of great importance to speak with still more circumspection of that which concerns matters of state and the interests of princes, to say no more than what is absolutely necessary, and to hold the scales even between God and Cesar, heaven and hell, the church and the court.

SECT. IV.—THE RESURRECTION OF THE DEAD.—THE ANGELICAL LIFE.

27. ¶ Then came to *him* certain of the Sadducees, which deny that there is any resurrection; and they asked him,

The devil never ceases to lay snares for the ministers of Christ and for his church, as he did continually for Christ himself during his mortal life. He never wants new stratagems, when the first have proved unsuccessful. We must not therefore ever grow supine and careless, but we must be always prepared to oppose his attempts, and to secure ourselves against his wiles.

28. Saying, Master, Moses wrote unto us, If any man's brother die, having a wife, and he die without children, that his brother should take his wife, and raise up seed unto his brother.

It is by the priesthood that the church is made fruitful, and that the bishops are the husbands of the church in Jesus

Christ, and become thereby his brethren in a particular manner. There are but too many who would fain espouse this holy widow; but alas, how few are there who are willing to bewail with her the death of her Lord, to lead with her a poor, desolate, and afflicted life, and to raise up children to her by labouring to raise them up to Christ! If to leave a brother's widow childless were a disgrace of infamy under the law, what shame will it be for you in the sight of God, ye slothful and idle ministers, if ye raise not up children unto Jesus Christ by the ministry of the word, by prayers, and by the labours proper to the hierarchy.

29. There were therefore seven brethren: and the first took a wife, and died without children. 30. And the second took her to wife, and he died childless. 31. And the third took her; and in like manner the seven also: and they left no children, and died.

Disorderly marriages, and such as proceed from incontinence, are frequently punished with barrenness. And the spiritual marriage between a bishop and his church is but too commonly attended with a deplorable barrenness when he brings along with him neither a call, nor virtues, nor talents, but only ambition, avarice, and other criminal passions. This long list of husbands dying childless, is a sad representation of the desolation and barrenness of so many dioceses whose lot is to have, for bishops, persons who contemn their spouses, and leave them barren.

32. Last of all the woman died also. 33. Therefore in the resurrection whose wife of them is she? for seven had her to wife.

With how many vain questions and fruitless curiosities does man fill his mind on these occasions, instead of making a Christian use of worldly events? God frequently confounds the designs which men frame beforehand, concerning children who are not yet come into the world. He obliges them to think rather of dying to this present world, than of immortalizing themselves by a numerous and flourishing posterity, the hopes whereof are so deceitful and uncertain. Nothing but the glorious resurrection can render us immortal; and nothing but the hopes we have of this, can yield us any comfort and consolation here below. It is by our fruitfulness in good works that we must do all we can to deserve it and attain unto it.

34. And Jesus answering said unto them, The children of this world marry, and are given in marriage: 35. But they which shall be accounted worthy to obtain that world, and the resurrection from the dead, neither marry, nor are given in marriage:

Who shall be accounted most worthy to obtain that world, but he who has most despised the present, and all its transitory advantages, and, by Christian hope, set his heart entirely upon invisible treasures and the years of eternity? The virtue of a good life, which makes us counted worthy of that which is eternal, being founded only upon the grace and mercy of God, does not in the least hinder it from being a pure gift of the divine bounty. Let us aspire to this angelical life of the saints after the resurrection, the first advantage of which is a virginal purity. Let us begin it even in this life, if we are able—every one according to his gift and the state whereunto he is called.

36. Neither can they die any more: for they are equal unto the angels; and are the children of God, being the children of the resurrection.

The second advantage of the saints after the resurrection is, to partake of the immortality of the angels. They will then have no more passions, no more occasion for food, and no more fear of dying, than pure spirits. The third advantage of the glory of the children of the resurrection is, a new birth, wherein they will have no other father but the Father of the world to come, who will restore life to the members as he has restored it to the Head, by the eternal and immortal Spirit working in them. The fourth advantage of the saints raised from the dead will consist in this, that they will no longer have any thing of the life of Adam, but will be wholly regenerated to a new life, and become entirely the children of God both in soul and body.

37. Now that the dead are raised, even Moses shewed at the bush, when he calleth the Lord the God of Abraham, and the God of Isaac, and the God of Jacob.

That which our Lord mentions here is a convincing proof of the resurrection. Neither the remembrance nor the reward of the righteous can be lost. God, who renders their piety immortal in heaven, owes to his justice the resurrection of their bodies, which make a part of themselves. The martyrs having lost the life of the body for the sake of God, it belongs to his justice to restore it to them again by the resurrection. The rest of the saints have also made a sacrifice thereof by the disposition of their hearts, which were prepared for every thing, as Abraham was to sacrifice himself in his son, Isaac to give up his own life, and Jacob to sacrifice that of his son Joseph in another manner.

38. For he is not a God of the dead, but of the living: for all live unto him.

They who are to rise again, only that they may die eternally, do not properly live unto him. Those live continually unto him who have lost their lives only for the short moment of this present world, and for whom God reserves an immortal life, which by means of hope they enjoy even already. Abraham received an earnest and figure of it in his son, who survived his sacrifice; Isaac in himself; and Jacob in his son Joseph. Lord, confirm and strengthen in me the faith and hope of this new life; and grant that I may always live unto thee and for thee.

39. ¶ Then certain of the scribes answering said, Master, thou hast well said.

To approve of truth is certainly a very good thing; but when we do it not at all times, we have reason to fear that we do not approve of it out of any love we have for truth itself, but either out of a fondness for our own opinion, or through a personal opposition to those who entertain a contrary, or from a mere want of power to contradict it, or a proud usurpation of the key of knowledge, and of the right to judge of every thing. We must give our approbation of the truth as disciples, and not as masters; with humility, and not with pride and ostentation, like these scribes.

40. And after that they durst not ask him any *question at all.*

The silence of the enemies of truth is no mark either of the conversion of their hearts or of the conviction of their minds. Oftentimes they cease to oppose it in the way of dispute, only that they may lay more dangerous snares for it, and oppress it either by open force or secret combination. God is the Lord and disposer of all things. It is always for his glory to render truth victorious in dispute; it is often for his glory to permit the defenders of it to sink under the artifices and violence of its enemies.

SECT. V.—CHRIST THE SON AND LORD OF DAVID.—PROUD AND COVETOUS SCRIBES.

41. And he said unto them, How say they that Christ is David's son?

Christ was born the son of David according to the flesh, to accomplish the promises; but he was not born of that royal family till after it was fallen into poverty and obscurity, to give us an example of humility, to teach us to despise all advantages of this kind, and to confound the vanity of men.

42. And David himself saith in the book of Psalms, The LORD said unto my Lord, Sit thou on my right hand,

David, in owning the Messias to be his Lord, owns him to be the Son of God, equal to his Father by his eternal birth, humbled under his almighty hand by his temporal birth, and exalted and placed at his right hand by his new birth to immortal life, which puts his human nature into possession of the rights belonging to his divine. Rest, glory, and an almighty power in heaven and on earth to form the kingdom of God, are denoted by this sitting. This ought to be the continual object of our adoration, our joy, and our confidence.

43. Till I make thine enemies thy footstool.

Jesus will be eternally the same; but even to the end of the world he will do no other thing but what he does at present, to form his church, to destroy sin, and to fight for and in his elect against the power of hell, and against concupiscence. Christ has now no other enemies besides those of our salvation and of the whole church. It is only for our sakes that he triumphs over them. When will it be, O Lord, that I shall behold every thing reduced under thy feet which in me opposes thy law; and, above all, my evil will and corrupt inclinations, which are my greatest enemies as well as thine?

44. David therefore calleth him Lord, how is he then his son?

Jesus Christ, that adorable compound of God and man, contains in himself both lowliness and greatness, dependency and sovereign independency, the creature and the Creator, the God who gave being and life to David, and the man who received a body derived from his blood, and united to the person of the divine Word. Let us steadfastly believe this mystery of a God who became the Son of man, that men might become the children of God: for on this very thing our salvation does depend; and this second mystery is annexed to the first.

45. ¶ Then in the audience of all the people he said unto his disciples,
46. Beware of the scribes, which desire to walk in long robes, and love greetings in the markets, and the highest seats in the synagogues, and the chief rooms at feasts;

Such pastors or teachers as are proud, ambitious, hypocritical, and covetous, are more dangerous than common and ordinary sinners. A bad example, supported by the authority, reputation, and majesty of religion, is a very subtle poison, from which it is very difficult for men to preserve themselves. It is a great misfortune for any people to be obliged to beware of those very persons who ought to be their rule and pattern. In vain do those preach humility by their words, whose whole conduct and behaviour preaches nothing but pride. When we see in those whom God enjoins us to respect such inclinations as are agreeable to self-love, it is very difficult for us not to approve of them, and not follow a guide authorized by his character, when he shows us a way to which natural propensity already carries us with violence.

47. Which devour widows' houses, and for a show make long prayers: the same shall receive greater damnation.

Christian widows, above all persons, ought to beware of the great pretenders to devotion. The necessity of seeking counsel and assistance abroad for want of that of a husband, the diligence and craft of a hypocrite who makes himself necessary, the easiness of their sex, the liberty they have to dispose of their estate, the impression which a religious appearance makes upon them, etc., render widows very capable of being deceived. They who sell their prayers and their advice at so dear a rate, shall pay dearly themselves for that whereof they rob the poor, by robbing pious widows, who are the common refuge of such distressed persons.

CHAPTER XXI.

SECT. I—THE POOR WIDOW GIVING OUT OF HER PENURY.

1. And he looked up, and saw the rich men casting their gifts into the treasury.

Christ even now beholds, with no less attention, the visible hand and the invisible heart, both of the rich and poor. We must desire to be seen by no other eyes but those of Christ, if we desire to receive the invisible reward of charity, and not the empty reward of vanity. Christ does not blame any thing in these rich men, to teach us not to judge of the intentions when the action is in itself good.

2. And he saw also a certain poor widow casting in thither two mites.

A poor man who gives to God even the necessaries of life, is a sight more worthy to attract the eyes of Christ, than a rich man who gives millions out of his superfluity. It is the same in proportion as to all other actions. They are not the eminent actions of the great which are great in the sight of God; but they are those which are done with a true Christian heart,—a heart which is thoroughly sensible of its own poverty, which, like a widow, bewails the death of the heavenly Bridegroom, and sighs only for him, which offers to God whatever it is, whatever it does, and whatever it possesses, and yet always believes it scarce offers to him any thing at all.

3. And he said, Of a truth I say unto you, that this poor widow hath cast in more than they all.

God judges of the greatness of the gift, not by the gift itself, but by the heart which offers it. The applause which the great gifts of the rich receive, the complacency they take in them, and the little religion wherewith they are frequently accompanied, degrade and lessen them in the sight of God. A poor person, rich in faith, charity, and humility, cannot possibly offer small gifts; because religion heightens, ennobles, augments, and multiplies the least things which it consecrates to God.

4. For all these have of their abundance cast in unto the offerings of God: but she of her penury hath cast in all the living that she had.

The rich man who gives a great deal, still reserves a

great deal to himself. Nothing remains to the poor man who gives all he has, but only confidence in God. God does not indeed reject the voluntary sacrifice of that which is superfluous: but for a man to offer even necessaries, is to offer his own life, is to sacrifice his own heart, which loves nothing so much as life. God manifests his greatness and the power of his grace in disengaging a soul even from that which is most necessary to life, and raising it above the fears of poverty, by the love of religion, and the belief of Providence.

SECT. II.—THE DESTRUCTION OF THE TEMPLE.—FALSE CHRISTS.

5. ¶ And as some spake of the temple, how it was adorned with goodly stones and gifts, he said, 6. *As for* these things which ye behold, the days will come, in the which there shall not be left one stone upon another, that shall not be thrown down.

That which appears most magnificent to the eyes of the flesh may amuse the curiosity of men, but it is not worthy of the observation of Christ or of the admiration of his members. They who have other eyes besides those of the body, have likewise another beauty to admire besides that which must perish. Christ, by his conduct, teaches us what use we ought to make of the sight of such objects as these; namely, to consider that in a very little time they will disappear and be no more, and that there is nothing solid and durable but that which is not seen. The wrath of God, which broke out with so much fierceness against this figurative temple, is but a shadow of that wrath which he frequently exercises upon kingdoms, possessions, and souls wherein he has been served and worshipped, and which have abused his greatest gifts.

7. And they asked him, saying, Master, but when shall these things be? and what sign *will there be* when these things shall come to pass?

Nothing is more useful and profitable than to discourse concerning the judgments of God, the destruction of every thing which makes the greatest figure in the world, and the end even of this sinful world itself: nothing is more unprofitable than to entertain and amuse our minds with the beauty of human works. Christ could not be induced to admire the latter; but he very readily enters into a conversation about the former.

8. And he said, Take heed that ye be not deceived: for many shall come in my name, saying, I am *Christ;* and the time draweth near: go ye not therefore after them.

If the apostles themselves had need of being warned not to mistake, in taking a seducer for a Saviour, a false Christ for the true, alas! what seducement have we not reason to fear? We find a false Christ whenever we find a deceitful guide, who directs us not to Jesus Christ, who leads us to a church which is not his, who inspires us with a doctrine which he never taught, who diverts us from the way of the gospel, and who, by his whole conduct, carries us at a distance from the cross and from salvation.

9. But when ye shall hear of wars and commotions, be not terrified: for these things must first come to pass; but the end *is* not by and by.

Wars are the forerunners of the last judgment, the beginning of the divine vengeance upon sinners, and an emblem of the destruction of the world. To punish sinners, God need only abandon them to their own passions, from whence proceed quarrels and lawsuits between private persons, and wars and revolts among states and princes. Those ambitious persons who lay waste whole provinces, who raise to themselves so great a name in the world, what are they but the executioners of God's justice, who already begins his judgment? Great armies are for the most part no other than great multitudes of criminals, whom God draws together to punish one another: the field of battle is only a great scaffold, where they are made a spectacle to the rest of the world; and fire and sword, the arms of his justice, which he puts into their hands that they may execute one another therewith. How dreadful, then, will it be when the end and consummation of this justice shall come, and both the fire and the sword shall be, as one may say, in the hand of God himself!

10. Then said he unto them, Nation shall rise against nation, and kingdom against kingdom:

Seditions, rebellions, and civil wars are fruits of hell and the work of the devil; but God makes use of those as he does of these, to punish both kings and people for their rebellions against him, and for that intestine war which the flesh wages against the Spirit in them both. None but God can bring good out of so great evils! but he makes them subservient to his mercy in a small number of elect, and to his justice in all besides.

11. And great earthquakes shall be in divers places, and famines, and pestilences; and fearful sights and great signs shall there be from heaven.

Let us fear sin and love God, and we shall not fear these evils. They are dreadful to none but those whose bad conscience hinders them from loving the coming of Christ. To such they are dismal presages of the end of all their false happiness, and of the beginning of an endless misery; to others they are blessed omens of their approaching deliverance, and of the kingdom of their Deliverer, and means whereby they purify and prepare themselves to appear before him with confidence. Happy is that person who makes this use of all public calamities, and who still finds something in them to nourish his faith, to strengthen his hope, and to increase his charity.

SECT. III.—PERSECUTIONS.—A MOUTH AND WISDOM GIVEN BY GOD.—PATIENCE.

12. But before all these, they shall lay their hands on you, and persecute *you*, delivering *you* up to the synagogues, and into prisons, being brought before kings and rulers for my name's sake. 13. And it shall turn to you for a testimony.

Persecution is useful and profitable, because it gives men an opportunity of making the truth known, of giving testimony thereto at the expense of that which is most dear to them, of trying their patience, of knowing their own hearts, and of adhering the more steadfastly to Christ the more the world despises and rejects them, and the more it endeavours to force them to hate him. We are very forward to appear before kings and great persons in order to receive benefits, and to pay them in praises and flatteries; but we are never so to appear before them to tell them the truth, or to speak in favour of innocence, which is the cause of Christ. Happy the martyrs and confessors whom God has chosen and rendered worthy to maintain the cause of truth and righteousness, which is his own! Unhappy their persecutors, not to know that those whom they treated so cruelly were the only persons who could have promoted their salvation, while those whom they loaded with their favours were only instrumental to their damnation.

14. Settle *it* therefore in your hearts, not to meditate before what ye shall answer:

It must necessarily be of very great importance, then, for us not to depend either upon any light or prudence with which our own understanding can supply us, or upon any strength or firmness which we may promise ourselves from our own courage. He who enjoins his servants to watch at all times, and to pray without ceasing, is far from designing here to forbid them to do either, since it is by means even of vigilance and prayer that this very thought is most deeply settled in their hearts. It is a great part of vigilance, and one of the chief fruits of prayer, for a man to learn therein to put his whole trust and confidence in God, and to rely only upon his grace.

15. For I will give you a mouth and wisdom, which all your adversaries shall not be able to gainsay nor resist.

No eloquence, no wisdom, except those which God gives, are victorious, and proof against those of the world. By faith, a man knows very well how to resign himself up entirely to God without tempting him. Can the Spirit of God then be less powerful over the heart of man, when he speaks to him immediately by himself, to cause him to do good, and when he rules the will of his creature by his own almighty will, to divert it from evil, than when he speaks to one man by the mouth of another? Let us be under no fear of any violence to be offered to the freedom of our will, when it is its God and its Creator who interposes to direct it; but let us fear lest we should gainsay and resist the truth, which assures us that nothing can gainsay or resist his Spirit when he is pleased to render his elect victorious over the enemies of their salvation.

16. And ye shall be betrayed both by parents, and brethren, and kinsfolks, and friends; and *some* of you shall they cause to be put to death.

Obstacles and hinderances to piety, and even the greatest persecutions, frequently proceed from our friends and relations. They do us less hurt when they strip us of all we have, and deliver us up to the executioner, than when they hinder us from following Christ, and from being obedient to his law and inspirations. In these days, men do not think they have any occasion to fear persecution from their friends and relations; and it is this very thing which renders it the more dangerous. Do they persecute us less when they deliver us up to ambition, vanity, and the torrent of worldly desires, by engaging us in dangerous employments, and advancing us to great places? Is eternal salvation of less value than the life of the body?

17. And ye shall be hated of all *men* for my name's sake.

Happy is that person who is hated by the world for the sake of Christ! It is a sign that he loves God, and is loved by him. Though a Christian, or a minister of Christ, be to live only among Christians, he must, notwithstanding, expect to see the world combined against him whenever he shall maintain the interests of Christ against the world. Not to resemble the world, is enough to draw upon us its hatred; but then it is likewise enough to make us resemble Christ, and to entitle us to his love and the protection of his grace. It is not the hatred of the world which sanctifies us, but the love of God which makes that hatred profitable to us, and the cause of Christ which heightens and ennobles it.

18. But there shall not a hair of your head perish.

Let us engrave these words upon our hearts, and be thoroughly sensible how adorable the providence of God over his servants is, and how great a source of consolation it is for them. That which is lost only for a moment, is looked upon as a loss by none but those who understand not the secret of the gospel. When we cast seed into the earth which will spring up, and in due season bear a hundred-fold, we do not lose it in any respect; but to be unwilling to lose any thing in this manner, is the certain way to lose every thing.

19. In your patience possess ye your souls.

It is patience alone which renders us masters of ourselves, under the loss of all things. Persecution, which deprives those of every thing whose heart is in their treasure, secures every thing to those who have the good treasure in their heart. Christian suffering is the price of salvation. It is by this that sinners obtain righteousness, that the just preserve it, that penitents recover it, that martyrs sacrifice themselves for it, and that the saints receive the crown thereof, and possess themselves in possessing God.

SECT. IV.—THE SIEGE OF JERUSALEM.—FLIGHT.

20. And when ye shall see Jerusalem compassed with armies, then know that the desolation thereof is nigh.

We know by fatal experience that armies carry desolation into all places; but we are not sufficiently sensible that they are the sins of men which draw them together, which keep them up, which regulate their operations in the council of the Lord of hosts, and which occasion the success of them. The only way either to disperse them or to make them instrumental to our salvation, is to be converted.

21. Then let them which are in Judea flee to the mountains; and let them which are in the midst of it depart out; and let not them that are in the countries enter thereinto.

The true way to flee from the wrath of God is to flee from the world by retirement, or at least to flee from sin by a speedy and sincere conversion. Happy they who, anticipating the time of wrath, have already fled to the mountain, the true church, leaving a reprobate society, and never more returning into it! Happy likewise is he who, profiting by wholesome admonitions, has recourse to God, whom we may suppose signified by these mountains, who separates himself from bad company and the occasions of sin, and never more engages himself therein!

22. For these be the days of vengeance, that all things which are written may be fulfilled.

Let us make the best use of the days of mercy, in punishing sin in ourselves by repentance and mortification, that we may anticipate the days of the divine vengeance. Is not that with which every sinner is threatened, in case he be not converted, without comparison more to be dreaded, though it be less the object of our senses? We must frequently think of it, if we would avoid it. We are afraid of representing this matter to our minds by serious reflection and meditation, lest it should give us too much disturbance and concern; and our greatest misfortune is, that we are not sufficiently disturbed and concerned about it. We endeavour to lull our faith asleep with respect to the threatenings whereof the Scripture is full, lest too lively a faith should render us uneasy: but can this insensibility hinder all things that are written from being fulfilled, if we continue unconverted?

23. But woe unto them that are with child, and to them that give suck, in those days! for there shall be great distress in the land, and wrath upon this people.

Miserable is that person whom natural tenderness hinders from avoiding the wrath of God! We are never sufficiently sensible how dangerous it is to bring ourselves under earthly ties, till we are forced either to break them or perish. Let us begin betimes to disengage ourselves from the incumbrances of the world, that death may not find us loaded with chains which we cannot shake off. The generality of persons at that hour, being either filled with anxious cares for their children whom they are about to leave, or wholly taken up with the concerns of a family of which they are extravagantly fond, have no time to flee from the wrath of God which is just ready to overwhelm them, and which will not end with death like that which is here spoken of.

24. And they shall fall by the edge of the sword, and shall be led away captive into all nations: and Jerusalem shall be trodden down of the Gentiles, until the times of the Gentiles be fulfilled.

What miseries do those undergo, even in this world, who have rejected Jesus Christ! The humiliation, slavery, and death with which the Jews have been punished, hindered not this miserable people from still hoping to be recalled and reestablished; but to those whom the wrath of God shall overwhelm at the last day, there will not remain even the least shadow of any hope. The Jews are dispersed into all nations, to proclaim and show to all the world what a people or a soul is without Jesus Christ; what it is to have let slip the time and opportunity of repentance; and what it is to have heard, without bringing forth any fruit, the Saviour and his gospel. That which has happened to this people happens to every one who is finally impenitent; but after a manner which is much more dreadful.

SECT. V.—THE SIGNS OF THE LAST JUDGMENT.—REDEMPTION NIGH.

25. ¶ And there shall be signs in the sun, and in the moon, and in the stars; and upon the earth distress of nations, with perplexity; the sea and the waves roaring;

All nature will be armed against the sinner at the day of judgment. God continually arms it against us by drought, excessive rain, the barrenness of the earth, the multitude of insects, the irregularity of the seasons, the malignity of the air, etc.; and we take no notice that his finger is in all this. All these convulsions of nature are no more than signs of the divine wrath: how then will it be when God himself shall appear, and pronounce the sentence of his judgment against the wicked? His goodness manifests itself in the midst of the most terrible presages of his fury, since it is by these that he would persuade us to avoid his anger by repentance.

26. Men's hearts failing them for fear, and for looking after those things which are coming on the earth: for the powers of heaven shall be shaken.

Let faith work in us now the dread and terrors of the last day. They will then be common to all, but profitable to few. The fear of temporal evils, of which men already see the beginnings, may cause indeed their hearts to fail them, but it cannot convert them of itself. The fear of invisible and eternal evils, which is excited by faith, accompanied with hope, and sanctified and perfected by charity, is that alone which is beneficial, and which is indeed more the fear of the Lord than the fear of the evils themselves. Give us, Lord, now in the time of our health, a calm and beneficial sight of thy justice, of which, at the last hour, the trouble and fear of death generally give but very imperfect notions, such as are false in themselves, unworthy of thee, and altogether unprofitable to the sinner!

27. And then shall they see the Son of man coming in a cloud with power and great glory.

Whoever has despised the Son of man in his humility, shall be forced to see him in all his majesty and power. Those to whom his state of weakness and humiliation, at his first coming, has been an occasion of scandal and incredulity, shall, in the power and glory of his second, behold their infidelity confounded. We must, by a true meekness and humility of heart, conform ourselves to the first, if we desire to partake of the greatness and glory of the second. It is just, O Jesus, that thou shouldst appear for thy glory, in thy own natural greatness and majesty—thou who, for my salvation, wast pleased to appear mean, abject, and contemptible to the eyes of men. Come then, Lord Jesus, in the glory which is suitable to the only-begotten of the Father!

28. And when these things begin to come to pass, then look up, and lift up your heads; for your redemption draweth nigh.

O day of affliction and confusion for the reprobate, how dreadful art thou! O day of redemption and confidence for the elect, how desirable art thou! At length the great mystery of the gospel is about to be made manifest. The deceitful and imaginary felicity of this world, and of the children thereof, is just going to disappear, and to be changed into a state of tears, despair, and misery to all eternity; and the light captivity, affliction, and momentary tears of the elect are going to be changed into the liberty, joy, and glory of the children of God. God of Israel! when will this veil, which hides thy children from the sight of the world, be taken away? When wilt thou appear openly with thy elect in glory?

29. And he spake to them a parable; Behold the fig tree, and all the trees; 30. When they now shoot forth, ye see and know of your own selves that summer is now nigh at hand. 31. So likewise ye, when ye see these things come to pass, know ye that the kingdom of God is nigh at hand.

As it is out of mercy that God gives presages of his wrath, to the end that men may escape it by repentance, so it is out of a particular tenderness toward his elect that he discovers to them the approach of his kingdom. It is the approach of this kingdom of eternal charity and justice, which enables them to endure with patience the afflictions they meet with under the reign of the iniquity and injustice of the world. To see the elect always persecuted in this world, their outward life appears no other than a frightful winter to carnal eyes. But whoever could behold their inward life, all of faith and hope, would see their heart, as it were, in a continual spring, wherein they look upon present evils as past, and future good as present. If this life be to the elect the time of spring, the life of heaven is a perpetual summer, which, without losing the flowers of the spring, without feeling the decay of autumn, or fearing the desolation of winter, possesses all sorts of fruit in abundance. Let us pursue the hint which Christ is here pleased to give us, by accustoming ourselves to look upon this present world, its elements and seasons, as a representation of the world to come. Sensual and sordid persons look upon the spring as a time which is favourable to their pleasures and their covetousness: true Christians look upon this general resurrection of nature as a slight draught of the resurrection of the children of God, and as a sign of the approach of the Sun of righteousness.

32. Verily I say unto you, This generation shall not pass away till all be fulfilled.

Neither the crime of the Jews, nor the dispersion of this nation, nor the destruction of Jerusalem, which Christ had just foretold, will hinder God from fulfilling his promises with respect to the body of this people. It is to this end that he still preserves them, in order to bring them into his church, and to conduct them to heaven, the true land of promise. My God, how faithful art thou to man! and yet man cannot be persuaded to trust in thee.

33. Heaven and earth shall pass away; but my words shall not pass away.

The stability and truth of the word of God, whether in relation to good or evil, is one of those perfections of which he is most jealous. It is the sin of bad Christians, as well as of the Jews, not to give credit to it. A king promises or threatens, and all obey: but in respect of God, men live as if the promises of eternal happiness, and the threatenings of the miseries of hell, were only the predictions of an almanac. Let us, therefore, take great care to fix and settle our faith upon the veracity of God and the immutability of his word, to receive this word, to hear and read it as the word of God, such as it really is, let the person be what he will who delivers it.

SECT. VI.—WE MUST AVOID THE PLEASURES AND CARES OF THIS LIFE.—WATCHFULNESS AND PRAYER.

34. And take heed to yourselves, lest at any time your hearts be overcharged with surfeiting, and drunkenness, and cares of this life, and *so* that day come upon you unawares.

Nothing more plainly shows how little faith men have as to the threatenings of God, of which his word is full, than to observe that security and that forgetfulness of death wherein the generality of Christians live, although God everywhere declares that we shall be surprised thereby. Almost all persons endeavour to shut their eyes against this truth: some by a life openly loose and disorderly, and by sensual pleasures; others by the multiplicity of affairs with which they are entirely taken up, and, as it were, oppressed. Christian watchfulness is to be found only in a penitential and retired life, or at least in a life disengaged from pleasure, business, ambition, and the desire of worldly riches.

35. For as a snare shall it come on all them that dwell on the face of the whole earth.

True Christians, who seek the things above, and not those on the earth, may be compared to the fowls of the air, which, so long as they keep at a distance from the earth, have no occasion to fear the fowler's nets. Wo unto those who, as it were, settle here below, and whom the care of worldly affairs, the desire of raising a fortune, and the love of this present life, and of the conveniences thereof, render perfectly men of the earth. Let us, with the wings of faith and hope, raise ourselves up to heaven, that we may not be caught in the net here below.

36. Watch ye therefore, and pray always, that ye may be accounted worthy to escape all these things that shall come to pass, and to *stand before the Son of man. [* *Fr.* Appear with confidence.]

Watchfulness and prayer are absolutely necessary to prepare us to appear with confidence at the last day. The one is inseparable from the other, and both are so from good works, since we cannot be attentive to our duty but through a desire of performing it, and since we pray only in order to obtain the grace of being faithful thereto. We must watch and pray always and at all times, because at all times we may be summoned before the tribunal of God. If our tongue cannot always pray, yet our heart can, for this prays to God when it desires God and his will, and when it hungers and thirsts after his righteousness and eternal happiness. A great part of our confidence and virtue consists in being diffident of ourselves, and in relying solely upon the grace and mercy of God, by acknowledging our own unworthiness and inability.

37. And in the daytime he was teaching in the temple; and at night he went out, and abode in the mount that is called *the mount* of Olives.
38. And all the people came early in the morning to him in the temple, for to hear him.

The usual division of our blessed Saviour's public life was, to instruct the people in the daytime, to pray to his Father during the night, to join mortification with prayer, and to be always ready to begin his labours again early in the morning. In how happy and flourishing a condition is a church, when a people, hungering after the word of God, meets with a pastor as desirous to feed them with it; and who joins to his instructions watchfulness and prayer, mortification and labour! The love and holy earnestness of a well-disposed people toward the word of God, animate the zeal of a pastor, and the pastor's zeal and assiduity encourage and animate the people.

CHAPTER XXII.

SECT. I.—THE BARGAIN AND TREACHERY OF JUDAS.

1. Now the feast of unleavened bread drew nigh, which is called the passover.

The unleavened bread for the passover is purity and innocence for the communion. The whole life of a Christian ought to be exempt from the leaven of sin, because he ought to be always in a disposition to celebrate the eucharistic passover, always ready to go to keep the eternal passover in heaven. It is always nigh in respect of that person who always desires it, and prepares himself continually for it. Cease not, O Lord, to purify my heart even to the end, thou who hast been pleased to make it, as it were, unleavened bread by baptism, in order to its being one day the bread of God in the glory of heaven.

2. And the chief priests and scribes sought how they might kill him; for they feared the people.

Ungrateful wretches! whose minds are wholly taken up with designs of death and destruction against Christ, while his is full of designs of life and salvation for the Jews and for all mankind. That person is in a very miserable state who is afraid of sin upon no other than human motives. This is not to hate sin, but only to love himself. When those who, by their profession, ought to breathe nothing but holiness and truth, are restrained only by temporal fear, that passion will soon be overcome by one more violent and powerful.

3. ¶ Then entered Satan into Judas surnamed Iscariot, being of the number of the twelve.

A priest, a minister of the Lord, is seldom corrupted only in part. If he be not a man of God, and a faithful instrument in his work, he has great reason to fear lest he should become a man of the devil, and an instrument in promoting his designs of darkness. Nothing gives more horror than the sight of a person possessed; and yet it had been a desirable mercy for Judas to have been delivered up to Satan to be tormented in his body, rather than to have his heart possessed by the devil, and abandoned to his temptation and illusion. It is avarice, or the desire of earthly riches, which generally lays open the heart of ecclesiastical persons to the devil, as it did that of this apostle. They deliver up the key of their hearts when they deliver up themselves to this passion.

4. And he went his way, and communed with the chief priests and captains, how he might betray him unto them.

He who has once given up his heart to sin, becomes capable of the greatest crimes. There may possibly be one Judas or more in the most holy society. We must not be scandalized, nor leave it on this account. The means and opportunities which the world seeks to invade the rights of the church, and to persecute its ministers, are generally furnished by ambitious clergymen, who are possessed with the spirit of the world as it were with a devil. The avarice and infidelity of one priest betrays and delivers up Christ to the envy and revenge of many others. That which was seen once in the Head will be seen very often in the members.

5. And they were glad, and covenanted to give him money.

It is a terrible judgment upon a sinner for him to find means of putting his wicked designs in execution, and for God to permit him to meet with no manner of obstacles therein. How many sins should I have committed, O Lord, if thou hadst not vouchsafed to oppose my corrupt will! Blessed be thy name forever, for not having left me to myself, as thou didst think fit to leave to themselves these ungrateful priests.

6. And he promised, and sought opportunity to betray him unto them in the absence of the multitude.

Whoever has a great desire to be rich, falls easily into the greatest crimes. A priest whose heart is corrupted by avarice does not wait till an opportunity to betray truth, justice, innocence, and Christ himself, is presented to him; but he goes to meet it, he seeks, he finds it, and delivers them up to their greatest enemies. Shut my heart, O Jesus, against the love of worldly riches, lest this love should set it open to admit the greatest treacheries against thee, or against the interests of thy glory.

SECT. II.—THE PASCHAL SUPPER.—THE EUCHARIST.

7. ¶ Then came the day of unleavened bread, when the passover must be killed.

The best disposition to qualify a man to undergo the greatest afflictions, and even death itself, is quietly to perform his duty in the usual manner, after the example of the Son of God, who sees every thing which his enemies are contriving against him. He prepares for the legal passover out of obedience to the law; and, by this very thing, he prepares to sacrifice himself as the true passover, by the appointment of his Father, and to give the type and figure its full verity and completion. O holy and truly sanctifying victim, I adore thee as the only person among all mankind worthy to be offered to God, being alone the true unleavened bread, the man without sin, and the lamb without spot or blemish.

8. And he sent Peter and John, saying, Go and prepare us the passover, that we may eat. 9. And they said unto him, Where wilt thou
that we prepare?

One of the greatest cares of a Christian ought to be, to prepare himself to celebrate the Christian passover, which is the holy communion, according to the appointment of God and the designs of its institution. The Jews are so faithful in keeping their figurative passover, in memory of a temporal deliverance; and sinners delivered from sin and hell by the sacrifice of Christ the true passover, either wholly neglect to celebrate the memorial thereof by a worthy communion, or perhaps, even while they do communicate, think but little either of the death of Christ who has delivered them, or even of the deliverance itself.

10. And he said unto them, Behold, when ye are entered into the city, there shall a man meet you, bearing a pitcher of water; follow him into the house where he entereth in.

Christ knows whatever lies most concealed and hidden in futurity. He by this gives his apostles a new proof of his divinity, to awaken their faith, and to prepare them for the belief of the mystery which he is going to institute. Let us learn to judge of this mystery, not by our own shallow reason, but by the idea of the divine omnipotence.

11. And ye shall say unto the goodman of the house, The Master saith unto thee, Where is the guest-chamber, where I shall eat the passover with my disciples?

Whoever is not a disciple of Jesus Christ, and has not learned of him to renounce sin, and to love his righteousness, cannot eat the passover with him, nor receive his body and blood. This is the passover of those who are delivered, and whose will cleaves no longer to the world and sin, and who, like true Israelites, have their staff in their hand, just ready to depart. He who is not, but whose will continues still enslaved to Egypt and Pharaoh, to the world and the devil through sin, cannot partake thereof; as the Jews did not eat the legal passover till they were just going out of Egypt, and were delivered from their bondage under Pharaoh.

12. And he shall shew you a large upper room furnished: there make ready.

A large upper room is a large heart extended by charity, furnished and adorned with all Christian virtues, and prepared and made ready by repentance and purity. It is in such a heart that Christ delights to keep his passover: but it belongs to him alone to form and prepare such a heart.

13. And they went, and found as he had said unto them: and they made ready the passover.

Men are never deceived when they obey the command of Christ. Peter and John prepare a passover for the Son of God and his disciples; but he himself is preparing another for them which they know not of, and disposing himself to render them capable of preparing it one day for the whole church, by making them priests to consecrate his body and blood, and to feed souls therewith.

14. And when the hour was come, he sat down, and the twelve apostles with him.

Christ confines himself to the accustomed hours, to teach us to comply with those of God, and to observe those appointed by the church for the times of divine service and prayer, and for the duties of religion. Nothing has a more godly appearance, or can seem more united than this society: but how great is the difference, in the sight of God, between the heart of Christ, just going to sacrifice himself to God his Father for the salvation of the world, and the heart of Judas, going to sacrifice himself to the devil in order to destroy even the Saviour of the world himself?

15. And he said unto them, With desire I have desired to eat this passover with you before I suffer:

This earnest desire of Jesus Christ does not relate to the legal and ceremonial passover, but to the eucharistic passover and the sacrifice of which he was going to be the victim. The eucharistic passover was celebrated once, by way of anticipation, before the bloody sacrifice of the victim of salvation, and before the deliverance it was appointed to commemorate; as the figurative passover had been likewise once celebrated before the going out of Egypt, and the deliverance of God's chosen people. Let us blush at our excessive coldness in relation to so precious a gift, when we consider the ardent desire and love with which Christ bestows it upon us. He desires to unite himself to us in so close and intimate a manner, as if he was to receive some advantage from this union; and those whose whole happiness depends upon it, seem to decline and avoid it. Put me, Lord, into such a disposition as to desire it more and more. Thou vouchsafest to give thyself to me, because thou lovest me; grant that I may love thee, to qualify me to receive thee.

16. For I say unto you, I will not any more eat thereof, until it be fulfilled in the kingdom of God.

The sacrifice of Jesus Christ, which is the completion of the figurative sacrifices, is itself entirely perfected and completed by that glory alone which qualifies the victim for the acceptance of God. One communion prepares for the other; and one effect which that of the eucharist ought to produce in us is, to make us desire the heavenly and eternal communion. We here partake but imperfectly of the mysteries and Spirit of Christ; we shall do it fully and perfectly in heaven.

17. And he took the cup, and gave thanks, and said, Take this, and divide *it* among yourselves.

Although this first cup belong not to the eucharist, but either to the ordinary supper or to the legal passover, yet it is sanctified by the thanksgiving of the Son of God. It is by praise and thanksgiving that we must prepare ourselves to receive the gifts of God, and to offer and present our duties unto him. He gives more than he receives, when he gives us the grace to offer as we ought.

18. For I say unto you, I will not drink of the fruit of the vine, until the kingdom of God shall come.

Jesus Christ exhibits and sets forth his death in giving us his body and blood in the eucharist, which is the memorial thereof; but he, at the same time, exhibits and sets forth the kingdom of God in its glory, of which his death is, as it were the seed and bud. Gratitude for the benefit of redemption, and hope of heavenly felicity, are two dispositions and duties with which we ought to have our minds and hearts filled in the holy communion. This is the true passover given to the church, both in the eucharistic sacrifice instituted in remembrance of the deliverance begun by grace, and in the sacrifice of heaven, which shall be offered in thanksgiving for the deliverance completed by glory.

19. ¶ And he took bread, and gave thanks, and brake *it*, and gave unto them, saying, This is my body which is given for you: this do in remembrance of me.

The institution of the priesthood, of the sacrifice, and sacrament of the altar of the new law, are three different benefits which deserve each of them a particular consideration and acknowledgment. What is it to celebrate the holy sacrifice, and to communicate in the remembrance of Christ? It is to do it in rendering his death present to us by faith. It is to do it with a heart overflowing with gratitude for his having redeemed us with his blood; and to show, by a life truly Christian, that we are dead to sin, to the world, and to ourselves, and that we really partake of the effects of his death and of the spirit of his sacrifice.

20. Likewise also the cup after supper, saying, This cup *is* the new testament* in my blood, which is shed for you. [* *Fr.* Covenant.]

Our sacrifice supposes three effusions of the blood of Christ: the first, representative upon the altar; the second, real upon the cross; and the third, virtual in our heart. This heart ought to be always a holy altar; and it is but too often a cross in respect of Jesus Christ. Would to God that this adorable blood were always the cement of a new covenant to souls; and that it were not frequently the occasion of removing them at a farther distance from God, or even of separating them from him to all eternity! To the end that thy blood, O Jesus, may unite me eternally to thee, grant that it may now separate me from myself, and from all my vicious inclinations.

21. ¶ But, behold, the hand of him that betrayeth me *is* with me on the table.

Before we approach this mysterious table, let us examine ourselves and see whether our hands, that is to say, our works, are the hands and works of a Christian or of a traitor. To hold intelligence with the enemies of Christ—namely, the world and sin, and, at the same time, to eat at his table,—this is no other than to betray him, even after we have taken an oath of fidelity to him in baptism.

22. And truly the Son of man goeth, as it was determined: but woe unto that man by whom he is betrayed!

It is blasphemy to say that the treachery of Judas, or that any other sin, is the work of God, as some heretics have done; but it is true that into what disorders soever sinners are carried by their own will, God is always more the master thereof than they are themselves. He is so good and so powerful, that he makes their wickedness subservient to his own designs; but the sinner is not at all the less punishable on this account, because he alone is the author of his own wickedness.

23. And they began to inquire among themselves, which of them it was that should do this thing.

No man knows into what temptation his own heart will permit him to be drawn. Jesus Christ alone can inform us. Prevent, O Lord, by thy grace, whatever my wretched will may possibly undertake contrary to thine! I cannot answer for my own heart: it belongs to thee, who art absolute master thereof, to answer for it, and to put a stop to the wickedness which thou perceivest in it!

SECT. III.—IMPERIOUSNESS FORBIDDEN.—GLORY PROMISED.

24. ¶ And there was also a strife among them, which of them should be accounted the greatest.

The apostles themselves received but little spiritual advantage from the sacrifice and sacrament of the eucharist, and from every thing which they had seen before the death of Christ and the mission of the Holy Ghost. Never had they greater cause to humble themselves than at this time, and yet they now contend for pre-eminence! The love of preference, so lively on this occasion in persons of no birth, without talents or temporal advantages, makes it evident that no man whatever is free from the wound of pride, and that humility is in all persons a gift of the grace of Christ.

25. And he said unto them, The kings of the Gentiles exercise lordship over them; and they that exercise authority upon them are called benefactors.

The true greatness of kings must necessarily consist in doing good to their subjects, since those whose government was most imperious and severe affected to have the name of benefactors. Those are great indeed, and truly benefactors, who make the happiness of their people their own glory, who never punish but out of necessity, who cause justice to reign and flourish, and who love more to command their own passions than their subjects.

26. But ye *shall* not *be* so: but he that is greatest among you, let him be as the younger; and he that is chief, as he that doth serve.

A pastor understands but little his place and office in the church, if he pretend to signalize himself therein by power, imperiousness, and grandeur. The advantage, above others, which the ministers of the church are permitted to desire, is to be more sacrificed to God by a true humility, and more devoted to the good of the church, and to the salvation of souls, by an active, laborious, and indefatigable charity. The marks of greatness and distinction are a burden to a holy bishop: he bears them indeed before men out of necessity, but he complains of them through humility before God.

27. For whether *is* greater, he that sitteth at meat, or he that serveth? *is* not he that sitteth at meat? but I am among you as he that serveth.

A pastor makes no manner of difficulty to stoop to the meanest of his flock, when he considers that he is really the servant, and not the lord of souls, and that He who is their Lord made himself their servant. One hardly dares propose such an example to the ministers of the church: but it is to no purpose for them to refuse to hear it; it is notwithstanding true, that the servitude of Jesus Christ is the pattern for that of pastors, how eminent soever they may be.

28. Ye are they which have continued with me in my temptations.

Christ glories in the fidelity of his servants, because it proceeds from himself. He is so good, that he is pleased to impute to them as merit the gifts of his grace, and to praise them for that perseverance which he works in them by his Spirit. It is Jesus Christ himself, who, throughout all ages, endures, in his church and ministers, the temptations of the world; and it is he also, who places to account the fidelity of those who continue with him, and forsake him not.

29. And I appoint unto you a kingdom, as my Father hath appointed unto me;

Whoever is not transported with joy at these words, has little faith and relish for the things of eternity. Who can comprehend the dignity and advantage of being a disciple of Christ, whom he vouchsafes to treat in the same manner wherein he is himself treated by his Father! How many truths are comprised under this comparison! What a promise is this! A promise unchangeable and free, which implies infallible means, but, at the same time, imposes a necessity of being conformable to Christ crucified.

30. That ye may eat and drink at my table in my kingdom, and sit on thrones judging the twelve tribes of Israel.

Glory is a state of joy, delight, power, and eternal communion in the great sacrifice of Jesus Christ. Thou, O Jesus, art pleased to assure us that the pleasures, riches, and honours which we renounce for thy sake, shall be restored to us a hundred-fold, by the holy delights of a table where we shall feed on God himself, by the infinite treasures of his eternal kingdom, and by a sovereign power over all creatures.

SECT. IV.—THE PRAYER FOR ST. PETER'S FAITH.—HIS DENIAL FORETOLD.

31. ¶ And the Lord said, Simon, Simon, behold, Satan hath desired *to have* you, that he may sift *you* as wheat:

These efforts of Satan against Peter are a warning to us, and an emblem of those which he is continually making against all Christians. Let us fear an enemy who is always desiring and never weary in soliciting for leave to tempt us. Let us comfort ourselves, however, since it is hereby manifest that he is not able to do any thing against us without the permission of God. Lord, what should we be in the time of temptation, but mere chaff which the wind scatters away, did not thy grace give us the firmness and solidity of wheat?

32. But I have prayed for thee, that thy faith fail not: and when thou art converted, strengthen thy brethren.

What would even the faith of Peter himself have been, had it not been strengthened by the prayer of Christ? It was likewise in Peter that the faith of all the faithful, of whom he was the pastor, that of all the pastors, of whom he was a principal one, and that of the whole church, of which he was a figure, were strengthened and fortified. No temptation is overcome but by the virtue of this prayer, which is even the oblation which this divine Mediator continually makes of his blood in heaven. Peter's sin did not proceed from infidelity, but infirmity. The experience which a pastor has had of his own weakness, and the acknowledgment which he makes of the assistance which upheld him, are a double engagement upon him to compassionate the weakness of others, and to apply himself to the supporting of them.

33. And he said unto him, Lord, I am ready to go with thee, both into prison, and to death.

How much presumption is there in man, before he has himself experienced his own weakness! The stronger he believes himself, the more weak is he: because his promising himself a great deal from his own strength, is a sign that God has already left him to himself. It is more difficult than we imagine, to know what love has gained the ascendant over our hearts. One of the chiefest of the apostles thought the love of his Master most prevalent, and it was the love of his own life.

34. And he said, I tell thee, Peter, the cock shall not crow this day, before that thou shalt thrice deny that thou knowest me.

The fall of Peter, thus foretold unto him, admonishes us to renounce our own light and knowledge, especially as to what regards the disposition of our heart. God and Christ, who is true God, know better than ourselves the use which we shall make of the freedom of our will; and yet this foreknowledge imposes no manner of necessity upon it. God foresees all the evil which he permits, as he predestinates all the good which he intends to perform in us.

35. And he said unto them, When I sent you without purse, and scrip, and shoes, lacked ye any thing? And they said, Nothing.

The providence of God is always watchful over such as forsake all to follow Christ, and continually mindful of their wants. It is of great use frequently to revolve in our minds the conduct of God toward us, because it ought to serve as a pledge and security for the time to come. Those who are grateful are always full of hope: none but the ungrateful distrust the divine providence. In friendship, it is a crime to be distrustful of a friend who has never failed us in our necessity: but let God anticipate all the wants of his creature ever so much, yet he still finds a heart subject to distrust and diffidence.

36. Then said he unto them, But now, he that hath a purse, let him take *it*, and likewise *his* scrip: and he that hath no sword, let him sell his garment, and buy one.

It is a virtue common to all true Christians to trust that nothing shall be wanting to them, either for their subsistence or their safety; but it is an apostolic virtue for a man to be ready, for the sake of Christ, to disclaim all human relief and assistance, and to expose himself as a mark to all men. It is this state which our blessed Lord foretells unto them, by intimating to them what is generally done by those who are either forsaken or assaulted by all the world.

37. For I say unto you, That this that is written must yet be accomplished in me, And he was reckoned among the transgressors: for the things concerning me have an end.

This is not the time for the true disciples of Christ to depend upon the good-will of men, when Christ himself is to be reckoned and treated as a transgressor and malefactor. It is just and reasonable that the members should share in the different conditions of the Head. To be persecuted, and to suffer as a heretic, as a wicked or an impious person, is generally the last trial, and the most meritorious, as being that which gives a man the greatest conformity to Jesus Christ.

38. And they said, Lord, behold, here *are* two swords. And he said unto them, It is enough.

This answer of Christ, "It is enough," ought to have made his apostles sensible of the greatness and nearness of the danger. These two swords were enough, and even too much, for him who designed to defend himself only by delivering himself up, to fight only by suffering, and to conquer only by dying. These were enough to give occasion to Christ to instruct the church, in one of the chief of the apostles, concerning the use she was to make of the sword, concerning the mildness we ought to show toward our enemies, and the submission we ought to have for authority; and to give Christ an opportunity of doing good to his persecutors, of making known his power to them, and of showing them plainly that his being seized by them, and his death, were altogether voluntary on his part.

SECT. V.—THE AGONY IN THE GARDEN.—THE ANGEL.—THE BLOODY SWEAT.

39. ¶ And he came out, and went, as he was wont, to the mount of Olives; and his disciples also followed him.

O holy mount, happy solitude, consecrated by the frequent retirement and prayers of the Lamb of God, by his last preparation for his sacrifice, by his sorrows, his agony, his prostration, his sweat, and his blood! Let our faith transport us thither in spirit, that we may with our heart follow Christ and the apostles thither, and there adore and contemplate all that was done for us, that we may reap the fruits and beg the spirit thereof, and there unite ourselves to Jesus Christ, praying for us, and bearing the punishment of our sins.

40. And when he was at the place, he said unto them, Pray that ye enter not into temptation.

We must not wait until the time of temptation before we pray, but we must pray before it comes. Christ prayed that the faith of the apostles might not fail; and his prayer was already heard by his Father: but it was necessary that the apostles likewise should pray, to complete in themselves that which was wanting to the prayer of their Head, according to the appointment of God, who had made their perseverance depend upon their own prayer, as well as upon that of Christ.

41. And he was withdrawn from them about a stone's cast, and kneeled down, and prayed,

These circumstances of our blessed Saviour's prayer are the pattern of a Christian prayer in affliction, under the apprehension of danger, and the expectation of death. In this condition, we must (1.) Separate ourselves even from our dearest friends, in order to open our hearts to God alone. (2.) We must humble ourselves, internally at least; and, if we are able, externally also. The custom of praying kneeling is derived not only from the apostles, but from Jesus Christ himself. Every knee must bow before the majesty of God, and at the sight of his justice: and nothing shows both more evidently than to see the Son of God upon his knees, and prostrate before his Father. Let us imitate him, and unite ourselves unto him.

42. Saying, Father, if thou be willing, remove this cup from me: nevertheless, not my will, but thine, be done.

If we would imitate Christ in his prayer, we must (3.) Lay our condition before God with plainness and simplicity. (4.) We must be full of trust and confidence. (5.) We must speak but little. (6.) We must resign ourselves up to the will of God, and choose rather to have that done than our own. (7.) We must persevere in praying. The sacrifice of our own will is that which God loves the most, and which ought ever to accompany all others. The more holy the will of Christ was, the more innocent and worthy to be preserved was the life for which he prays; and, on this account, the sacrifice which he makes of it to the will and designs of his Father is so much the more worthy of his majesty and holiness.

43. And there appeared an angel unto him from heaven, strengthening him. 44. And being in an agony he prayed more earnestly:

We must, (8.) After the example of Christ, not reject those external consolations which God sends us in our troubles. (9.) We must fight valiantly against every thing within us which opposes the will of God. (10.) We must pray the more earnestly, and redouble our fervency, when the affliction or temptation is redoubled. The divine nature, without separating itself from the human, leaves it to the weakness common to other men, to the end that the Head may be the consolation of the weakest of his members and the instruction of the strongest. Christ receives assistance from an angel, to teach us to receive comfort, support, and instruction in our troubles, even from our inferiors, when God causes us to have a dependence upon them in that respect. What relief soever we may receive from the creatures, we must, notwithstanding, continually have recourse to the God of all consolation.

—And his sweat was as it were great drops of blood falling down to the ground.

To the end that our prayer may be effectual, like that of Christ, we must (11.) Be prepared to resist even unto blood in fighting against sin. How adorable is this bloody sweat, which the violence of Christ's grief and sorrow for our sins forces out of his veins! The first Adam was condemned to a common and ordinary sweat; the second, to perform and finish that penance in a manner truly worthy of God, endures a sweat which had never any parallel or example. He submits to the marks of the greatest weakness, in order to merit for his members the greatest strength. The most humble ways are those which Christ still prefers before others. That which seems to us most unsuitable to his majesty and greatness, appears to him most suitable to his love for God and for his church. Let us adore this blood shed for us, which falls down to the ground, and seems to be lost there. Oh let not the fruit of it at least be lost as to us!

45. And when he rose up from prayer, and was come to his disciples, he found them sleeping for sorrow,

Lastly: In these circumstances of trouble and affliction, which oblige us to pray, we must not forget even the wants of those who are intrusted to our care. The disciples receive at present the impression of Christ's infirmities and sorrows, as it were, by reflection from him; they will one day receive the fruit and the strength procured by them, when the time of suffering for him is come. Our strength depends upon the will of God, and not upon the instrument of which he makes use to convey it to us. An angel visits and comforts the Son of God; the Son of God himself visits and comforts his apostles: and yet the latter continue still under their weakness, whereas the former receives as it were fresh courage.

46. And said unto them, Why sleep ye? rise and pray, lest ye enter into temptation.

It is one fruit of prayer to be able to encourage others thereto, and to assist them in it. The necessity of prayer in temptation, shows us the necessity of a new grace in order to overcome it. To fall asleep when we ought to pray, is to yield already to temptation. And by our not resisting sloth, this temptation draws on such as are more dangerous, if we do not wake and rise immediately. It is good to have a charitable monitor, who may awake us from our slumber, and encourage us under our dejection. Be thou mine, O Jesus, as thou wast pleased to be that of thy apostles!

SECT. VI.—THE KISS OF JUDAS.—MALCHUS.—THE HOUR OF DARKNESS.

47. ¶ And while he yet spake, behold a multitude, and he that was called Judas, one of the twelve, went before them, and drew near unto Jesus to kiss him.

The impious person, blinded by his audacious impudence, imagines that God is blind too. To flatter the consciences of men, and thereby ruin them eternally,—what is this but to give a kiss like that of Judas to Christ in the persons of his members? It is no other than to offer to give one to himself in person, for a man to go to receive him in the holy sacrament with a heart like that of Judas, with a conscience burdened with deadly sin, and with a will continually disposed to sin, and ready to deliver Christ up thereto on the first occasion. It is a most deplorable disposition when any one loves these occasions, when he will not withdraw himself from them, but on the contrary seeks them, and, as much as in him lies, carries Jesus Christ to them after the communion. If this be not actually to betray Jesus Christ with a kiss, it is something which comes very near it.

48. But Jesus said unto him, Judas, betrayest thou the Son of man with a kiss?

There is need of a very great degree of virtue, and of a charity long rooted in the heart, to keep a man from losing the meekness of his temper in the midst of the greatest outrages. To bear the deceitful caresses of a false friend, requires more virtue than to endure the most violent attacks of a known and declared enemy. This kindness, this gentle reproof, this usual familiarity, and this discovery which he makes of the bottom of this traitor's heart, make it evident that nothing external is sufficient to convert a sinner, if God vouchsafe not to speak to the heart itself.

49. When they which were about him saw what would follow, they said unto him, Lord, shall we smite with the sword?

They know Christ but little who are for defending him by force of arms. He is very far from desiring to save his own life by exposing that of others, since he came on purpose to shed his blood, and to die for all mankind. This question of the apostles is a sign of their doubtfulness, and at the same time of their ignorance, as to the designs of God concerning his Son, in which they had been so often instructed; but this ignorance does not excuse Peter, and this doubtfulness condemns him. There are abundance of persons in the world who, like Peter, consult God, and yet suffer themselves to be hurried away by their passion or their false zeal before they know his will.

50. ¶ And one of them smote the servant of the high priest, and cut off his right ear.

The blind and indiscreet will, which is not guided by the will of the eternal wisdom, exposes itself so much the more to offend God, the more ready and eager it is to follow its own violent motion, even in seeking to serve him.

51. And Jesus answered and said, Suffer ye thus far. And he touched his ear, and healed him.

Jesus permits evil, in order only to bring out of it a greater good. He teaches us to return good for evil. The Spirit of Christ and of his true disciples does not allow private persons to repel by force any violence authorized by the name of lawful magistrates, how unjust soever it may be. Private revenge and public rebellion are things unknown to true Christians, who count it their glory rather to lose their own lives than to take away those of other men. The only miracle which appears not to have been asked of Christ, is this in favour of an enemy and an unjust aggressor; and he works it, not to deliver himself, but by the sole motive of his own inclination and charity.

52. Then Jesus said unto the chief priests, and captains of the temple, and the elders, which were come to him, Be ye come out, as against a thief, with swords and staves?

The reason why Christ is treated as a thief, is because sinners are really such, in robbing God of his glory, and of every thing which they owe him. The best of persons are more sensibly affected by the ill usage which wounds their reputation and honour, (this usage being most proper for thieves,) than they are by any other kind of injustice. It is in order to secure us from that excess to which this sense of human honour is apt to carry us, that Christ is willing to be treated as a thief,—even he who has divested himself of all, and who is now just going to lay down his life.

53. When I was daily with you in the temple, ye stretched forth no hands against me: but this is your hour, and the power of darkness.

Christ determines the hour of his death, as a voluntary victim, who offers himself not out of necessity, but out of choice and love. Such is the blindness of sinners, who think they reign and triumph when they accomplish their wicked desires; whereas they are only the instruments of the devil, who makes them serve his design, as the devil is himself an instrument whom God makes subservient to his. This is, in truth, much more thy hour, O Jesus, than that of these impious wretches,—the hour of thy great work, to which thou makest both the power of darkness and the malice of men subservient and instrumental.

SECT. VII.—CHRIST LED TO CAIAPHAS.—THE DENIAL AND REPENTANCE OF PETER.

54. ¶ Then took they him, and led *him*, and brought him into the high priest's house. And Peter followed afar off.

O Jesus! made a captive on purpose to deliver captives! break the chains of my sinful habits by that invisible power which cannot be bound or confined by men! Let this captivity, which expiates all the ill use of the corrupt freedom of my will, and merits for me the cure, deliverance, and good use thereof, be the object of my religion, my gratitude, and my love!

55. And when they had kindled a fire in the midst of the hall, and were set down together, Peter sat down among them.

He who loves danger, and takes no care to avoid the occasions of sin, runs the hazard of perishing eternally. It is infinitely better for a man humbly to retire, acknowledging his weakness, and having recourse to Him who is the strength of the weak, till he vouchsafe to show him mercy, than wilfully to persist in performing a presumptuous promise, by endeavours which are still more presumptuous. The stronger we would fain appear, out of a confidence merely human, the more destitute are we of the strength of God.

56. But a certain maid beheld him as he sat by the fire, and earnestly looked upon him, and said, This man was also with him.

Every enemy is formidable to a person not supported by God. An occasion which we entirely disregard is sometimes very fatal to our virtue. If every thing be dangerous to us when we do not distrust ourselves, how much more is it so when we are possessed of an opinion of our own strength! Peter was extremely desirous to distinguish himself from the rest of the apostles, who humbly laid hold of the permission which Christ gave them to flee, intimated by those words, "Let these go their way," (John xviii. 8;) but he distinguishes himself from them by nothing but a most shameful fall.

57. And he denied him, saying, Woman, I know him not.

This denial of which Peter is guilty is a dreadful example

of human infirmity. The love of life and the fear of death make men forget the best resolutions when they have not been formed by God, and are not supported by an humble prayer. One of the chiefest of the pastors, overcome thus by a servant maid at the very first blow, warns us to be upon our guard against every thing, especially in a place and company to which neither our vocation nor our duty calls us.

58. And, after a little while, another saw him, and said, Thou art also of them. And Peter said, Man, I am not.

One sin hardens the heart, and disposes it for the commission of another. God permits Peter to fall more than once, that he may have no room to excuse his sin as proceeding from surprise; and that he may seek the cause thereof in his own presumption. Such a one is surprised at the cowardice of Peter, who, upon a hundred occasions, wherein his duty obliges him to declare for the innocent, says, either by his words or his actions, "I am not of them."

59. And about the space of one hour after, another confidently affirmed, saying, Of a truth this *fellow* also was with him; for he is a Galilean.

One temptation, when not resisted, draws on another. The space of one hour is allowed Peter to recover himself, and he makes no use of it: in vain God gives men time for repentance, if he do not give them likewise a penitent heart. The patience of God serves only to harden the sinner, when it is not accompanied with the internal operation of grace. Without this, it is both ineffectual toward his recovery, and frequently the occasion of a new fall.

60. And Peter said, Man, I know not what thou sayest. And immediately, while he yet spake, the cock crew.

Let us not be weary of considering the deplorable infidelity of the heart of man when left to himself. These three falls are, as it were, three witnesses of human weakness; and show plainly that none but God knows perfectly how great it is. He permitted these falls in one of the chiefest of the pastors, to the end that all the sheep may behold in him what they are of themselves, and what they are by grace.

61. And the Lord turned, and looked upon Peter: and Peter remem-

bered the word of the Lord, how he said unto him, Before the cock crow, thou shalt deny me thrice.

How powerful is the internal look of Christ! Without it, nothing external can convert. With it, even the hardest hearts melt into tears. The cock had crowed, and yet Peter did not recollect himself, because Jesus had not yet looked upon him. He casts but one look of mercy upon this sinner, and his heart is pierced with grief. Oh turn not away from mine, O Lord, those eyes of mercy, on which my salvation and eternal happiness depend!

62. And Peter went out, and wept bitterly.

All that we know of this apostle's repentance is, that he immediately quitted the occasion of his falling, that he lamented his fall, and lamented it bitterly. All the rest follows a true sorrow and a true hatred of sin, because these can proceed from nothing but a love to God, and this love pardons itself nothing, and spares nothing to please him. It is always a time to weep, because it is always a time to love; but it is not always a proper time to endeavour to make satisfaction for our sin in the sight of men. We must sometimes wait for a fit opportunity, as Peter did.

SECT. VIII.—CHRIST MOCKED, ABUSED, AND CONDEMNED.

63. ¶ And the men that held Jesus mocked him, and smote *him*.

God becomes the sport of his creatures, and he is pleased to endure it to merit for us the grace to bear contempt with patience. Can the sinner suffer himself to be carried out into resentment, complaints, and revenge, when he beholds his Saviour and his God, innocence and holiness itself, in these circumstances retaining the meekness of a lamb, who could have lifted up his voice like a lion, and crushed all his enemies by the sole motion of his will?

64. And when they had blindfolded him, they struck him on the face, and asked him, saying, Prophesy, who is it that smote thee?

Christ is willing to be deprived of the use of his bodily eyes, to open those of our mind. His divine sight is exposed to mockery and contempt, to expiate the abuse which human pride makes of knowledge. These soldiers insult and abuse the Son of God, but without knowing him; and Christians affront the God whom they know as audaciously as if he were blindfolded, and could only guess at those who insult him. Thou seest every thing, O my God; and the very bottom of all hearts is known to thee. Cause me, therefore, to do every thing as under thy immediate inspection and in thy presence.

65. And many other things blasphemously spake they against him.

Christ suffers these abuses and blasphemies to atone for ours. Grant, Lord, that I may forget all occasions of complaint which relate to myself, and employ my thoughts wholly upon the contempts and abuses which thou wast pleased to undergo for my sake. Thou sanctifiest these things by enduring them in thy divine person; thou makest of them a sacrifice to thy Father, a pattern of patience and humility for me, and a fountain of grace for thy whole church. Grant me, I beseech thee, the grace to adore this divine object, to offer this sacrifice, to imitate this pattern, and to draw continually from this fountain-head!

66. ¶ And as soon as it was day, the elders of the people and the chief priests and the scribes came together, and led him into their council, saying, 67. Art thou the Christ? tell us.

Authority, sacerdotal dignity, and learning, without grace, serve often to destroy Christ and his church, whereas they ought to contribute solely to the establishment of his kingdom therein. If these men had been willing to have believed, they should have asked the prophecies concerning Christ, and the miracles which he had wrought; and these would have answered for him, that he was the only Son of God. But they would fain induce him to speak with no other design but to destroy him. Preserve me, Lord, from being ever guilty of so heinous an outrage! grant, that I may never ask thee any thing, O eternal Truth, but only in order to follow and obey thee!

—And he said unto them, If I tell you, ye will not believe: 68. And if I also ask *you*, ye will not answer me, nor let *me* go.

Let us here learn of the Son of God to show always modesty and respect toward our superiors, how unjust soever they may be. We ought to be very reserved in the discovery of truths, when men are not well disposed to hear them; that we may prevent their being contemned, and the other ill uses the wicked are apt to make of them, as much as we can.

69. Hereafter shall the Son of man sit on the right hand of the power of God.

Christ is faithful to his ministry to the very last, in declaring to those who are going to put him to death the power of that state wherein his resurrection would place him. He preaches indeed to the deaf, but he instructs his church, and honours the truth, by bearing witness to it before the enemies thereof and his own judges. He does not in the least insult them, by threatening them with his power: he only declares to them, that, instead of that mortal life they are going to take from him, he shall receive a new one, full of power and glory.

70. Then said they all, Art thou then the Son of God? And he said unto them, Ye say that I am.

The incarnation and resurrection of the Son of God being the fundamental mysteries of the Christian religion, which were to make so many martyrs, it was necessary that Jesus Christ, as the head of them, should be himself a martyr for those truths. He knew very well that they would cost him his life; but he knew likewise, that life is a debt which all men owe to the truth, and that to sacrifice it to God is not to lose it.

71. And they said, What need we any further witness? for we ourselves have heard of his own mouth.

How different is the joy of these men, upon hearing the truth out of the mouth of Christ, from that of his true disciples! These find therein the words of eternal life; but those convert it into words of death, both for Christ and themselves, by the abuse they make of it. Preserve me, Lord, I beseech thee, from abusing it; for without thy grace I can do nothing else!

CHAPTER XXIII.

SECT. I.—CHRIST ACCUSED BEFORE PILATE.

1. And the whole multitude of them arose, and led him unto Pilate.
2. And they began to accuse him, saying, We found this *fellow* perverting the nation, and forbidding to give tribute to Cesar, saying that he himself is Christ a king.

Christ, who was accused of blasphemy against God, of treason against Cesar, and of sowing sedition among the people, affords those abundance of consolation who suffer under calumny, and admonishes judges and princes not to give credit to it very easily. There is certainly no conduct or behaviour in the world, how upright and innocent soever it may be, which can secure a man from accusations of this nature, since that of Christ could not secure him from them.

3. And Pilate asked him, saying, Art thou the King of the Jews? And he answered him and said, Thou sayest *it*.

Christ is still willing to be called the King of this people, though they are so disloyal and ungrateful to him as to solicit his death. Let men do all they can to shake off the yoke of Christ's sovereignty, yet he will ever preserve his rights. He exercises his power over all men, either in punishing or in changing their rebellious wills. Grant, O Jesus, that I may be the subject of thy mercy and grace; vouchsafe to reign in my heart by thy love!

4. Then said Pilate to the chief priests and *to* the people, I find no fault in this man.

A judge who is neither corrupted nor prepossessed, finds it not at all difficult to discover innocence in the midst of calumnies. Let us to our shame acknowledge that there is often more equity and integrity to be found in a layman, and even in a heathen, than in a Christian or a clergyman who is blinded by envy or interest. It is something, indeed, for a judge not to suppress and stifle the knowledge which he has of innocence; but he becomes the more guilty upon this account, if he abandons the defence of it, and delivers it up to its enemies.

5. And they were the more fierce, saying, He stirreth up the people, teaching throughout all Jewry, beginning from Galilee to this place.

The peaceable doctrine of Jesus Christ, represented as seditious, is matter of comfort and consolation to those evangelical preachers who are aspersed. It is the common artifice of those whose bad doctrine or hypocrisy is discovered and laid open by others, to decry their accusers as turbulent and seditious persons. To hinder such false teachers from corrupting every thing by their pernicious maxims and calumnies, is, if you will believe them, to trouble the consciences of men, and to disturb the peace of church and state.

SECT. II.—CHRIST SENT TO HEROD.

6. When Pilate heard of Galilee, he asked whether the man were a Galilean. 7. And as soon as he knew that he belonged unto Herod's jurisdiction, he sent him to Herod, who himself also was at Jerusalem at that time.

How many Christians are there who, like Pilate, make Christ subservient to their temporal affairs and designs! What will not a judge do, rather than let a cause go out of his hands from which he hopes to reap advantage! On the contrary, a man endeavours to clear his hands of any cause, when he has so much honour as to be unwilling to betray innocence, but has not courage enough to defend it, to the hazard of his fortune, or of losing the friendship of the great. Christ never went to court of his own accord: he is led thither. And he appears there in bonds, to signify to us that truth is there seldom free from captivity and insults.

8. ¶ And when Herod saw Jesus, he was exceeding glad: for he was desirous to see him of a long *season*, because he had heard many things of him; and he hoped to have seen some miracle done by him.

Thus many people of the world learn the truths of Christianity with a joy arising only from curiosity, and not from any desire of being instructed in them, and of putting them in practice. Christ makes every thing instrumental to the accomplishment of his designs. Herod's curiosity gives our blessed Saviour an opportunity to increase the number both of his humiliations and of the witnesses of his innocence, and likewise to draw from the mouth even of a Jewish king the condemnation of the Jews. The great men of the world always want some new sight for their entertainment and diversion. This was all the use which Herod and his court made of Christ.

9. Then he questioned with him in many words; but he answered him nothing.

Christ hears not those who seek him only out of curiosity. The curiosity of men of corrupt minds, with regard to mysteries, is much to be suspected; and we should not amuse ourselves in endeavouring to give them satisfaction. It is difficult for a man to come off with advantage, when he engages in discourse concerning religion with persons who have no more than what human policy gives them. A respectful silence is an instruction for some, and a refuge against others. That person says a great deal who speaks by his modesty, his humility, and his patience.

10. And the chief priests and scribes stood and vehemently accused him.

Corrupt priests and teachers are generally the most implacable enemies of Christ and of the truth. The passions betray those who are slaves to them. An affected moderation would have rendered these accusers less suspected, their accusations more probable, and their envy less visible, than this vehemence; but envy seldom or never consults prudence. And God permits this to be so for the honour of truth and innocence.

11. And Herod with his men of war set him at nought, and mocked *him*, and arrayed him in a gorgeous robe, and sent him again to Pilate.

The curiosity of those who apply themselves to the reading of the Holy Scripture and to religion only through this spirit, is most commonly turned into contempt—contempt produces libertinism, this leads to atheism, and atheism to damnation. There are scarce any places to be found in the gospel, wherein we do not learn of Christ that it is the lot and portion of true Christians, as well as of their Head, to be contemned and despised by the world. It is not in the courts of princes that faith and a reverence for holy things are most conspicuous. It is not from carnal men that we can ever learn how much silence and humility are to be esteemed, since they look upon these things as no better than folly.

12. ¶ And the same day Pilate and Herod were made friends together; for before they were at enmity between themselves.

Irreligious men and heretics, though ever so opposite to one another, frequently unite together against Christ, his truth, and his church. Worldly interest divides carnal men, and worldly interest makes them friends again; but religion rather suffers than gains by this reconcilement. In a very little time, O Jesus, thy death will reconcile and unite together not only a Gentile and a Jew, but Jews and Gentiles, by one and the same faith, in one and the same body, and under one and the same head.

SECT. III.—BARABBAS PREFERRED TO CHRIST.

13. ¶ And Pilate, when he had called together the chief priests and the rulers and the people, 14. Said unto them, Ye have brought this man unto me, as one that perverteth the people; and, behold, I, having examined *him* before you, have found no fault in this man touching those things whereof ye accuse him: 15. No, nor yet Herod: for I sent you to him; and, lo, nothing worthy of death is done unto him.

God is pleased to make use of all sorts of means to manifest the innocency of his Son, as he does to cause his truth to triumph and to enlarge his church. Pilate, who here strongly insists upon the conduct of Herod as an argument in favour of Christ, will certainly condemn those Christian judges who do not hold out in defence of calumniated innocence even so long as this heathen. But this heathen condemns himself, in declaring Christ innocent of that very crime against the state for which he is just going to deliver him up to be crucified. That man is in a very miserable condition indeed, who is not at all the better even for that little good which he does among abundance of evil.

16. I will therefore chastise him, and release *him*. 17. For of necessity he must release one unto them at the feast.

If Christ be guilty, why should he be released? If he be innocent, why should he be chastised? We see here a representation of the corrupt management of a judge who would fain please everybody, instead of having regard to justice alone. For a man to expose it to suffering at the same time that he knows and publishes it, is to dishonour and disgrace it: as if it did not deserve to have every thing sacrificed for its sake.

18. And they cried out all at once, saying, Away with this *man*, and release unto us Barabbas:

There is nothing in the world which the wicked man will not prefer before truth in order to satisfy his passion. How false is the judgment of the world! Who can have any regard for it after that which it passes upon Jesus Christ? Let us judge of the injury here done to Christ, by our own disposition and resentment when we are placed beneath some contemptible person. Let us be ashamed of being so apt to complain of unjust preferences. Can quarrels, revenge, and deadly hatred, arising from disputes about rank and punctilios of honour, subsist any longer after such an example?

19. (Who for a certain sedition made in the city, and for murder, was cast into prison.)

To what degree does not the Son of God abase himself? A robber preferred before the Saviour of the world, a seditious villain before the Prince of peace, and a murderer before the Author of life, to purchase for us salvation, peace, and life eternal. These wretches make a great outcry concerning the public good, the rights of the prince, and the royal prerogative, in order to oppress our blessed Saviour; but they entirely forget and neglect all this in begging the releasement of a seditious person, and an enemy to peace and the public good. Thou seest, Lord, the corruption of man's heart. Since it is in order to cure this heart that thou art pleased to bear the effects of its corruption, vouchsafe to apply this remedy to mine.

20. Pilate therefore, willing to release Jesus, spake again to them.

The voice of our sins, which requires the death of Christ, is more strong and prevalent than that of Pilate, which intercedes for his life. The world is full of these imperfect good wills, which never proceed to execution, and which serve only to render sinners more inexcusable, because they sin with knowledge and a full sight of their duty. Give us, Lord, an active and efficacious will to perform our duty; and abandon us not to the weakness of our own desires.

21. But they cried, saying, Crucify *him*, crucify him.

See here the inconstancy of the friendship of the world!

The very same persons, but six days ago, cried out, "Hosannah to the Son of David," who now cry out, "Crucify him, crucify him." What a strange forgetfulness was here of so many benefits! What strange ingratitude was this in a people who had been eye-witnesses of so many miracles! But how great the goodness and charity of Christ, who foresaw all this ingratitude at the very time when he heaped his blessings upon them; and who loses nothing of his meekness even now, when they demand his death.

22. And he said unto them the third time, Why, what evil hath he done? I have found no cause of death in him: I will therefore chastise him, and let *him* go.

Strange condition this of the Son of God, given up by the justice of his Father to the discretion of his creatures! He meets with no good will but in his judge, and this has no other effect but to make him suffer the more. How often has he turned into good the evil which men were contriving against us? And the justice of God permits that very good which Pilate designed to do him, to be turned to his disadvantage.

23. And they were instant with loud voices, requiring that he might be crucified: and the voices of them and of the chief priests prevailed.

The confederacy and clamour of the wicked often prevail against the reasons of those who speak in behalf of truth and justice. Injustice and envy have more perseverance in their wicked designs, than the good intention of Pilate has in endeavouring to save Jesus Christ. In the perverse and stubborn wills of these hardened wretches I plainly perceive what mine would certainly be, if thou, Lord, should abandon it to its own natural obduracy.

SECT. IV.—CHRIST DELIVERED UP TO THE JEWS.—SIMON THE CYRENIAN.—THE DAUGHTERS OF JERUSALEM.

24. And Pilate gave sentence that it should be as they required. 25. And he released unto them him that for sedition and murder was cast into prison, whom they had desired; but he delivered Jesus to their will.

He who loves any thing more than truth, will abandon it sooner or later. Christ is delivered up to the will of man, that man may deliver himself up to the will of Christ through his grace. Lord, I see myself in this criminal as in a glass;

thou takest my place in taking this, and in setting him at liberty by thy death. O may thy Father see and own me in thee! Grant that he may behold me covered with thy blood, nailed to thy cross, and obedient even unto death, like one of his children, like one of thy members!

26. And as they led him away, they laid hold upon one Simon, a Cyrenian, coming out of the country, and on him they laid the cross, that he might bear *it* after Jesus.

God never leaves any person alone who bears his cross for the sake of him. It is a great favour to be chosen of God to accompany an afflicted soul, and to keep it from sinking under the burden of its cross. Nothing affords greater consolation to one who feels the weight of it, and fortifies him more, than the example of another who bears it with constancy and courage. Lord, abandon not those whom the world crucifies for defending thy cause—give them that strength, consolation, and support of which they stand in need!

27. ¶ And there followed him a great company of people, and of women, which also bewailed and lamented him.

Happy that person who follows Christ, bearing his cross; who compassionates his pains, and sheds tears over him! We see here none but the meaner sort of people touched with compassion for Christ, and bearing him company while he carries his cross. All the rest—the king of the Jews, the Roman govenor, the high-priest, the chief priests, doctors of the law, scribes, and soldiers—all these concern themselves no otherwise about Christ than only to contribute to his sufferings. That compassion which shows itself by outward expressions, is not the most perfect; but the simplicity and sincerity of those souls who thus take part in the pains and sorrows of the Son of God, supplies what is defective in them. God assembles together about Christ, as he carries his cross, the pious souls which were in Jerusalem, on purpose that they may reap the fruits of this painful journey of Christ, of the example of this adorable victim loaded with the wood of his sacrifice, and likewise of the instructions which this dying Saviour has yet to give them.

28. But Jesus turning unto them said, Daughters of Jerusalem, weep not for me, but weep for yourselves, and for your children.

At the court Christ kept a perfect silence: he vouchsafed not to honour King Herod with so much as one word; and he here speaks in public to the meanest of the people. How ought this preference to humble the great! How ought it to comfort those whom they generally look upon as mere worms of the earth, unworthy of their notice, but whom Christ thinks worthy of his notice, his acknowledgment, and his last instructions! One of the fruits of our applying our minds to the contemplation of Christ's sufferings, and raising in ourselves a compassion for them, is to receive instruction concerning those crosses and afflictions which will in all probability happen to us, to prepare ourselves to bear them like Christians, and to enter into the spirit of repentance for our sins. In vain do we weep for Christ, if we do not weep for ourselves when we consider the justice of God. A man must have a heart as good as that of this good Shepherd, to forget the evils which he suffers himself, and to be mindful of those of others, though as yet at a great distance. This ungrateful city cannot be blotted out of his mind to his very last breath. How terrible an example is this against the revengeful!

29. For, behold, the days are coming, in the which they shall say, Blessed *are* the barren, and the wombs that never bare, and the paps which never gave suck.

We have not indeed any reason to fear those very evils which were to happen at the siege and destruction of Jerusalem; and yet these words are directed likewise to us, because these calamities prefigure those of the damned, who shall seek death without being able to find it, and shall suffer an eternal confusion. Nothing but repentance can prevent these miseries. It is a very great mercy, that Christ vouchsafes thus to warn and persuade us to avoid the wrath of God; but it is a very great misery, and a most deplorable blindness in men, to receive no manner of advantage from it by continuing still in impenitence. Every sinner ought to apply to himself in particular this general admonition.

30. Then shall they begin to say to the mountains, Fall on us; and to the hills, Cover us.

Thus an insupportable confusion shall fall on all those who have been ashamed to perform the duty of repentance. All desires to escape the wrath of God will be altogether fruitless and ineffectual when the time of mercy is past. The state and condition of a person who dies without any repentance, or with one which is late, imperfect, and doubtful, has something in it very dreadful: but how much more dreadful will it be, when he finds himself at the tribunal of his Judge without any other refuge than these wishes of despair! Let us prevent them by an efficacious will; and let us earnestly beg this will of God. Let us hide ourselves in the holes of the rock, in the wounds of Jesus Christ, while they continue open to us.

31. For if they do these things in a green tree, what shall be done in the dry?

If Christ, the tree of life, full of the juice of grace, truth, and righteousness, is treated with so much rigour for the sins of men, let us not wonder to see the most holy persons suffer in this life. What have not the wicked to fear, who are no other than dry and barren branches, cut off from the stock, when they see holiness itself overwhelmed with sorrows and afflictions? It is only at the foot of the cross that we can frame true ideas of the justice and anger of God. All that we see beside is no more than a shadow of them.

32. ¶ And there were also two others, malefactors, led with him to be put to death.

My God, into what company hast thou brought that Son, who lives and reigns eternally with thee in the society and unity of the Holy Spirit! By this thou art pleased to comfort those who, being oppressed by the calumnies and injustice of men, are confined to the company of malefactors, in a dungeon, in the galleys, and perhaps on a scaffold. Cause them, O my God, by the perception of a lively faith, to be sensible of the consolation arising from the conformity of their state with that of thy beloved Son.

SECT. V.—CHRIST CRUCIFIED AND INSULTED.—THE TITLE ON THE CROSS.

33. And when they were come to the place, which is called Calvary, there they crucified him, and the malefactors; one on the right hand, and the other on the left.

Christ, in submitting to the punishment of slaves, joins the greatest of ignominies with the most violent of all pains, that nothing may be wanting to the example of patience and humility which he intends to give us in his death, and to the remedy which he prepares thereby for the cure of all our wounds. Apply this remedy to me, O adorable Physician! Cause me to imitate this example, and vouchsafe to imprint thyself in my soul as my pattern, O thou Head of the truly humble and the truly penitent!

34. ¶ Then said Jesus, Father, forgive them; for they know not what they do.

These are adorable words of the oblation of the grand sacrifice of Christ, spoken by him while they were nailing him to the cross, where this new Priest, laid upon this new altar, offers himself as a victim for the ignorances of the people. If a God must die, it must be out of an excess of love, and carrying it to its highest perfection, in offering his blood for those who shed it, in making himself the mediator and advocate of sinners, and in interceding for grace and salvation for his enemies and executioners. He dies as the martyr of his own divinity, confessing and sealing with his blood this fundamental truth of the Christian religion which has made so many martyrs, namely, that he was truly the Son of God, which he declares by using the term, "Father." Settle and establish in thy church, O Lord, this double foundation of its faith and morality—thy divinity and thy love—against the new enemies of both! If these men sin out of ignorance, this does not excuse them any more than it does thy executioners; but it renders them, however, more worthy of compassion, through the extremity of their misfortune.

—And they parted his raiment, and cast lots.

That which is done here by the avarice of these soldiers,

was guided and directed by the same Spirit who had foretold it, to give the greater authority to these mysteries by the completion of the least circumstances. Lord, thou abandonest and givest up to thy executioners these garments, made by the hands of men; but thou leavest us garments far more precious than these, since thou vouchsafest to clothe us with thyself in baptism, and to give us thy virtues, mysteries, grace, and holy Spirit, to cover the nakedness of our heart. Grant, O Jesus, that we may be always clothed therewith, both within and without.

35. And the people stood beholding. And the rulers also with them derided *him*, saying, He saved others; let him save himself, if he be Christ, the chosen of God.

As long as this life lasts, the righteous continue exposed to the insults of the world: and, what is worse, it does what it can to rob them of their trust and confidence in God, and to cause them to murmur against his Providence. Our churches are to us instead of Calvary; our altars, instead of the cross; and the eucharistical sacrifice, instead of the sacrifice of the death of Christ, of which it is the most lively representation. Would to God, that those who here made of the mystery of the cross only a spectacle of curiosity and an occasion of dishonouring Jesus Christ, had not still imitators in these days! I adore thee, O Jesus, both upon the cross and when I approach the altar, as the Saviour who has delivered us from our sins; as the Christ, who pourest upon us of the fulness of the unction of thy Spirit and thy grace; and as the only chosen of God, in whom all the rest are elected, sanctified, and glorified as his members.

36. And the soldiers also mocked him, coming to him, and offering him vinegar,

See here the comforters whom Christ finds on earth in the day of his sufferings, and in the extremity of his sharpest pains! He thirsts, and no man offers him so much as one drop of water! They give him vinegar, while sinners gratify their taste with the most delicious liquors. Lord, apply to our sensuality the remedy which thou preparedst for it by this particular suffering!

37. And saying, If thou be the King of the Jews, save thyself.

O my God, how true is it that carnal men cannot comprehend the dispensations of thy wisdom and thy Spirit! Jesus is the king of the Jews, in reigning by his grace not over Jews according to the flesh and the letter, but over Jews according to the Spirit and the truth; and this grace is the fruit of his cross and death. It is by dying that he establishes his kingdom, gains his people, and saves them. Let this be to the Jews a stumbling-block, and to the Gentiles foolishness,—it shall ever be the object of my adoration, my gratitude, my hope, and my love!

38. And a superscription also was written over him in letters of Greek, and Latin, and Hebrew, THIS IS THE KING OF THE JEWS.

Pilate, from being the judge of Christ, seems to become his first apostle to the Greeks, Romans, and Hebrews, publishing to them his reign upon and by the cross. It is just, O Jesus, that every tongue should confess that thou art a king upon the cross, as well as in thy glory, until the time come when every knee shall bow at thy adorable name. Give me that reverence, obedience, religion, gratitude, and love which I owe thee in this quality and this state of suffering. Let my submission to whatever afflictions may befall me for thy sake, or by thy appointment, be to me a pledge and assurance of my fidelity toward thee, O my crucified King!

SECT. VI.—THE PENITENT THIEF.

39. ¶ And one of the malefactors which were hanged railed on him, saying, If thou be Christ, save thyself and us.

Dismal and irrecoverable estate indeed, when even the last punishments of sin do not open the sinner's eyes! Let us adore the justice of God, and his judgments upon sinners. He who suffers, blaspheming God, without faith, hope, and submission, suffers as a reprobate. It is a favour to be punished in this life, when a man knows how to make a good use of his sufferings; but how rarely is this grace to be found! Whoever suffers altogether by constraint, both without accepting of his sufferings in the spirit of repentance and without the benediction or unction of the Spirit of God, suffers doubly, without comfort and without benefit. Miserable is he who makes this choice!

40. But the other answering rebuked him, saying, Dost not thou fear God, seeing thou art in the same condemnation? 41. And we indeed justly; for we receive the due reward of our deeds: but this man hath done nothing amiss. 42. And he said unto Jesus, Lord, remember me when thou comest into thy kingdom.

The elect, by accepting their cross, suffer abundantly the less, are comforted by God himself, and receive an infinite reward. The penitent thief is the first confessor of Christ's heavenly kingdom, the first martyr who bore testimony to the holiness of his sufferings, and the first apologist for his oppressed innocence. He consecrates to Christ whatever he has at liberty—his heart to believe in him, and his tongue to confess him. The first fruit of faith, in a penitent punished for his sins, is, to consider the difference there is between the sufferings of Christ, entirely innocent, and those of sinners. The second is, to acknowledge that he himself suffers justly. The third is, to have compassion on those who lose all the fruit of their sufferings by receiving them ill, and to exhort them to repentance. The fourth is, not to be offended or scandalized at the humiliations of Christ. The fifth, to expect his eternal kingdom. The sixth, to pray humbly to him. And the seventh, to have no other ambition than to be remembered by him, for his memory is his heart; and all is well when we have a place therein.

43. And Jesus said unto him, Verily I say unto thee, To-day shalt thou be with me in paradise.

Let us admire how exceedingly God comforts true penitents at the time of death by a lively hope. Whoever perseveres, united in heart to Christ in his sufferings, shall be united to him in his glory. One sinner is converted at the hour of death, that we may hope—and but one, that we may fear! Christ, the sovereign dispenser of his own grace and glory, gives it to a thief at the last moment of his life, to show us that he does not give it to merit. The bounty of God surpasses the utmost hopes of true penitents. The person before us here begged only to be "remembered," without presuming to mention a word relating either to time, or to any thing else; and Jesus promises him heavenly repose, the joy of possessing it together with himself, and the enjoyment of it that very day. What sinner will not be attracted by a goodness so bountiful, preventing, and divine!

SECT. VII.—DARKNESS.—THE DEATH OF CHRIST.—THE CENTURION.—THE HOLY WOMEN.—JOSEPH.—CHRIST'S BURIAL.

44. And it was about the sixth hour, and there was a darkness over all the earth until the ninth hour.

How much thicker was the darkness which covered the hearts of the Jews, since they did not perceive by this miracle that they had crucified their King and God! Let it admonish us at least to return the humblest thanks to Christ, for having merited for us, by his death, the light of faith and the grace of his covenant.

45. And the sun was darkened, and the vail of the temple was rent in the midst.

God speaks even yet by inanimate creatures to this obdurate people, who refused to hear his Son. He makes use of every thing to awaken the sinner; but the sinner, by his obduracy, renders every thing ineffectual when God works not an internal and invisible miracle upon his heart. How is it, that they do not now at least know that it is the Sun of their souls, whose light and life they have extinguished and put out, and that his death rends the vail of types and shadows, discovers the truth, and opens heaven! But the time is not yet come.

46. ¶ And when Jesus had cried with a loud voice, he said, Father, into thy hands I commend my spirit: and having said thus, he gave up the ghost.

The cry of Jesus shows the reality of his human nature, the extremity of his pains, and the ingratitude of men. This is the cry of the true Abel, whose blood intercedes for mercy toward sinners. One fruit of these last words is to teach us to resign ourselves up willingly to God as our Father, at the time of death, after the example of Jesus Christ. He lays down his life of himself, as a voluntary victim. Let us learn, in imitating him, to be always ready freely to sacrifice our own. As the true wheat of the elect, he dies here on earth in order to bring forth much fruit in heaven. How large a field of meditation does every one of these last words afford us! How much is there in them to be adored and imitated! How many other duties are we obliged to perform toward a God who dies for us such a death, and by such a love:

47. Now when the centurion saw what was done, he glorified God, saying, Certainly this was a righteous man.

The first fruits of the death of Christ are not for a priest, a doctor of the law, a Pharisee, or for any Jew, but for a Gentile, a soldier, who was present at it merely by the duty of his post. How far are thy judgments, O my God, above the reach of our understandings! The Jewish priests, notwithstanding all the helps they had from the law and the prophets, from the miracles and preaching of Christ, could see nothing of his holiness; and thy mercy supplies the want of all those things in the heart of this centurion, and causes him to know and confess the Saviour of the world. Let us adore these judgments of God—his justice toward some, and his mercy toward others.

48. And all the people that came together unto that sight, beholding the things which were done, smote their breasts, and returned.

The second graces are for the common and illiterate people, who were not so much set against Christ, and had not contributed to his death out of any malicious design, as others had done. Many of these people, but a few hours since, had cried out, "Crucify him, crucify him!" and yet Christ vouchsafes to touch their hearts, and to give them the grace of repentance. On the contrary, with how much difficulty does a revengeful person pardon an injury; and how long must one wait for some small testimony of reconciliation! Let us adore the readiness of Christ in pardoning those who were instrumental in his death, and condemn our own slowness and backwardness in forgiving the least offences.

49. And all his acquaintance, and the women that followed him from Galilee, stood afar off, beholding these things.

Christ has often curious and inquisitive spectators of his mysteries, who are only present in body; but love and fidelity are the things which keep these holy women here, as they were those which caused them at first to follow Jesus Christ. His grace drew them to him; his grace detains them. Effect in my heart, O Jesus, that which thou didst effect in theirs! Grant that I may never contemplate thee fastened to the cross but with reverence and religion, never but with a crucified heart!

50. ¶ And, behold, *there was* a man named Joseph, a counsellor; *and he was* a good man, and a just:

Fidelity in taking part in the humiliations of Christ is a thing very rare in a person of quality. Joseph is the first confessor of Christ in his state of death. It was for this particular office that God prepared him by that goodness and justice which are here praised by the evangelist, and of which it is the reward. The majesty and magnificence of God, and his design of setting off the humiliations of his Son, are the cause of his reserving to himself some great persons, to be peculiarly applied and consecrated to the mystery of his burial. We do not enough consider this mystery, though it be particularly set down in the Scripture and in the creed. It is the emblem of baptism, wherein we are buried with Christ.

51. The same had not consented to the counsel and deed of them: *he was* of Arimathea, a city of the Jews; who also himself waited for the kingdom of God.

God has servants of several sorts; and graces, the measure and quality whereof are little known to men. We must not proceed rashly to judge in this matter, nor to condemn those who may seem to us to be too reserved on some particular occasions. There are some persons of whom God requires no more, with respect to public acts of injustice, than only not to join in them, and to live according to the rules of Christian faith and hope, unless they are particularly obliged, by their state of life or their ministry, to oppose injustice, and to speak in behalf of innocence. We know that Joseph "consented not to the counsel and deed of them;" but we do not know whether he spoke on this occasion or not.

52. This *man* went unto Pilate, and begged the body of Jesus.

Faith draws even from the death of Christ the courage to declare for him. On such dangerous occasions a man may easily know whether he has been silent through cowardice and fear, or according to God's will, and by his Spirit. To beg "the body of Jesus," is to beg the victim of the world, the most precious relic which can possibly be imagined, and the source of all graces. Happy he who begged it, received it, and disposed of it as God required him to do.

53. And he took it down, and wrapped it in linen, and laid it in a sepulchre that was hewn in stone, wherein never man before was laid.

God causes his Son to receive the honour of a burial that it may serve as a declaration of his innocence, and as a proof of the reality of his death and resurrection. Christians are well enough disposed to honour the death and resurrection of Christ, but few are mindful of his burial. This, according to Paul, is the model of a Christian life, which is a life hid from the world, a life wherein we labour not only to crucify, but likewise to bury the old man; so as that nothing may any longer appear but the new man, and such things as are worthy of him.

54. And that day was the preparation, and the sabbath drew on.
55. And the women also, which came with him from Galilee, followed after, and beheld the sepulchre, and how his body was laid.

Jesus Christ being dead, draws to his sepulchre those holy women who had continued faithful to him at the cross. These souls, devoted to the service of his sacred humanity, to feed and support him during his life, seek him after his death, that they may serve him as long as they know him to remain on earth. Let us bury and serve him in the poor, since he has left them in his place, and has in them continual wants and necessities to be supplied.

56. And they returned, and prepared spices and ointments; and rested the sabbath day according to the commandment.

The honour which these pious women prepare for the body of this divine victim, is a mark of its sanctity and of the consecration of this holy flesh, by its being offered as a sacrifice. It is upon this account that we likewise pay some honour to the bodies of Christians, as being the temples of the Holy Ghost, and parts of that adorable victim.

CHAPTER XXIV.

SECT. I.—THE HOLY WOMEN AT THE SEPULCHRE.—THE INCREDULITY OF THE APOSTLES.

1. Now upon the first *day* of the week, very early in the morning, they came unto the sepulchre, bringing the spices which they had prepared, and certain *others* with them.

The diligence and earnestness of a soul which seeks God, is represented in these holy women. All sloth must be shaken off when the doing something for Jesus Christ is the matter in question. There are two conditions which ought to precede the good works which we would offer to God: we must prepare ourselves to perform them with holy dispositions; and we must set about them without delay.

2. And they found the stone rolled away from the sepulchre.

When persons have a true confidence in God, obstacles do not hinder them from undertaking whatever they have reason to believe he requires; and the removal of them they leave to him. All manner of difficulties vanish before those who are led by a lively faith and a sincere desire to please God.

3. And they entered in, and found not the body of the Lord Jesus.

God sometimes tries those who seek him, when they think to find him in the exercises of piety. It is no small mortification to a soul which loves God, to lose an opportunity of serving him when it imagines itself so happy as to have one present.

4. And it came to pass, as they were much perplexed thereabout, behold, two men stood by them in shining garments:

The absence of Jesus Christ ought always to give us some perplexity, and to make us fear lest this has happened through our own fault. God never leaves those souls in trouble long whom he exercises by withdrawing himself from them: if he do not send them comforters from heaven, he causes them to meet with visible angels upon earth for their support and consolation. The only way is to be faithful to him; and he will certainly be so on his part.

5. And as they were afraid, and bowed down *their* faces to the earth they said unto them, Why seek ye the living among the dead?

We never seek Jesus Christ without benefit and comfort when we seek him sincerely and with our whole heart. How full of consolation is this gospel of life to those souls who are wholly taken up in contemplating the death and burial of their Saviour! The mysteries of the cross and death of Christ, to those who apply themselves thereto with faith and devotion, are a means of arriving at the joy of his new life.

6. He is not here, but is risen: remember how he spake unto you when he was yet in Galilee,

Whoever by mortifying himself seeks Jesus Christ dead, shall find him risen again, by receiving the Spirit and participation of his new life. The belief of mysteries is founded chiefly upon the word of Christ. It is to this word that the angels refer these very souls, whom they instruct with their own mouth by the direction of God. Render our minds intent, O Jesus, and make us always remember, that thou art no longer visible here below, that heaven is the place where we must seek for thee, and that thou art to be found only by faith.

7. Saying, The Son of man must be delivered into the hands of sinful men, and be crucified, and the third day rise again.

Strange necessity of the humiliations and sufferings of Christ! How can sinners then pretend to be exempted from suffering? It was not indeed absolutely necessary in itself that the Son of God should be the victim of his Father; but it was necessary that he should be so, supposing the designs of God concerning the satisfaction of his justice and the salvation of men. Since Christ, according to the divine decrees, was to be the principle of our life and righteousness, and the head of the elect, it was necessary that, after he had appeased the wrath of God by his death, he should receive a new life by his resurrection.

8. And they remembered his words,

The remembrance of the words of Christ on proper occasions, is a grace which proceeds from Christ himself. It was he who assisted the memory of these pious women, and who worked in their hearts, at the same time that the angels exhorted them to remember.

9. And returned from the sepulchre, and told all these things unto the eleven, and to all the rest. 10. It was Mary Magdalene, and Joanna, and Mary *the mother* of James, and other *women that were* with them, which told these things unto the apostles.

These women, who had more courage than the apostles at the time of Christ's passion, receive the first news of his resurrection, and are the persons who inform them of it. It is the duty of those pious souls whom God visits with particular graces, to acquaint their pastors or directors therewith, and to submit them to their judgment. Obedience preserves those graces which piety has obtained, and gains a new degree of grace to make use of them.

11. And their words seemed to them as idle tales, and they believed them not. 12. Then arose Peter, and ran unto the sepulchre; and stooping down, he beheld the linen clothes laid by themselves, and departed, wondering in himself at that which was come to pass.

The wonder of Christ's resurrection infinitely surpasses the hopes and understandings of men. God did not perhaps require of the apostles that they should believe so great a mystery upon the bare word of two or three women; but he only begins to awaken their faith by this first account. Peter, as one of the chiefest of the apostles, runs to the sepulchre, believes, wonders, and is thereby disposed to receive with greater faith the visit of our blessed Lord.

SECT. II.—THE TWO DISCIPLES GOING TO EMMAUS.

13. ¶ And, behold, two of them went that same day to a village called Emmaus, which was from Jerusalem *about* threescore furlongs. 14. And they talked together of all these things which had happened.

If the faith of these two disciples was somewhat weakened, yet they were at least filled with the remembrance of Christ's mysteries; and for persons to love to discourse of holy things, is one means to raise and revive their hope. Would to God, that Christians would in their journeys and conversations imitate them, instead of entertaining one another with trifles, as they generally do.

15. And it came to pass, that, while they communed *together* and

reasoned, Jesus himself drew near,* and went with them. [* *Fr.* Came and joined them.]

How profitable and advantageous is it to discourse of Jesus Christ! If, when we speak of him with piety, he do not become visibly present indeed, yet he becomes more present to our heart by an increase of grace. Let us admire and adore the charity of the good Shepherd, who, as soon as ever he is risen again, labours to gather his dispersed flock, and to bring back his sheep which were gone astray! Vouchsafe, O Lord, to join thyself to us, to act and go along with us, in all our undertakings and journeys to sanctify them by thy Spirit.

16. But their eyes were holden that they should not know him.

If grace open not our minds, they will continue eternally shut with respect to the mysteries of Christ. God has his secret and wise designs when he sometimes hides himself from those whom he loves the most. The ignorance to which God, out of his just anger, abandons the wicked by way of punishment, is one thing; that into which he permits the righteous to fall, only to exercise and try them, is another. We may have Jesus Christ with us, and not know him. We may walk along with him in his ways, and yet not see clearly into his conduct.

17. And he said unto them, What manner of communications *are* these that ye have one to another, as ye walk, and are sad?

Christ compassionates the sorrows of those who have a sense of his. This grief and sadness for having lost him, though weak and imperfect in itself, is notwithstanding pleasing to him, and prepares them for something more perfect. It is even the weakness and imperfection of the disciples which occasions this visit, and draws upon them the comfort and consolation of so good a Master. Who will not hope in him?

18. And the one of them, whose name was Cleopas, answering said unto him, Art thou only a stranger in Jerusalem, and hast not known the things which are come to pass there in these days?

How many Christians are such strangers in the church that Christ and his mysteries are almost utterly unknown to them, after so many ages of predictions, miracles, and instructions! Let our faith render the mystery of the cross so familiar to our minds, that we may never be surprised whenever the cross presents itself unto us.

19. And he said unto them, What things? And they said unto him, Concerning Jesus of Nazareth, which was a prophet mighty in deed and word before God and all the people: 20. And how the chief priests and our rulers delivered him to be condemned to death, and have crucified him.

Death and glory cause a forgetfulness of what has been suffered during this mortal life. Christ seems to be such with respect to the apostles, as they themselves were with respect to him. He forgets, as it were, his state of infirmity, as they had forgotten his divinity. The praise of a bishop, or of a minister of the church, cannot be real and substantial, unless it include these two things—deeds and words, doing and teaching. It is a matter of small moment, to charm the ears with fine discourses, or to dazzle the eyes with remarkable and shining actions; it is only by the works of a holy life, that a man is in the sight of God such as he ought to be. If an extraordinary mission be not authorized by miracles, we are not obliged to have any manner of regard to it. If piety do not support preaching and ecclesiastical labours, a man either labours altogether in vain, or at least in vain as to himself.

21 But we trusted* that it had been he which should have redeemed Israel: and beside all this, to day is the third day since these things were done. [* *Fr.* Hoped.]

Alas, what is the spirit of man without the Spirit of God, even in those who were appointed to be the founders of the church and the preachers of the faith! It hopes for every thing when there is the least foundation imaginable; and it despairs of every thing in the time of the greatest hope. True faith waits for God's proper time, without any concern or anxiety: Christian hope is such only by patience and perseverance. The deliverance and salvation of the heart are the things which both aim at and expect.

22. Yea, and certain women also of our company made us astonished, which were early at the sepulchre; 23. And when they found not his body, they came, saying, that they had also seen a vision of angels, which said that he was alive.

Early in the morning of the third day the sepulchre is found empty, angels descend from heaven to publish the resurrection, and the apostles themselves find not Christ's body in the tomb: is not all this enough to put these wandering pilgrims again into the right way, who had been instructed by the preaching of the Son of God? But nothing external is sufficient to inspire men with faith and hope; this is the work of internal grace, which operates in the heart. This incredulity of the apostles is mysterious, it makes a part of the economy of the divine dispensations, and is instrumental in promoting the faith of all people. God frequently permits faults in others for our instruction; and the falls of the most perfect are useful in supporting the most weak.

24. And certain of them which were with us went to the sepulchre, and found *it* even so as the women had said: but him they saw not.

For this very reason they ought to have believed he was risen; for he could not have been so if they had found him there. But without grace, that which should contribute to awaken and fortify faith and hope serves only to weaken them the more; whereas, with grace they are nourished, and increase by those very things which seem most violently to obstruct and oppose them.

25. Then he said unto them, O fools, and slow of heart to believe all that the prophets have spoken:

This reproof from Christ seems somewhat harsh and severe, but it is extremely charitable, and necessary to awaken their faith. A flattering mildness or gentleness, which lulls the sinner asleep, is no other than a real cruelty; whereas, on the contrary, a sharp word is a kind instance of severity, and a necessary remedy to open the eyes of a friend. The mystery of the cross is the salvation of the world. Whoever does not believe it, disowns all the prophets, or does not understand them at all.

26. Ought not Christ to have suffered these things, and to enter into his glory?

The necessity of suffering is unavoidable: there is no other gate by which we can enter into glory. This is the way of salvation for the whole church; it is that of every one of the elect: it was the way of the Head, and it must be that of the members. In vain would men hope to find out another way, more easy, and better suited to the inclinations of nature.

For the more it is flattered, the more it is corrupted and rendered more unworthy of God. It cannot possibly be either sanctified or saved but by mortification, which makes one part of the cross. No, Lord, I desire no salvation but through the virtue and by the participation of thy sufferings; and it is in these very sufferings that I find the grace and strength to partake of them in thy Spirit.

27. And beginning at Moses and all the prophets, he expounded unto them in all the Scriptures the things concerning himself.

All the Scriptures, even those of the Old Testament, are full of Jesus Christ. We find him in them when we know how to seek him as we ought; and this we must do by the light of faith, and of the love of Jesus Christ himself. Let us pursue the intimation here given us by Christ, in order to attain to the true knowledge of his mysteries. How worthy is this study of a Christian, instead of those vain sciences with which the mind is generally filled! Vouchsafe, great God, to give us a relish and love for thy Scriptures, and a perfect understanding of them. Let it be our delight to seek, to find, and to taste Christ in them; and to admire therein the holiness and wonders of thy conduct in relation to him, to his church, and to all his elect!

28. And they drew nigh unto the village, whither they went: and he made as though he would have gone further.

God tries the charity of his servants as well as their faith. He seems sometimes to be withdrawing himself from a soul when he is ready to manifest and communicate himself thereto in the fullest manner. The fear of losing him increases our esteem both of God and of his gifts, and kindles in us a more ardent desire of them; and it is by this desire that he causes us in some sense to deserve not to lose them, and to receive a more abundant participation of them.

29. But they constrained him, saying, Abide with us; for it is toward evening, and the day is far spent. And he went in to tarry with them.

The love of truth, and the influence of charitable instructions, cause charity to grow and increase in the heart. In this manner ought we to use a holy violence toward Christ in the persons of the poor, and, as it were, constrain him to receive our hospitality and our alms. We must likewise use this holy violence toward him in prayer, that our imperfections may not constrain him to forsake us Happy is that person who fully knows what it is to possess him by faith and charity, and by the holy eucharist! The time of receiving this, is the proper time to importune him more earnestly to make his abode in us. How much greater reason have we to redouble our importunities, when we see the Sun of righteousness begin to decline, and the light of faith to grow dim in ourselves, in our brethren, or in the church, and more especially when the day of life is likewise far spent?

30. And it came to pass, as he sat at meat with them, he took bread, and blessed *it,* and brake, and gave to them.

Christ himself feeds those who feed him in the poor. We may know religious persons not only in the exercises of religion, but even in the most common actions of life, which they convert into holy actions, by the holiness of their dispositions, by prayer which sanctifies every thing, and by the oblation which they make thereof to God. The meals of Christians ought to resemble those of Christ, who here teaches them never to sit down to them till they have invoked the divine blessing by thanksgiving and prayer, which must be performed with faith, attention, and reverence, and not carelessly, by rote, and only for fashion's sake.

31. And their eyes were opened, and they knew him; and he vanished out of their sight.

The eucharist is a bread of life and of knowledge. God diffuses his light, and manifests himself when he pleases, by this sacrament, to such souls as are a little wavering in the faith, and begin to grow weak in piety. One communion alone sometimes opens the eyes more with respect to matters of faith, than all the discourses and instructions of men. The practice of God's word is often more enlightening to souls which have a true simplicity, than constant study is to the learned. It happens, on some certain occasions, that we possess God without knowing him; and that when we do know him, we lose the sensible enjoyment of him. We have then great need of an enlightened guide, who can both discern and follow the ways of God, and who will neither lead souls astray, nor disquiet and disturb them.

32. And they said one to another, Did not our heart burn within us, while he talked with us by the way, and while he opened to us the Scriptures?

The word of Jesus Christ is a fire which inflames him who feeds thereon; whereas the conversation of the world serves only to distract and to cool the heart. Pious discourses, the truths of the Scripture, and the explication of the mysteries of our salvation, when retained in the memory, kindle the love of God in our heart, and feed and preserve it there. We do not always perceive immediately the good effects produced in us by the word of God and by sermons, but we find them afterward. Let us but love to hear God spoken of, and we shall soon be sensible that God himself speaks to us, warns us, and changes our hearts.

33. And they rose up the same hour, and returned to Jerusalem, and found the eleven gathered together, and them that were with them, 34. Saying, The Lord is risen indeed, and hath appeared to Simon.

There sometimes wants but one Christian conversation, one pious discourse, or one devout communion, to cause a soul to return into the way of perfection, which it was just going to leave. The faith of these disciples grew weaker the farther they removed from Jerusalem; by returning thither, they find sufficient matter to strengthen and increase it. We may observe two circumstances very common in the failings of the elect,—that God does not permit them to fall away very far, and that they are ready to return whenever he recalls them. Christ distinguishes Peter, and favours him with a particular visit, because he is a penitent whose heart is under great affliction and humiliation; and likewise to teach us to respect and honour authority in the pastors, notwithstanding all their faults and imperfections. It is a very great consolation to the disciples recovered from their errors, but continuing still weak, to learn so soon that Christ does not reject sinners, and that he has even a compassion and tenderness toward penitents.

35. And they told what things *were done* in the way, and how he was known of them in breaking of bread.

We may here observe the wonderful effects of the eucharist, of the practice of works of mercy, and of the word of God, which are—(1.) To recover us out of dangerous ways and errors. (2.) To bring us back to unity. (3.) To confirm us in the faith. And, (4.) To open our eyes, that we may know Christ more perfectly. O heavenly bread, broken upon the cross for my salvation, in the eucharist for my spiritual nourishment, and in the Scriptures for my instruction, save, feed, and enlighten me; and grant that I may everywhere know and acknowledge thee to be the bread of God, of life, and of my soul.

SECT. III.—CHRIST APPEARS TO THE APOSTLES, CONFIRMS HIS RESURRECTION, AND PROMISES THE HOLY GHOST.

36. ¶ And as they thus spake, Jesus himself stood in the midst of them, and saith unto them, Peace *be* unto you.

Jesus is present in the midst of those who discourse of his mysteries. O good Shepherd, thou seekest thy sheep in all places, to comfort them, to strengthen their faith, and to show them, by thy visible presence, that thou knowest the means to render thyself present to them in their wants, and whenever they are assembled together in thy name and according to thy word. May thy charity be praised by all Christians, may it be imitated by all pastors in their proper manner. Whenever Jesus enters into a heart, he brings peace into it. He produces it there by only wishing or willing it, because his will is omnipotent, and is even his omnipotence itself

37. But they were terrified and affrighted, and supposed that they had seen a spirit.

The spirit of man, incapable of itself to discern the things of God, is ready on all occasions to lay itself open to the illusions of the devil, and to take the peculiar favours and visits of God for no other than illusions. The devil flatters men at first, to take away all diffidence and distrust, and to keep them from examining any thing: on the contrary, the Spirit of God imprints a fear and amazement on the mind, because he would have nothing which is extraordinary received without examination.

38. And he said unto them, Why are ye troubled? and why do thoughts arise in your hearts?

The mind of man is strangely fruitful in such thoughts as are contrary to faith. In all extraordinary visits from God, it is good to be somewhat fearful and diffident, but not to such a degree as to be troubled, and to suffer all sorts of thoughts to rise in our hearts. It is not sufficient that we receive extraordinary measures of grace from God; it is likewise necessary that he should make them known, and hinder our minds from turning them to our own disadvantage.

39. Behold my hands and my feet, that it is I myself: handle me, and see; for a spirit hath not flesh and bones, as ye see me have.

A body raised from the dead is a real body, which is solid, and capable of being touched. We must settle and confirm ourselves in the belief of the resurrection of our bodies by the resurrection of that of our Head. Whoever expects to have his own body enjoy the rights which are enjoyed by the body of Christ, must, after his example, take upon himself the yoke of mortification here below. Those marks and prints of his sufferings, which still remain in the midst of his glory, serve to put us in mind that it was by the cross that he merited it, and that we must bear it after him in order to be glorified with him.

40. And when he had thus spoken, he showed them *his* hands and *his* feet.

Christ retains the scars of his wounds, (1.) To encourage us to suffer for him, by showing us how much he loves sufferings. (2.) For the comfort and consolation of his elect. (3.) For the confusion of the damned. (4.) To afford us a sanctuary or refuge in our temptations and troubles. And, (5.) To show us fountains of grace continually open to us in our wants. Grant me, Lord, the fidelity to improve to these purposes the contemplation of thy sacred wounds. Let them not be closed against me, I humbly beseech thee. And let my heart enter into thine by that passage which thou hast been pleased to keep open for it.

41. And while they yet believed not for joy, and wondered, he said unto them, have ye here any meat?

God produces faith by degrees in the heart, that men may be the more sensible that it is his work. The slowness and backwardness of the disciples shows plainly that they did not believe lightly and rashly. Every thing here seems to oppose the belief of the resurrection—amazement, fear, a prepossessed imagination, joy, and admiration; the evidence alone of the proofs here given bears down all before it, and establishes the belief of this truth. For a man not to yield to these, is to resolve to shut his eyes, and to be wilfully blind.

42. And they gave him a piece of a broiled fish, and of a honeycomb.
43. And he took *it*, and did eat before them.

To instruct and heal a soul, a pastor must stoop to the lowest condescensions. If he eat with his sheep, he must do it only out of charity, not often, and with the indifferency of a man raised from the dead, chiefly to comply with their weakness, and to strengthen them without weakening himself. Happy that pastor who, even by the meanest and most natural actions, shows plainly that he is risen again, in performing them in the spirit of the new life, and as a person altogether heavenly.

44. And he said unto them, These *are* the words which I spake unto you, while I was yet with you, that all things must be fulfilled, which were written in the law of Moses, and *in* the Prophets, and *in* the Psalms, concerning me.

Would to God that those entertainments or repasts at which pastors and spiritual directors are engaged to be present, were, like this, only an occasion of instructing others, of making known the truths of religion, of replenishing souls with Christ and his mysteries, of inspiring into them a love for the Scriptures, of sanctifying conversation with pious discourses, and of settling and confirming the wavering faith of the weak. Let us be careful to seek Jesus Christ in the Old Testament, as well as in the New. He is in all parts thereof; and in all he frames the heart of a Christian. The Prophets exercise our faith, the Psalms nourish our hopes, and the Law tries and makes known our charity.

45. Then opened he their understanding, that they might understand the Scriptures,

We cannot penetrate into and understand the true sense of the Scriptures, but only by Jesus Christ. In vain would he himself have instructed the apostles in the truths contained in them, if he had not likewise given them the understanding thereof. It is a strange delusion under which heretics are, in flattering every private person with this gift of understanding, which even the apostles themselves, though sanctified, did not receive till after the resurrection, and that by a peculiar grace and favour. It is the fruit of humility, prayer, true spiritual poverty, and of fidelity in bringing the mind into subjection to the yoke of faith. O Jesus, it is thou who hast the key of the knowledge of the Scriptures, as well as that of our understandings and hearts. Cause us to understand, to love, and to practise them.

46. And said unto them, Thus it is written, and thus it behoved Christ to suffer, and to rise from the dead the third day:

"It behoved Christ to suffer," because God had so ordained it; because he could not content his mercy without satisfying his justice, which was not to be done but by a victim worthy of himself; and because "It became him, for whom are all things, and by whom are all things, in bringing many sons unto glory, to make the Captain of their salvation perfect through sufferings." (Heb. ii. 10.)

47. And that repentance and remission of sins should be preached in his name among all nations, beginning at Jerusalem.

Repentance on the part of sinners, and mercy on that of God, are the summary of the whole gospel. Christ has purchased the whole earth by his death, and by preaching he takes possession thereof; but he both purchased it and possesses it only in order to sanctify and consecrate it to God. True repentance and remission of sins are inseparable. Whoever refuses to make any satisfaction to justice by repentance, has not the least right to mercy. God leads to both by his word. He gives the spirit of repentance to those whose sins he intends to pardon; and causes those to obey his word to whom he designs to give the grace of repentance.

48. And ye are witnesses of these things.

All Christians are not designed to be witnesses of the mysteries and doctrine of Christ, by preaching them and dying for them, as the apostles were; but all ought to be witnesses of them by their life and conversation. Our faith renders these things present to ourselves; let our manners and behaviour publish them to others.

49. ¶ And, behold, I send the promise of my Father upon you: but tarry ye in the city of Jerusalem, until ye be endued with power from on high.

Comfortable promise this, and which follows the preceding discourse very seasonably. For who could believe that a God died and rose again, who could hope for the remission of his sins, who could love repentance and the cross, without this gift which the Father promises and sends us by the Son? Retirement and repose were by Jesus Christ judged necessary for the apostles and disciples, in order to their receiving the Holy Ghost, who is the strength of the weak: and can we judge otherwise by ourselves? These words should teach us neither to expose ourselves to the world and its temptations, nor to undertake the work of God, until we be endued with power from on high.

SECT. IV.—CHRIST BLESSES HIS APOSTLES, AND ASCENDS INTO HEAVEN.—THEIR JOY AND CONTINUAL PRAYER.

50. ¶ And he led them out as far as to Bethany, and he lifted up his hands, and blessed them.

Jesus blesses his disciples as their Father, their Head, and their sovereign Priest; and this benediction supports them till the descent of the Holy Ghost. These adorable hands, lifted up, stretched out, pierced, and nailed to the cross as hands of malediction, did by that very means become the fountain of benediction to the whole earth, and of all kind of graces to his church. Lift up, and extend over me, O Lord, from the height of heaven, these divine hands, on which my eternal portion and happiness depends.

51. And it came to pass, while he blessed them, he was parted from them, and carried up into heaven.

The love with which Christ loves his own continues unto the end. He parts from them, only to unite them more closely and holily to himself. He ascends into heaven, to prepare the way and to open the gate thereof unto them. Bless me, Lord, with that kind of benediction which unites those to thyself who are as yet separated from thee in this world; and let thy heart, in leaving the earth, separate mine from it, and draw me after thee into heaven.

52. And they worshipped him, and returned to Jesusalem with great joy:

Christ, in receiving the adoration of his disciples, gives them his joy. It is good to unite ourselves in heart to the apostles, that we may worship Jesus Christ with them, and, in imitation of them, to obey him in seeking retirement, and in continuing in Jerusalem, which is the church, there to expect the divine promises which are received only in her bosom. It is very probable that this last adoration imprinted on the minds of the disciples a reverence toward Christ, and left them in such a temper of devotion, in respect of him, as did not forsake them during their whole life; and that the joy which they felt in their losses and tribulations was the consequence of this joy, which Jesus gave them at the time of his parting from them.

53. And were continually in the temple, praising and blessing God. Amen.

Christ, who obliged his disciples to prepare themselves for the coming of the Holy Ghost by the exercise of praise, thanksgiving, and prayer, thereby teaches us how we ought to prepare ourselves for the same. Temples and churches are the house of God; there he loves to receive our homage, to shed forth his Spirit, and to communicate himself to his creatures. If the apostles had so much reverence for a temple wherein Christ was present only in figure, how much more ought we to have for those temples where he really resides; where the representative sacrifice of his death is offered continually to his Father; where that alliance or union, which he vouchsafes to have with us to all eternity, is formed; and where pastor and people, met together to praise and bless God, afford a comfortable emblem of the heavenly Jerusalem to all those whose hearts are entirely set upon that celestial country!

THE

GOSPEL OF JESUS CHRIST,

ACCORDING TO

J O H N.

CHAPTER I.

SECT. I.—THE WORD GOD.—THE LIGHT SHINING IN DARKNESS.—GRACE AND TRUTH BY JESUS CHRIST.

1. In the beginning was the Word, and the Word was with God, and the Word was God.

What sublimity and majesty, what beauty and instruction, are there in these first words, which are the gospel of the most holy Trinity! Our knowledge thereof ought to begin by that of the Son of God, to whom it properly belongs to make his Father known, as being his resemblance, image, and substantial Word, coeternal, and equal to him in all things. It belonged likewise to the Holy Ghost to bring us to the knowledge of the Son, and to discover to us his glory, (chap. xvi. 13, 14,) as he does in this place, by beginning first with what he is in himself. He thinks it sufficient to propose to our faith his eternity, his existence in his Father, and his divinity, without unfolding these mysteries to us. Our faith ought likewise to think this sufficient; and to believe rather than to dispute, to adore rather than to explain, to be thankful rather than nicely to examine, and to love rather than to know.

2. The same was in the beginning with God.

The eternal Word, sole offspring of the divine understanding, and only Son of the Father, is from all eternity in the bosom of him who produced him by an eternal generation; neither was the Father ever without the Son. O eternal Word, inseparable from thy eternal principle! adorable Son, who never leavest thy Father's bosom! let me be never separated from thee, and unite me in thee to thy Father!

3. All things were made by him; and without him was not any thing made that was made.

The Holy Ghost, in the second place, declares to us the glory of the Word according to what he is in respect of the creatures in general. They all owe him homage, both on the account of their being, whereof he is the fountain, by that power which is common to him with the Father; and likewise on the account of their manner of being, whereof he is the divine idea and pattern, as being the eternal wisdom from whence all the creatures receive whatever beauty, order, and proportion they have, either in relation to one another or to the designs of God. O eternal Wisdom! lively image of all thy Father's perfections, and adorable pattern of all created excellency! cause me to seek, to contemplate, and to adore thee in all thy creatures! Grant that they may continually remind me of thee; that I may always ascribe to thee all the glory of them, and that I may never be deaf to so many voices, which incessantly inform me that thou hast made them, and that I ought to adhere to thee alone.

4. In him was life; and the life was the light of men.

The Holy Ghost, in the third place, declares to us the glory of the Word with respect to living, spiritual, and intelligent creatures. He is not only a living being which has light, but he is both life and light itself by his eternal generation, the principle of all created life, and the fountain of all the light and knowledge which is in the soul. O uncreated wisdom, eternal truth, holy and sanctifying light, happy and blessed life, and even happiness and blessedness itself! Without thee there is nothing but folly and falsehood, darkness and sin, death and misery. Open and enlighten my understanding, penetrate and inflame my heart, since my whole felicity consists in knowing and loving thee.

5. And the light shineth in darkness; and the darkness comprehended it not.

The Holy Spirit, in the fourth place, declares to us the glory of the Word in relation to men fallen by sin into the darkness of ignorance and concupiscence. That small remainder of the knowledge of what is good, and of natural light in sinners—namely, reason itself, is no other than a communication of the eternal light of the Word; and yet the generality of men are either altogether ignorant of it, or at least unmindful of rendering to him the glory thereof. The Word incarnate, dwelling unknown among men, is the light which shineth in darkness. Let us take great care that we be not, even at this day, under the same darkness, at least in some degree. How often do we know this light, only to reject it when it shows us our duty.

6. ¶ There was a man sent from God, whose name *was* John.

The Holy Ghost, in the fifth place, declares to us the glory of the Word in respect of the Jews, among whom he appeared as a light shining in darkness. It is a peculiar instance of mercy toward a sinner, a city, or a people, when a holy man is sent from God to prepare them for the reception of salvation. But this great and peculiar mercy requires a suitable compliance and return. John's mission is without miracles, because it is ordinary, and he only preaches repentance to men in order to fit them to receive the Messias; which was likewise the gospel of all the prophets.

7. The same came for a witness, to bear witness of the Light, that all *men* through him might believe.

Let us honour John as the first witness of Jesus Christ, the first apostle of the light, and the first minister of the faith. How far soever those who have contributed to our faith and salvation may be from having any relation to us, let us look upon them as our fathers, our benefactors, and our patrons. We inherit all the graces and favours showed to the Jews, and therefore we owe to God all that grateful acknowledgment for them which they did not pay him.

8. He was not that Light, but *was sent* to bear witness of that Light.

It is not any mere man who can enlighten us, though he

were another John. The Word of God, the eternal truth, alone is our light. How much is it to be feared, lest those who are sometimes called the lights of the church, should either be too easily persuaded themselves that they are so, or at least not be at all unwilling to be thought so by others. John had but one thing to do, which was to bear witness of the truth and the light; he confined himself to this, and employed his whole life and his death therein. Where is that minister of Christ to be found who follows his example?

9. *That* was the true Light, which lighteth every man that cometh into the world.

Let us adore the Son of God as the true Light, and the supreme, original, and substantial Reason, which lighteth every man that cometh into the world, since the soul cannot either think, or argue, or discern truth from falsehood, or good from evil, of itself, but only by that light which is communicated to it from this eternal Reason. How many other ways, O true Light, dost thou enlighten man by being incarnate! What darkness dost thou not disperse by thy coming into the world! Vouchsafe to shine still more and more in my soul, so as to drive out thence all the remains of false light and of real darkness. Grant that I may love, follow, and prefer thee to every other light!

10. He was in the world, and the world was made by him, and the world knew him not.

The love of the world hinders men from knowing him who made it—though he made it only to make himself known! Sin blinds men, and shuts his eyes against the true light, which is his God; and the more he resigns himself up to sin, the more his knowledge of God diminishes, and his darkness continually increases. It was this darkness which drew down on the earth the true light in the incarnation. The Word, seeing that the world by human wisdom knew not God in the works of his divine wisdom, came on purpose to save man by the foolishness of preaching. And the world does not know him even yet.

11. He came unto his own, and his own received him not.

Let us tremble at these words. Not to receive Jesus Christ

is the greatest of misfortunes. The Jews rejected him, not knowing who he was; and we, how often have we done the same thing after having known and received him, after having been loaded with his benefits! To receive Jesus Christ, is to obey his word, to follow his light, and to live according to his gospel. O my God, how great is the number of those who have never received thee as they ought, and who reject thee by their wicked lives, though they profess themselves to be thine by partaking of thy sacraments! Christ, rejected by his own, is the consolation of all such as suffer at the hands of their near relations.

12. But as many as received him, to them gave he power to become the sons of God, *even* to them that believe on his name: 13. Which were born, not of blood, nor of the will of the flesh, nor of the will of man, but of God.

In the last place, the Holy Ghost declares the glory of the incarnate Word, with respect to Christians, in his communicating the quality of son of God, and his rights, to those who receive him with a faith which is lively and fruitful in good works. The true nobility, and that which alone ought to be esteemed and valued by a Christian, consists in being a child of God. This quality comprehends every thing; but, alas, few understand it, few preserve it, few live like children of God! A gentleman of the lowest rank values himself upon his not degenerating from his birth; and yet a Christian, by leading a carnal life, degenerates from a birth which is altogether holy, spiritual, and divine. It is by the choice of the will of God, and by his love, that we are made partakers of his divine nature, and appointed to enjoy his heavenly inheritance. It is this will, therefore, and this love, which we must take for the rule of our life, and not the will of the flesh nor the will of man—namely, a human or carnal love.

14. And the Word was made flesh, and dwelt among us, and we beheld his glory, the glory as of the only-begotton of the Father, full of grace and truth.

It is no less impossible to comprehend here the humiliation and abasement of the Word, than it is to comprehend his dignity and glory. Here are five degrees of abasement opposed to the glories above-mentioned:—God became man; the Son of the Father, the son of man; the Word, a child;

the Life, a mortal man; and the Light, by dwelling among men, shone in the midst of darkness. Is it then so small a matter that carnal man should become the child of God, when, in order to this, it was necessary that the Son of God should be made flesh? To set our hearts upon the objects of sense and upon worldly greatness, is to oppose the design of the incarnation, since it was on purpose to withdraw our affections from such objects, and to raise them to the love of things invisible, that God was pleased to become visible, and to humble and abase himself. It is highly just and reasonable that we should every day adore and contemplate, with gratitude and thanksgiving, the humble birth and appearance of the Word in human nature, since this is the foundation of our own adoption. Let the great persons of the world learn from him, not to avoid and shun the poor and miserable; and let the poor, on their part, learn to bear with patience and willingness the want of honours and riches. Christ is the fulness of truth, of grace, and of glory: of truth, to verify the types and figures of the Jewish church; of grace, to complete the righteousness of the Christian church; of glory, to crown the holiness of the elect, and to perfect and consummate the church and religion in heaven.

15. ¶ John bare witness of him, and cried, saying, This was he of whom I spake, He that cometh after me is preferred before me; for he was before me.

A preacher ought to determine not to know or to preach any thing save Jesus Christ humbled, after John's example; and Jesus Christ crucified, after Paul's. He must be very careful to fix the minds of his audience upon the excellency of our blessed Saviour, by hiding and concealing himself. John is not a timorous witness; he preaches Christ openly, and with a loud voice, and is under no apprehension that, by extolling his Master's greatness, he shall lessen his own reputation. Men are not, generally speaking, very forward to praise those who appear in the same rank and have the same employment with themselves. The praise which John here gives to Christ is plain and simple, because it is sincere; very different from that of a hypocrite, who proclaims the merit of others only out of pride, to hide his own envy, and to gain esteem by an appearance of equity, penetration, and humility.

16. And of his fulness have all we received, and grace for grace.

All grace which tends to salvation was given peculiarly to Jesus Christ. Whatever we receive of that nature is no other than a gift of his bounty, and an emanation from his fulness. Let us adore him as our Head, that, in quality of his members, we may be filled out of his abundance. The more closely we are united to him, the more do we receive of his double fulness, who, as God, is the fountain of all good, and as the head of Christians and of the elect, is the principle of all their holiness, and of every grace which contributes thereto. Head for head—the second Adam for the first: "grace for grace;" namely, an extraordinary, efficacious, powerful, and divine grace, such as is that of our blessed Saviour, for the ordinary, weak, and perishing grace of Adam, which was subject to free-will, suited to man in the state of innocence, and productive of nothing but human virtues. Legislator for legislator—Jesus Christ for Moses: "grace for grace;" instead of external grace of the law, a law of fear, threats, types, and shadows, which affected only the senses,—an internal grace, a law of love, which converts the heart, which, writes in it the law of God, and puts us in possession of the true promises. Let us be sensible of our own privileges and advantages, let us praise God for them, and not do any thing to render ourselves unworthy of them.

17. For the law was given by Moses, *but* grace and truth came by Jesus Christ.

The law was given to awaken, admonish, and enlighten the sinner, and to cause him to seek after grace. Grace is given to perfect and fulfil the law by charity; and truth, to disperse the darkness of idolatry, the shadows of Judaism, and the hypocrisy of wicked Christians. The servant can do no more than barely publish the law and declare the will of his Master: it belongs to Jesus Christ, the true God and Saviour of souls, to take full possession of them by his grace, to cause them to love him as he pleases, and in them to accomplish the truth of his promises, by changing hearts of stone into hearts of flesh.

18. No man hath seen God at any time; the only begotten Son, which is in the bosom of the Father, he hath declared *him*.

God, in his own nature invisible to mortal man, rendered himself visible by the incarnation. He has but one only Son, and he makes us members of him, that he may have in him as many children as Christians: a favour so great and inconceivable this, that none but he who confers it upon us can make us thoroughly sensible thereof. The bosom of the Father is the source from whence all truth is derived, and where, at the same time, it resides; and as the Son alone, the eternal truth, is in that adorable bosom, it is by him alone that all truth must be conveyed to us,—some by the natural channel of reason, some by the supernatural means of revelation. O divine Light! O eternal Truth! grant that my heart may become like a glass, always fit to receive the impression of thy image! Grant that neither the dust of the earth nor the breath of pride may ever tarnish or deface that purity and brightness which thy Holy Spirit has vouchsafed to communicate thereto!

SECT. II.—THE TESTIMONY OF JOHN.

19. ¶ And this is the record of John, when the Jews sent priests and Levites from Jerusalem to ask him, Who art thou?

What shall we be able to answer, when God himself shall ask us, and that perhaps very soon, "Who art thou?" A Christian? A priest? A bishop? Where is the life of one? Where are the proper works? Let us present this dreadful question, and let us frequently ask ourselves, Who we are. Let us by no means stay for an answer from our self-love. That is a flatterer and seducer, whom we should neither hear nor suffer to speak. Let us also have the same diffidence of others in this respect: for we deceive them, and they in their turn deceive us. Let our heart answer us as sincerely as it will be one day forced to answer God.

20. And he confessed, and denied not; but confessed, I am not the Christ.

A person who is truly humble is very glad to find an opportunity of showing himself what he really is, by removing the false opinions which have been entertained concerning him. He does this in very plain, distinct, and strong terms, without leaving the least room for any doubt. He has no notion of that kind of faint denials whereby a man retains with one hand that which he rejects with the other, and, without receding from the honour of that place which he unjustly keeps in the esteem of others, would likewise fain enjoy the reputation of humility.

21. And they asked him, What then? Art thou Elias? And he saith, I am not. Art thou that prophet? And he answered, No.

The humble man speaks very little, no more than is just necessary, for fear of doing some prejudice either to humility or truth. Humility conceals from the humble man all personal advantages, and persuades him that he is nothing. John has the spirit and power of Elias—is a prophet, and more than a prophet; but has no inclination to discover it, since he may conceal it without any prejudice to truth. He whose mind is fully taken up with the greatness of his Master, thinks of nothing but how to abase and humble himself before him.

22. Then said they unto him, Who art thou? that we may give an answer to them that sent us. What sayest thou of thyself?

To an humble person nothing is more ungrateful than to speak of himself; but he is far from showing that it is so, out of a desire to reap the honour due to his modesty. True humility uses no artifice, and seeks not to discover itself by an affected resistance. It loves to be constrained; but it always yields to authority with a wise and discreet simplicity.

23. He said, I *am* the voice of one crying in the wilderness, Make straight the way of the Lord, as said the prophet Esaias.

The preacher is only the voice of Jesus Christ, which is to prepare the hearts of men by repentance for his coming. Let him therefore take great care not to speak any thing but what may be spoken and avowed by Jesus Christ himself. Every thing in a minister of Christ ought to speak, and that concerning Jesus Christ himself, and the ways he has appointed of returning to God. How much good would a preacher do, if he was but, as it were, a voice not to be seen, but only heard! To see, and to be seen too much, often destroys more than the word edifies. A voice which cries aloud, is a preacher who teaches the ways of the gospel without weakening the truths thereof, himself, or his ministry. They may be said to preach in the wilderness who preach with as little awe upon them from their audience, and with as much boldness, as if they saw nobody.

24. And they which were sent were of the Pharisees. 25. And they asked him, and said unto him, Why baptizest thou then, if thou be not that Christ, nor Elias, neither that prophet?

It is one mark of a lawful mission, for a man to be always ready to give an account thereof to those who have authority to demand it. The devil is very expert in deceiving and causing men to mistake their way. He puts them upon amusing themselves, and disturbing holy men with unprofitable questions and inquiries, instead of profiting by their doctrine, admonitions, and the example of their virtues. It is by these that they should form a judgment of them.

26. John answered them, saying, I baptize with water: but there standeth one among you, whom ye know not;

Men are not easily determined to undervalue themselves and their employments, in order to please and keep fair with those from whom they have nothing either to hope or fear. There is a holy artifice or address in turning the minds of men from a vain and useless curiosity to that religious and necessary one which fixes their thoughts upon Jesus Christ. Hitherto the ignorance of the Jews was excusable; but how highly culpable are multitudes of Christians who know not Christ! He is treated like an unknown person by all such as have no regard to his presence, who live in a forgetfulness of his mysteries, and are as negligent in representing to him their wants as if he were not their Saviour.

27. He it is, who coming after me is preferred before me, whose shoe's latchet I am not worthy to unloose.

If the greatest of saints be unworthy to render to Christ even the meanest service, how much more unworthy beyond all comparison is the sinner to adore and love God, which is the highest action which a creature can perform toward him!

Reverence, fear, and humiliation, before the holiness of God and Christ, must always accompany our addresses in prayer. Let us learn to put a vast difference between the honour we pay to Jesus Christ and that respect which we pay to the memory of the greatest among the saints. This is one of the first instructions which God thought fit to give us by John, and we cannot act contrary thereto without overturning every thing in religion.

28. These things were done in Bethabara beyond Jordan, where John was baptizing.

A word, in appearance altogether insignificant, is sometimes full of mysteries. John made choice of this place, because it was the passage of Jordan, over which the people about that time began to travel in their way to Jerusalem to keep the feast of the Passover. It was likewise by that very place that Jesus or Joshua led the people of God into the promised land, by a second miraculous passage through the midst of the water, which was a kind of second baptism, followed soon after by the second circumcision and the second passover. It was, lastly, the place where the manna ceased. And all this prefigured that which Jesus Christ was come to perform in truth and reality, by washing his people from their sins, in order to put them into possession of heaven, where the perfect adoption is completed—the second circumcision of the whole old man, where all types and figures cease, and where he himself is the true Lamb and the eternal Passover.

SECT. III.—ANOTHER TESTIMONY OF JOHN.—JESUS THE LAMB OF GOD.

29. ¶ The next day John seeth Jesus coming unto him, and saith, Behold the Lamb of God, which taketh away the sin of the world!

Behold here, not the lamb of the legal and figurative passover, but Him who was typified and represented thereby; not one of those sacrifices which God rejects as incapable of pleasing him, but the sole sacrifice which he himself has chosen, and in which he is well pleased; not the lamb which, being offered every year and every day, could not take away sin or justify the sinner, but Him who, being once sacrificed on the cross, taketh away all the sins, not only of the Jews, but of all the world. I adore thee, O Jesus, as the proper and peculiar victim of God, alone worthy to adore him, and to render him a homage suitable to his greatness and majesty! It is in, by, and with thee alone that we are permitted to praise and adore him, to give him thanks, to satisfy his justice, to implore his mercy, to hope in him, and to perform toward him the other duties of religion.

30. This is he of whom I said, After me cometh a man which is preferred before me; for he was before me.

Christ, as man, was after John; as God, he was before him. He who knows the worth and value of humility, can never be weary of humbling himself when it is necessary to exalt others. John teaches the ministers of the word that they owe their people an example of humility in particular; because they, as well as he, are the ministers, and, as it were, the forerunners of a God who stooped to the form of a servant.

31. And I knew him not: but that he should be made manifest to Israel, therefore am I come baptizing with water.

The only design of John's being sent into the world was to make Christ manifest to Israel; and yet he lived even to the time of his own preaching without so much as knowing him. An eager and impatient desire to know what will become of us, and for what we are designed, is contrary to perfection. When God leads and conducts a soul by himself, he does it by ways so pure and holy, that it is supported by nothing but his Spirit and his grace. For a man to spend thirty years of retirement in a desert, in a course of almost incredible mortification, and under a total destitution of all human relief and consolation, without knowing to what end; to have but once the comfort of speaking to Christ, and to see him only as he passed by; and yet to continue faithful to God, and entirely satisfied with his conduct,—this is indeed no other than to serve God for God's sake.

32. And John bare record, saying, I saw the Spirit descending from heaven like a dove, and it abode upon him.

Christ is the only person worthy to receive the fulness of the Holy Spirit; and John, to receive the first knowledge of so great a mystery. The more a man is filled with the Holy Spirit, the better is he able to judge in what fulness Christ received it in order to communicate it. Innocence, purity, sincerity, meekness, charity, fruitfulness in good works, etc.—these are the virtues with which Christ and the Holy Ghost would inspire us, by taking to themselves, the one the emblem of a lamb, the other that of a dove. Grant, O Jesus, that I may not be of the number of those upon whom thy Spirit only descends, but does not abide.

33. And I knew him not: but he that sent me to baptize with water, the same said unto me, Upon whom thou shalt see the Spirit descending, and remaining on him, the same is he which baptizeth with the Holy Ghost.

Men may here learn to impart to souls, and to the directors of them, the necessary knowledge of truth, with due measure and in proper season. God seems to have given John, for thirty years together, no more light than was necessary to his personal perfection, with intent, perhaps, to establish him thereby in such a substantial humility as might keep him from being puffed up by those greater degrees of light and knowledge which were to be given him for the salvation of others. John is very far from the temper of those who are ashamed of having been a long time ignorant of some truths, and who boast of their intimacy with great persons, and of their early knowledge of some secret. It is very rare for a man to be willing to contribute to the glory of others by his own abasement. Whoever the person be who administers the baptism of Christ, it is always Christ himself who baptizes internally. Let us praise him for having not permitted our sanctification to be at all obstructed by the insincerity or wickedness of any minister.

34. And I saw, and bare record that this is the Son of God.

It is the duty of a servant of God freely and willingly to bear witness to the truth, more especially if he have received a particular commission to do it from God or the church, as preachers, priests, teachers, etc. Christ must necessarily have been the Son of God, because he gave the Holy Ghost, and washed man clean from all his sins. Wonderful is the divine wisdom: it obviates the perverseness of the Jews by the testimony of John, who calls Jesus Christ the Son of God before Christ declares that he is so.

SECT. IV.—TWO OF JOHN'S DISCIPLES FOLLOW CHRIST.—ANDREW BRINGS PETER TO HIM.

35. ¶ Again, the next day after, John stood, and two of his disciples;
36. And looking upon Jesus as he walked, he saith, Behold the Lamb
of God!

One duty incumbent on pastors is to make the sufferings and sacrifice of Christ thoroughly known, and to inspire sinners with a firm trust and confidence in him as the victim of their salvation. This quality is the meanest of all belonging to him, because it puts him in the place of all sinners, and gives God a right over his life as many times as there are men whose lives are forfeited to the divine justice. John here gives him the appellation of Lamb, rather than that of any other kind of victim, because the lamb was the proper victim for the deliverance of God's people, and because the Jews were perhaps at that very time going up to the paschal sacrifice. How much better title and greater obligation have we to adore Christ under this name, we whom he has delivered by dying for us as our passover! What a comfort is it, that, in casting our eyes upon the representative sacrifice of Christ, we can every one say, "Behold the Lamb of God," whose blood is my deliverance, my life, my strength, and my salvation! Unhappy they who deprive themselves of this support and consolation, by rejecting this commemorative sacrifice, wherein this Lamb is spiritually present, and offered up to his Father for us!

37. And the two disciples heard him speak, and they followed Jesus.

We ought to follow this victim as his members, desiring to be sacrificed with him by humiliations, sufferings, and death. Oh let it not be in vain, that we have this sacrifice so often represented before our eyes: let it be also present to the eyes of our faith. Let us follow the path marked with Christ's blood, imitate his patience, and clothe ourselves with his meekness.

38. Then Jesus turned, and saw them following, and saith unto them, What seek ye? They said unto him, Rabbi, (which is to say, being interpreted, Master,) where dwellest thou?

The holy curiosity of these disciples is not long without its reward. How profitable is it to seek Jesus Christ! but in order to find him, we must seek him by his own direction and assistance. The law shows him to us, and inclines us to take some steps toward him; but we can take none to any purpose, nor by any means go to him, unless he prevent us with his grace, by turning toward us, looking upon us with the eyes of his mercy, and speaking even to our hearts. The first quality which we are obliged to own and acknowledge in him, is, that he is our Master, of whom we are to learn the way of salvation, and how to walk therein.

39. He saith unto them, Come and see. They came and saw where he dwelt, and abode with him that day: for it was about the tenth hour.

The church is the house of Christ. How great a happiness is it to abide with him therein! It is matter of continual gratitude and acknowledgment for all those who enjoy it. "Come and see," all ye who do not yet belong to it, and you will soon discover and own that those have no other design than to impose upon you who would frighten you from this house of truth and unity. Christ, notwithstanding his poverty, used hospitality: a man has always enough to do this, if he have but charity. Happy day and happy night for these two disciples!

40. One of the two which heard John *speak*, and followed him, was Andrew, Simon Peter's brother. 41. He first findeth his own brother Simon, and saith unto him, We have found the Messias, which is, being interpreted, the Christ.

When we have once found Christ, and the way which leads to him, we must not hide this treasure, but we must communicate it to others. Fidelity in obeying the voice of a master or spiritual director, obtains the grace and favour of finding one more enlightened, even Jesus Christ himself. Andrew is the first disciple and apostle of Christ, according to the order of vocation, and performs the office of an apostle toward his own brother Simon.

42. And he brought him to Jesus. And when Jesus beheld him, he

said, Thou art Simon the son of Jonas: thou shalt be called Cephas, which is by interpretation, A stone.

It is not enough to preach Jesus Christ; a man must likewise conduct and bring souls to him. Happy he whom Christ beholds! His looks are saving, and reach the heart. True friendship between friends or relations consists in mutually assisting one another in the business of salvation. A person who admits his friend or his brother into a share of his fortune, and of his favour with the great, is very frequently instrumental in poisoning their hearts with the love of the world or of riches, and in ruining their souls forever. But to procure them the knowledge and favour of Christ, is to promote their eternal salvation.

SECT. V.—PHILIP AND NATHANAEL.

43. ¶ The day following Jesus would go forth into Galilee, and findeth Philip, and saith unto him, Follow me. 44. Now Philip was of Bethsaida, the city of Andrew and Peter.

Let us by no means accuse this disciple of levity in obeying so readily, without knowing the person who commanded him; but let us adore the power of this Master, who holds, as it were, our wills in his own hand. There are three sorts of calls to the knowledge of the truth. The first is, of those who seek it by the advice of their spiritual director or pastor, as Andrew did. The second, of such as are brought to it by the advice and example of some pious relation, as Peter was. The third, of those who did not at all think of it, and whom God calls thereto in an extraordinary manner, as he called Philip. In whatever way this happens, the call always comes from God.

45. Philip findeth Nathanael, and saith unto him, We have found him, of whom Moses in the law, and the prophets, did write, Jesus of Nazareth, the son of Joseph.

Philip's knowledge in the law and the prophets is a proof of his earnest application to the business of his salvation, and to the discovering the Messias; and this application, which was no other than a gift of God, was perhaps the very thing which drew down upon him that of his vocation. The joy of these two disciples at having found the Messias in the person of Jesus, shows plainly that they desired him, sought after him, and had their hearts entirely taken up with him. Let us imitate them if we really desire to find Jesus Christ, to preserve him in our hearts, and to receive new graces.

46. And Nathanael said unto him, Can there any good thing come out of Nazareth? Philip saith unto him, Come and see.

It is necessary to taste Christ in order to know him. We must not judge of the things of God by appearances or human prejudices. What is it to "come and see," but only to examine and believe, according to the principles of faith, those things which relate to salvation? God has compassion on such whose simplicity engages them in prejudices contrary to the truth; but he confounds those who take them up through envy and malice, and communicate them to others.

47. Jesus saw Nathanael coming to him, and saith of him, Behold an Israelite indeed, in whom is no guile!

He who is solicitous, and takes the pains to inform himself concerning any thing, shows that he is sincere in his error; but he who is not desirous of any better information, gives us sufficient grounds to believe that his prejudice is not free from all guile and dissimulation. The character of great sincerity is a very great character, not indeed in the world, but in the gospel and in the church.

48. Nathanael saith unto him, Whence knowest thou me? Jesus answered and said unto him, Before that Philip called thee, when thou wast under the fig tree, I saw thee.

The divine knowledge of Christ sees into every thing. It is the comfort of the sincere, that he knows the uprightness of their hearts; and it ought to be the terror of the crafty and deceitful, that the disguise and dissimulation of their minds cannot be concealed from him.

49. Nathanael answered and saith unto him, Rabbi, thou art the Son of God; thou art the King of Israel.

A beginning of grace, which perhaps appears very small and inconsiderable in the eyes of men, is capable of bringing us entirely to God, when he sheds abroad his light and love in our hearts. This faith of Nathanael is much to be admired; and yet it is but a small specimen, as it were, of that which the Son of God was to produce in the hearts of so many Jews and Gentiles. Let us show toward this divine Master, the docility proper to disciples; toward this only Son of God, the respect and reverence of true Christians; and toward this king, the obedience and submission of faithful subjects.

50. Jesus answered and said unto him, Because I said unto thee, I saw thee under the fig tree, believest thou? thou shalt see greater things than these.

When a man has once opened his heart to faith, his faith continually grows stronger by means of new proofs. God at first makes faith depend upon very small things, to subject and humble the minds of men, and to convince them that it is a gift of God; he afterward comforts and encourages them, by giving them a sight of the greater wonders of religion, to manifest his goodness and magnificence toward those who resign themselves up entirely to him.

51. And he saith unto him, Verily, verily, I say unto you, Hereafter ye shall see heaven open, and the angels of God ascending and descending upon the Son of man.

The homage and service of angels paid to Christ, both before his death and at his resurrection and ascension, show plainly that he is more than Son of man. The more men put their trust and confidence in God, like true Israelites, the more he is pleased to increase it by the hopes of the greatest blessings. What good news, what mighty consolation is this, for us as well as for this new disciple, that heaven, shut up so long, is now going to be opened to men in favour of this heavenly person, who is Son of God as well as Son of man; that the correspondence between heaven and earth is about to be restored; that this man who converses on earth is King of heaven, since the angels who dwell there pay him homage; and that he is himself the way which leads thither, the truth which promises and secures to us the enjoyment, and the life which makes the happiness and felicity of that place!

CHAPTER II.

SECT. I.—THE MARRIAGE IN CANA.

1. AND the third day there was a marriage in Cana of Galilee; and the mother of Jesus was there:

This is a blessed marriage indeed, at which the greatest example of purity, modesty, and humility is present, and inspires these three virtues; whereas, generally speaking, immodesty, excess, and pride render marriages criminal and unhappy. The mother of Jesus is there the first, because she is the pattern of all Christian mothers, whose discretion contributes most to make a holy and Christian marriage by the good education of their daughters. They who enter into this state ought to take her for their pattern, as being the most discreet and modest of virgins, the most holy of all wives, and the first Christian mother.

2. And both Jesus was called, and his disciples, to the marriage.

To call Christ to our marriages is to draw down his Holy Spirit on them by prayer: to invite his disciples thereto, is to observe in them his maxims and doctrine, to use such behaviour as becomes his disciples, and to follow the rules of his church. How unhappy generally are marriages when Jesus Christ is not at them, when they are entered into upon nothing but human and carnal motives, upon views of ambition, pleasure, or covetousness, and with a conduct and behaviour altogether profane and heathenish! To do thus is to drive Christ from them, instead of inviting him to them. A good Christian takes care, in like manner, to invite him to all other assemblies or meetings, either for entertainment, for public or domestic, civil or ecclesiastical affairs, or which relate either to learning or to charity.

3. And when they wanted wine, the mother of Jesus saith unto him, They have no wine.

It is an excellent disposition for persons to represent only their real wants and necessities to God in prayer, after her example, with plainness, modesty, charity, and confidence.

Does not the conduct of the blessed virgin on this occasion give us reason to think that she used to represent to her Son the necessities of the poor, or those of her own family? Let us profit by this example which she has given us, of confidence in God under wants and necessities, and of fidelity in employing our credit in behalf of the poor when we are not able to relieve them ourselves.

4. Jesus saith unto her, Woman, what have I to do with thee? mine hour is not yet come.

In this answer of Christ we behold an example of a perfect disengagement from flesh and blood, and even from the most pious parents, with respect to divine matters and the ecclesiastical ministry. He chooses rather to treat his holy mother with some seeming harshness, than to neglect giving in her person this important advice to all parents, that they must not pretend to direct the actions of their children in those things which relate to their vocation or ecclesiastical functions, or to put them upon doing something very eminent and remarkable, merely to gain honour and reputation to themselves. Let us admire and imitate this edifying humility of the blessed virgin, who speaks not one word in her own justification, submitting to this reproof with silence, but without losing her confidence in him. Jesus, on his side, is faithful in his dependence upon God, even to a moment. This moment was not anticipated, but was made to depend on the request of the blessed virgin, and the obedience of the servants.

5. His mother saith unto the servants, Whatsoever he saith unto you, do *it*.

Confidence increases by a humiliation received as it ought, and is weakened or destroyed by the contrary.

6. And there were set there six water pots of stone, after the manner of the purifying of the Jews, containing two or three firkins apiece.
7. Jesus saith unto them, Fill the water pots with water. And they filled them up to the brim. 8. And he saith unto them, Draw out now, and bear to the governor of the feast. And they bare *it*.

These people want wine, and Jesus calls for water: but he who speaks is the Creator both of water and of wine, and changes every year the former into the latter in the vine. An implicit and ready obedience obtains the greatest favours and graces, of which men often render themselves unworthy, by despising or neglecting things which seem either trivial or improper, upon which God has notwithstanding been pleased to make those favours and graces depend.

9. When the ruler of the feast had tasted the water that was made wine, and knew not whence it was, (but the servants which drew the water knew,) the governor of the feast called the bridegroom,

Let us humbly offer up our addresses to Christ, to obtain, not the change of water into wine, but the conversion of our corrupt heart into one truly Christian; not temporal advantages and enjoyments, which are flat, insipid, unstable, and glide away and are lost in earth like water; but the gifts of grace, that fruit of the vine, of the blood and merits of Christ, that wine which renders virgins fruitful in good works. Lord, thou knowest what my soul of itself is, even weakness itself, and that the wine of thy grace is its whole strength.

10. And saith unto him, Every man at the beginning doth set forth good wine; and when men have well drunk, then that which is worse: *but* thou hast kept the good wine until now.

God gave at first the old vine of the law, without strength, spirit, or taste; and in the fulness of time he gave the new wine of a strong and powerful grace, which enables us to fulfil the law, which inebriates the heart in a holy manner, and causes it to forget all present things. Let us desire, pray for, and taste this wine of our heart, which is so necessary to our salvation. This is the wine of the marriage of the Lamb—a marriage begun in the incarnation, by the union of the Word with our nature; continued and brought to perfection in the sanctification of sinners, by their being incorporated with Christ; finished and consummated in heaven, by the union of all the elect with their Head, and the completion of the adoption of God's children in the bosom of the Father.

11. This beginning of miracles did Jesus in Cana of Galileee, and manifested forth his glory; and his disciples believed on him.

We must honour this adorable beginning and these first-fruits of the miracles of Christ. The end of miracles is not to satisfy the curiosity of men, nor to support and comfort the body, but to promote the glory of God, and to establish the faith. This miracle was wrought for the new disciples of the Christian church, and to establish the belief of Christ's almighty power as the foundation of the gospel.

SECT. II.—THE BUYERS AND SELLERS DRIVEN OUT OF THE TEMPLE.— THE BODY OF CHRIST.—HE DOES NOT TRUST HIMSELF TO ALL MEN.

12. ¶ After this he went down to Capernaum, he, and his mother, and his brethren, and his disciples; and they continued there not many days.

Jesus leaves his own country, to teach his ministers, as the first thing, to wean themselves from theirs, that they may be ready to go any whither. He chooses Capernaum, to instruct them that they ought not to prefer those places where they are likely to find most convenience, but those where there is most need of their presence. His mother and his brethren follow his example, to show that his ministers ought rather to draw their relations after them by their good example, than to suffer themselves to be drawn aside by their carnal affection; and that, in things pertaining to their ministry, they should rather govern their relations than be governed by them.

13. ¶ And the Jews' passover was at hand, and Jesus went up to Jerusalem,

The constant attendance of Christ, even on the external duties of religion, has the force of a law obliging us constantly to attend on them. He observes the feasts and obeys the law, when he could at the same time time have dispensed with it; and thereby shames those who value themselves upon seeming to be above these duties, through licentiousness, pride, or negligence. He gives us, in his own person, the pattern of a good parishioner and master of a family, who obliges his children and domestics to an exact observance of these duties. What business can excuse those who make that a pretence for not performing the duties of a parishioner, since the Son of God himself has set them such an example? We must imitate it, by applying ourselves on these occasions to such things as will promote the glory of God and the good of our neighbour.

14. And found in the temple those that sold oxen and sheep and doves, and the changers of money sitting:

It is very remarkable, that both the first and the last time that our blessed Lord was in the temple, after he was baptized, he signalized his zeal against the irreverence and profanation which the Jews were guilty of therein. Will not the example of our High-Priest awaken the zeal of all those who are invested with his authority, against so many profaners of the churches, where the majesty of God resides, and the true sacrifice is offered? Profane, unprofitable, and criminal discourse, indecent postures, a scandalous unseemliness in dress, lascivious glances, meetings about business, sinful assignations, and vain, extravagant, and wicked thoughts,—these are much more insupportable in the sight and in the temple of God, than either those creatures which were designed for sacrifices, or than the bare trading in things of the like nature.

15. And when he had made a scourge of small cords, he drove them all out of the temple, and the sheep, and the oxen; and poured out the changers' money, and overthrew the tables;

Nothing kindles the wrath of Christ more than the merchandise and profanation of holy things, and the insolence of those who dare be guilty thereof, even in the house of God. For a man to go on purpose to commit new sins in that very place whither he ought to go to bewail and expiate the old, is no other than to mock God Almighty. If all those who profane the Christian temples by their irreverence were to be driven out thence, how few would remain therein!

16. And said unto them that sold doves, Take these things hence; make not my Father's house a house of merchandise.

Can we believe this truth, and avoid trembling out of respect and reverence, when we enter into churches? Whatever either has no relation, or is contrary to religion, prayer, adoration, the worship of God, and the sanctification of souls, ought to be banished from those places which are consecrated to the divine Holiness alone. They who come into them to sell the word of God, the exercise of the sacred ministry, prayer, and the praise of God, having nothing in view but human glory, recompense, temporal advantages, and raising a fortune,—these are no other than sacrilegious sellers and changers, who ought to be cast out of the true temple.

17. And his disciples remembered that it was written, The zeal of thine house hath eaten me up.

We must not, in the heat of zeal, lay aside Christian meekness; but then we must likewise take great care that we do not grow lukewarm and indifferent, under the specious pretence of meekness and charity. Christ here informs us, that the zeal of God's house is, as it were, the proper virtue belonging to pastors. A man is a Christian for himself: he becomes a pastor for the benefit of his neighbour, but without zeal he can do him no service. The church is the house of God, and whatever tends to promote the holiness and interests thereof is the proper business of his ministers. If a pastor, as he ought, looks upon the soul of the meanest of his sheep as the house of God, can he possibly see the disorder and filthiness thereof and not use his utmost endeavour to cleanse it? To be only zealous, is not sufficient in a pastor; he must have an ardent zeal, which, as it were, continually feeds upon and eats him up; but such as is guided and directed by the wisdom of God.

18. ¶ Then answered the Jews and said unto him, What sign shewest thou unto us, seeing that thou doest these things?

Pastors must expect to meet with contradiction when they endeavour to correct disorders and to reform abuses. Everybody has a right to exclaim against public and visible disorders when the pastors, instead of opposing them, countenance and promote them. The Jews require a sign or miracle; and is it not a very great one, that Christ should, without any visible authority, make men obey him so readily, and strike such a terror into them only with a scourge of small cords! Is not this enough to show the presence of the divinity? The miracle which must authorize and justify the zeal of all pastors, is an exemplary and truly apostolic life.

19. Jesus answered and said unto them, Destroy this temple, and in three days I will raise it up.

See here a terrible judgment upon those who oppose that which is good! God leaves them in their darkness and ignorance, with respect both to that good and to their own sins. Men show very plainly that they love sin, when they will not suffer any one to put a stop to it, to remove the occasions thereof, and to reprove and punish the sinner. This is a sin which draws after it greater sins, and punishments proportionable to them; and especially that of not knowing either the one or the other. The destruction of the true temple of God, by the death of Jesus Christ, was the punishment of the pride, envy, and avarice of the Jews, which made them take the part of these profaners of the figurative temple.

20. Then said the Jews, Forty and six years was this temple in building, and wilt thou rear it up in three days?

It is not at all surprising that the Jews understood not the figurative words of Christ; but it was the hardness of their hearts which rendered them unworthy to be more clearly and plainly instructed. Christ, at the very beginning of his preaching, establishes beforehand the belief of his death and resurrection. It frequently happens that an instruction proves of more advantage to others in succeeding times, than to those to whom it was first addressed.

21. But he spake of the temple of his body.

The body and soul of Jesus Christ are the true temple of God, in which he dwells, where he receives the true worship and adoration, and where all religion is to be found in its truth and reality. How much light does this obscure and figurative expression contain and afford to all those who have the eyes and attention of faith! Whatever respect, zeal, and affection the Jews had for their temple, that, and infinitely more, ought Christians to have for the humanity of Christ, the true and adorable temple of his divinity. Let us present ourselves before it in spirit, let us be united to it in heart; let us turn all our thoughts, desires, and sighs toward this temple during our banishment and captivity, as the Jews, while they were captive, directed all theirs toward the temple at Jerusalem.

22. When therefore he was risen from the dead, his disciples remembered that he had said this unto them; and they believed the Scripture, and the word which Jesus had said.

The completion of mysteries opens the understanding to

the knowledge of the Scriptures, and strengthens faith. Truths bring forth fruit in their season. The slowness and backwardness of some understandings should not hinder us from instructing them whenever we have an opportunity. Truth is a seed which grace will cause to blossom at God's appointed time. Now is the proper time to read the Scriptures, and therein to adore with comfort the mysteries fully accomplished, the veracity of God in his word, and his faithfulness in respect of his promises—and yet we neglect to read them! The Jews will rise in judgment against us, and condemn us.

23. ¶ Now when he was in Jerusalem at the passover, in the feast *day*, many believed in his name, when they saw the miracles which he did.

Christ here keeps his passover in his own manner, and causes some of his elect to keep it also, in causing them to pass from incredulity to faith, by the anticipated merits of his blood. This is to communicate in the Christian passover by way of anticipation. The miracles which Christ so lately refused to the obstinacy and envy of the Jews, he now vouchsafes to grant to his elect, in order to accomplish his designs concerning them. Let us learn to do all the service we can to souls, when God is pleased to give us opportunity; and let us not be at all concerned at the offence taken by such pharisaical persons as shut up the way of salvation against themselves.

24. But Jesus did not commit* himself unto them, because he knew all *men*, [* *Fr.* Trust.]

Mysteries are not to be revealed but with wisdom and discretion, in measure and by degrees; nor the body and blood of Christ to be given to men without great judgment. Christian prudence requires that we should neither hastily condemn any one, nor inconsiderately trust all upon specious appearances. Man does not thoroughly know, but frequently deceives himself; how then should others avoid being often deceived by him? We have no right to search into the heart; but we have a right, through the grace of Christ, to beg of him some portion of his light, to secure us from being deceived, and to enable us to know our neighbour so far as our duties and necessities require.

25. And needed not that any should testify of man; for he knew what was in man.

It would be the vainest thing imaginable for any one to pretend to hide himself from Christ: he sees the very bottom of the heart, and knows us better than we do ourselves. What respect and caution should a person observe in all his actions, who is assured that God continually beholds his heart! It is a double kindness and advantage to man, that he has no knowledge of the secrets of the heart, which his curiosity would cause him to abuse, and that he is capable of receiving as much as is necessary at the hand of Him who dispenses every thing with a sovereign wisdom.

CHAPTER III.

SECT. I.—NICODEMUS.—WE MUST BE BORN OF THE SPIRIT. —THE WIND BLOWETH WHERE IT LISTETH.

1. THERE was a man of the Pharisees, named Nicodemus, a ruler of the Jews: 2. The same came to Jesus by night, and said unto him, Rabbi, we know that thou art a teacher come from God: for no man can do these miracles that thou doest, except God be with him.

We must not discourage those who come to Christ, though they may lie under a great many imperfections, and have not yet courage enough to serve him openly; but we must endeavour to instruct them, and to manage prudently the first beginnings of their faith or piety. This received principle among the Jews, that it is God who speaks by miracles, and that an extraordinary mission ought to be authorized thereby, will condemn heretics. When a man seeks truth sincerely and in earnest upon such principles as are generally acknowledged, he is not far from finding it. The corruption of the heart is a greater obstacle thereto than the prepossession of the mind. Christ is indeed the teacher of the true righteousness promised by the Scriptures, and foretold by the prophecies; but he teaches it in a manner very different from that which this ruler imagines, since he does it by putting it into the heart, and causing the heart to enjoy and love it. He does not only teach it as a person come from God, but he teaches it as God; and God is not only with him, but he himself is God. Teach me in this manner, O Jesus, my Saviour, my Master, and my God

3. Jesus answered and said unto him, Verily, verily, I say unto thee, Except a man be born again, he cannot see the kingdom of God.

The first step toward returning to God is to renounce our birth derived from Adam, and to be born again in Jesus Christ. We must afterward renounce ourselves, our will, our inclinations, and the presumption we have of our own strength, that we may receive new from Jesus Christ. The knowledge of the corruption of our nature, and of the necessity of our being renewed by Christ, is the very first thing which we must learn in the Christian religion.

4. Nicodemus saith unto him, How can a man be born when he is old? can he enter the second time into his mother's womb, and be born?

Let us not at all wonder that our reason is very difficultly persuaded to submit to the belief of mysteries. The ways of God are incomprehensible, and his mysteries full of contradictions to carnal minds and to a Jewish understanding. It is good for a man at first to comprehend little or nothing in religion, that he may be convinced of the necessity of a light superior, but not contrary, to that of reason. We have here a plain proof that man is become altogether carnal, in that this ruler thinks of nothing but a natural mother and a birth according to the flesh, instead of reflecting, that he whom he owns to be a teacher sent from God, for the salvation of souls, could not speak of any other thing but the new birth of the soul and the reformation of the heart.

5. Jesus answered, Verily, verily, I say unto thee, Except a man be born of water and *of* the Spirit, he cannot enter into the kingdom of God.

In this new, divine, and spiritual birth, God himself, by the virtue of his Holy Spirit, is to us as a father; and the church, represented by the water, receives us into her bosom as our mother. Baptism gives us a right to the kingdom of God, provided we live like children of God and members of Christ, in being obedient to his Spirit.

6. That which is born of the flesh is flesh; and that which is born of the Spirit is spirit.

Let us always remember that our spiritual birth obliges us to lead a spiritual life. We consist of two men, which make but one: the one carnal, born after a carnal, the other spiritual, born after a spiritual manner. What a shame is it that "that which is born of the flesh" should subject and govern the spiritual man, and render it carnal, instead of our subduing and mortifying whatever there is in us which is carnal and corrupt!

7. Marvel not that I said unto thee, Ye must be born again.

Adam, being a sinner, could beget only sinners, and propagate no other inclinations but such as tend to sin. It belongs to thee, O holy Jesus! as the principle of our new life, to give us thy Spirit, and to inspire into us thy spiritual and holy inclinations. He who is thoroughly sensible of the corruption of the heart of man, is far from wondering that it is necessary for him to be changed into a new man, and that he must receive a new spirit, a new heart, and a new principle of life and action. It is this new birth which gives us a right, on all occasions, to pray for the new Spirit.

8. The wind bloweth where it listeth, and thou hearest the sound thereof, but canst not tell whence it cometh, and whither it goeth: so is every one that is born of the Spirit.

He who is fully convinced of this truth, that grace is due to no person whatever, and that the distribution of the gifts of God's Holy Spirit, in order to make us his children and spiritual men, proceeds solely from his will and mercy,—such a person takes the greatest care to live in a constant course of humility and gratitude. A true Christian is a great wonder and an incomprehensible mystery; for we see such a one renouncing and hating himself, and continually opposing all his inclinations, without seeing either the principle which puts him in action, or the end at which he aims, or the reward for which he hopes. That person who sees with no other eyes but those of the flesh, cannot possibly perceive that which the Spirit works in the heart of him who is born of the Spirit. Lord, it is from thee that this Spirit proceeds, which alone searches the deep things of God, which renders invisible mysteries visible to the eyes of faith, makes future enjoyments present to our hope, and causes charity to perform things otherwise impossible.

9. Nicodemus answered and said unto him, How can these things be?

The spirit of man is always opposing and contradicting the Spirit of God, and would fain know the manner of his conduct and operation in the heart. It is not for them who believe in an almighty God to be under any apprehension lest he should find something impossible to be accomplished in his designs concerning our salvation, and in the methods of his grace. Nicodemus was excusable, considering the time in which he lived: Christians cannot have the least excuse, after so many ages of miracles and wonders.

10. Jesus answered and said unto him, Art thou a master of Israel, and knowest not these things?

The learning of men is always accompanied with great ignorance; and yet they are puffed up therewith. The gospel humbles the learned and comforts the simple. The humble and teachable faith of the poor in spirit make all difficulties easy; whereas the presumptuous confidence of the masters of the law blinds them, and renders every thing incredible to them. Would to God there were not many to be found who pass their lives, like this Pharisee, in the study of the Scripture, and yet, like him are ignorant of the true intent, mysteries, and end thereof, which is Jesus Christ!

SECT. II.—CHRIST ALONE HATH ASCENDED UP TO HEAVEN.—THE BRAZEN SERPENT A TYPE OF CHRIST.—THE SON SENT TO SAVE THE WORLD.—HE WHO DOETH EVIL, HATETH THE LIGHT.

11. Verily, verily, I say unto thee, We speak that we do know, and testify that we have seen; and ye receive not our witness.

Christ alone knows, and can teach the mysteries of eternity, and the conduct of God in respect of souls. Whenever we read the gospel, we must remember that it is the Son of God who speaks therein concerning the things of God; that, by the prerogative of his eternal birth, he is light of light, truth itself, and the fountain of all knowledge; and that, in his mission and temporal birth, and in virtue of the union of his soul with the eternal Word, he received a perfect knowledge of the designs and ways of God, and of the whole economy of grace, of which he is the sovereign dispenser. It is a shame and reproach to human reason that it frequently admits and receives, without any difficulty, the witness of a stranger and an impostor, and yet cannot be persuaded to receive that of truth itself.

12. If I have told you earthly things, and ye believe not, how shall ye believe, if I tell you *of* heavenly things?

In order to obtain the gift of understanding, we must humble ourselves, and submit our reason to the yoke of faith, without which there is nothing but darkness with respect to mysteries. Those which come to pass in time, though they be spiritual, are yet earthly in comparison with those which are eternal. One of the first doubts and first evangelical instructions recorded by John, relates to the wonderful and mysterious operation of the Spirit of God in changing the heart of man—of so great importance is it to be instructed in this matter. Let us not imitate the incredulity of this disciple. That which we believe concerning the heavenly mysteries concealed in the bosom of God, should dispose us to believe that which he is able to perform in the heart of man upon earth.

13. And no man hath ascended up to heaven, but he that came down from heaven, *even* the Son of man which is in heaven.

The secrets of heaven do not come within the compass of human reason. He only among men has the key of them who, as the Son of God, is in heaven. We must therefore unite ourselves to him by faith, which alone transports us to heaven, and discovers to us the mysteries of that place. No person is born again, raised to a new life, and ascends up to heaven, but only in Jesus Christ, of whom he is made a member by baptism, and together with whom he makes but one Christ. O union! O unity! which we shall never be able to comprehend, to esteem, and to love enough!

14. ¶ And as Moses lifted up the serpent in the wilderness, even so must the Son of man be lifted up:

This is the second prediction of the undeserved death of Christ on the cross, by his applying to himself the type of the serpent which had neither life nor venom. Though he bore only the resemblance of sinful flesh, yet he bore the real curse denounced against it in his body upon the cross. But, O God! into how great a blessing is this curse changed for all those sinners who put their whole trust and confidence therein! It is by the virtue of the cross of Christ that we receive faith, that we are made his members, and that we have a right to heaven; but it is by our crucifying ourselves with him that all this is accomplished in us.

15. That whosoever believeth in him should not perish, but have eternal life.

The fruit of Christ's death and passion is the life of faith; and the fruit of faith is to cause us to find in him a deliverance from the death of sin and of hell, and whatever is necessary to our attaining to that life which he has merited for us by his cross. O cross of my Saviour, my only refuge, the cradle as it were of my faith, the origin of my salvation, and the source of eternal life! Ungrateful is he, and an enemy to his own happiness, who loves not to turn his intellectual eyes toward thee, there to adore his life crucified, and to find there the death of all his passions.

16. ¶ For God so loved the world, that he gave his only-begotten Son, that whosoever believeth in him should not perish, but have everlasting life.

How many, how great and important truths, how many mysteries are here presented to the faith of a Christian! Somewhat more than faith is requisite to comprehend them; there must be more than all the love we can possibly have on earth to answer the love of God, who gives not an angel, but his only-begotten Son; who gives him to his creatures, to sinners, and to his enemies; and who, by giving him, reduces him as it were to nothing, that they may not perish by his justice. It is in the bosom of God himself that we must seek for the reason of his mercies, and for the causes of salvation. The first of God's gifts is his love; the first gift of his love to the sinner is his Son; the first gift of his Son is faith; and faith is the root of all other graces, the principle of the new life, and the key which shuts up hell, and opens the gate of heaven.

17. For God sent not his Son into the world to condemn the world; but that the world through him might be saved.

The first coming of the Son of God is in order to save the world: miserable is that person who renders it ineffectual to himself, and turns it into a judgment by his infidelity! It is our own sin which condemns us; it is the grace of Christ which saves us: in him alone then must we place our whole trust and confidence. Lord, this world which through thee is to be saved, seek it, I beseech thee, at the very bottom of my heart.

18. ¶ He that believeth on him is not condemned: but he that believeth not is condemned already, because he hath not believed in the name of the only begotten Son of God.

Whoever by means of faith is not in Jesus Christ, continues still in Adam, and is under his condemnation. The true justifying faith is neither the false confidence of heretics, nor the dead and barren faith of such among the orthodox as lead wicked lives; but it is that which changes the heart, and causes it to love and embrace the maxims of the gospel. We do not believe in the name of our blessed Saviour as we ought, if we walk not in the way of the gospel: we have nothing but a false and deceitful confidence in Christ, when we are not obedient to his word.

19. And this is the condemnation, that light is come into the world, and men loved darkness rather than light, because their deeds were evil.

The greatest misfortune of men does not consist in their being subject to sin, corruption, and blindness; but in their rejecting the deliverer, the physician, and even light itself. Nothing more plainly discovers the corruption of the world, and affords greater cause to dread the wrath of God, than to see men's opposition to the light continually increase, the more abundantly he is pleased to diffuse and manifest it abroad. The love of darkness is always disguised under a pretended love of light; and it is the great and just judgment of God, both upon particular persons and whole nations, to give them over to this reprobate mind, which takes light for darkness, and darkness for light.

20. For every one that doeth evil hateth the light, neither cometh to the light, lest his deeds should be reproved.

There are three degrees of blindness: The first is, when passion causes men to prefer the darkness of sin before the light of truth. The second, when the love of sin renders truth itself disagreeable and odious to us. And the third, when men keep at a distance, fly from it, persecute, suppress, and stifle it as a dangerous evil. The love of the gospel, and of the great principles of Christian morality, grows and increases in a heart in proportion as it disengages itself from sin, and as it really loves and practises virtue. On the contrary, men always find the gospel too severe, the most necessary truths too hard, and the Christian morality carried too high, and full of mortifying discouragements, when they will not renounce those passions which are condemned thereby. A man who is notoriously profligate frequently judges better in this case than a proud hypocrite, who would at the same time enjoy both the reputation of piety and the pleasure of his passions.

21. But he that doeth truth cometh to the light, that his deeds may be made manifest, that they are wrought in God.

True Christians are the children of light and the disciples of truth; and it is their joy continually to walk by the most pure light of the gospel, and to regulate their actions by the most substantial truths of Christianity. He who seeks God alone, and resolves to do nothing but according to his Spirit, is very far from having any apprehension that he shall know the law of God too well, and discover too much of the holiness of his ways. Those who seek the glory and applause of the world come to the light thereof, and expose their actions thereto: those who, in performing good works, love only the grace of God, which is the principle, his will, which is the rule, and his glory, which is the end of them, are likewise desirous to have them examined by his light, that they may praise him for what is found good in them, that they may condemn what is bad, and that they may improve and complete whatever is defective and imperfect.

SECT. III.—JOHN THE FRIEND OF THE BRIDEGROOM.—THE SPIRIT GIVEN TO THE SON WITHOUT MEASURE.

22. ¶ After these things came Jesus and his disciples into the land of Judea; and there he tarried with them, and baptized.

Jesus trains his disciples up to labour, and does not suffer them to continue in idleness. It is he who baptizes by his disciples, because they do it by his appointment, in his presence, and perhaps with his baptism; how much more certainly does he baptize, when his baptism is given by the ministers of his church, which is his body, which acts by his Spirit, and which lives and subsists only in him! It is of great use for men to have this truth present to their minds whenever they either administer or receive the sacraments that they may bring along with them that faith and reverence which they ought.

23. ¶ And John also was baptizing in Enon: near to Salim, because there was much water there: and they came, and were baptized. 24. For John was not yet cast into prison.

We ought to labour in the work of God until we fall under an impossibility of performing it, according to John's example. His labours are terminated by imprisonment and death; and he foresaw that this would be the consequence of them. How few evangelical workmen would there be in the church, if they expected nothing else from the world! Imprisonment, which is the fruit of a holy freedom in preaching the truth, is the seed of that perfect liberty and freedom which we shall enjoy in the very source and fountain thereof.

25. ¶ Then there arose a question between *some* of John's disciples and the Jews about purifying.

Emulation between the disciples of different masters, how holy soever those masters may be, is an evil which is always to be feared. It is not a new thing for persons to be divided by disputes concerning repentance, instead of agreeing to perform it in the spirit of charity. To discover who is in the wrong in these disputes, we need only observe on which side emulation and interest may chiefly lie.

26. And they came unto John, and said unto him, Rabbi, he that was with thee beyond Jordan, to whom thou barest witness, behold, the same baptizeth, and all *men* come to him.

How difficult is it to secure ourselves from too human a fondness and affection for a spiritual guide or director, when he has gained a considerable reputation! This affection appears plainly to be such, when we do not rejoice so much at the good which is done by others, as at that which we see him do. Self-love divides and distracts the heart with contrary desires. One sort of vanity would fain have imitators and followers; another cannot endure them: charity and humility agree to desire none but for the sake of God. "All men come to him:" these are words of envy and emulation. Alas! what mischiefs has this vice caused in the church; and how many does it still cause therein! How much good has it obstructed! How many souls has it destroyed!

27. John answered and said, A man can receive nothing, except it be given him from heaven.

Let us never forget this great principle of Christian humility—that every good thing comes from God. If there were any good in man, any pious motion in his heart which is not "given him from heaven," it would be sufficient to entitle him to ascribe to himself all the consequences thereof. Every grace, every vocation has its bounds and limits; and no person ought to raise himself above his own. An humble and wise director of souls ought frequently to inculcate into his disciples this rule—that they must not set their affections upon him or his talents, but upon God, from whom they are derived.

28. Ye yourselves bear me witness, that I said, I am not the Christ, but that I am sent before him.

How great honour soever it may be for a minister of the church to be sent as the ambassador of God and the harbinger of Jesus Christ, he has still more reason to humble himself than to be puffed up on that account; for this office is not merely a post of honour, but a laborious commission and employment. A man is not made a bishop to receive the homage due to God; but to see it paid to him, and to prepare his way by instruction, prayer, and good example.

29. He that hath the bride is the bridegroom: but the friend of the bridegroom, which standeth and heareth him, rejoiceth greatly because of the bridegroom's voice: this my joy therefore is fulfilled.

The church belongs to Christ, and not to particular pastors. Spiritual directors ought to look upon souls as the spouses or brides of Christ, and to hearken to his voice, that they may guide and direct them as they ought. They must not be jealous on the account of any extraordinary favours which he shows them; and they must rejoice when he either puts them into the hands of others, or takes them under his own immediate direction, and guides them in such a manner as is above their reach, and by ways which, though they do not comprehend, yet they see plainly are the ways of God. There can be no greater joy to a pastor than to see, by the edification of his flock, that the Bridegroom speaks to the hearts thereof, and that it is really his in quality of his spouse.

30. He must increase, but I *must* decrease.

A true pastor has nothing at heart but the increase of the glory of Christ: his own consists in promoting that at the expense of all things. The more he is humbled for his master's sake, the more serviceable and useful is he both to him and his work. Humiliation never surprises or afflicts him who, like John, continually expects it, and is disposed to sacrifice his reputation, as well as his life, to advance the kingdom of the Son of God.

31. He that cometh from above is above all: he that is of the earth is earthly, and speaketh of the earth: he that cometh from heaven is above all.

The divinity, birth, and divine mission of Christ are the three sources of the holiness and authority of his words. Man of himself has nothing but what is low and mean in his words and thoughts; and nothing but what is great, sublime, and heavenly, when, leaving himself and his own darkness, he by faith enters into Jesus Christ and his light. We all carry within ourselves two men of a different nature: the one heavenly, the other earthly; and it is the great design of God to make them one, in renewing, sanctifying, and rendering the earthly man happy, by the spirit, in the body, and according to the pattern of the heavenly man. Grant, Lord, that I may shut my ears against every thing which the children of this world have to suggest to me concerning earthly things; and that the ears of my heart may be continually open to those divine truths which thou camest from heaven to reveal to us, O heavenly Man, who art also God!

32. **And what he hath seen and heard, that he testifieth; and no man receiveth his testimony.**

These words afford us a true idea of faith and of incredulity. To believe, or not to believe, is no other than to receive or reject the testimony which the Son of God gives concerning what he has seen and heard; that is, concerning what he knows, by that divine knowledge which he received from his Father, when, by his eternal birth, he received of him his essence—a knowledge communicated by the incarnation to the God-man, in whom are hid all the treasures of divine knowledge and wisdom. What punishment does not the incredulous person deserve who judges the Son of God less worthy of credit and belief than the most inconsiderable eye-witness among men?

33. **He that hath received his testimony hath set to his seal that God is true.**

The faith of the elect and of the whole church is, as it were, the seal of the truth of God's word, and of his fidelity in his promises. What blasphemy is there more horrid than to give the lie to truth itself, and to say that God is a liar! And does not every man do this who refuses to receive the truth delivered by the Son of God, whose miracles evidently proved him to be such?

34. **For he whom God hath sent speaketh the words of God: for God giveth not the Spirit by measure *unto him*.**

Observe here the excellency of Christ's mission, and how it differed from that of the prophets. The first difference is, that God spoke to them by intervals; whereas he speaks continually in his Son, because this Son is God. The second difference is, that the prophets spoke by an inspiration which was borrowed, transient, and "given by measure;" whereas he spoke by the Holy Ghost, who is his own Spirit, who inseparably dwells in him, and by the possession of whose fulness he receives his unction and consecration. What respect and reverence ought we to have when we read the gospel! To do it as we ought, we must beg a portion of this Spirit, whose fulness is the source of the divine, adorable, and sanctifying word.

35. The Father loveth the Son, and hath given all things into his hand.

The third difference between the mission of Christ and that of the prophets is, that God loved the prophets as his servants; but that he loves Christ as his only Son, and communicates himself to him in proportion to his love. The fourth difference is, that the prophets had only particular commissions, limited to a certain time, and to certain purposes; but that Christ has full power given him, as the general disposer of all his Father's works, the executor of his designs, the head of his church, the universal high-priest of his good things to come, the steward and dispenser of all his graces, the Saviour of all his people, and the only way which leads to truth and life. Lord, I desire not either to take any step toward these, or to arrive at them any other way than by thee. My salvation is in thy hand. My joy is to depend upon thee.

36. He that believeth on the Son hath everlasting life: and he that believeth not the Son shall not see life; but the wrath of God abideth on him.

It is by faith that Christ dwells in our hearts; and to have him there, is to have everlasting life. To believe in Jesus Christ, is not barely to give credit to what he reveals; but it is to put our whole trust and confidence in him, as the only Mediator of salvation, by the merits of his blood, and by the power of his grace. This faith is the seed of everlasting life; and both consist in knowing and loving God imperfectly here below, perfectly in heaven. A lively faith renders the enjoyments of the world to come present even in this life; but glory will render them visible. There is no salvation, in any state whatever, but only by Jesus Christ. Without him, the sentence of death, pronounced against all mankind in Adam, would be put in execution without mercy; because there is no mercy to be had but through Jesus Christ. It is through thee alone that I entreat, hope for, and expect it, O thou my only and almighty Mediator!

CHAPTER IV.

SECT. I.—THE WOMAN OF SAMARIA.—THE WATER SPRINGING UP INTO ETERNAL LIFE.—THE WORSHIPPERS IN SPIRIT AND TRUTH.

1. When therefore the Lord knew how the Pharisees had heard that Jesus made and baptized more disciples than John, 2. (Though Jesus himself baptized not, but his disciples,) 3. He left Judea, and departed again into Galilee.

It is prudence and charity to take away all occasions of envy and sin from the weak, and even from the wicked, as much as we possibly can. There is a time to give away to the enemies of the truth, and a time to render it triumphant over them. It is a very great grace not to mistake in this matter, and to do nothing out of season. To avoid dangers on some occasions is a thing not only permitted, but it is frequently according to God's appointment, for the interest of his glory, and consequently a part of perfection. To make an humble retreat is a thing sometimes more difficult to nature than a stout and glorious resistance. That person follows God who does not expose himself to suffering before the time. The residue of a pastor's life shows plainly enough whether he retired out of fearfulness or out of faithfulness to his ministry.

4. And he must needs go through Samaria. 5. Then cometh he to a city of Samaria, which is called Sychar, near to the parcel of ground that Jacob gave to his son Joseph.

One soul alone of the number of the elect, though as yet buried in corruption, sometimes invites Christ, and draws down the blessings of God upon a whole country. Let us adore the zeal of the true Pastor, who comes on purpose to seek his lost sheep. When a man has no longer any opportunities of serving God in a country, he must endeavour to find them in some other place. It is no other than necessity, in all appearance, which obliges Christ to pass by this city; but, in reality, it is the eternal love of God toward some particular souls therein, which he intends to save. All ages are full of instances of this nature; but to observe the secret conduct of God in them an attentive faith is necessary.

6. Now Jacob's well was there. Jesus therefore, being wearied with *his* journey, sat thus on the well: *and* it was about the sixth hour.

Christ by his toils and weariness obtains rest for us. They are not mentioned without design. What a sight to the eyes of faith is a God wearied by his incessant labours for the salvation of his creatures! What return of duty does he not justly require of us! Let us at least be so faithful as to adore him in this condition; to give him thanks for wearying himself in seeking us; and to imitate him, as occasion requires, in bearing the fatigues of our employment or state of life; and sometimes even those of journeys in union with his, and in reflecting on them with reverence and respect. The rest of Jesus Christ is as mysterious, and as full of kindness and beneficence, as his weariness: for he waits for a soul which was tired in the ways of sin, in order to give it rest. It is a great matter for a man to learn how to rest himself without being idle, and to make his necessary repose subservient to the glory of God.

7. There cometh a woman of Samaria to draw water: Jesus saith unto her, Give me to drink. 8. For his disciples were gone away unto the city to buy meat.

Jesus asks in order to give. A cup of cold water, (where there is not ability to give more,) which he asks and receives by the hand of a poor man, is perhaps the occasion of salvation to him who gives it: perhaps his salvation depends upon so small an alms. Christ honours and sanctifies the state of those who are forced to ask charity, by asking it himself. He voluntarily reduces himself to such circumstances as to want the assistance of his creatures, that we may not be ashamed to have our dependence on them. He here shows us the way, by common and ordinary conversation, insensibly to introduce discourses concerning piety and salvation. His divine thirst and earnest desire to save souls is that which is most vehement, and to which he makes his bodily thirst subservient. They are both to be adored and imitated.

9. Then saith the woman of Samaria unto him, How is it that thou, being a Jew, askest drink of me, which am a woman of Samaria? for the Jews have no dealings with the Samaritans.

When a soul is to be saved, we must not refuse our cares

and endeavours to the greatest sinners. If we cannot be instrumental to the salvation of heretics, and have reason to apprehend that our own will be endangered by them, the law of nature obliges us to avoid them. Error, as well as vice, is a contagious disease. To converse familiarly with such as may infect us with either, when we lie under no necessity nor obligation to do it, is no other than to be willing to perish. How many precautions do we generally take to secure the body!—how few with regard to the soul!

10. Jesus answered and said unto her, If thou knowest the gift of God, and who it is that saith to thee, Give me to drink; thou wouldest have asked of him, and he would have given thee living water.

Jesus Christ is the great gift of God, and the source of all other gifts. Such as this Samaritan woman is, such is every sinner before the first ray of divine light has shone in his heart. So far is she from being able to deserve it, desire it, or ask for it, that she rejects it, and has not the least suspicion imaginable that she has any want of it. To be admonished of our ignorance signifies but very little, if God do not perform the rest. To know Jesus Christ and the necessity of his grace, is the first step toward conversion. His grace is living water, which quenches our thirst after worldly riches and pleasures. Who would not incessantly desire and long to drink thereof? Frequent opportunities of receiving this water present themselves to us, and we are not sensible of them. Disgrace, sickness, poverty, and affliction often bring along with them this precious gift, and yet we refuse them. Cause us, Lord, to know this gift on all occasions, that we may esteem, desire it, and pray for it, and that we may give all we have to purchase and preserve it.

11. The woman saith unto him, Sir,* thou hast nothing to draw with, and the well is deep: from whence then hast thou that living water? [* *Fr.* Lord.]

The term "Lord," of which this woman makes use, shows that when God begins to speak to the heart he disposes it to hear, by making it sensible of his presence, and imprinting thereon a great degree of respect and reverence. And then it begins to discover the greatness of his promises, and to perceive that they cannot possibly be only carnal and temporal; it sees plainly the weakness and inability of nature, and the absolute necessity of supernatural assistance.

12. Art thou greater than our father Jacob, which gave us the well, and drank thereof himself, and his children, and his cattle?

What is the greatness of Jacob in comparison with that of Christ, which Jacob himself adored in the sign of the greatness of his son Joseph, a prophetic sign of the kingdom of the Messias! How deep, O Jesus, is that well from whence thou drawest without measure the water of wisdom and grace, the fulness whereof thou possessest, and of which thou givest thy children and the whole flock of God to drink!

13. Jesus answered and said unto her, Whosoever drinketh of this water shall thirst again: 14. But whosoever drinketh of the water that I shall give him shall never thirst;

Christ here teaches us not to be diverted from the subject in debate by personal reflections, when we are engaged in conferences about religion, but to go on convincing and instructing. These are terrible words for those who are continually parched with thirst after earthly riches and enjoyments! Of what water have they drunk?

— But the water that I shall give him shall be in him a well of water, springing up into everlasting life.

The dead and muddy water of earthly things only inflames our thirst: grace, which is a clear and living stream, and which alone can extinguish it, comes from and returns to God, carrying us along with it, and uniting us to him to all eternity. These words are full of comfort to all such as have renounced the love of false riches, and set their affections upon those of heaven: for this is a proof that this water is already in their heart, and a just ground for them to hope that it will "spring up into everlasting life."

15. The woman saith unto him, Sir, give me this water, that I thirst not, neither come hither to draw.

To desire and pray for the grace and Spirit of Christ, are the first steps toward conversion. This desire, how imperfect soever it be in this woman, is, notwithstanding, the effect of the internal operation of grace, though nothing but what is merely human appear in the manner of Christ's exciting this desire in her heart. Let us admire this mixture and union of the Spirit of God with external and human appearances, which honours the union of the divine and human nature, and the divinely human operations of the God-man. Do thou thyself, O Lord, raise in me the desire of this divine water, that thou thyself mayest also satisfy the desire which thou hast raised!

16. Jesus saith unto her, Go, call thy husband, and come hither.

After these first desires, which began to stir and awaken the sinner, God causes him to enter into his own heart to take a full view of himself, and to lay his hand upon his own sores. That which is done here by the words of Christ, is effected by accidental meetings, reflections, and sermons in other sinners, who find themselves most exposed to their own sight when they endeavour to flee from themselves with the greatest care.

17. The woman answered and said, I have no husband. Jesus said unto her, Thou hast well said, I have no husband: 18. For thou hast had five husbands; and he whom thou now hast is not thy husband: in that saidst thou truly.

It is to no purpose to endeavour to turn away our eyes from ourselves that we may not see our own corruption. God sets it plainly before our eyes when he has undertaken to give us an abhorrence of it. Every sinner in proportion is very glad to conceal his failings from himself as much as possible, and to avoid considering and reflecting upon them. Self-love always blinds us in something or other which regards our own persons, and continually opens to us some secret door, to give us means and opportunity to steal away from our own sight, and to make our escape from ourselves. But to what purpose is it to flee from ourselves, if we cannot possibly avoid either the sight or justice of God?

19. The woman saith unto him, Sir, I perceive that thou art a prophet.

This woman perceives at last, and confesses her sins. How powerful and full of mercy is this ray of grace, which at one and the same time opens our eyes that we behold our own wickedness and the holiness of God, draws from us an acknowledgment of our own slavery, and causes us to know our deliverer! Lord, thou art indeed a prophet, and more than a prophet, since thou dost not only discover the heart, but dost likewise work and operate therein.

20. Our fathers worshipped in this mountain; and ye say, that in Jerusalem is the place where men ought to worship.

In order to repent and think effectually of salvation, a person must, in the first place, be assured of the true church, out of the pale of which neither the grace of repentance, nor the spirit of prayer, nor the true worship of God, nor salvation, is to be found. The prejudice of birth and education in the greatest part of sectaries, is the cause of their false way of worship. They have nothing to say in vindication of it, any more than the Samaritan woman, but only that it is the religion of their fathers. But it is necessary to trace both the true and the false religion up to their very original.

21. Jesus saith unto her, Woman, believe me, the hour cometh, when ye shall neither in this mountain, nor yet at Jerusalem, worship the Father.

It is the advantage of the Christian religion to be able, by the oblation of the external representative sacrifice, to worship God in every place.

22. Ye worship ye know not what: we know what we worship; for salvation is of the Jews.

The sinner knows not what God he worships, because he worships what he loves, and he loves whatever flatters his passions—to-day one thing, to-morrow another. The true knowledge of God is not mixed with errors, nor the true worship with superstitions authorized by the body of the pastors, or adopted by the whole church. Where Jesus Christ is represented in sacrifice as the victim and salvation of the world, there is the true church, the true knowledge of God, and the true worship.

23. But the hour cometh, and now is, when the true worshippers shall worship the Father in spirit and in truth; for the Father seeketh such to worship him.

The true church is the church of the true worshippers; the true worshippers are those who worship God, (1.) By sacrifice. (2.) By an external sacrifice. (3.) By a sacrifice which is the representative body and blood of Christ. (4.) By a sacrifice which is offered to God as the Father, the almighty principle of every created and uncreated being, of all divine and human life, and of all natural and supernatural good. (5.) In the spirit of love, which is the spirit of children and of true Christians. And, (6.) In the truth and purity of the faith. Where, O my God, wilt thou find these worshippers which thou seekest, unless thou thyself form them by thy grace? Blessed be thou, for having caused us to be born in the times of the spirit and the truth! Do not suffer us to bring along with us to the Christian sacrifice a Jewish or Samaritan disposition.

24. God *is* a Spirit: and they that worship him must worship *him* in spirit and in truth.

There are three sorts of sacrifices, suited to the three different states of the church and of religion. The first, external and corporeal, for the Jewish church, which was merely typical and prophetic. The second, both internal and external, corporeal and spiritual, for the Christian church on earth. The third, purely internal and spiritual, for the church of the elect in heaven. The first and second, as far as they are external and corporeal, are only preparatory, and instituted merely on the account of sin, and for the transitory state of the church; or only to prefigure the spiritual sacrifice, as the former; or to be subservient thereto, as the latter. The second, as far as it is spiritual, together with the third, is the sacrifice which is most agreeable to the nature of God, who is a pure Spirit. A spirit and heart sacrificed and consecrated to God by adoration and a sincere humiliation before his majesty, a submission and absolute dependence on his will, a lively acknowledgment of his goodness and benefits, and a zeal and ardent love for his glory,—this is the sacrifice, in some measure, worthy of that eternal and infinitely perfect Spirit, and of that supremely holy and unchangeable will, which is God himself. It is by this internal sacrifice that that of Jesus Christ himself is a sacrifice in spirit and in truth, and acceptable to God. Without this sacrifice of the mind and heart by charity, the external sacrifice, which ought to be the sign, effect, and representation of the other, is only an empty sign, a deceitful representation, and a Jewish sacrifice.

25. The woman saith unto him, I know that Messias cometh, which is called Christ: when he is come, he will tell us all things.

Jesus then came at a time when the expectation of the Messias was so common among the Jews that even a poor Samaritan woman, without the assistance of the prophets, whom her sect did not receive, does not stick to declare that he was upon the very point of appearing in the world. She will condemn the Jews and all incredulous persons who have seen in him the works and marks of the Messias. Yes, Lord, it is really thou from whom we are to learn all things. It is to thee that I ought to have recourse in all my doubts, and it is from thee that I must receive sufficient light to understand the Scriptures.

26. Jesus saith unto her, I that speak unto thee am *he*.

How great comfort and consolation is it, in our doubts and miseries, to know that we have Jesus Christ for our Saviour and Master! He confounds the vanity of proud and conceited doctors or teachers by discovering himself to this poor woman, though involved in error, schism, and immorality, rather than to the Pharisees, persons of great learning and an austere life. It is a great mistake to imagine that the knowledge of the mysteries of religion ought not to be imparted to persons of her sex by the reading of the sacred books, considering this instance of the great confidence Christ reposed in this woman by his manifestation of himself unto her. The abuse of the Scriptures, and the rise of heresies, did not proceed from the simplicity of women, but from the conceited learning of men. The more religion and piety any persons have, the more right have they to feed on the word of God, and on his truths.

SECT. II.—THE WILL OF GOD THE FOOD OF THE SOUL.—THE PROPHETS SOWED, THE APOSTLES REAP.—THE FAITH OF THE SAMARITANS.

27. ¶ And upon this came his disciples, and marvelled that he talked with the woman: yet no man said, What seekest thou? or, Why talkest thou with her?

Christ conversed but very little with women, since his disciples marvel at his doing it: this affords an example of great weight for the clergy. We must not immediately sensure good men, though they seem to us to do something contrary to decency. We run no risk at all in suspending our judgment, and waiting until some further discovery may be made; but we hazard a great deal when we expose ourselves to the violation of justice and charity by a rash and precipitate judgment.

28. The woman then left her waterpot, and went her way into the
city, and saith to the men, 29. Come, see a man, which told me all
things that ever I did: is not this the Christ? 30. Then they went out
of the city, and came unto him.

Wonderful effect this, of one word of our blessed Saviour upon the heart of a woman who becomes the apostle of her country! He must needs have spoken to other ears than those of the body, since he has a greater influence on her heart than she has herself, insomuch that she forgets every thing through her great haste to carry tidings of him to her countrymen. Let us learn of her that, in order to give ourselves up to God, it is necessary we should forget temporal things, that we should withdraw from our ordinary employments for some time, that we should be full of acknowledgment for the grace we have received, that we should seriously meditate upon Christ, and by zealous discourses bring those to him who either do not know him or offend him, whenever we have an opportunity of doing it.

31. ¶ In the mean while his disciples prayed him, saying, Master, eat.
32. But he said unto them, I have meat to eat that ye know not of.

Christ cannot lose sight of this soul whom he has just gained over to his Father; he follows her in mind and heart; he acts in hers; he is taken up with reflecting upon the zeal which carries her back to the city; he attends upon her tongue to bless the word of eternal life which she delivers to them; and he seeks among that people those whom his Father has given him, that he may draw them to him; he offers them up to him, prays to him for them, and works in their hearts to render them tractable and obedient to the voice of this woman. This is the food of him who is himself our bread and sustenance.

He teaches the apostles and ministers of the gospel that they must not easily be induced to give over any work which they have begun, on the account either of bodily wants or temporal concerns. From this indifference of Christ in respect of food, after his having walked till noon, it is easy to infer from whence this woman received the forgetfulness of her bodily thirst. This forgetfulness is a participation of that of Jesus Christ.

33. Therefore said the disciples one to another, Hath any man brought him *aught* to eat?

Men, as yet carnal, find it difficult to conceive how much strength a zeal for the glory of God gives even to the body. The work of God supports the workman, and an evangelical labourer does not live by bread alone, but by the same word of God which proceeds out of his mouth for the nourishment and support of others. God has in store for his servants such meat and delicious food as the mind of man knows not of.

34. Jesus saith unto them, My meat is to do the will of him that sent me, and to finish his work.

A pastor ought to have nothing at heart but the work of God and the salvation of souls. This ought to be his delight, his meat, and his life. There is nothing greater in the world than this apostolical employment; yet we must not love the dignity and eminency thereof, but the doing the will of God. We ought to apply our minds thereto not because it pleases us, but because it pleases God; and to esteem the work not on the account of the part we have in it, but because it is God's, and for his sake. Though a man labour therein till he has quite spent himself, yet it is still more the work of God than of man, since it is his Spirit which speaks by the preacher's mouth, and which produces faith in the heart of the auditor. While we are carrying on the work of God in others, let us take care that the devil do not carry on his work in us by means of vanity. In this employment our humility must be equal to our zeal. We have reason to tremble under the weight of these three words—the will, the mission, and the work of God.

35. Say not ye, There are yet four months, and *then* cometh harvest?

behold, I say unto you, Lift up your eyes, and look on the fields; for they are white already to harvest.

The multitude of the nations whom God calls to the faith, and the vast number of sinners who are to be brought to repentance, are a harvest always ready for the evangelical labourers. It belongs to them to labour at all times, and to God to give his blessing to their labours when and as he pleases. Let us often lift up our eyes, and awaken our zeal, either to beseech him to send forth labourers among so many sinners, among so many people who know him not, or to go among them ourselves if he vouchsafe to call us forth.

36. And he that reapeth receiveth wages, and gathereth fruit unto life eternal: that both he that soweth and he that reapeth may rejoice together.

Observe here three fruits, which ought to serve as motives to encourage an evangelical workman in his labour. The first is, salvation and an eternal reward for himself. This is fully sufficient to oblige us to expect no other; but we must not hope to have it till after the harvest. The second is, the salvation of souls converted. And the third is, the perfection of the body of the elect, and the consummation of the saints in God, by eternal joy and glory, in which the full harvest does consist. If to have contributed to the salvation of one soul be a cause of joy and comfort, what will it be for a man to see heaven, as it were, peopled by his labours! The salvation of an evangelical minister frequently depends upon that of other men: in labouring for them he labours for himself.

37. And herein is that saying true, One soweth, and another reapeth.
38. I sent you to reap that whereon ye bestowed no labour: other men laboured, and ye are entered into their labours.

It is no small comfort to those who labour much in the church, and see no fruits thereof, to be assured that they shall lose no part of their reward. It often happens that the fruit does not appear till a long time after the death of the labourers: but all are equal in the sight of God, both they who sow and they who reap, when their charity is equal. It is a motive to humility for these ecclesiastical workmen, to consider that the plentifulness of their crop is perhaps the fruit and recompense of the piety of their predecessors. A second guide or spiritual director pleases himself with seeing the progress made by a soul under his care; whereas it is perhaps the effect of the prayers, labours, and patience of another person.

39. ¶ And many of the Samaritans of that city believed on him for the saying of the woman, which testified, He told me all that ever I did.

God frequently converts a soul in order to make it instrumental in converting others. By making use of the ministry of a poor woman for the conversion of these people, who were at so great a distance from the truth, he shows plainly that all instruments are alike to him to whom none is necessary, and who of himself turns the heart of man as he pleases. We must not disdain to receive from a woman that instruction of which we stand in need. God is pleased sometimes to humble learned men, by giving them a further insight into their duty by the means of pious ladies on whom he has conferred a great degree of light and knowledge, to reward their charity, fidelity, and zeal for his glory.

40. So when the Samaritans were come unto him, they besought him that he would tarry with them: and he abode there two days.

Christ finds more openness of heart and more teachable dispositions among the Samaritans than among the Jews; and yet he forbids his disciples to preach the truth to them. Oh the depths of the judgments of God! Christ here teaches us to despise none, to instruct all without distinction, and not to judge what fruit the divine word will produce by the present disposition of sinners. God alone knows those who are his, and on whom he intends to show the great instances of his mercy.

41. And many more believed because of his own word;

The word of Christ in his own mouth is more powerful and efficacious than in that of another. In like manner greater blessings attend the reading divine truths in the gospel itself, than when we read the very same truths in other books: to do the former is to receive them, as it were, immediately from the mouth of wisdom itself. As a lively and reverential faith supplies Christ's corporeal presence in us, so will he, by the power of his grace and the abundance of his blessings, supply us with the beneficial and saving effects of that presence.

42. And said unto the woman, Now we believe, not because of thy saying: for we have heard *him* ourselves, and know that this is indeed the Christ, the Saviour of the world.

How much light and knowledge does faith infuse, in a little time, into those hearts which God vouchsafes to open to his word! Had these men rejected this word when it was first delivered to them by this woman, they would then have never heard it from the mouth of Christ himself. Nothing is to be slighted when our salvation is concerned: one single step at first is frequently attended with very great consequences. Happy this people, in having been the first-fruits of the faith among the Samaritans; in having learned, in so short a time, the need which the whole world had of a Saviour, and consequently the corruption of nature, and the necessity of grace to repair and restore it; in having been the first who owned, reverenced, and proclaimed on earth that amiable quality and name of Saviour, which the angel had proclaimed from heaven to the Jews; and in having been the only persons who, before the apostles, published this truth, that Jesus is the Saviour of the world! Who can tell but that this was a reward for their having invited, received, and kept Jesus Christ among them; and was perhaps conferred as a blessing upon that hospitality which they had shown toward him, without having any regard either to the aversion of the Samaritans or to the hatred of the Jews?

SECT. III.—THE RULER'S SON HEALED.

43. ¶ Now after two days he departed thence, and went into Galilee.

What! so short a stay in a place where he met with nothing but kind reception and obedience, and where he saw so much fruit of his labours! The reason is, because the conduct of a minister of the gospel is not to be regulated by such considerations, but by God's appointment. To do the work enjoined is not enough; we must examine whether we do it according to his will and the order of his mission. It is an instance of self-denial which is very uncommon and extraordinary, to leave those who respect and applaud us that we may go to preach among others from whom we have reason to expect a quite different treatment.

44. For Jesus himself testified, that a prophet hath no honour in his own country.

It is seldom known that a man is very serviceable to his friends and acquaintance in the business of salvation, and yet inclination always leads us that way. When we decline going among them for fear of being despised, it is pride; but when we do it because we would not have the word of God exposed to contempt, it is prudence and discretion. In the mean time we must take care not to be mistaken in our motives. The safest way is to keep to the advice and example of Jesus Christ in relation to this matter.

45. Then when he was come into Galilee, the Galileans received him, having seen all the things that he did at Jerusalem at the feast: for they also went unto the feast.

To believe without miracles, is the excellency of the faith of the Samaritans; to believe on the account of miracles, is at least to do more than the generality of the Jews, and to yield to the authority of God as the Galileans did. These miracles are for us, as well as for those who saw them, since the gospel renders them present to us. Let them serve therefore to increase our faith and confidence in Christ, especially since they have been confirmed by the grand miracle of his resurrection, and by so many others which have followed it. The Galileans would perhaps have rejected Christ and his word, if they had not seen his miracles; and they would not have seen them if they had not gone unto the feast. Of so great advantage is it faithfully to perform the duties of religion. So great is the blessing which attends the constant appearance at our parish church on days set apart for the honour of God!

46. So Jesus came again into Cana of Galilee, where he made the water wine. And there was a certain nobleman, whose son was sick at Capernaum.

Christ does not come to this place to seek any new applause on the account of his miracle, but to reap the fruit of it in the confidence of this ruler, and to strengthen the faith of these people by showing them another. An evangelical labourer, after the example of Christ, must be careful to keep up and confirm the good which he has done among souls by the ministry of the word.

47. When he heard that Jesus was come out of Judea into Galilee, he went unto him, and besought him that he would come down, and heal his son: for he was at the point of death.

Afflictions are useful, since they oblige us to have recourse to God. We should very often be extremely fond of a son, a friend, or an estate, and place our whole happiness therein, if the danger of being deprived of every one of them did not put us in mind that they are all but perishing things, and that we must seek our happiness in something which cannot be taken away from us. Neither the fondness of this father toward his son, nor his too great forwardness in desiring a miracle to secure his enjoyment of him, nor his false notion of the omnipotence of God, nor the imperfection of his faith, gives any disgust to Christ. Thus God bears with our prayers, how imperfect soever they be.

48. Then said Jesus unto him, Except ye see signs and wonders, ye will not believe.

Would to God there were not abundance of persons in the world who, like this nobleman, do not believe miracles because they do not see them! It is great ingratitude not to think ourselves concerned in those signs and wonders which God has wrought at distant times or remote places, to establish the faith of the church which everywhere and in all ages is one and the same. It is a shame and reproach to the understanding of man, that it is seldom averse to the belief of strange and extraordinary things, unless it be when God is the author of them. It is not enough just to believe them: we must preserve the remembrance of them; we must not suffer the impression they have made upon our mind to be lost; but we must draw from them their just consequences, and reap that fruit which they ought to produce.

49. The nobleman saith unto him, Sir, come down ere my child die.

The power of Jesus Christ is not confined either to time

or place. Men are very far from desiring miracles with as much earnestness to secure their faith and salvation, as to secure to themselves the enjoyment of some temporal advantage, which may possibly extinguish their faith, and rob them of salvation. The presence of Christ is a very great and desirable blessing: but to confine his power and goodness to his presence, is a piece of infidelity which seems very common even in the present age. The eagerness and confusion of our desires, which are too natural and carnal, often hinder us from understanding that which God speaks to us. Christ intends to cure this father of his want of faith, in order to make him worthy to receive the cure of his son; but he is hitherto wholly taken up with the thoughts of that which he is afraid of losing. Alas, how many fathers are there in the world who nearly resemble him!

50. Jesus saith unto him, Go thy way; thy son liveth. And the man believed the word that Jesus had spoken unto him, and he went his way.

Let us observe here the double miracle, wrought by the word alone of Christ: the one on the distant body of the son, the other on the invisible heart of the father, who is himself cured of his incredulity by believing the cure which he did not see. We admire the first, but we take scarce any notice at all of the second, which is yet more worthy of God, affords a greater proof of the divinity of Christ, belongs more peculiarly to his mission, and is less communicable to prophets and other holy men. It is of this miracle, O Lord, that I stand in need; it is this which I beg of thee, as being the Saviour of my soul and the sovereign Physician for all the diseases of my heart.

51. And as he was now going down, his servants met him, and told *him*, saying, Thy son liveth. 52. Then inquired he of them the hour when he began to amend. And they said unto him, Yesterday at the seventh hour the fever left him.

The efficaciousness of the word of Christ, even absent, taught his disciples thus early that his departure into heaven ought not in the least to diminish their trust and confidence in his assistance. His word performs that which it signifies, because it is the sign of his will, and his will is his omnipotence itself. The fevers which affect the body are generally healthful to the soul; and therefore we ought to be more earnest in praying for a good use of them than for their cure, and much less should we desire a miracle to this purpose. Those fevers only which affect the soul are obstacles to salvation; and nothing must be spared to obtain their cure. Say to me, O Jesus, after an effectual manner, Thy soul is healed? Say to the church, who pours out her sighs before thee in behalf of so many weak and diseased children, "Thy son liveth."

53. So the father knew that it *was* at the same hour in the which Jesus said unto him, Thy son liveth: and himself believed, and his whole house.

It is not sufficient that we ourselves are convinced of the miracles which God has wrought for us: we must likewise assert the truth of them to others, that God may be glorified thereby, and that the church may reap that fruit from them which he designed she should. This family had not been converted, if this father had contented himself with only believing the miracle, and returning thanks to God in the private recesses of his heart. The publication of the divine graces and favours is an engagement to gratitude and acknowledgment; and, considering our own unfaithfulness, we cannot lay ourselves under too many engagements to perform any duty. This nobleman is an example of a master of a family intent on making all the favours and mercies which God has showed him instrumental to the spiritual advantage thereof. The piety of a father or of a superior is a grace belonging to the head, which should be diffused throughout all the members: and when God intends to save a family or society, the seed of this grace is generally sown in the head thereof.

54. This *is* again the second miracle *that* Jesus did, when he was come out of Judea into Galilee.

The exactness of the evangelist is serviceable to the faith, and tends to confirm the truth of the miracles of Jesus Christ. The first, wrought at Cana, established the faith of the heads of the church; the second gained a whole family thereto. Both were designed to instruct the people of Nazareth at a distance, and to show them plainly who he was, without exciting either their envy or contempt by his presence.

CHAPTER V.

SECT. I.—THE POOL.—THE MAN WHO WAS DISEASED THIRTY-EIGHT YEARS.

1. After this there was a feast of the Jews; and Jesus went up to Jerusalem.

We find our blessed Saviour, at all times and on all occasions, exact in observing the laws and usages of religion, in celebrating the festivals, in edifying his neighbour by a constant performance of the duties of piety, and in seeking all opportunities to prove his mission, to instruct the people, and to comfort the elect, by showing them the Saviour so much desired and expected.

2. Now there is at Jerusalem by the sheep *market* a pool, which is called in the Hebrew tongue Bethesda, having five porches. 3. In these lay a great multitude of impotent folk, of blind, halt, withered, waiting for the moving of the water.

A great number of diseases and diseased persons are necessary to represent the state and condition to which man is reduced by sin: so miserable is he, and full of infirmity from his very birth. He is nothing but weakness, corruption, and blindness, utterly unable to do the least good, and in him all grace and virtue are exhausted and withered away. This, O my Saviour, is what I should have been eternally in thy sight, if, after having been so long expected, thou hadst not come down among us by thy incarnation. How great is the debt which I owe thee for having moved this water in my behalf, which has made me whole! Finish, Lord, what thou hast begun.

4. For an angel went down at a certain season into the pool, and troubled the water: whosoever then first after the troubling of the water stepped in was made whole of whatsoever disease he had.

We must wait for the moments of grace and mercy, which God has reserved to his sovereign power for the conversion of souls, not passing our time in idleness, but in labour, humility, and vigilance. The grace of repentance is a thing very rare: a true penitent, who in every respect deserves that name, is almost as difficult to be found as a phœnix. To wait for the angel's coming down, either by the pool's side or in one of the porches, is to desire, implore, and wait for the spirit of repentance, in order to perform it every one in his proper state. Whoever fully understands the value of this grace should make great haste, should use violence toward himself, and not lose a moment in casting himself into this healing pool. It is a holy ambition in a person to be desirous of stepping first into it, as looking upon himself to be the first or chiefest of sinners. The trouble which we meet with in repentance is a trouble of grace, which the dread of the divine judgments raises in our minds to no other end but to procure us a substantial peace and an everlasting calm. O peace of a good conscience! O perfect cure! what ought we not to do in order to obtain and enjoy thee?

5. And a certain man was there, which had an infirmity thirty and eight years.

God often makes choice of the greatest sinners, to show forth in them the greatness of his mercy and the power of his grace. The more destitute we are of human aid and assistance, the more right have we to hope for that of God. Though the disease of our soul be inveterate and incurable, yet it is not so in respect of the almighty Physician. This is a very great comfort even for the greatest sinners. Pastors ought to apply themselves with the greatest care to those who have the greatest need: to these the preference is due.

6. When Jesus saw him lie, and knew that he had been now a long time *in that case*, he saith unto him, Wilt thou be made whole?

The look which Christ casts upon this paralytic is an emblem of that internal look of mercy which he casts upon a sinner while he lies grovelling on the earth through the corruption of his heart, and depressed under the weight of his sins. In vain would the sinner endeavour to conceal from him the wounds and ulcers of his heart: Christ knows them better than he himself does. When the body is out of order, the will has no need of a physician to dispose it to desire health, because it is not that which is indisposed, unless it be perhaps in desiring health either too eagerly or to a bad purpose. But in the disease of the soul, it is the will itself which is indisposed; and its greatest illness is, that it loves its disease, and hates and avoids health. We cannot therefore be made whole and cured of our sins unless we be willing: but it is God who produces in us both the will and the effect; he causes us to desire that which he designs to give.

7. The impotent man answered him, Sir, I have no man, when the water is troubled, to put me into the pool: but while I am coming, another steppeth down before me.

It is the first beginning of a cure, for a man to know the need he has of a good director of the conscience, to guide him to the healing pool of repentance, and to put him into it. The more uncommon such persons are, the more care must be taken in choosing well. Before a sinner makes this choice, he ought frequently to address himself to God after this manner:—Lord, I have no man to whom I can intrust my heart; who knows how to manage and improve those motions of attrition by which it is stirred and troubled; who will not flatter my contrary passions and inclinations, but has knowledge and prudence, vigilance and application, strength and resolution, sufficient to put me into the exercises of a penitential life.—It is necessary to wait for such a man, to delay our choice rather than to make a bad one; but above all, to implore the assistance of that invisible man without whom no other is able to do any thing

8. Jesus saith unto him, Rise, take up thy bed, and walk.

Observe here three effects of the cure of the soul: (1.) It forsakes its sin. (2.) It lays aside the marks, and declines all the occasions thereof. (3.) It performs the contrary actions. It is in this respect that a spiritual director ought to show some courage and resolution, and to make use of his authority, but to do it with mildness and the discreet methods of charity. Christ causes the sinner to do that which he commands. He gives the heart strength to rise from the earth, arms to undertake works of mortification, and feet to walk in the way of God's commandments and of penitential exercises. A spiritual guide or director cannot give these feet, these arms, or this strength; but he ought to beg them for the person under his care, and that with so much the greater earnestness and perseverance, as the penitent is less able to do it, and does it less himself.

9. And immediately the man was made whole, and took up his bed, and walked: and on the same day was the sabbath.

It is a miracle which happens very seldom, for a man to be delivered in an instant from his sins and evil habits, and from the weakness which generally attends them. God sometimes works this miracle to manifest his power, and to inspire confidence into sinners; but he most commonly lets them feel their weakness, and struggle with their vicious habits, on purpose to humble them by the remembrance of their sins, to make them apprehensive of a relapse, and to oblige them to be diffident of themselves, and to have recourse to him by prayer. Tractableness and obedience to the directions given, is a virtue very necessary to a penitent who is in good hands. It gives strength to the weak, settles them in a state of great peace and satisfaction, and draws down upon them abundance of graces.

10. ¶ The Jews therefore said unto him that was cured, It is the sabbath day; it is not lawful for thee to carry *thy* bed.

The most discreet directors of the conscience always meet with persons who control and censure their conduct, and who know how to cover their spirit of malice, envy, and self-interest with the specious pretence of religion, and a feigned love of the divine law. It is the property of Pharisees to decry the pastors of the church, and to raise a distrust in the mind of penitents by vain scruples and a false tenderness of conscience. All the notice we are to take of such malicious persons is to despise, to leave them to themselves after Christ's example, and to persevere in doing our duty.

11. He answered them, He that made me whole, the same said unto me, Take up thy bed and walk.

True obedience consists in complying rather with the author and the spirit of the law than with the letter. He who has a good director of his conscience, has a good warrant for his conduct. A real cure of a man's passions, received in following his directions, is the best assurance he can have of the approbation of God. It is a right way of reasoning to argue thus:—This spiritual director has cured me of my vanity, of my fondness for the world, of my inclination to gaming, luxury, and sloth, and of my other vicious habits: I ought therefore to rely upon his conduct, and despise whatever is alleged against him without proof in order to render him suspected to me. As it is by real cures that true physicians are distinguished from quacks, so it is by the change of the manners of penitents that good directors of the conscience are known.

12. Then asked they him, What man is that which said unto thee, Take up thy bed and walk?

We are too often apt to make inquiries of this nature, which proceed from envy, jealousy, and self-interest, concerning a spiritual guide who is faithful to his ministry, only that we may find out somewhat for which we may decry him. "What man is that," who causes others to renounce ambition and pleasure, and would have them walk so uprightly in the ways of God? His works speak for him: and those likewise of these impertinent inquirers show plainly what they are.

13. And he that was healed wist not who it was: for Jesus had conveyed himself away, a multitude being in *that* place.

Christ, by conveying himself away, admonishes his ministers not to expect applause after the doing some remarkable action, but to hide and conceal themselves. A disinterested director of the conscience studies only how he may be serviceable to souls for the sake of God, and never thinks of making the least temporal advantage to himself by the direction of them. Spiritual guides and penitents should not know one another any further than in what relates to the cure of the soul; nor should directors of the conscience make their relation too much known, or employ to their advantage that interest which the nature of their office necessarily gives them.

14. Afterward Jesus findeth him in the temple, and said unto him, Behold, thou art made whole: sin no more, lest a worse thing come unto thee.

Let us learn from these words, (1.) That diseases and afflictions are punishments of sin, and, consequently, that the best remedy we can apply to them is repentance and conversion. (2.) That these punishments ought to serve as instructions;

and that, after the cure either of our bodies or our souls, we are obliged to manifest a very great humility and a profound gratitude toward God. (3.) That relapses are more dangerous, and more severely punished. (4.) That one of the chief cares of a spiritual guide or director, who has laboured in the conversion of a soul, and been blessed with success, is to remind it from time to time of the great favour it has received, of the sad condition out of which it has been recovered, and to secure it against relapses. (5.) That a spiritual director ought not to lose sight of a soul which he has converted; but that he ought even to seek it out, to improve the beginnings of its new life. And, (6.) That it is in the temple, and at the foot of the altar, that a penitent soul ought to be found, in prayer, in performing the duties of religion, in the presence of God, and in recollection. It is there that it will find Jesus Christ, and receive new graces and instructions.

15. The man departed, and told the Jews, that it was Jesus, which had made him whole.

It requires abundance of prudence to speak of the graces we have received, and of those by whose ministry we have received them. Men sometimes think to gain new admirers of the works and mercies of God, and they only stir up envy, and kindle a persecution against his servants.

16. And therefore did the Jews persecute Jesus, and sought to slay him, because he had done these things on the sabbath day.

Every thing conspires to make Christ suffer; and even the gratitude and acknowledgments of those who love him contribute thereto. It belongs to the fidelity of a Christian not to abstain from doing good, and especially from works of charity, for fear either of giving a seeming occasion of offence to others, or of receiving ill treatment from them. Whenever God visibly authorizes an action which appears contrary to his law, he himself interprets his own law, or dispenses with it. A strange way this of judging of the conduct of Christ, as well as of his ministers!—to fix only upon that which is blamable in appearance, and to consider no part of that which God does in justification of it. Blind wretches! not to discern the works of God's omnipotence from the actions of men; nor, among the latter, to distinguish those of necessity and charity, which could not possibly be prohibited, from common and ordinary actions, which the law forbade on the sabbath day.

SECT. II.—CHRIST'S SERMON TO THE JEWS.—THE SON DOES WHATEVER THE FATHER DOETH, IS JUDGE, AND RAISES THE DEAD.

17. ¶ But Jesus answered them, My Father worketh hitherto, and I work.

See here a most high and divine apology for the pretended violation of the Sabbath. Let us here admire how God makes the perverseness of the enemies of the truth subservient to the manifestation of the most sublime truths of religion, and how he instructs his elect while in all appearance he speaks only to his enemies. The first reason which Christ here gives of his conduct on this occasion is, that he is God, and that the Jewish Sabbath is not at all obligatory with respect to him. That rest and complacency which he took in his works after the creation of the world, and which he intended should be honoured by the rest of the Sabbath, does by no means hinder either the eternal operations of his divine understanding and adorable will, which terminate in the generation of the Son and the procession of the Holy Ghost; nor the operation of his providence, which preserves, governs, and makes all creatures act; nor the operation of his Spirit, either as to the miraculous effects produced on corporeal beings, or the effects of grace in spiritual. The Son, being God equally with the Father, does all things as well as he: they having eternally but one and the same virtue, majesty, substance, power, will, operation, etc. The creatures, every one according to its state and condition, ought by a quiet and constant labour to honour that God who is continually working amid his eternal rest. A soul who knows to what end it was created, is incessantly aspiring after that unity of action in heaven which is to succeed the variety and multiplicity of our actions here on earth. Let us take great care, by a union of mind and will with God in whatever we do, to prepare ourselves for that unity which is promised us for all eternity.

18. Therefore the Jews sought the more to kill him, because he not only had broken the sabbath, but said also that God was his Father, making himself equal with God.

Christ is the martyr of truth and charity, who exposes himself to the danger of death, rather than abandon the miserable, or not assert his divinity, when the glory of his Father required it. Is this the gratitude and acknowledgment which men owe thee, O Saviour of the world! for having vouchsafed to manifest thyself unto them, and to reveal a truth upon which their salvation entirely depends? This is the lot and portion of truth upon earth. Those who preach the most saving truths, must expect to be contradicted and exposed. This contradiction is instrumental to the sanctification of the preacher, the glory of God, and the triumph of truth itself; but it tends to the condemnation of the world, and is the cause of the judgments of God.

19. Then answered Jesus and said unto them, Verily, verily, I say unto you, The Son can do nothing of himself, but what he seeth the Father do: for what things soever he doeth, these also doeth the Son likewise.

The second reason of the conduct of Christ in the pretended violation of the Sabbath, and by which he confounds the malice of the Jews, in revealing the most sublime truths of Christianity, is, that he may make known that he is not only God, but likewise the Son of God, who receives from his Father, together with his divine essence, his whole knowledge, will, designs, and power, as also a holy and adorable necessity of doing by him what things soever he doeth himself. O inability, almighty and infinitely perfect, whereby God is unchangeably all that he is eternally, without any possibility of being otherwise! The Father cannot act any otherwise than of himself, as being the beginning without beginning. The Son cannot act of himself, since he receives of the Father his essence, power, and will, by his eternal origin and birth, yet without any imperfection or dependence. To whom does it belong to adore this mystery of the Word proceeding from the understanding of the Father, but to those for whose sake he humbled himself in stooping to be born in and of the flesh? To do that which he seeth the Father do, is to do it by a will and power flowing from the Father by way of light and knowledge. Let us adore these incomprehensible mysteries, and, like true children of God, love to imitate them in doing nothing merely of our own will, but with a dependence upon God and Jesus Christ as the principle and pattern of all our actions.

20. For the Father loveth the Son, and showeth him all things that himself doeth: and he will show him greater works than these, that ye may marvel.

The third reason of the conduct of Christ in the pretended violation of the Sabbath, is because, that as Son of God incarnate, and the sole object of the love and confidence of his Father, he observes only his commands, being the person who executes all the designs of his love toward his church, of which he is the head. In this quality he has received of him a full knowledge, and as it were a draught of all his designs, which he is punctually to follow in order to accomplish them by his human nature, as by the instrument of his divine, united to the divine nature itself. How adorable are these two communications made to the Son in his two different births: the one eternal, by the natural and necessary fruitfulness of the Father's understanding; the other temporal, by the free and gratuitous kindness and mercy of his will! The miraculous cures performed by Christ are but an introduction to the wonders of his mission. These are for us rather than for the Jews. Let us admire, adore, thank, and praise God, for all the great things he has done for us by his Son.

21. For as the Father raiseth up the dead, and quickeneth *them;* even so the Son quickeneth whom he will.

The proof of these three reasons of Christ's conduct in the pretended violation of the Sabbath—namely, because he is God, the Son of God equal to his Father, and the general dispenser of his designs concerning men, is drawn from his prerogatives and functions in these three qualities. For his first prerogative and function is to give life. The prophets both healed sick persons and raised the dead, but not one of them did either to prove that he was the Son of God, ascribing to himself a power of raising the dead equal to that of the Father, or asserting that he quickened whom he would, or foretelling miracles a long time before they came to pass. Of what nature soever the life be, it comes from thee, O Jesus, as the author and principle of all life in conjunction with thy Father, and as the first-fruits of life both in time and eternity. I adore thee, therefore, as restoring life to the dead even in the days of thy mortal life. I give myself to thee as restoring the life of grace to sinners from the highest heavens. And I wait for thee as the fountain and pattern of the eternal life of thy elect at thy second coming.

22. For the Father judgeth no man, but hath committed all judgment unto the Son:

The second prerogative and function of Christ is, to be the universal Judge of the quick and the dead. To him belongs all judgment, visible and invisible, particular and general, temporal and eternal, either by withdrawing grace, or inflicting punishment. I own and adore thee, O Jesus, as my judge, and as the sovereign disposer of life and death. My lot is in thy hands; for thou dispenseth thy graces according to the measure which thou hast settled, and appointest punishments according to the degree and demerit of the sins. Judge me, O Lord, not in thy anger, but in thy mercy. Punish me in this world, not in the other: not by withdrawing thy Holy Spirit from me, or casting me out of thy sight, but rather by depriving me of the carnal satisfactions of this life, and the fatal prosperity of this corrupt world.

23. That all *men* should honour the Son, even as they honour the Father. He that honoureth not the Son honoureth not the Father which hath sent him.

The third prerogative of Jesus Christ is, to be honoured with the same honour which is paid to his Father; as being his only Son, appointed by him heir of all things according to his human nature, and Lord of all things according to his divine; as being his envoy and ambassador, not barely representing his adorable majesty, but possessing it indivisibly with him; and as being his living image, an honorary image which does not by some particular features just give a faint idea of his greatness, but which really contains all his perfections, is the very brightness of his glory, and the eternal and subsisting character of his essence. It is the design of God to cause his Son Jesus Christ to be honoured, to receive honour himself only in and by him, and to own none for his true worshippers but Christians who bear the name of his Christ; and yet the generality of Christians apply themselves less to him than to his servant. Great God! awaken in this age, I beseech thee, a spirit of devotion toward thy Son, and cause him to be honoured in the church as he ought.

24. Verily, verily, I say unto you, He that heareth my word, and believeth on him that sent me, hath everlasting life, and shall not come into condemnation; but is passed from death unto life.

The fourth prerogative and function of Christ is, to bring the word of his Father to men; to make his own word the seed of faith, and to cause it by faith to become the necessary means of escaping the condemnation of Adam, of rising again to the life of grace, and of enjoying that which is eternal. Observe here the chief points necessary to salvation: (1.) To hear the word of the gospel of Jesus Christ. (2.) To believe and put our trust in God. (3.) To believe the doctrine of the Trinity—a God who sends, a God who is sent, and a God who is the Spirit and love of both—one only God in three persons. (4.) To believe the incarnation of the Son sent by the Father. (5.) To believe the fall of Adam, his condemnation to the death of body and soul, and original sin, which renders his fall and condemnation common to all his posterity. (6.) To believe the necessity of a Redeemer in order to our passing from death unto life. (7.) To hope for everlasting life. Grant, O Jesus, that I may truly honour thee in adhering steadfastly to thy word with a lively faith, in feeding upon it in hope of the blessed life hereafter, and in practising it by charity.

25. Verily, verily, I say unto you, The hour is coming, and now is, when the dead shall hear the voice of the Son of God: and they that hear shall live.

The (8th) point necessary to salvation is, to believe the resurrection of the body and the immortality of the soul.

Christ makes his voice to be heard equally by the dead and by the most hardened sinners, and restores to the latter the life of the soul, and to the former that of the body. O Jesus, who art the word of life, the life itself made manifest to men, life eternal which was in the Father as the first production of intellectual life in God himself, and as the principle of the living, subsisting, and consubstantial love of the divine Persons,—to thee only it appertains to be the life of the children of God, and the source of all life in men, whether spiritual or corporeal, natural or supernatural, mortal or immortal, of grace or of glory; and such thou art by the ministry of thy word, to honour thyself as the eternal life and word, and to teach us to honour thee as such, and to depend upon thee in all the uses and effects of life and of the word, which thou hast been pleased to communicate to us out of thy abundant fulness.

26. For as the Father hath life in himself; so hath he given to the Son to have life in himself; 27. And hath given him authority to execute judgment also, because he is the Son of man.

The authority of Jesus Christ as head of the church and envoy of his Father, is comprised in these two qualities of Saviour and Judge. As Saviour, he delivers from death and bestows life; and he bestows it as being essential life, and the fountain of all life in quality of Son of God. As Judge, he punishes and condemns to death, and will alone exercise this power of judging the world in a plain and sensible manner; because he alone rendered himself visible by the incarnation, and he alone is Son of God and Son of man together. I adore thee, O Jesus, who judgest both the quick and the dead invisibly with thy Father, as Son of God, and who wilt judge them visibly in thy Father's name, as Son of man.

28. Marvel not at this: for the hour is coming, in the which all that are in the graves shall hear his voice,

No, Lord, my faith scruples not in the least to believe that death heard thy voice from the bed of Jairus's daughter, from the coffin of the widow's son, and from the grave of Lazarus; because I believe likewise, without the least scruple, that dust and ashes will hear it from the centre of the earth and from all parts of the world, and that death will obey thee everywhere and forever. Let my heart, O Jesus, not be deaf to thy voice, when thou vouchsafest to speak to it in order to destroy in it some part of the death of sin! Happy is that person whom Christ has caused to hear the voice of his grace from the very lowest abyss of his sin, and who has been obedient to his call! What gratitude and acknowledgment is due to him for so great a benefit!

29. And shall come forth; they that have done good, unto the resurrection of life; and they that have done evil, unto the resurrection of damnation.

According to these words of Christ, there is no medium between good and bad actions, with respect to salvation; between the resurrection of life and the resurrection of damnation. There are but two sorts of love, from which all our desires and actions proceed: the love of God, which does every thing for his sake, and which is rewarded by him; and the love of ourselves and of the world, which does not ultimately refer that to God which ought to be referred to him, and which for this very reason becomes bad. Let us think seriously upon this matter: we shall come forth out of our graves such as we enter in, destined either to a blessed and eternal life for our good works, or to eternal death for our sins. Who would not courageously apply himself to good works, which will make so prodigious a difference and distinction between men?

30. I can of mine own self do nothing: as I hear, I judge: and my judgment is just; because I seek not mine own will, but the will of the Father which hath sent me.

The sovereign power is given to Jesus Christ, as head of the church, to form it in succeeding ages by the infusion of his Spirit and life, and to judge mankind at the end of the world, in raising them either to life or condemnation. But this sovereign power of this divine Head of the church depends originally upon the knowledge and will of the Word, which are those of the Father. Christ, as man, has no thoughts, designs, desires, or inclinations of himself; and he neither quickens nor judges any one by a choice which is arbitrary, and independent on the inspiration, conduct, and direction of the Word to whom he is united. The injustice of our judgments and actions proceeds either from the darkness of our understanding or from the corruption of our will. Every thing is just in Christ, because every thing in him is conformable to the truth and the will of his Father. Render me, O divine Word, attentive to that which thou speakest to me, and so faithful as to desire nothing but what is agreeable to thy will! Hinder by thy grace, I beseech thee, any secret design of doing always my own will, from darkening my judgment in relation to the things of God and eternal salvation!

SECT. III.—CHRIST DOES NOT BEAR WITNESS OF HIMSELF.—JOHN A BURNING AND A SHINING LIGHT.

31. If I bear witness of myself, my witness is not true.

How false then is the testimony or witness which the proud person bears to himself in his own heart, without having the testimony of his works, and having against himself that of his own infidelities and miseries? Those reformers who have no other testimony of their mission than that which they give to themselves, do they deserve to be so much as heard! No witness whatever ought to be more suspected by us, and is more justly liable to exception, than ourselves, when we are the only persons who speak to our own advantage. We imagine we see in ourselves the good which we have not; and we do not see the evil which we really have.

32. ¶ There is another that beareth witness of me; and I know that the witness which he witnesseth of me is true. 33. Ye sent unto John, and he bare witness unto the truth.

John is the first witness of Jesus Christ, by a wonderful dispensation of the providence of the Father in relation to his Son, causing another to bear witness of him before he should bear witness of himself. Humility does not allow us to be the first in speaking in our own behalf, without great necessity. It is one mark of a divine mission for a person, before his appearing in the world, to have some declaration from God concerning him: a mark which no authors of heresy ever had. There are several circumstances in John which render his testimony unexceptionable:—(1.) He is consulted by the very enemies of Christ as a holy and extraordinary person. (2.) He is perfectly free from all self-interest, having declined making the least advantage by his own reputation. (3.) He is sincere, undaunted, and so averse to all kinds of flattery that he reproves Herod at the hazard of his liberty and life. (4.) He was so far from having been solicited or courted by Christ, that he had not yet so much as seen him.

34. But I receive not testimony from man: but these things I say, that ye might be saved.

We ought never to omit any thing which may be instrumental to the salvation of souls; yet we must avoid ostentation in whatever we do. It is the part of prudence, as well as humility, not to be forward in endeavouring to engage others in favourable discourses concerning us: it belongs to God to open their mouths in our commendation. A pastor should not be jealous of his own reputation, but only so far as it concerns the salvation of his flock and the honour of the church: to promote these is the sole end to which he ought to make the esteem of men subservient.

35. He was a burning and a shining light: and ye were willing for a season to rejoice in his light.

Only to shine is but vanity; to burn without shining is not sufficient. To burn with the love of God, and to enlighten our neighbour by instruction and good example,—this is the perfection of the pastoral charity, and the completion of the ministry. Wo to those extinguished lamps, in which neither the light of truth nor the heat of charity can be found! Wo to those people and souls who find both these qualities in their pastors only to their own condemnation, like the Jews! When a light rises in the church, it darts forth at first a lustre, at which the world itself rejoices; but this lasts not long. The world always loves its own darkness better than light, and endeavours to extinguish, in the end, the light which opposes its darkness. We have great reason to fear lest we should be of the number of those souls who rejoice at the brightness of the light or reputation of a preacher or spiritual director, and perform not that which he requires of them in order to their salvation.

36. ¶ But I have greater witness than *that* of John: for the works which the Father hath given me to finish, the same works that I do, bear witness of me, that the Father hath sent me.

The miraculous works of Christ are the second witness which bear testimony of him. The testimony of men, when not supported by that of works, is of little or no account. The opinions of men change, and ours change concerning them, as those of the Jews did in respect of John; but works continue always the same. Let us never grow weary of reminding our brethren who are wandered out of the way of what God is never weary of reminding us in his word, namely, that their apostles were only seducers, having had neither forerunners to introduce them, nor miraculous works to authorize them, nor voice of God to approve them, nor Scripture to foretell and point them out.

37. And the Father himself, which hath sent me, hath borne witness of me. Ye have neither heard his voice at any time, nor seen his shape.
38. And ye have not his word abiding in you: for whom he hath sent, him believe ye not.

God the Father is the third witness who bears testimony of Jesus Christ. He speaks to men by his incarnate Word. He who will not own and receive the Son, and the word of salvation which he delivers, shall never know God, whom we cannot possibly either hear with the ears or see with the eyes of the body, but only with the ears and eyes of faith in his word. If we have the word of God in our mind and mouth alone, and have it not abiding in our heart, we have it only after a Jewish manner, and to our own condemnation.

SECT. IV.—THE SCRIPTURES.—THE LOVE OF HONOUR HINDERS FAITH.—MOSES CONDEMNS THE JEWS.

39. ¶ Search the Scriptures; for in them ye think ye have eternal life: and they are they which testify of me.

All the Scriptures, which are full of Jesus Christ, are a fourth witness in his favour. They are mines of gold: we must search and, as it were, dig very deep in them, by means of study, prayer, and meditation, in order to find Jesus Christ. The ill use which these people made of the Scriptures hinders not our blessed Lord from encouraging and pressing them to read them all with care. They do indeed contain eternal life—not for those who, like the Jews, mind only the letter, are intent on carnal promises, and put their whole confidence in them knowing nothing of their spirit and design—but for those who by a deep search discover Christ in them, and place all their hopes of salvation in him alone. Teach me thyself, O Lord, to seek, to find, and to relish thee in these divine books.

40. And ye will not come to me, that ye might have life.

It is a dreadful proof of hardness of heart in the Jews, that they should choose rather to adhere to a law of death, than to go to Christ, to whom this very law refers and guides them, as to the author and fountain of life. How much more hardened, then, is the heart of a Christian who has already received it, and tasted the fruits thereof, if he still prefer the death of sin before it! What discouragement, what despair will not so soft a reproof, so tender and preventing a love, remove! But every thing is hard and difficult to him whose heart is hardened. To keep at a distance from Christ, is to avoid and fly from life: it is in vain to seek it anywhere else.

41. I receive not honour* from men. [* *Fr.* My glory.]

To see the earnestness of the Son of God in soliciting us to put our trust and confidence in him, and in drawing sinners after him, one would imagine that this honour and glory depended upon their faith, and that he could not be happy unless they were so. No, Lord, thy glory has not the least dependence on ours; and the esteem of men cannot possibly either tempt thee or increase thy happiness. But we are those who, without thee, must necessarily be eternally miserable.

42. But I know you, that ye have not the love of God in you.

To see the great zeal of the Jews for the observance of the Sabbath, and for the law of God, should we not be apt likewise to imagine that their hearts were inflamed with the love of him. And yet all this was nothing but the love of themselves, and of human glory, which they would fain acquire from the gifts of God. How common is this false zeal! How deceitful is it! There is in these persons abundance of pride, vanity, and delusion; but they have not the least degree of the love of God in them. Do thou vouchsafe, O Lord, to shed abroad this love in our hearts—thou, whom the extreme want thereof, which thou sawest in mankind, drew down from heaven!

43. I am come in my Father's name, and ye receive me not: if another shall come in his own name, him will ye receive.

See here some plain and evident marks that they were never animated with the love of God, and that they are fallen under great delusion. The first is, that they have received persons who came in their own name, having no mark of a divine mission, at the same time that they have rejected those who were authorized by sanctity of life, by the gifts of the Holy Ghost, etc.

44. How can ye believe, which receive honour one of another, and seek not the honour that *cometh* from God only?

The second mark is, that pride, and the love of vain-glory—two vices most opposite to faith and salvation—have been the distinguishing character of these heads of a party; whereas that of the apostles, and of apostolical men, consisted in humility, and in carefully avoiding all human glory.

45. Do not think that I will accuse you to the Father: there is *one* that accuseth you, *even* Moses, in whom ye trust.

The third mark, which shows that these men are mistaken, and likewise have not the love of God, is, that the very Scripture alone, in which they put their whole confidence, is sufficient to accuse, convict, and condemn them as seducers and corrupters of the word of God. A real delusion and error is sometimes concealed under a false reverence for the word of God, a false confidence in Christ, and a false love of religion. Suffer yourselves, dear brethren, to be convinced and condemned by the truth of the Scripture. Whoever does not follow the example of the saints, must expect to have them for accusers.

46. For had ye believed Moses, ye would have believed me: for he wrote of me.

The fourth mark or proof of delusion and error is, that they have not, and cannot possibly have, a right understanding of the Scriptures. The law and the Scripture speak only of Jesus Christ. He is the key of the books of the Old Testament, which we can never understand nor relish unless we read them with a view to him, and that entire, as consisting of head and members, and observing in them every thing which concerns his body the church.

47. But if ye believe not his writings, how shall ye believe my words?

The fifth mark or proof of delusion is, that they have assumed to themselves a power to believe or not believe what they think fit, to despise the authority of the church and of Christ himself, and to subvert the whole foundation of the faith. Enlighten, Lord, these blind people, and lead them back into the way of faith which they have forsaken. They will believe whatever thou speakest to them by thy word, if thou vouchsafe to write it in their hearts by thy Spirit.

CHAPTER VI.

SECT. I.—THE MIRACLE OF THE FIVE LOAVES.—JESUS RETIRES TO AVOID BEING MADE A KING.

1. After these things Jesus went over the sea of Galilee, which is *the sea* of Tiberias. 2. And a great multitude followed him, because they saw his miracles which he did on them that were diseased. 3. And Jesus went up into a mountain, and there he sat with his disciples.

Jesus here shows his wisdom, in not provoking the envious any longer by his presence; his charity, in removing from them the occasions of sin; his humility, in withdrawing himself from the world after such remarkable actions; his piety, in recollecting himself in retirement after his preaching; his goodness, in not hiding himself from those who follow him; and his preference of the mean and illiterate people, who hearken to the voice of miracles while the learned continue altogether deaf thereto. Let us hearken to that of his virtues, which gives us a more useful lesson than all the miracles which he wrought on the body.

4. And the passover, a feast of the Jews, was nigh. 5. ¶ When Jesus then lifted up *his* eyes, and saw a great company come unto him, he saith unto Philip, Whence shall we buy bread, that these may eat?

When human means fail, God causes his power to appear.

Christ does not work miracles till he has showed the necessity there is for them, to teach us never to ask or desire any without an absolute necessity. He takes occasion from this want, and from the approaching passover, to give his disciples an emblem of the miraculous passover which he is preparing for his church. Since his different miracles denote his different qualities, it is necessary there should be some to show that he is in all respects the pastor of his sheep. Too faithless, too ungrateful is he who distrusts his goodness, providence, and almighty power, for the support and nourishment either of the body or of the soul.

6. And this he said to prove* him: for he himself knew what he would do. [*Fr.* Tempt.]

God tempts us, to prove and exercise our faith; the devil, to weaken and extinguish it. Let us carefully observe and consider these two sorts of temptations, that we may reap profit from them. That of the devil, through the disposal of the divine mercy, tends to make us sensible of our own weakness, and to cure us of having any presumption of our own strength. That of God, has a tendency in itself to make us conceive a more lively belief of his majesty and greatness, and to clear our minds of those mean ideas and human notions which we are apt to entertain concerning his almighty power. Grant that I may know thee, O my God, and that I may know myself.

7. Philip answered him, Two hundred pennyworth of bread is not sufficient for them, that every one of them may take a little.

Infinitely less will be sufficient to satisfy them all, because he who made them all of nothing can likewise feed them all out of nothing. Observe here the common failing and defect of men under their wants: their minds are more intent on the wants themselves, than on the goodness, wisdom, and power of God, who commands us to put our trust in him. It is a sin against the established order of his wisdom, to expect that he should, without any necessity, dispense with the ordinary rules of his providence. It is a sin against the belief of his omnipotence, to desire to subject it to human methods.

8. One of his disciples, Andrew, Simon Peter's brother, saith unto

him, 9. There is a lad here, which hath five barley loaves, and two small fishes: but what are they among so many?

Five loaves and two small fishes are more than enough in his hands who continually multiplies the corn of the earth a hundred-fold, and raises out of her bosom so many good things for the food and nourishment of mankind, of little birds, and of the smallest insects. Whoever is faithful in adoring and praising God for all the benefits he does us by the ordinary methods of his providence, will not find his faith and confidence stagger when he stands in need of extraordinary assistances. The latter are as easy to God as the former; but they afford us a plainer proof of his mindfulness with respect to the wants of particular persons, and of his continual vigilance. It is his will that we should be made sensible of the greatness of our want, that we may set the greater value upon his assistance.

10. And Jesus said, Make the men sit down. Now there was much grass in the place. So the men sat down, in number about five thousand.

It is not so much for the sake of these five thousand men that Christ is going to work this miracle, as for the sake of all those who live in continual submission to the laws of providence. He who feeds here five thousand men in an extraordinary manner, and by a visible miracle, cannot he find means to support this numerous family, which raises in the mind of this father and mother so many uneasy and distrustful thoughts? God works more invisible miracles than visible; and the latter are designed only to strengthen the belief of the former in those persons to whom providence is, as it were, obliged to give some present security. Does not that abundance of grass which God bringeth forth continually for the cattle, justly upbraid men with their infidelity or their distrust?

11. And Jesus took the loaves; and when he had given thanks, he distributed to the disciples, and the disciples to them that were set down; and likewise of the fishes as much as they would.

Every thing wastes in the hands of men: but every thing multiplies in those of the Son of God. Before Christ feeds the body, he feeds and nourishes the soul by the good example of his gratitude and thankfulness to his Father. There is often found in a good pastor greater acknowledgment for that which God confers upon him for the benefit and advantage of his people, than in the people themselves who receive that advantage. Christ feeds only those who, in sitting down, give a proof of their trust and confidence in him by their obedience. Let us in this emblem contemplate our duties with respect to the word of God and to the communion, the fruit whereof is answerable to the disposition of our heart. The more earnestly we hunger after them with a sincere hunger of heart and will, the more benefit do we still receive from them.

12. When they were filled, he said unto his disciples, Gather up the fragments that remain, that nothing be lost.

Every thing which Christ has consecrated by his word or his Spirit ought to be precious to us, and nothing should be lost. We ought to manage our temporal riches to the best advantage, not out of covetousness, but out of respect to the gifts of God. These fragments left by the poor are yet more precious: Christ does not take care about saving them, till the poor have eaten and are satisfied. It is not out of indigence that he causes these fragments to be gathered up, since nothing is beyond the reach of his power; but it is to make known the greatness of the miracle, and to teach the rich themselves not to squander away unprofitably that which they have received at the feast of reading the divine word. Let us lose nothing, let us make some advantage of every thing; for even the least things are precious and nourishing.

13. Therefore they gathered *them* together, and filled twelve baskets with the fragments of the five barley loaves, which remained over and above unto them that had eaten.

The power and bounty of God surpass our wants. The incredulity of man is happily disappointed, when God gives him that which he could not presume either to hope for or to ask. It often happens that the wealth of the rich is diminished and lost, because they neglect to sow in the hands of the poor; while the poor themselves become rich, because they have been liberal and generous, even in the midst of poverty, to those who were in greater want. A pastor, being obliged to feed his flock at all times and seasons, ought to be in a disposition to give that which he has not perhaps at present, but which he will find in the hands of the sovereign Pastor of souls. God pours down his blessing upon such a confidence as this in time of necessity, and the pastor enriches himself while he feeds his people.

14. Then those men, when they had seen the miracle that Jesus did, said, This is of a truth that Prophet that should come into the world.

Miracles are the true marks of an extraordinary mission from God. Christ is that prophet foretold by Moses, (Deut. xviii. 15,) whom God was to raise up from the midst of this people as one of their brethren; to which prediction it is probable Christ himself lately referred the scribes and Pharisees, (chap. v. 46.) Passion shuts their eyes; but gratitude opens those of this illiterate multitude. The worthy receiving of the communion is a source of light for us to know Christ, and of courage to own and confess him. How long, O Lord, hast thou vouchsafed to feed me in this desert, and I neither know nor confess thee yet as I ought! I am daily at thy table, fed with thy word and truth, nourished with thy body, and animated with thy blood, and I yet hesitate to declare myself thy disciple by my life and conversation.

15. ¶ When Jesus therefore perceived that they would come and take him by force, to make him a king, he departed again into a mountain himself alone.

The fruit of receiving the holy communion, or of reading the gospel, must not be for us only to know and make profession of following Christ: they must likewise cause him to reign in our hearts. It is not this reign or kingdom which he avoids: he came on purpose to establish it, and, in order thereto, to teach us by his own example to condemn the pomp of human grandeur, and to decline high stations and dignities, and whatever proceeds from the spirit of the world. Lord, how few are there whose hearts are open to this example, and who, by a holy retirement, disappoint the designs which men have of raising and advancing them in the world!

SECT. II.—CHRIST WALKS UPON THE SEA.—THE PEOPLE FOLLOW HIM.

16. And when even was *now* come, his disciples went down unto the
sea, 17. And entered into a ship, and went over the sea toward Capernaum. And it was now dark, and Jesus was not come to them.

Christ, who was very rarely absent from his disciples, leaves them only in order to pray in the mountains, or to avoid worldly greatness. There are two reasons which not only give pastors a right, but likewise sometimes oblige them to separate themselves from all which is most near and dear to them: (1.) The great occasion they have to seek God, and to unite themselves to him by prayer. (2.) The necessity they may be under of avoiding worldly employments, by a life entirely free not only from all ambition, but from the very suspicion thereof.

18. And the sea arose by reason of a great wind that blew.

Nothing is more to be dreaded than the great wind of temptation, when we are without Jesus Christ, in the darkness of sin, or in the midst of the stormy sea of this world. The devil never fails to assault us with his wicked suggestions, and to use his utmost endeavours to destroy us, when he sees that Christ is not with us, and that our hearts are left in darkness by his absence. Happy are we when this absence and darkness are designed only to try us, when the one does not proceed from anger, nor the other is inflicted upon us as a punishment.

19. So when they had rowed about five and twenty or thirty furlongs, they see Jesus walking on the sea, and drawing nigh unto the ship: and they were afraid.

It frequently happens, that what is designed for our good makes us afraid by the reason of the weakness of our faith. This often falls asleep in the midst of benefits and favours, and requires temptations, dangers, and afflictions to awaken it. We are more sensible how much we stand in need of God and Christ when we fall into want, than when we live in plenty; when we are under the apprehension of evils, than when we continue in the undisturbed enjoyment of good things. Trouble and disorder of mind generally attends temptation in the weak, and is really more dangerous than the temptation itself: because the devil, taking advantage of that trouble and disorder, assaults our faith, raises in our minds a dread of Christ, and renders that suspicious to us which we ought to look upon as our whole light and strength.

20. But he saith unto them, It is I; be not afraid.

The presence and word of Christ remove all fears; but he himself must make men sensible of both, otherwise he is present only to the blind, and speaks only to the deaf. What is man? Nothing but darkness and weakness, when he is in dangers; full of distrust and apprehension of being deceived, when assistance is vouchsafed him; and utterly incapable of doing any thing without Christ at all times, and in all states and dispositions. Lord, what conduct soever thou art pleased to observe toward me, vouchsafe always to speak to me these comfortable words, "It is I;" and thereby secure me both from presumption and despair.

21. Then they willingly received him into the ship:* and immediately the ship was at the land whither they went. [**Fr.* Barque.]

We make a great progress in piety in a very little time, when God is pleased to shed abroad in our hearts his love and grace in great abundance. The barque receives much more assistance from Christ when he enters into it, than he does from the barque. Thus it is with respect to the service of God and Christ: the Master is more useful to the servant than the servant to his Master; and the labours of the ministers of the church more necessary to the salvation of the ministers themselves than to the glory of God. Come, Lord, I beseech thee, to this soul, and vouchsafe to enter into it by new assistances, that it may soon reach the perfection to which it tends. Come to thy church, animate thy ministers with thy Spirit, perfect the saints, gather thy elect together, and give thy whole body its complete fulness and stature, that it may quickly arrive at its own country, its centre, and its eternal rest, which is thyself.

22. ¶ The day following, when the people, which stood on the other side of the sea, saw that there was none other boat there, save that one whereinto his disciples were entered, and that Jesus went not with his

disciples into the boat, but *that* his disciples were gone away alone;
23. Howbeit there came other boats from Tiberias nigh unto the place
where they did eat bread, after that the Lord had given thanks: 24. When
the people therefore saw that Jesus was not there, neither his disciples,
they also took shipping, and came to Capernaum, seeking for Jesus.

Can we forbear seeking Christ with earnestness when we are sensible that we have lost sight of him some time? It is no unprofitable labour to inquire how he came to withdraw himself, why those who fed us in his name have been taken away from us, and frequently to revolve in our minds the graces and benefits we have received from him. Let us be very careful not to neglect those opportunities which God is pleased to give us of finding him again, and of reuniting ourselves to him.

SECT. III.—THE MEAT WHICH PERISHES NOT.—CHRIST THE TRUE BREAD OF HEAVEN.—DOES NOT HIS OWN WILL.—SAVES HIS ELECT.

25. And when they had found him on the other side of the sea, they said unto him, Rabbi, when camest thou hither?

These people desire to be assured of the certainty of his miraculous passage; and it is a holy curiosity and a rational zeal in them, not to suffer the wonderful works of God to be buried in silence.

26. Jesus answered them, and said, Verily, verily, I say unto you, Ye seek me, not because ye saw the miracles, but because ye did eat of the loaves, and were filled.

Few persons seek Jesus Christ for his own sake: the generality do it out of interest. It is good frequently to examine our own hearts and intentions in this respect. We ought to seek God and not his gifts. The common inclination and disposition of people in relation to miracles, was to think only of enjoying the present temporal advantages arising from them, without endeavouring to penetrate into the designs of God in working them. The contemplation of miracles ought to strengthen our faith, to raise our minds up to God, and to fill us with admiration of his greatness and goodness. It is the proper business of pastors, after the example of Christ, to make their people sensible of their failings, and to rectify their faith.

27. Labour not for the meat which perisheth, but for that meat which endureth unto everlasting life, which the Son of man shall give unto you: for him hath God the Father sealed.

The life of a Christian is not an idle and inactive life. Application, fervency, and good works are necessary to nourish piety, and to obtain it of Christ. If we take a view of all states and conditions in the world, is it not true that we shall find almost all mankind entirely taken up either with the care of providing for themselves "the meat which perisheth," or with the thoughts of raising a fortune yet more vain and perishing, as if life were bestowed upon them to no other end and purpose! Who is there who seriously applies his thoughts to "that meat which endureth unto everlasting life?" What man makes it his business to be a Christian, and to live by faith? This is a gift of God, but man must co-operate with it. It is the will of man which believes, but it is God who forms therein the act of believing. None but God can confer this gift upon us; and the Son of man is here said to give it because he is really and truly God, being the express image and character of the Father's substance, and authorized as such by the seal of miracles. Vouchsafe, O Jesus, to be continually in my heart, and to work therein as the author and finisher of my faith!

28. Then said they unto him, What shall we do, that we might work the works of God?

Faith admonishes us to have recourse to God, and to implore his assistance; and the first effect of this assistance is, that the darkness of our understanding is enlightened. So great is this darkness, that we frequently mistake works merely human for works of God. To make works really such, it is necessary that the Spirit of God should be the cause and principle of them: his will their rule, and his glory their end. We have always sufficient occasion to see and acknowledge our own ignorance in the ways of God, and to beseech him to direct us in them. Without his light, the most clear-sighted are but darkness.

29. Jesus answered and said unto them, This is the work of God, that ye believe on him whom he hath sent.

The great work of God in us is that of a lively faith, which worketh by love. Let us, without ceasing, importune him to perfect and complete this work in us. The multiplicity and diversity of the works of the law, which served only to prefigure Christ, and could not justify the sinner, are now reduced to one single means of salvation, namely, Jesus Christ. Thus the law of works, which only exalted and puffed man up, is now entirely reduced to the sole law of faith, which humbles him, and excludes all boasting; because faith, which is the principle of the righteousness of God, is no other than the work of God in us. When will it be, O Jesus, that thou wilt perfect this work in me, by rendering me uniformly obedient to whatever thou requirest of me by faith?

30. They said therefore unto him, What sign shewest thou then, that we may see, and believe thee? what dost thou work? 31. Our fathers did eat manna in the desert; as it is written, He gave them bread from heaven to eat.

What unaccountable blindness, what hardness of heart is this, to ask such a question after so many signs and miracles! And yet this is but a shadow of the present blindness and hardness of sinners, after the accomplishment of all the mysteries of Christ, and after having received so many favours and graces at his hands. Man, full of himself, extols his own works as much as possibly he can. His want of attention, and his insensibility with respect to those of God, cause him either wholly to forget, or little to regard, the greatest wonders of the divine power. To undervalue benefits received is a high instance of ingratitude, and an indignity which makes the patience of Christ appear more eminent and illustrious. It is the atheist who is still seeking after proofs of a Deity, though he walks every day amid apparent miracles, which, having continued from the beginning of the world in one and the same course and order, and with an unchangeable exactness and regularity, are on this very account more to be admired than those which were only transient.

32. Then Jesus said unto them, Verily, verily, I say unto you, Moses gave you not that bread from* heaven; but my Father giveth you the true bread from* heaven. [* *Fr.* Of.]

What strange mildness is this toward such brutish and ungrateful people! We see here in Christ no manner of application and endeavour to set off the greatness of his miracle; but his only care is, to instruct them in the mystery of his incarnation, whereby the bread of angels became the bread of men. He here teaches pastors not to leave their people in error, and under false notions of religion, by showing the Jews that the manna was neither the bread of heaven, nor yet given by Moses. It is the duty of a pastor to use his utmost endeavours to raise the minds of his flock from sensible and corporeal objects to things invisible and eternal; as Christ here raises those of these people from the figure to the truth, from the food of the body to that of the soul. Christ is that wonderful and divine bread which faith alone can discern and know. He is, (1.) The gift of the Father. (2.) An eternal gift, which he never resumes. (3.) The true bread, which gives and sustains the true life. (4.) The true bread of heaven, where he received his celestial and eternal origin, and from whence he came down to have a temporal beginning here on earth.

33. For the bread of God is he which cometh down from heaven, and giveth life unto the world.

He is, (5.) The bread of God, which he alone can give, because he alone begets him of his own substance. He is, (6.) That bread which restores life to sinners, and causes the children of God to live eternally. O bread of God! thou art life indeed, true life, life eternal, the life both of the body and of the soul, and the life not only of one people, but of all nations! Grant that we may seek thee, that we may feed upon thee here below, and be thou ever the nourishment and delight of our hearts!

34. Then said they unto him, Lord, evermore give us this bread.

My God, how closely shut against the truths of salvation is the mind of man before it is enlightened by faith! No dulness, no defect whatever of understanding, should be able to discourage a pastor, according to the example set by the Prince of pastors. This bread is present before their eyes, but it is far from their hearts; and they ask for it without knowing it. Our prayers, O Lord, are perhaps more imperfect sometimes, and yet thou dost not reject them!

35. And Jesus said unto them, I am the bread of life: he that cometh to me shall never hunger; and he that believeth on me shall never thirst.

In the seventh place, Christ is the bread which sustains, strengthens, and perfects life. (8.) He fills and satisfies all his members. There is but one life which deserves this name, and that is the life which we have in Jesus Christ, and of which he is himself the principle and the food to all eternity. We must of necessity be incorporated into this bread in order to receive life from it; and it is by means of a lively faith that we approach Christ, that we enter, as it were, and are changed into him, that we may become a part of this living bread, and be eternally offered therein upon the table and altar of the living God. O eternal Bread, who camest to us by means of the incarnation—eternal Truth, which art alone the end of all our desires, and the only bread which can satisfy my soul—thou fillest me with hope, by discovering thyself so clearly to persons so unworthy as these here before us were! Thou findest in those whom thou quickenest no merit at all, but by quickening them thou createst some in them.

36. But I said unto you, That ye also have seen me, and believe not.

Neither the preaching of Christ, nor his presence, nor his miracles, are sufficient to induce men to believe in him. To effect this, he must speak and preach to the invisible ears of the heart; he must render himself present to it by the gift of faith, and work internal miracles therein. There are abundance of persons in the world whom Christ might justly upbraid in the same manner, after having made himself, as it were, continually visible in his church for so many ages, by the wonders which his Holy Spirit has wrought in it.

37. All that the Father giveth me shall come to me: and him that cometh to me I will in nowise cast out.

Adorable secret this, relating to the gift or present which God makes of his elect to his Son!—a gift which is neither preceded nor caused by any merit, but which is the principle and source of that share which all those who are given to Christ are to have in his merits, that they may obtain some in and by him. None of all these will fail to come to Jesus Christ, and to remain and continue in him by a persevering charity. This is a gift which includes and comprehends in it all others. There is no other reason to be given for the continuance of other persons in incredulity, but only the corruption and voluntary hardness of their heart; but the reason why their corruption is not removed, nor the hardness of their heart surmounted, is a profound and incomprehensible secret. Let us not amuse ourselves with disputing concerning this subject, but let us be contented to admire and adore. A pastor or minister of the church, after the example of Christ, ought to receive all those whom God sends unto him, and to use his utmost endeavours to save them all.

38. For I came down from heaven, not to do mine own will, but the will of him that sent me.

In this life we have, after the example of Christ, but one thing to do, but one thing to seek, and that is the will of God. Let us, in this wise and adorable will, and nowhere else, seek after the reason of the choice of his elect, and of the preference which he gives them in the distribution of his graces. Christ confines himself to this will, and yet human presumption would fain proceed further, and sound the depth of his councils and the secrets of his wisdom. O intolerable rashness! Observe here three main points in relation to bishops and other pastors: (1.) A pure and blameless entrance into the ministry, by a lawful call from God, and by the mission of the church. (2.) The sole end of the ministry, which is to promote the designs and will of God. (3.) The manner of exercising it conformable to the humility of the sovereign Pastor. How low ought that person to stoop, in order to set forward the salvation of souls, who holds the place of a God who came down from heaven!

39. And this is the Father's will which hath sent me, that of all which he hath given me I should lose nothing, but should raise it up again at the last day.

Every bishop, every pastor, ought to look upon all the souls in his diocese or parish as given to Jesus Christ, and frequently to say to himself, that "it is the Father's will that he should lose none of them." Let us with confidence believe that we are of the number of those whom the Father has given to his Son; and let this confidence, which is a part of Christian hope, cause us to serve God with courage, and with the joy of children who expect and wait for an inheritance in heaven. We are in the hands of Christ, as a gift or a trust which God has deposited therein; and have nothing to fear except from our own will. But, Lord, art not thou the absolute master thereof? Christ, in raising up his elect to restore them to his Father, will evidently show the world, which imagined that it had deprived them of all life and destroyed them irrecoverably, that their loss was no other than their salvation.

40. And this is the will of him* that sent me, that every one which seeth the Son, and believeth on him, may have everlasting life: and I will raise him up at the last day. [**Fr.* My Father.]

All those whom God, by an absolute and efficacious will, intends to save through Jesus Christ, are infallibly saved. Observe here three infallible effects of predestination, and of the Father's will as to the salvation of his elect: (1.) Their being called, according to the purpose of his will, and incorporated into Jesus Christ, (ver. 37, 38.) (2.) Their final perseverance, the grace and gift whereof will be infallibly conferred upon them, (ver. 39.) (3.) Everlasting life, which will crown the other gifts, (ver. 40.) Let us often adore this sacred will, which is the principle and source of our sanctification and happiness. It is not without design that mention is here made of it three times together. It is in this will, and not in our own, that we must put our whole trust and confidence. Cause me, O Jesus, to co-operate therewith by mine; and grant that I may have no other will but only to render myself conformable to that of thy Father!

SECT. IV.—THE MURMURING OF THE JEWS.—HE WHO HATH LEARNED OF THE FATHER COMETH TO THE SON.

41. The Jews then murmured at him, because he said, I am the bread which came down from heaven.

Great truths disturb the weak, and blind the wicked, at the same time that they give comfort and consolation to the children of God. Neither the great number of dogs who rend the preachers of the truth, nor the multitude of swine who trample it under their feet, ought to be any obstacle to the feeding of the lambs and the doves. There will be ever in the very church itself murmurers, who will lift up their voice to interrupt the progress of Christian and evangelical truths; but there will be likewise still some religious worshippers and undaunted lovers of them. Let us rather die than be of the number of the former.

42. And they said, Is not this Jesus, the son of Joseph, whose father and mother we know? how is it then that he saith, I came down from heaven?

The meanness of Christ's temporal birth renders the greatness of his eternal birth incredible to carnal men; as the majesty of his divine being has made others question the reality of his human nature. Reason is always mistaken when it pretends to judge by itself, or to make the senses judges of the mysteries of religion, instead of having recourse to the authority of the word of God.

43. Jesus therefore answered and said unto them, Murmur not among yourselves. 44. No man can come to me, except the Father which hath sent me draw him: and I will raise him up at the last day.

See here the admirable meekness and gentleness of Christ toward those very persons who blaspheme him. Who is there among us who could thus patiently endure to have his rights and chief dignity contested? Let us earnestly endeavour to imitate Christ, in not suffering ourselves to be transported with anger against those who oppose the truth. Whoever is thoroughly sensible from whence the difference proceeds, which there is between a teachable and an obstinate person, in respect of the divine word, humbles himself, and adores in secret the power of God's grace over him to whom he shows mercy, and the justice of his conduct in reference to him whom he leaves under his obduracy and perverseness. We cannot obey the voice which calls us to Jesus Christ, except he himself draws us to him in causing us to will that to which we were averse before. Men come to Christ by means of faith and charity; but either of these is a singular and free gift of God. This consideration ought not to discourage us, but to excite in us ardent desires and fervent prayer. It is at the time of the general resurrection that the great distinction and separation will be made in the sight of men, and that the whole business of salvation will be perfected and consummated. It is on this account that Christ repeats these words so often, "I will raise him up at the last day," that we may not undertake to judge before that time.

45. It is written in the prophets, And they shall be all taught of God. Every man therefore that hath heard,* and hath learned of the Father, cometh unto me. [**Fr.* The Father's voice.]

It is the peculiar privilege of the new law, that men are taught and moved by the internal and almighty voice of God. Those who were so before Christ's appearance in the world, belonged to his covenant, and, having received of his Spirit, were Christians by way of anticipation. Grace is therefore that voice of the Father which teaches and instructs men inwardly, and causes them to come unto Jesus Christ. Whoever comes not unto him, after having heard the outward voice of the Son, is not taught by the Father. It is the property of his adorable voice to open of itself the ear of the heart, and to make itself heard by the most deaf, in curing their spiritual deafness. Vouchsafe, O my God, to make us even here below disciples of thy school, that we may be such to all eternity.

46. Not that any man hath seen the Father, save he which is of God, he hath seen the Father.

The school where the Father instructs mankind is a school which is concealed and hidden from the senses, and known only to the Son. God is visible only to the invisible eyes of the heart: these are they which we must open, purify, and expose to this invisible and eternal light. Christ, by the prerogative of his eternal birth, is the witness and channel of all truth, and the source from whence all our knowledge of God is derived. It is therefore in and by thee, O Jesus, that we must seek it; it is from thee alone that we can receive it.

47. Verily, verily, I say unto you, He that believeth on me hath everlasting life.

Christ is the everlasting life of his members: it begins in

this world by faith and charity, and is consummated in the other by glory. Faith is the root, and eternal happiness the fruit: grace gives a right to the treasures of heaven, and glory puts us into possession of them. We have here the earnest, pledge, and first-fruits of them in the Holy Spirit; we shall have the fulness and all the advantages thereof in heaven, by the perfection and consummation of his love in us. Everlasting life is comprised in Jesus Christ; and faith, whereby he dwells in our hearts, gives them eternal life, but hidden like him, and, as it were, wrapped up in the veil of faith.

48. I am that bread of life.

How great and comprehensive is this sentence in its brevity! Christ is life in all respects, and every thing is life in him. He is life eternal by his divine essence; the word of life by his birth from and in the bosom of the Father; the bread of life for the angels from the creation of the world; the bread of life in respect of his own sacred humanity, by means of his incarnation; and the bread of life to men by faith in this world, and by glory in the world to come. He is the principle and author of life, substituted in the place of Adam, who became the principle and author of death to all his posterity. He is the bread of life, which not to eat is sufficient to cause us to die eternally, God having made the life of men to depend upon it; which to eat but once as we ought, would be sufficient to keep us from ever dying, and which we ought to be eating continually, because we ought to believe in him continually, and to be united to him in the most close and intimate manner.

49. Your fathers did eat manna in the wilderness, and are dead. 50. This is the bread which cometh down from heaven, that a man may eat thereof, and not die. 51. I am the living bread which came down from heaven:

What could the Jews expect from a kind of food which was dead and inanimate, but only that it should leave them subject to the death both of the soul and of the body? Such as their law and religion were, such was their food: dead, figurative, and of no manner of virtue or efficacy toward the attainment of the true righteousness, which is the life of the soul. Thou alone, O Jesus, art the true bread! not formed in the air like the manna, and spread upon the face of the earth by the ministry of angels, to preserve this people alive for some time, but born in heaven, sent down to men by the incarnation, ever living and giving life, continually infusing the life of faith and charity into thy members in the wilderness of this world, and a continual source and principle of immortal life in thy saints, on which they will feed eternally without wasting it, without being cloyed therewith, and without desiring any other thing whatever.

SECT. V.—THE LIVING BREAD: THE FLESH OF CHRIST IN THE EUCHARIST.

— If any man eat of this bread, he shall live forever: and the bread that I will give is my flesh, which I will give for the life of the world.

The love of Jesus Christ is liberal and communicative, and that to such a degree that it is not contented till he has given himself; and that not for his own satisfaction or happiness, but for ours. It is not sufficient to thy heart, O Jesus, to unite itself to mine in one respect alone; thy love causes thee to find means of giving thyself to me both many times and in divers manners, and still with new advantage: as my Head, and the Fountain of my life in the incarnation; as my Saviour, and the Victim of my salvation upon the cross; and as my bread and food in the eucharist. O infinite gift! O incomprehensible ways of giving thyself! O divine contrivances of the love of Jesus! O ungrateful, and worse than ungrateful heart of a Christian, if he do not live more to Christ than to himself!

52. The Jews therefore strove among themselves, saying, How can this man give us *his* flesh to eat?

By much reasoning and disputing in a manner altogether human, concerning the mysteries of God, men lose both the faith and the fruit of them. This language of the Jews is that of all those who amuse themselves with vain disputes concerning the gifts of God, instead of receiving them with faith and gratitude. We would fain comprehend the effects of the love and power of God; and these effects are suitable to the love and power of the Creator, on no other account but because they are incomprehensible to the creature. Let us, without the least hesitation, believe the word and promises of God; let us use our utmost endeavours to render ourselves worthy of them; and let us leave to him the care of finding out the proper means to accomplish them.

SECT. VI.—THE FLESH OF CHRIST GIVES LIFE AND IMMORTALITY.

53. Then Jesus said unto them, Verily, verily, I say unto you, Except ye eat the flesh of the Son of man, and drink his blood, ye have no life in you.

Nothing less than the body and blood of Christ is sufficient to sustain the divine life of a Christian. Of what words should Christ have made use to confirm his promise of giving us his flesh to eat and his blood to drink, if these are not sufficient? It is by faith that we live upon this food, though it is by the mouth that we eat it: but it is only by a life and by actions of faith, that we can know whether we live by that which we eat or not.

54. Whoso eateth my flesh, and drinketh my blood, hath eternal life; and I will raise him up at the last day.

He who thoroughly understands the economy of the Christian religion, the main part of which is the sacrifice of Jesus Christ, is sensible of the necessity of this eating of his flesh and drinking of his blood. The church militant of all ages could not possibly have communicated and partaken outwardly of the Victim of the cross, if this Victim had not been represented in all ages by real sacrifices, which promised a communion still more real in a real and subsisting sacrifice. This is the thing, for which, O Jesus, thou hast been pleased to provide by the wonderful contrivance and institution of the eucharistic communion, which is, as it were, a supplement to the sacrifice of the cross, (to which communion was wanting,) a communion which cannot be expressed, and which is necessary to salvation by an implicit desire at least, every grace of Christ having a relation to and dependence upon the holy eucharist. We communicate in this life by a spiritual communion, that we may partake of the mysteries, the merits, and Spirit of Jesus Christ. We shall communicate by a spiritual communion in heaven, that we may partake of the eternal life and immortal glory of Christ, in a soul perfectly happy, and a body raised up at the last day.

55. For my flesh is meat indeed, and my blood is drink indeed.

Yes, Lord, I believe that thou by thy flesh and blood art the true food which preserves my soul from death, and will restore life to my body. Oh, let me not be so unhappy as by the corruption of my heart to turn this bread of life into deadly poison, and to cause this plant of immortality to bring forth fruits of death. Since thy flesh and blood are the meat and drink of my soul, grant me, Lord, the grace not to deprive it of this food by my own negligence. Let my greatest care be to prepare myself for it. Let it be my only grief to see myself deprived thereof for my repeated acts of infidelity!

56. He that eateth my flesh, and drinketh my blood, dwelleth in me, and I in him.

He who eats the flesh of Christ is most closely joined and united to him by charity, and by a union which is, as it were, natural and corporeal. For it is a natural and reciprocal communion between the head and the members, between Jesus Christ and his church. He gives himself to us, and dwells in us: we give ourselves to him, and dwell in him. He is the fulness of his church, and his church of him. He, as it were, feeds on us, and fills himself with us, and grows in us as in his members, that he may arrive at that fulness and perfection which his mystical body ought to have. Grant, O Jesus, that by desiring and engaging thee to come, and dwell, and grow in me, I may answer the desire which thou art pleased to manifest that I should dwell in thee; and let me raise no obstacle in thy way by my irregular desires, and my hunger after earthly things!

57. As the living Father hath sent me, and I live by the Father; so he that eateth me, even he shall live by me.

The Father, in begetting his Word or Son, communicates to him his life; in sending this Son by the incarnation, and uniting him to flesh and blood, he communicates this divine life to the sacred humanity of Christ, who receives this life of, in, and for his Father. Thus the faithful Christian, in receiving the flesh and blood of Jesus Christ, is made partaker of his divine nature, his life, his inclinations, etc., in, by, and for Jesus Christ himself. O my God! what wilt thou bestow upon man in heaven, since even here on earth thou causest him to live so divine a life? O divine life of a Christian soul, which hast thy first original in the bosom of the living Father, who lives of himself, and communicates his life to the Son, and by him to the flesh and blood to which he is united, and by the most lively representation of this adorable flesh and blood to his members, conveying it by this channel into their hearts! This is not the ingenious thought of a mystical divine, who lets his fancy take a flight; it is a plain and literal truth, delivered by the eternal truth itself, and which alone ought to disengage us from every thing which is capable of rendering us unworthy to receive this life, of causing us to lose it, or of weakening it in us.

58. This is that bread which came down from heaven: not as your fathers did eat manna, and are dead: he that eateth of this bread shall live for ever.

The eucharist is the manna of Christians in the desert of this world. Wretched is that person, who, either through disgust or slothfulness, feeds not on it; but more wretched still is he, who, receiving it in sin, or under the habit and love thereof, eats his own judgment and condemnation. If we eat this adorable manna with the ingratitude, infidelity, disgust, murmuring, and untractableness of the Jews, this manna, instead of preserving us from dying, will give us a double death, and instead of leading us toward the promised land, and introducing us thereinto, will carry us at a farther distance and exclude us from it. O living Bread! cause me to live upon and in thee. Bread of heaven! vouchsafe to conduct me thither. O eternal Bread! inspire me with a true desire of eternity, till thou art pleased to put me into possession of that blessed life.

SECT. VII.—THE DISCIPLES OFFENDED.—THE APOSTLES CONTINUE STEADFAST.—ONE OF THEM IS A DEVIL.

59. These things said he in the synagogue, as he taught in Capernaum.
60. Many therefore of his disciples, when they had heard *this*, said, This is a hard saying; who can hear it?

The words of eternal truth are hard sayings, but they are such only to those who have a hard heart. Men must submit their understanding to the yoke of faith, and soften their heart by a tractable disposition. The most saving words are not to all persons words of salvation. The school of Christ is not to all his disciples a school of light and truth. It is to every one of us such as our heart is; because the heart itself is this school. It happens very frequently that those very truths which men would not dare contradict in the gospel, and in the mouth of the Son of God, they are not at all afraid to censure as hard and carried too far, when they meet with them in the writings, or hear them from the mouth of the disciples.

61. When Jesus knew in himself that his disciples murmured at it, he said unto them, Doth this offend you?

Jesus knows the bottom of the heart, and by that means condemns the impiety of his unbelieving disciples. Let us be ashamed to complain that we are not always favourably heard, since we see the most sacred truths exposed to murmuring and contradiction, and made an occasion of scandal or offence. This will ever be the case as long as the world continues what it is, namely, a society of enemies to the truth, and the school of scandal and infidelity. Doubts and scruples in relation to some certain truths may possibly arise in the minds of true disciples; but then, they either suppress them by faith, or humbly propose them with the temper of a disciple, but never murmur, or are offended at them.

62. *What* and if ye shall see the Son of man ascend up where he was before?

When we are perplexed with any doubts concerning matters of faith, we must raise our minds from the humiliations of Christ to the contemplation of his greatness, power, immortality, and divinity. The ascension is a full proof of all the mysteries and truths delivered by the Son of God, and particularly of the incarnation, whereby the bread of God came forth from God, and came down from heaven in becoming man.

63. It is the spirit that quickeneth; the flesh profiteth nothing: the words that I speak unto you, *they* are spirit, and *they* are life.

The flesh of Jesus Christ is, to the children of Adam, the principle of a new life by means of the incarnation, on no other account but only because it is united to the divine Word, which is essentially spirit and life. It is the bread and fountain of life in the eucharist to none but those who have the spirit and life of faith. The body and letter of Christ's words become the bread of life and understanding, when we receive them with the spiritual discernment of faith, and feed upon them with the relish of charity. What abundance of spiritual riches are treasured up in this ark of Christ's body! How many mysteries are concealed under this sacred veil! How much grace and light under the external figures of Christ's word!

64. But there are some of you that believe not. For Jesus knew from the beginning who they were that believed not, and who should betray him.

It is therefore faith which opens this ark, which pierces through this veil, which unfolds these sacred signs, and finds therein the spirit and the life; while infidelity sees nothing but what is carnal, and, consulting only the senses, receives from them an answer only of death. There are two sorts of sacrilegious communions in respect of the body and of the word of Jesus Christ: one by infidelity, which believes nothing therein; the other by sin, which betrays, delivers up, and crucifies Christ, by the abuse either of his body and blood, or of his word. Suffer not, I beseech thee, the least degree of either of these in my heart, O Lord, who searchest the very bottom of it. A man is not necessarily holy for being in the company of holy persons, or even of the most holy Jesus himself; but he must needs be exceeding holy, who endures with so much patience and mildness the company of a traitor, and of other unbelieving persons.

65. And he said, Therefore said I unto you, that no man can come unto me, except it were given unto him of my Father.

The exercise of faith is no less difficult than the practice of other virtues. The grace necessary to both is given to some, and not to others. He who has received it ought to fear, because he may possibly lose it. He who has not received it should hope, because he may yet receive it. Christ describes this by three different characters: being drawn by the Father, (ver. 44,) being taught by the Father, (ver. 45,) and being given of the Father, (ver. 65.) The first denotes the efficaciousness of this drawing or attraction of God. The second shows, that it is an attraction of light and love, which causes us to know the truth, and to love it. The third assures us, that it is altogether free, and is no other than the pure gift of God.

66. ¶ From that *time* many of his disciples went back, and walked no more with him.

Temptation gives an opportunity of discerning true disciples from hypocrites, and such as are disciples only for a time. A preacher or spiritual director may be deserted without his own fault. This is a slight humiliation, which yet is not always borne without concern and trouble. Our blessed Lord, in bearing it himself, sanctifies it, and teaches us to bear it without disturbance. We ought to pity and lament those who loathe and grow weary of truth or virtue, and to humble ourselves through the apprehension either of our having contributed thereto, or of our falling into the same fatal distaste and aversion ourselves.

67. Then said Jesus unto the twelve, Will ye also go away?

Christ stands in need of no man in the world himself; but there is no person in the world who does not stand in need of him. This is a just ground for us to fear, and to humble ourselves under the apprehension, lest we should do something which may oblige him to forsake us. He is not a master who has no concern for his servants, but he would have none but such as engage themselves in his service freely and of their own accord. His only design in trying them, is to give them an occasion of reflecting upon the happiness of their vocation, and to cause them to value it the more. Lord, leave me not thus to my own will. To be willing to go away and leave thee, is to be willing to perish; and I shall infallibly be willing to do it, if thou leavest my will to itself.

68. Then Simon Peter answered him, Lord, to whom shall we go? thou hast the words of eternal life.

There is no master like Jesus Christ. His school is that of eternal life. But what a school, what a master, what doctrine is this! He is himself the very truth which he teaches, the eternal and subsisting, the living and quickening truth; he is life itself, and life eternal, who teaches both truth and life, inspiring them into our understanding by his light, and into our heart by his love. To whom then shall we go, O Jesus, that we may learn to live, and live eternally on the truth? He well deserves to find nothing but delusion and death, who seeks for truth and life from any but from thee alone.

69. And we believe and are sure that thou art that Christ, the Son of the living God.

This is a most perfect profession of faith, which it is of great use frequently to make. There is a faith which is simple and illiterate; and there is one which is more enlightened, and which amounts almost to evidence; but it is such evidence as proceeds from the supernatural light of God, and not from the things themselves, nor from human understanding. There is one sort of learning which is hurtful to faith, namely, worldly learning, which is nothing but pride and ostentation; and there is another sort which edifies, and which supports and strengthens faith: such was that of Paul, who saw Jesus Christ in the Scriptures, and him alone; and to whom the whole order and economy of the events, laws, ceremonies, actions, and circumstances of the Old Testament, served as a picture wherein he beheld Christ drawn as it were at full length, while the common sort of Christians saw him only in miniature, and in the short representation of a plain and simple faith. Unspeakably happy is he who has such a faith, and lives up thereto. But miserable are those learned persons who study and know every thing except Jesus Christ.

70. Jesus answered them, Have not I chosen you twelve, and one of you is a devil?

The being duly called to the ecclesiastical office is not sufficient, if a man live not suitably to that holy vocation. There never was a call more certain than that of Judas; and yet never was any man more unworthy and unfaithful. The life of a brute, the mind of a devil, in a person called to an angelical state of life, is indeed a monster, but not so uncommon as those of nature. People ought not to take offence and to be scandalized at the disorders either of priests or Christians: neither the church nor the priesthood is less the true church or priesthood of Christ on that account.

71. He spake of Judas Iscariot *the son* of Simon: for he it was that should betray him, being one of the twelve.

An apostle, chosen by Christ himself, is a traitor and a devil! what ecclesiastical person has not reason to tremble! Adorable is the conduct of Jesus Christ, in leaving his apostles so long under so dreadful an uncertainty; every one of them having cause sufficient to mistrust himself, and being obliged not to judge his neighbour, nor even to suspect that he intended to commit so heinous a crime. Fear and distrust of our own weakness; an obligation to watch over our heart, and carefully to observe ourselves; a dread of sin, and Christian humility: these are the fruits of this holy solicitude which God produces from it by his grace.

CHAPTER VII.

SECT. I.—CHRIST'S RELATIONS AMBITIOUS.—THE WORLD HATES THOSE WHO REPROVE IT.

1. After these things Jesus walked in Galilee: for he would not walk in Jewry, because the Jews sought to kill him.

Christ avoids persecution by withdrawing himself, and not by interposing his power: and this on purpose to confound the pride of men. He does not fly from death; but, by declining it at present, he seeks to do the will of his Father, and waits his proper season. To be eager and impatient to suffer, is not always a sign of perfection ; and it is often a great fault not to retire from persecution. For a man to sacrifice his life for the sake of God, is no other than a work of God ; but for this very reason it must be done only according to the appointment, at the time, and in the Spirit of God.

2. Now the Jews' feast of tabernacles was at hand.

The feasts of the Jews are still, with greater reason, the feasts of Christians; because they set before their eyes the benefits of God, and the principal points of their duty. The Passover is our deliverance from the bondage of sin by Jesus Christ; the feast of Pentecost, God's eternal covenant with us through the Spirit; and that of Tabernacles, reminds us of the continual protection of his grace, of his watchfulness and providence over his church militant in the wilderness of this world, and in our passage through this life; and of that state of travel, sojourning, and warfare, wherein we must continue till our entrance into the promised land of heaven, and into the eternal rest of God, which will be our perfect deliverance from sin, and the consummation of the divine covenant.

His brethren therefore said unto him, Depart hence, and go into Judea, that thy disciples also may see the works that thou doest.

This conduct of our blessed Lord's relations, is a lively emblem of the ambition and vanity of those parents, who put their children upon undertaking eminent employments in the church, and showing their talents in the world, under pretence of promoting the glory of God. Happy is that person who gives no ear to them! Blind rashness this of flesh and blood! which, without knowledge, virtue, or authority, subjects to itself the vocation of the ministers of the altar, and pretends to direct all their steps in the exercise of the sacerdotal office. False prudence, sacrilegious avarice, barbarous ambition this of carnal parents! to put out as it were to use (but what dreadful use!) the good qualities of their children, their talents, their ecclesiastical revenues, their call, their employment, their life, and their salvation, or rather their eternal damnation! The voice of self-love alone does but too often excite ministers whose labours in places less exposed to the world are attended with certain and visible success, to leave them in order to exercise their office in a station more suitable, as they imagine, to their great capacities; but in reality more full of rocks and shelves to destroy their own souls, without promoting the salvation of others.

4. For *there is* no man *that* doeth any thing in secret, and he himself seeketh to be known openly. If thou do these things, shew thyself to the world.

That person is no better than mad who takes no care to shut his ears against the voice of pride, which is continually crying out to us that we must show ourselves to the world. How full of rashness, injustice, and ignorance is this speech! as if God, in the distribution of his talents and spiritual graces, could have any other end besides his own glory; and his servants might propose to themselves some other end, form quite different designs, and put their own glory in the place of his! My God, how little do the children of men comprehend the holiness of thy ways, since they perceive not in thy Scriptures, and in thy whole conduct toward thy apostles and servants, that it is upon the abasement of the creature, and upon the humiliation of Christ and his ministers, that thou art pleased to raise thy glory and thy church!

5. For neither did his brethren believe in him.

See here the source of that blind ambition which carnal parents have in respect of their children who have been bred up clergymen; it is because they have no faith, and lay no stress at all upon the truths of the gospel, or upon the promise and hope of eternal salvation. No persons whatever give their advice in ecclesiastical and spiritual matters with greater confidence and assurance, than those who have not even any degree of faith at all. Those selfish and worldly designs which parents form in relation to their children in holy orders, to their benefices and their talents, are in some the effect of the extinction of their faith, in others the cause and beginning of this extinction. Lord, vouchsafe to put a stop to the torrent of this carnal love in parents. Thou seest how thy church is almost overwhelmed with it.

6. Then Jesus said unto them, My time is not yet come: but your time is always ready.

We must be extremely careful not to anticipate God's appointed time, especially in undertaking the more eminent and remarkable actions. The world, which has no other rule of acting but its own will, is always ready to act: the Christian, who is desirous to perform the will of God, waits till he is pleased to make it known to him, and then makes it the spring of all his motions. A man is as ready to ruin himself as he is to act, when the forwardness and activity of his will does not proceed from the sovereign will of God. It is the part of man to be attentive to the will of God; because it belongs to God to prepare the will of man. This is a state of dependency in which true liberty does consist; as the contrary independency is real slavery. The more a man desires to have the government and direction of his own will, the more is he a slave thereto. The time of Jesus Christ is the time of his sacrifice; because, to offer that was the very end for which he was sent, and the chief object of his desires. It is in a very different sense, and from a quite contrary disposition, that the sinner—never willing to sacrifice himself, never willing to die—says continually to himself, "My time is not yet come."

7. The world cannot hate you; but me it hateth, because I testify of it, that the works thereof are evil.

The hatred which the world bears against those whose lives are a reproach to it, will last as long as the world. It is a great misfortune to have nothing which deserves this hatred; but, alas! there are few who are not well satisfied under this misfortune. An unfaithful pastor, who leaves sinners in the quiet enjoyment of a false peace of conscience, applauds himself perhaps for carrying it fair with all sorts of people; whereas this peaceable way of living, in neither condemning the world, nor being condemned by it, is no other than his own condemnation and death. A pastor is the vicegerent of Christ, to reprove the evil works of the world. He deceives himself, if he pretend either to do his duty without reproving it, or to reprove it without being hated by it. Jesus Christ himself did not think fit to reconcile these two things.

8. Go ye up unto this feast: I go not up yet unto this feast; for my time is not yet full come. 9. When he had said these words unto them, he abode *still* in Galilee.

How admirable, how edifying is this faithfulness of Christ, in observing so exactly all the times and seasons appointed by his Father! The disciples of Jesus Christ, namely, all true Christians, go to the festivals of the church, and celebrate them with dispositions very different from those of the world. We should decline associating ourselves with such persons as carry a worldly spirit along with them to the most holy solemnities, and into the very sanctuary itself; we should separate ourselves from promiscuous and tumultuous conversations, and not turn holy days into days of visiting, entertainment, and diversion, among our worldly friends or relations. When a man applies himself to the most exact and faithful observance of the will of God, abiding in that place where the order of his vocation requires his presence, and in an easy and quiet expectation of the feast; then it is that he imitates Christ and his religion.

SECT. II.—CHRIST NEITHER TEACHES HIS OWN DOCTRINE, NOR SEEKS HIS OWN GLORY.

10. ¶ But when his brethren were gone up, then went he also up unto the feast, not openly, but as it were in secret.

Christ acts in this manner that he may avoid making a noise; that he may not provoke the envious by a crowd of relations eager to show him to the world, and ambitious to raise his reputation; and that he may teach the great not to affect to distinguish themselves at church by a great train of attendants, but to keep within the rules of modesty, and to avoid every thing which may disturb either their own devotion or that of others.

11. Then the Jews sought him at the feast, and said, Where is he?

How many are there in the world who seek Jesus Christ on the greatest festivals, only to crucify him by sacrilegious confessions and communions! It is generally during these great solemnities that the secret enemies of Christ distinguish themselves from his true disciples; those who have faith from those who have none; and who, for want thereof, cannot find him present, and therefore say, "Where is he?" He hides and conceals himself from those who do not seek him as they ought.

12. And there was much murmuring among the people concerning him: for some said, He is a good man: others said, Nay; but he deceiveth the people. 13. Howbeit no man spake openly of him for fear of the Jews.

Christ will be always thus exposed to the contradiction of men, even to the end of the world. Let us observe with wonder how blind the judgment of the world is to which Christ is exposed! We show ourselves to be really Christians when, in serving God, we are very willing to be treated as our divine Head was. The chief freedom which men have in the world, is to speak ill of Jesus Christ and his religion. What esteem then ought we to have for the world? That which Christ suffered in his own person from the Jews during the time of his life, he now suffers in his church, his truth, and his servants, at the hands of infidels and heretics, and frequently of wicked livers among the orthodox. A profligate person generally finds some protection and some persons to speak in his favour; whereas a good man is abandoned, and nobody dares open his mouth in his behalf. The reason is, because the worldly man is more faithful to the world than Christians are to Jesus Christ. How desirable is it to be thus abandoned, since it gives us so great a conformity with our Head, and secures the protection of God in the day of his wrath!

14. ¶ Now about the midst of the feast Jesus went unto the temple, and taught.

The time is now at length come, the moment appointed by the Father, for which Christ waited, in order to declare himself to the priests, and to manifest himself for the first time in the temple of God, as the publisher of the new law, and the expected Messias. Here are several instructions for a preacher who is rightly and duly called to that office. First, He ought to avoid all eagerness and forwardness to preach, after the example of the Son of God, who lets half the octave of the feast be past before he begins. Second, He must not exercise so holy a function at the instance of his relations, or upon motives of flesh and blood. Third, He must not make the first day of his preaching a mere festival among relations. Fourth, He should imitate Christ, who sets apart as much time for prayer as for preaching, and prays four days in order to preach as many. Fifth, He must not, under pretence of preparing himself to preach, excuse himself from keeping the festivals in a Christian manner. Sixth, His sermons must be instructions, and not declamations; he must teach, and not trifle away time in displaying fine thoughts, or playing upon words.

15. And the Jews marvelled, saying, How knoweth this man letters,* having never learned? [**Fr.* The Scriptures.]

Seventh, It is necessary that a preacher should have laid in beforehand a large stock of knowledge as to the truths of religion, by the study of the Scriptures. Eighth, He must likewise learn them otherwise than by study. The unction of the Spirit is a great master in this science, and it is by prayer that we become his scholars. Much prayer and little study advance the work of God more than abundance of study without prayer. An ordinary degree of knowledge in the Scriptures may be sufficient for others; but, in the sacred ministers of the divine word, this knowledge ought to be so great as to cause admiration.

16. Jesus answered them, and said, My doctrine is not mine, but his that sent me.

Ninth, A preacher, following the example of Christ, must not preach his own doctrine; he must impart to others nothing but what he receives, nothing but what he can refer to God as the author of it. The ministers of the word are not sufficiently sensible of the great dependence which they have upon Christ. If we consider only the common track in which the generality of them proceed, we may be apt to imagine that their office is merely arbitrary, to be performed as they themselves shall think fit; but if we consider the conduct of Christ, who is the model and example they are to follow, we find every thing prescribed and pointed out. A preacher, who lays aside the truths and thoughts of God, to pursue and utter his own, is like an ambassador who suppresses the orders and instructions of his prince, and substitutes in their stead his own designs, and the imaginations of his own heart. The mission of the clergy is the rule of their function; and that comes to them from God by Jesus Christ. And therefore God in Jesus Christ ought to be the principle, the pattern, and the end of all the rest.

17. If any man will do his will, he shall know of the doctrine, whether it be of God, or *whether* I speak of myself.

Tenth, A man ought to preach in such a manner, that those who are really the servants of God, and can relish and discern his word, may know it to be so in the mouth of the preacher. It is of very great importance to hear or read the word of God with a heart which truly and earnestly seeks him. His light discovers itself to those who are willing to follow it; but it seems obscure to those whose heart is darkened by the clouds of a bad intention, or of a wicked life. Lord, let thy love influence my will, that my understanding may not meet with darkness in the midst of thy light.

18. He that speaketh of himself seeketh his own glory: but he that seeketh his glory that sent him, the same is true, and no unrighteousness is in him.

Eleventh, A preacher must not seek his own glory, but he must seek only that of God. It is pride, and the love of their own glory, which made false prophets, who, speaking and coming of themselves, pretend that God has sent them. Humltity, and the declining every thing which may raise and heighten a man's character, is one mark of a divine mission. To preach and teach the inventions of our own mind, and attribute them to the Spirit of God, is no other than vanity, hypocrisy, unrighteousness, and imposture.

19. Did not Moses give you the law, and *yet* none of you keepeth the law.

Twelfth, A preacher must not be discouraged at the hardness of sinners' hearts. The word of God, in the mouth of even Moses himself, was barren and unfruitful. It is the minister's part to sow the seed of his word; but it belongs to God to cause it to bring forth fruit. God frequently suffers a holy preacher to wait a long time without seeing the fruit of his instructions, on purpose to let him know that he ought not to boast of the success of his discourses, to oblige him to pray very much, and to humble himself for his failings, which perhaps are the obstacle, and to make him sensible how much he stands in need of grace. For the law, without grace, causes us only to prevaricate, because it does not give us the principle of love.

—Why go ye about to kill me?

Thirteenth, A preacher ought not, through fear either of ill usage or of death itself, to dissemble such truths as are necessary, be they ever so disagreeable to sinners. He who is called to the ministry of the word, is called to suffer the contradictions of the world, and to seal with his own blood, if occasion require, both the truth which he preaches, and his own fidelity in preaching it. Why? Lord, thou hast just now informed us. It is because none of us keepeth the law, because the whole world is corrupted, and because we have need of such a victim as may redeem us, sanctify us, and merit for us that grace which enables us to keep the law.

20. The people answered and said, Thou hast a devil: who goeth about to kill thee?

Fourteenth, A preacher must not expect to see himself justified before the world. The most modest complaint is, in the world's opinion, a new crime. Every man is a liar, and yet no one can bear to have the lie given him without demanding satisfaction: what pride is this! Christ is truth itself, and yet suffers the imputation of being possessed with the spirit of lying, error, and calumny, and even with the devil himself, without seeming to take the least notice of it: what humility is this! A soft complaint, which proceeds no further, which makes no severe reply, nor returns any injurious reflection, is much more edifying than a silence which may be attributed to ignorance, insensibility, fear, or to an excess of wrath and passion.

21. Jesus answered and said unto them, I have done one work, and ye all marvel. 22. Moses therefore gave unto you circumcision; not because it is of Moses, but of the fathers; and ye on the sabbath day circumcise a man.

Fifteenth, A preacher ought to slight and disregard personal affronts and injuries, but never to desert the cause of God. To maintain the doctrine of truth, and to vindicate those works which God does in confirmation thereof, are two duties which are inseparable. Christ omits nothing to acquit himself of both. After that sublime apology for the pretended violation of the Sabbath, recorded in chap. v., ver. 17, he here makes use of one better suited to vulgar capacities, that he may become all things to all men. As a Christian, a man may patiently suffer an act of injustice; but as a minister of God, he ought, by discovering it, to hinder it from being prejudicial to the work of God, or hurtful to his neighbour.

23. If a man on the sabbath day receive circumcision, that the law of Moses should not be broken; are ye angry at me, because I have made a man every whit whole on the sabbath day?

By performing good works we sanctify festivals; so far are we from violating and profaning them thereby. And if to inflict a bleeding wound be esteemed a good work, how much more is it such to make a man every whit whole by one single word? Envy blinds men, and causes them to condemn in others that which they do themselves. Anger, envy, rash judgment, parricide conceived in the heart against the Son of God, and a spirit of opposition to the divine works—all this is allowable on festivals, if these men are to be believed; but to give assistance to a neighbour, overturns and destroys all religion. A way of reasoning this, which we too often meet with in the conduct not only of Christians, but of priests.

24. Judge not according to the appearance, but judge righteous judgment.

Man, who sees not the heart, ought to be very cautious in judging his brother. How much cause have we to fear, lest, in our judgments concerning others, we should be influenced, either by the advantages of nature and fortune, or by our own prejudices or interests, and at the same time imagine that we proceed upon just grounds and reasons! It is not the action in itself, or the external part of it, which is pleasing or displeasing to God, innocent or criminal: to judge rightly of it, we should know the principle from which it proceeds, the end at which it aims, all the circumstances attending it, and the true frame and temper of the will. It is unjust to form our judgments upon the outward appearance of any action, or by the love or hatred we bear toward the person who has done it. To judge uprightly and justly, we must love justice: and since our love for it is but small, let us never judge but when it is absolutely necessary, and let us then do it with fear and caution.

25. Then said some of them of Jerusalem, Is not this he, whom they seek to kill? 26. But, lo, he speaketh boldly, and they say nothing unto him. Do the rulers know indeed that this is the very Christ?

The tongues and ill-will of men are always subject to the power of God. This is matter of great consolation to those whom they persecute. He watches continually over his faithful ministers, who, without disquieting themselves about the designs of the wicked against them, are intent on performing their duty. To neglect it through fear of temporal evils, is to choose rather to expose ourselves to the wrath of God, than to the displeasure of men.

27. Howbeit we know this man whence he is: but when Christ cometh, no man knoweth whence he is.

It belongs to God to give the true understanding of his own Scriptures; otherwise human reason does but make every thing in them more intricate. The senses which see nothing but external and corporeal objects, are very bad guides to lead us to the belief of invisible and supernatural mysteries. That which is here said by these Jews of Jerusalem, gives us a lively representation of the boldness and confidence with which carnal men, by their own private spirit, frequently determine the sense of Scripture. It often happens that men think themselves very knowing in the Scriptures and in the ways of God, when they are really as blind in respect of them, as these very Jews.

28. Then cried Jesus in the temple as he taught, saying, Ye both know me, and ye know whence I am: and I am not come of myself, but he that sent me is true, whom ye know not.

Lastly, A preacher must not give over instructing those whom God has committed to his care, let the world say and do what it will to the contrary. Christ raises his voice on purpose to teach his ministers that it is a dishonour to divine truth to preach it in a timorous manner. His Father who sent him is true, (1.) Because he is the source and origin of the eternal and subsisting truth, and as such sent him by the incarnation. (2.) Because he thereby made good the truth of his promises. (3.) Because he gives testimony to the truth of the incarnation of the Word by miracles, which are the seal of his divine mission.

29. But I know him; for I am from* him, and he hath sent me. [* *Fr.* Born of.]

The Word receives by his generation his knowledge of his Father, in receiving his nature. He does not know him by a simple manner of existing, or by means of ideas distinguished from himself; but because, as being his Son, he is the subsisting term of his Father's knowledge, the eternal character and substantial idea of his essence, and of all his divine and eternal perfections. Let us adore the three mysteries, couched under the three different expressions used in this verse—his eternal birth, the manner of his birth, which is by knowledge, and his temporal birth and mission.

30. Then they sought to take him: but no man laid hands on him, because his hour was not yet come.

Christ delivered up himself when it was his will to do it; but to determine that, he waited with submission till the hour of his sacrifice came, which had been appointed by his Father. We are in the hand of God, both as we are his creatures, and as we are the members of his Son. Nothing can happen to us but what is permitted by this omnipotent hand. We sometimes, as it were, take ourselves out of his hand, by seeking protection elsewhere, and putting our trust and confidence in precautions altogether human, and directly contrary to that fidelity which we owe him. We equally take ourselves out of his hand, when we either rashly advance without his orders and direction, or shamefully retreat through fear contrary to his law.

31. And many of the people believed on him, and said, When Christ cometh, will he do more miracles than these which this *man* hath done?

God chooses the poor of this world, to make them rich in faith, and heirs of the kingdom, (James ii. 5,) rather than the great and the learned. Humility and simplicity open the mind and heart to divine truths; whereas pride and arrogance of mind shut it up against all manner of proofs, and harden the heart against them. All the learning and subtlety of the scribes and doctors of the law, does not come up to this plain and conclusive argument: miracles are necessary, and withal sufficient to authorize the mission of a prophet; those which, according to the Scriptures, are to authorize the Messias, can be neither greater nor more in number than those of Jesus: therefore Jesus is the Messias, since in working such miracles he plainly declares and proves himself to be so.

32. ¶ The Pharisees heard that the people murmured such things concerning him; and the Pharisees and the chief priests sent officers to take him.

All the attempts of men against the will of God are vain and ineffectual. No confederacies in the world, let them be ever so strong and powerful, can oppose his designs or break his measures. It is a very great temptation, to see the most sacred authority and the most holy and edifying profession, united in a conspiracy against Christ and doctrine. That which was here done against him, is done sometimes against his truth and his servants. It is still a far more dangerous temptation to the wicked, to behold in them they persecute, miracles only of meekness, virtue, and charity; and to see no instance of vengeance and justice, nor any thing which may raise in them a dread and apprehension of punishment.

33. Then said Jesus unto them, Yet a little while am I with you, and *then* I go unto him that sent me.

Those who neglect to receive Jesus Christ, are at length deprived of this opportunity. The time of grace is short; it is an extreme folly not to know how to improve it. Death, in respect of the righteous, is no other than a return to their father's house,—and this return will quickly be. It is the comfort of the righteous under oppression, that they expect every moment to be called home, where they will be forever placed beyond the reach of the wicked. The short term of this present life passes still more swiftly with respect to those who enjoy every thing here below according to their heart's desire. True wisdom consists in regarding as nothing whatever passes away so soon, be it either good or evil.

34. Ye shall seek me, and shall not find *me:* and where I am, *thither* ye cannot come.

It is absolutely necessary to seek God in this life by a true conversion and by good works, in order to find him at the time of death. What will he who finds not Jesus Christ at that hour find, except his own condemnation, despair, and eternal misery? A terrible judgment this upon the wicked whom God leaves in their infidelity! Blessed be thy name, O Jesus, who hast showed us mercy in giving us faith! Grant, Lord, that this faith, which thou hast planted in my heart, may continually seek thee, find thee, raise my heart up to thee, unite it to thy Spirit, and at last conduct me where thou art.

35. Then said the Jews among themselves, Whither will he go, that we shall not find him? will he go unto the dispersed among the Gentiles, and teach the Gentiles? 36. What *manner of* saying is this that he said, Ye shall seek me, and shall not find *me:* and where I am, *thither* ye cannot come?

The reprobate, insensible both to admonitions and threatenings, make only a jest of them. Without the precious gift of faith, men see nothing but absurdities in the mysteries of religion and in the most sacred words of Scripture. It concerns us very highly to avoid the company of those who ridicule that which ought to make them tremble. How strong soever we may think ourselves, we have still reason to fear lest we should be influenced by a regard to men, and that we are not sufficiently settled in the truths of faith, for fear of being reputed enthusiastical by a libertine, or a person who has none.

SECT. III.—WHOEVER THIRSTS LET HIM COME TO CHRIST.—RIVERS OF LIVING WATER.—CHRIST THE OCCASION OF DIVISION.

37. In the last day, that great *day* of the feast, Jesus stood and cried, saying, If any man thirst, let him come unto me, and drink.

In order to come to Christ, a man must have a thirst after grace and eternal life. But it is he who gives this thirst; it is he himself who draws those after him who come unto him. This thirst is inconsistent with a thirst after honours, riches, pleasures, and the amusements of the world. In vain do we seek among the creatures for something to satisfy our desires, and to allay our thirst. Our drought continually increases, so long as we do not seek Jesus Christ. It is not sufficient that we are sensible how much we stand in need of Christ; we must go to him by faith, we must drink the wholesome waters of his grace, and we must draw them even from our blessed Saviour's fountains, from his mysteries, his cross, his sacred wounds, etc. The larger and deeper the vessel of our faith is, the greater quantity shall we receive and bring away of this water which sanctifies and makes us fruitful.

38. He that believeth on me, as the Scripture hath said, out of his belly shall flow rivers of living waters.

He who has the Spirit of God, and a lively and obedient faith, has within his heart continual springs of graces, good works, and blessings, sufficient to water the whole earth. If the marks and characters of faith are not seen in our life and actions, it is undoubtedly either because there is no faith at all in our hearts, or because it is either quite dead or in a very declining condition. The water of faith is not a standing water, but a living water which runs perpetually. My God, vouchsafe to bless thy church, by sending it those men of faith, full of thy Spirit, whose hearts may overflow like rivers, and bring a fruitful inundation upon thy field by their labours, prayers, instructions, and good examples.

39. But this spake he of the Spirit, which they that believe on him should receive: for the Holy Ghost was not yet *given;* because that Jesus was not yet glorified.

The gift of the Holy Ghost is the fruit of all the mysteries of Jesus Christ. It was requisite that our adorable Head, the principle and pattern of our new life, should receive it himself, before he communicated it to his members; that he should be regenerated by his resurrection, before he sent the Spirit of the Christian regeneration; that he should be entirely separated from this present world, before he became, by means of his Spirit, the Father of the world to come; that whatever remained in his body of the image and resemblance of the first Adam, should be swallowed up in glory before he became, in quality of the second Adam, the new principle of a divine and heavenly life; and that his sacrifice should be completed by the resurrection, (which puts the victim of God into a condition fit to be received into his bosom,) before his church and members could partake of this sacrifice, by receiving the Holy Spirit which is the fruit thereof; and that even with respect to those who received him before the incarnation, by an anticipated spiritual communion, as also in respect of the sacramental communion of the apostles, which preceded the immolation of the victim.

40. ¶ Many of the people therefore, when they heard this saying, said, Of a truth this is the Prophet. 41. Others said, This is the Christ.

If the bare promise of the gift of faith, of the effects thereof, and of the effusion of the Holy Ghost, drew from the mouth of these people this confession, how blind is the heart of unbelievers in our days, after his promises have been so manifestly accomplished, after the effusion of the gifts of the Holy Ghost continued in so incontestable a manner, without intermission, for seventeen ages, and after the conversion and faith of all nations, which is so plain and convincing a proof of that effusion! Let us likewise take care, lest our faith have some degree of distrust, lest it be too timorous or faint-hearted.

—But some said, Shall Christ come out of Galilee? 42. Hath not the Scripture said, That Christ cometh of the seed of David, and out of the town of Bethlehem, where David was?

How great assistance does the implicit, but rational obedience of faith afford! How many false reflections, unprofitable inquiries, and vain disputes does it prevent! The difficulties and seeming contradictions of some places of Scripture, ought to be no obstacle to the belief of such truths as are elsewhere sufficiently attested, both by the Scriptures themselves and by miracles. God, in his adorable wisdom, dispenses the sacred light and darkness of his word together, to hide from the profane those truths of which they are utterly unworthy, to exercise the faith of his true disciples, and thereby cause them, in some measure, to deserve the understanding of them. Pride and irreligion meet with darkness in the midst of light; humility and religion arrive at the light even by the means of darkness itself.

43. So there was a division among the people because of him.

Jesus Christ and his doctrine will ever be, through the malice of men, an occasion of division in the church. We ought to prepare ourselves for this misfortune, and not be at all scandalized or offended at it. There are some divisions which are necessary. That person betrays and abandons the truth, who ceases to defend it, or to oppose the professed adversaries thereof, either for fear of giving occasion of scandal, or through a false love of peace. Truth is the patrimony of the widow and the orphan, of the church and the Christian; we surrender and deliver up this patrimony, whenever we suffer it to be either taken away, or wasted by any unnatural relation, under pretence of avoiding suits at law, and of preserving peace and good understanding in the family.

44. And some of them would have taken him; but no man laid hands on him.

Happy is that person who is in the hands of God! those of the world have no power over him. The ill-will of men is less to be feared by us than our own will. The former serves only to engage God more and more on our side, provided our own perverse will do not make us his enemies. The wicked are the scourges and instruments of God's justice: if he permit their ill-will to be in action, it is either to punish sinners, or to exercise the righteous, and increase their virtue.

SECT. IV.—THOSE WHO BELIEVE IN CHRIST CALLED ACCURSED.—NICODEMUS VINDICATES HIM.

45. ¶ Then came the officers to the chief priests and Pharisees; and they said unto them, Why have ye not brought him? 46. The officers answered, Never man spake like this man.

How many rude and ignorant people, who submissively receive the word of Christ, will rise up in judgment against the wits, against the learned men of the age, and against the great persons of the world! They who execute unjust orders merely on the account of their office, and without knowing the injustice of them, are not at so great a distance from salvation as those who, to satisfy their passions, either give such orders themselves, or cause them to be given by others. God gives what efficacy he pleases to his word. Whenever he vouchsafes to open the heart, be the light of the understanding ever so small and inconsiderable, we then see the beauty of his word, we taste its sweetness, and we feel and admire its power. But whenever he permits the heart to be closed against it, even the light of nature becomes an obstacle to our understanding and embracing it, and we perceive nothing therein which is more than human.

47. Then answered them the Pharisees, Are ye also deceived?

So corrupt is the world, that it hates those who will not join with it in the persecution of good men. Whoever desires to be the servant of God, and to continue faithful to him, must contemn not only the judgment of the world, but sometimes even that of those who pass for the great masters and examples of piety. No man is willing to be thought seduced; and this is frequently the very thing which causes us to fall into seduction: we dread the shadow and name of error, and we receive and embrace the real substance.

48. Have any of the rulers or of the Pharisees believed on him?

Worldly greatness and false devotion are more likely to make us lose the true faith, than to assist us in obtaining it. That person has already a very wrong notion of the spirit of faith, who imagines that external quality is of any advantage to it. If Christ have but few followers and true disciples among the great, the reason is, because human grandeur agrees but ill with the humility of his gospel. And those who are puffed up with the reputation of their learning, and an outward show of piety, are still less disposed to admit into their heart the simplicity of his word.

49. But this people who knoweth not the law are cursed.

The pride of men is so great, that they choose rather to be eternally lost with the great, than to be saved with the poor and simple. The poverty and simplicity of the elect is a matter of scandal and offence to the reprobate. The vainglory manifested in these words, is sufficient to satisfy us that, with regard to salvation, it is much better to lie obscure and concealed amid the crowd of a believing populace, than to be distinguished by great talents, and by any excellency which is apt to fill the mind with pride. It is not the bare knowledge, but the spirit of the law, which leads to him who is the end thereof. We have then the true knowledge of it, when we have the love of it in our hearts, and manifest our obedience by showing the works of it in our lives. The curse of the law falls on all those who have nothing but the letter of it.

50. Nicodemus saith unto them, (he that came to Jesus by night, being one of them,)

The courage of Nicodemus is the effect of the conversation which he had with Christ. The word of the Son of God gives a man zeal and resolution to do good. He has disciples in all states and professions of life, because he has everywhere an absolute power over the heart. He finds means to have witnesses of the truth, and defenders of innocence, in the most corrupt societies; because he himself forms those witnesses and defenders by his grace. There sometimes wants but one such person to reclaim, or at least restrain all the rest; but it is extremely difficult for a man to resolve to be that one person.

51. Doth our law judge *any* man, before it hear him, and know what he doeth?

All sorts of laws are violated in respect of Christ: this is matter of comfort and consolation to those who meet with the same treatment for his sake. It is a rule of natural equity, as well as of the written law, which is of great importance, and of use to everybody, That we must not condemn any one, either in conversation, or in our own thoughts, (where every one presumes to judge his neighbour,) without knowing the case. Much less ought persons in authority to punish or condemn the accused, either by juridical sentence, or by arbitrary proceedings, without hearing them, and giving them means and opportunity to defend themselves. Let us never imitate these great pretenders to zeal for the law, who are the first who violate it themselves.

52. They answered and said unto him, Art thou also of Galilee? Search, and look: for out of Galilee ariseth no prophet. 53. And every man went unto his own house.

If we would not be deceived, we must never expect to meet with a good reception from the world, when we take the part of truth and justice against powerful and passionate men. Envy convicted, and put to a nonplus, is strangely at a loss. Nothing comes amiss to it, so Christ be but looked upon as a false prophet. It is the usual way with the enemies of his doctrine, to endeavour to draw the defenders of it off from the question, that they may hide their own confusion, and avoid yielding to the truth.

CHAPTER VIII.

SECT. I.—THE WOMAN TAKEN IN ADULTERY.

1. Jesus went unto the mount of Olives. 2. And early in the morning he came again into the temple, and all the people came unto him; and he sat down, and taught them.

In the heat of persecution or evangelical labour, it is necessary to have frequent recourse to retirement and prayer, in order to receive new strength, and then return to the combat and to the sacred functions. Neither danger, nor hardness of heart in the flock, ought to discourage a pastor from labouring in the work of God. On the contrary, these are motives to him to redouble his care, his prayers, and his application. He who has his mission at heart, finds the repose of the night too long, as our blessed Lord did. The sheep answer the pastor's zeal. We always find the people very forward and eager to hear the word of Christ, while it was despised by the rich, censured by the learned, and persecuted by the priests and the Pharisees.

3. And the scribes and Pharisees brought unto him a woman taken in adultery; and when they had set her in the midst, 4. They say unto him, Master, this woman was taken in adultery, in the very act.

It is a double impiety to divert the Son of God from the

sacred functions of his ministry, and to do it with a design to destroy him. Envy and rage never want new contrivances to ruin the ministers of God: the devil takes care to suggest them to the mind, and to furnish his agents with them. He does his work by their hands, in seeking the death of sinners; while Jesus carries on his, in labouring to save them.

5. Now Moses in the law commanded us, that such should be stoned: but what sayest thou?

Ye hypocrites, if the law commands it, why do you question it? And if it does not, why do you say so? It happens very frequently, as it did in the case before us, that men make no difficulty of acting directly contrary to the spirit and design of the law, under pretence of a more than ordinary exactness in observing it. To make it subservient to our passions, is to violate the whole law together. This woman had transgressed only one commandment; but these great pretenders to zeal transgress and subvert the very foundation of the whole—namely, the spirit of charity, mildness, and justice.

6. This they said, tempting him, that they might have to accuse him. But Jesus stooped down, and with *his* finger wrote on the ground, *as though he heard them not.*

There is nothing which hypocritical and corrupt zealots will not put in practice, and value themselves upon. Under pretence of discovering an impostor, of surprising him in his discourse, of exposing his dangerous maxims, and of finding matter to convict him, they forbear no kind of deceit, artifice, and treachery. Jesus acts a quite contrary part, in giving them time by his silence to recollect and recover themselves. He stoops down, to avoid adding to the shame and confusion of the adulteress by his looking upon her, while her merciless accusers expose her to the public view of the people.

7. So when they continued asking him, he lifted up himself, and said unto them, He that is without sin among you, let him first cast a stone at her.

An answer full of wisdom, which confounds the devices of these wicked men, without any violation of truth, charity, gentleness, or justice. We are not always obliged to answer those who have a design to ensnare us. We may evade it by some innocent artifice; and such is never wanting when we keep our hearts open to the Spirit of God. Let those whose duty it is to punish offenders, take great care that they be not moved thereto by passion, hypocrisy, false zeal, or ill will; but let them do it with reluctancy, and a deep sense of their own sins and miseries, which perhaps render them more guilty in the sight of God.

8. And again he stooped down, and wrote on the ground.

Since Jesus Christ (1.) never wrote but once in his whole life; (2.) since he did it only in the dust; (3.) since it was only to avoid condemning a sinner; and, (4.) since he would not have that which he wrote so much as known,—let men learn from hence never to write but when it is necessary or useful, to do it with humility and modesty, upon a principle of charity, and not out of malice. Christ writes his divine thoughts on the ground; and we would willingly have ours written upon cedar, and engraved upon brass.

9. And they which heard *it*, being convicted by *their own* conscience, went out one by one, beginning at the eldest, *even* unto the last: and Jesus was left alone, and the woman standing in the midst.

Christ could have dispersed this crowd of accusers by his authority and power, but he has a regard to the law and to justice, the execution whereof they eagerly pursued. Men ought to use their interest in behalf of criminals with great prudence and caution, and that more in persuading the accusers to desist from their prosecutions, than in diverting the judges from their duty, which they have no power to neglect. It is both prudent and charitable to give persons an opportunity to extricate themselves, without noise and confusion, out of a business wherein they have rashly engaged themselves through passion. To provoke and shame them publicly, does but engage them in it more deeply. Happy is that misery which finds itself left alone with mercy!

10. When Jesus had lifted up himself, and saw none but the woman, he said unto her, Woman, where are those thine accusers? hath no man condemned thee?

Jesus lifts up himself victorious and triumphant over his

enemies by his silence and gentleness. There are some occasions wherein these two, joined with humility and prayer, are more effectual than any other means whatever. When men have only a false zeal for justice, it immediately vanishes when self-interest makes them apprehend that their own persons are in danger. Nothing is a more proper remedy to cure us of that itching desire which we have to accuse and condemn others, than to place our own sins before our eyes, and to consider how obnoxious we are to the divine justice.

11. She said, No man, Lord. And Jesus said unto her, Neither do I condemn thee: go, and sin no more.

It ill becomes the ministers of reconciliation and the dispensers of the mercy of God, to appear in criminal prosecutions, and to solicit the condemnation of sinners, when Christ has given them such an example to the contrary. It is more suitable to their ministry to use all their endeavours to gain them time, that they may be converted, and punish themselves by a true repentance. When we have once recovered any person out of the hands of justice, to prevent this grace and favour from being prejudicial to him, we must apply ourselves to him, in order to prevail with him to make a good use thereof, by renouncing sin, and leading a Christian life. Christ does not condemn this woman; but then he does not meddle with the law which did condemn her; to teach his ministers to pay a due regard to those laws from the severity of which they endeavour to save some guilty persons. He is on all occasions mild and merciful—on all occasions prudent, just, and equitable.

SECT. II.—CHRIST IS THE LIGHT OF THE WORLD.—HIS FATHER BEARS WITNESS OF HIM.—THE IMPENITENCY OF THE JEWS.

12. ¶ Then spake Jesus again unto them, saying, I am the light of the world: he that followeth me shall not walk in darkness, but shall have the light of life.

Every person ought to say to himself, There are but two ways, one of which is certainly mine: the first is the way of light, which leads to life; the second is the way of darkness, which leads to death. The latter is the life wherein men follow their passions, a life which is nothing but wandering, darkness, and death, both in itself and in its consequences. The former is the Christian life, of which Jesus Christ is himself the way, the light, and the life. The way—by the merits of his sacrifice, and by the dignity of the mysteries of his life, and of his death upon the cross, which comprehend all his actions, privations, and sufferings. The light—by the truth of his word, which contains his saving instructions, his edifying virtues, and his internal dispositions. The life—by the holiness of his Spirit, from which fountain is derived the infusion of his love, the operation of his grace, and the communication of his glory. How great comfort must it needs be to one who sincerely desires to be saved, to find thus in Jesus Christ whatever is necessary to salvation! But how dreadful is it, not to follow this only light, and to choose rather to follow the darkness of our own passions!

13. The Pharisees therefore said unto him, Thou bearest record of thyself; thy record is not true.

Nothing shows more plainly that men walk still in darkness, than their disputing against the light. Those who are resolved not to believe, forget even miracles, and all the proofs which have been brought in confirmation of the truth, and insist on every thing which seems to oppose and contradict it. Obstinacy and indocility are pharisaical vices, which gradually shut the heart more and more against the light.

14. Jesus answered and said unto them, Though I bear record of myself, *yet* my record is true: for I know whence I came, and whither I go; but ye cannot tell whence I come, and whither I go.

The light manifests itself by its own brightness, without any other assistance—but not to the blind. And such they are, whose passions shut their eyes against the truths of the Scripture and against miracles. An ambassador is believed upon his own word, when it is once known from whence he comes, and his credentials have been read; but men cannot read them unless they open their eyes. In like manner, they must have the eyes of their mind free from passion, in order to judge of the mission of Jesus Christ by his miracles, which are his credentials. Eternal thanks be rendered to thee, O

Jesus, for that thou hast vouchsafed to keep us from shutting our eyes against the wonders of thy life and the miracles of thy power!

15. Ye judge after the flesh; I judge no man.

No ambassador is more worthy to be received and credited than he who, offering magnificent promises as conditions of an alliance or covenant, confirms them by innumerable miracles, does good to all, condemns none—no, not even an adulteress taken in the very act—and suffers himself to be judged and condemned by carnal men, who judge only by passion. Irreligious persons generally consider nothing in divine truths and mysteries, but that which appears therein contrary to sense and shallow reason. It is even because these truths come from God, that they are therefore above the understanding of man.

16. And yet if I judge, my judgment is true: for I am not alone, but I and the Father that sent me.

Ambassadors are invested with the authority, but not with the dignity and sovereignty, of their princes; but Jesus Christ, inseparable from his Father, and one and the same God with him, can equally do all things, is equally to be believed, and is as just and righteous in all his judgments. Let us adore Jesus Christ as the adorer, apostle, and preacher of the most holy Trinity. We commonly pass over such places of Scripture as this very slightly, and yet there is nothing more holy, more sublime, and more worthy to be adored, than that which is therein contained. This is the mystery of Christians; whatever is taught us concerning it by Christ ought to be precious to us, and requires our adoration, thanksgiving, attention, love, etc.

17. It is also written in your law, that the testimony of two men is true. 18. I am one that bear witness of myself, and the Father that sent me beareth witness of me.

None but Jesus Christ can bear witness of himself. Man, who has nothing derived from himself but falsehood and sin, has more reason to suspect himself than any other. Even Jesus Christ did not bear witness of himself, until his Father had borne witness of him by his Spirit at the time of his baptism, and by his miracles; and until his own freedom from self-interest, his aversion to pride and vanity, his meekness, charity, patience, etc., were become publicly known. The testimony of good works and Christian virtues, is that with which his ministers ought always to support their ministry.

19. Then said they unto him, Where is thy Father? Jesus answered, Ye neither know me, nor my Father: if ye had known me, ye should have known my Father also.

A man may desire and ask for the knowledge of God and of his mysteries, either by an humble and hearty prayer, as Philip did, (chap. xiv. 8,) or by a criminal way of inquiry, full of artifice and infidelity, as the Pharisees here did, and as the learned men of the world very often do. Nothing so clearly discovers and makes known the goodness and love of God toward mankind, as his giving them his Son; and they, in rejecting the belief of this gift, show plainly that they have no true notion of the sovereign goodness of the Father toward them. The abusing the light of the Holy Scriptures, and rejecting the miracles of Christ, which are the voice of God, are punished with ignorance and darkness of mind.

20. These words spake Jesus in the treasury, as he taught in the temple: and no man laid hands on him; for his hour was not yet come.

At what advantage soever the wicked may have the good whom they intend to destroy, they cannot make use of that advantage without the permission and appointment of God. A man enjoys the greatest peace of mind, when he has once settled himself in a firm and steadfast belief of God's providence, and an absolute dependence upon his designs and will. This is that which gives an evangelical minister so much freedom and boldness, while he considers nothing but his duty, and fears no other evil, but only lest he should not faithfully discharge that duty in all respects.

21. Then said Jesus again unto them, I go my way, and ye shall seek me, and shall die in your sins: whither I go, ye cannot come.

Have we not just reason to fear when we see the Jews abandoned to their obduracy? That man alone has no occasion to tremble at these words, who is certain that he shall never have this disposition of the Jews in any degree whatever. Here are four dreadful truths which ought to be the cause of fear to all, but of despair to none:—(1.) That there are some persons from whom God withdraws himself, in leaving them to themselves. (2.) That then they seek God to no purpose, because they do not seek him as they ought. (3.) That they die in their sins. And (4.) That they shall be eternally separated from God. The only end and design of Christ in assuring us that there are such persons is, that we may earnestly endeavour, by a sincere conversion and a true repentance, not to be of the number. We never seek Christ either too late, or to no purpose, when we seek him with sincerity, humility, and a penitent heart. He may be found indeed at the last moment; but who knows whether he shall be then in a condition to seek him? And who does not know that it is by grace alone that we are enabled to do it?—which grace is not due to any one, much less to those who have so often contemned and despised it.

22. Then said the Jews, Will he kill himself? because he saith, Whither I go, ye cannot come.

To what blasphemies are not men transported by envy, by the spirit of contradiction, and by a contempt of God's word! Let us earnestly beg of God the grace never to fall into any of these sins. The righteous profit by God's admonitions, and even by his threatenings to the wicked; but the wicked turn to their own destruction the most wholesome warnings which are more immediately directed to them. They verify, by the hardness of their heart, that very thing which Christ has just now foretold. My God, what is a heart which is not possessed and ruled by thy Spirit!

23. And he said unto them, Ye are from beneath; I am from above: ye are of this world; I am not of this world.

What obduracy and perverseness soever a good pastor finds in his flock, he is never discouraged. The mysteries of the Trinity and the incarnation are such as these hardened wretches were most unworthy to know; but then they are likewise such as are most necessary: and this is what ought chiefly to be regarded. Let us remember that we also are from above, as members of this heavenly person by our new birth. Let those who are of this world love the things of this world; but let the Christian, whose birth and spirit are from above, have no inclinations but for the things above, and judge of every thing only by the Spirit of heaven.

24. I said therefore unto you, that ye shall die in your sins: for if ye believe not that I am *he*, ye shall die in your sins.

Let us seriously and attentively consider how dangerous it is to reject Jesus Christ. Sinners ought frequently to be told what it is to die in their sins, and how much a state of final impenitence is to be dreaded. It is a mistaken prudence to hide these dreadful truths from sinners, for fear of casting them into despair by the terror of God's judgments. We ought, on the contrary, to force them, by the sight of their danger, to throw themselves into the arms of Christ, the only refuge of sinners. How positive and severe soever these threatenings are, yet Christ at the same time informs us that our conversion may hinder their being put in execution, and that this conversion has for its foundation the belief of a Saviour who is an almighty God, and a full trust and confidence in his mercy.

SECT. III.—CHRIST DOES NOTHING OF HIMSELF.—THE TRUTH MAKES MEN FREE.—ABRAHAM'S CHILDREN.—THE CHILDREN OF THE DEVIL.

25. Then said they unto him, Who art thou? And Jesus saith unto them, Even *the same* that I said unto you from the beginning.

Jesus is the Son of God, the eternal Word, the eternal principle and source of all things, and the light of the world. Every thing in him proclaims this, both his word and works; but envy shuts both the eyes and ears of the Jews. He has one life which never had a beginning, and which all the attempts of his enemies cannot bring to an end. Thou hast another, O Jesus, the loss of which is the salvation of men. I adore thee in all thou art from eternity, and in all thou didst begin to be for my sake in time.

26. I have many things to say and to judge of you: but he that sent me is true; and I speak to the world those things which I have heard of him. 27. They understood not that he spake to them of the Father.

Jesus Christ speaks nothing but what his Father directs

him to speak: his ministers, in like manner, ought to preach nothing but what they have learned of Jesus Christ. He teaches those who have ears to hear, that all the good things of eternity are contained in his person: but he conceals from them the evil which he saw in the heart of man. It is a matter of great importance, for a man to be able to imitate, as he ought, this moderation of the Son of God, in publishing that which it is the part of charity to make public, and in suppressing that which it requires should be concealed. Truth, charity, fidelity, is the motto of an ambassador of God, of a minister of the gospel. Let us adore God the Father, as the fulness, source, and eternal origin of the eternal truth; and his adorable bosom, as the fountain of all the truths of salvation. This is the school, as it were, in which the Word himself (who was never ignorant of them) learns them, in order to teach them to mankind as their master.

28. Then said Jesus unto them, When ye have lifted up the Son of man, then shall ye know that I am *he*, and *that* I do nothing of myself; but as my Father hath taught me, I speak these things.

How many Christians are there, who, in like manner, do not know him until they have crucified him by their sins! How just cause of humiliation is this! As the bosom of the Father is the school of the Son, where he learns all truth, in being himself born therein as the subsisting truth, so the bosom of the Son crucified in our flesh, is the school of Christians, begotten on the cross, and adopted in Jesus Christ crucified. We may here observe three parts of the doctrine of this divine school:—The first contains the mysteries of the Trinity and of the Son of man, expressed by the term, "I am." The second, denoted by the term, "I do," includes the actions of Christ's life, and his death upon the cross. The third, signified by the term, "I speak," comprehends his doctrine and maxims. The three fundamental points or tenets taught in this school are, (1.) That Jesus Christ is perfect God, and perfect man, in one single person. (2.) That his actions are divine—of an infinite merit and dignity. (3.) That his doctrine is truth itself, and the infallible rule of our life and conversation. O sublime and divine schools, raised infinitely above human sense and understanding! How much are ye neglected! how little are ye known in comparison of the schools of the world! Grant, O Jesus, that I may know no other school but thine. Give me, I beseech thee, the eyes of a lively faith, the ears of a teachable heart, and the understanding of an attentive charity, that I may be able to read in the book taught there, which is thyself; to hear the master who teaches there—namely, thy Spirit; and to comprehend the lessons there given, which are truth and charity.

29. And he that sent me is with me: the Father hath not left me alone; for I do always those things that please him.

Christ was pleased by his obedience to merit the continual assistance and protection of his Father, as likewise a state of glory for his human nature, though he had already a right to both by his hypostatical union. Let us, after his example, be faithful to God, and we shall always find him with us. One man cannot send another without being separated from him: God sends his Son, by uniting the human nature to the divine in the person of the Word, by a union, of all others, the most intimate and inseparable. The hierarchical mission honours and imitates this divine mission, which is the source and pattern thereof. It unites the subordinate minister to his bishop, and by him to Jesus Christ; admits him to a share of the priesthood, authority, grace, and spirit of his bishop; renders him an instrument entirely one with the bishop in the sacredotal operations and sacred functions; and makes the bishop, in some sense, present wherever the minister is, who acts by his power and orders, and does what is pleasing to him, according to the spirit of the heavenly High Priest.

30. As he spake these words, many believed on him. 31. ¶ Then said Jesus to those Jews which believe on him, If ye continue in my word, *then* are ye my disciples indeed;

It is not then sufficient, barely to believe in Christ; we must likewise "continue in his word," in order to be his "disciples indeed." To continue therein, is not to have only a transient taste of it, not to love some of its truths, nor to practise some one part of it, nor to observe it only externally, or for some days, or even months; but it is to love all its truths, to persevere in the practise of them throughout the whole course of our lives, and that upon a principle of love to God, and to make his law our joy and delight. O divine word of Jesus Christ, habitation of the Christian, mansion of delight, joy, and repose, retirement where we enjoy true peace, fortress where we are secure from all the insults of our enemy, sacred temple where we adore God, and palace wherein we possess all the treasures of the divine wisdom and knowledge! Happy is that person who really continues in thee by an assiduous meditation, and an inviolable adherence to thee, and who, in every state and condition of life, either remains in thy bosom, or retreats into it!

32. And ye shall know the truth, and the truth shall make you free.

The Jews learned nothing but types and shadows in the school of Moses; the Gentiles, only falsehoods and lies in the school of the devil; but Christians, in the school of Christ, learn the truth, which confounds falsehood, disperses shadows, and fulfils the law. We never learn or know the truth perfectly, except when we love it; and we never love it, but only when the love thereof is graven in our hearts by the finger of God, which is his Spirit. And this love makes us free, in delivering us from the heavy yoke of the letter and ceremonies of the law, from criminal inclinations, from deceitful pleasures, and worldly fears, which render us slaves to sin. O Spirit of Truth, vouchsafe to teach me the truth, in that way which is peculiar to thyself—thou, who art the only master and teacher thereof!

33. They answered him, We be Abraham's seed, and were never in bondage to any man: how sayest thou, Ye shall be made free?

O vanity of the children of Adam! They boast of their nobility, because they are ignorant how much sin has degraded them. How great is the blindness, for men to be in bondage, and not to know it! And yet how common is this blindness! This is the great wound of a heart not yet set at liberty by the truth—to be in bondage and misery, and yet to think itself free and happy. Cause me, Lord, to know my bondage, make me sensible of my misery; for fear lest, like the Jews, I should despise the promise of liberty, and insolently reject the hand which offers to make me free.

34. Jesus answered them, Verily, verily, I say unto you, Whosoever committeth sin is the servant* of sin. [* *Fr.* Slave.]

Sin renders us slaves to the law of sin and of the devil; and so much the more slaves, the more we believe ourselves masters of our own will, and free from all law. Miserable is that person, who, being a slave by birth through original sin —a slave by right of war, having suffered himself to be overcome—and even a slave by choice, having voluntarily sold himself—still loves his bondage, and flies from his deliverer! If we doubt whether we be slaves, let us but enter into ourselves, and consider the corruption of our will, of which we have made for ourselves as it were a chain of iron. Break this chain, O Lord, I beseech thee, and resume that which belongs to thee alone!

35. And the servant abideth not in the house for ever: *but* the Son abideth ever.

The law cannot possibly restore to the sinner the right which he had to live eternally with his God in heaven, because it cannot deliver him from the slavery of sin. It is only the Spirit of the divine adoption which can revive that right within us, by delivering us from sin, and making us children of God, members of his Son, and coheirs with him to whom alone the inheritance belongs. As we regain this right only by charity, so we preserve it only by preserving charity, which alone opens heaven, because this alone never sins, this alone makes a good use of the creatures, and this alone fulfils as it ought the law of God.

36. If the Son therefore shall make you free, ye shall be free indeed.

There is now no freedom in respect of that which is good, but only through the grace of the Son of God, which alone sets the sinner's will free from the dominion of concupiscence. In vain do men seek, by means of riches and reputation, of authority and preferment, of study and philosophical wisdom, to free themselves from any particular subjection and slavery of mind; they labour only to make themselves new chains, while the heart is not freed from the bonds of iniquity, and from the slavery of the passions, by the only deliverer Jesus Christ. The freedom of my will itself, O Jesus, is the most servile thing in me, and the most enslaved, so long as it is not set at liberty by thee. The more thou leavest it to itself, the less will it be free!

37. I know that ye are Abraham's seed; but ye seek to kill me, because my word hath no place* in you. [* *Fr.* Nor entrance in your heart.]

It is only to his shame that a wicked man glories in being descended from holy men, whose example he will not imitate. The true children of Abraham have their hearts open to evangelical truth, because it is the completion of the promises of which they are heirs. It is a dismal omen, to be only deaf thereto; it is more so, to be provoked against it; but to persecute and endeavour to destroy those who preach it, is the last degree of perverseness and obduracy. The word of God requires a heart which is empty. A heart filled with earthly projects, carnal interests, ambition, thoughts of raising a fortune, worldly business, and with the love of the pleasures and superfluities of life, is not fit to receive the evangelical seed. When a man shuts his heart against it by his passions, he opens it, at the same time, to the greatest crimes.

38. I speak that which I have seen with my Father: and ye do that which ye have seen with your father.

The children of God imitate their Father; the wicked imitate the devil, whose children they show themselves to be, in following his inclinations and desires, and acting by his spirit. Who can forbear trembling, when he considers this division of two models or examples so opposite to each other, and between which there is no medium—God or the devil? Whoever does not conform his life to the will of God, whose child he pretends to be, suffers himself to be led and drawn away at the will and pleasure of the devil, and chooses him for his father. It is the property of the children of God, after the example of their Head, to study the will of their Father, and to make that the constant rule of all their actions.

39. They answered and said unto him, Abraham is our father. Jesus

saith unto them, If ye were Abraham's children, ye would do the works of Abraham.

In vain do we glory in being called Christians, if we do not the works of Christians. It is neither the name, nor faith alone, nor one good work, which will cause us to be owned for the children of God; but it must be the general tenor of our works and actions, our whole life and conversation: it is according to this that we are either Christians or worldly persons. Whoever desires to know whether he belong to Christ, must consider and examine whether his life be really Christian, and conformable to the gospel of Jesus Christ.

40. But now ye seek to kill me, a man that hath told you the truth, which I have heard of God: this did not Abraham.

Nothing is so contrary to salvation as to hate those who preach the truth to us. It was the distinguishing virtue of Abraham, to receive the truth with faith and obedience: it is this disposition which is the mark and character of his children according to the Spirit. A sick person, who rejects his physician, and will take neither remedies nor food, is past all hopes of recovery. The truth contains both; it heals and nourishes the heart of those who receive it; but it is not the truth taught by philosophers which has this virtue, but the truth of God.

41. Ye do the deeds of your father. Then said they to him, We be not born of fornication; we have one Father, *even* God.

That man who has delivered himself up to sin is, in the sight of God, no other than a child of the devil, though he bear the quality of a child of God in the sight of men. A sick person who conceals his disease, has no desire to be cured. And a sinner who is intent on nothing but his own justification, labours only to render himself more criminal. An humble acknowledgment of our faults and miseries is the first remedy which God would apply to the wound of our pride; and this is that which pride itself will by no means endure. It is no very common thing for a man to be humble upon his having fallen into sin, and to forbear adding hypocrisy to his other faults. Let us take great care, lest the fear of losing the esteem of men hinder us from discovering our sins to those of whom God thinks fit to make use in order to heal and raise us up. This is a very dangerous temptation, especially for those who have always made profession of greater piety and religion than others. It is by this humiliation that God designs to secure their salvation.

42. Jesus said unto them, If God were your Father, ye would love me: for I proceeded forth and came from God; neither came I of myself, but he sent me.

One of the first fruits of the faith of true Christians, is love and devotion toward Jesus Christ, a singular respect and reverence for his word, and a particular application to honour his incarnation, whereby he was given and sent to us by his Father, and proceeded forth from his bosom without ever leaving it. When men really love God, they have a respect for all those who speak from him, and they honour him in his ministers. For what reason does Christ, our sovereign High Priest, repeat this truth so often—that he came not of himself, but was sent by his Father—if it be not to teach us the necessity of ecclesiastical vocation and mission?

43. Why do ye not understand my speech? *even* because ye cannot hear my word.

Carnal man does not understand the speech of God, and has no manner of relish for his word. As love disposes men to hear those favourably whom they love, and to enter readily into their thoughts, so envy and hatred inspire them with a spirit of contradiction, and shut the mind against the discourse of those whom they do not love. It therefore concerns us highly not to suffer ourselves to be prejudiced against the ministers of God's word: for prejudice passes easily from the persons to the truths which they preach. This prejudice was of fatal consequence to the Jews, and ruined them irrecoverably. Who can tell whether his own will not have the same effect, if he do not earnestly endeavour to lay it aside? It is no small sin for a man to oppose one single truth, or to reject it merely in opposition to certain persons.

44. Ye are of *your* father the devil, and the lusts of your father ye will do: he was a murderer from the beginning, and abode not in the truth; because there is no truth in him. When he speaketh a lie, he speaketh of his own: for he is a liar, and the father of it.

The wicked person imitates the devil, falls in with his lusts and desires, and serves for an instrument to accomplish his designs. That man who violently opposes the truth, which is the life of the soul, and endeavours to root it out of the heart of its disciples, is no other than a murderer. We have here two characters of the devil, and of the Jews, his children. The first is, contempt and opposition with respect to truth. The second is, envy and persecution against those who continue faithful. To adhere firmly to it, it is necessary to have the love thereof engraved deeply in our heart. Truth is the proper stock, as it were, of Jesus Christ; and when he teaches it, he finds it in himself: for he is truth itself, and the fountain and father of it in respect of us. That which Christ is in relation to truth, the same is the devil in relation to lies. O truth! what does a man become when he forsakes thee? what is a mind and heart delivered up to falsehood, after having been fed with the truth and sustained by it?

45. And because I tell *you* the truth, ye believe me not.

The truth is but little hearkened to and ill received, even from the mouth of Jesus Christ himself, if his grace do not touch the heart. The most evident mark of the corruption of any heart is, when, instead of thankfully receiving the truth for which it was made, it shows the greatest sharpness and bitterness against those who teach it, and is filled with the gall of envy and hatred. The truth has always a very dangerous and deplorable effect upon men when it only occasions them to have no confidence in those who preach it.

SECT. IV.—HE THAT IS OF GOD HEARETH GOD'S WORDS.—CHRIST SAID TO HAVE A DEVIL: REFERS HIS HONOUR TO HIS FATHER: IS BEFORE ABRAHAM.—THE JEWS ATTEMPT TO STONE HIM.

46. Which of you convinceth me of sin? And if I say the truth, why do ye not believe me.

A preacher or pastor ought to be unblamable in his life and conversation. Is he who shows in his manners plain and evident works of the infidelity of his heart in respect of the truths of the gospel, a likely person to induce others to believe them? It belongs to none but the Prince of pastors to be entirely free from sin, and to join to the priesthood a perfect innocence: but his ministers ought to be at least free from heinous crimes. O Jesus, the only priest truly innocent, without spot, and separate from sinners, vouchsafe to confer upon thy ministers some part of that holiness and sanctity with which thou art filled.

47. He that is of God heareth God's words: ye therefore hear *them* not, because ye are not of God.

The disposition with which a man hears the word of God, and the use which he makes thereof, show whether he is the servant of God, and how far he is so. What can be said of so many Christians who take so little care either to hear or to read the word of God, or who do it only by way of ceremony and for fashion's sake, but that they are Christians by way of ceremony, and use some small endeavours after salvation only for fashion's sake? We are never tired with hearing a friend speak, or with hearing him spoken of; and shall we pretend to be the friends of God, and yet have a negligence, disgust, and perhaps a continual forgetfulness of the word and of the blessings of God? What! "not to be of God!" Lord, can we have the least degree of faith, and not choose to do and suffer every thing rather than expose ourselves to this misfortune?

48. Then answered the Jews, and said unto him, Say we not well that thou art a Samaritan, and hast a devil?

This is matter of instruction and consolation, and a fit subject of meditation for all those who are calumniated. Deplorable blindness this, and dreadful hardness of heart! that men should abandon themselves to the greatest blasphemies and to the most horrid crimes, not only without hesitation, without remorse, without any consideration either of their duty or their sin, but even with an erroneous persuasion of the goodness of their actions, and applauding themselves for their great knowledge and judgment! There is a false kind of evidence, a persuasion arising from error, an acquiescence under seduction, which make human reason easy, and the conscience secure, even when it takes Christ for a reprobate, and for a seducer animated by the spirit of darkness. A state which was common to almost all the people of God, to almost every priest, Pharisee, and doctor of the law then alive, is not perhaps so very uncommon at this time as we imagine. Is it not a still greater degree of blindness, to endeavour to excuse these blind wretches from the guilt of sin?

49. Jesus answered, I have not a devil; but I honour my Father, and ye do dishonour me.

In vain should we seek among all the philosophers for such a pattern of meekness in bearing injuries, and of wisdom in justifying himself from the most outrageous calumnies. It is necessary, after Christ's example, always to distinguish exactly those calumnies which fall upon the ministry, and undermine the very foundation of the Christian mission and doctrine, from those which are only personal; and among the latter such as are indefinite, as a general accusation of Samaritanism, heresy, etc., from a particular accusation of some certain error, or of some criminal action. A man may neglect and despise all personal and indefinite calumnies; but he ought to vindicate himself from the other. The reputation of a minister of the church is not his own, but the church's; as that of an ambassador, or of a minister of state, belongs to the prince and to the state. The more an ambassador honours his prince by his fidelity, wisdom, and address, and the more he is approved and authorized by him, the more any injury which is done him, is done to the prince himself, and to the state. A minister sent from God would be unworthy of his character, if he should tamely suffer himself to be represented as an emissary of the devil, and an apostle of lies. Even Jesus Christ, who suffered all that could possibly be suffered, teaches him to justify himself from such calumnies as these, after his example and in his spirit.

50. And I seek not mine own glory: there is one that seeketh and judgeth.

The care of a minister of Christ for his own reputation has its proper bounds, which he ought perfectly to know, and which he must not transgress under pretence of seeking the glory of God and the honour of his ministry. He ought to vindicate, but not revenge himself. It is sufficient to have repelled the calumny with a moderation becoming a Christian and a priest: his exemplary life, and the prudence of his conduct, are to perform the rest. What they cannot effect, he must leave to God; lest, from being a minister of his mercy, he become the minister of his own revenge.

51. Verily, verily, I say unto you, if a man keep my saying, he shall never see death.

The keeping or observing the word of God gives eternal life. It is a great mistake to imagine that it must needs be a failing and imperfection to have that in view, and as a motive to our endeavours; whereas we ought to be thankful to God for his goodness in affording us such a support to our weakness, and such an incentive to quicken our sloth. A minister of Jesus Christ may suffer himself to be humbled; but he must never suffer either the ministry, or the word of truth of which he is the minister, to be decried and undervalued. Can he possibly do better than to imitate his Saviour, who here extols the excellency of his word and truth so much the more, the more the Jews villified it in endeavouring to make it pass for the word of the devil!

52. Then said the Jews unto him, Now we know that thou hast a devil. Abraham is dead, and the prophets; and thou sayest, If a man keep my saying, he shall never taste of death.

The greatest meekness cannot win the hearts of the declared enemies of truth: but this does not excuse us from exercising it toward them even to the last, after the example of Jesus Christ. This declaration, which proceeded just now from the mouth of Christ, and which is so full of comfort and consolation to the lovers of evangelical truth, serves only, through the just judgment of God, and the inherent malice of these Jews, to harden them the more, and to increase the delusion of their false evidence and persuasion. Let us be very careful to secure ourselves from falling into so miserable a state as this: it begins sometimes by a very small matter.

53. Art thou greater than our father Abraham, which is dead? and the prophets are dead: whom makest thou thyself?

The world knows no other death beside that which separates the soul from the body, and has no notion of that which separates it from its God, which the patriarchs and prophets avoided by keeping his word, and adhering to Christ before his coming. Every thing becomes obscure to those who have once delivered up their hearts to incredulity. Their remembrance of the prophets ought to have applied their minds to consider and observe in Christ the miracles and other marks of the Messias, contained in their prophecies; and they remember them only to lessen him and set him below all the prophets. Lord, let me never be so unfortunate as to know thee no better.

54. Jesus answered, If I honour myself, my honour is nothing: it is my Father that honoureth me; of whom ye say, that he is your God:

Who will dare to glorify or honour himself, since Jesus Christ did not? It belongs to the creature to humble itself: God alone has a right to exalt it. Human glory or honour is nothing, were it even in Jesus Christ himself. He sets a value only upon that which he received from his Father by the mouth of John, by the voice heard from heaven, and by miracles.

55. Yet ye have not known him; but I know him: and if I should say, I know him not, I shall be a liar like unto you: but I know him, and keep his saying.

Observe here three duties with respect to God: (1.) To know him. (2.) To confess him. (3.) To obey him. Christ spares not the pride of these persons, who boasted that they alone had the key of the knowledge of God, whom they ought indeed to have known better than any others. This is a judgment which should make us tremble: to see that the light of the Scripture, the knowledge of God, and all the assistance of the law, became the source of blindness to these wicked Jews, even to the priests and doctors themselves, through the ill use which their pride made of them all. Since we cannot worship and adore God unless we love and obey him, let us not flatter ourselves that we know him as our Master and Father, so long as we despise his law and do not perform his will.

56. Your father Abraham rejoiced* to see my day; and he saw *it*, and was glad. [* *Fr.* Desired ardently.]

There was no true joy under the Old Testament, but only

in the hopes of the coming of Jesus Christ. The piety of the patriarchs, prophets, and other holy persons before the incarnation, consisted in desiring, praying, and looking for the Saviour who was to be born, and in earnestly endeavouring to render themselves worthy to have a share in the favour and blessing of his coming. Is insensibility or coldness toward Jesus Christ to be endured in Christians, who do not now behold his mysteries at a distance, and have not only the promise of them as Abraham had, but have received this inestimable gift, have been washed in his blood, nourished with his flesh, filled with his Spirit, and loaded with his benefits? Let the faith, the ardent desire, and the joy of this holy patriarch inspire us with the same sentiments and affections toward Christ, cause us to love his interests, and engage us constantly to discharge our duties to him in spirit and in truth.

57. **Then said the Jews unto him, Thou art not yet fifty years old, and hast thou seen Abraham?**

The more light is offered to a blind and obdurate heart, the blinder does it still grow. It has no eyes but only for sensible and corporeal objects. Every thing contributes to the nourishment of the faith and piety of the elect: every thing serves to increase the infidelity of the wicked, who turn every thing into ridicule. It is the common way of those who affect the character of strong reasoning, to believe nothing but what they can comprehend, and to reject whatever is above their understanding. A man passes with them for no other than whimsical, when he believes what they despise; but what signifies their judgment to those who are so much the more esteemed in the judgment of God the more they disregard the judgment of the world?

58. **Jesus said unto them, Verily, verily, I say unto you, Before Abraham was, I am.**

This answer of Jesus Christ is a proof of his divinity and eternity. He was in God his Father as his Word and wisdom, and he was pleased to think of giving himself to us. He is come, he has given himself, and yet we perhaps think very seldom of him: so far are we from giving and consecrating ourselves to his divine person, incarnate for our sakes. Thou,

O Jesus, art before Abraham, not only in the designs and decrees of God thy Father, as the enemies of thy divinity say, for in that sense every thing is eternal; but in his bosom, as his coeternal, consubstantial Son, and together with him the Creator of Abraham. I adore thee according to what thou art from eternity in God thy Father; and all the vain subtleties of the wit of man are not able to stagger my faith.

59. Then took they up stones to cast at him: but Jesus hid himself, and went out of the temple, going through the midst of them, and so passed by.

Persecution is the reward of evangelical preachers in this life: and there are few such, because there are few who are willing to suffer. The retreat which Christ here makes is humble, prudent, and instructive. He does not refuse to die for the truth of his divinity; he will be a martyr for it in a very little time: but he reserves himself for a more ignominious and cruel punishment, and waits for the moment appointed by his Father, that he may make his death a sacrifice of obedience. He goes out of the temple, because it was designed only for the victims of the Jewish people, and not for the victim of the world—a victim which requires a new altar, and is to be sacrificed in the sight of the whole earth. If the crime of the Jews be already committed in their mind by their purpose and design of stoning our blessed Saviour, the sacrifice is likewise accomplished in the heart of Christ by his disposition and desire. Let me learn of thee, O victim of God, thus to sacrifice myself on all occasions, and to anticipate the sacrifice of my death, in keeping myself continually disposed and prepared for it by the spirit of sacrifice.

CHAPTER IX.

SECT. I.—THE MAN BORN BLIND RESTORED TO SIGHT.

1. AND as *Jesus* passed by, he saw a man which was blind from *his* birth.

Blindness of body is not only one of the punishments of sin, but also an emblem of spiritual blindness, in which all the children of Adam are born by reason of sin. It is a small matter not to behold this light, which is common to inferior animals: but what is it to be deprived of that light which is my life, my happiness, and my God! which is thyself, O eternal light! without which every thing is but darkness, wandering, and death, and even in this life a beginning of hell! Everlasting thanks be rendered to thee, O Jesus, for that, in passing through this mortal life, through ignominies and sufferings, from the manger to the cross, thou didst vouchsafe to see me before I was capable of seeing thee, and didst cast upon me those eyes of mercy which, of a child of darkness, have made me become a child of light!

2. And his disciples asked him, saying, Master, who did sin, this man, or his parents, that he was born blind?

It is plain, from hence, that it was a common opinion even among the Jews, that the diseases of man take their rise from sin, and that from his birth he is guilty of a sin of which this blindness might be the punishment. Every child of Adam ought to accustom himself, when under afflictions, to contemplate the justice of God, who can render none miserable but those whom he finds sinners. There is danger in seeking after the cause of the miseries of others in personal sins, which we may perhaps rashly impute to them; but we cannot possibly do amiss in seeking in our own the cause of that which we ourselves suffer.

3. Jesus answered, Neither hath this man sinned, nor his parents: but that the works of God should be made manifest in him.

There are some afflictions which God sends only for his own glory; and he who endures them is but too highly honoured, in being subservient thereto at the expense of every thing which is most near and dear to him. Though God never afflict the innocent, and though afflictions always serve either to punish sin or to purify the sinner, yet this is not always the first, and never the principal design of God. He intends here to honour and authorize his Son; but it is to his own glory that the miracles, authority, and glory of his Son ultimately tend. Happy is that minister of this Son, who imitates his example, in never seeking his own glory in the most eminent and remarkable works which God is pleased to perform by his hands. Let us always remember that it is the work of God, and not our own, which shines forth in us; and that it ought to shine forth only to his glory.

4. I must work the works of him that sent me, while it is day: the night cometh, when no man can work.

It is a holy and apostolical disposition in a pastor or evangelical labourer to be entirely employed in the work of God, to have no other business besides that of his mission, and never to be tired with working as long as the day of his life lasts; the time of rest comes not till the day is at an end. When Christ, the Sun of Righteousness, either withdraws himself from us, or takes us out of the world, it is a night which is much more to be feared than that of nature. This night cometh, and it cometh very fast, wherein nothing more can be done in order to salvation; when nothing shall remain to us but what we have done in the day of this life; when whatever is not the work of God in us shall be the subject of his judgment; and when every work of God which we have turned to our own glory shall turn to our own condemnation. What a dreadful misfortune is it to suffer ourselves to be surprised by this night!—a night which will never have an end in respect of all those who are thereby surprised.

5. As long as I am in the world, I am the light of the world.

The bodily presence of Jesus Christ on earth made the day or light of the world; and his spiritual presence in the church and in a heart, by faith and grace, makes the day or light of that heart, and of the whole church. He is just going to show, by enlightening this one person, that it is he who lighteth every man who comes into the world; and that he likewise came on purpose to enlighten the world, which lay buried in the darkness of ignorance and sin. It is a great misfortune to the Jews to have changed, in respect of themselves, this day into night, this light into darkness, by not making any spiritual advantage of the time of his preaching; but this misfortune is common to all those who reject the light of truth, and who spend the short time of this life in doing any thing rather than what concerns their salvation;

and this in the midst of the instructions, good examples, and all the other assistances which are to be found in the church.

6. When he had thus spaken, he spat on the ground, and made clay of the spittle, and he anointed the eyes of the blind man with the clay,

He who made man out of the earth cures him with earth. That which, in the hand of another person, would cause blindness, serves to restore sight in the hand of Jesus Christ; because the creature is nothing, and can do nothing but what the Creator is pleased to make it be and do. Spittle being a figure of wisdom, we have here an emblem of the union of the eternal wisdom with the earth and clay of our flesh, and of the wonderful virtue of that union. Let us, in this blind man, behold as in a glass the blindness of our own soul, through its fondness toward the creatures. Earthly things, the works of the divine wisdom, of which they bear so many evident marks, do, notwithstanding, blind the minds of men. They hinder them from seeing heaven and heavenly things, though they are, as it were, laid open to their sight. Put thy hand, O Lord, I beseech thee, upon the eyes of my heart, and let thy divine unction cure its blindness.

7. And said unto him, Go, wash in the pool of Siloam, which is by interpretation, Sent. He went his way, therefore, and washed, and came seeing.

This pool of Siloam is an emblem of the baptism of Jesus Christ, sent by the Father, which cures the blindness of sin in all those who are obedient to the word of faith. If we admire in this pool the supernatural virtue which God gives it to enlighten the eyes of one blind man, how can we continually behold the baptismal fountain with so much indifference? Is it more to open the eyes of the body than to penetrate into the very soul of all baptized persons, not only to enlighten the eyes thereof, but to heal it entirely, to restore it to life, to sanctify it, and to consecrate it to God? I return most humble and hearty thanks to thee, O Lord, for that which thou hast wrought in me by means of this sacred pool; and I admire that miracle of illumination, which is continually performed in thy church, and which is evident to the eyes of faith.

8. ¶ The neighbours therefore, and they which before had seen him that he was blind, said, Is not this he that sat and begged?

The blindness of the body is not always accompanied with poverty; but that of the soul is inseparable from it. Whence comes it to pass, that, when we hear of a returning sinner, instead of unprofitable discourse, we do not say one to another, in admiration and acknowledgment of the goodness of God, "Is not this that poor, miserable, and blind wretch, who but just now sat in the darkness of sin, being an enemy of God, a slave of the devil, and a child of wrath? And behold, he is become a child of light and benediction, a child of God, a member of Christ, and an inheritor of the kingdom of heaven!" The reason why we do not entertain one another in this manner, is because we have but little inclination to apply our minds to spiritual things, and because our faith is almost always asleep, and, as it were, buried in flesh and blood.

9. Some said, This is he: others *said*, He is like him: *but* he said, I am *he.*

A sinner, whose heart God has enlightened and changed by his grace, is not easily known again. He is no longer the same man—that child of Adam, who was entirely governed by his passions: he is now a true Christian, in whom there appears nothing but the humility, charity, and meekness of Christ; in whom there is no longer the least sign of the love of the riches, pleasures, and vanities of the world. How would it be if one could see his heart? That man is much to be lamented who is one of those false penitents who are not at all different from what they were, but only as they outwardly make use of the sacrament, and whom we always know to be the same by every thing else. A true penitent is ever difficult to be known by others, never by himself: he is full of gratitude and acknowledgment for his recovery; but has always before his eyes his past diseases and miseries, and the root and cause of them which he carries in his own heart. I am, by the grace of Christ, a person altogether different; but of myself I am always the same.

10. Therefore said they unto him, How were thine eyes opened?

It is a holy and useful curiosity, and such as tends to the

glory of God, to inquire of a person whom he has newly enlightened, how he wrought in his heart; how his eyes were opened so as to see the vanity of the world, of all its honours, pleasures, amusements, fashions, maxims, etc.; and how his mind, blind as it was to the things of God and of salvation, became so fully persuaded of the truths of religion and of the gospel, so attentive and open to the word of God, and so firmly fixed on every thing that is good.

11. He answered and said, A man that is called Jesus made clay, and anointed mine eyes, and said unto me, Go to the pool of Siloam, and wash: and I went and washed, and I received sight.

Many doubt concerning Christ through infidelity, or are silent through fear, or ask him questions out of curiosity, or persecute him through malice: one single person alone confesses him with faith, and owns him out of gratitude. It is a good sign of these virtues, when a man is always ready to open his mind to his neighbour in relation to the miseries from which he has been freed, the mercies he has received from God, and the methods of his conduct; provided that this tend to the glory of God and to the edification of his neighbour, and that he do it with the necessary precautions, so as neither to fall into vanity, nor to renew odious ideas, nor to rake into the filth of past sins.

12. Then said they unto him, Where is he? He said, I know not.

It is good to desire and endeavour to know a man of God, to whom we see by experience that he gives a blessing for the illumination of souls. Men seek with earnestness a skilful physician for the health of the body, or a learned person to instruct their children: but they neglect, they are afraid to find, they avoid, and reject a man who has the knowledge of God for the salvation of the soul. It is always the safest way to withdraw from the esteem of the world, as Jesus Christ did; and at least to let the heat of the first applause be past. It is not always (as in the case before us) that a sinner, enlightened of God, does, without any fault of his own, find himself in a little time in such a state as not to be able to tell what is become of Christ in reference to himself: for this often happens because he did not take care to retain him in his heart by his fidelity and gratitude.

SECT. II.—THE INQUIRY OF THE PHARISEES.—THOSE WHO CONFESS CHRIST PUT OUT OF THE SYNAGOGUE.

13. ¶ They brought to the Pharisees him that aforetime was blind.

See here the spirit of the world, where it is often a crime to give men the true light, and one almost as great to have received it. It is a temptation to a virtuous man to see himself pursued and sought after for a good action, while crimes are committed by the wicked with impunity. One could have no comfort under this great disorder, were it not for the good which God brings out of it. A sinner is exceedingly to blame when he complains of being exposed to this calamity, which was endured by the Holy One of God.

14. And it was the sabbath day when Jesus made the clay, and opened his eyes.

Festivals were not instituted for men to spend them in idleness, but to sanctify themselves on those days by charity, which is the true sabbath and the true rest. The sabbath was one of the most mysterious observances of the Jewish religion. Christ chose to heal the sick on that day, to signify what he was come to do with respect to sinners; and to show that he was the same God who created man, that he was carrying on by the redemption his first designs and work, and that he had a right to join the second where the first had ended.

15. Then again the Pharisees also asked him how he had received his sight. He said unto them, He put clay upon mine eyes, and I washed, and do see.

Happy had these blind persons been, had they made this inquiry and search only out of a desire to find the light, that they might be cured of their blindness! This light was hid in that body of clay which was sanctified by its union with the divinity; and this was the very thing which blinded their pride instead of enlightening it. We must seek the light humbly, if we would not be blinded thereby. How much does their blindness increase who seek after it maliciously, out of envy, and to make a bad use thereof!

16. Therefore said some of the Pharisees, This man is not of God, because he keepeth not the sabbath day. Others said, How can a man that is a sinner do such miracles? And there was a division among them.

As that which the Pharisees here said concerning Christ is a dreadful instance of a judgment proceeding from envy, where a false appearance of evil prevails above the most convincing proofs of integrity and piety: so that which others said is an amiable instance of a judgment formed by honesty and good sense, where solid and substantial proofs correct all disadvantageous appearances. Envy judges of the works by the persons who do them; equity judges of persons by their works. The judgments of men will ever be divided with respect to the best of men, so long as the world is divided by different passions and interests.

17. They say unto the blind man again, What sayest thou of him, that he hath opened thine eyes? He said, He is a prophet.

Strange malignity this of the children of Adam! They are always ready to believe what is evil, not only without, but even contrary to plain and evident proof; but they never have sufficient proof to induce them to believe what is good concerning those whom they do not love. A sincere and Christian heart makes no difficulty of speaking according to truth, even before the enemies thereof. To bear witness to the integrity, virtue, and innocence of those by whom God has been pleased to enlighten us, is the least acknowledgment which we owe both to him and them.

18. But the Jews did not believe concerning him, that he had been blind, and received his sight, until they called the parents of him that had received his sight. 19. And they asked them, saying, Is this your son, who ye say was born blind? How then doth he now see?

God makes the injustice of men subservient to his goodness. The more the Pharisees examine this miracle in order to raise doubts concerning it, the more indubitable do they render it. By all this we see how much it concerns us not to suffer our minds to be prepossessed; since passion closes the eyes against things the most evident. What pains and trouble do men give themselves, only to avoid receiving the truth! There is no avenue, whereby it can approach them, which they leave unshut. They refuse to receive it only because it displeases them; and it displeases only because they will not receive it out of obstinacy, interest, or blindness. These Jews have very faithful followers in the persons of heretics, and of those among the learned, who, by much examining things, bring themselves to that pass as to reject that as incredible which is in itself the most evident.

20. His parents answered them, and said, We know that this is our son, and that he was born blind: 21. But by what means he now seeth, we know not; or who hath opened his eyes, we know not: he is of age; ask him: he shall speak for himself.

Few persons are willing to expose themselves to danger in bearing witness to the truth, because few really love it. Men always find reasons to shift this obligation off upon others, and to clear themselves of the trouble: but the question is, how they will clear themselves before God. It is dangerous for parents to give this bad example to their children; superiors to inferiors; masters to their disciples. The nearer relation we bear to those who have received signal blessings from God, the more ought we to look upon ourselves as concerned in their obligations, and to assist them in discharging them. When any worldly advantage is to be gained, a man is very willing to make one: but when there is somewhat to be hazarded, he will have nothing to do in the matter. A father is always ready to receive all the honour and advantage he can from the talents of an understanding son, whom the world applauds; but he is the first who draws back, when the use of those talents is likely to bring him into any trouble from the great.

22. These *words* spake his parents, because they feared the Jews: for the Jews had agreed already, that if any man did confess that he was Christ, he should be put out of the synagogue. 23. Therefore said his parents, He is of age; ask him.

Neither the fear of being deprived of any office, employment, or temporal advantage, nor even the dread of an unjust excommunication, ought ever to hinder us from performing our duty. A sentence of excommunication never hurts the person against whom it is pronounced, unless he have done somewhat to deserve it; and it always falls back upon those who pronounce it, when they do it unjustly. We never are without the pale of the church, no, not even when we seem to be driven out of it by the wickedness of men, so long as we continue united to God, to Jesus Christ, and to the church itself by charity. The Holy Ghost, to whom it principally belongs to bind and loose, never renders himself the minister of the passion or blindness of men.

SECT. III.—THE BLIND MAN ABUSED AND CAST OUT FOR THE SAKE OF CHRIST.

24. Then again called they the man that was blind, and said unto him, Give God the praise: we know that this man is a sinner.

The pretence of zeal for God's glory often serves to cover the purpose and design of committing the greatest crimes. A perverse and obstinate endeavour to force a man, contrary to his conscience, to condemn one whom he knows to be innocent, was employed against Christ himself: against whom then may it not be employed? The positive assertion of persons of credit, that our neighbour is an ill man, is not sufficient to give us a right to condemn him when we have either any proofs of his innocence, or any reason to doubt of the truth of their information. A blind obedience on such occasions is so far from giving glory to God, that it is an act of disobedience to his law.

25. He answered and said, Whether he be a sinner *or no,* I know not: one thing I know, that, whereas I was blind, now I see."

It is more easy to find among the poor than among the rich such a generous, plain, and persevering acknowledgment as that here made by this blind man who had received his sight. Nothing should ever induce us to disown the favours God has conferred upon us, when his glory is concerned. With how much greater gratitude ought a converted sinner to say, "I was born blind by reason of Adam's sin; and thou, Lord, hast vouchsafed to make me a child of light: I was under the blindness of my own sins, and thou hast enlightened me: I was in darkness, and had no sight at all of my duties; and now I see them perfectly. Thy name be glorified for this, O my God!"

26. Then said they to him again, What did he to thee? how opened he thine eyes?

Envy is indefatigable, and infidelity persists obstinately in its wicked designs. They spare not even the works of God. The world is full of such persons as seem seriously to consider these works, who yet apply their minds thereto with no other purpose but to contradict them, to rob God of the glory of them, and to make them the subject of their cavils and disputes. Let me learn, O Lord, to consider them with reverence; let me therein admire thy power and greatness, and contemplate those other perfections, the marks and characters of which are so visibly impressed on them.

27. He answered them, I have told you already, and ye did not hear: wherefore would ye hear *it* again? will ye also be his disciples?

We ought never to be weary in recounting the wonders of God's power and goodness, when we meet with persons who love to hear them; but obdurate and malicious hearts, which will certainly abuse this knowledge, are altogether unworthy of it. To receive spiritual advantage thereby, men must bring along with them the minds of disciples, such as are humble, teachable, and obedient, not such as set themselves up to be judges of the divine works.

28. Then they reviled him, and said, Thou art his disciple; but we are Moses' disciples.

The greatest blessings are frequently looked upon as curses by the wicked; or would at least be counted a grievance by abundance of people of fashion, as they are called. There are a great many of them who would take it as an affront if we should think them devout; and who would be highly offended if we should exhort them to show themselves the servants of God, and to make profession of Christianity in their life and conversation. A Christian is but too happy, when the affronts and injuries of carnal men have no other effect upon him but only to make him more intent on following Christ. It is my glory, O Lord, to be thy disciple; and such I am resolved to continue even to my last breath.

29. We know that God spake unto Moses: *as for* this *fellow*, we know not from whence he is.

It is extremely dangerous to know some certain truths, and

not to know them well. God spoke indeed to Moses; but the most important truth he taught him was, that he was no more than only a type or shadow of our blessed Saviour, and that his law was given to no other end but to lead men to Jesus Christ: and this was the thing which these Pharisees, these great pretenders to learning, knew nothing of. It was, in some respects, an advantage to the Gentiles, that they had no eminent person to whom they could be devoted, and that they were under no temptation of pursuing a wrong path in following only types and shadows.

30. The man answered and said unto them, Why, herein is a marvellous thing, that ye know not from whence he is, and *yet* he hath opened mine eyes.

A man has abundance of strength and courage when he has the truth on his side. An ignorant person undertakes here to argue with men of learning and doctors of the law, and confounds them: the reason is, because the truth fights in him, and his adversaries fight against the truth.

31. Now as we know that God heareth not sinners: but if any man be a worshipper of God, and doeth his will, him he heareth.

The prayers of a professed libertine, of a seducer, and of such sinners as will not think of conversion, are rejected of God; but those of a sinner, who, through love to God, hates sin, never are. A penitent sinner is no longer a sinner in the sight of God. He can never despise the prayer of an humble and contrite heart; since it is his Spirit who causes it to pray, and forms the very prayer itself.

32. Since the world began was it not heard that any man opened the eyes of one that was born blind. 33. If this man were not of God, he could do nothing.

God never works miracles to authorize an impostor, or to declare any person innocent and holy, who is not really so; neither does he ever work any by the hands of those who desire them only for the support of errors or of a false mission. It cannot be pretended by any that it is according to the method of the divine dispensations to work any miracles by the wicked, publicly known to be such; much less in so great a number, and of so extraordinary a nature as those of Christ.

34. They answered and said unto him, Thou wast altogether born in sins, and dost thou teach us? And they cast him out.

We may observe here three marks or characters of wicked pastors. The first is, to treat their sheep, and especially the most harmless of them, with haughtiness, and even with contumelious language. The second, to be altogether impatient that any one should remind them of their duty. And the third, to have no love of unity, but to be always ready to drive those out of the fold who are already in it, instead of inviting and bringing those into it who do not belong thereto. That is a happy separation which divides us from the world, and from the society of the wicked, to unite us to Jesus Christ. It is the privilege of this poor man to be a professor of Christ, even before he is a Christian. He loses the communion of the Jewish church, without having the consolation which Christians unjustly excommunicated enjoy, who are more closely and strongly united to the church on that account: but Christ is just going to make him full amends another way.

SECT. IV.—THE BLIND MAN INSTRUCTED BY CHRIST.—THEY WHO THINK THEY SEE MADE BLIND.

35. Jesus heard that they had cast him out; and when he had found him, he said unto him, Dost thou believe on the Son of God?

When the world rejects us, and casts us out, then Christ finds us, discovers himself to us, and gives us comfort. The very least degree of grace and favour which God vouchsafes to confer upon us, is sufficient to support and comfort us under all the evils which men can bring upon us. They who separate good men from their society by an unjust excommunication, do in reality excommunicate themselves, by separating from the communion of saints, and unite those the closer to Jesus Christ by rendering them more conformable to him.

36. He answered and said, Who is he, Lord, that I might believe on him?

Docility opens the heart to faith: but it is God who gives both. Not to believe immediately, but to desire to be first instructed, is agreeable to the prudence which faith itself requires. When we are once thoroughly persuaded of the almighty power of God, we are disposed to believe every thing as soon as it is sufficiently propounded to our understanding as coming from him. This new convert, who saw only one miracle, will rise up in judgment against those incredulous persons who never have enough.

37. And Jesus said unto him, Thou hast both seen him, and it is he that talketh with thee.

O comfortable, instructive, efficacious, and, as it were, sacramental words! which manifest Christ to the mind, and imprint on the heart the belief of his divinity, effecting that which they signify. Fidelity to Christ is well rewarded when it is honoured with the particular confidence of Christ himself. The grace which was rejected by those who were puffed up with their own learning, is here given to the simplicity and sincerity of an ignorant person, to confound the pride of human understanding.

38. And he said, Lord, I believe. And he worshipped him.

A lively faith is always accompanied with humility and religion; and the first duty performed by these is adoration or worship. This faith, though very suddenly produced, cannot be justly suspected, being followed by an act of worship which few persons then paid to Christ as the Son of God. That faith is sufficiently tried which has showed itself not to be influenced by any human regards.

39. ¶ And Jesus said, For judgment I am come into this world, that they which see not might see; and that they which see might be made blind.

Let us with fear and trembling adore this dreadful judgment of God, which makes known who are, and who are not his. He blinds the eyes of those who are puffed up with their own learning and knowledge, by leaving them in their darkness, and declaring to them truths and mysteries which they reject through the hardness of their hearts; and he enlightens those who are humble in their ignorance, by communicating to them his own light. Let us tremble under the hand of God; since it is his mercy which makes this distinction, by giving us that grace which he by no means owes us, and leaving others in their blindness by a judgment which they deserve.

40. And *some* of the Pharisees which were with him heard these words, and said unto him, Are we blind also?

It was a plain and evident sign of the blindness of these men, that they did not know that they were blind: more unhappy in this respect than he who wanted bodily sight, since he was sensible of his blindness, and desired earnestly to be cured. Nothing is more dangerous than to think ourselves enlightened; because then we never humble ourselves on the account of the darkness which is within us, we are puffed up with the conceit of that light which we have not, and are not at all solicitous to obtain that of God which we imagine we already have.

41. Jesus said unto them, If ye were blind, ye should have no sin: but now ye say, We see; therefore your sin remaineth.

That light or knowledge which is not accompanied with humility, serves generally to no other end but to increase our sins. It is nothing but a false persuasion of being sufficiently instructed and enlightened, which causes so many persons to continue in their sinful prejudices, and which hinders them from hearing and informing themselves better, and from avoiding a multitude of rash judgments, and of other sins. It is always good to distrust our own light, and to be in a constant disposition to receive instruction from others. How knowing soever some may be in Scripture and divinity, there is a certain manner of knowing what they do know, which depends only upon God, and without which they are still blind with all their learning and knowledge, either natural or acquired. Humility, docility, and prayer are the way which leads to that certain method of knowledge; but we take no care to put ourselves into this way in order to arrive at it, when we imagine we have no occasion for it.

CHAPTER X.

SECT. I.—THE SHEPHERD AND THE THIEF.—CHRIST IS THE DOOR.

1. Verily, verily, I say unto you, He that entereth not by the door into the sheepfold, but climbeth up some other way, the same is a thief and a robber.

Every thing spoken by Christ is infallibly true; but whenever he delivers any truths with a particular asseveration, it is either because they are of greater importance, or because the mind of man is more averse to them, or because the small number of those who will practise them may render them incredible. Strange and terrible alternative! There is no possible evasion: Christ himself assures us that he is this door, (ver. 7.) Whoever, therefore, entereth not by Jesus Christ into the pastoral office, is no other than a thief and a robber in the sheepfold. And he enters not by Jesus Christ, who enters with a prospect of any other interest beside that of Christ and of his church. Ambition, avarice, love of ease, a desire to be distinguished from the crowd, to enjoy the conveniences of life, or to promote the interest of one's family, and even the sole design of providing against want,—these are all ways by which thieves and robbers enter: and whoever enters by any of these ways, or by simony, solicitation, craft, violence, etc., deserves no better name.

2. But he that entereth in by the door is the shepherd of the sheep.

Observe here the marks, qualities, and duties of a good pastor. The first mark of a good pastor is, a lawful entrance into the ministry by the internal call of Christ—namely, by an impulse proceeding from his Spirit, upon considerations which respect only his glory, and upon motives which aim at nothing but the good of his church, the salvation of souls, the doing the will of God, and the sacrificing himself entirely to his service, and to that of the meanest of his sheep. How many are there in the church who go under the name of pastors, and whom in that quality we are obliged in conscience to obey, who are no other than thieves and robbers in the sight of God! Let us not judge rashly of them; but let us beseech God that they may judge themselves.

3. To him the porter openeth; and the sheep hear his voice: and he calleth his own sheep by name, and leadeth them out.

The second mark of a good pastor is, an external call, which is then lawful, and comes from the Holy Ghost, when it is conveyed by a lawful mission, and by the apostolic authority of bishops, with a concurrence of the necessary talents and qualifications according to the rules of the church, and in conformity to the spirit of the canons. The Holy Ghost being the fountain and original of all these things, it is by them that he is, as it were, the porter of the fold, and thereby opens the door to pastors, and shuts it against thieves and robbers. Third, It is not sufficient that a pastor has the gift of word; he must likewise make use of it for the instruction of the sheep: and, in so doing, he must speak in such a manner as is suited to their capacity, that it may be truly said that the sheep hear his voice. A dumb pastor is not properly a pastor, but an image. A pastor who speaks without being understood, is rather an actor or a mountebank than a preacher. Fourth, It is the duty of a good pastor to know his sheep perfectly, (for men call only those by their names who are well known to them;) to be thoroughly acquainted with their wants and necessities, both inward and outward, and with their good and bad inclinations; to endeavour to discover the will of God concerning them; to visit them in their poverty, and in their bodily or spiritual diseases; to be intent and vigilant, and ready to assist every one of them in particular; to call his own sheep, not those of others; and to forbear invading another man's flock, or affecting to gain the good opinion and confidence of those sheep which are not committed to his care. Fifth, He must use his utmost endeavours to bring souls out of the family of Adam, and to admit them into that of Christ; to bring them, as it were, out of themselves and their sins, out of their evil habits and inclinations, out of the diversions of the world and the pomps of the devil; and to lead them into the wholesome pastures of God's word, and into the ways of a Christian life.

4. And when he putteth forth his own sheep, he goeth before them, and the sheep follow him; for they know his voice.

In the sixth place, it is not sufficient for a pastor to have shown his own sheep the way, and put them into it: he must go before them, he must be the first to practise what he teaches, he must lead such a life as they may follow without any fear of going astray, and he must enliven and animate his instructions by his actions. It is enough for the rest of the faithful to preach by example only; but it is not so for a pastor, whose sheep can never follow him unless they hear his voice. In him, preaching the word, and setting a good example, must always be inseparable. True Christians have always more regard to the word of truth than to the example of life; because it is by the former that they are to be one day judged.

5. And a stranger will they not follow, but will flee from him; for they know not the voice of strangers.

In the seventh place, a good pastor is never deserted by the elect sheep. They are able to discern, by the light of the Prince of pastors, and by the marks which he has been pleased to give, true pastors from thieves and robbers. As all the several parts of the church of God make but one flock, so all the different pastors make but one pastor in Jesus Christ, and not one of them is a stranger to another. Those are strangers who teach a strange doctrine.

6. This parable spake Jesus unto them; but they understood not what things they were which he spake unto them.

These men neither understand, nor desire to understand. They show plainly that they are blinder than they imagine, and that the light which is in them is nothing but darkness. God frequently punishes, by the thickest darkness, the presumption of those who pretend to have a perfect knowledge of the Scriptures. These men understand not the words of the Shepherd, because they are not of his flock. And the just punishment of men's having rejected the truth of Christ when it was most plain and evident, is to find themselves unable to penetrate that sacred obscurity which he is sometimes pleased to cast about it.

7. Then said Jesus unto them again, Verily, verily, I say unto you, I am the door of the sheep.

Eighth, A pastor who has entered into the ministry by the door—namely, by Jesus Christ, must have this truth deeply imprinted on his heart, that he himself is not the door of the sheep, but Jesus Christ; that it is by him that the sheep find entrance into the church, and are admitted to the grace of faith, of the sacraments, of charity, of good works, and of salvation; and that it is he who, by his merits and grace, shuts the wolf out of the fold, and secures the flock against the temptations, insults, and wicked designs of the enemy. Lord, it is my only comfort to know that without thee I can do nothing, and that by thy assistance I can do all the good which thou requirest of me, and avoid all the evil which thou hast forbidden.

8. All that ever came before me are thieves and robbers: but the sheep did not hear them.

Ninth, A pastor ought to remember, that whoever boasts of being the way of salvation and the gate of heaven, shows himself to be a thief and an impostor; and that though few are arrived at this degree of folly, yet that there are many who rely too much upon their own talents, eloquence, and labours, as if the salvation of their sheep depended necessarily thereon: in which respect they are always robbers, since they rob the grace of Christ of the glory of saving the sheep. God often disappoints and puts presumptuous pastors to shame, in not opening the hearts of their flock to hear and receive their instructions; but he blesses such as are humble, in causing them to be heard with attention, and in giving them the unction of his Spirit, that they may move and convert souls.

9. I am the door: by me if any man enter in, he shall be saved, and shall go in and out, and find pasture.

In the tenth place, a pastor ought to conduct souls to Jesus Christ, and by him, as the door of salvation. Life, and an abundant plenty of all sorts of good things, are in his hands, that he may bestow them on those who have a full trust and confidence in him, and rely solely upon his grace. Will Christians never be persuaded that Christ is their treasure, and that it is in and by him that they are to seek all graces and all assistances, spiritual and temporal? Yes, Lord Jesus, thou art the door both of grace and glory. It is by thee that we enter into the church, to find there the pasture of thy word and of thy heavenly doctrine, of thy mysteries, of thy sacraments, and of thy precious body and blood. It is by thee that, when we go out of this world, we enter into heaven, there to find that only pasture of eternal truth in which thou wilt feed thy sheep forever.

10. The thief cometh not, but for to steal, and to kill, and to destroy: I am come that they might have life, and that they might have *it* more abundantly.

In the eleventh place, the sole end which a pastor ought to propose to himself, after the example of the Prince of pastors, is to use his utmost endeavours to procure his sheep eternal life by the means of the life of grace. He, as well as Jesus Christ, is a pastor only to this purpose. Whoever does not apply himself to this is a thief, who enters into the ministry only to steal the revenues of the church, to kill and murder souls by his errors, his pernicious maxims, his scandalous example, or his negligence, and to lay waste and destroy every thing in the flock of God. That which men may imagine they have no intent on doing, the devil really designs; and these thieves are his instruments. What judgment have patrons of benefices reason to expect, who, instead of presenting pastors to the flock of Christ, present thieves and robbers, who come only to plunder and destroy all in the church! O Jesus, the true pastor, give me life, I beseech thee—that superabundant life of which thou art the only source, by thy death and by thy new life, by thy body, thy blood, and thy Spirit!

SECT. II.—THE GOOD SHEPHERD AND THE HIRELING.—CHRIST GIVES HIS LIFE FOR THE SHEEP.—HE IS SAID TO BE POSSESSED AND MAD.

11. I am the good shepherd: the good shepherd giveth his life for the sheep.

Twelfth, The good pastor ought to sacrifice himself for his sheep either by labouring in his ministry, or, if there be occasion, even by exposing his life for the benefit and advantage of his flock. What strange disorder and confusion does it make, when pastors act directly contrary, and are always ready to sacrifice their sheep to their passions, their avarice, their ease, and their resentments! It is no other than to sacrifice them, for a man to choose rather to see them perish than to put himself to the expense which is necessary to procure them instructions, or to undergo some fatigue in constant application, visits, and the other duties of his ministry. That person is very far from giving his life for the salvation of souls, who refuses to give up even his time and application to that end.

12. But he that is an hireling, and not the shepherd, whose own the sheep are not, seeth the wolf coming, and leaveth the sheep, and fleeth; and the wolf catcheth them, and scattereth the sheep.

In the thirteenth place, a good pastor must carefully distinguish between a mercenary spirit and the pastoral charity: the former causes a man to look upon the sheep as his own property, that he may lord it over them, and make what advantage he can of them; by the latter, a man looks upon them as his own on no other account but only because they are Christ's, whose interests are the same with his own. The hireling counts them his own no longer than they are profitable to him; the shepherd looks upon them as his as long as he himself can be serviceable to them. There never is a more proper time to discern true pastors from hirelings, than when persecution, poverty, pestilence, or some other distemper has seized the flock. Never is the shepherd more constant in his attendance on it; never is the hireling more ready to leave and abandon it.

13. The hireling fleeth, because he is a hireling, and careth not for the sheep.

A pastor ought, in the fourteenth place, to consider, that to flee when he ought to stand his ground, to yield up the interests of his flock when he ought to maintain them, to hide himself when he ought to appear, and to be silent when he ought to speak—that to act thus, is a plain indication that a man has either no concern at all for the welfare of his sheep, or more regard to his own temporal conveniencies than to their eternal salvation. From the time that a man is mercenary, he has within him a certain criminal indifference for every thing relating to the interest of God and his church, and is ready to give it all up for any shadow of worldly fortune and advantage.

14. I am the good shepherd, and know my *sheep*, and am known of mine. 15. As the Father knoweth me, even so know I the Father: and I lay down my life for the sheep.

In the fifteenth place, a good pastor ought not only to know his sheep, but likewise to employ his thoughts continually upon them, and to bear them always in his heart, in imitation and honour of the eternal Father and Son, who are incessantly employed in contemplating each other with a certain knowledge of love: for a good pastor is a father, and his sheep are his children. This knowledge which the Father has with respect to his Son, as the Head of his elect, and the Pastor or Shepherd of his sheep, comprehends within it all his designs concerning the Head and the members, and all his eternal purposes relating to the redemption of the sheep by the death of the Pastor, and to their sanctification and eternal salvation by him and in him. The knowledge which the Son has with respect to his Father, is a knowledge of adherence to his designs, and of obedience even unto death for the sake of his sheep. And as he never was one moment without this knowledge of love, obedience, and sacrifice, so he never was one moment without giving his life for the sheep, which is here signified to us by these words, "I know," and "I give," etc. Good pastors adore this knowledge of love and election in the Father, and of adherence and obedience in the Son; they devote themselves to him to be subservient to the Father's designs concerning the elect; they dedicate themselves to their service, sacrifice themselves continually for them, and, with reverence and adoration, conform themselves to all the dispositions of Christ toward them; saying with Paul, "We endure all things for the elect's sake."

16. And other sheep I have, which are not of this fold: them also I must bring, and they shall hear my voice: and there shall be one fold, *and* one shepherd.

In the sixteenth place, a good pastor never thinks he has

gained souls enough over to God; he is continually desirous to bring in more, and labours incessantly to fill up the number of the elect, which is known only to God, and to complete and perfect at length the body of Christ. Both Jews and Gentiles are reunited in the church, which alone is the mystical body of Jesus Christ. The church is one by the unity of the God whom she worships, of the Head who governs her, of the Holy Spirit which animates her, of the gospel which directs her, of the baptism which purifies her, of the sacrifice which she offers, of the bread which feeds her, of the faith which supports her, of the hope which exalts her, of the country to which she tends, and of the charity which unites her at present to God, and will perfect her eternally in him. Let us comfort ourselves under those divisions which afflict us here on earth, by the hope and prospect of that unity which we wait for and expect in heaven.

17. Therefore doth my Father love me, because I lay down my life, that I might take it again.

In the seventeenth place, nothing renders a pastor more amiable in the sight of God, nothing draws down upon him more graces and blessings, and more speedily advances the work of his sanctification, than a contempt of all earthly things, of the conveniencies of life, and of life itself, that he may approve himself a faithful minister of Christ. A man may justly be said to lay down his life, when he lays down the love thereof; when he offers it up sincerely to God, to be spent in his service; and when he is disposed and ready to lose it in any manner whatever for his glory. The hope of finding and taking it again by means of the resurrection, is so far from lessening this sacrifice, that it completes and perfects it: it being the end of sacrifice to reunite us to God for his glory.

18. No man taketh it from me, but I lay it down of myself. I have power to lay it down, and I have power to take it again. This commandment have I received of my Father.

In the eighteenth place, the sacrifice of a good pastor must be altogether voluntary. He is not indeed master of his own life and death, as the sovereign Pastor was, but he must be willing to lay down his life, though he could preserve it. It was entirely in the power of Christ to die or not to die, as well as to rise again; and yet he delivered himself up to death. This is the thing which renders his love more worthy of our gratitude and our love. He was sacrificed, because he was willing to be sacrificed; and he was willing out of love to us, and out of obedience to his Father. Admirable alliance this, of a free and voluntary obedience, arising from love, with an absolute incapacity of disobeying! We shall never resemble him in this respect until we come to heaven. Nineteenth, A pastor ought to have the will of God continually before his eyes, and to join the virtue of obedience to that of charity. His first sacrifice is that of his will.

19. ¶ There was a division therefore again among the Jews for these sayings.

The more Christ endeavours to make himself known, the more blind and obdurate the Jews become. How many truths so sacred, necessary, and divine, are ill received by men! Grant, Lord, that I may reap that fruit and advantage from them which the Jews refused to reap! Let us, at least, frequently adore in Christ this quality of being the good pastor or shepherd, and this excessive love which caused him to give his life for us. The more we have strayed from the fold, the more ought we to love him in the quality of pastor, and to have recourse thereto in our wants. If we are thoroughly sensible of them, we shall, without ceasing, offer up our prayers to the good Shepherd, beseeching him to seek us, to find us, to lead us, to carry us, to defend us, to feed us, etc.

20. And many of them said, He hath a devil, and is mad; why hear ye him? 21. Others said, These are not the words of him that hath a devil. Can a devil open the eyes of the blind?

Christ is now the third time treated as a demoniac and a madman. What man is there who could bear it even once without some emotion and complaint? And yet, in the twentieth and last place, this usage is what a pastor must expect to meet with in this world after abundance of toils and labours. The reward of his instructions and of his zeal in preaching the truth, is to be despised, calumniated, and abused, even for the truth's sake, as Jesus Christ was. If the eternal wisdom, and the fulness of the divine Spirit which dwells in Christ, did not secure him from being treated as a person possessed by the devil, as a madman, and as one not worthy to be heard, who, then, can presume to complain?

SECT. III.—CHRIST'S SHEEP HEAR HIS VOICE, AND CAN NEVER PERISH.—THE RAGE OF THE JEWS AGAINST HIM.

22. ¶ And it was at Jerusalem the feast of the dedication, and it was winter.

The feast of the dedication of a temple or church is one of those which ought to be kept most religiously; and it is generally very much neglected in some places, and in others most abominably profaned. This is the feast of God's holiness, which is his temple wherein he dwells, (Ps. xxii. 3,) and where he is separated from all the impurity of the creature. Temples or churches are emblems of this eternal temple, and of all the things which God consecrates to himself, in order to reside therein by a particular communication of his holiness; of the sacred humanity of the Son of God, that temple of the divinity, consecrated by the divinity itself; of the Christian, consecrated by the Spirit of God; and lastly, of the church of Christ, which is founded and built here on earth, but the dedication of which will be performed in heaven, where it will be entirely consecrated to God by his holiness, no longer veiled, but shining forth in all its majesty and glory. O divine Holiness, grant me grace to perceive and adore thee; sanctify me; excite in me a lively sense of thy presence in churches where thou art graciously pleased to communicate thyself to us; and let their consecration remind me always of my own!

23. And Jesus walked in the temple in Solomon's porch.

The walks of our blessed Saviour are not such as proceed from idleness, irreverence, and irreligion, accompanied with discourse of the same nature, and such as we sometimes see in holy places, to the shame of Christians, and even of the ministers of the church: but they are profitable and religious walks, such as tend to salvation. He is a pastor who shows and presents himself to his sheep, to feed them with the word of God, and to edify them by his own example; and who does all this not within the temple only, but likewise when he is out of it.

24. Then came the Jews round about him, and said unto him, How long dost thou make us to doubt? If thou be the Christ, tell us plainly.

Impatience to know the truth proceeds sometimes from a hatred thereof, and a design to persecute it. This crafty, hypocritical, and malicious importunity is the effect of the greatest corruption of heart; whereas a sincere, humble, generous, and fervent zeal for truth is a certain sign of great purity of heart, and of a soul which aims at nothing but truth itself. Why did these men persecute Christ for this truth, if they knew nothing of it? And if they did know it, why do they pretend to be ignorant concerning it? Thus many pretend not to have sufficient proofs of the divine Being, that they may not be obliged to live according to his laws. Others endeavour to render the truths of the gospel obscure, that they may excuse themselves from putting them in practice.

25. Jesus answered them, I told you, and ye believed not: the works that I do in my Father's name, they bear witness of me.

A Christian, and more especially a minister of Christ, ought to speak more by his works than with his tongue, in imitation of the example of his Head. The injustice, ingratitude, malice, insincerity, and insolence of the request which the Jews here made, well deserved that Christ, to complete their blindness and obduracy, should grant them that abundant light which they asked with no other design but to destroy him. Such a prayer as this made by wicked persons is a new sin, and that which God grants thereupon is a new effect of his judgment and his wrath.

26. But ye believe not, because ye are not of my sheep, as I said unto you.

Those who are not of the flock do not hear the voice of the pastor. When a man's heart is open to receive the word, it is an infallible sign that he belongs to the truth; but he whose heart is shut against it has not in the least degree the mark and character of a sheep, which is docility. It is by faith that we become part of the flock, are united to the Shepherd, and enter into the fold.

27. My sheep hear my voice, and I know them, and they follow me:

Here are three marks whereby we may know that we are of the number of the elect sheep. The first is, when the Son of God gives us a love, relish, and obedience in respect of his word. The second, when he seems mindful of our sanctification by the care which he takes concerning it. The third, when we imitate his life and virtues. He who bears these three characters to the end, is what we call a predestinate person. By these we may judge, not with certainty indeed, but with confidence, that we are of the happy number. But without these, to flatter ourselves with any such thoughts is no other than presumption. Lord, open my heart to the gospel, that I may love it; to thy saving hand, that I may submit to be guided by it; and to the example of thy virtues, that I may follow it.

28. And I give unto them eternal life; and they shall never perish, neither shall any *man* pluck them out of my hand.

Neither the devil, nor the world, nor concupiscence, can cause those finally to perish for whom God has prepared eternal life, though they may cause them to fall. That blessed life which God designs for his elect is a gift which he even now confers upon them in conferring that of his grace, and in preserving them from every thing which might otherwise occasion their ruin. Wo to the presumption of man, if he pretend to be more secure in his own hands than in those of his Saviour! Wo likewise to that presumption, if he expect that his Saviour will keep and preserve him, without his own endeavours to preserve himself from the snares of the devil, of the world, and of his own will!

29. My Father, which gave *them* me, is greater than all; and no *man* is able to pluck *them* out of my Father's hand.

The elect are in the almighty hand of God; and their Head, to whom they were given to be the members of his body, does himself possess the almighty power of his Father, having received it from him, together with his divinity, by his eternal birth and by his incarnation. This is the foundation of our comfort and our confidence. That which secures the salvation of the elect is, (1.) That they belong to Christ, out of whose hand no power is able to pluck them. (2.) That they are a gift which is irrevocable. (3.) That they are the gift of the Father to his Son, and therefore the gift of an infinite love. (4.) That they are the gift of a Father who is greater and more powerful than all created things together. And, (5.) That, by consequence, even the will of man (which certainly is of the number of those things) cannot withdraw itself forever from God, when he has given it to Jesus Christ for eternity: because grace, by which he works in that will, is no other than the operation of his own omnipotent will. I have this confidence, O my God, that thou wilt always exert thy power over my will, and that thou wilt not suffer any creature whatever to separate me from thee.

30. I and *my* Father are one.

All religion is built upon this immovable foundation, That he who has undertaken to save us and to conduct us to God is one and the same God with his Father, though he be a person really distinct from him. These truths, although they be common, are notwithstanding infinitely above our reason. It is our duty to adore them, to exercise our faith upon them, and to return most humble thanks to Christ, for that, being one with his Father from all eternity, he is graciously pleased to become one with us to all eternity.

31. Then the Jews took up stones again to stone him.

This is now the third time that the Jews have attempted to cast Christ down headlong, or to stone him. There would be but few preachers, could they foresee as Christ did, that they should frequently meet with nothing but ill usage in the exercise of their ministry. They are often discouraged at less; and, what is more deplorable, there is no occasion for so frightful a prospect to make them change the truth into lies and flatteries, and disguise the word of God in a most shameful and scandalous manner.

32. Jesus answered them, Many good works have I shewed you from my Father; for which of those works do ye stone me?

Christ, being persecuted, justifies himself, to show that his members ought to justify themselves on some occasions. A mildness so extraordinary as this, in return for such prodigious ingratitude and hardness of heart, is a very instructive and powerful sermon for preachers, and for all those who are treated ill for the sake of truth. Christ did not always observe the same conduct. He sometimes withdrew himself from the like treatment, by becoming invisible; here he preserves himself by the power of his word. Thus the conduct of one holy person is very different from that of another, even on a like occasion, though they are both acted by the very same spirit. We ought therefore to honour equally both the humble wisdom of him who makes a prudent retreat, and the wise constancy and resolution of him who maintains his ground, and withstands the wicked to their face.

33. The Jews answered him, saying, For a good work we stone thee not; but for blasphemy, and because that thou, being a man, makest thyself God.

Abundance of persons desire and ask to be instructed, and then are scandalized and offended at the truths which are taught them. Thus it is sometimes that God, through a kind of mercy, leaves people in their blindness; because they would otherwise become more wicked, and more worthy of punishment by their blasphemies. Have we any reason to wonder, that the most certain truths now delivered by the lips of men are frequently taken to be errors, when we see that Jesus Christ himself was charged with blasphemy, for declaring such truths as were supported by all the power of the Spirit which was in him, and confirmed by so many miracles?

34. Jesus answered them, Is it not written in your law, I said, Ye are gods? 35. If he called them gods, unto whom the word of God came, and the Scripture cannot be broken; 36. Say ye of him, whom the Father hath sanctified, and sent into the world, Thou blasphemest; because I said, I am the Son of God?

A priest is obliged to assert and maintain his character and mission, after the example of the sovereign Priest of the Christian church. Though every priest be admitted to a participation of the mission of Jesus Christ, yet there is still an infinite difference between one who is only consecrated and sanctified by the external word of God, and him who is himself the consubstantial and eternal word of the Father, who does not sanctify him by any thing external or created, but by himself. For, (1.) He begets him in the fulness of his own sanctity or holiness. (2.) He consecrated and sanctified his humanity by the divinity itself. (3.) He ordained him to be the High Priest of his religion. (4.) He separated him from sinners, and appointed him to be his own victim, holy in himself, and sanctifying others. And, (5.) He declared him to be holy by a vast number of miracles, and by many other proofs. Christ insists on nothing but his sanctity and his mission, in answer to the accusation of blasphemy, to teach priests and pastors that nothing so effectually disarms calumny and detraction as a lawful call and mission, and a holy and edifying life. Let us remember, after the example of Christ, that we are holy in respect of our state and vocation; but withal, that our condemnation will be the more dreadful on this account, if we be not likewise holy in all manner of conversation.

37. If I do not the works of my Father, believe me not.

Since Jesus Christ himself was willing not to be thought the Son of God if men did not see in him the works of his Father, let us not expect to be looked upon as ministers or children of God if we do not show forth in our lives the works which become such persons. A man's life and actions ought to answer his profession. A minister of state talks of nothing but of the interests of the government and of the service of his prince: to these his whole life is dedicated; these are the end of all his actions. Such, in proportion, ought a minister of the kingdom of God to be in respect of God, of Jesus Christ, and of the church. A Christian, a clergyman, and one devoted to the service of religion, ought to do none but Christian, ecclesiastical, and religious actions: for even their most common actions should be heightened and animated by the spirit of Christianity, of the ministry, and of religion.

38. But if I do, though ye believe not me, believe the works; that ye may know and believe that the Father *is* in me, and I in him.

A true pastor has no other design, throughout the whole course of his life, but only to bring his sheep to the knowledge of God and of Jesus Christ; and to give birth, growth, and action, strength, perfection, and perseverance to their faith. Plain and evident miracles are unexceptionable witnesses. A man may disguise the truth of them, or pretend not to see their force; but he cannot avoid being inwardly sensible of it. An atheist, an unbelieving person, may give his heart the lie, and hinder it from openly owning its conviction; but he cannot entirely suppress that conviction, nor rob himself of the evidence of those proofs which arise from the wonderful works of God, and from the miracles of Jesus Christ, of his apostles, and of other holy persons. Let us learn from Jesus Christ himself the adorable mystery of the most blessed Trinity, according to which the divine persons are in each other by the unity of one and the same essence, will, and spirit. It is to the imitation of this admirable unity that we are called here on earth. It is in the consummation of this unity that we shall find our eternal happiness in heaven.

39. Therefore they sought again to take him; but he escaped out of their hand, 40. And went away again beyond Jordan, into the place where John at first baptized; and there he abode.

Truth confounds the wicked, but does not convert them. Christ, by a just judgment, leaves these obdurate and impenitent wretches to themselves. When a man sees plainly that there is no admission for the truth, and that nothing but violence is to be expected, his only way is to escape out of the hands of the enemies of truth, that he may serve it in retirement and prayer, and there wait for the accomplishment of God's designs, for the judgments of his mercy or his justice, and for the moment of his own consummation. That man continues in peace, and is undisturbed amid troubles and persecutions, who frequently calls to mind his baptism, and considers that he was therein sacramentally and mysteriously crucified with Christ, to no other end but in order to be really crucified with him by sufferings during this life, and to die in them as he did.

41. And many resorted unto him, and said, John did no miracle:

Miracles are not the things which denominate men saints, since the greatest among them wrought none; but they are such by charity and good works. Miracles and prophecies are the proofs of an extraordinary mission; but John had no need of either, having only the ordinary mission of prophets. This saint, as the revived voice of all the prophets, and the interpreter of their prophecies, points out the end and accomplishment of them all in Jesus Christ; and Christ confirms, authorizes, and verifies all, by his word, his life, and his miracles. One of the best means to be convinced of the truth of religion is, to compare the miracles with the prophecies.

—But all things that John spake of this man were true. 42. And many believed on him there.

Christ seeks his elect in the midst of the reprobate; and it is for the sake of the former that he exposes himself so often to the rage of the latter. It is likewise for their sakes that he retires to a private place, to favour their good disposition by removing them at a distance from their enemies, and from all other obstacles. The faith of so great a number, notwithstanding the rage and fury of those in power, is a miracle of grace, and the end of all external miracles.

CHAPTER XI.

SECT. I.—THE DEATH AND RESURRECTION OF LAZARUS.

1. Now a certain *man* was sick, *named* Lazarus, of Bethany, the town of Mary and her sister Martha.

The Son of God here gives us an emblem of the fall, the conversion, and the justification of a hardened heart. To raise Lazarus, he made use only of prayers and tears: but to restore to us the life of the soul, it necessarily cost him the most precious life by the most cruel death. Let us fill our hearts with this truth in reading this history, which gives us a lively representation thereof. Let us adore all the different ends and designs our blessed Lord had in working this miracle, as particularly that he might give occasion to his sacrifice by the malice of his enemies, that he might strengthen the faith of his disciples against the scandal of the cross, that he might represent to them his power in raising the soul, etc.

2. It was *that* Mary which anointed the Lord with ointment, and wiped his feet with her hair, whose brother Lazarus was sick.

The memory of good works never perishes. They draw down the graces of God upon sinners. One person of piety in a family is a treasure of more value than the greatest riches: these may be the occasion of eternal perdition to it; that person, of eternal salvation. This house is a figure of the church, which is the house of prayer and of charity. To pour out our heart before God in prayer, is to pour out a perfumed oil upon our blessed Lord; and to relieve the poor with alms, at least out of what is superfluous to us, is to wipe his feet with our hair. There is a mixture of several sorts of persons in the church: there are Marys who pass their life in prayer; there are Marthas who are continually employed in good works; and there are Lazaruses who are sick and in a languishing condition. Some of these actually die by the death of sin, and are raised again by virtue of the tears, the prayers, and the powerful word of Christ.

3. Therefore his sisters sent unto him, saying, Lord, behold, he whom thou lovest is sick.

When Jesus Christ withdraws himself from a soul, and leaves it to itself, it certainly falls into temptation and sin. It is only to the prayers of the church and of her children that God grants the conversion of sinners. In order to obtain this, such a prayer is necessary as is full of faith, reverence, humility, and confidence; which, without prescribing to God, only lays before him the sinner's wants, and what the infinite love of our blessed Saviour caused him to do for our sakes. The conduct of these two sisters exhibits to us the model of a Christian family, which takes care to pray for all who are akin to it, and yet has no regard to the relation of flesh and blood, but considers only what the grace of Christ has made them, and is concerned only for the diseases of their souls, in consideration of him who has redeemed them out of his exceeding love. A sinner, who is sensible of his own unworthiness and misery, ought frequently, after the example of these two sisters, to address himself to Christ in this manner, "He whom thou lovest has sinned," or is tempted: an address very proper to support the sinner's hope, to cover him with a salutary shame and confusion, to implore the divine mercy more effectually in his behalf, etc.

4. When Jesus heard *that*, he said, This sickness is not unto death, but for the glory of God, that the Son of God might be glorified thereby.

The infirmity, the death, and even the sins of the elect, through the infinite mercy of God, turn to his glory, to that of Jesus Christ, and to the salvation of the sinner. God looks upon the diseases of men, and upon the prayers which are made for their recovery, after a manner very different from the generality of relations and of other persons. He has no regard either to the temporal wants of the former, or to the importunity of the latter; but considers only his own glory, and their salvation. My God, I am heartily willing that thou shouldst not hear either my own prayers, or those which are offered up for me, but only so far as is consistent with thy glory and my salvation.

5. Now Jesus loved Martha, and her sister, and Lazarus.

The love of Jesus Christ for his church and its members is the source of all his mercies. This love is not like human affection, which is for securing the objects of it as much as possible from diseases, afflictions, and from death itself. He suffers those whom he loves most to be exposed to all these like other men; but his love causes them to make a better use of them. John makes mention here of this love, to teach us that distempers are not always marks of God's displeasure, and that we ought not upon their account to imagine ourselves either neglected or forgotten by his providence, or deprived of the blessing of his love.

6. When he had heard therefore that he was sick, he abode two days still in the same place where he was.

God frequently refuses to grant a less favour, in order to confer upon us a greater. He permits sin, that he may make the power of his grace and the excess of his love more conspicuous in the conversion of the sinner. It is through want either of knowledge or of power, that physicians do not save the lives of their patients; but it is through a sovereign wisdom, a perfect knowledge, and an infinite power, that the Physician of our souls suffers his friend to die: for he is able to restore him to life, and knows what use he purposes to make of the patient's death, of which all other physicians can make no use at all.

7. Then after that saith he to *his* disciples, Let us go into Judea again.

It appears very plainly that it was neither the love of life, nor the fear of death, which caused Christ to leave Judea, but only a design to suspend the rage of the Jews by his absence, while he obediently waited for the precise time appointed for his sacrifice. That time is now approaching; and he goes into Judea again, as much to meet his own death as to restore Lazarus to life. He leads his disciples thither, not to expose them to danger, but to preserve them from it in such a manner as might add strength to their faith, to give one of them an opportunity to betray him, to make another an eyewitness of his death, and, with all these mysterious preparations, to celebrate that grand sacrifice, etc.

8. *His* disciples say unto him, Master, the Jews of late sought to stone thee; and goest thou thither again?

Life is of no account to him who thinks of nothing but doing the will of God, let the event be what it will. That which is here done by our divine Master, in order to raise a dead person, teaches his ministers that nothing ought to hinder them from using their utmost endeavours to raise those souls which God either particularly intrusts or providentially recommends to their care. If a minister on such occasion is likely to suffer and to hazard his life, it is upon his suffering perhaps, and his exposing himself to every thing for the sake of a single soul, that the salvation of this soul depends. The apostles are amazed at this forwardness of our blessed Saviour; as if a true pastor could be long absent from the chief place of his mission, and where the designs of God concerning him require his residence.

9. Jesus answered, Are there not twelve hours in the day? If any man walk in the day, he stumbleth not, because he seeth the light of this world. 10. But if a man walk in the night, he stumbleth, because there is no light in him.

He who acts in the light, and by the grace of Jesus Christ, is continually doing good; without this grace there is nothing but darkness and sin. While it was day, that is, during the time of Christ's mortal life allotted by his Father, his enemies had no power at all over it; but when the time of night—namely, of his death, was come, he delivered himself into their hands. The will of God is the light by which we ought to be guided. Nothing grievous can ever happen to us so long as we follow it. When we walk without this light, in the night of our own will, we cannot avoid either stumbling or going astray. Let thy will, O Lord, be always the lamp which may enlighten my steps, and the light which may direct me in thy ways!

11. These things said he: and after that he saith unto them, Our friend Lazarus sleepeth; but I go, that I may awake him out of sleep.

Those who speak by the Spirit of God use, even in common matters, expressions which are instructive, and which add light to the understanding. This which our blessed Saviour here uses, teaches us that death is a kind of rest or sleep to the friends of Christ: that to the just man it is as desirable as rest after the labours of the day; that the hope of the resurrection should make us despise death, which is to last as it were no longer than the space of one night; that it is as easy to the Son of God to raise a dead person, as it is to awaken one who is asleep; that the disciples of faith ought to be accustomed to the language of faith, which is useful to preserve and revive the notions thereof in their minds, etc.

12. Then said his disciples, Lord, if he sleep, he shall do well. 13. Howbeit Jesus spake of his death: but they thought that he had spoken of taking of rest in sleep.

How could these men imagine that our blessed Lord would undertake so dangerous a journey as this, to no other purpose but to awaken a man out of a common and even a healthful sleep! This was a very great instance of stupidity, and showed plainly how sensual and carnal their minds still were. The knowledge of this is very useful, to convince incredulous persons, that the apostles were not of themselves at all capable either of converting the world, or of inventing those wonderful things and those sublime discourses which they relate. To make use of metaphorical ways of speaking, which are very common in the Scripture, and which deceive only those who, through their own dulness, deceive themselves, is not to be guilty of lying or falsehood, when we take this method only in order to their spiritual advantage, and leave them under their mistake but a very little time.

14. Then said Jesus unto them plainly, Lazarus is dead. 15. And I am glad for your sakes that I was not there, to the intent ye may believe; nevertheless let us go unto him.

That which here happened to Lazarus, is an emblem of God's withdrawing his grace, which is often instrumental to the salvation of many, though it be attended with the fall of a just person. All things work together for good to the elect; every thing tends to promote their faith and their salvation, when God is pleased it should be subservient to that end. He frequently permits the fall of some of them, on purpose to strike the most holy with a salutary dread; to render those who fall more humble, vigilant, and penitent; to edify the church by their repentance; and to encourage the greatest sinners to have recourse thereto. Christ could have cured Lazarus at a distance, his divinity being present in all places; but this was the proper time of honouring his human nature as the instrument of his divine, to which it was united in his person. He gently blames the little faith of his apostles, that he may make them more attentive to the miracle which he is going to perform.

16. Then said Thomas, which is called Didymus, unto his fellow-disciples, Let us also go, that we may die with him.

These words of Thomas are very proper to be used by a true disciple, always ready to die with his Master, as a proper form wherewith he may encourage himself to follow his example, and to expose himself to every thing, depending upon his grace, and conforming himself to his holy dispositions, and to his spirit of sacrifice. A priest who is filled with this spirit, will, as he goes to the altar with his mind fixed upon Christ crucified, excite and animate himself by these words to unite himself to him, and offer himself with him in sacrifice, in what manner soever God shall please to dispose of him, of his life, his repose, etc.

SECT. II.—MARTHA'S DISCOURSE WITH JESUS.

17. Then, when Jesus came, he found that he had *lain* in the grave four days already.

A habit of sin is the grave of the soul: the soul cannot come out of it without a miracle. There is no sepulchre so loathsome and insupportable as the conscience of an inveterate sinner, in which he has buried himself alive. Christ was pleased that the greatest of his miracles should be an emblem of the conversion of such sort of sinners, to the end that none of them might be without hope from his mercy to recover the life of his soul. He is able to raise them all, let them have lain ever so long buried in their vicious habits, because his mercy and his power have no bounds: but he actually raises very few, for reasons which it belongs not to us to dive into; and perhaps, too, because he would not have us take occasion from thence to have less abhorrence of sin, and to continue long in it with a false peace, by rashly presuming upon the mercy of God.

18. Now Bethany was nigh unto Jerusalem, about fifteen furlongs off.
19. And many of the Jews came to Martha and Mary, to comfort them concerning their brother.

We condole with a person who has lost a brother by death; but we do not compassionate a soul which has lost its God by sin. Where is our faith? Had these comforters but looked into the grave of their own heart, they would there have found souls more dead than Lazarus, through their incredulity and envy. Every one ought to search into his heart on the like occasions. A man who is dead in sin cannot comfort himself any otherwise than by the hopes of being converted, and by having recourse to God to beg of him the grace of conversion through Jesus Christ; for there is no other comfort or consolation under the death of the soul.

20. Then Martha, as soon as she heard that Jesus was coming, went and met him: but Mary sat *still* in the house.

We must go to meet Jesus by our desires, we must wait for him in retirement with patience and peace of mind. What a comfort must it needs be to a poor sinner, when, by the first inspirations and motions of conversion, and by a disgust for the world, an aversion to its pleasures, and a clear sight of the deformity of sin, he plainly perceives that Jesus Christ is coming toward his heart! Then is the time for Martha to go to meet Jesus by works of charity and a liberal distribution of alms; and for Mary to continue still in the house, by prayer, meditation, and recollection, and by searching into the heart to examine its most secret thoughts, inclinations, and disorders.

21. Then said Martha unto Jesus, Lord, if thou hadst been here, my brother had not died.

Martha says nothing here but what is very consistent with Christ's own words, (ver. 15.) Her experience of his continual goodness, her belief of his almighty power, and the rule he seemed to have prescribed himself, (of refusing no cures which should be asked of him while he was present by his sacred humanity,) persuade her that he would have been moved by the prayers and tears of her and her sister, as well as by those of so many other persons. And in this she judged rightly, for he wept at the sepulchre of Lazarus, though he shed no tears when he first knew of his death.

22. But I know, that even now, whatsoever thou wilt ask of God, God will give *it* thee.

The just person believes that God can work a miracle at any time: but he does not always ask one, because he does not know whether it may be useful and expedient. Let us not tax this holy person with want of faith, since Christ himself speaks even to the same purpose, (ver. 41.) It is her faith in this divine Mediator which causes her to speak in this place, as it is her belief of his divinity which makes her do it a little lower, (ver. 27.) Let us learn from her, that we are to ask nothing of God but through Jesus Christ our only mediator; that we can obtain nothing without him, and that by him we obtain every thing; but that he gives as God whatever he asks as God-man, as high-priest, and as advocate with the Father, in virtue of the rights of his divine person and merits.

23. Jesus saith unto her, Thy brother shall rise again.

How just soever the praise was which Martha here gave to Christ, he takes no notice at all of it. By making her a general promise, he gives her occasion to reflect upon a resurrection much more desirable than that which she desired for her brother. God generally allows time for our too great earnestness in seeking any temporal blessing to abate and cool, that we may not receive it in the imperfection of nature, but with the submission and purity of faith.

24. Martha saith unto him, I know that he shall rise again in the resurrection at the last day.

The belief of a general resurrection was, it seems, settled among the Jews by Scripture and tradition; but it had been particularly confirmed in this family by the instructions of the Son of God. The fidelity of Martha in preserving in her heart this fundamental truth, ought to excite us to reflect frequently upon it.

25. Jesus said unto her, I am the resurrection, and the life; he that
believeth in me, though he were dead, yet shall he live: 26. And whosoever liveth, and believeth in me, shall never die. Believest thou this?

Christ, after his usual manner, takes occasion, from the favour which is asked of him, to deliver such truths as have relation thereto. There is no person who has not some opportunities of imitating this zeal and pastoral care. What Christ is, what he does, and what he will do, are three foundations upon which Martha ought to build the hope of her brother's resurrection. (1.) He is the principle of all resurrection and life in his members, being the life by his divine essence and his eternal birth. (2.) He is the source of the resurrection from infidelity to faith, by the inspiration of faith itself into the soul; and from sin to grace, by the infusion of charity. (3.) He is the author and model of the resurrection to a glorious and immortal life, by the communication of his own. It is by our believing these truths that we prepare ourselves to receive the accomplishment of them. A sinner who desires the resurrection of his soul, or the perfection of that resurrection, ought to have a firm belief of the power of grace over his heart.

27. She saith unto him, Yea, Lord: I believe that thou art the Christ, the Son of God, which should come into the world.

The exercise of faith, which is the source of prayer, is very often too much neglected. Christ recommends it more than the exercise of other virtues, because it is the seed of them. Nothing seems incredible or too great to be hoped for from Christ, when there is a lively belief of his divinity; but when this foundation is shaken, the whole building falls to the ground. The faith of Martha comprehends all in a few words, and is a direct and full answer to the question of Christ. It soars up to the very bosom of the Father, the living God, the principle of a living God, and who, by this very Son, is the fountain of all life; and from thence it comes down again into the world, to the virgin's womb, where Christ was formed, by the union of the Son of God with flesh, that he might become the head and the principle of life to the children of God.

SECT. III.—JESUS GROANS, WEEPS, PRAYS, CRIES OUT, AND RAISES LAZARUS: THE APOSTLES UNBIND HIM.

28. And when she had so said, she went her way, and called Mary her sister secretly, saying, The Master is come, and calleth for thee. 29. As soon as she heard *that*, she arose quickly, and came unto him.

It is necessary that both Mary and Martha—both the prayers and good works of the church—should concur to the conversion of a sinner. It is to both that Christ is pleased to promise and grant the resurrection to grace and glory. In this family Christ has no other name but Lord and Master, because it is a family of faith and obedience, wherein nothing is learned but Jesus Christ, and that from Jesus Christ himself, and nothing is done but what he commands and desires. Happy is that Christian family which resembles this! Mary, without the least delay, leaves those comforters who do but add to the weight of her grief, and goes to seek the only true Comforter. It is only at his feet that we can find that sovereign consolation which reaches even the heart.

30. Now Jesus was not yet come into the town, but was in that place where Martha met him. 31. The Jews then which were with her in the house, and comforted her, when they saw Mary, that she rose up hastily and went out, followed her, saying, She goeth unto the grave to weep there.

This crowd of Jews know not that Christ was the person

who drew them to the place, and brings them out of this house to be witnesses, on the part of the whole nation, of the last and most remarkable proof of his mission. This will be a miracle of mercy for some few, for the rest a miracle of judgment: to the former it will be the last influence of grace to complete and finish their conversion—to the latter, the filling up of their measure, and, as it were, the seal of their obduracy. We must pray on all occasions. It frequently happens that people think they are only going to make a visit of civility or curiosity, when they are perhaps going to meet with that which will decide their portion for all eternity.

32. Then when Mary was come where Jesus was, and saw him, she fell down at his feet, saying unto him, Lord, if thou hadst been here, my brother had not died.

The feet of Christ are the usual retreat of Mary. They are a throne of grace, and a sanctuary or refuge both for the just and for sinners. Mary and Martha use the same language, (ver. 21;) which represents to us that the prayers and good works of a Christian proceed from the same faith in Christ, and produce a firm confidence in him. Mary, well instructed in the secret methods of Christ's conduct, knows that he intends to act and work upon the hearts of men by the presence of his Spirit, after his ascension into heaven; but that his abode on earth was designed to make their bodies sensible of the power of his adorable flesh, and of the quickening virtue of his sacred humanity. These souls, which are consecrated thereto, do in a particular manner depend upon it for all sorts of graces. God honours his sacrifices, and shows us beforehand that we have from thence the life of the body as well as that of the soul. The soul communicates or partakes of this sacrifice in a manner proper to itself, by receiving from thence its sanctification and perfection; and so will the body likewise communicate or partake of it in another manner, by receiving its own perfection by the communication of the glorious life thereof. The resurrection of Lazarus is a specimen, as it were, of this communion, and of the communication of the life of Christ's body.

33. When Jesus therefore saw her weeping, and the Jews also weeping which came with her, he groaned in the spirit, and was troubled,

The Jews here weep, and out of compassion bewail a death in which they had no particular concern; and yet are just going to murder, in a most barbarous manner, the Author of Life himself. Thus we often bewail the misery of others, and are altogether insensible of our own. Christ, by his infinite power, takes upon himself all the impressions of human infirmity, in order to sanctify them. He groans in the spirit, when he considers the nature of sin, the consequences, effects, and punishment thereof, which are pain and death. The ill use which he foresees the Jews will make of the miracle he is going to work, and a full purpose of following his Father's order in restoring Lazarus to his sisters, raise in Christ this contest, which causes him to groan in the spirit. He groans in us, when faith excites in our minds a holy indignation, and a salutary trouble on the account of our sins, to that degree that the habit of sin yields to the violence of our sorrow and repentance. Let us adore in Christ these divine motions of human nature, which in him have nothing but what tends to the honour of God.

34. And said, Where have ye laid him? They said unto him, Lord, come and see.

Christ does not ask out of ignorance, any more than God did, when he said, "Adam, where art thou?" Where is the sinner, when he is no longer in the hands of his God? To what a miserable condition is he reduced, when by his sin he has taken away the life of his soul! The sinner forgets God, and God forgets the sinner. If God vouchsafe not to seek him, to come unto him, and to cast an eye of mercy upon him, he will never seek his God, never move one step toward him, and consequently never find him. Here is an humble and efficacious prayer, "Lord, come and see." A hardened sinner is a dead person, not able so much as to ask for life; others therefore must do it for him. Lord, come to this soul which has forsaken thee, and see its misery. Come to these inveterate sinners; come to the sepulchre of their heart, and see how thy work is disfigured by the corruption of sin.

35. Jesus wept.

Jesus weeps, and laments the death of all mankind, and the blindness of the Jews. By his tears, (1.) He sanctifies ours. (2.) He wipes them from our eyes. (3.) He dries up the fountain of them, which is sin. (4.) He expiates our vain and criminal joys. And, (5.) He procures us such as are substantial and eternal. Let us adore, unite ourselves with, and return most humble thanks to Jesus Christ weeping for us. Thou, O Jesus, bewailest the sinner, and the sinner does not in the least bewail himself! Let thy tears be to him a source of penitential and Christian tears. Let me never, I beseech thee, lament the loss of things which must perish; but let me lament the loss of thy grace and thy love, and of every degree of both, which, through my own fault, I have not received!

36. Then said the Jews, Behold how he loved him!

Men judge like men concerning the actions of the Son of God, and seek for the cause of his tears in friendship and natural tenderness. The God-man, the Saviour of mankind, does nothing but what has for its principle or motive the glory of God and the salvation of men. These very people are themselves the object of these sacred tears, while they seek the cause of them in another person. Thus we frequently attribute to others public or private calamities of which our own sins are the true cause. How sweet, how comfortable is it, when we contemplate Christ nailed to the cross, where he pours out not only his tears, but even his blood, upon our souls, to say, in the deepest sense of gratitude, "Behold how he loved them!"

37. And some of them said, Could not this man, which opened the eyes of the blind, have caused that even this man should not have died?

Every thing is useful and advantageous to the righteous: to the wicked, hurtful and prejudicial. Envy turns the most wholesome things into poison. When Christ works no miracles, these men insult him; and as soon as ever he has wrought this, they do all they can to stifle and suppress the knowledge of it. Blind censurers of the conduct of God, to whose infinite wisdom they would prescribe rules! Rash and presumptuous judges, who would fain know the times and seasons, the disposal and knowledge whereof God has, by his sovereign power, reserved solely to himself! The world is full of these crafty and malicious insinuations which tend either to decry the best actions of holy persons by hinting at some passages of their former life, or to render these odious, by comparing them with the lustre and reputation of the other. So dangerous is it to give any admission to envy, prejudice, hatred, etc.

38. Jesus therefore again groaning in himself cometh to the grave. It was a cave, and a stone lay upon it.

The indignation which Christ conceived against sin, envy, and the abuse of his favours, is the cause of his groaning this second time. He lets it be just perceived, without suffering it to break out; to teach us, that we must often suppress within ourselves those motions of indignation and zeal which the sight of the vices and disorders of men is apt to raise in us. The heart of an obdurate sinner may very properly be called his sepulchre, which, by means of a long habit of sin, is shut and closed up against grace as it were by a hard and heavy stone, and in which there is nothing but darkness and corruption. It is a very great and extraordinary mercy when the deliverer comes to this prison, when the light shines in this darkness, and holiness itself visits this corruption. Every person in the world has his stone of evil habits, which is more or less hard and heavy as these are more or less inveterate and sinful. Lord, I feel the weight and hardness of mine: vouchsafe to come near it by thy grace, and to open this sepulchre!

39. Jesus said, Take ye away the stone. Martha, the sister of him that was dead, saith unto him, Lord, by this time he stinketh: for he hath been *dead* four days.

Our blessed Lord could have taken away the stone by speaking only one word; but he does not think fit to multiply miracles without necessity or without use. It is necessary that men should work their part toward their own salvation, and that they should endeavour chiefly to remove all outward obstacles, and whatever serves to indulge their evil habits. This is what depends most upon man; for grace alone changes the inward part, namely, the spring and bent of a depraved will. Bad example is, as it were, the stench of sin: it is very difficult to go near open and inveterate sinners without being infected by them. It is a part of the duty of charity to advise others, especially those who are innocent and know little of sin, to beware of them; but to conceal the danger, for fear of wounding the reputation of such sinners, is a false and irregular exercise of charity. Pastors, whom our blessed Lord here represents, are not, however, on this account, excused from going to sinners and doing all they can to procure the resurrection of their souls: they must put their trust in the divine protection, and proceed with the greater care and caution.

40. Jesus saith unto her, Said I not unto thee, that, if thou wouldst believe, thou shouldst see the glory of God?

God proportions his liberality toward his servants according to the measure of faith which he gives them to deserve it. The difficulty there is in prevailing upon an inveterate sinner to forsake his vicious habits, causes us almost to despair of his conversion; but it is in surmounting this very difficulty that God places his glory, even more than in working external miracles. It is often our infidelity, or the weakness of our faith, which hinders us from obtaining of God the conversion of great sinners. We can hardly persuade ourselves to ask it at all, or we do it in a very careless and negligent manner, because we do not sufficiently rely upon the power of grace. To expect only common and ordinary effects from it, is to have but very little knowledge thereof. That which is proportioned only to our narrow conceptions, is not worthy of God.

41. Then they took away the stone *from the place* where the dead was laid. And Jesus lifted up *his* eyes, and said, Father, I thank thee that thou hast heard me.

Thankfulness for benefits received, draws down new. It plainly appears that Christ had already prayed in the secret recesses of his heart, and thereby prepared himself for this miracle. This is what a good pastor ought to do, especially when he is to labour in the conversion of some great sinner.

Christ being about to conclude his public life and his preaching by the last and most illustrious of his miracles, returns solemn thanks to his Father, for the power given to his human nature to prove the authority of his mission by miracles.

42. And I knew that thou hearest me always: but because of the people which stand by, I said *it*, that they may believe that thou hast sent me.

Jesus Christ is always heard; because, according to his different natures, he is at the same time the person who both makes and hears the prayer. A pastor, whose duty it is to set a good example to others, (1.) Ought not always to pray in secret. (2.) He ought to have that familiarity with God by prayer, (if that expression may be used,) and so much trust and confidence in him, as to hope that he will grant him his request. (3.) He should show, by a perfect disengagement from all worldly interest, his integrity in undertaking the sacred ministry. (4.) He should manifest a very great dependence upon the Spirit of God. And, (5.) He ought to humble himself in the sight of God before he performs any act of power and authority.

43. And when he thus had spoken, he cried with a loud voice, Lazarus, come forth.

The loud voice of our blessed Saviour is an emblem of his all-powerful grace, which is absolutely necessary to bring the sinner out of the sepulchre of his hardened heart, and to make him confess his sin. With how great difficulty does a man rise and recover himself, when he has sunk under an evil habit, and been, as it were, overwhelmed by it! The sinner, being at so vast a distance from God, has need that God should speak to his heart in a very loud voice to make him hear. Jesus Christ omitted nothing in order to raise this dead person: he underwent the fatigue of a journey, having come a great way to seek him; he wept, he groaned, he prayed, he cried out with a loud voice, and commanded the dead to come forth. What ought not a pastor then to do, in order to raise a soul, as far as he is able, and especially a soul which has been a long time dead!

44. And he that was dead came forth, bound hand and foot with grave-

clothes; and his face was bound about with a napkin. Jesus saith unto them, Loose him, and let him go.

He whom the grace of Christ has converted and restored to life, must come forth, as it were, out of himself, by renouncing sin, and must leave the darkness and corruption of his wicked habits. An habitual sinner does not easily get clear of all those bands with which he has bound himself, even though he have received the life of grace. It is God who justifies him internally by his grace: it is the church who looses him externally by her ministers. After this, a wise and charitable director of the conscience takes pains to free him from the difficulty he has contracted of walking in the way of God's commandments, and of performing good actions; and assists him in renewing the image of God in his soul, which he has defaced and blotted out thereof by his sins.

45. Then many of the Jews which came to Mary, and had seen the things which Jesus did, believed on him.

See here how profitable and beneficial it is to visit virtuous persons, and to frequent their company. Salvation sometimes depends upon such an opportunity as this. A man meets with Jesus Christ in some Christian family, he begins to know him there by the works of his grace, and he receives at length the precious gift of faith. To comfort the afflicted is a work of mercy, which draws after it a blessing, provided it be done not with a Jewish or Pagan, but with a Christian heart.

SECT. IV.—THE JEWS TAKE COUNSEL TOGETHER TO DESTROY CHRIST.—CAIAPHAS PROPHESIES.

46. But some of them went their ways to the Pharisees, and told them what things Jesus had done.

The devil finds means to make some advantage of the most holy actions; and it seldom happens that he has not his part in good works. He has his ministers, who carry on his business in ruining themselves eternally. There are always flatterers to be found, who make their court to persons in authority by decrying virtuous men and their good actions. It is a very hellish employment for a man to be a professed accuser of God's elect, and to inform against them for their holy actions, as others inform against notorious villains for their crimes; and yet some of that employment are to be met with in the world.

47. ¶ Then gathered the chief priests and the Pharisees a council, and said, What do we? for this man doeth many miracles.

We always find the wicked intent on the destruction of others, without ever thinking of their own salvation. Who would not have been apt to imagine, that the governors of the Jewish church, and the most religious sect among that people, assembled together after such a miracle as this, were consulting and deliberating only on the proper means of having Christ acknowledged for the Messias, yielding at last to such convincing proofs of his mission? And yet they are doing the direct contrary: under so thick a darkness are these priests! so strangely hardened are the hearts of these Pharisees! They here own the miracles, which are an evident token of the divine approbation; and yet they think of nothing but destroying the person who wrought them. What a dreadful instance is this of the extremities to which men are insensibly led by prejudice, obstinacy, self-interest, and the love of human glory!

48. If we let him thus alone, all *men* will believe on him; and the Romans shall come and take away both our place and nation.

Thus abundance of persons are mindful of nothing but temporal things, entirely forget eternal, and so lose both. Deplorable blindness this, for men to think of taking precautions against God Almighty, and against his designs! Senseless reasoning! as if the faith of a people, to whom Christ preached a morality so disagreeable to nature, could be any other than the work of God; and as if he could be unable to defend those who believed in him! From the time that passion has gained the ascendant in the mind, it has no longer reason, good sense, or understanding; but a wretched and fallacious policy takes their place. It happens daily that, in order to prevent some inconsiderable or imaginary evils, men plunge themselves into such as are real, and are attended with an irreparable loss. Grant, Lord, that I may never be of the number of those who, either to gain or secure some little temporal advantages or conveniencies, expose themselves to eternal misery.

49. And one of them, *named* Caiaphas, being the high priest that same year, said unto them, Ye know nothing at all, 50. Nor consider that it is expedient for us, that one man should die for the people, and that the whole nation perish not.

The public good will ever be the pretence with which the ambitious and the covetous will endeavour to conceal their wicked designs. These men dare not say plainly, "It is more expedient that truth, justice, and innocence should perish, and that we should crucify this worker of miracles rather than lose our credit and reputation, the esteem of the world, and all the advantages arising from them." But they actually do what they have not the confidence to speak. Let worldly men but seriously examine themselves, and they will find something of this nature in their own conduct. They copy in miniature that original which the Jews drew at full length.

51. And this spake he not of himself: but being high priest that year, he prophesied that Jesus should die for that nation;

All those who foretell future events are not saints. The priesthood, even in a wicked man, has virtue and efficacy. God sometimes puts the greatest truths into the mouth of a wicked man, that others may neither be puffed up with their knowledge, nor think themselves the holier on that account, nor attribute to themselves those truths which come from God. The very same words have an impious and sacrilegious meaning in the intention of a wicked person; and one which is religious, sound, and altogether divine, as they were intended by the Holy Ghost. We may therefore very justly seek after a sense which is spiritual, mysterious, and edifying, in historical relations, and in words which, according to their common signification, express nothing extraordinary.

52. And not for that nation only, but that also he should gather together in one the children of God that were scattered abroad.

The words of Caiaphas are a prophecy not only of the death of Christ, but also of the fruit and effect of his death in the forming of his church, which is one, holy, and universal. His death, breaking down the wall of partition, gathers together Jews and Gentiles into the unity of his body; destroying the spirit of bondage, renders us the children of God by the spirit of love, which produces holiness; and bringing in all nations to Christ, gives universality to his church. How is it, that these blind wretches have no eyes to perceive the power of him who forces them to proclaim the glory of his kingdom, arising from the faith of all nations, and from that very death which they are contriving to inflict upon him, on purpose to hinder all men from believing on him! We cannot sufficiently admire and adore the wisdom of God, who thus confounds the false policy of men.

53. Then from that day forth they took counsel together* for to put him to death. [**Fr.* Thought of nothing but.]

A strange employment this for the chief ministers of the true religion, to whom the oracles of God were committed, to entertain in their minds so detestable a design against their benefactor, even though he had not been their God. Let us also think of this design, and of this adorable death; but let it be in order to make it our life, in devoutly meditating upon it, in applying to ourselves the fruits thereof by a lively faith and a holy desire, and in imitating it by the mortification of our heart and our senses. How happy are Christian priests who have this quickening death continually present to their minds; who preserve the memory of it in the church by the representative sacrifice, which is the sacred memorial thereof; and who convey the remembrance and effects of it even into the hearts of the faithful, by causing them to partake [spiritually] of that victim of salvation which was sacrificed upon the cross!

54. Jesus therefore walked no more openly among the Jews; but went thence unto a country near to the wilderness, into a city called Ephraim, and there continued with his disciples.

It is the divine appointment that we should decline persecution, till a necessity of obeying God, or charity for the souls of men, oblige us to appear. Happy the country which affords a retreat to the Son of God persecuted. But more happy the heart which opens itself to him while the world persecutes him, which adores him, which is wholly taken up with him, which fills itself with his word, which is nourished by his truth, and which continually excites and quickens its faith and love by meditating upon his mysteries. Ye worthy disciples of Jesus Christ, who by frequent retirement follow him, as it were, into the wilderness, who there continue united to him, and, like him, wait there for the time of your sacrifice; bless God for that happy lot and portion which is fallen to you by his grace, while the world is intent on nothing but to crucify the Son of God afresh by their sins.

55. ¶ And the Jews' passover was nigh at hand; and many went out of the country up to Jerusalem before the passover, to purify themselves.

How much more necessary is it for Christians to purify themselves in order to celebrate the Christian passover! For want of due preparation to receive the fruit of Christ's mysteries at this feast, it becomes to a great number an occasion only of greater defilement.

56. Then sought they for Jesus, and spake among themselves, as they stood in the temple, What think ye, that he will not come to the feast?
57. Now both the chief priests and the Pharisees had given a commandment, that, if any man knew where he were, he should shew *it*, that they might take him.

The devil finds means of ruining souls on the greatest festivals, which were instituted for their sanctification. For whereas some, in order to this end, seek Christ at such seasons, others do it only to crucify him in their hearts by the commission of new sins. What numbers are there in respect of whom Christ does not come to the feasts of the church by his grace and his Spirit, though they then receive even his representative body and blood! But how few are there who are at all sensible of his absence, and who put this question to themselves, "What is the cause that he is not come to the feast?" Is it not on the account of that sinful habit, which we always confess, but never forsake?

CHAPTER XII.

SECT. I.—MARY ANOINTS THE FEET OF CHRIST.—JUDAS MURMURS AT IT.—THE JEWS CONSULT TO KILL LAZARUS.

1. THEN Jesus six days before the passover came to Bethany, where Lazarus was which had been dead, whom he raised from the dead.

A good pastor, whose labours to procure the resurrection of a soul God has blessed with success, ought not presently to leave it; but he must visit it, and watch over it, to assist it in preserving the life of grace. It is chiefly before Easter that he ought to inquire and examine whether those under his care be duly prepared to celebrate the sacred banquet, and to approach the holy table. When a pastor finds himself near his end, his concern for the souls which he has newly taken off from their evil habits, or which he has brought near to God, as it were, begins afresh; and he applies himself to them in a particular manner, endeavouring to strengthen and confirm the former, and to advance the progress of the latter. What then ought we not to believe concerning the pastoral charity of Christ, who never visited any but for their advantage.

2. There they made him a supper; and Martha served: but Lazarus was one of them that sat at the table with him. 3. Then took Mary a pound of ointment of spikenard, very costly, and anointed the feet of Jesus, and wiped his feet with her hair: and the house was filled with the odour of the ointment.

The true house of obedience, signified by the word Bethany, is the church. It is there that Jesus Christ sups with his friends, where an active charity, which is mindful of the wants of others, serves him in his members; where sinners raised to life, and purified by repentance, sit at the table with him; and where a contemplative charity, devoted to God and Christ, pours out its faith, religion, prayers, and its whole soul in his presence, and at the same time its alms upon the poor, making use of temporal riches to wipe off their tears, and to alleviate their wants and miseries. These perishing things are, in the nature of hair, to be cut off in proportion as they grow and increase, that we may not make ourselves a vain ornament or a superfluous burden of that which is necessary for others.

4. Then saith one of his disciples, Judas Iscariot, Simon's *son*, which should betray him, 5. Why was not this ointment sold for three hundred pence, and given to the poor?

Wretch, who is just going to sell the only Son of God for thirty pence, and values at three hundred a little ointment, perfume, and vapour! When a man has once delivered up his heart to sin, he makes small account of Jesus Christ. All divine things become vile and contemptible to him who does not weigh them in the balance of faith. A covetous person counts every thing lost which is not sacrificed to his avarice. This vice frequently covers itself with the pretext of charity, and cannot endure that any thing should be expended for the service of God. Good works are often an occasion of murmuring to those who are possessed with the spirit of the world: we must give them leave to talk, and go on ourselves in the performance of our duty.

6. This he said, not that he cared for the poor; but because he was a thief, and had the bag, and bare what was put therein.

Christ trusts a thief with his money, because he sets no value upon it; but he keeps souls in his own custody, and redeems them with his blood, because, having received them of his Father, he values them more than all the world besides. He suffers his money to be stolen from him, but never his sheep. What a shame is it for so many of those to whom he has intrusted them, to leave them to perish for want of due care; while they themselves are entirely taken up with temporal affairs, and eagerly intent on the improvement of their revenues! Our blessed Lord shows us, by his own example, that it is not inconsistent with a life of perfection to have some small reserves of money in common; but that the care and management thereof is not to be given to the most perfect. Would to God that those who enjoy ecclesiastical benefices, and are on that account the stewards of the poor, would always be mindful of that quality and condition, and employ their revenues as faithful stewards, and not, like Judas, make use of the name of the poor in so loud a manner, when some little temporal interest is concerned, or the repairing of their churches is the thing in question.

7. Then said Jesus, Let her alone: against the day of my burying hath she kept this.

What mildness and gentleness was this toward a wretch who was a vile hypocrite! Christ suffers him to deceive him as far as it lay in his power, to lie unto him, and to steal from him. Men are never willing to suffer any thing of this nature. He makes no discovery of the avarice of Judas: whereas men seldom spare their own brethren the shame of their vices when it is at all for their interest to discover them. Love is of a foreseeing and preventing nature. The love of the Father toward Jesus Christ causes men to pay him beforehand, at the time of his entry into Jerusalem, the honour of a triumph, for the victory he was just going to gain by his death over death itself, over sin, the world, and the devil. The love of Christ toward his church causes him to anticipate his own death by the institution of the eucharist, which figuratively represents him as dying for us. And the love of the church towards Christ causes her to give him beforehand the honour of embalming and burial by the ministry of Mary, by whom she is represented. The design of Mary is to honour her Saviour's sacred humanity as the source of the life of her own soul, and of that of her brother's body. The design of the Holy Ghost is to prefigure the death and burial of Christ, and to do honour to them by way of anticipation. Thus the ceremonies of the law did, by the sole intention of the Holy Ghost, admirably well signify some future mysteries: and many ceremonies of the Christian church contain under them, and represent Christian mysteries, truths, and virtues, not by the mere design of those who instituted them, but chiefly by the intention of the Holy Spirit, who directs every thing in the church. We ought to be very careful to resign ourselves up to this Spirit, in order to penetrate into his gracious purposes, and to co-operate with his designs.

8. For the poor always ye have with you; but me ye have not always.

Mary's love teaches her how to improve the opportunity of Christ's presence to her own benefit and advantage: we shall likewise improve it to ours in proportion to the love we bear him. We never fail of finding him in the poor. We have him always present in the pastors, to pay him the duty of obedience; in his word, to follow his light: but we have him not always present in a visible manner, to pay him the honour due to the Son of God living upon the earth. Every duty has its proper time and virtue; and one does not interfere with another. The Holy Spirit, who regulates the order of them in religion, inspires some persons with an inclination to some particular exercises and devotions, and others he directs to follow a different method, thus dividing his gifts to every one severally as he will.

9. Much people of the Jews therefore knew that he was there: and they came not for Jesus' sake only, but that they might see Lazarus also, whom he had raised from the dead.

Jesus had hitherto always declined appearing much in the company of those whom he had cured miraculously, when the receiving of honour and applause could be the only consequence thereof: now he chooses to appear in such company, and draws together much people of the Jews, because this miracle is to cost him his life, and because the time of his sacrifice is come. To be earnestly desirous to see the works of God is a very commendable curiosity; but it is a very ill disposition to be satisfied with barely seeing them, and not to glorify God on their account by all the ways in our power, every one according to his state and his measure of grace.

10. ¶ But the chief priests consulted that they might put Lazarus also to death; 11. Because that by reason of him many of the Jews went away, and believed on Jesus.

Few persons seek Christ for his own sake; many do it out of curiosity, and others out of malice. Happy are they who come and give themselves to him, by whatever motive they were induced! But miserable are those who make no other use of the knowledge of his wonderful works, but only to set themselves at a greater distance from him! How impious, rash, and extravagant soever this design be of putting Lazarus to death because his resurrection was the work of Christ, it has notwithstanding some imitators in a different way. There are even Christians who endeavour to destroy such works as are manifestly of God and for his sake; and he, for their misery or punishment, suffers their designs to succeed; which he did not do with respect to the Jews in their design upon Lazarus. Nothing but the very spirit of the devil, and an envy which is truly his, can prompt men to do all they can to subvert the works of the Holy Spirit, merely out of hatred to those whom he has been pleased to use as his instruments, and because these works gain them reputation, and are prejudicial to the worldly glory and carnal interest of such envious wretches.

SECT. II.—CHRIST'S ENTRY INTO JERUSALEM.

12. ¶ On the next day much people that were come to the feast, when they heard that Jesus was coming to Jerusalem, 13. Took branches of palm trees, and went forth to meet him, and cried, Hosanna; Blessed *is* the King of Israel that cometh in the name of the Lord.

All the chief priests and magistrates, those who make the greatest figure and appearance, have their minds wholly taken up with their malicious designs against our blessed Lord, and are intent on finding out some means to rid themselves of him: on his side he has only one part of the common people, who came from abroad. This affords us an emblem of that which happens in all ages, in which the common people have always shown most sincere affection toward Christ and his gospel. The zeal and affection of those who are not yet rooted and grounded in love, are of short duration; and the glory which the world bestows, is but like a flash of lightning. It was to our blessed Lord a fresh occasion of sorrow, because he knew the inconstancy of these people.

14. And Jesus, when he had found a young ass, sat thereon; as it is written, 15. Fear not, daughter of Zion: behold, thy King cometh sitting on an ass's colt.

Let us not disdain to learn from hence that tractableness, humility, and meekness with which we must receive and bear the yoke of Christ. In showing the Jews how easily he could have drawn the people to him if he had thought fit, he likewise shows Christians with how much power and gentleness he would effectually draw to him all nations. He leaves pomp and magnificence to earthly kings; they stand in need of it to hide and conceal their weakness. Humility and simplicity compose the whole equipage of a King whose only design is to encounter pride and to triumph over sin and death. Fear not, O people of the Jews, oppressed with the weight of legal ceremonies, this King comes not amid the terrors of thunder and lightning, to impose upon you the insupportable yoke of a law of fear and death: he comes to bless you with a law of life and love, which is received only in proportion as it is loved, and which, with a most winning gentleness, engages us to love and embrace it. Reign in me, O Lord, by causing me to love thy law!

16. These things understood not his disciples at the first: but when Jesus was glorified, then remembered they that these things were written of him, and *that* they had done these things unto him.

The resurrection and glory of Jesus Christ enlightened the eyes of his disciples, which the infirmities of his flesh had dimmed and weakened. When a man is intrusted with the instruction of others, he must not be discouraged by their slowness of apprehension, but must proceed in the discharge of his duty; God, in his due time, will open the understanding of those in whom he designs his word shall bring forth fruit. We often read the Scripture without comprehending any thing of the mystical senses which it contains; let us notwithstanding adore it, continue to read it, and wait with patience. The light will at last shine out, will disperse this darkness, and remove the veil which hinders us from seeing Jesus Christ and his mysteries in the divine oracles. Grant me, Lord, I beseech thee, a persevering love of thy word; and let the sacred obscurity thereof, instead of lessening my veneration for it, increase and heighten it!

17. The people therefore that was with him when he called Lazarus out of his grave, and raised him from the dead, bare record. 18. For this cause the people also met him, for that they heard that he had done this miracle.

In vain do men use their utmost endeavours to drown the voice of God speaking by miracles: it is impossible to frustrate his designs. Christ does not now withdraw himself from the concourse and applause of the people; because he knows in what it will all end. He now receives their praises, and the marks of their esteem, while he is under the expectation of ignominy and reproach; as he will in a very little time receive humiliation in hopes of glory.

19. The Pharisees therefore said among themselves, Perceive ye how ye prevail nothing? behold, the world is gone after him.

The greatest miracle of Christ is that which exasperates his enemies the most. They resolve upon his death for an action which ought to convince them that he is the resurrection and the life. When the first motions of envy and hatred are not restrained, it is at last impossible to keep them within bounds. The plain and evident fruitlessness of all their endeavours transports these men into rage and despair, but does not in the least alter their purpose. They discover, even against their will, the bottom of their hearts, and the true occasion of their envy: they would have had the world gone after them, and they see it is gone after Christ. How much reason have we to fear lest we should run into the like excess, if we love the praise of men, and should happen to stand in competition with others! A reputation to be supported and maintained, is a dangerous snare to those who have but a small degree of love for God.

SECT. III.—SOME GENTILES DESIRE TO SEE JESUS.—THE GRAIN IS BARREN EXCEPT IT DIE.—LIFE MUST BE LOST TO SAVE IT.

20. ¶ And there were certain Greeks among them that came up to worship at the feast: 21. The same came therefore to Philip, which was of Bethsaida of Galilee, and desired him, saying, Sir, we would see Jesus.

It is a privilege peculiar to the Christian church, that out of her bosom there is no salvation nor religion. God had some worshippers out of the synagogue, whom he had reserved to himself, and kept undefiled amid the corruption of paganism, to manifest the power of his grace, and to hinder the devil from pleading a sort of prescription against the rights of the Creator. In proportion as the Jews shut the door of salvation against themselves, the Gentiles begin to knock at that door, which is Jesus Christ. This temple, to which these came to worship, is no more than a type or shadow of the church, into which they are shortly to come in crowds to acknowledge the true God; and this desire to see Jesus, is the first fruits of that ardent thirst which the Holy Ghost will raise in them after the faith in Jesus Christ. How adorable are thy counsels, O my God! how divinely terrible in this vicissitude of grace and religion!

22. Philip cometh and telleth Andrew: and again Andrew and Philip tell Jesus.

How pleasing to God is this union, when the ministers of his church agree, and, as it were, conspire together to bring souls to Christ, and to instruct them in the truths of his religion! True disciples have no notion of envy and emulation, and of any forwardness to show their own credit and interest in preference to others; because they seek not their own glory, but that of their common Master.

23. ¶ And Jesus answered them, saying, The hour is come, that the Son of man should be glorified.

Christ is sought to with zeal and earnestness, and yet he makes no manner of advances toward those who appear to have so great an esteem and value for him. The children of Adam take much more care to improve all opportunities which are favourable to their self-love, and to answer the good opinion of others, by giving them such a reception as may preserve and increase it. It is not only the humility of Christ which causes him to act in this manner, but also his wisdom. He shows no affection toward the Gentiles, that he may not provoke the Jews. When a man is in some eminent station, and exposed to the censures of others, he ought to take great care that he be not drawn into any wrong measures by a false appearance of good. The glory of Christ is the manifestation of his name to all nations, and the calling of them to the faith: and yet he speaks but very obscurely concerning it, that he may show, even to the last, some regard toward those who act without the least toward him.

24. Verily, verily, I say unto you, Except a corn of wheat fall* into the ground and die, it abideth alone: but if it die, it bringeth forth much fruit. [* *Fr.* Be cast.]

Christ and his members bring forth fruit only by mortification and the cross. Jesus is the bread of the elect, but he is wheat before he becomes bread; and he is a corn of wheat in respect of his seeming smallness, his solidity, and his virtue to nourish and satisfy. Let us adore this corn of wheat, which being cast, by the incarnation, into the field of this world, as the seed of the elect and of the whole church, and being dead and buried in the earth, sprung up and brought forth much fruit by his resurrection and ascension; and is to be the eternal food of his church in heaven, after having fed her under the symbol of bread here on earth. Whoever desires to belong to the harvest, must be likewise of the seed. Whoever would be an ingredient of this heavenly bread, ought to prepare himself first to be a grain of wheat cast into the earth by humiliation, buried by the oblivion or contempt of the world, winnowed in the floor, and bruised under the mill-stone, and to pass through the water and fire of affliction, tribulation, and repentance. A pastor or minister of Christ has no reason to hope that he shall be able to produce much fruit, if he be not mortified and disposed to suffer, and to give even his life for his sheep and for the church. When persecution takes away a holy pastor, his flock seems, in all human appearance, to have lost all; but to the eyes of faith it appears in a very hopeful and prosperous condition. The corn of wheat is dead: there is good cause to hope that it will bring forth fruit.

25. He that loveth his life shall lose it; and he that hateth his life in this world shall keep it unto life eternal.

The inordinate love of the present life, and of the conveniencies thereof, extinguishes, in the generality of mankind, the belief and love of life eternal. Few persons examine themselves concerning their love of life; and yet Jesus Christ assures us that there is one kind of this love which is the occasion of eternal death. We love life in the sense here intended, when we are fond of it for its own sake, and for the sake of the carnal satisfactions and temporal advantages which accompany it. Let us carefully avoid being desirous to preserve it on this account, and to enjoy it to the prejudice of what we owe to God, to the church, and to our own salvation. This would be no other than to invert the proper order of our love: to prefer the creature to the Creator, the flesh to the Spirit, temporal things to eternal; to use the gift contrary to the intention of the giver, and to make the end subservient to the means. There is now very seldom any opportunity of martyrdom, which is the highest proof of that love which prefers God before all things: but a Christian finds an opportunity of giving this proof in a life of mortification; and a pastor in the labours of his ministry, which separate him from the pleasures of life, which cause him to sacrifice it to God, to the church, and to the business of salvation, and often shorten the course of it. How happy is it to lose it thus for a moment, since it is to keep it for eternity—as the way to love it in reality, and in God's account, is to hate it for his sake!

26. If any man serve me, let him follow me; and where I am, there shall also my servant be: if any man serve me, him will my Father honour.

Here are three motives which ought to induce a Christian to despise life, and to reconcile him to labour and mortification. The first is, the obligation under which he lies to imitate the Master to whom he has engaged his service, and to follow him in all things. In vain does any man flatter himself with the imagination that he serves Christ, if he do not follow his example, if he do not love what he loved, and despise what he despised. The second motive to the contempt of life, and to the love of labour and mortification, is the hope of following Christ into glory, and of partaking of his reward. A prince who is to ascend a throne, men are ready to follow wherever he goes, and at the expense of every thing—what would they not do, if they entertained any hopes of ascending it with him, as Christ has promised they shall who follow him! Had we but a firm and lively faith in this promise, we should then likewise have this hope; and this hope, like an anchor of the soul both sure and steadfast, would keep our hearts and desires fixed upon the eternal possessions of that heavenly kingdom. The third motive to persuade us to despise life, and to apply ourselves to labour and mortification, is, because the Father will crown all those with honour and glory who have followed his Son, and will even receive them as his children. What master should we not be willing to serve on this condition, in hopes of dividing the inheritance with his children, even though we had no other security than the deceitful word of a worldly man? Lord, let thy infallible word have that influence upon my heart which it ought to have; and do thou cause me to rely upon thy promises without the least doubt or hesitation. They surpass indeed all human comprehension—but thou also art infinitely above the reach of every human understanding. It is a God who loves us, and who loves us with the tenderness of a father, because he loves us in his Son; and nothing can set bounds to his love, or to the gifts which he designs to confer upon his children.

SECT. IV.—THE INWARD TROUBLE OF CHRIST.—A VOICE FROM HEAVEN.—THE POWER OF THE CROSS.—WE MUST WALK WHILE WE HAVE THE LIGHT.

27. Now is my soul troubled; and what shall I say? Father, save me from this hour: but for this cause came I unto this hour.

Few Christians ever apply their minds to adore in Christ this part of his inward sufferings. He shows us in his own person that, in order to hate life in the sense designed above, it is not necessary that we should be altogether insensible of the natural dread of death. Christ, by being thus troubled at the very bottom of his soul, and under a kind of uncertainty what resolution to take, informs us to our comfort that it is the disposition and choice of the will, not the affections of nature, which God considers in us, and by which he will judge us. Christ is sensible in himself of the infirmities of our nature; but it is by his power that he suffers them to make any impression upon himself. We must not conceal from souls the difficult and rugged ways of perfection, but support and encourage them therein by his example. The infirmities which the strong sometimes feel but for a moment, serve to comfort and fortify the minds of the weak. Whenever the dread of the cross and of death dejects us, we ought, after Christ's example, to address ourselves to God in prayer, to adore his purposes and designs, and to make an absolute submission of nature to them.

28. Father, glorify thy name. Then came there a voice from heaven, *saying*, I have both glorified *it*, and will glorify *it* again.

The great means to obtain and enjoy peace of mind, is to seek nothing in life and death but the glory of God alone. To be in this happy disposition upon unforeseen occasions, is the fruit of a holy life. The troubles and anxieties of faithful souls end at length, in leaving God to choose that for them which he shall judge most conducive to the glory of his name. This is what we must always do in the time of sickness, under any danger of death, and in all difficult circumstances which trouble and perplex the mind. The way to be always heard, is to ask nothing of God but his will, and that which tends most to his glory. Christ finds his own glory in that of his Father, as in its ultimate end. The Father finds his in that of his Son, as in the general means and instrument which he has chosen to establish it, by the forming of his church, by the calling of the Gentiles, by miracles, etc.

29. The people therefore that stood by, and heard *it*, said that it thundered: others said, An angel spake to him.

How very unusual a thing is it to know the voice of God perfectly, especially amid the noise and hurry of the world! It does not belong to every one to distinguish it and to judge of it. We must at least take great care that we do not pretend to do it rashly and inconsiderately.

30. Jesus answered and said, This voice came not because of me, but for your sakes.

Every thing is for the elect. To apply to ourselves in particular that which is spoken in general to all persons, is the sure means to profit by the word of God. This voice, this truth is for us, since it directs us into the way of our salvation. It is certainly for us, if we make a good use of it: it is against us, if our lives be not answerable thereto. The nearer our blessed Lord's sacrifice approaches, the more does God prepare and dispose things for it, and prevents the scandal of the cross by the highest testimonies of his approbation.

31. Now is the judgment of this world: now shall the prince of this world be cast out.

Is it not rather, on the contrary, the world which is going to judge the Son of God, and the prince of this world who is going to triumph over the Saviour thereof, and to cast him out of it by death? This seems to be true to the eyes of the flesh—but to the eyes of faith the former is so. What comfort and consolation do these words afford to righteous persons, when oppressed by carnal men! When they sink under their injustice, then it is that they become their judges; and when they are reduced by them to the last extremity, then are they victorious, and triumph over them. My God, how differently does the world appear to those who live by faith and to those who live by sense! In time of temptation, the safest way to arm ourselves against the world and the devil, is to do it with faith, and with the contemplation of Christ's death and passion; since it was by these that they were overcome. The most heinous and flagitious attempt of the devil, is the end of his reign: it is often the same case with respect to wicked men.

32. And I, if I be lifted up from the earth, will draw all *men* unto me. 33. This he said, signifying what death he should die.

The cross is not only the tribunal on which Christ judges the world, and pronounces the sentence of condemnation upon the devil: it is likewise the throne of his mercy toward sinners, the source of all blessings, the cause of our deliverance, the instrument of our salvation, and the meritorious original of an almighty grace, by which he draws all men unto him. Nothing yields greater comfort to Christ, under the dismal prospect of his sufferings and death, than to consider that the salvation of sinners is to be the fruit thereof. Let but pastors be zealous for the salvation of souls, and they will count all labours, pains, and even the loss of life itself, as nothing. It is one of their duties, by frequent prayers to beseech Christ, who draws all men to him by his cross, that he would be pleased to draw sinners to him, and overcome all the resistance of their hearts by the power of his death. O Jesus, lifted up upon the cross for my sins, to thee I offer my heart upon it: lift it up to thyself, and place it out of the reach of all earthly things!

34. The people answered him, We have heard out of the law that Christ abideth forever: and how sayest thou, The Son of man must be lifted up? who is this Son of man?

Faith easily reconciles those seeming contradictions which the mind of man discovers in the mysteries of Jesus Christ, and in the life of his members. The law foretells and declares the humiliations and death of the Messias, as well as the magnificence and eternity of his reign; but self-love stops at that which flatters its vanity and tenderness, and passes by whatever is not agreeable to its carnal notions and inclinations. Men are very unwilling to be acquainted with that path which leads to glory by ignominy, and wherein they must die in order to arrive at immortality. But, O Saviour of the world, who can refuse to take this path, since thou thyself hast walked therein! To read the Scriptures with a carnal and unmortified heart, is a very great obstacle to the understanding of them. We shall plainly perceive the cross in all parts of them, if we love it: it is the cross which takes away the veil of the law, and opens our minds to understand mysteries.

35. Then Jesus said unto them, Yet a little while is the light with you. Walk while ye have the light, lest darkness come upon you: for he that walketh in darkness knoweth not whither he goeth.

Without the true light, which is Jesus Christ, what can we do but wander, fall into the snares of the enemy, go off still more and more from our centre and chief end, stumble, hurt ourselves, meet with frequent falls, and at last tumble down the precipice? We often depend upon the present light we enjoy as much as if it were either our due or at our own disposal; and perhaps it is this very thing which will bring darkness upon us. If we desire to preserve the light, let us dread the loss of it. A traveller, who is apprehensive that the day is drawing to an end, ought to mend his pace, and to hasten forward as fast as he can. It is not enough for our security, that darkness do not come upon us while we are doing ill: it is enough to ruin us, if it should overtake us either doing nothing at all, or not doing all we ought to do. Not to walk, not to advance, is to do ill; since it is to refuse obedience, and to resolve not to arrive at our proper end. Would to God there were no instances to be found, of persons whose light has been turned into darkness for not having made that use of their light which God required of them! Let us take great care that we ourselves never increase the number; let us walk while we have the light, and prevent the night of death by a speedy and perfect conversion.

36. While ye have light, believe in the light, that ye may be the children of light. These things spake Jesus, and departed, and 'did hide himself from them.

Scarce can we forbear trembling, when we see this poor people just going to lose the light forever, because they had preferred the darkness of their passions before it; and yet we are under no apprehension lest our own should deprive us of the same light, which is given us in the gospel. Faith is the great means whereby the divine light enters into our hearts, and which causes the light to shine in darkness. Ever since the fall of Adam, our soul is like a dying lamp, which the eternal light revives and feeds again by means of faith, and which will one day be reunited to the fulness of that eternal light. The perfect light of glory will be communicated only to those who, by the light of faith, have followed Jesus Christ and his maxims. Lord, who hast taught us that faith is the work of God in the soul, preserve and perfect, I beseech thee, in mine, this work of thy mercy.

SECT. V.—THE JEWS CONTINUE INCREDULOUS.—FAITH SUPPRESSED BY FEAR.

37. ¶ But though he had done so many miracles before them, yet they believed not on him:

No miracles, no benefits, no instructions are able to soften the heart of man, without the internal and actual grace of Christ. The more plentifully God bestows upon us his outward gifts, the more carefully ought we to beg of him the grace to make a good use of them by faith; since otherwise they will serve only to our condemnation. Whatever Jesus did before the Jews, he has done before us, since we believe it: and how many other miracles has he done since, which we have no less reason to believe! They will rise up in judgment against us, as much, nay more, than against them, if we do not believe with that obedient faith which engages us to practise according to our belief.

38. That the saying of Esaias the prophet might be fulfilled, which he spake, Lord, who hath believed our report? and to whom hath the arm of the Lord been revealed?

God sees from all eternity the evil which he thinks proper to suffer the corrupt will to commit, by leaving it to itself; but neither his foreseeing, nor his foretelling this evil, imposes any necessity upon the will: God having no part in the corruption and disorder of it, which is the sole cause of sin. Whatever God foretells, is so exactly fulfilled that it seems to happen on purpose to verify the prophecy; whereas, in reality, this was delivered only because the event would certainly come to pass. There are but few who believe; and among those who do, few have so perfect a faith as to be altogether unconcerned in this reproof of the prophet. Jesus-Christ being of the same substance with the Father, being his word and power according to his divine nature, is as it were his arm, since by him he made the world and all things therein; and it is likewise by him, in his human and created nature, that he repairs and restores all things, and saves the world. The sacred humanity of Christ is the instrument of all the miracles which God wrought by his Son, of the merit of all his graces, and of all the works of holiness and mercy. It is a dreadful, but withal a just and adorable judgment, when God, for the punishment of past offences, abandons the sinner to infidelity and to the obduracy of his corrupt will. The Jews see the miracles, but they do not see the arm which works them, having a veil upon the eyes of their heart. Pride spreads this veil over the heart: humility removes and takes it away.

39. Therefore they could not believe, because that Esaias said again,

It is impossible that what God has foreseen and foretold should not come to pass; because it is impossible that he should either deceive us, or be deceived himself. We must steadfastly adhere to the truth of the Scriptures, which are of infallible certainty. Let us bewail ourselves under this inability of the will, with which, by reason of the sin of Adam, we are all born, and which, by our own sins, we daily increase. Let us continually have recourse to him who has said, "Without me ye can do nothing," and "No man can come to me, except the Father draw him."

40. He hath blinded their eyes, and hardened their heart; that they should not see with *their* eyes, nor understand with *their* heart, and be converted, and I should heal them.

The voluntary inability of a blind and obdurate heart has three causes: (1.) The devil, who suggests. (2.) Man, who consents. (3.) God, who either leaves the sinner to his own corrupt inclination, or heaps up benefits upon him, which to him are no other than fresh occasions of sin, as both admonitions and miracles were to Pharaoh, and here to the Jews. Blindness and obduracy have several degrees: whoever either does not see and understand the truths which are necessary to his good conduct and behaviour, or is not directed by those he does understand, on such occasions wherein they ought to be his rule and guide, is blind and hardened with respect to them. Let us take care that these words do not induce us to murmur against God, or to presume to censure his proceedings, instead of humbling ourselves, and adoring him with fear and trembling.

41. These things said Esaias, when he saw his glory, and spake of him.

The prophets spake only of Jesus Christ. Whoever has not him in his mind and heart when he reads them, finds in them no manner of relish at all. If Esaias saw Jesus Christ in his glory, then is he really and truly God: and it was of him, as well as of the Father and the Holy Ghost, that he sung that hymn of his holiness, "Holy, holy, holy is the Lord of hosts: the whole earth is full of his glory," (Isaiah vi. 3.) It was he also who blinded this people, by showing them light in darkness, his divinity in the meanness of our flesh; who hardened them, by working so many miracles, which served only to increase their envy and hatred toward him; and who rendered their diseases incurable, by exposing himself to their rage, and suffering them to crucify him. Lord, prepare my heart, that it be not blinded and hardened by the reading of thy word, and by the consideration of the wonders of thy life!

42. ¶ Nevertheless among the chief rulers also many believed on him; but because of the Pharisees they did not confess *him*, lest they should be put out of the synagogue:

When I see these chief rulers believe in the midst of so many obstacles, I give glory to God, and admire the power of his grace. But when I see them afraid to own their faith, I am ashamed of the cowardice of men, and their weakness makes me afraid. God could have removed their timorousness as he did their incredulity; but he delays the last gifts, that men may not attribute to themselves the first. In whatever state and circumstances we are, we must take great care not to set our hearts too much upon them. The fear of a disgrace, or of an unjust excommunication, is enough to ruin us eternally; since it was probably the cause of the damnation of abundance of Jews, who were convinced of the innocence and divinity of Christ. We must not pertinaciously adhere to any thing which it is in the power of man to take away, if we desire to secure that which none but God can confer upon us. He can save a soul without the use of the sacraments, and out of the external communion of the church; but he cannot save it so long as it prefers these things before its duty, and the obligation it lies under to own and confess him.

43. For they loved the praise* of men more than the praise* of God. [**Fr.* Glory.]

How common are these four obstacles of faith! (1.) Too great a regard to men. (2.) Riches and temporal advantages. (3.) The fear of disgrace. (4.) The love of the praise of men. Faith and charity may be separate from each other; since these Jews had the former, but not the latter, which alone causes men to love the glory of God. Abundance of persons persuade themselves that they love God more than the world, until some trying occasion fully convinces them of their mistake. It is a very great misfortune, for a man not to know himself but only by his falls and acts of infidelity; but it is the greatest of all, not to rise again and recover himself. This is generally occasioned by the love of the praise and glory of men: because in their account it is more shameful to rise again than it was to fall.

SECT. VI.—THE LIGHT OF FAITH.—THE WORD OF GOD JUDGES MEN.—CHRIST SPEAKS NOTHING BUT WHAT HIS FATHER HAS SAID UNTO HIM.

44. ¶ Jesus cried and said, He that believeth on me, believeth not on me, but on him that sent me.

Christ raises his voice on purpose to conclude his public preaching in a more remarkable manner; to show that the hatred and power of his enemies do not in the least dismay him; to upbraid those with their cowardice who dared not openly declare for him, and to encourage them by his example, etc. In this and the following verses Christ himself gives us an encomium of faith: and he must needs know it perfectly, being the author and finisher thereof. First, He shows the dignity and excellency of it. For that which the eyes of the flesh see of Christ is not the ultimate object of our faith, but the means which makes that object known to us, namely, God his Father. Christ brings his Father's word to men, as his ambassador; and therefore the injury of not believing falls ultimately and chiefly upon the Father himself. Christ here magnifies his office and mission, because he perceives, in the hearts of these timorous magistrates, that they are afraid it will be a disgrace to them should they adhere to a person who seemed to have nothing more in him than other men.

45. And he that seeth me, seeth him that sent me.

The knowledge of the Father is inseparable from that of the Son, who is his image according to his divine nature, and who, by his whole life, conduct, and miracles, rendered the wisdom, goodness, greatness, and power of his divinity (which he has in common with his Father) visible to the eyes of men. Grant, Lord, that I may imitate thee, in always raising my mind up to the very fountain of that good which God has infused into me, and in desiring that others may see and consider him alone in all his gifts. We are the images of God, both by the gifts of nature and of grace; let us be so likewise by our godliness and the holiness of our lives, that whoever sees us may plainly see God in us.

46. I am come a light into the world, that whosoever believeth on me should not abide in darkness.

Second, Christ shows the usefulness and advantage of faith, in that it is the only way whereby we can get out of darkness. What unaccountable madness is it, to choose rather to abide in the darkness of sin than to admit the light which comes to seek us—a light which was before the world began, and which came down even into the darkness thereof! There is not one of all the sons of Adam who was not born in darkness, and whom Christ did not find plunged therein, when he came to him by the first ray of his grace. But, alas! how many did he leave in that state of darkness by his justice, when he vouchsafed to draw us out of it through the tenderness of his mercy! Let us not pass by this, or any other opportunity, without returning thanks to God for this inestimable favour, and without seriously considering the fidelity it requires of us.

47. And if any man hear my words, and believe not, I judge him not: for I came not to judge the world, but to save the world.

Third, Christ specifies the nature and quality of the faith which God requires of us, which must be such as shows itself by our obedience to his law. Not to believe what Christ declares to men, is an indignity toward him which deserves an eternal punishment: but how much greater is the indignity, to believe his words, and yet to despise them! My God! what numbers of Christians does this truth arraign, and perhaps us too who are reading it at this time! The first mission of Christ is all grace and mercy: he comes as a Saviour, and not as a Judge. It belongs not to an envoy or ambassador to revenge the injuries he receives; but to the prince who sent him, and who is affronted in his person: and Jesus Christ both appears and preaches no otherwise than in the name of his Father. Those who are commissioned to deliver his word to men, ought to imitate his example in this respect.

48. He that rejecteth me, and receiveth not my words, hath one that

judgeth him: the word that I have spoken, the same shall judge him in the last day.

Fourth, Christ shows the necessity of faith in order to avoid the wrath of God; since he who continues in darkness is already judged as a child of darkness. The ministers of Christ ought never to revenge the injuries which are done them; nor should they ever be provoked because their preaching is disregarded and despised. It is the word of God, and not their own which they deliver; and therefore they must leave the care of punishing the contempt thereof to him alone. A pastor is sent to no other end but to save; and if he be obliged at any time to inflict punishments, they must be only such as are healing and salutary. The truth will judge that person whom it does not justify. Christians will certainly be judged by the gospel; and yet few practise it, many despise it, and the greatest part know little or nothing of it.

49. For I have not spoken of myself; but the Father which sent me, he gave me a commandment, what I should say, and what* I should speak. [**Fr.* How.]

Fifth, Christ teaches us that faith has two immovable foundations. The first is, that the word we believe is the word of God. The second, that the mission of the person who preaches it is sufficiently authorized of God by miracles. That person preaches with a well-grounded confidence, who speaks or advances nothing merely of his own head. God gives a blessing to his word in the mouth of an obedient pastor or preacher, who teaches nothing but what he has received from God, and does not disguise it by such a way of expression and delivery as savours too much of the world. Every thing was appointed and prescribed to Christ by his Father, even to the very manner how he should speak: and his obedience was so much the more perfect, free, and meritorious, the more incapable he was of disobeying his Father. The disciples and ministers of Christ ought to deliver nothing but what they have learned from him, and not the inventions of their own wit; and are obliged to manifest in themselves the holiness of him in whose name they speak by a plain, modest, and Christian way of behaviour.

50. And I know that his commandment is life everlasting: whatsoever I speak therefore, even as the Father said unto me, so I speak.

The law of God fulfilled by charity or love, has a quickening virtue in it, and is the source of life everlasting. This is the sum and substance of all evangelical preaching; with this Christ concludes his exercise of the public ministration of the word; and to this all the cares and endeavours of a preacher or pastor ought to tend. For he ought to make it his whole business to inspire his people with the love of God's law, to convince and satisfy them that the true devotion of a Christian consists in the keeping of his commandments, and not in arbitrary performances which are the choice of inclination; that there is no other way besides this to everlasting life; and that the pastor himself ought to set them an example of a perfect obedience to God, by doing his duty in the manner which God has enjoined. Since life everlasting is annexed to the commandments of God, those men shut the gate of the former against Christians, who give them false notions of the latter, and weaken their obligation by pernicious ways of softening the rigour of them. Grant us, Lord, the grace to show a perfect submission to thy law; and be pleased likewise to give thy church such pastors as may make known the holiness of that law, and teach it in the purity of thy Holy Spirit.

CHAPTER XIII.

SECT. I.—CHRIST WASHES THE FEET OF THE APOSTLES.

1. Now, before the feast of the passover, when Jesus knew that his hour was come that he should depart* out of this world unto the Father, having loved his own which were in the world, he loved them unto the end. [* *Fr.* Pass.]

Hitherto the work of Jesus Christ, the establishment of the Christian religion, is only marked out, as it were, in a platform; and the minds of men prepared by his preaching, by the example of his life, by his miracles, which evidently proved his mission, and by the cures which he performed on their bodies. He is now going to give the highest proofs of his love, by the last and greatest instances of humility and patience; by the prescription of the great remedies for sin, of the great means of salvation, of Christian grace, and of the new sacrament; by the forming of his ministers, by the institution of the grand sacrifice, and the celebration of the grand passover, upon which and its consequences God has made the salvation of the world depend. By making this reflection upon our blessed Saviour's love, John requires of us fresh attention, and a new increase of our love and gratitude. This sacrifice, which must cost him so dear, seems no more to him than a passage or departure to his Father. Whatever passes away is nothing: the reward of the most painful obedience, consisting in the enjoyment of God, is eternal; and to one who really loves him, the very expectation of enjoying him is sufficient to make him forget every thing beside. A good pastor, who is about to leave his flock, makes it his last care to form good labourers who may supply his place: this is the work to which our blessed Lord devotes the remaining part of his life. How comes it to pass that we are so inconstant in our love toward Jesus Christ, since he loves us with so constant a perseverance unto the end?

2. And supper being ended, the devil having now put into the heart of Judas Iscariot, Simon's *son*, to betray him;

How dreadful is the devil's power over the hearts of sinners who have laid themselves open to him, since it extends so far as to make them betray Jesus Christ! My God, what exceeding difference is there between that which the love of Christ puts into his heart in favour of sinners, and that which self-love and blind concupiscence put into their hearts against him! Nothing could have any influence upon this ungrateful wretch, or soften the hardness of his heart—neither those marks of kindness and friendship which he had lately received, nor even the sight of his Master just going to fall down at his feet. On the contrary, nothing can hinder Christ from showing toward him his love and patience to the very last. Where, then, are those who cannot bear the sight of a person whom they dislike, or who has been wanting in the discharge of some duty toward them?

3. Jesus knowing that the Father had given all things into his hands, and that he was come from God, and went to God;

Man is so corrupt, that neither the knowledge of his own miseries, nor the experience of his extreme frailties and infirmities, is capable of humbling him under the hand of God. On the contrary, Christ is so holy, that the knowledge of his own divine perfections, and of the sovereign power God has given into his hands, cannot hinder him from humbling himself even at the feet of the vilest of his creatures, of a sinner whose heart is under the possession of the devil. Let the great come to this school, there to learn, by seeing the inconceivable humility of the only Son of God, not to be puffed up with the splendour of their birth and family, or with the vast hopes of still increasing their wealth and honour. This humility of Christ proceeds not from any ignorance of what he is in himself, as it often does in men, but from the choice of his will, and from the knowledge of the greatness and majesty of God. Let us adore his sovereign power, his sublime perfections, his descent from his Father, and his glorious return into his bosom, with so much the more reverence and devotion the more he has been pleased to humble and abase them for our sakes.

4. He riseth from supper, and laid aside his garments; and took a towel, and girded himself. 5. After that he poureth water into a basin, and began to wash the disciples' feet, and to wipe *them* with the towel wherewith he was girded.

When the children of Adam humble themselves, there is always some deficiency in their humiliation; pride still finds a way to creep in, and shows itself in some respect or other; but the humiliation of Christ is complete in all its circumstances, since he makes no use of the assistance or service of any one either to lay aside his garments, or to gird himself, or to pour out the water. And yet this is but a shadow of that more perfect and abasing humiliation whereby the Son of God, as it were, stripped himself of all his majesty and glory, to clothe himself with the nature of servants as with a napkin or towel, with which he wiped away our sins and earthly affections after having washed us in the water of his tears and his blood. Having condescended and stooped thus far below himself, he now stoops even below Judas—it being impossible for him to stoop lower than the feet of that monster. It is from Jesus Christ, in this posture, that men must learn to cleanse themselves by humiliation and penitential exercises, in order to prepare themselves for the priesthood, for the Christian sacrifice and communion, for which Christ hereby prepared his apostles.

6. Then cometh he to Simon Peter: and Peter said unto him, Lord, dost thou wash my feet?

The humility of Christ is incomprehensible even to one of the chief of the apostles. The first in dignity ought to be the first also in purity, humility, faith, and religion. Had not Peter, when he saw Jesus at his feet, greater reason to say to him, as he did once, being himself prostrate at his, "Depart from me, for I am a sinful man, O Lord?" On the contrary, it is for this very reason that Christ must not depart from him; since none but he can cleanse him from his sins. Expressions of reverence and respect, and testimonies of religion, are sometimes sincere and unfeigned, and yet for all that are not well-timed, and conformable to the will of God.

7. Jesus answered and said unto him, What I do thou knowest not now; but thou shalt know hereafter.

There is a sort of resistance or refusal which seems to be humble and respectful, and yet proceeds from our ignorance, and even from our presumption. Men are sometimes desirous to show themselves humble in their own way, contrary to the settled order of their duties, and so oppose the will of God before they are aware. It is this will which ought always to regulate the external exercise of humility. We frequently know the will of God without knowing the reason thereof; and the first thing we have to do is to submit to it, since in this the true obedience of faith does consist. God sometimes puts into a spiritual office a person in many respects very imperfect, and places one of great holiness at his feet: in a little time we shall know the reason of this; for the darkness of this world will soon pass away. All the outward actions of Christ are full of mysteries: a patient and obedient faith attains to the understanding of them.

8. Peter saith unto him, Thou shalt never wash my feet. Jesus answered him, If I wash thee not, thou hast no part with me.

How admirable a sight, and how instructive a lesson do we here behold in this contest between the humility of Christ, and the faith, reverence, and love of Peter! These virtues, when not accompanied with obedience, are as nothing in the sight of God. The greatest fervency and zeal of devotion, attended even with some outward signs of humility, are but mere delusion when not regulated by that obedience which is due to the church and to our superiors. There is no threatening more terrible to a soul which loves God, than that of being separated from him. Whatever degree of purity we may imagine we have, if we be not cleansed by Christ, we are unworthy of his table, of the participation of his body, and of the glory of his new life. Lord, imprint this truth deep in my heart, that I may be sensible how much I stand in need of thee to make me clean in thy sight, and that I may have recourse to thee, O thou fountain of true purity.

9. Simon Peter saith unto him, Lord, not my feet only, but also *my* hands and *my* head.

A ready obedience is a certain sign of a sincere humility, and of a true faith. Let us leave Christ to do with us according to his good pleasure, that we may partake of his grace, his mysteries, and his kingdom. How unworthy soever we may be of the divine gifts, we must accept them when God offers them to us. It is a false kind of humility to refuse the goodness of God too long; and it is no other than presumption to pretend to set rules to his liberality toward us, and to know how far we stand in need of him. The great difficulty in the way to perfection is to know how to resign up our will and desires to the guidance of him who knows us better than we do ourselves. We always desire either too much or too little when our will is not directed by him. We must learn of Peter not to persist in our resolutions, as soon as we know that they are not from God, and that they are obstacles either to salvation or to perfection.

10. Jesus saith unto him, He that is washed needeth not, save to wash *his* feet, but is clean every wit: and ye are clean, but not all.

The head is an emblem of faith, which is the source of all

good thoughts in the mind, and of all pious motions in the will; the hands denote good works, and the feet the affections. When even our faith is pure, and our life truly Christian, there is still a great deal to be cleansed in the affections and dispositions of the heart. This is the work of our whole lives, to the performing of which we continually stand in need of the assistance of Christ as well as to the preserving of the other gifts of his mercy. There are some scrupulous souls who, from a principle different from that of Peter, are always fancying that they have occasion to wash either their head or their hands; and thus amusing themselves with imaginary wants, take no manner of care to wash their feet, to correct their affections, and to oppose their imperfect or disorderly inclinations.

11. For he knew who should betray him; therefore said he, Ye are not all clean.

It belongs to Christ alone to judge of inward piety. The perfect knowledge which he shows the traitor he has of his heart and of his designs, has not the least influence upon him, because his avarice has taken full possession of him. The desire of earthly riches renders men deaf to the word of God, to inspirations, and internal admonitions. We should take care to enter again into the bottom of our own hearts, instead of having the presumption to imagine we can prevail with Christ to enter into them, when the reproach of our own conscience assures us that they are not clean enough to receive him. Christ, by this admonition, afflicts the rest of the apostles; but it is much better to give holy persons some uneasiness and disquiet, of which they know how to make a good use, and which will increase their vigilance, than either not to warn a sinner at all who is running headlong into perdition, or to ruin his reputation by open and public reproof.

12. So, after he had washed their feet, and had taken his garments, and was set down again, he said unto them, Know ye what I have done to you?

That person does not know the mysteries of Christ who knows only the outward part of them. The good Shepherd, intent on forming the pastors who are to supply his place, teaches them, by his example, to instruct their flocks in the spiritual meaning of the institutions of the church, which is the life and soul of them. It is chiefly either just before or after the use of these institutions, or when they are most present to the mind, that a priest ought to make this inquiry: "Know ye what I am going to do, or what I have done to you? what it is has been done to this child by all these institutions of baptism?" etc.—How holy is that table, how becoming a Christian and a priest, where men entertain and instruct one another in the life of Christ, and in the institutions of the church, by means of curious questions in religion! This is a method which might supply the want of those lectures of piety with which the councils enjoin even bishops to sanctify their tables and meals. It is a shame and reproach to Christians, that their tables are often more profane than those of moral heathens were.

13. Ye call me master and Lord: and ye say well; for *so* I am.

The humility of a bishop does not consist in not knowing or not owning the greatness and authority of his dignity; but in not insisting upon it to any other purpose but the salvation of souls, and in sacrificing all external and temporal advantages for their sakes. It concerns us highly to consider seriously all those rights which these two qualities of Master and Lord give Jesus Christ over us. If we are his disciples, let us study, publish, love, and follow his maxims. If we are his servants, let us serve none but him; let us imitate his virtues, which are the proper badges which show that we belong to him; let us direct all our labours to the advancement of his interests and his glory; let us be always ready to obey him, and to do his will, etc.

14. If I then, *your* Lord and Master, have washed your feet; ye also ought to wash one another's feet.

If holiness itself stoop so low even as the feet of Judas, what ought not a bishop or a priest to do for the sake of souls? A master whose business it is to teach the virtue of humility, and such every pastor ought to be, should not undertake to teach it till he has first practised it himself. If our circumstances do not require us to imitate literally the example of Christ, in washing the feet of our brethren, let us do it at least spiritually, in exercising charity and humility toward them, and even toward our enemies. Christ has annexed to some sensible signs and visible sacraments those truths, virtues, and mysteries, the memory whereof he would have us preserve with the greatest care, as being the most necessary for us: particularly to the washing of feet he has joined the remembrance of his humility; to the sacrament of the eucharist, the remembrance of his love.

15. For I have given you an example, that ye should do as I have done to you.

Christ was pleased to become our pattern and example, chiefly as to the practice of humility and charity. It is even of greater use and advantage to observe the spirit of this ceremony than the letter, in humbling ourselves below our neighbours, to gain them over to God. Every one ought to endeavour, in his proper station, to cleanse and purify his brother by good example, by fraternal reproof, by wholesome advice and exhortations, by forgiving the injuries he has received, and by humbling himself for those he has done. A pastor who is always ready to serve his neighbour, always intent on cleansing him from his sins, endeavouring by his tears to wash away the filth which sinners have contracted from their conversation with the world, etc., is a true imitator of the holy and adorable servitude of the Prince of pastors.

16. Verily, verily, I say unto you, The servant is not greater than his lord; neither he that is sent greater than he that sent him.

Who are we, that we should expect to be treated better than Jesus Christ? Nothing can be more just and equitable than this fundamental maxim of Christianity; and yet there is nothing with which we are less willing to comply. It is great injustice in a sinner, to be unwilling either to humble himself or to be humbled; but it is much greater in a person whom Christ has admitted to a share of the sacerdotal service with himself, which requires a more exact and faithful imitation of his humility. To see Jesus Christ thus embrace humiliation, is matter of great consolation to the humble; but to those who are enemies thereto, it is a reproach, a subject of shame and of condemnation. Let us often repeat that to ourselves which Christ here speaks to us; and then we shall never complain of ill usage, afflictions, or humiliations.

17. If ye know these things, happy are ye if ye do them.

It is not light or knowledge which makes a man happy in this life; but the good use of knowledge, and the love of the cross of Christ. The knowledge of our duties, without the practice of them, serves only to expose us to a severer judgment. The more we know concerning Christ, and the more plainly it appears to us that he embraced a state of poverty and humiliation, not out of weakness or necessity, but out of choice and love, the more abominable in the sight of God is our love of grandeur, luxury, and of a soft and sensual life. It is neither by thoughts nor words, nor by mere external acts of worship, that we really own Christ to be our Master, and ourselves to be his servants, but by doing his will, and imitating the example of his humility. Men often talk loudly of the names of vicars, vicegerents, and ambassadors of Christ; but they think but little of the obligations which those names lay upon them, they avoid what he loved, they seek what he despised, they desire to live in friendship with the world, and are willing to succeed the sovereign Pastor in his authority, but not in his humility.

SECT. II.—THE TREACHERY OF JUDAS FORETOLD.

18. ¶ I speak not of you all: I know whom I have chosen: but that the scripture may be fulfilled, He that eateth bread with me hath lifted up his heel against me.

It is not easy to honour and imitate this calmness and tranquillity of mind and heart with which Christ speaks of the person who was to betray him, and of his own death. But he can do in us whatever he did in himself. Those who are betrayed by their friends, undergo this misfortune through ignorance, and because they are not aware of it; but Christ from the beginning saw all the wicked designs of Judas, and could have avoided them. The Psalms of David are to be understood literally concerning Christ, as well as the other prophecies; and the history of the treason committed against David, did prophetically describe that which was to be committed against Jesus Christ. That holy king was not only a prophet in respect of his Psalms, but he was a man entirely prophetical by his life, his persecutions, his battles, his victories, his reign, etc. He is a picture of Jesus Christ, in which we see him represented in a lively manner when we behold it with the eyes of faith.

19. Now I tell you before it come, that, when it is come to pass, ye may believe that I am *he*.

A good pastor ought to prepare Christians for temptation, and to arm them beforehand against any occasion of scandal or offence which he foresees will happen. Christ neither does nor says any thing in vain, because he has several designs both in his actions and his words. He does not convert Judas indeed by his prophetical admonitions, on the contrary he hardens him the more; but he makes known his divinity, strengthens the faith of his disciples, gives them means of engaging others to acknowledge him to be what he really is, and affords even us an occasion to adore his conduct, wisdom, meekness, patience, and intent application to the work of his Father, and his great care to prevent the scandal which the treachery of one of the apostles must necessarily have given all the rest, had he not showed them that he was not ignorant of it even when he chose him, and that he knew of his treachery before he put it in execution.

20. Verily, verily, I say unto you, He that receiveth whomsoever I send receiveth me; and he that receiveth me receiveth him that sent me.

So close and strict is the union between Christ and his members, that he himself receives the good which is done to them. But stricter still is that between him and his ministers, by the unity of his priesthood, to a share in which he vouchsafes to admit them. Their mission makes a part of his. It is his place which they sustain; his authority which they exercise; a portion of his divine unction which they have received; and they are the functions of his priesthood which they continue. It is an error which is attended with dreadful consequences, for a person either to reject Christ while he thinks he rejects only a mere man; or to receive a false prophet or an impostor, imagining that he receives

Jesus Christ. The mission is the thing which we must chiefly regard. To assure us that we receive an ambassador of God, sent by Jesus Christ, it must appear that the mission which is pretended to is derived from Christ.

21. When Jesus had thus said, he was troubled in spirit, and testified, and said, Verily, verily, I say unto you, that one of you shall betray me.

Christ having showed in the preceding verse what it is to be an apostle, and to how high a degree of honour such a person is advanced, he now discovers at last of what excessive ingratitude toward him one whom he had raised to that honour was capable. Nothing gives us a juster idea of a God betrayed by his apostle, by him whom he had honoured with his particular confidence, than to see this divine constancy and resolution, as it were, shaken, and this sovereign peace and tranquillity of mind disturbed and troubled in Jesus Christ. The sins of priests and pastors, especially when they betray Jesus Christ in betraying the church, the truth, and the interests of souls, are capable of troubling the soul of Christ himself, so much does he abhor sins of that nature. How few are there of that profession who are so deeply affected with the sins and with the loss of souls as to be troubled in spirit on that account, and whose charity toward their enemies is never wearied out!

22. Then the disciples looked one on another, doubting* of whom he spake. [**Fr.* Being in pain to know.]

There is no greater pain or more rigorous penance to souls which really love God, and hate sin for his sake, than these doubts and uncertainties in which he sometimes leaves them concerning the state of their conscience. We have reason to dread every thing, when we are once thoroughly sensible what the heart of man is under those dismal circumstances into which the sin of Adam has brought it. We neither avoid any thing which is evil, nor do any thing which is good, without a kind of miracle, since it is by a supernatural assistance: and to think ourselves sure of this miracle would be such a degree of presumption as would alone render us unworthy of it. The very name of sin ought to make us tremble, whatever the testimony of our conscience is.

23. Now there was leaning on Jesus' bosom one of his disciples, whom Jesus loved.

The virginal purity of John gives him so free an access to the bosom of Christ; and it was from his bosom that he drew the sublime truths of his gospel, and that ardent love for his Master. Chastity and modesty are inseparable. It is this modesty which hinders John from naming himself, when he relates the particular favours which his Master conferred upon him. His gratitude causes him to forget, as it were, his own name, that he may make himself known by nothing but the kindness of his Saviour toward him; and he forgets even all his other gifts, that he may remember that only of his love, the most precious of all, and the fountain of all the rest. Where should that disciple whom Jesus loved rest, if not in the bosom, and on the heart of Jesus, where this love resides? Let us by no means envy the happy lot of John: let us be faithful imitators of the purity, modesty, and charity of Christ, and we shall be all of us his beloved disciples. When we receive the communion worthily, we are in the bosom of Christ, and Christ is in ours; we dwell in Christ, and Christ in us: of this we are assured by his word.

24. Simon Peter therefore beckoned to him, that he should ask who it should be of whom he spake.

Charity and authority ought to conspire together in the church to discover the disorders and irregularities of its ministers, and mutually to assist each other, to hinder them from being hurtful and prejudicial to souls. The primacy or first place in love has the advantage of the first place in power, with respect to prayer and a near access to Christ. He discovers his secrets to those whom he loves most. Those who are the highest in authority ought not to think they debase themselves when they have recourse to the prayers of those who surpass them in the love of God.

25. He then lying on Jesus' breast saith unto him, Lord, who is it?

Purity and charity give men a right to use a sort of holy freedom with God and Christ. The divine gifts and talents must be employed under the guidance and direction of authority. Piety obeys power with simplicity of mind, as power ought with humility to command piety. A person may be said to pray "lying on Jesus' breast," who offers up his prayers relying on his fatherly love, with trust and confidence in his merits, and with the spirit of a child, which is love. We ought not to have any curiosity to know who are wicked, but only for the advantage of the church, and that we may be upon our guard against them.

26. Jesus answered, He it is, to whom I shall give a sop, when I have dipped *it*. And when he had dipped the sop, he gave *it* to Judas Iscariot, *the son* of Simon.

The gifts of God, received by hypocrites, give admission to the devil into their heart. How dangerous is it to receive unworthily the very best things from the hand of Christ himself! If there be so much danger in thus receiving a morsel of bread, how much more is there in unworthily receiving the consecrated elements which represent his body and blood? A man is in a very desperate condition indeed, when the divine gifts serve only to manifest the corruption and wickedness of his heart. It would perhaps be more profitable to a wicked person to receive chastisements at the hand of God rather than benefits; but it is in this respect that his justice is extremely terrible, in that he bestows such good things upon him as do but harden him the more, instead of punishing him in order to open his eyes. My God, overwhelm me with temporal punishments rather than ever permit me to fall into so deplorable a state and condition.

27. And after the sop Satan entered into him. Then said Jesus unto him, That thou doest, do quickly.

It sometimes happens that some temporal benefit from God, or a sacrilegious communion, of which this sop is an emblem, completes the obduracy of a sinner, and renders him as it were incurable. All sense of every thing is extinguished in this traitor: he has neither understanding, nor remorse, nor shame: the devil has taken full possession of his heart, to make it the instrument of his intended work. There are three causes which concur to the hardening of any person: (1.) The benefits of God received with a traitorous, perfidious, and ungrateful heart. (2.) The devil, who enters into such a heart, wherein there is no longer any thing to resist him, and hinder him from making it his slave. (3.) God, who abandons this heart to its wickedness and hardness, since it has so often rejected the charitable hand of its Physician. Fatal liberty this of doing evil! Happy those to whom God refuses it, and whom he obstructs and opposes in their wicked designs.

28. Now no man at the table knew for what intent he spake thus unto him.

A pastor ought to preserve charity toward the greatest sinners, and to use them with tenderness to the very last. Christ makes himself understood by whom he pleases, and in what manner he pleases. Judas understands him to his condemnation: the rest of the apostles do not understand him at all, to the end that peace may be preserved among them, that the traitor may be concealed, and that no obstruction may be given to the sacrifice upon which the salvation of the world depends. Their simplicity serves as a veil to hide Judas. Charity is not apt to be suspicious and distrustful: it never sees what is evil, but only when it is forced to see it.

29. For some *of them* thought, because Judas had the bag, that Jesus had said unto him, Buy *those things* that we have need of against the feast; or, that he should give something to the poor.

It appears, from hence, that Christ left the care of his money, and the management of his common and ordinary expenses, to Judas, but that he reserved to himself the giving particular directions in what concerned his sacrifices, and in whatever related to the worship of God in his family, or to the relief of the poor. Who will pretend to excuse himself from the duty of giving alms, when he sees that Jesus Christ and his apostles gave even out of their poverty? He sanctified the festivals by charity, and, in so doing, teaches us to distribute our alms in greater abundance on those days whereon God is pleased more abundantly to shed abroad his graces in our hearts. This is a retribution due by justice: but all the advantage is on our side.

30. He then, having received the sop, went immediately out; and it was night.

The extraordinary favours of God received unworthily, his

admonitions despised, and his inspirations rejected, serve only to precipitate that person into sin who has delivered up his heart to the devil. The devil is an imperious master, who will be served immediately, and gives the sinner no time to recover himself. Nothing is a plainer indication of the sinner's blindness, than the pleasure he takes in serving a tyrant after having left a Master endued with so much gentleness and goodness. The night which this miserable wretch has in his heart is, without comparison, blacker and darker than that which he chooses for his work of darkness. O night the most criminal, dreadful, and dark, and yet at the very same time the most holy, amiable, and bright!—since as, on the one side, the Son of God is therein betrayed, sold, and delivered up by the most execrable sacrilege and parricide, so, on the other, he therein gives, delivers up, and sacrifices himself by the most religious action that ever was, leaves the most divine pledge of his love, and teaches therein the brightest and sublimest truths of that religion which he then institutes!

SECT. III.—THE SON OF MAN GLORIFIED.—THE COMMANDMENT OF LOVE.—PETER'S DENIAL FORETOLD.

31. ¶ Therefore, when he was gone out, Jesus said, Now is the Son of man glorified, and God is glorified in him.

Christ, who was so much concerned and troubled in spirit while Judas was present, and in company with the rest of his apostles, seems to have recovered the peace and freedom of his mind immediately upon the going out of that man of sin. A bishop, a pastor, or a superior, is very grievously afflicted when he sees a soul ruin itself, and a member tear itself from the body from which, being separated, it cannot possibly have any life. But when there is no remedy, he adores God in the depth of his judgments, and joins peace and tranquillity of mind with fear and trembling. It is matter of great joy to those who are intrusted with the care of any society, to see it purged of the leaven which might corrupt the new lump. Judas, on his side, speaks concerning the death of Christ, and speaks of it in his own way; Christ likewise, on his side, speaks concerning it—but in how different a language! He sees nothing but glory where others discover nothing but humiliation and ignominy!

32. If God be glorified in him, God shall also glorify him in himself, and shall straightway glorify him.

Christ finds his glory in his humiliations, and in his obedience even unto death, because God finds his therein. In like manner the Christian will always find his true honour in honouring God, in what way soever it be, and whatever it cost him. The men of this world, and those who follow the business of war, talk of nothing but glory or honour, because this is their end and design; and the more dangers they have undergone in order to arrive at it, the more glorious do they esteem themselves. Of what then should Jesus Christ speak, who is the man of God, and the God-man, if not of the glory of God, which is his end, and that of all things? We ought to value nothing besides, but only so far as it leads and conducts us to this. The hope of our own glory, such as God has designed for us, is very consistent with our seeking the glory of God, since it is a means conducing thereto. But the most excellent and powerful means of all others, is the glorious resurrection of Christ. It is to publish and proclaim this mystery, that Christ appoints his apostles; it was in being confessors and martyrs for it, that the fidelity of Christians appeared. It is likewise, next to God, the great object of our piety and devotion, and the grand solemnity of the church.

33. Little children, yet a little while I am with you. Ye shall seek me; and as I said unto the Jews, Whither I go, ye cannot come; so now I say to you.

The wonderful tenderness of Christ toward his disciples teaches us that true piety is not hard-hearted and insensible. The more perfect charity is, the more does it compassionate the troubles and infirmities of others. It is a great consolation to the Christian sheep or children, to see that their Father, as well as themselves, is sensible of the concern which attends a necessary separation: and to give them this consolation is a pastoral and paternal duty. The tenderness of a pastor ought to have a freedom and generosity in it, so as not to hinder him from delivering disagreeble truths, and giving such advice as is necessary. The state of the life after the resurrection is altogether spiritual; and Christ is not then known according to the flesh, or according to the usual manner of conversation.

34. A new commandment I give unto you, That ye love one another; as I have loved you, that ye also love one another.

The commandment of love is a new commandment, in that it has the love of Christ for its pattern, and is newly engraved in the heart by the Holy Ghost. We must love one another only for heaven, and with a view to eternal happiness. This was undoubtedly a new kind of love to the Jews, who had only carnal hopes and expectations, and whose dispensation was altogether temporal; but the Christian, who is made such only in order to attain to heaven, cannot be ignorant of this truth. The generality of the friendships of the world are wholly Jewish and temporal. There are very few which are truly Christian, and which tend to a union in and for God by the Spirit of Jesus Christ. Lord, engrave deep in me this love, which renews the heart, which makes the new man, and which loves nothing but in thee, according to thy will, and for thy sake!

35. By this shall all *men* know that ye are my disciples, if ye have love one to another.

Love is the proper mark and character of a Christian; but such a love as is altogether free, which has neither self-interest for its foundation nor benefits for its motive, and which is proof against injuries. To love because we are loved, is a friendship which is merely human, and which is common to us with heathens: but to love because God enjoins it upon us, and to do it for his sake, this is the spirit of the new religion of Christ. The mutual love or charity which shows us to be the disciples of Christ, must be conformable to his; for he has taught us nothing but what he practised himself: and in order to resemble him, we must love our very enemies, and be ready to give up our temporal life to secure their eternal salvation. A disciple of Moses is known by a timorous, servile, and strict observance of a great number of precepts, which the Jews were not able to bear: on the contrary, we know a disciple of Christ by a free, voluntary, and faithful observance of this one commandment of our blessed Saviour, which includes all the rest.

36. ¶ Simon Peter said unto him, Lord, whither goest thou? Jesus answered him, Whither I go, thou canst not follow me now; but thou shalt follow me afterwards.

Peter's fondness for the visible presence of Christ fixes his mind upon his preceding words, which mentioned his departure from them, instead of making him attentive to the commandment of love, which joins us closely and intimately to Christ, and renders him present in our hearts. An irregular curiosity follows an affection which is not perfect, and temptation follows curiosity. God has his proper times and seasons, and he enables us by his grace to do that at one time which we could not do at another. Whatever sense we may have of our own weakness, let us always hope, that although we be not yet in a condition to follow Christ in his ways, yet we shall one day be able to do it. All have not the assurance of this from the very mouth of Jesus Christ, as Peter had; but all ought to have the same hope and confidence in this respect.

37. Peter said unto him, Lord, why cannot I follow thee now? I will lay down my life for thy sake.

There are very few who know the measure of their own strength. We must not rely upon that which we perceive in ourselves, or which we imagine we have; but we must pray much, and promise nothing from ourselves. Peter asks why he cannot follow Christ now; and the reason is, because he believes he can. Presumption gives imaginary strength, and hinders men from asking and receiving that which is real. When God assures us of any thing, let us not pretend to argue about it; but let us be so far from contradicting him as to believe without the least hesitation. Peter was not yet strong enough to renounce his own opinion and judgment, and to submit entirely to the word of God—and yet he thought he could renounce the love of life, and die for the sake of his Master! Thus a deceitful zeal makes us believe we could do great things for God, while, at the same time, we do not even easy things which he actually requires of us. Strange delusion this!

38. Jesus answered him, Wilt thou lay down thy life for my sake? Verily, verily, I say unto thee, The cock shall not crow, till thou hast denied me thrice.

How deep and how little known is the wound of pride and presumption in respect of our own strength, since Christ, in order to lay it open to our sight, and to heal it, permits so grievous a fall in an apostle whom he loved so much! Christ must lay down his life for Peter, before Peter can lay down his for him. The Son of God must confess his own divinity before the tribunal of men, to the end that Peter may confess it; because the Son of God is the head of the martyrs, and the first of the confessors, from whom must be derived the courage to declare for him, and the strength to suffer for his name. Peter, who refuses to hearken to the voice of Christ in order to know himself, will learn, from the crowing of the cock, that too great a confidence leads to a precipice.

CHAPTER XIV.

SECT. I.—CHRIST THE WAY, THE TRUTH, AND THE LIFE.—HE WHO SEES HIM, SEES THE FATHER ALSO.

1. Let not your heart be troubled: ye believe in God, believe also in me.

A pastor who has been obliged to give the minds of his flock some trouble and disturbance, either by acquainting them with some dreadful truths, or with his own departure, ought to use his endeavours to strengthen and support them. Our blessed Lord never gives human consolations. All his ways are ways of faith, and he never takes souls out of them, but still causes them to walk more and more therein. He does not forbid the trouble of the senses, which nature cannot always restrain, but the trouble of the heart, which generally proceeds either from want of faith in the providence of God, or from want of trust in the grace of Christ, which are the two foundations of Christian hope. Is it not sufficient to calm and assuage all our troubles, to know that we have God for our Father, and his Son for our Mediator? We can lose nothing so long as we retain faith, because this renders even Jesus Christ present to us in a more holy and powerful manner than if he were only visibly present. We must often pray for this faith, which quiets and fortifies the heart. It is by Jesus Christ that we have access to God, and that God comes to us; let us therefore never separate our faith and confidence in Christ from those which we have in God.

2. In my Father's house are many mansions: if *it were* not *so*, I would have told you. I go to prepare a place for you.

The weak must be encouraged with the hope of reward, which is not designed only for the most perfect. The reward is answerable to the virtue, and the different degrees of glory to those of charity. What more solid comfort and consolation can we possibly have, than to hope that Christ will vouchsafe to share with us the habitation which he enjoys in heaven, in the very bosom of his Father! How could we have ever hoped for so sublime and advantageous a place, had not Christ undertaken to prepare it for us! How many mysteries are contained in this expression! It is thus, to avoid afflicting his disciples, that he hides from them that painful and humbling preparation, which is the sacrifice of the cross—a sacrifice truly preparatory, because it merits every thing, and applies nothing; as that of the eucharist merits nothing, and applies every thing, by means of the Holy Ghost and of his grace.

3. And if I go and prepare a place for you, I will come again, and receive you unto myself; that where I am, *there* ye may be also.

The death of the righteous is nothing else but their reunion with Jesus Christ their head. This is the thing for which all these mysteries prepare us, and for which we ought to prepare ourselves by his grace. The first preparation is upon the cross, by means of the sacrifice. The second is in heaven, by the ascension and the mission of the Holy Ghost, which is the fruit both of the sacrifice and of the ascension. Both the resurrection and ascension, which seem to be only for Jesus Christ, are designed also for us as much as the mysteries of humiliation and suffering. The third preparation is in ourselves, which ought to answer the two former, of which it is both a participation and an imitation, by the mortification and destruction of sin, (which are the effect and imitation of the death on the cross,) and by the internal sanctification of charity and other Christian virtues. This sanctification is the beginning of our participation of the glorious parts of Christ's sacrifice—namely, the resurrection and ascension, (Eph. ii. 6,) which will not be fully accomplished in us until his return, when he will receive us unto himself, when he will fix us in the place which he has prepared for us, and when we shall be with him where he is. Let us not lose the time of this preparation if we desire to have any share in this reunion.

4. And whither I go ye know, and the way ye know. 5. Thomas saith unto him, Lord, we know not whither thou goest; and how can we know the way?

God frequently out of mercy conceals his graces while he bestows them on us; but it is also frequently our own ingratitude and infidelity which conceal them from us. There are a great many particular truths comprehended under the faith in Christ, which are unfolded and become clear as occasion requires, and in proportion as piety applies our minds to them, or as God opens our understanding. Our continual application to sensible objects easily causes us to forget those spiritual truths which have been often taught us. The Spirit of God gives us sometimes only a small glimpse of certain truths, on purpose to raise in us a desire to know them, and to cause us to fit and prepare our minds for the knowledge of them by prayer, application, and an humble confession of our own weakness.

6. Jesus saith unto him, I am the way, the truth, and the life: no man cometh unto the Father, but by me.

Jesus is the way by his example; the truth by his word; and the life by his grace. The new and living way, wherein faith causes us to walk; the infallible truth of good things to come, for which we must hope; and the eternal life, which must be the sole object of our love. Out of this way, there is nothing but wandering; without this truth, nothing but error and deceit; and without this life, nothing but death. By means of sin, the heart has lost the life of righteousness;

the understanding, the light of truth; and the senses, the assistance of the creatures which served as a way to lead us to God. All three are restored to us in Jesus Christ: the way of heaven discovered and laid open to our senses by his life and mysteries; the truth, which enlightens our understanding; and the life, which reanimates our heart. Let us take great care not to transfer to any creature that which Christ appropriates to himself exclusively of every thing besides. He alone is our way, as our Mediator by his blood; he alone is the truth of the promises, which are fulfilled only in him as the Head of the elect, and in us as his members; and he alone is our life, as being the principle of the Christian life, and of all the actions thereof by his grace. That man well deserves to lose himself, to be deceived, and to be deprived of life, who keeps not close to thee alone, O eternal way, in which alone those find themselves who have gone astray; incarnate truth, which alone enlightenest those who are in darkness; celestial and divine life, which alone givest immortal life to the dead! Thou art the divine way, which camest to weary thyself in seeking sinners; the truth, which didst vouchsafe to descend into our darkness; and the life, which didst humble thyself so low as to die for us!

7. If ye had known me, ye should have known my Father also: and* from henceforth ye know him, and have seen him. [* *Fr.* Quickly ye shall.]

Who could hear the heavenly doctrine, and behold the miraculous works of Christ, without being convinced that he spoke the truth in assuring them that he was the Son of God; to be convinced of which was the same thing as to know that he had a Father of whom he was begotten. We well deserve to be upbraided in the same manner by Christ, we who make it appear so little in our lives that we know him as our Master, our Saviour, and our all. What hope, what love ought to answer our faith, were it as lively and active as it ought to be! Our knowledge in this life is very obscure and imperfect: we can only comfort ourselves with the hope of enjoying that divine light which is to disperse all our darkness. How desirable is this "quickly," and how long a time does it seem to those who are impatient to leave their state of childhood, and to arrive at the knowledge of the perfect man! Come quickly, O thou light of my heart; but haste likewise to prepare this heart of mine, and to purify it in that manner which is worthy of thyself!

8. Philip saith unto him, Lord, show us the Father, and it sufficeth us.

Whoever sees the Son sees the Father also, by reason of the essential relation between their persons, and of the unity of their nature. Yes, Lord, it belongs to thee alone to show us the Father, since thou alone knowest him, since thou only art his co-eternal idea, the character of his substance, the invisible image of his perfections, the light which comes from that light, and which alone can shine into created minds. Show us the Father now by a lively faith, and in such a manner as may cause us to love him, to the end that thou mayest show him to us one day in his glory, in causing us to possess him. God only is necessary to man, and he alone is sufficient for him. It is the greatest mark of the corruption of man's heart, to see him continually pursue false happiness, and despise the only true good and the only felicity of his soul. When, O my God, shall I cease wearying myself in these unprofitable searches and pursuits? Say to my soul, I am thy salvation and thy life, I am the supreme good which thou seekest elsewhere, and which thou canst never find but in me alone.

9. Jesus saith unto him, Have I been so long time with you, and yet hast thou not known me, Philip? he that hath seen me hath seen the Father; and how sayest thou *then*, Show us the Father?

God has been so long time with us, so long has he showed himself to us by his benefits, and made his power, wisdom, and goodness manifest in his creatures; and so long has he urged us by his inspirations, his chastisements, and his word, to own him for our God, and to obey him as our Father and our Lord, and do we not yet know him? Let us open the eyes of our faith, and not those of our flesh. We cannot see him that is invisible but only with invisible eyes; and we see his same divine essence, his same power, and his same perfections, in the Father, the Son, and the Holy Ghost. I believe this, O Jesus, and yet I still make this address to thee, "Show me the Father," because I see him only as in a glass or through a veil. When will this veil be taken away?

10. Believest thou not that I am in the Father, and the Father in me? the words that I speak unto you I speak not of myself: but the Father that dwelleth in me, he doeth the works.

Here is nothing human, nothing which is carnal. Let reason submit itself to the yoke of faith, to adore mysteries which it cannot comprehend. A God, who is the very same being with his Son, and yet is not the same person; a Son, who dwelleth in his Father, and his Father in him, and who yet are really distinct one from the other. A Son, who receives every thing, even being itself from his Father, without the least indigency, dependence, or posteriority; and a Father, who gives and communicates whatever he is to his Son, without giving him beginning, and without parting with any thing which he gives to his coeternal and consubstantial Son, and working together with him by the same almighty power. These are truths, in attempting to fathom which reason loses itself. Let us learn from truth itself not to speak as of ourselves, since of ourselves we have nothing but falsehood and sin. Let us likewise learn to refer ultimately to God all the good we do, since it is he who does it in us, and who does all the good works which we do by a kind of unity of principle and operation, which represents and honours that between the Father and the Son: the same good action being entirely God's by his grace, and entirely our own by our will.

11. Believe me that I *am* in the Father, and the Father in me: or else believe me for the very work's sake.

The power with which Christ spoke in testifying the truth of his divinity, and in showing plainly that he knew the bottom of the heart, might have been sufficient to prove the truth of his incarnation; but his external works were invincible proofs thereof. Let us make it appear by our life and actions that the Spirit of God lives and works in us; that the works of the members are not unworthy of the Head; and that the manners of the children evidently show that God is their Father. An excellent method to increase and strengthen our faith, or at least to keep it from growing weak, is to read in the gospel the miracles of Jesus Christ with respect and reverence.

12. Verily, verily, I say unto you, He that believeth on me, the works that I do shall he do also; and greater *works* than these shall he do; because I go unto my Father.

Faith puts as it were the power of God into our hands. Our blessed Lord reserves the greatest miracle for his apostles and other holy persons on the following accounts: (1.) That there might be less room to attribute those miracles to them. (2.) To show that he has not less power on earth than when he was present here in a visible manner. (3.) To supply the want of that impression which was made by the visible presence of his sacred humanity. (4.) Because his state of glory, and the establishment of his kingdom among the nations which had not known God, required more illustrious effects of his power; in like manner as he had given such extraordinary instances thereof in bringing his people out of Egypt, and in establishing the Jewish religion. (5.) Because it is only in a certain sense that by his death he merited to be the mediator and advocate of men, and that by his resurrection he entered upon his functions of priest, of intercessor, and of head. The mysteries of his resurrection, ascension, and sitting at the right hand of God, are mysteries which ought to be the foundation of great trust and confidence in Christians; but they do not sufficiently apply their minds to the contemplation of them.

13. And whatsoever ye shall ask* in my name, that will I do, that the Father may be glorified in the Son. [**Fr.* The Father.]

Whatever we ask, and whatever we do in the name of Christ, he himself does it in us. He here lays down three conditions for the obtaining of miracles: (1.) They must be asked of the Father with the hope and confidence of children; in the name of Christ, as belonging to him; and by his merits, his mysteries, and in consideration of his love for his Father, of his zeal for his glory, and of his sacrifice offered for his church. (2.) Men must be far from imagining that the miracles are wrought by the holy persons themselves; but must believe that it is God who works them by Jesus Christ. (3.) They must have no other aim but the glory of God in Jesus Christ, and no sinister views of interest and of passion. For God will never make his power subservient to any thing but his own glory.

SECT. II.—LOVE.—THE COMFORTER.—THE KEEPING OF THE COMMANDMENTS.

14. If ye shall ask any thing in my name, I will do *it*.

We must pray to God only through Jesus Christ, by his Spirit, by his merits, and in his person, as being his members. It is a great indignity to Christ, and an instance of irreligion, to put more, or even as much confidence in the saints as in him who is the Holy One of God. It is but an ill way of making our address to him who is able to do whatever we ask of him, to ascribe his power to his servants. Pastors do not instruct the people sufficiently in this great truth, that Christ promises to give only to those who ask in his name, nor inform them what it is to pray in that manner.

15. ¶ If ye love me, keep my commandments.

Let us not flatter ourselves that we love God, if we do not keep his commandments; neither let us flatter ourselves that we can fulfil his commandments, if we do not love him. The observance of the law is the proof of our love; but love is the principle of that observance. A mercenary person who keeps the law only for the sake of some temporal interest, and a slave who does it merely for fear of punishment, are hypocrites, who love only themselves, and not God; and who give God nothing but external actions, and devote their heart to the creature. Examine your hearts, examine your works, if you are desirous to know what you are in the sight of God. The one must be answerable to the other.

16. And I will pray the Father, and he shall give you another Comforter, that he may abide with you for ever;

The Holy Ghost comforts the faithful, in inspiring them with confidence to address themselves to God as to a Father full of kindness and goodness; in shedding abroad in their hearts the love of the good things of eternity, which only can afford true consolation; and in rendering them victorious over the temptation of sin, which is the only evil which ought to afflict us. Can this double advantage, arising from the return of Christ to his Father, be sufficiently esteemed and valued by us? He performs, in the presence of God, the office of Mediator and Advocate on our behalf; and from thence he sends his Spirit into the world to supply his place therein, and to act and fight for us. He still sends this Comforter daily into our souls; and he will never leave or forsake us if we do not first forsake him. This is not only the fruit of the labours, the prayers, and the death of Christ, as the victim of God slain upon the cross; but likewise of the prayer which he offers continually for us in heaven as our High Priest. O divine Spirit, who art the Comforter, render us worthy of thy consolation! and since this is only for those who love Jesus Christ and keep his law, render us faithful in the performance of these duties.

17. *Even* the Spirit of truth; whom the world cannot receive, because it seeth him not, neither knoweth him: but ye know him; for he dwelleth with you, and shall be in you.

The Spirit of truth can have no concord with the spirit of the world, which is governed by the spirit of error. He is perfectly known only by those who have him in their heart. The world cannot receive him, because the spirit of lying, double-dealing, and deceit, which reigns therein, is utterly inconsistent and irreconcilable with the Spirit of truth, sincerity, and uprightness. The Holy Ghost was at first promised to the church as the Spirit of truth, because truth is the foundation of the church. He is the internal teacher of truth by his operation in the heart, as Jesus Christ was the external teacher thereof by his word. It is he who gives to the church the truth of the promises, of which the synagogue had only the types and shadows. Carnal men have no other eyes but those of flesh; they know and love nothing but sensual and carnal objects; and it is the corruption of their hearts which renders them unworthy to receive this incorruptible Spirit. But nothing can render them worthy to receive him but that only which proceeds from him either residing or working in the heart.

18. I will not leave you comfortless: I will come to you.

The church then, our mother, so long as she does not see her Lord, is a widow; and we are orphans so long as we continue without seeing our Father. If we are insensible of this absence, we deserve not the name of children. Our Father is invisible, but he is notwithstanding continually present with his children, if they have faith. Our duty as orphans is to weep with our mother, to lift up our hands toward our Father, to depend upon him, to invoke him, and earnestly to desire his return. Come then, Lord Jesus, and leave us no longer orphans in this vale of tears and miseries.

19. Yet a little while, and the world seeth me no more; but ye see me: because I live, ye shall live also.

As the absence of Christ during the time of his burial, being only three days, was but a little while in respect of the apostles, so, with respect to ourselves, it is but a little while to the end of our life, or even to the end of the world. For every thing passes away as a dream, a shadow, or a flash of lightning. It is a matter of great importance to all persons whatever, frequently to meditate upon the shortness of time: to the righteous, to comfort them under the persecutions of the world; to the wicked, to excite them to prevent the wrath of God by repentance. We shall see God: what tears ought not this hope to wipe away from our eyes! The world shall not see him: what good things of this life can afford it any comfort under so great a misfortune! Because Christ lives, we shall live also. Our life and glory are joined to those of our Head. His resurrection is the cause and the pattern of ours, and our life a participation of his. Cause me therefore to live in, by, and according to thee, O Jesus, my life and my eternal glory!

20. At that day ye shall know that I *am* in my Father, and ye in me, and I in you.

This verse is an abridgment of the Christian theology, by the knowledge which it gives us of the Trinity, of the Incarnation, and of our own Sanctification: (1.) Of the Trinity: because it is here declared that the Son is in the Father by the unity of his nature with him, and by the eternal birth which his Father gives him in his bosom, wherein he is, together with him, the principle from which the Holy Ghost proceeds. (2.) Of the Incarnation: because we here learn that our nature is in the eternal Word, the Son of God, by a personal union; that the church is in Christ, as his body, and that all Christians are his members incorporated with him. (3.) Of Sanctification: because Jesus Christ is in us by his Spirit of adoption, to sanctify and to govern us, and to communicate to us, as the head to its members, the life of grace and of glory. Accomplish in me, O my God, these last mysteries of thy love and thy mercy! Vouchsafe to work that quickly in my heart which thou intendest to work in it at that day! When will that blessed day come wherein nothing shall continue veiled from our eyes, but we shall have a clear and distinct view of all things?

21. He that hath my commandments, and keepeth them, he it is that loveth me: and he that loveth me shall be loved of my Father, and I love him, and will manifest myself to him.

The love of God toward us is both the cause and the reward of our fidelity in keeping his law. He will love none but those eternally whom he loved first. His love will crown only those whom it supported in the combat, and rendered faithful in their obedience to his law. Our love of God is the source of the true light, and of the saving knowledge of Jesus Christ in this world, and of the beatific sight of him in the world to come. It is neither study, nor wit, nor learning, which renders us acceptable to God; but fidelity in performing his will. A soul which walks exactly in the way which God has pointed out to it, has, by means of a practical and sanctifying knowledge, a deeper insight into divine things, than those learned men of the world who know every thing except how to love God and to save their own souls.

22. Judas saith unto him, not Iscariot, Lord, how is it that thou wilt manifest thyself unto us, and not unto the world?

There are abundance of Christians, even at this day, who, like this apostle, have very gross notions concerning the mysteries of religion. When the things of God are the subject of discourse, we must raise our minds above the senses and all the objects thereof. It is to the soul that the manifestation here spoken of by Christ is to be made. It is in the heart that his kingdom must be established by his Spirit. The world, which has no soul nor heart but only for sensible and perishing things, can neither receive this Spirit, nor have any share in this kingdom.

23. Jesus answered and said unto him, If a man love me, he will keep my words: and my Father will love him, and we will come unto him, and make our abode with him.

A faithful obedience to the law of God, which is the effect and mark of our love, is likewise the thing which increases and improves it. It is not a transient love, nor the keeping of God's word in some particular instances, which can engage him to make his abode in us as in his temple; but it is the constant practice of his precepts, and the faithful performance of all his commandments. God counts not those among the number of his faithful and constant friends who make no difficulty of betraying him frequently by sin. This great and divine visit, which God makes to none but the elect, and by which he draws them to himself, is only for those who love him to the end. A soul which, by a holy ambition, aspires to be the eternal temple of the ever-blessed Trinity, ought to have, as it were, an eternal disposition of doing the will of God. Whatever sanctity we desire in visible temples, let us preserve the same in our hearts; let us do in the latter what is done in the former, and banish out of the one whatever is not suffered in the other. God alone can enable us to comprehend what it is to contract as it were a friendship with him, to receive him into our heart, and to entertain him there in all his majesty and greatness. Let us serve the world, if it have any thing to confer upon us which is comparable to this. If none but God can advance us to such honour, let us serve him alone.

24. He that loveth me not keepeth not my sayings: and the word which ye hear is not mine, but the Father's which sent me.

See here the question of Jude resolved. The world shall not see God, because it does not love him nor keep his word.

Whoever imagines that he can please God, and keep his commandments, without loving him, directly contradicts the very words of truth itself. Let us ultimately refer every thing to God, as the Fountain of all good, after the example of his only Son. His fidelity in observing the commands of his Father is a just ground of shame and confusion to all those who do not obey him. A God becomes obedient, and a creature absolutely refuses subjection. The obedience which we yield to the gospel is a homage which we pay to the truth and the will of God, to the mission of his Son, and to the foundation of that mission—namely, his eternal generation.

SECT. III.—THE HOLY GHOST TEACHES ALL THINGS.—THE PEACE OF GOD NOT OF THE WORLD.—THE LOVE AND OBEDIENCE OF CHRIST.

25. These things have I spoken unto you, being *yet* present with you.
26. But the Comforter, *which is* the Holy Ghost, whom the Father will
send in my name, he shall teach you all things, and bring all things to
your remembrance, whatsoever I have said unto you.

The Holy Ghost, who, proceeding from Christ as the head, diffuses himself into his members, is sent from the Father by the Son, to enlighten their inward parts, and to teach them all things. In whatever relates to salvation, we depend upon the Holy Ghost, as the Spirit of Jesus Christ, sent in his name, and through his merits, and given to him alone for himself and his members. There is no grace but what is given in the name and for the sake of Christ; for God cannot look upon us as we are in ourselves or in Adam, to any other end than to punish us; nor can he show us any mercy and favour, but only as he looks upon us in Jesus Christ. The Holy Ghost and his grace are necessary for us in all respects. The understanding has need of him, in order to know the will of God, and to receive comfort and consolation in this state of exile. The heart stands in need of him; because it is this Spirit alone who can teach it to do the divine will, by inspiring into it a love thereof. The memory has likewise as much need of him, to bring all things to its remembrance, and to fill it with the knowledge of salvation.

27. Peace I leave with you, my peace I give unto you: not as the

world giveth, give I unto you. Let not your heart be troubled, neither let it be afraid.

The peace of the world consists in rest, joy, plenty, and delights; the peace of Christ, in submission to the will of God, in the joy of charity, and in the hope of good things which are invisible. The carnal man is troubled, afraid, and ready to despair, when he is deprived of temporal satisfactions in which he places his happiness and finds his peace; the heart of a Christian preserves its peace and tranquillity, even when it is deprived of Christ, as to his most sensible presence and consolation. The world either gives peace only in fruitless and barren desires, or else gives only a false and counterfeit peace; but Christ performs what he speaks, and his words produce their effect even in the heart, by fortifying it against the threats of the world, and against every thing which may disturb or interrupt its friendship with God. Let those who love the world seek that peace which it gives; thine, O Jesus, is sufficient for me! Put me into possession of it, I beseech thee, since thou art pleased that I should enjoy it by a legacy of thy will, by a deed of gift made in thy lifetime, and by right of inheritance.

28. Ye have heard how I say unto you, I go away, and come *again* unto you. If ye loved me, ye would rejoice, because I said, I go unto the Father: for my Father is greater than I.

The interests of Christ ought to be dearer to us than our own; but we can never seek the former without finding the latter. It is our duty to rejoice, in that God has more power to take away the ignominies and humiliations of his Son, than men had to bring them upon him; that he has more power to glorify his Son, than even his Son had to humble himself. His glory is ours, since we are his members; but then for this very reason his humiliations and sufferings ought likewise to be ours by imitation, as they are by the application which he makes of them to us. O inconceivable love of our blessed Master, thus to conceal from his disciples that which was most grievous and afflictive in his departure, and to show them only the advantages thereof! There is nothing wherein the greatness and magnificence of God shine forth more illustriously, than in the resurrection of his Son and of his members, by which he has found out a way to raise dust and ashes even to the throne of his majesty, and to communicate his glory to a piece of earth: for of this the very body of Christ is composed; and it was in clothing himself therewith that he became less than his Father.

29. And now I have told you before it come to pass, that, when it is come to pass, ye might believe.

Faith is the end of prophecies. Nothing is more proper to strengthen our faith in relation to those good things to come which we expect, than to consider how every thing which we have already received was foretold. The prediction of future events is one proof of the divinity of Christ. All the ancient prophecies, and even those of Christ during his life, tend to establish the belief of his resurrection; and this resurrection being come to pass exactly as it was foretold, gives the strongest security imaginable for all which is to follow, even till the resurrection of his members and the full completion of his mystical body. Nothing happens from time to time but what has been foretold; but we take no notice of it, though it was foretold on purpose to strengthen and increase our faith.

30. Hereafter I will not talk much with you: for the prince of this world cometh, and hath nothing in me.

They are not in the least mistaken who attribute to the devil whatever is done by the spirit of this world, since Jesus Christ himself attributes it to the same author. He is the prince and the head of all those who follow his maxims, and act by his spirit: as Christ, though in a very different manner, is the Head of those who live according to his gospel, and follow the impulse of his grace. The men of this world imagine that in following their passions they do their own will; whereas in reality they only obey that of the prince of this world, whose desires and designs they gratify and fulfil. A man therefore who is devoted to the world, and who follows the spirit thereof, how great soever he may appear to carnal eyes, is but a very vile and miserable object to the eyes of faith; since he belongs to the devil, and is a slave to his will.

The prince of this world can claim nothing in Christ, because Christ is not of this world—none being of it but by sin. He submitted his temporal life to the power of the devil, that he might by his death deliver us from slavery and eternal death. That which renders holy persons victorious over the devil, is their constant opposition to the world, and their fidelity in renouncing every thing which is according to its spirit.

31. But that the world may know that I love the Father; and as the Father gave me commandment, even so I do. Arise, let us go hence.

Christ goes to die and to sacrifice himself out of love, out of obedience, and with courage. For whom are this example and this sacrifice both of love and of obedience designed, if not for Christians? That which he manifested at the time of his death, he likewise made manifest throughout the whole course of his life; and if we desire that our death should, like that of our Head, be a sacrifice of love and obedience, we must take care to make our life so too. This is not a counsel exhorting us to perfection, but a law which lays upon us an indespensable obligation: since all our actions ought to have the love of God for their principle and motive, his glory for their end, and his will for their rule; which plainly shows us in what we should seek and glorify him, and by what we ought to testify the sincerity of our love toward him.

CHAPTER XV.

SECT. I.—CHRIST THE VINE, AND THE FAITHFUL THE BRANCHES.—LIFE AND JOY IN HIM ALONE.

1. I AM the true vine, and my Father is the husbandman.

Christ is the true vine, the excellent, spiritual, and heavenly vine, of which all others are but types and shadows: the vine planted by the hand of God in the womb of the virgin, in the field of the world, and cultivated by the same hand. This vine does not produce a bitter kind of fruit like that of the synagogue; but a wine by which the world is redeemed, washed, sanctified, nourished, strengthened on earth, and, as it were, inebriated in heaven. Christ resigned himself up to the hand of his Father, to be cultivated and pruned according to his will. Let us adore this heavenly husbandman; and since we are branches of his vine, let us submit ourselves entirely to his care and management: for if he do not cultivate us after his divine manner, we can be nothing but unprofitable branches.

2. Every branch in me that beareth not fruit he taketh away: and every *branch* that beareth fruit, he purgeth it, that it may bring forth more fruit.

Christian professors without works are branches without fruit. That person has no faith who chooses rather to be one day cut off and taken away from the body of Christ, than to be exercised and purged by the afflictions of this life, in order to bear the fruit of good works. Both good and bad branches are joined to the vine, but both do not bear fruit: the latter will not be separated from the vine forever, till the great day of separation comes. There is no branch but what must feel the pruning-knife; but wo to those branches which the husbandman passes by in this life, and about which he will use the pruning-knife to no other end but to cut them off entirely from the stock. The sufferings of the righteous and those of the wicked produce very different effects: the one are the better for them, and the other the worse. Whoever refuses to be pruned or purged, refuses to bear any fruit, and is willing to be cut off and taken away. Let us take great care that we do not reject the hand of this charitable husbandman.

3. Now ye are clean through the word which I have spoken unto you.

The word of Christ cleanses and purifies the heart of a Christian by enlightening it, by showing it the true happiness, and the means of arriving at it, and by inducing it to renounce and amend its faults. It is a sort of knife, which serves to cut off from the branches all superfluous shoots, and which we must always have in our hand during this life. When God does not prune his vine by afflictions, he does it by his word and his grace, in causing it to prune itself by mortification and repentance. We are indeed clean already, when Christ has washed us in his blood; but even in the fairest branch there still remains something to be pruned and taken off. Nothing is more dangerous than to think ourselves altogether clean and pure in this world, and to imagine that we have finished the whole work which is to be done in our heart.

4. Abide in me, and I in you. As the branch cannot bear fruit of itself, except it abide in the vine; no more can ye, except ye abide in me.

Observe here two things absolutely necessary:—The one, that we continue closely united to Jesus Christ by faith and charity, that we may live in and of him; the other, that we receive from him the power to do good, because we cannot possibly do any of ourselves without the influence of his grace and his Spirit. It is not enough to be united to Christ our head by baptism, we must likewise unite ourselves to him by prayer, by good desires, by meditation, and by the practice of his gospel, which renders him more effectually present to us. It is very proper, in order to renew in us the spirit of baptism, to offer up on all occasions this address of the primitive Christians:—"I renounce thee, Satan, with all thy pomps and works; and I unite myself, O Jesus, to thee, and give myself entirely to thy Spirit." To separate ourselves from his church, which is his body, is to separate ourselves from him and from his Spirit. And what fruit can we possibly bear in a state of separation from this body, and without this Spirit, but only the fruit of malediction and of death?

5. I am the vine, ye *are* the branches. He that abideth in me, and I in him, the same bringeth forth much fruit; for without me ye can do nothing.

Admirable unity this of the Head with its members, of Christ with his church; which make but one—one only body as it were—one man and one vine. Christ causes his members to bring forth much fruit, when he causes them to lead a life truly Christian; when he animates all their actions with his Spirit, even such as are most ordinary and common; and when he engages them in the constant performance of good works. To this end he continually infuses his virtue into them, as the head into its members, and as the vine into its branches, a virtue which always precedes, accompanies, and follows their good works, and without which they can be in no manner acceptable to God. The grace of Christ, the efficacious principle which produces all kind of good, is necessary to every good action, great or small, easy or difficult, and that both to our beginning, continuing, and finishing thereof. Without it, we not only do nothing, but it is certain that we can do nothing.

6. If a man abide not in me, he is cast forth as a branch, and is withered; and men gather them, and cast *them* into the fire, and they are burned.

Whoever abides not in Christ, and dies in that state, is fit for nothing but the fire, like a branch cut off and withered. That person who does not continue united to the Head, will, (1.) Be severed from the body, and have no share in the good things belonging to it. (2.) He will be deprived of the juice and sap of grace. (3.) He will be abandoned to the devil. (4.) He will be cast into the eternal fire. And, (5.) He will burn there continually, without ever being consumed. Whoever presumes he can bear fruit of himself, is not in the vine; and whoever is not in the vine, is not in Jesus Christ; and whoever is not in Jesus Christ, is not a Christian: (St. Augustine.) Can any man without horror reflect on this threatening of the Son of God? And yet the world is full of these withered branches,—namely, professed libertines, atheists, bad Christians, schismatics, and heretics. Let us bewail the condition of these blind wretches, who will not so much as take the pains to examine whether they be in the vine, or be cut off from it; or who even flatter themselves that they are in it, and bear fruit, when in reality they are nothing but withered branches, ready to be cast into the fire. Let us likewise bewail, or at least fear our own condition.

7. If ye abide in me, and my words abide in you, ye shall ask what ye will, and it shall be done unto you.

Observe here three sorts of union, or three conditions, in order to obtain from God that which we desire: (1.) We must be united to Christ by a lively faith, and by charity. (2.) We must be united to him by a love of his truth, and a frequent meditation upon his word, which is the rule of our desires, as being the book of God's designs, to which all our prayers and desires ought to be conformable. It is not sufficient to have faith and charity; we must continually nourish them with the word of God. To read it carelessly, and for fashion's sake, is directly contrary to that reverence which is due to it, and to our own spiritual advantage. It must be imprinted strongly on our minds, or, as it were, engraved deep in our hearts, that it may abide therein. Nothing but love can perform this, as nothing but love can cause us to practise it. (3.) The third condition necessary to our being heard is prayer. It is by this that the branch draws the juice and sap of the vine, and receives from thence more plentiful nourishment. God leaves to those who love him the liberty to ask, and promises to give them every thing; because they neither love nor ask any thing but his will; and because the Spirit who prays in them is the very same who hears their prayers.

8. Herein is my Father glorified, that ye bear much fruit; so shall ye be my disciples.

Here are three motives which cause our prayers to be heard: the glory of God, the edification of the church, and the sanctification of souls. These are three conditions always included in a true Christian prayer. Wherever the first is, which comprehends the other two, God always grants whatever is asked of him. All the glory which God is pleased to have out of himself is chiefly reduced to that which he procures himself, by the operation of his grace in the hearts of men on earth, and by the manifestation of his glory in heaven. And indeed the production of the fruits of his Spirit in a soul, and the forming of one single Christian, are more to his glory than the creation of the material world, and the production of that wonderful variety of flowers and fruits; because it is by the former that the mystical body, the spiritual world, is formed, in and by which he designs to be eternally glorified, of which his Son is the Head, and his Spirit the soul. Let us be under no uneasiness how to find out ways of glorifying God: there is none better or more necessary than to use our utmost endeavours in promoting our own sanctification and salvation, and likewise that of others. This is the great means chosen and appointed of God for the promoting of his glory, and is the fruit of the labours of the apostles, and the triumph of the grace of Christ. We cannot neglect this means without neglecting to glorify God.

9. As the Father hath loved me, so have I loved you: continue ye in my love.

We owe every thing to the free love of Christ toward us, as Christ owes every thing to that of his Father, by which he filled him with all the fulness of the Godhead. He chooses us to be his members, and on purpose to work in and by us all the good we do; as his Father chose him to be our Head, and on purpose to work in and by him the miracles which he wrought. God loves his Son, and us in him. Christ loves his Father, and us for his sake. Let us, in like manner, love God in Christ, and Christ for the sake of God. The love of God, of Christ, and of a Christian, make, as it were, a triple knot which shall never be broken in heaven, being that wherein eternal life and the great mystery of a blessed eternity do consist. Miserable is he, even in this world, who does not part with all to continue in this love! Thou God of my heart, who didst first love me, cause me to continue with perseverance in thy love, that thy love may continue eternally in me!

10. If ye keep my commandments, ye shall abide in my love; even as I have kept my Father's commandments, and abide in his love.

The keeping of God's commandments is the only means to establish his love in us to all eternity. God inseparably annexes his love, and the eternity thereof, to the fulfilling of his law, and that even with respect to Jesus Christ himself. Observe here the love and obedience of the Son toward his Father, which could not possibly cease nor be interrupted for one single moment, and which, notwithstanding, merits the eternal continuance of the Father's love toward the Son. The more absolute and infallible the direction of the Word was in relation to the human will of Christ, and the more efficacious and all-powerful the operation of the Holy Ghost was in his heart, the more free was his will, his love the more worthy of God, and his actions the more meritorious. The fidelity of my love toward God, and the adherence of my heart to his law, can be nothing but the effect of thy almighty grace, O Jesus: vouchsafe, I beseech thee, to produce this effect in me, in honour of that which thy Father produced in thee.

11. These things have I spoken unto you, that my joy might remain in you, and *that* your joy might be full.

As the love of God is always followed by the observance of his law, so the observance of his law is inseparable from true joy of heart. This is the joy of Christ, the Christian joy, the effect of his grace, the fruit of his Spirit, and the seed and bud of that eternal joy which he will diffuse into his members, with which he will, as it were, inebriate his elect, and overflow their hearts. This joy will not be full and perfect till charity be so too, and the law fully and perfectly accomplished, and engraved so deep in the heart as never to be erased or blotted out. If we desire to rejoice as true Christians, let us make the law of God our delight and joy; not a transient joy which proceeds from a barren and unfruitful reading, but that solid and substantial joy which arises from a sincere and real love, and from an exact and persevering practice. Senseless and stupid is that person who sacrifices this joy, and the hope of that in heaven, to a joy which is only carnal and momentary, and is the source of a thousand vexations and inquietudes even in this life.

SECT. II.—THE COMMANDMENT OF LOVE.—FRIENDS, NOT SERVANTS.—CHRIST'S CHOICE OF THE ELECT.

12. This is my commandment, That ye love one another, as I have loved you.

Let us then carefully remember, that the commandment which is Christ's in the most peculiar manner is, That we love one another as Christ has loved us; that is, that we do it in and for God, to that degree, as even to lay down our lives one for another. Eternal happiness then, does not cost so much as we imagine, since all the commandments are reducible to this concerning loving: to our loving our brother for the sake of God, and God himself in our brother. The school of God is a school of love and charity, where Jesus Christ as man is himself the first disciple of his Father. Christ's love for us has his Father's love to him for its pattern, (ver. 9,) and he teaches us, as our Master, to form our love toward our brethren by that love which he has manifested toward us. What a pattern is this to follow! who can ever come up to it? Let us comfort ourselves; the divine Person who gave us this pattern will cause us to imitate it, if we fix our eyes upon him by faith, and pray to him with humility, and with a sincere desire of following his example.

13. Greater love hath no man than this, that a man lay down his life for his friends.

How great then is the love of Christ, who laid down his life for his enemies, and who made them his friends by so doing, and treated them as the dearest of his friends! In the world there is nothing which a man will not do to regain the favour of a powerful enemy of whose assistance he stands in need, or of whose hatred he is afraid: but for a man to do this is not to love an enemy, it is only to love himself; it is an earnest desire and endeavour to preserve life, instead of a disposition to lay it down for the sake of another person. Thou alone, O Jesus, hast really had for thy enemies the love of a disinterested friend, without being influenced by any motives either of fear or of hope, and even foreseeing the ingratitude with which mankind would repay thy love. Such an example as this can only make those despair who do not place their hopes in thy grace: but, Lord, thou knowest that thy grace is, through thy grace itself, all my hope, and that I despair only of myself.

14. Ye are my friends, if ye do whatsoever I command you.

The whole of religion consists in doing the will of God, and in observing his law; this has been, at all times and under every dispensation, the inviolable condition of the covenant and friendship of God with men. Inconceivable goodness this! He has a right to require of us life for life; and he is pleased to require nothing but our obedience! Blind perverseness, and incomprehensible ingratitude of the sinner, who rejects this condition which makes his happiness; who prefers a yoke of iron, the grievous yoke of his own will, or rather of that of the devil, to the light and easy yoke of the will of his God; and chooses rather to be under the tyranny of the devil than to have Jesus Christ for his friend! Could we ever have presumed to aspire at such a friendship, if Jesus Christ had not promised it us of his own accord? And yet such kind advances as these are not able to gain our heart! This heart, so corrupt and disorderly when it rejects the friendship of its God, is often so even when it accepts it. He has made the keeping of his commandments the necessary qualification for the honour of his friendship, and we would have him be satisfied with something quite different.

15. Henceforth I call you not servants; for the servant knoweth not what his lord doeth: but I have called you friends; for all things that I have heard of my Father I have made known unto you.

The new law does not make slaves by fear, but friends by love. The knowledge of mysteries is reserved for Christians. The Jews had them all in the Scripture, but then the Scripture was as a letter in cipher, made up and sealed, of which they were only the bearers, as being no better than servants or slaves. It belongs to the Lamb to open this book of mysteries, to break the seals, to decipher this mysterious letter, and to unfold the secrets of it. If we desire to know them perfectly, let us be the friends of the Lamb. Let us become humble disciples of his word, as he himself became the disciple of his Father. All the truths of salvation were committed to the apostles as to trustees, that they might leave them to their successors. All truths are revealed to the church; but a great many will not be perfectly unfolded till we come to heaven. The knowledge which we shall attain in our heavenly country will only perfect and complete that of this life.

16. Ye have not chosen me, but I have chosen you, and ordained you, that ye should go and bring forth fruit, and *that* your fruit should remain; that whatsoever ye shall ask of the Father in my name, he may give it you.

Let us here take notice of the conditions which are necessary to make men the friends and confidants of Christ, and, as it were his ministers of state: (1.) They must not intrude themselves, but wait for the choice of Christ. (2.) They must be ordained to the ministry by a lawful mission. (3.) Not in order to lead an idle life, but to go and labour. (4.) They must not wait till some work is offered them, but they must go and seek souls. (5.) They must labour so as to bring forth not leaves, but fruit; not in order to please, but to convert. (6.) They must ultimately refer all the fruit to God, and not to themselves out of vanity, self-interest, etc. (7.) They must do all for the sake of the elect, who are the fruit which remains always, because it has the eternal love of God for its root, and stands on the firm foundation of his divine election. (8.) They must take care to fortify them against the trials and afflictions of this world, and to prepare them for them, that they may stand their ground in the time of temptation. (9.) They must devoutly offer to God in prayer both their labours and the fruit of them. (10.) They must present to God his elect, as to a Father who begets them by his word and his Spirit. (11.) They must present them in the name and through the merits of Jesus Christ, in whom the Father has chose them, and by whom he has purchased them. (12.) They must render themselves so devoted to the interests of God in their labours, and so familiar with him in their prayers, as to have the confidence to ask, and the hope to obtain, all things of him, for his glory, the good of the church, and the salvation of souls.

17. These things I command you, that ye love one another.

They must, (13.) Keep up a good understanding between ecclesiastical labourers. This is very forcibly recommended as absolutely necessary in order to bring forth much fruit. It is easy to maintain and preserve it when all the servants have no other interest but that of their Master. But it can never subsist and continue when some of them seek their own glory, and have their own particular views. If, instead of a true, pure, and disinterested charity, there be nothing among them but an outward political peace, this is not the thing which Christ requires. Division among the evangelical labourers is one of the devil's artifices which is most successful against the work of God. In proportion as we love this work, we ought likewise to love the union which Christ recommends to his disciples as the only thing; to foment division is to carry on the devil's work, and to join with him.

SECT. III.—THE WORLD THE ENEMY OF THE FAITHFUL.—THE JEWS INEXCUSABLE.

18. If the world hate you, ye know that it hated me before *it hated* you.

In order to be the friends of Christ, it is necessary, (14.) That men should expect to be hated and persecuted by the world. The great consolation of those who are persecuted because they are not of the world, is to see themselves treated as Christ was. Those whom he vouchsafes to associate to his priesthood and mission, ought to have the same friends and enemies with him. Let us always remember the hatred the world bore to the sovereign Pastor of souls, and we shall not be at all surprised to see the implacable hatred it shows against its servants. Where now is that world which hated and persecuted Christ? And what was it able to do, but only to promote and advance his glory and designs? The world which is at present, will have the same success and portion; and we shall partake of the glory of Christ if with him we suffer the hatred of the world. The first motive to induce us to suffer it patiently, is the example of our blessed Master, and the union we have with him.

19. If ye were of the world, the world would love his own; but because ye are not of the world, but I have chosen you out of the world, therefore the world hateth you.

The second motive to incline us to bear the hatred of the world is, that it is a means whereby we may be assured that we are not of the world, that we do not follow its maxims, and are not guided by its spirit. The third motive is, that whenever the world forces us to separate ourselves from it, or hates us because we do it, we have a certain sign that God loves us with that eternal love by which he chooses and separates whom he pleases from the corrupt mass of mankind. Infinitely happy is he whom it costs nothing but the friendship of the world to purchase that of Christ! According to this word of truth, what other thoughts can we entertain of those who are courted by the world, and loaded with its favours, but only that they are of the world, and are adversaries to Christ, if their hearts be set upon these false and imaginary good things? To be of the world, and to be a Christian—to be a Christian, and yet be loved by the world,—these are two strange paradoxes, and two propositions utterly irreconcilable with the gospel.

20. Remember the word that I said unto you, The servant is not greater than his lord. If they have persecuted me, they will also persecute you; if they have kept my saying, they will keep yours also.

A fourth motive to engage us to endure the hatred of the world is, this necessary alternative—either we must not be the servants of Christ, or else we must be hated and persecuted by the world. We ought always to have this maxim in our minds, as a preservative against any fears or apprehensions of what the world can do to us. It is the truth which is the occasion of all the persecutions raised against the ministers of the gospel by carnal men. To pretend to preach it without offending and provoking them, is to pretend to be more wise and powerful than our blessed Lord himself. Let us, with patience and peace of mind, and adoring in secret the judgments of God, bear the contempt and neglect of his word, and the storms which are raised against the truth; since this behaviour is peculiar to the most holy and religious persons, who treasure up in their hearts the maxims of Christ, and carefully observe the rules of his conduct. Impatience, murmuring, and vexation, proceed from the spirit of man, not from the Spirit of God.

21. But all these things will they do unto you for my name's sake, because they know not him that sent me.

A fifth motive to induce us to bear the hatred of the world is, because it is a great honour in the sight of God to be exposed as a mark to the malice of the world for the sake of Christ and of his truth. Persecution ought to give us a higher degree of esteem, affection, and acknowledgment for the grace of having known and received the truth, because we see plainly in persecutors what a misfortune it is for men not to have received it, and to be abandoned to their own darkness. Let us compassionate them and their ignorance, and be very far from insulting or despising them. We may possibly become what they are, and they may become as happy as ourselves. We deserved the very same judgment which they did, and did not deserve that mercy which alone distinguishes us from them. If ignorance does not hinder them from being guilty, how much more guilt do those contract who sin in the very midst of light and knowledge, and wickedly abuse even these by employing them against the truth itself?

22. If I had not come and spoken unto them, they had not had sin; but now they have no cloak for their sin.

Miserable is that person whom the divine benefits only render inexcusable! This is often the effect of outward blessings, which the sinner abuses by his own infidelity. The greatest of all gifts, which was that of Christ incarnate, and the peculiar favour of hearing him preach, rendered those inexcusable who ought to have expected and known him by the prophecies which had pointed him out. They did not want light, since that shined in the midst of their darkness; and it was only by reason of that darkness of their mind, or the hardness of their heart and the violence of their passions, that they rejected it. That God did not soften their heart, nor change their corrupt will, as he could have done, was a judgment which did not in the least excuse their sin, since it was the punishment of some other sin, and since God owes the sinner nothing but punishment.

23. He that hateth me hateth my Father also.

The good or evil which is done to Christ, or to his members, reaches even God himself. To reject the Son is to reject the Father, who is one and the same God with him. To affront an ambassador is an indignity offered to the prince whom he represents. To despise a preacher is to despise him from whom he derives his mission. The sins which are committed against the pastors and ministers of the church have a peculiar guilt in them. God is thereby dishonoured as the author and institutor of religion, and Christ as the priest and universal high-priest, of whom the other are only the representatives and vicegerents.

24. If I had not done among them the works which none other man did, they had not had sin ; but now have they both seen and hated both me and my Father.

The more new and extraordinary any mission is, the more reason have we to reject it if new and extraordinary miracles do not prove it to be of God. Jesus Christ himself did not think fit that his miracles of charity, meekness, humility, and other virtues, or his divine manner of preaching the word of God, should of themselves oblige men to receive him, when he declared himself sent from God to reform religion. That man puts his salvation into the hands of an impostor, who believes a new apostle without miracles; but, on the other side, he shuts his ears against the voice of God who does not yield to the evidence of miracles, by which God alone can speak to men. Our having received Christ does not fix us in a state of security; we have reason to fear lest we should be condemned for not having made sufficient use of his mysteries.

25. But *this cometh to pass,* that the word might be fulfilled that is written in their law, They hated me without a cause.

It is no other than to hate God, for a man to refuse to obey him, and to oppose the establishment of his kingdom and religion; because to do this is to declare himself an enemy to his glory, which depends upon that establishment. This expression, "To hate God," raises horror, and more still, "To hate him without a cause." And yet we certainly hate him, when we do not love his law, his government, the dispensations of his providence, etc. We have no such direct thought or formal purpose; but actions include all this. What cause can there possibly be to hate a God who is goodness itself, and who never did any thing but good to us? But in sin there is neither reason nor justice.

26. But when the Comforter is come, whom I will send unto you from the Father, *even* the Spirit of truth, which proceedeth from the Father, he shall testify of me:

Let us humble ourselves in the lowest manner imaginable before this adorable mystery of the Trinity of the divine Persons, in which our faith has for its object a Father without beginning, who begets a Son—a Son who, together with him, and by the fruitful nature which he receives from him, produces the Holy Spirit, who is the substantial and consubstantial love of the Father and of the Son, and equal in all respects to them both. Let us adore the incarnation of the Word, which is likewise here intimated to us; since, if Jesus Christ were not God, he could not send the Holy Ghost, for he could send nothing but what he produced; neither could he receive the testimony of the Spirit of truth, if what he had said concerning his divinity were false. Let us with gratitude admire the mystery of the mission of the Holy Spirit into the church, in order to form it; into the ministers thereof, that they might co-operate with him in the forming of it; and into the faithful, to enable them to overcome the world, and to cause them to enter into the structure of Christ's body. What have we to fear? The Spirit who is in the church and in our hearts, is stronger and more powerful than he who is in the world and in the wicked. He is a Spirit of comfort, who is proof against all the tribulations, persecutions, and afflictions of the world: a Spirit of truth, who is proof against all delusion, artifice, and lying. He is a Spirit of comfort to those who deprive themselves of all worldly comforts on purpose to follow Christ; he is a Spirit of truth, because he gives men a love and relish for it, forms the preachers and disciples thereof, and bears testimony to the incarnate Truth by his external gifts and his internal operation, by miracles and Christian virtues, by his light which makes this incarnate Truth known, and by the strength and courage he inspires into martyrs and confessors to enable them to own and confess it. In vain do men use their utmost endeavours to suppress errors by human methods alone, without the assistance of the Spirit of truth. To do this is his peculiar work; it is in him that we must put our whole confidence, in order to have him in our heart, in our mind, and in our mouth. We should frequently invoke him as the Spirit of truth, in opposition to the spirit of error and seduction.

27. And ye also shall bear witness, because ye have been with me from the beginning.

There are two inseparable witnesses of the Son of God—his Spirit and his word; or his Spirit working both inwardly and outwardly in the church, and his Spirit speaking by the mouth of his apostles and ministers. This is the settled and established way of God, with which he very rarely dispenses. There is no truth but what comes to us by the testimony of the apostolical word, by Scripture, or by tradition; nor any necessary ministry but what the apostles received of Christ, in order to leave it to the church. It was on this account that the church was founded by those who had been with Christ from the beginning, that by them and their successors the channel of truth and of mission might be derived down to us in an uninterrupted course from Jesus Christ, the source and fountain thereof. Let us keep to the channel if we desire to keep to the fountain.

CHAPTER XVI.

SECT. I.—PERSECUTIONS FORETOLD.—THE COMFORTER PROMISED.

1. These things have I spoken unto you, that ye should not be offended.

The word of God is the true consolation of Christians under afflictions, and a powerful preservative against scandal or offence. When we expect the worst, we are surprised at nothing: but we are always deceived when we persuade ourselves that we shall find the world favourable to the truths of the gospel, and that we shall be able to reconcile it to the maxims of Jesus Christ. The only safe precaution we can take, is to hope for no quarter from it, and to rely upon nothing but the power and goodness of the Spirit who is promised to us. Human foresight has no other way of encouraging men, than in raising them above dangers by the hope of avoiding them; the prediction of Christ gives them no other hopes of overcoming the world, but only by assuring them that they shall sink under the malice thereof. The motto of the carnal man is, Overcome, that you may not suffer; but that of the Christian is directly contrary,—Suffer, that you may overcome; be trampled upon, that you may not fall; die, that you may live.

2. They shall put you out of the synagogues: yea, the time cometh, that whosoever killeth you, will think that he doeth* God service. [* *Fr.* Offers a sacrifice to God.]

That is certainly a very deplorable time, when men think they honour God by persecuting the truth and the disciples thereof. That time is come; and will end only with the world: and therefore our patience must not end until the term of our lives expire. We are always in hopes of seeing impiety humbled, and innocence victorious: but we deceive ourselves; for time in its whole extent is the season of this world, that of Christians is eternity. The fear of death is sometimes a less dangerous temptation than that which proceeds from the love of religion. It is very grievous to be looked upon and treated by the ministers thereof as an impious wretch, unworthy of all commerce with God; as a rotten member, capable of spreading a general corruption in the society of the saints: this is, to a devout person, a death more terrible than that of the body. In vain do those who persecute good men with fire and sword, flatter themselves with the uprightness of their intentions, and their zeal for religion, if they are either blinded with their own passion, or hurried on by that of others, for want of due examination. Men often think they sacrifice to God a wicked person, when at the same time they are sacrificing to the devil a servant of God.

3. And these things will they do unto you, because they have not known the Father, nor me.

Ignorance in the true worship of God, and in his designs concerning his Son, has been the cause of a great number of crimes and sins; but was itself the effect and punishment of other sins. If such an ignorance can excuse from sin, we may justify the persecutors of the apostles. When men have once rejected the light, as the Jews had, there are no sins of which they are not capable. That penal darkness which sin spreads over the heart does not only occasion it to run precipitately into crimes, but even persuades it that it serves God in committing them. A double injustice and misery this, for men to affront God by persecuting his servants, and endeavouring to destroy his worship and religion, and at the same time to expect that he will reward them for it. My God, how dismal is that state, wherein men think they follow the divine light when they have no other guide but their own darkness; wherein they take evil for good, and sin for virtue!

4. But these things have I told you, that, when the time shall come, ye may remember that I told you of them.

Truths bring forth fruit in their proper season, though, when they are first taught, they frequently seem to be cast away. It is a pernicious complaisance toward our friends, to conceal from them mortifying and afflictive truths when it is expedient and profitable for them to know them. Christ does not afflict his disciples merely for the sake of afflicting them, but to show them how much they stand in need of him, and to oblige them to watch and pray, and to distrust both the world and themselves. It is an invincible proof of the truth of the Christian religion, that Christ foretold exactly whatever was to happen both to himself and to his church; and that his church, being opposed by all the powers of the world, should yet triumph over them all by the sole strength of the word and the Spirit of God.

—And these things I said not unto you at the beginning, because I was with you. 5. But now I go my way to him that sent me; and none of you asketh me, Whither goest thou?

A discreet pastor knows how to give his admonitions and consolations seasonably, and according to the wants of persons. We ought to fix and settle the minds of men in a lively belief of the almighty power of God, and of the grace of Jesus Christ, before we show them the difficulties, dangers, and temptations which they will meet with in the ways of God: as Christ confirmed his apostles in the belief of his divinity by the miracles and wonders of his life, before he clearly discovered to them the mystery of his death, and the persecutions which they themselves were to undergo. We have but little curiosity as to the things of eternity; our hearts are more taken up with the good or evil things of this life, than with those which are reserved for the world to come. We have not Jesus Christ now visibly present to ask him any question: but he is present in the Scriptures and in his church to answer us; and he renders himself present in prayer, to speak to those who know how to render themselves present therein to him by a lively, intent, and reverential faith.

6. But because I have said these things unto you, sorrow hath filled your heart.

How rare and uncommon a thing is the love of the cross, and how few are there whose minds are not dejected at the sight of its approach! There is no sensible enjoyment whatever which we fear to lose, which does not take up our mind and heart more than all the invisible good things which are the objects of our hope: so little are we yet settled and established in faith. Joy and sorrow are the two passions which generally employ the whole application of the mind and activity of the heart: it is therefore a matter of great importance to choose a proper object for those passions, and to be no otherwise affected with it than we ought. That sorrow which is according to faith is not an idle, languishing, and inactive sorrow; but a sorrow which is intent on God and on the things of eternity; a sorrow which knows how to ask what is proper of God in prayer, and to beg of him light and information concerning our present state, and grace to make a good use of that light, that it may be a means to guide us in following him to that place whither he is gone before. Christian sorrow may enter into the heart, and affect it very much; but it ought never to fill it, or entirely to take it up. It may dwell, but must not command there, nor assume an absolute dominion. Faith and hope ought still to have the ascendant over it.

7. Nevertheless I tell you the truth; It is expedient for you that I go away: for if I go not away, the Comforter will not come unto you; but if I depart, I will send him unto you.

Death, according to the language of Christ's love, is no other than a kind of journey. It is a passage or going from earth to heaven. He hides from his disciples whatever is grievous and afflictive in the sacrifice of his death, and shows them only how necessary and expedient it was for them. Order must be strictly observed: earth, defiled and profaned by the sin of Adam, and by so many crimes and sacrileges, must be purified by the sacrifice of the cross before it can receive the Holy Spirit; the sin of man must be expiated by the death of the true victim before he can be reconciled to God by his Spirit; and the heart of man must be washed in the blood of his Saviour before it can become the temple of the Holy Ghost, and contract with God the new covenant, of which Jesus Christ is the mediator by his blood, and the bond and surety by his Spirit. We cannot have, at one and the same time, the comforts both of earth and of heaven: we must make our choice. The engagements of affection even to the most holy persons are obstacles to holiness, and to spiritual consolations which are more pure, solid, and advantageous. How much more then do carnal passions and criminal affections render man unworthy of God!

8. And when he is come, he will reprove the world of sin, and of righteousness, and of judgment:

Faith discovers to us three different states of man: (1.) Under sin, in which there is nothing but infidelity toward God, because there is no faith in Jesus Christ. (2.) Under grace, in which state sin is overcome, and righteousness acquired by faith in Jesus Christ risen from the dead, and by the hope of invisible treasures. (3.) In the peace and glory of heaven, where Christ will reign with his members—the devil with all the reprobate being banished into hell by the last judgment. Thus faith shows us three principal and fundamental truths, taught here by Jesus Christ, and explained by Paul, Rom. iii. 9, 22; i. 17, 18; v. and vii., which comprehend the whole Christian theology, which is designed not for one people alone, like that of the law, but for the whole earth. The first is the general corruption of nature in Adam, and in consequence of that the reign of sin until the coming of Jesus Christ. The second is the reparation of our nature in the new Adam, and the reign of Christian righteousness by his grace. The third is the condemnation of sinners, and the total destruction of the kingdom of sin, and of all the power of the devil, by the last judgment. None but the Holy Ghost can give us a certain knowledge and an indubitable proof of the wound of original sin, and of the disorder it has caused in the world. The mysteries of the establishment of the true righteousness by Jesus Christ, are still more impenetrable without faith. And the judgments of God in the temporal and eternal punishment of sin are, to human understanding, a profound and unfathomable abyss.

9. Of sin, because they believe not on me;

Nothing is more capable of giving us a true notion of the great corruption of the world by sin, than the incredulity of the Jews, who were only hardened by so many benefits, prophecies, and miracles, and provoked and exasperated even by the meekness of Christ. Envy, obduracy, and opposition to the known truth are, in those who have received a greater portion of light, a plain and evident token of the dominion of concupiscence. And yet we cannot from thence arrive at this knowledge without the assistance of the Holy Ghost. The consideration of the incredulity of so many people ought to convince us that we as well as they were no other than children of wrath. The sins of others show us what we ourselves should be without the grace of Christ.

10. Of righteousness, because I go to my Father, and ye see me no more;

It is the fruit of the descent of the Holy Ghost, that we know both the unprofitableness of the legal and carnal righteousness, and the necessity of the righteousness of God, by faith in Jesus Christ raised from the dead, ascended into heaven, and there hid from the sight of men, to be the object of their faith and confidence until his manifestation at the last day. If the true righteousness consists in setting our affections upon nothing which is visible, ye sons of men, how long will ye suffer your hearts to be bowed down toward the earth? What advantage is it to you to love vanity and to seek after lies? "Seek those things which are above, where Christ sitteth on the right hand of his Father." It is from thence that true righteousness comes. It is there that true happiness is to be found.

11. Of judgment, because the prince of this world is* judged. [* *Fr.* Already.]

It is the gospel, preached by the mission of the Holy Spirit, which discovers to us the wrath of God, which will one day break forth against the impiety and unrighteousness of men. It was by publishing the last judgment, and proclaiming Jesus Christ to be the Judge of the quick and dead, that the apostles began the preaching of the gospel. The prince of this world is already condemned, and the sentence of his condemnation is executing every day since that of the descent of the Holy Ghost, when three thousand souls were taken away from him as from a usurper. Idolatry destroyed, the Gentiles converted, the possessed delivered in the name of Jesus, the gospel everywhere received, and the martyrs sacrificing their lives rather than offer incense to the devil,—all this evidently shows that he stands condemned, and is stripped of all. Ye blind men, who still cleave to the world, and place therein all your hopes and expectations, what will become of you, since your prince is already judged and condemned to eternal punishment?

12. I have yet many things to say unto you, but ye cannot bear them now.

Christ here practises that which he teaches, giving only milk to children, and proportioning his truths to the apprehension of his auditors. He sows the seed of the most sublime truths, and of the whole system of ecclesiastical knowledge, which the Holy Ghost will one day unfold and particularly explain to them; just as we now proceed with respect to children, whom we teach the mysteries of the Trinity and of the incarnation only in general. It is the duty of a good pastor to instruct his people according to their capacity. A director of the conscience must explain and lay open the truths and ways of God to the souls under his care in proportion as God is pleased to open their understanding and their heart, and as far as it is useful and profitable for them. He must study this wise and prudent conduct of Christ, and beg of him the grace to imitate it on proper occasions.

13. Howbeit when he, the Spirit of truth, is come, he will guide* you

into all truth: for he shall not speak of himself; but whatsoever he shall hear, *that* shall he speak: and he will shew you things to come. [* *Fr.* Teach you.]

Since every truth of faith and salvation was delivered to the apostles to be consigned to the care of the church, whatever they have not taught in the Scripture, is neither a matter of faith, nor necessary to salvation; and whatever is contrary to that which they have taught, is false and erroneous. It belongs to the Holy Spirit to cause those seeds of truth, which Christ sowed in the hearts of his apostles, to spring up and bear fruit, to enlarge and explain them, and to make them both understood and loved. The method of teaching the truths of religion which is peculiar to the Spirit of truth, is to inspire them into the mind and heart, and to give men both the understanding and the love of them. The Spirit of truth is the internal, almighty, and infallible teacher thereof, only because he proceeds from the eternal truth and wisdom, and in receiving from thence his essence, together with it receives all truth; as the eternal truth and wisdom receives it from his Father by his eternal generation. In like manner the church, when she teaches her children, does not speak of herself, but speaks only that which she has heard from the Spirit of truth by the Scripture. Whoever is particularly called to study, explain, and defend the truth, ought to depend very much upon this Spirit; he ought to adore, to invoke, and to draw him down by ardent desires and good works, that he may by his assistance be able to penetrate into the truths of Christianity. To expect that he will satisfy our curiosity concerning future events, is to tempt and dishonour him; the truths, the mysteries, and the hopes of the other world are the things which he comes to show us, and they are these which we must beseech him to cause us both to believe and love.

14. He shall glorify me: for he shall receive of mine, and shall shew *it* unto you.

As the mission of the Son was for the glory of the Father, so the mission of the Holy Ghost is wholly designed to glorify the Son, in establishing his kingdom which is the church, in making his name known throughout the world by the preaching of the gospel, in forming his members by the new birth and the new life which he gives them in him, and in manifesting his power and glory by miracles, by the gift of tongues, by prophecies, and by all the other effects of the gifts of this Holy Spirit. All effects whatever of holiness and piety, and all the works of grace, come from the Holy Ghost, as the Spirit of Jesus Christ; a Spirit, who, proceeding from him, does from all eternity receive every thing from him, and who was in time sent and given only to him and to his members, for the sake of his merits alone, and only for the accomplishment of his designs and the formation of his body. The divine persons even honour those from whom they proceed; and whatever proceeds from God, either does actually honour him, or at least ought to do it. We ought, therefore, to make no use of the gifts of our Creator but what tends to his honour, by ultimately referring them all to his glory, and using them only according to his will and his design in bestowing them upon us.

15. All things that the Father hath are mine: therefore said I, that he shall take of mine, and shall show *it* unto you.

The Holy Ghost proceeds from the Father and the Son, as from one and the same principle. Whatever the Father hath is the Son's, and it is from the Father that the Son receives power to produce the Holy Ghost, by communicating to him whatever he himself receives from the Father, namely, his essence. Every thing which was showed to the apostles and to the church, came from the Son, and by him from the Father. Christ repeats what he said before, on purpose to admonish us the more earnestly that we ought not to teach the faithful any other doctrine but what the apostles learned of the Holy Ghost, or which is included therein. God showers down his blessing in a very plentiful manner upon the words of a good pastor, who preaches nothing but what he receives from Jesus Christ, not solely by the study of his word, but likewise by prayer and meditation.

SECT. II.—JOY AFTER SORROW.

16. A little while, and ye shall not see me: and again, a little while, and ye shall see me, because I go to the Father.

Joy succeeds sorrow. Christ sometimes hides himself from those whom he loves most, but not for any long time. The whole term of this present life is but a little while; and therefore all the joy or sorrow thereof can be but little: every thing therein is of very short continuance. Neither that which is agreeable and pleasant, nor that which is painful and afflictive in this world, deserves to be regarded. Christ having given his apostles the preceding comforts and consolations, he now speaks more plainly to them concerning his departure; but then he adds to those consolations the hope of the resurrection, which is the foundation of them all. He is snatched away from us by death only in order to be restored to us in the fulness of power and glory, and in a condition to be the object of our joy and of our eternal felicity.

17. Then said *some* of his disciples among themselves, What is this that he saith unto us, A little while, and ye shall not see me: and again, a little while, and ye shall see me: and, Because I go to the Father? 18. They said therefore, What is this that he saith, A little while? we cannot tell what he saith.

Men will not understand either the necessity of suffering or the shortness of this life. The words of Christ are sometimes obscure, on purpose to oblige us to apply ourselves more diligently to the study of them, and to have recourse to him in order to understand them. That which he had so often told them concerning his death, and very lately concerning the treacherous design of one of the twelve, ought to have prepared their minds for these words: but the time of light and understanding was not yet come. The obscurity or difficulty of religious matters does not dishearten or discourage true disciples, but, on the contrary, excites them to seek after light and understanding, in humbly acknowledging their own ignorance; whereas the proud take occasion from that obscurity, either to ridicule the things of God or to neglect the study of them, or to murmur against God, and blaspheme him on that account. It is the settled order of Providence, that we should depend one upon another for our instruction in truths which are obscure, and should all of us together have recourse to God when men are not able to explain them to us.

19. Now Jesus knew that they were desirous to ask him, and said unto them, Do ye inquire among yourselves of that I said, A little while, and ye shall not see me: and again, a little while, and ye shall see me?

Christ goes to meet those who sincerely desire to know the truth. He anticipates their questions, because the desire of the heart is a prayer which God hears distinctly; but he grants it only in the manner and measure which he thinks fit. A good pastor ought to rejoice, when he sees the faithful take delight in discoursing concerning the mysteries and truths of Christianity, and in humbly desiring to be informed concerning that which they do not understand. He ought, on his side, to take delight in entertaining them on such subjects, in preventing them in their doubts, and in explaining to them whatever it is useful for them to know.

20. Verily, verily, I say unto you, That ye shall weep and lament, but the world shall rejoice; and ye shall be sorrowful, but your sorrow shall be turned into joy.

The world rejoices for a moment, while the righteous are in tears: but the joy of the latter shall be eternal, while the former shall be eternally in sorrow. That which passed at the death and resurrection of Christ is a lively representation of what his members suffer in this life, and of what they will enjoy in the glorious life hereafter. The present life is, as it were, three days, wherein the world triumphs in oppressing the righteous, and the righteous groan under the power of the world. Christ himself assures us, that sighs and tears are our lot and portion; and yet it is our chief care how to avoid them. If we eagerly desire and seek after the joy of the world, we show ourselves willing to weep and lament with it eternally. All tears are not Christian tears: concupiscence has hers as well as charity. For a man to weep because he is deprived of the object of his passion, is to weep like a reprobate, if faith do not correct this unhappy motive, and cause the heart to acquiesce and submit. Happy is the penitent who changes his vain or criminal joys into holy and salutary tears, through the hope that God will change his momentary sorrow into eternal joy!

21. A woman when she is in travail hath sorrow, because her hour is come: but as soon as she is delivered of the child,* she remembereth no more the anguish, for joy that a man is born into the world. [**Fr.* A son.]

Jesus Christ is this Son, born to a new, glorious, and immortal life by means of his resurrection, which is his third birth. The pangs of travail are endured on the cross, where the old man suffers to bring forth the new. Can we ever forget this mystery of our salvation? The church, as also every one of us, was brought forth upon the cross amid the pains and by the death itself of Jesus Christ. Let us remember that we were born upon the cross; and that our regeneration or new birth being at present imperfect, the proper time for our joy is not yet come. As this whole life is, as it were, the travail of child-birth, so it will be followed by eternal joy when Christ entire shall be perfectly regenerated or born again in his glory, that only Son consisting of the Head and the members, of whom the Father will say to all eternity, "This is my beloved Son," etc. Let us, by the hope and expectation which the Christian faith gives us, but take a foretaste of that joy which is to succeed our pain and sorrow, and these will appear as nothing. Such is the law of childbirth; and there is no dispensation, not even for Jesus Christ himself.

22. And ye now therefore have sorrow: but I will see you again, and your heart shall rejoice, and your joy no man taketh from you.

The apostles partook of the joy of our blessed Saviour's resurrection, because they had partaken in the sorrows of his death. The greater share we have in the latter during this life, the greater shall we have of the former in heaven. The joy of the world affects only the senses or the imagination; the joy which penetrates and fills the heart, is the joy of God. This is the only joy which cannot be taken from us; because God is the only good of which we cannot be dispossessed against our will. The godly sorrow of repentance and mortification attracts the eyes of Christ toward our hearts; and these gracious looks produce therein a solid and substantial joy which tends to salvation. None but God can raise in the hearts of his servants a real and unfeigned joy, even amid the sharpest sorrows and afflictions of this world. The sinner has no kind of joy but what may be taken from him against his will, because it all comes from without: the Christian is under no apprehension of losing his joy, because the only object of his love is in his own heart.

SECT. III.—PRAYER IN THE NAME OF CHRIST.—CONFIDENCE IN HIM.

23. And in that day ye shall ask me nothing. Verily, verily, I say unto you, Whatsoever ye shall ask the Father in my name, he will give *it* you.

In order to obtain every thing of the Father, we must pray in the name and through the merits of Jesus Christ as the Redeemer, Mediator, and Head of the church. In this manner the church prays, and thus all her children ought to pray. The sinner, as a child of Adam, deserves only to be rejected of God. He has no right to offer up any prayer, but only as he is a child of God and a member of his Son; nor to speak to God, but by his Spirit. But then he begins to become such whenever he earnestly desires it. When a man presents himself before God in prayer, full of his own perfections and deserts, he is but little disposed to expect every thing only through Jesus Christ. No man can possibly pray too much like a beggar and a criminal, like one who has nothing, who is unworthy of every thing, and who has not even a right to pray but by and in Jesus Christ alone. Prayer is the business of the heart: he therefore who asks only with his lips, without the desire which is of faith, well deserves not to be heard.

24. Hitherto have ye asked nothing in my name: ask, and ye shall receive, that your joy may be full.

There are abundance of Christians who deserve the same reproach; few prayers being truly Christian, and offered in the spirit of faith, with due confidence, and through Jesus Christ. There are some who are always ready to put their trust and confidence in some saint recommended to them by men as a proper object of their devotion, and who neglect what Christ himself recommends to them, which is to place their devotion in adoring, praising, returning thanks, and praying to God through Jesus Christ, and in expecting no manner of grace or blessing but through him alone. Every thing is promised to the performance of the single duty of prayer: because prayer, truly so called, includes in it a sincere desire to be the servant of God; this desire necessarily produces a diligent application to the means of being so; and this application excludes whatever is not conformable to the will of God. He grants to the prayer of those who love him not that which may give them a transient and imperfect satisfaction, but that which is instrumental to them in attaining to the full and perfect joy of eternity, and in gaining even here below the joy of faith and hope, which alone fills the heart, supports it, and gives it peace.

25. These things have I spoken unto you in proverbs: but the time cometh, when I shall no more speak unto you in proverbs, but I shall show you plainly of the Father.

The time of the gospel is the time of light, of truth, and of mercy; because every thing is revealed, though it be not yet placed in the broad and open day. The Jews were in the light in comparison of the Gentiles, but they were in darkness if compared with Christians: and the faith of Christians is but darkness in comparison of that light which the blessed enjoy. The truths which our blessed Lord taught his apostles during his life were for the most part obscure to them, because their heart was not then illuminated with the light of the Holy Ghost. Christ could have given them this light before; but it was expedient for them not to receive it till after his death and resurrection, that they might know it was the fruit and effect of those mysteries. Whenever we open the sacred book we may assuredly expect to find nothing therein but parables, as they may be called, unless God vouchsafe to open our understanding with a ray of his light. When, O my God, will that happy time come, when nothing shall be obscure to us; when we shall behold every thing in the clearest and brightest light?

26. At that day ye shall ask in my name: and I say not unto you, that I will pray the Father for you:

It was not clearly and fully known that Jesus Christ was the Mediator between God and man, and that every thing was to be asked and granted in his name, till after he had shed his blood, opened heaven, and sent down the Holy Spirit upon his church, and till so many gifts of that Spirit, and so many miracles wrought by the apostles, had appeared in the world. It seems as if the time of praying to God in the name of Jesus Christ was not yet come in respect of a very great number of Christians; so little are they disposed to receive and to act according to this truth. From the time that we are assured that Christ is our Mediator, we must not in the least doubt but that he prays for us, since this is the very function of a Mediator. I am very sensible, O Lord, that thou prayest for me, since I find in myself the powerful effects of so many graces and mercies, which none but thou couldst obtain for me.

27. For the Father himself loveth you, because ye have loved me, and have believed that I came out from God.

God's loving us with the love of a Father is a certain sign that we are ingrafted into the body of Christ by faith and charity; for he loves none after that manner but only in his Son. And Christ's dwelling in our hearts by faith and love is a certain sign that God loves us; since his love is the first of all his gifts, the source of our faith and our love, and even of the gift of his beloved Son, which he gave us by the incarnation. We may justly think, that our being in Jesus Christ by a lively and active faith, is a state of continual prayer, or a state which attracts the love and favour of God, unless the sallies of concupiscence are an obstacle thereto; as the state of Jesus Christ, both God and man, is an eternal prayer, which continually solicits the love and mercy of God in behalf of sinners.

28. I came forth from the Father, and am come into the world: again, I leave the world, and go to the Father.

The eternal generation of the Son in the Father, his humble incarnation in his mother, and his glorious life in his resurrection and ascension, are three divine births worthy of our frequent adoration, as comprehending all the greatness and dignity of Jesus Christ. Let our faith pierce the veil of these plain and common words, which contain under them the two greatest mysteries of Christ, the incarnation and the resurrection—his humiliation and his exaltation. Let us adore these mysteries; let us imitate the humiliation of Christ, and we shall then partake of his exaltation. This incomprehensible self-denial of the Son of God, whereby he stripped himself as it were of all the greatness, riches, and glory of his eternal birth, to stoop so low as to our meanness, poverty, and misery, is but very badly imitated by us if our hearts be set upon the greatness, riches, and glory of this world. Christ, by his resurrection and ascension, teaches us to separate ourselves from this present world, and to disengage our affections from earthly things. Every thing in him preaches this doctrine, but it is a doctrine which we cannot resolve to put in practice.

29. His disciples said unto him, Lo, now speakest thou plainly, and speakest no proverb.

When God himself vouchsafes to resolve our doubts, and to disperse our darkness, we are as it were transported into a region of light. This vicissitude of darkness and of light is useful and advantageous to us: the former humbles us, and the latter gives us comfort. The one teaches us not to attribute the light to ourselves; the other, not to be dejected under darkness: and both cause us to adhere to Christ, and to depend upon him. His grace is necessary in order to our endeavouring to get out of darkness, and to keep us from leaving and forsaking the light.

30. Now are we sure that thou knowest all things, and needest not that any man should ask thee: by this we believe that thou camest forth from God.

A person whose conscience is perplexed with fears and apprehensions, and who cannot discover to men the temptations to which his faith is exposed, and the inquietudes which disturb his heart, is never more sensibly convinced that God is the God of his heart, than when he comes himself of his own free grace to dart his light into it, and thereby to show him plainly that he continues in God's favour, that his faith is pure, and that his heart is devoted to his service. Show, Lord, I beseech thee, that thou art my God. Prevent the wants of a heart which knows not even how to lay them open before thee; which does not so much as think of doing it; and which frequently shuts out from itself that light and consolation of which it stands most in need. It was in order to come into my heart that thou camest forth from God thy Father.

31. Jesus answered them, Do ye now believe? 32. Behold, the hour cometh, yea, is now come, that ye shall be scattered, every man to his own, and shall leave me alone: and yet I am not alone, because the Father is with me.

A man sometimes thinks himself proof against every thing, who is very near his fall. The divine favours and consolations make us sometimes forgetful of our own weakness. It is a double instance of God's mercy to any person, when with one hand he fills his soul with the sweetness and comfort of his love, and with the other infuses into him a salutary dread of the unfaithfulness of his own heart. This reproof was a seasonable admonition for the disciples; but they did not thereby apprehend that they were shortly to leave and forsake him in his tribulations who was so careful to prevent their afflictions by his divine consolations. How ungrateful are we! always ready to receive benefits at the hands of God, and always ready to desert him for the sake of every trifle. It is the comfort of holy persons, when forsaken by men, to consider that God is with them in their tribulation, though they be not always sensible thereof.

33. These things I have spoken unto you, that in me ye might have peace. In the world ye shall have tribulation:* but be of good cheer; I have overcome the world. [* *Fr.* Afflictions: but have confidence.]

The ground of our confidence in Jesus Christ is, that he has overcome the world and all its temptations, for himself and for his members. Let us seriously meditate upon this admirable conclusion of his last sermon. The peace which he leaves to his servants does not consist in having nothing to suffer from the world, but in despising every thing it can make us suffer, through a full trust and confidence in him. He declares that in the world we shall have tribulation; but all the tribulations or afflictions of the world are as it were blunted, and have lost their strength and power, by the victory which Christ has gained over it. It is one of the last and dying cares of Christ to make us sensible of the necessity of our having afflictions in this world; and yet the whole care of a great many is to have none at all. They choose rather to have peace with the world, than to have peace with and in Jesus Christ; because they love the good things of this world, and are afraid of temporal evils. We must expect the worst which can happen to us from the hands of men, and hope for the best from the grace of Christ: this is the only way to possess our soul in peace. It is the peace of Christ which overcomes sin in us, and the malice of men for us, by the same power whereby he overcame the devil and the world. No, my Saviour, I desire no peace but that which is the fruit of thy victory; I am resolved to have none but what is altogether consistent with thine.

CHAPTER XVII.

SECT. I.—CHRIST PRAYS FOR HIS GLORIFICATION.

1. These words spake Jesus, and lifted up his eyes to heaven, and said, Father, the hour is come; glorify thy Son, that thy Son also may glorify thee:

Our blessed Saviour teaches us to join prayer to our words of comfort and exhortation, which reach no farther than the ear if God vouchsafe not to accompany them with the unction of his grace and his Spirit. It is the order observed by the church in her liturgy, that the reading and expounding of the words of Christ and his apostles should precede the prayer of consecration. Christ's lifting up of his eyes represents to us that lifting up of the heart, which makes one of the principal parts of prayer. The first condition of the Christian sacrifice is obedience; for the first sacrifice is that of the will. The obedience of our adorable victim is exact, even to the very hour of his sacrifice: for that it belongs not to the victim to choose the hour of its immolation, but to wait for it. It belongs only to him who is the absolute disposer of life to prescribe the term and limits of it. It is the glory of every creature to be sacrificed to its Creator: but the life of Christ, sacrificed to his Father, is the meritorious cause of our glorification both of his natural and mystical body, and the great means which God himself chose in order to establish his kingdom and his glory. A priest or a bishop ought not to consider his own honour, or the dignity of his ministry, any otherwise than in conjunction with the glory of God, and this in imitation of Jesus Christ, who looks upon his Father as the beginning and end of all his own glory. Happy are those members of his, who, after his example, desire no other glory but that which comes from God, and desire it only for his sake. The first intention and end of the sacrifice of Christ is the glory of his Father.

2. As thou hast given him power over all flesh, that he should give eternal life to as many as thou hast given him.

The second intention and end of the sacrifice of Christ is the salvation and glory of the elect. The lot and portion of all mankind is in the hands of Jesus Christ. All nations are his inheritance. He will save and glorify them all in those whom his Father has given him, and drawn to him, by the preaching of the gospel. Christ's zeal for the accomplishing of his Father's designs, and his love toward us, cause him to refer his death and resurrection to the salvation and glory of his members. What a shame is it to see Christians so cold and indifferent in the business of eternal life, when the Son of God sacrificed himself to purchase it for them! They are so far from entering into the way which leads to it, that they are even ashamed to speak concerning it: as if they were designed for somewhat else, and as if it was for others that Christ died and rose again!

3. And this is life eternal, that they might know thee the only true God, and Jesus Christ, whom thou hast sent.

If life eternal consist in the knowledge and love of God and of his Son Jesus Christ, then none are happy in this world but those who make it their business to know and to love God. All other knowledge is but vanity and vexation of spirit, when it is not ultimately referred to that knowledge in which our whole felicity ought to be placed. Who would not pity those fine wits who know every thing except the gospel; whose memories are stored with all the actions of antiquity, except those of Jesus Christ; who make a thousand discoveries in arts and sciences, and neglect the art of sanctifying themselves, and the science of salvation? To know God without Jesus Christ, is to know life eternal without knowing the way which leads to it, the guide who conducts us thither, and the source of that knowledge and love which puts us into possession thereof. Grant, O my God, through Jesus Christ thy Son, that I may neither love, nor ardently desire any thing but this knowledge, and that I may know thee only in order to love thee.

4. I have glorified thee on the earth: I have finished the work which thou gavest me to do.

To glorify God is to finish the work which he has given us to do, and not to undertake any other merely of our own head, how great and considerable soever it may possibly be. We have no other business on earth but to glorify God: and in order to this, every one has his particular work appointed him. Wo to that person who seeks his own glory in the work of God! How great is the difference between Jesus Christ and the generality of Christians! His work is finished together with his life; ours is scarce begun when we are forced to leave this world. Christ, who was sent to preach the gospel to the poor, has discharged his mission and fulfilled his ministry, and is now going to seal them with his blood. My God, how much reason is there to fear that very few preachers can at the time of death have a confidence bearing any proportion to this! Such a confidence at the last hour is the portion of a good pastor, who has spent himself in the labours of his office, and more especially of him who dies a sacrifice for the truth which he has preached or defended.

5. And now, O Father, glorify thou me with* thine own self, with the glory which I had with* thee before the world was. [**Fr.* In.]

Blind is that person who seeks any other glory besides that which God is pleased to give to us in himself, as well as to our adorable Head: to our Head, by diffusing upon his human nature, and even upon his body, the brightness of that glory which the Word always had in God; to us, by causing us to receive of his fulness. In Christ, this is the perfection of the incarnation; in us, it is the consummation of Christian sanctification: and the one as well as the other is the execution of God's eternal decrees, and of the free predestination of the head and of the members in God, wherein the present and the future time are both equally present. God glorifies those in heaven and in himself who glorify him on earth and in themselves. In Christ, as well as in his members, God crowns nothing with his glory but the gifts of his grace: but through his grace and goodness these very gifts become in his sight the merit which deserves eternal glory.

SECT. II.—CHRIST PRAYS FOR HIS APOSTLES.

6. I have manifested thy name unto the men which thou gavest me out of the world: thine they were, and thou gavest them me; and they have kept thy word.

Christ would have no ministers associated to his priesthood but those who are chosen, sanctified, and given him by his Father. Men cannot appoint themselves to that office, nor dispose of their own persons, since they belong to God who made them, who by his eternal election more particularly appropriated them to himself, who delivered them from the slavery of the world, and gave them to his Son. What is man, that he should be made the gift of God to his own Son? What is a soul, that Christ should glory in having received it of his Father, and should vouchsafe to claim it as his proper right? But then, what is that soul which disdains to belong to Christ, and which chooses rather to be the slave of sin, and to return to the bondage of the world? We are Christ's not only by the single title of his Father's donation—we are his likewise by the title of his labours and his preaching, whereby he has manifested his Father's name unto us; by the title of his grace, which has kept us from ruining ourselves in transgressing his law; by the title of faith, the gift of which he has bestowed upon us; and by that of charity, which he has shed abroad in our hearts, to enable us to keep the word of God. How unjust, how ungrateful must that person be, who refuses to belong to Jesus Christ!

7. Now they have known that all things whatsoever thou hast given me are of thee.

The Christian faith causes us to know God as the fountain of all good, even of that which is in Jesus Christ himself, of his divinity, his mission, his word, his miracles, and his virtues. This acknowledgment and confession which Christ makes so often, that he has nothing but what he has received, is a very great and important lesson for Christians. The pride and presumption of the sons of Adam put them continually upon seeking after some good in themselves which is not a gift of God, that they may make it a foundation of merit in respect of all the gifts which God has bestowed upon them. Our blessed Saviour does not act after this manner.

8. For I have given unto them the words which thou gavest me; and they have received *them*, and have known surely that I came out from thee, and they have believed that thou didst send me.

The knowledge of the incarnation and mission of Christ is a very great gift of his to us; and the word by which we know them, is a gift of God to Jesus Christ, and of Jesus Christ to men, which requires abundance of gratitude and acknowledgment. An evangelical labourer ought to set a value upon his vocation and mission not so as vainly to pride himself in it in the sight of men, but to humble himself in the sight of God on the account of his own unworthiness. To the end that the Word may be received, a twofold gift is necessary: the one external, by preaching; the other internal, by the operation of grace: there being in the heart no docility with respect to the divine word, if God do not produce it therein by his Spirit.

9. I pray for them: I pray not for the world, but for them which thou hast given me; for they are thine.

Christ prays particularly for his apostles; and he teaches us to pray often and with great earnestness for the pastors, and for all those who labour in the church. It is his love toward her which causes him to pray for them, and because they are consecrated to God for her benefit and advantage. Our love toward God our Father, and toward the church our mother, is extremely weak when our spiritual governors are not remembered in our prayers. The world, that body of wicked persons, which does and always will subsist, though some of its members be taken from it, lies under a continual curse, and is treated as one excommunicated, who has no share in the sacrifice of Christ any more than in his prayer. What opinion then ought we to entertain of the world for the future?

10. And all mine are thine, and thine are mine;* and I am glorified in them. [* *Fr.* Whatever is mine is thine, and whatever is thine is mine.]

The interests of God and of Jesus Christ are the same; but Christ regards them more as they relate to his Father than as they relate to himself: and he has so great a concern for his apostles, more because they are God's, than because they are his own; more because they are to be the instruments of his Father's glory, than because he himself will be glorified in them. Kindle, Lord, I beseech thee, this pure zeal in the hearts of thy ministers. Let thy glory be the end of all their labours, as the glory of thy Father was the only thing which thou soughtest upon earth. Happy is that pastor, who, through a perfect freedom from all self-interest, and a real disengagement from every thing, can with Jesus Christ truly say to God, "Whatever is mine is thine;" and who can, from a sincere and ardent love, add, "Whatever is thine is mine!" Miserable is that minister of Jesus Christ in whom Christ is not glorified!

11. And now I am no more in the world, but these are in the world, and I come to thee. Holy Father, keep through thine own name those whom thou hast given me, that they may be one, as we *are*.

The invisible protection of God is never wanting to his servants, when he deprives them of his visible protection. It would be something very dreadful to faith, for a man to see himself in the midst of the world without Jesus Christ, did not faith itself assure us that he is with us in temptations and afflictions. Christ asks of his Father that which he himself will do together with him, to manifest his eternal origin from him as God, his dependence upon him as he is man, and the necessity of praying to God to support us in our conflict with the world, and, when that is over, of ultimately referring to him the glory of the victory. Let us imitate Jesus Christ, who addresses himself to the different perfections of God according to the different occasions which have relation to them. Let us adore and invoke the holiness of God against the corruption of the age; the almighty power of his name, against the power of the world and of hell; his unity, against that multiplicity of objects which divide and distract our minds here below: and so of the rest. Holy Father, keep us, we beseech thee, by thy holiness and thy divine unity; and conduct us at last to that perfect and consummate unity which has for its original and pattern that of the Trinity itself.

12. While I was with them in the world, I kept them in thy name: those that thou gavest me I have kept, and none of them is lost, but the son of perdition; that the Scripture might be fulfilled.

A pastor ought, after the example of Christ, to be in the world to no other end but only to seek and to keep the elect of God. It is a matter of great comfort to such a pastor to be able to say that he has kept those who have been intrusted but not absolutely given to him. On the contrary, it is a great misfortune to a flock when it has a pastor who pretends to keep it in his own name, as belonging to himself, for his own glory, and by his own virtue and power. The loss or perdition of the wicked always afflicts a man of God; but he adores his judgments and unsearchable counsels, and humbles himself under his almighty hand. The word of God is fulfilled in his judgments, since it is so frequently declared therein that he will destroy those who break his law, and that he will exercise his justice against slanderous and perfidious persons.

13. And now come I to thee; and these things I speak in the world, that they might have my joy fulfilled* in themselves. [**Fr.* The fulness of my joy.]

Christ comforts his servants, not in giving them the joy of the world, but in making them partakers of his own. It is a very great consolation under the apprehension of afflictions and persecutions, to hear a holy pastor pouring out his soul in prayer, with all the tenderness of a Father toward us, and with all the confidence of a son toward God. The joy of hope passes easily from a father's heart into that of his children. The joy of the world is an empty thing, and empties the heart only that it may fill it with vanity; but the joy of Christ is full of the divine unction, which fills, supports, and comforts the heart. It has its fulness even in this life; what then will it be in the other, when perfect love shall give our heart its full dimensions, that we may receive the plenitude of the divine gifts, and "be filled with all the fulness of God!"

14. I have given them thy word; and the world hath hated them, because they are not of the world, even as I am not of the world.

Fidelity in following and preaching the word of God in its purity is inconsistent with the friendship of the world. There is no danger of being hated by the world, when, through fear of displeasing it, we abstain either from following the way of truth or from teaching it; for from the time that we act thus, we ourselves are of the world. The gift which God gives of his word, in the manner wherein he gave it to the apostles, is inconvenient and grievous to those who love the comforts and conveniences of this life; but how advantageous is it to those who know how much better it is to be hated by the world with Jesus Christ, than to be loved by it!

15. I pray not that thou shouldest take them out of the world, but that thou shouldest keep them from the evil.

Those who love the church, and are called to the service of it, must continue in the world, notwithstanding its contrariety and opposition to Christ, out of submission to his will, in order either to promote the salvation of the world or to be crucified in it. There is reason to hope that God will keep those from the evil and corruption of the world who remain in the midst of it by his order and appointment, or on the account of the duties of their state and vocation. But we run a great risk of perishing, when we are under no engagement or obligation from God to continue therein. There are abundance of persons who ought earnestly to beseech God to take them, as it were, out of the world, that they may perform the great work of repentance, and that they may, in the retirement of some proper place, be secure from the corruption of the world: there are others, whose duty it is to beg of him the grace to remain in the midst of it without being corrupted thereby. This last must be the subject of those prayers which the faithful are to offer up in behalf of their pastors.

16. They are not of the world, even as I am not of the world.

Let the repetition of this truth make the clergy sensible how different their life ought to be from that of worldly persons, and how much they ought to abhor the maxims of the world! To resemble Christ in this respect is a very great proof of a call to the ministry. What is the design and meaning of this "as," but only to inform us that we must hate the world, resist and oppose its lusts, and be ready to be crucified by it as Jesus Christ was?

17. Sanctify them through thy truth: thy word is truth.

The sanctity or holiness which Christ asks for those whom his Father has given him, is a Christian holiness, spiritual, internal, and conformable to the spirit of his religion, instead of the Jewish sanctity, which was only carnal, external, etc. The truth and the immutability of the word of God are the seal of all his designs concerning them and his whole church, and the rule of true and substantial piety. The clergy, whose lives are to be a pattern to others, ought to take greater care than others to form their piety by the word of God and the spirit of the church. It is not enough not to be of the world, to keep at a distance from its vices, and not to follow its maxims; we must be the servants of God by a true holiness and by all Christian virtues. The renouncing whatever remains in us of the corruption of the world, is the beginning of true holiness—which consists in faith, hope, and charity, whereby we are united to God.

18. As thou hast sent me into the world, even so have I also sent them into the world.

None ought to be more opposite to the world, or to be more truly and substantially holy, than he who is sent into the world to labour toward the sanctification of souls. Why are so few ecclesiastical persons strictly holy? It is because they are generally sent into the world before they have ceased to be of the world, and before they have taken any pains about their own sanctification. It is not at all strange, that those who are already corrupt should, by their conversation with the world, proceed to the highest degree of corruption; since even the most holy persons are sometimes corrupted thereby, and lose their own souls. The mission of Christ is the source and the pattern of all mission in the church. How can those who take upon them the ministerial office without being called and sent, look upon Jesus Christ as their pattern, and as the original of their ministry?

19. And for their sakes I sanctify myself, that they also might be sanctified through the truth.

How can Christ possibly fail of obtaining the sanctity for which he prays, since he asks it in consideration of his own sacrifice, which is the great and solemn prayer of our Mediator, and the infinite price of our sanctification? We can be truly sanctified only by charity; and this charity could be purchased for us by nothing but the sacrifice of the cross. For a man to sanctify and to sacrifice himself are one and the same thing. Both consist in destroying the old man, either by death or by mortification, for the sake and the honour of God, and in order to be united and consecrated to him alone. The sacrifice of martyrdom is the most excellent way of sanctification, for that it manifests the greatest disengagement from the old man, and the greatest contempt both of life and of pain—the one the most dear, and the other the most dreadful thing to human nature; and because this contempt proceeds from the strongest and sincerest desire of being united and consecrated to God. O Jesus, sanctify me in truth! O good Shepherd, grant to thy church a great number of pastors who may be able every one of them to say, I sanctify myself for thy sheep, that they also may be truly sanctified!

SECT. III.—CHRIST PRAYS FOR THE SALVATION OF ALL THE ELECT.

20. Neither pray I for these alone, but for them also which shall believe on me through their word;

The success of the preaching of the gospel, and the faith of those who hear it, are the effect of the prayer of Christ, and of his sacrifice, which is the most holy and efficacious of all prayers. There is no manner of grace, no degree of faith whatever, which is not the fruit of the prayer and of the sacrifice of Jesus Christ. There are no Christians in any age whatever, who do not owe their faith to the word of the apostles, who are apostles even in respect of those who are at this day converted to the faith: because it is their very word which has been conveyed down to us by the hands of their successors. If it were not the same word, it could not be the same church; since it is upon the word that the church is founded. A bishop, a priest, and indeed every ecclesiastical minister, ought to imitate the example of Christ in offering up frequent and fervent prayers in behalf of the church, and in offering himself in sacrifice for her sake.

21. That they all may be one; as thou, Father, *art* in me, and I in thee, that they also may be one in us: that the world may believe that thou hast sent me.

The unity of faith tends to the unity of charity; and both together terminate in the wonderful and eternal unity of the mystical body of Jesus Christ in heaven. We shall there all be one, not in or by ourselves, but in God, and in the very unity of the ever-blessed Trinity. Who can possibly comprehend the dignity of the church and of her children, and how the unity of the Father and of the Son in the Holy Ghost is the source, the pattern, the cause, and the end of the unity of Christ's members in the spirit of sanctification? "One in us;" namely, in the Father, who, by adopting and regenerating us as his children, makes us partakers of the divine nature, to honour and imitate that inexpressible communication which he makes of his essence to his own Son in his eternal generation: in the Son, of whom we are all members, composing together with him but one and the same body, of which he is the sole Head, which he rules and governs, and to which he communicates his life, that he may honour both the communication which he, together with the Father, makes to the Holy Ghost of the life received from the Father himself, and likewise the communication which he, by the Holy Ghost, makes of his own life to man, to whom he united himself in unity of person by the incarnation, which communication is in honour and imitation of that unity: in the Holy Ghost, who is as it were the soul and life of this body, the bond which unites all the members to one another and to their Head, and the love with which they love one another; and this in order to honour what he is with respect to the Father and the Son, namely, their bond of union, the foundation of their complacency, and their eternal and consubstantial love.

22. And the glory which thou gavest me, I have given them; that they may be one, even as we are one:

Christians receive by baptism the glorious quality of being the children of God, which belonged to none but the only Son of God. He was the only Son in all respects, but he was pleased not to continue so, having associated us to his person by the divine adoption, in order to unite us to himself by the strictest and most tender union. He gives us likewise his glory, in giving us for our spiritual food and sustenance his glorious flesh, which changes our corrupt nature, and as it were mixes us with his, and renders us one flesh, one blood, and one and the same spirit with him. Christ no doubt intended by this repetition to raise in our minds a serious and attentive consideration of this divine unity to which we are called. Though we be not able to comprehend it, it is not at all the less credible, and it is the more valuable on this account. Let us render ourselves as worthy of it as we can, by carefully maintaining peace and union with our brethren, and endeavouring to the utmost of our power to preserve the unity of the church. Nothing does more plainly show that the church is the work of God incarnate, than that spirit of unity and charity which reigns therein, even among the most distant members: ver. 21. The spirit of schism, and whatever bears any resemblance thereto, ought to be abhorred by all true Christians.

23. I in them, and thou in me, that they may be made perfect in one; and that the world may know that thou hast sent me, and hast loved them, as thou hast loved me.

All religion, and all the designs of God, tend to unity. Christ becomes the bond and centre thereof by his incarnation. All the fulness of the Godhead dwells in him substantially, really, and perfectly, by the person of the Word; he dwells in Christians spiritually by faith; and all men, in some manner, dwell in him bodily by the flesh which he took of them. It is through Jesus Christ, that those who are incorporated with him receive the perfection and consummation of that unity which they have with God and with one another. The love which God bears toward us as his children, in adopting us in and by Jesus Christ, is the source of Christian unity: as his eternal love of Christ is the cause of his predestinating him to that adorable unity which makes him both God and man. The consummation of unity is the perfection of charity; and those incomprehensible methods which God has chosen to establish a perfect charity among men, are a proof of the incarnation, and the effect of his exceeding love toward us. The more our unity with Christ resembles his unity with his Father, the more does the love of the Father toward us resemble that love which he has for his only-begotten Son. Grant, O my God, that all our thoughts and actions may have a constant tendency to promote unity and charity with our brethren; and reunite us all in thyself, O thou adorable unity and charity!

24. Father, I will that they also, whom thou hast given me, be with me where I am; that they may behold my glory, which thou hast given me: for thou lovedst me before the foundation of the world.

How full of consolation, both to the afflicted apostles and to all Christians, is this confidence, with which Christ, as Mediator, and in virtue of the blood he is going to pour out, desires that his faithful servants may be where he himself is, to be made happy by the sight and participation of the glory of his divine and human nature! This is a consequence of the unity concerning which he has just now spoken. Christ entire, consisting of the Head and the members, and composing but one body, and, as it were, one only Son of God, cannot be anywhere but in the bosom of the Father; neither can he possibly be there without being glorified, and, as it were, overflowed with the glory of God. Christ ultimately refers both the glory which he has received by his incarnation, and that which he is to receive by his resurrection, to the love with which his Father loved him before the foundation of the world, as to its source and original. It is in him that we are predestinated to the same glory; and we can never arrive at it but only by the same way of humility and mortification.

25. O righteous Father, the world hath not known thee: but I have known thee, and these have known that thou hast sent me.

Faith, by which we know the mission of Jesus Christ, and by him his Father, is the foundation of all the other gifts of God. The world, abandoned to its darkness and ignorance, remains therein only because it loves its own darkness more than the light of God. To think of this should make us tremble, and cause us to humble ourselves under the almighty hand of God; since we ourselves were once of the world, and may be so again, if God vouchsafe not to support us with the same grace by which he separated us from it. Let us with Jesus Christ adore the justice and righteousness of God, in rewarding the good and in punishing the wicked.

26. And I have declared unto them thy name, and will declare *it;** that the love wherewith thou hast loved me may be in them, and I in them. [* *Fr.* Made known thy name unto them, and will still make it known.]

Let us not be puffed with the knowledge which we have of God. It proceeds not from ourselves, but from the goodness of God, and the grace of Jesus Christ. The word of Christ makes God known; the Holy Ghost perfects this knowledge, and renders it useful to us by charity or love; and love establishes Christ in us, and us in him, in order to our consummation with him in God to all eternity. Christ, in ascending into heaven, did not abandon his church. His Spirit and grace make known his Father's name in all succeeding ages.

Whatever conceptions of the greatness and majesty of God we may here frame from faith and from the Holy Scriptures, that knowledge which is reserved for us in heaven is of a quite different nature. Grant, O my God, that I may have no other knowledge of thy name and thy perfections but what may serve to confirm thy love toward me, to increase mine toward thee, and still more and more to form Christ in my heart, till thou vouchsafe to glorify me in him, and him in me!

CHAPTER XVIII.

SECT. I.—THE GARDEN.—THE JEWS FALL TO THE GROUND.—CHRIST TAKEN AND LED TO ANNAS.

1. When Jesus had spoken these words, he went forth with his disciples over the brook Cedron, where was a garden, into the which he entered, and his disciples.

Every circumstance of our blessed Lord's passion which the Holy Ghost has delivered to us, must needs contain something which is instructive and useful. This brook, over which David passed at the time of his humiliation and flight from his unnatural son Absalom, puts us in mind that the ingratitude of that person was but a type or shadow of that of the Jews in after ages, and of all sinners. Into this garden of tears and sorrows does Christ now go, to expiate with his blood the sin of Adam, committed in a garden of delights. Far is he from desiring to avoid death, since he goes freely and voluntarily to cast himself into the hands of his enemies, and in retirement and prayer to wait for their coming.

2. And Judas also, which betrayed him, knew the place: for Jesus ofttimes resorted thither with his disciples.

The remembrance of the prayers in which our blessed Lord had so often passed whole nights in this place, and of which this traitor had been himself a witness, is not capable of softening his heart. When the sinner is fully possessed with his passion, all external means which God uses to prevail with him have no effect upon his mind.

3. Judas then, having received a band *of men* and officers from the

chief priests and Pharisees, cometh thither with lanterns, and torches, and weapons.

Let us fear and tremble, when we see Judas desert from the Son of God, to go into the service of the devil; leave the company of Christ's disciples, to put himself at the head of his enemies; and renounce the office of an apostle, to perform that of a traitor. He chooses to make himself a slave to these corrupt priests and great pretenders to zeal for the law, and to be the minister of their passions, rather than to be the minister of the charity and the priesthood of Jesus Christ. This being a slave to one single passion, as Judas was to his avarice, is enough to render a man a slave to the passions of all other men. Could this wretch have possibly imagined that these weapons and soldiers could prevail against Christ, had not his covetousness entirely blotted out of his mind the remembrance of what his Master had done before his eyes to render all the former attempts of the Jews against him fruitless and ineffectual?

4. Jesus therefore, knowing all things that should come upon him, went forth, and said unto them, Whom seek ye?

The Holy Ghost has been very careful to prevent the scandal or offence which the weak might take at the sufferings of our blessed Saviour, by informing us expressly that he suffered nothing but what he clearly foresaw, and what he chose to suffer. Men are bold in dangers on no other account but only because they do not foresee the consequences: Christ exposes himself to that very danger which he foresees, and can avoid. This question, "Whom seek ye?" was a very great admonition to these persons, had but their minds been open to receive it, since it plainly showed the power of that person who blinded them so far as to hinder them from knowing him whom they sought; but it is one effect of this sort of blindness, not to be sensible of the blindness itself.

5. They answered him, Jesus of Nazareth. Jesus saith unto them, I am *he*. And Judas also, which betrayed him, stood with them.

He who came to seek sinners on purpose to give them life, is here sought by sinners in order to be put to death. In this every sinner may behold a lively representation of his own ingratitude and perfidiousness. The token of the kiss having been rendered insignificant, the Jews are not now able to distinguish and to know Christ. Thus God, whenever he pleases, renders all the precautions of men vain and ineffectual, and breaks all their measures and designs.

6. As soon then as he had said unto them, I am *he*, they went backward* and fell to the ground. [* *Fr.* Were thrown down.]

They all fall to the ground, and yet not one of them perceives and owns the hand of God or the omnipotent voice of Christ. Thus God often ruins the fortune, the designs, the health, etc. of the wicked; but none are converted by making a good use of this judgment, except those whose hearts he vouchsafes to touch with the powerful influence of his love. Judas, an apostle, an eye-witness of Christ's miracles, nourished so long with his word, and preobliged by so many favours, is thrown down, but not converted: Saul, a persecutor of the apostles and of the church, who had never known Christ, who still breathed out threatenings and slaughter against his disciples, is no sooner thrown down but he yields, and becomes meek and gentle as a lamb. The reason is, because the latter is inwardly pierced with such light and grace as it is in vain to resist, and the former is abandoned and given up to his own reprobate mind. O my God, how profound and unsearchable are thy judgments! I adore them, and submit myself to them.

7. Then asked he them again, Whom seek ye? And they said, Jesus of Nazareth.

God allows the sinner time to recover himself, and gives him opportunity to make useful reflections upon his fall. But something else besides time and opportunity is necessary, otherwise his heart will only grow more obdurate. These miserable wretches seek that which they ought: they seek the Saviour of the world, but it is in order to destroy him—and by this they destroy their own souls. It is but too true, that we often seek with greater industry and perseverance occasions of ruining ourselves, than we do those of attaining to salvation. Of how much use and advantage would it be for every one of us frequently to put this question to himself,

"Whom seekest thou?" Jesus Christ or the world? If the former, is it in order to adore him, or to crucify him by thy sins?

8. Jesus answered, I have told you that I am *he:* if therefore ye seek me, let these go their way:

Christ, forgetting the care of his own life, is solicitous only how to save the lives of his apostles. The very same word in the mouth of Christ has very different effects: at one time it is like a thunderbolt, which strikes down all it meets; at another, it is like a gentle breath of air, which passes by without doing the least harm. Thy power, O Jesus, is triumphant whenever thou pleasest: and thou art now just going to subject it to thy enemies, because it is thy will and pleasure so to do. Christ gives a plain and evident proof of his absolute power, by giving law to this band of soldiers, and obliging them to do what he thinks fit.

9. That the saying might be fulfilled which he spake, Of them which thou gavest me have I lost none.

This saying, which has two proper and literal meanings—the one relating to temporal, the other to eternal life—plainly shows the copiousness of the word of God. Whoever is in the hand of Christ, is in perfect safety. Happy the person who continues therein! but how can we do this, if Christ himself vouchsafe not to take hold of us, to guide us, and to unite us to himself? Lord, I hope I am of the number of those sheep which thou wilt never lose! Let thy eyes, thy Spirit, and thy heart be always watchful over my conduct and my salvation! For without thee there is nothing to be expected but dangers, perils, and inevitable destruction.

10. Then Simon Peter having a sword drew it, and smote the high priest's servant, and cut off his right ear. The servant's name was Malchus.

This action of Peter is a representation of the vain endeavours of the pride of man without grace. Nature is very earnest, zealous, and presumptuous; but all earnestness or zeal which does not proceed from the Spirit of God, is of no long duration. Christ guides Peter's hand, and permits him not to do any other harm to this servant but only what was requisite to give himself an opportunity of doing good to his enemies, of instructing his disciples, and of edifying all persons. The right ear is an emblem of docility, obedience, and a true understanding of the Scriptures, which will not be found any more, either in the priests or the people of the Jews, until Christ shall one day restore them to them by his grace.

11. Then said Jesus unto Peter, Put up thy sword into the sheath: the cup which my Father hath given me, shall I not drink it?

Christ here teaches the clergy to abstain from all violent proceedings. He sometimes heals the wounds which the precipitate conduct of the chief pastors has made without his orders. He restores to its former state what they cut off through a rash and inconsiderate zeal; and commands them to put ùp the sword which they use unseasonably. God must be obeyed, whatever the event may be. He who loves him, cannot endure to be deprived of any opportunities of suffering for him. To dispose a man to look upon these as a gift and present from the hand of God, it is necessary for him to be a true disciple of Christ, who first made sufferings honourable, and discovered the value of them. Let us take great care that we be not of the number of those sinners who decline the cup of repentance and mortification, and who are overjoyed to meet with such spiritual guides as dispense with them, and by their conduct hinder them from looking upon this cup as a great favour, and a precious gift of the divine mercy. What knowledge, what authority soever in the church those may have who divert us from performing repentance in the strictest manner, or without reason dispense with our performance of it, let us rather believe Christ, who enjoins us to do it, and teaches us to love and practise it in a spirit of obedience. Happy is that penitent who says to one of these imitators of Peter, the cup which God out of his fatherly love has given me, shall I not drink it, to avoid that sentence which he will one day pronounce with the utmost severity of an inexorable judge?

12. Then the band and the captain and officers of the Jews took Jesus, and bound him.

O adorable captivity, O sacred bonds of our blessed Saviour! By these, (1.) He expiates the ill use of our liberty. (2.) He obtains for us the grace to use it well. (3.) He sets us free from sin, and makes us become the servants of righteousness, in which consists the glorious liberty of the children of God. (4.) He sanctifies the imprisonment and confinement of his disciples, and even of criminals. How honourable to the ministers of Christ are bonds, which he endured before them, if they endure them for his cause and in his spirit! How delightful is a prison, when a man considers that he is the prisoner of Jesus Christ, that his present condition has been sanctified by him, and that he is chosen of God to honour him particularly in that state; to be consecrated to him in it, and to reap the spiritual advantage peculiar thereto! Grant, Lord, I beseech thee, that thy bonds may be endured with this spirit, both by the innocent and by the guilty!

13. And led him away to Annas first; for he was father-in-law to Caiaphas, which was the high priest that year.

This appearance of Christ before a person who had no authority is one part of his humiliations. He submits to this, that he may multiply the number of them, and add to the shame which he bears in the stead of sinners, and in order to their salvation. The iniquity of Christ's enemies triumphs in this; but his humility triumphs abundantly more. There are in the world many of these fatal alliances, which engage men to have a hand in many acts of injustice, and sometimes even in the most heinous crimes. Of how great importance is it to contract an alliance only with virtuous persons! An alliance is often attended with very great consequences; and is sometimes the occasion of salvation or damnation.

14. Now Caiaphas was he, which gave counsel to the Jews, that it was expedient that one man should die for the people.

It is matter of great joy to the wicked to see their advice followed; but this joy, which is an effect of the wrath of God, will last but a short time, and will be punished with an endless sorrow. It is a judgment still more terrible upon them, when God permits their designs of oppressing innocence and justice to succeed according to their desire. But this judgment is most of all terrible, when priests are the objects of it. If there be any bad advice or counsel to be given against the interests of Christ, of his church, his truth, or his servants, it is frequently one of his ministers who gives it. So dangerous is it for a man not to be holy in a holy dignity or office.

SECT. II.—PETER FOLLOWS CHRIST TO THE HIGH PRIEST'S PALACE.—CHRIST EXAMINED CONCERNING HIS DOCTRINE, RECEIVES A BOX ON THE EAR.—PETER'S DENIAL.

15. ¶ And Simon Peter followed Jesus, and *so did* another disciple: that disciple was known unto the high priest, and went in with Jesus into the palace of the high priest.

In vain does any man pretend to follow Jesus when he has no other guide but presumption, and no other strength beside that of nature. The command Christ gave to the soldiers, that they should let his disciples go their way, was an admonition to these to retire. But Peter has a mind to distinguish himself by doing more than others, and will thereby plunge himself into a misfortune which he would have avoided had he followed the rest. He would not believe his master, when he told him that he could not follow him then; and he will find the truth of it by a sad experience. Ecclesiastical persons are not to follow Christ into the house of the great. He goes thither only by compulsion, and in order to be humbled. Whoever goes to such places merely upon human motives, and contrary to God's appointment, will meet with nothing there but occasions of falling, as Peter did.

16. But Peter stood at the door without. Then went out that other disciple, which was known unto the high priest, and spake unto her that kept the door, and brought in Peter.

Men sometimes imagine they do a considerable piece of service to their friends who are clergymen, by introducing them to the great; and thereby they undesignedly expose them to sin and to eternal damnation. It is of much greater advantage to find a true friend who persuades us to go back, than those false friends who incite us to proceed, and who procure us admittance. Peter, while he stood at the door, had perhaps some inclination to retire, and to avoid the danger: but a convenient opportunity drives away abundance of good thoughts, and renders holy inspirations fruitless and insignificant. The devil is but too careful in opening to us a way to those places where he can hold us captive to his own advantage.

• 17. Then saith the damsel that kept the door unto Peter, Art not thou also *one* of this man's disciples? He saith, I am not.

That man thinks himself as firm and immovable as a pillar, who is weaker than a reed. Whoever does not own himself a disciple of Christ, denies him. We imagine ourselves faithful, because we do not speak the very same words Peter did. But what is our refusing to follow the maxims of the gospel, but a plain denial of Christ, and a disowning ourselves to be his disciples? What would not Peter have said in the presence of Caiaphas, and before his judgment-seat, since even at the door of his house, and only before a servant-maid, his courage fails him, and he gives ground so easily? This first fall even at the threshold, ought to have been of use to him, to humble him, to open his eyes, and to prevent his falling again: but he was entangled in the snare.

18. And the servants and officers stood there, who had made a fire of coals, for it was cold; and they warmed themselves: and Peter stood with them, and warmed himself.

We ought, especially if we are weak, to avoid all bad conversation: to expose ourselves thereto is a presumption which often costs us dear. Curiosity and idleness frequently cause us to seek and to meet with companions as inquisitive and idle as ourselves, and this combination of idleness and useless curiosity seldom fails of producing abundance of faults, and of giving occasion to a great many sins. The devil generally presides at assemblies of this nature, and furnishes matter of discourse out of his own stock. He makes one in all conversations which have no manner of relation to God, and sometimes even in those wherein men seem to propose to themselves no other end but what is good.

19. ¶ The high priest then asked Jesus of his disciples, and of his doctrine.

In this examination, Jesus Christ, the sovereign priest and

the eternal truth, is humbled in respect of both these qualities, being obliged to give an account of his doctrine and his disciples, as one suspected to have conspired with the latter against the government, and to have designed to destroy the law of Moses by the former. Conspiracy and innovation, imputed at random and without proof, are generally the two crimes of which the innocent are supposed to be guilty. Christ was graciously pleased to be accused of all manner of crimes, that he might be the consolation and strength of all those who are unjustly accused by the world. Let us particularly reverence in him every thing which was humbled for our sakes.

20. Jesus answered him, I spake openly to the world; I ever taught in the synagogue, and in the temple, whither the Jews always resort; and in secret have I said nothing.

Those who broach strange doctrines seek darkness: whereas truth seeks the light; and those who preach it are not afraid to publish it in the open day. It is a very great proof of innocence, when the person accused has the confidence to appeal to the testimony even of his enemies, and they can take no manner of advantage from it. Christ gave particular instructions to his disciples for the conduct of their lives, and for the direction of the church; but he gave them no secret maxims, no private doctrines which he designed should be concealed.

21. Why askest thou me? ask them which heard me, what I have said unto them: behold, they know what I said.

We cannot possibly learn more perfectly than from Jesus Christ, how to join modesty and resolution together in asserting and maintaining the truth to the very last. It is peculiar to him who has a good conscience, to possess his soul in patience under the most unjust and heinous accusations, without breaking out into any reproachful and injurious language. An evangelical preacher ought to preach the gospel in such a manner that he need not fear to appeal indifferently to all those who have heard him.

22. And when he had thus spoken, one of the officers which stood by struck Jesus with the palm of his hand, saying, Answerest thou the high priest so?

There are always flatterers to be found who make their court to the great at the expense of justice and innocence. It is a reproach to a judge to have such officers as violate even in his presence the most common and general laws, by which the greatest criminals are protected from the insults of private persons. A wicked judge who finds himself stopped in his proceedings by the plainest proofs of innocence, is glad to be relieved by any incident, whatever the innocent person may suffer thereby. There is not a more grievous and unpardonable affront, in the opinion of the world, than a box on the ear: and it was for this very reason that Christ chose to suffer it, that he might confound and humble the pride of man, and leave the proud an example of patience which, if not imitated, will certainly condemn them. With what shame and confusion ought we to be covered, how ought our hearts to be affected, when we read so surprising a circumstance as this, of which we ourselves are the occasion by our sins?

23. Jesus answered him, If I have spoken evil, bear witness of the evil: but if well, why smitest thou me?

It is more difficult on such occasions as this to speak with truth, mildness, and justice, as Jesus did, than it is to turn the other cheek. They do no other than give Jesus Christ a new blow, who abuse and persecute his ministers for having preached his doctrine, and rebuked vice with a freedom becoming evangelical labourers. These, after the example of Christ, must not abate any thing of their sacerdotal freedom and boldness on the account of their sufferings, but must vindicate themselves, as he did, by convincing reasons. It is for the interest of superiors that we should not be silent, but that we should justify ourselves when we are accused of being wanting in respect toward them. To act otherwise, would be to give encouragement by our own example to those who are glad of all opportunities to dishonour them.

24. Now Annas had sent him bound unto Caiaphas the high priest.

It is thus, O Jesus, our new Adam, that thy hands, bound and tied fast with cords, expiate the daring presumption of our first parents in reaching out their hands to the forbidden fruit. It is thus likewise, that thou condescendest to do penance for so many ill uses in which sinners employ their hands, making them the instruments of so many crimes, sacrileges, and impurities. The sight of the bonds with which our blessed Saviour was bound weakens the faith of his apostle still more, who sees that his Master makes no use of his power to break them; and therefore gives him over for lost. But faith ought not to look upon them in this view. It is not so much to the power of men that Christ yields, as to the power of his love toward us. Nothing ought to give me more confidence than these voluntary bonds which he endures on purpose to break those which my will has made for itself of its own iniquities and vicious habits.

25. And Simon Peter stood and warmed himself. They said therefore unto him, Art not thou also *one* of his disciples? He denied *it*, and said, I am not.

It is not good to receive any thing of the world, or to grow familiar with it; for familiarity leads to compliance and too great a regard to men, and these lead to sin. The fall of one of the chief of the apostles shows us plainly that salvation cannot be built upon any thing which is in man, whom a bare word or two shakes and immediately throws to the ground. The weakness of the first preacher of the faith, when left to himself, makes it evidently appear that it was a Spirit very different from that of man which spoke by the mouth of the martyrs, and a strength far superior to theirs which enabled them to withstand tyrants, and to surmount the fears of death. It was not it seems enough, that Christ should inform us by his word, concerning the necessity of his grace, in order to overcome the least temptation in such a manner as might be profitable to our salvation: it was requisite that we should read this truth written in the largest characters in the fall of one of the most favoured apostles, and in the weakness of one of the chief pillars of the church. When a man has once experienced his own weakness on any particular occasion, he must quit that occasion if he have any regard to the salvation of his soul.

26. One of the servants of the high priest, being *his* kinsman whose ear Peter cut off, saith, Did not I see thee in the garden with him?

When grace supports us, the more the danger increases,

our strength and courage exert themselves the more. But when man is left to himself, his weakness appears the more visible; and his fall becomes so much the more fatal, the greater the danger is. There was some little reason to fear this servant-maid; there was more to be afraid of the men; but one of the high priest's servants, in the high priest's own house, a kinsman of him whom Peter had wounded, who was an eye-witness of the action, who saw him with Christ, and who mentions the very place and circumstances, makes this poor apostle dread the worst which could happen, who had by his own imprudence involved himself in this danger. Let us learn, from the example of his misfortune, to fear danger, and to flee from it.

27. Peter then denied again; and immediately the cock crew.

It is a very great misfortune for a man not to be convinced of his own weakness without grievous falls. Those of Peter answer exactly to his presumption; his three denials to his three presumptuous promises: but three humble protestations of love for Jesus will make amends for both. It is high time for the cock to crow, and for thee, O Lord, to begin to open the eyes and ears of this sinner, who is already blinded by his falls, and begins to grow hard and obdurate. The sins of Peter afford matter of consolation to such sinners as have had frequent relapses, since he received mercy after three acts of infidelity. But that which may administer hope to penitents, does by no means justify the presumptuous security of sinners.

SECT. III.—CHRIST BROUGHT BEFORE PILATE.—HIS KINGDOM IS NOT OF THIS WORLD.—HE WAS BORN TO BEAR WITNESS TO THE TRUTH.—BARABBAS.

28. ¶ Then led they Jesus from Caiaphas unto the hall of judgment: and it was early; and they themselves went not into the judgment hall, lest they should be defiled; but that they might eat the passover.

Let us consider Christ's appearance before an idolatrous judge. What unaccountable blindness is this in the Jews, to fear being defiled by entering into the house of a heathen, and not to fear being so by soliciting him against the innocent, and by their own wickedness! We sometimes find the like superstition in the great pretenders to devotion. This is a new indignity to Christ, to be delivered up to the Gentiles, which had been foretold by the prophets and by Christ himself; but it is at the same time a new right which he acquires over them, to subject them to his dominion; and, perhaps, for this reason it is expressly mentioned in the creed, that Christ suffered under Pontius Pilate. The Gentiles have no more cause to boast than the Jews, since both are guilty of the death of Christ. There is no man in the world who has not crucified Jesus Christ, since there is not one who has not offended God and transgressed his law, either by himself or in Adam.

29. Pilate then went out unto them, and said, What accusation bring ye against this man? 30. They answered and said unto him, If he were not a malefactor, we would not have delivered him up unto thee.

There cannot possibly be a higher act of injustice, than to desire that a judge should suppose the accused person guilty of the crime without any further examination; and this is what Jesus Christ suffered. All the forms of justice are tedious and troublesome to those who are afraid lest an innocent person should escape their malice and revenge. To be delivered up and brought to the bar is enough to make a man guilty, when envy and passion are his accusers. It is no strange and extraordinary thing to see innocent persons oppressed by arbitrary proceedings, without any legal process: but for a man to be brought before a judge in order to be delivered up directly to execution, without any proof of his crime, or any examination concerning it, is a new way of oppression first invented and contrived against the Saviour of the world. In thee, O Jesus, we find matter of comfort and consolation under every hardship and affliction!

31. Then said Pilate unto them, Take ye him, and judge him according to your law. The Jews therefore said unto him, It is not lawful* for us to put any man to death: 32. That the saying of Jesus might be fulfilled, which he spake, signifying what death he should die. [**Fr.* Permitted.]

All things conspire against Jesus Christ; and even the prudence of the Roman emperors, who had taken from the Jews the power of life and death, is the occasion of his being condemned to the cross. The Jews were not permitted indeed to put criminals to death; but they were permitted, and even obliged in conscience, to acquit the innocent, and to examine the justice or injustice of the accusers. Can men ever complain of the injustice which is done them, and of the rash judgments which are cast upon them, if they pretend to follow the footsteps of their Master, and to imitate his patience?

33. Then Pilate entered into the judgment hall again, and called Jesus, and said unto him, Art thou the King of the Jews?

Jesus is humbled in his character of King, and delivered up by his own people and by the priests, that he may be a pattern of patience and humility to persons in all states and conditions. That which earthly kings will least of all endure, and which indeed they have reason least of all to endure, is, that any one should question whether they be kings. Christ, in suffering this, shows plainly that his humility is as extraordinary as his royalty. He is the King both of the Jews and the Gentiles; but the one kingdom which these two people are to compose, is far above the reach of Pilate's apprehension. These carnal Jews are unworthy of thee, O my King and my Saviour! make us, we beseech thee, true Israelites according to the Spirit, and vouchsafe to bring us by thy grace into subjection to thyself. They are hearts which thou seekest, in order to establish thy kingdom in them; and thou knowest where to find them.

34. Jesus answered him, Sayest thou this thing of thyself, or did others tell it thee of me?

Christ teaches us to behave ourselves modestly and respectfully toward magistrates and earthly powers, even when they do not discharge their duty. The judge has the interest of his sovereign at heart, because his own fortune depends upon it; but he is perfectly indifferent and unconcerned about the interest of this just and innocent person, against whom he admits of the highest accusations without proof or witness; and this because he neither hopes nor fears any thing from him. Judges ought to examine every thing, and, above all, their own heart.

35. Pilate answered, Am I a Jew? Thine own nation and the chief priests have delivered thee unto me: what hast thou done?

Observe here the surprising wisdom of our blessed Saviour, who, by the question he asks of his judge, draws from his mouth an answer which justifies his innocence: for this judge plainly slights and drops the accusation relating to the state, grounded upon the dubious acceptation of the name of king, of which the Jews maliciously made use to destroy him. This is not therefore now any cause in which the state is concerned; it is only a question of religion. It was the proper business of the Jews, and not of the person accused, to declare what he had done, and likewise to prove it. This is an instance of prevarication in the judge, not to take full cognizance of the crime before he proceeds to examine the party accused.

36. Jesus answered, My kingdom is not of this world: if my kingdom were of this world, then would my servants fight, that I should not be delivered to the Jews: but now is my kingdom not from hence.

The kingdom of Jesus Christ is not of this world; and shall a Christian then seek after honour, riches, and power here below? We are called indeed to reign, but it is in heaven, and not upon the earth. As the kingdom of Christ, being not of this world, does not intrench upon the kingdoms of earthly princes, so these are not of the spiritual world, which is the church. We must not be of this world, if we desire to belong to the kingdom of Christ; and he receives us into the number of his subjects by baptism, only on condition that we renounce the world and all its pomps and vanities.

37. Pilate therefore said unto him, Art thou a king then? Jesus answered, Thou sayest that I am a king. To this end was I born, and for this cause came I into the world, that I should bear witness unto the truth. Every one that is of the truth heareth my voice.

It is the property of Jesus Christ, the eternal truth, and it is the duty of his disciples, to bear witness unto the truth at the hazard of life. The kingdom of God is the kingdom of truth: Christ came on purpose to preach and to settle it by faith; and this faith is a gift of God, which those only preserve to the end who belong to this kingdom by the eternal and unchangeable choice of God. Every Christian, in his proper way, is obliged to bear witness to the truth on all occasions which present themselves. Pastors, as the deputies of Christ, ought, after his example, to look upon themselves as persons born and continuing in the world to no other end and purpose but to bear witness to the truth all imaginable ways, and at the expense of all things. The more violently it is attacked, either in itself by the errors of heretics, or in its ministers by the calumnies of worldly men, the more is any one obliged to speak in its defence. There is no surer sign of our being in the way of salvation, than our having for the word of God that love, docility, and application, and obedience which are due to it.

38. Pilate saith unto him, What is truth? And when he had said this, he went out again unto the Jews, and saith unto them, I find in him no fault *at all.*

How many are there in the world who, after Pilate's example, either will not learn the truth, or despise it, or pretend not to know it, that they may not be obliged to expose themselves to danger in the defence of it! The innocence of Christ is at one and the same time acknowledged and abandoned by his judge. He speaks to the truth itself, he asks it questions, and then turns his back upon it. That will not allow us to interrogate it in a cold, indifferent, and careless manner, or with a double heart: we must do it with respect, love, sincerity, and perseverance. Would to God the great would earnestly seek to know it, and would patiently attend while it is discovered to them! But they are more afraid to know it than to be ignorant of it.

39. But ye have a custom, that I should release unto you one at the passover: will ye therefore that I release unto you the King of the Jews?

Christ meets with more humanity from a heathen than among the Jews: so strangely does the abuse of the divine favours and benefits corrupt and harden the heart. These commendable endeavours in behalf of innocence serve only to increase the humiliation of Christ, and the condemnation of him who uses them. When a man has power and authority in his hands, he does by no means discharge his duty if he only perform good offices, if he only entreat and solicit persons in favour of the innocent who lie under calumny or persecution:

he ought to resist iniquity to its face without any regard to men, and to declare himself boldly and vigorously for the cause of justice. It is thy mercy, O my God, toward thy enemies, which is the cause that thy Son finds no mercy or compassion at all in the hearts of men. We could never have been released or delivered, if our blessed Saviour had. It is not he, it is mankind which is the criminal to be released at the passover, at that passover whereof he himself is the victim. It is his glory and our salvation that he dies innocent, instead of being released and set at liberty as a criminal and malefactor.

40. Then cried they all again, saying, Not this man, but Barabbas. Now Barabbas was a robber.

We compare and prefer Barabbas to Jesus Christ whenever we choose to follow our own passions rather than the gospel; the spirit of the world rather than that of God; and the inclinations of the first Adam, a sinner, rather than those of the second, who is holiness itself. We abhor that which the Jews did but once; and we do the same every day without remorse or concern, and even without considering what it is we are doing. The Jews renounced Christ: but it was before they had received his Spirit, or were made members of his body. The ingratitude of a Christian who has known and tasted his heavenly gifts, has nothing which comes near it. Let us cast our eyes upon the life of the generality of mankind, and see whether there are any great number whose actions do not continually cry out, "We will not have Jesus Christ! we will have none of his humility, his poverty, his mortification, his cross!" etc.

CHAPTER XIX.

SECT. I.—CHRIST SCOURGED AND CROWNED WITH THORNS.—BEHOLD THE MAN.—CRUCIFY HIM.

1. THEN Pilate therefore took Jesus, and scourged *him*.

Let us not wonder to see Jesus Christ undergo the punishment of rebellious slaves, since he stands in the place of sinners, and expiates the disobedience and rebellion of Adam. It is a very wrong piece of policy to design to prevail upon the world by granting it one part of its demands, and, by refusing it the other, to think we discharge our own duty. There is no dividing our fidelity between God and the world; and our infidelity is arrived at its utmost height when once we have begun to sacrifice innocence to calumny. Sensuality reigns in all parts of the sinner's body; and it is in order to expiate and remove it that Christ submits to this scourging, which tears his adorable body, and makes it all but one wound. Shall we not then be ashamed of our love of ease, and of that tenderness with which we indulge our rebellious flesh, seeing his holy and innocent flesh is treated in so barbarous a manner for our sakes?

2. And the soldiers platted a crown of thorns, and put *it* on his head, and they put on him a purple robe,

Christ is crowned with thorns and arrayed like a king out of mockery, to expiate the crime of Adam in affecting an independency even in respect of God: for there is no person whatever who does not inherit from Adam the love of preeminence and the spirit of dominion. We see the proper remedy for them in our adorable Head, crowned with thorns, humbled, mocked, and insulted in the quality of King. He refused once to accept of the regal dignity from men, because it was not attended with any humiliation, and because the crown they offered him was without thorns; he now accepts it, because it is very proper for him who came on purpose to reign by the cross. A Christian who is placed in the high station of honour and authority, has great reason to fear and tremble, if he find therein nothing of the thorns or humiliation of Christ to serve as a counterbalance. Grandeur and authority are so infected with the poison of human pride, that there is an obsolute necessity of an antidote and preservative against it.

3. And said, Hail, King of the Jews! and they smote him with their hands.

Christ suffers in his sacred countenance that which those persons deserve who take so much pains in adorning their faces that they may draw others into sin. This is the mystery which Christian princes ought more particularly to consider. In this they ought to study the art of ruling in a Christian manner, and how to sanctify in themselves grandeur and regal power. The court of Jesus Christ, crowned with thorns, is not a court of flatterers, but of mockers; by suffering whose abuses and insults he expiates that love of praise and flattery from which it is extremely difficult for princes to secure themselves in the midst of a court where all strive to outvie each other in offering them this poisonous incense. Though it be not indeed consistent either with their dignity or with the public good, that they should bear with insolence and affronts, yet their piety and salvation at least require that they should not bear with flatteries. This is the least homage which they owe to the royal dignity of Christ, treated in so base and ignominious a manner.

4. Pilate therefore went forth again, and saith unto them, Behold, I bring him forth to you, that ye may know that I find no fault in him.

See here another part of Christ's humiliations, his appearance before his own people. A strange way this of clearing the innocence of an accused person, to punish him in order to acquit him! But stranger yet is the hard-heartedness of this people, whom the cruelty of this judge does not soften! Lord, since thy Father, who is justice itself, suffers thee to be treated in this manner, thou must of necessity have crimes of which Pilate knows nothing at all: and these crimes are mine, and those of all mankind. Grant, Lord, that I may have the fidelity and gratitude at least to adore thee, and to endure with thee the shame and confusion which thou endurest for my sake.

5. Then came Jesus forth, wearing the crown of thorns, and the purple robe. And *Pilate* saith unto them, Behold the man!

Behold here the state and condition to which the sinner has reduced his King! changing, by his crimes, the lustre of his regal dignity into a spectacle of pain and ignominy. These thorns, with which the King of the Christian is crowned, are more precious than the gold and diamonds which sparkle in the crowns of earthly kings, since they are the ransom of the world, and the price of eternal salvation. Other crowns are only a vain show, which is often nothing but the effect and the occasion of sin. The pride which fills the head of a person who is puffed up with his dignity, reputation, or learning, especially when he appears in public, is the disease which Christ designs to heal by means of these thorns which pierce his sacred head. Let these thorns, O Jesus, sanctified by touching thy adorable flesh, and endued with a divine and efficacious virtue by being stained in thy blood, pierce the tumour of my pride and vanity, and let out the imposthume of the passions of my heart! This purple robe, which is instrumental to the humiliation of Christ, expiates the profuseness and ostentation of the children of Adam in their apparel, and merits and procures for us the grace to despise that magnificence and excessive niceness therein which the rich affect. "Behold the man," who is the victim of God for men, and the true offering of men still offered up representatively to God. How sensibly does it touch sinners, and how insupportable is it to them, to be named or pointed out publicly by any thing in them which exposes them to disgrace and contempt! This, O Jesus, is the very thing which thou intendest to expiate, and to cure in me by these words!

6. When the chief priests therefore and officers saw him, they cried out, Saying, Crucify *him*, crucify *him*. Pilate saith unto them, Take ye him, and crucify *him*: for I find no fault in him.

What strange acclamations are these, from a people upon whom this King has heaped so many favours! Can we, after this, refuse to suffer the ingratitude and infidelity of those to whom we have done the greatest service? This is a kind of homage, and an honour which we owe to Jesus Christ, who for our sakes suffered both those heinous provocations at the hands of the Jews. Our sins cry out even louder than the Jews, and they were those which prevailed against the innocence of our blessed Saviour. Nothing is more shameful than the base cowardice of a judge who is not willing to commit a crime himself, and yet suffers it to be committed. Light or knowledge renders a judge the more criminal, who deliberately yields to the passion and power of men, and abandons innocence.

7. The Jews answered him, We have a law, and by our law he ought to die, because he made himself the Son of God.

Who can bear with the hypocrisy of the sinner, who makes even his crimes a matter of conscience and religion? But who can satisfy himself that he is entirely free from this temptation? Calumny always suppresses whatever may be of advantage to those whom it designs to ruin, and conceals all the proofs of their innocence. Christ "made himself the Son of God" indeed; but then he likewise plainly proved himself to be so, by doing the works of the Son of God, and restoring life to the dead. There is another law—namely, the law of the divine justice and mercy, which requires that the Son of God should die to satisfy the justice of his Father, and to merit and effect the salvation of men. It was thy eternal love toward us, O Saviour of the world, which made this law; and nothing but thy own transcendent charity constrained thee to do it!

SECT. II.—PILATE'S FEAR.—CHRIST'S SILENCE.—ALL POWER COMES FROM ABOVE.

8. ¶ When Pilate therefore heard that saying, he was the more afraid;

How miserable is the condition, and how vain are the endeavours, of that person who would fain please both God and the world! A small degree of love for justice causes a man to struggle for some time; but it is too weak to prevail. To persevere and continue true to it, he must love it with all his heart; but he certainly loves it less than his own fortune, when he sacrifices it thereto. When a man knows his duty, and has not yet sold himself to iniquity, he cannot do a wicked action without some remorse; but these remorses are only so many witnesses against the sinner.

9. And went again into the judgment hall, and saith unto Jesus, Whence art thou? But Jesus gave him no answer.

How many complaints, murmurings, and justifications of ourselves, proceeding from self-love, ought this silence to stifle and suppress! It is a virtue which was never heard of before Christ came, and which has been very rarely practised ever since, for a man to have it in his power to justify himself, and yet to continue silent. Christ confounds the eagerness and impatience of the children of Adam to justify themselves from the least suspicions and the slightest accusations, by suffering himself in silence such as are of the highest and most heinous nature. But had he justified himself and avoided death, we could never have been justified or delivered from that which is eternal. Thou hast loved us, O Lord, more than thy own life; and we, ungrateful as we are, prefer not only our life, but even our criminal will and inclinations, and every trifling interest, before thy glory and thy holy will.

10. Then saith Pilate unto him, Speakest thou not unto me? knowest thou not that I have power to crucify thee, and have power to release thee?

Christ has another Judge, who is invisible, whose judgments he adores in silence, under whose omnipotent hand he humbles himself, and whom he looks upon as the sovereign disposer of every thing which men do against him. A good judge cannot boast of his power; he can do nothing but what he can do justly. He has no other power but only to make the laws take place, by yielding obedience to them first himself. The judge before us has no cause to glory in his authority, but rather to humble himself for the corruption of his own heart, since he punishes without having any obligation to do it from law or justice. He is not the master, but the minister of the law; and therefore ought to make it subservient to the public good, and not to his own private interest. A good judge ought never to make himself feared by his power and authority, but rather to tremble himself through the fear of abusing it. Great authority, with little or no virtue, is a very dangerous state.

11. Jesus answered, Thou couldest have no power *at all* against me, except it were given thee from above: therefore he that delivered me unto thee hath the greater sin.

In what hands soever lawful authority is lodged, we ought always to look upon it as coming from above. The righteous know that the very hairs of their head are all numbered. Nothing surprises, much less amazes them, because they have their eyes always intently fixed upon him who has his continually open upon them. Besides the general providence which appoints good and permits evil, which establishes all lawful authority and regulates the good or bad use thereof, the eternal counsels and decrees of God concerning Christ, his church, and his elect, ought to yield matter of great comfort and confidence to those who suffer in his name. If to abandon an innocent person to the calumny and malice of men be a great crime in one who has authority in his hands, and consequently has a right, and is under an obligation both to speak and to act in his behalf; how much more guilty is he who delivers up an innocent person, when he knows not only his innocence, but likewise the great designs of God concerning him, and the works he intends to effect by his means, having been fully informed of these mysteries by the Scriptures and by private instructions! Every one may apply these words to particular cases.

12. And from thenceforth Pilate sought to release him: but the Jews cried out, saying, If thou let this man go, thou art not Cesar's friend: whosoever maketh himself a king speaketh against Cesar. 13. ¶ When Pilate therefore heard that saying, he brought Jesus forth, and sat down in the judgment seat, in a place that is called the Pavement, but in the Hebrew, Gabbatha.

God having condemned his Son to death, it is not in the power of any man to deliver him from it. Whoever is possessed with a design of making or improving his fortune, will never perform his duty. A judge, that he may not abuse his authority, must be free from passion. He is no longer master of his own conscience, from the time any private interest has gained the ascendant there. When once a judge, a magistrate, or any great person has discovered his weak side, the wicked know very well how to draw him into their designs. Nothing but an extraordinary grace can secure a man from their snares, when it is his interest to keep fair with them.

14. And it was the preparation of the passover, and about the sixth hour: and he saith unto the Jews, Behold your King!

All that passed here was truly the preparation of the grand passover, the passover of the Christians, which was just going to be sacrificed. Would to God there were not priests to be found even now, who, as it were, prepare themselves for the Christian passover and sacrifice by calumniating and persecuting their brethren, or by other sins, in the habitual practice of which they allow themselves! Since it is by humiliations and sufferings that Christ is pleased to establish his kingdom, this is the very time wherein we ought to adore and receive him as the king of our hearts. Yes, Lord, I know thee by these marks, and own thee for my King. Cause me by thy grace so to imitate thy example that thou mayest likewise own and acknowledge me for thy subject!

15. But they cried out, Away with *him*, away with *him*, crucify him. Pilate saith unto them, Shall I crucify your King? The chief priests answered, We have no king but Cesar.

Whoever suffers avarice, ambition, or any other sinful desire to reign in his heart, is very far from owning or having Jesus Christ for his king. Our tongues and our hands do even now continually crucify him afresh, when our words and our works are contrary to his law. These men require the death of the Messias whom they had desired, sued for, and expected, during so many ages; and they submit to the yoke which they had so much detested and abhorred: an unaccountable instance this of what envy and hatred can do, when they are resolved to satisfy themselves. When this double passion has once taken full possession of the heart, a man knows no other happiness but to revenge himself, and no other misery but to have before his eyes the object of his hatred and his envy. Piety only knows how to reconcile the royal authority of Christ with that of Cesar, the spiritual power with the temporal. The more Christ reigns in our hearts, the greater are our fidelity, submission, and obedience to our temporal sovereigns.

SECT. III.—CHRIST DELIVERED UP TO THE JEWS, CARRIES HIS CROSS, AND IS CRUCIFIED.—THE TITLE ON THE CROSS.

16. Then delivered he him therefore unto them to be crucified. And they took Jesus, and led *him* away.

How many persons in the world side with Christ at first, and abandon him afterward to the wicked, through cowardice, too great a regard to men, and bad example! There are more than we imagine, whose hearts are like that of this pretended lover of justice, who delivers up the person accused to his enemies not only without pronouncing sentence, without any proof of his crime, but even owning and acknowledging his innocence. Importunity and solicitation prevail at last upon a judge who hearkens to worldly hopes or fears. The fear of displeasing his prince is the main spring of all the actions of a courtier who has not the fear of God; and he is always ready to sacrifice every thing to his master's favour, and to deliver up every thing, rather than run the least hazard of losing that.

17. ¶ And he bearing his cross went forth into a place called *the place* of a skull, which is called in the Hebrew Golgotha:

The true Isaac, as the victim of God, carries the wood for his sacrifice; as a conqueror, the arms with which he is to vanquish sin, the world, and the devil; and as a king, the sceptre with which he is to rule his people. This cross, the emblem of our sins, with which Christ is loaded, is now immediately to be the remedy and atonement for them. Let us contemplate ourselves in our head and pattern: he appears in our stead, and suffers that which we ought to suffer. This spectacle, which seems so ignominious to the eyes of the flesh, is justly looked upon by the eyes of faith as the object of our love and our imitation throughout the whole course of our life. Let us remember that this is what our blessed Lord had in view when he said, "Whosoever will come after me, let him deny himself, and take up his cross, and follow me." We must follow, and not go before him; for it is after his example that we must bear the cross; it is his cross which must attract and draw us; and it is only by that grace which this cross has merited for us, that we are enabled to bear it.

18. Where they crucified him, and two others with him, on either side one, and Jesus in the midst.

Truth is always crucified in the midst of sinners, as Christ was between two thieves. In like manner virtue is placed between two opposite vices. The Christian must follow Christ even upon the cross: it is not enough only to bear it—he must also be fastened to it. There are some crosses which are honourable, and are attended with a glory which makes the person crucified amends for what he suffers: but such is not the cross of Christ, which is as humbling as it is painful. It is humbling in itself, being an object of malediction; it is so, likewise, in respect of the company in which he suffers, namely, two thieves; and of his being placed between them as the greatest criminal. How many important truths are there to be learned at the foot of this cross! How many duties to be paid! How many graces to be received! Let us at least learn what our sins deserved. Christ suffers, that he may cause us to suffer with him in a holy manner, by his grace, and according to the example of his humility and patience.

19. ¶ And Pilate wrote a title, and put *it* on the cross. And the writing was, JESUS OF NAZARETH THE KING OF THE JEWS. 20. This title then read many of the Jews; for the place where Jesus was crucified was nigh to the city: and it was written in Hebrew, *and* Greek, *and* Latin.

The regal power of Jesus Christ on the cross was attested and published even by his judge, to those three different people of whom the church was chiefly to be composed, and who at that time shared between them the religion, learning, and empire which Christ has united in his church. Those whose design it is to humble Christ, proclaim his greatness and his glory without being sensible of it themselves. God will always confound those who endeavour to humble his elect. And the greater share these have in the sufferings of their Head, the greater will they have in the glory of his kingdom. The royal dignity of Christ can be neither destroyed nor impaired by the ignominy of the cross, since this very ignominy is the foundation thereof. I adore thee, O Jesus, under this external appearance so unworthy of thee, as the only victim of God worthy to be offered to him, as the sovereign High Priest of good things to come, and as the King of everlasting glory.

21. Then said the chief priests of the Jews to Pilate, Write not, The King of the Jews; but that he said, I am King of the Jews. 22. Pilate answered, What I have written I have written.

God by his wonderful power so disposes even of the heart of the wicked, as to make them subservient to his truth and his mysteries. Had Christ been crucified merely as a false king, he could not have been the victim of his people and the salvation of the world. This title, written in three different languages, proves, by three eternal witnesses, the perfidiousness and sacrilegious wickedness of the Jews against their King. The remembrance and remorse of sin are an executioner which the sinner has always before his eyes, and which he carries in the bottom of his own conscience. No sooner has he committed the sin, but he begins to be tormented by it. Could he entirely blot out the remembrance of it upon earth, it would signify nothing; it would still subsist before God, and therefore it is out of his remembrance that he must earnestly endeavour to blot it, which can be done by nothing but a true conversion and repentance.

SECT. IV.—CHRIST'S GARMENTS.—HIS COAT.—THE BLESSED VIRGIN AND JOHN AT THE FOOT OF THE CROSS.

23. ¶ Then the soldiers, when they had crucified Jesus, took his garments, and made four parts, to every soldier a part; and also *his* coat: now the coat was without seam, woven from the top throughout.
24. They said therefore among themselves, Let us not rend it, but cast lots for it, whose it shall be: that the scripture might be fulfilled, which saith, They parted my raiment among them, and for my vesture they did cast lots. These things therefore the soldiers did.

The nakedness of Jesus Christ upon the cross, is a circumstance which plainly shows us that he refused no kind of humiliation for our sakes. He endures this shame that he may cover our sins from his Father's sight. The first Adam by his sin deserved this shame; the second Adam bears it, to merit our deliverance from it; to expiate the crime of those who either are not ashamed of it, or even take a pride therein; and to strengthen us against the temptations which arise from this quarter. Every thing here tends to make known the mysteries of the cross and of the church. These upper garments, divided into four parts, represent to us the vast extent of the church into the four parts of the world; the under garment without seam, and which is preserved entire, denotes the unity of the church and of the preaching of the word of the cross. Every thing contributes to establish the belief of Christ's being the Messias. The fulfilling of the prophecies demonstrates that he is really the King of the Jews who was therein foretold, and whose name and memory they in vain endeavour to abolish. Those who divide the church are more cruel than these heathen soldiers, who would not divide the seamless coat of Christ.

25. ¶ Now there stood by the cross of Jesus his mother, and his mother's sister, Mary the *wife* of Cleophas, and Mary Magdalene.

The blessed virgin is present at the foot of the cross. She prefigures and foreshows the fidelity of the church, the courage of the martyrs, and the constancy even of the weaker sex, which death itself will not be able to separate from the love of Christ, through the grace received from his cross and passion. The first fruits of this victorious grace are given to the three Marys. Peter, left to himself, denied Christ through fear of a maid and of some men-servants; Pilate delivered him up out of a groundless apprehension of falling under some disgrace: but these women surmount the fearfulness of their sex, the horror of such a spectacle, the tenderness of nature, the sense of the ignominy and disgrace in having a son and a master crucified between two thieves, and the danger to which they are exposed from the brutality of an enraged populace. What inward strength and courage do persons receive at the foot of the cross, when they render themselves present there by a lively faith and with a Christian confidence!

26. When Jesus therefore saw his mother, and the disciple standing by, whom he loved, he saith unto his mother, Woman, behold thy son!

Christ sanctifies, teaches, and encourages filial love in Christians, by his faithfulness in performing the duties of a son toward his holy mother in the midst of all the ignominies and horrors of death. It is a practice worthy of a Christian, to reverence, to contemplate, and to imitate this courage and resolution of Christ expiring on the cross, and to have recourse to this mystery in order to obtain that strength, that presence of mind, and that judgment which are necessary to enable us to discharge our duties upon the bed and at the approach of death. How great a privilege is it to John, to be substituted in the place of Christ by the appointment of Christ himself! This privilege is likewise for us, since it is a mysterious and prophetical substitution of all the sons of the church, who are all the brethren of Jesus Christ. It would have been but a small consolation for the blessed virgin, under the loss of a son who was God, to have received John in his stead, had not this apostle been to her a pledge, and, as it were, a sign and visible sacrament of that invisible presence which Christ would always continue in her heart.

27. Then saith he to the disciple, Behold thy mother! And from that hour that disciple took her unto his own *home*.

John, in recompense of his virginal purity, receives the blessed virgin for his adopted mother: and from hence we learn how much Christ loves that virtue, and how much we ought to love and value it. What may and ought we not to believe concerning the gratitude and acknowledgment with which John received this precious trust concerning the veneration and filial obedience he showed toward her, and concerning his fidelity, in profiting by a domestic example so wonderful and extraordinary! The faithful attendance of John at the cross of Christ is likewise rewarded with this inestimable gift: by which we are plainly informed that Christ vouchsafes to share his richest treasure with those who imitate his purity and charity, who are not ashamed of his humiliations, and who love his cross.

SECT. V.—CHRIST THIRSTS.—ALL THINGS ACCOMPLISHED.—HIS DEATH.—NO BONE OF HIM BROKEN.—HIS SIDE PIERCED.

28. ¶ After this, Jesus knowing that all things were now accomplished, that the Scripture might be fulfilled, saith, I thirst.

The thirst of Jesus Christ expiates the intemperance of Adam and of his children. The thirst of his heart after the glory of his Father, and the salvation of sinners, was without comparison more vehement. Is that excessive tenderness toward themselves supportable in some Christians who, even upon days of fasting, cannot endure a little thirst by way of mortification, when they see Jesus Christ endure a thirst so vehement that he complains thereof, though he suffered so many torments without opening his mouth? Ought the false maxim of a casuist, who tells us that a draught of any thing does not break our fast, to have more influence upon us to induce us to transgress the law of fasting, than the example of Jesus Christ to encourage us to endure hunger and thirst? Christ complains of thirst only that he may suffer the more, that he may prove the reality of his incarnation and his sufferings, and fulfil the prophecies in the minutest circumstance. Let thy adorable thirst, O Jesus, extinguish our thirst after the false enjoyments of this world, and all those vain desires which continually prey upon our hearts.

29. Now there was set a vessel full of vinegar: and they filled a sponge with vinegar, and put *it* upon hyssop, and put *it* to his mouth.

The tongue of Jesus Christ undergoes its particular torment to atone for the ill use which men make of theirs by blasphemies, evil-speaking, vanity, lying, gluttony, and daintiness. See here the comfort and refreshment which men give to him who lays down his life for them. A true representation this of the ingratitude, sourness, envy, and of the total corruption of the heart, which is all we have of our own stock to give in return for the transcendent love of our blessed Saviour. What an exchange is this! a vessel full of vinegar for the effusion of his blood upon us. Can we after this complain of the ingratitude of men toward us, and of the little comfort we sometimes receive from our friends?

30. When Jesus therefore had received the vinegar, he said, It is finished: and he bowed his head, and gave up the ghost.

This action of Jesus Christ is an adorable example of fidelity, which we ought to imitate in bearing mortification to the time of our death, and in drinking whatever Christ has reserved for us of the sourness and bitterness of his cup. My God, what comfort and consolation is it to a faithful soul, in the midst of the sharpest pains to be able to say at the hour of death that all is finished, that all the designs of God concerning it are accomplished by its obedience! It is requisite that our life should not be torn from us, as it were, by violence, but that we should, after the example of our Head, render it up with a willing mind to him who gave it us. It is a sacrifice, it must therefore be voluntary. It is a homage, it must be full of submission. It is a restitution, and must be made with a love of justice. And it is a satisfaction, and therefore it must be humble. The death of Jesus Christ is the accomplishment of the Scriptures. It teaches us to resign ourselves up to God at the hour of death. In order to obtain the blessing of a happy death, it is of the greatest use imaginable frequently to honour that of Jesus Christ, which is the source from whence the grace enabling us to die well is derived.

31. ¶ The Jews therefore, because it was the preparation, that the bodies should not remain upon the cross on the sabbath day, (for that sabbath day was an high day,) besought Pilate that their legs might be broken, and *that* they might be taken away.

In vain does the sinner endeavour to bury the memory of his crimes; his sins will always rise up against him. The greatest joy of these persons but a few hours ago, was to see Jesus Christ upon the cross: now they cannot endure the sight of him there. The pleasure of revenge is soon changed into an abhorrence of the crime which it has caused a man to commit. There are even at this day some such hypocrites as these, who make no scruple of preparing themselves for the great festivals of the church by crucifying the Son of God by their sins, and who are never ashamed of them but only in the sight of men. They are careful how to conceal, but not how to expiate their crimes.

32. Then came the soldiers, and brake the legs of the first, and of the other which was crucified with him. 33. But when they came to Jesus, and saw that he was dead already, they brake not his legs:

We must take the greatest care to preserve always the unity of Christ's mystical body in the midst of persecutions, and even in death itself; as he here preserves his natural body whole and entire. This body, by being sacrificed, is become the victim and holocaust of God; and therefore men have no longer the least pretence of right in it, nor is it in their power from henceforth to make any attempt upon it. Christ, by preventing this new design of his enemies, intended to make it evident that he gave up his life freely and voluntarily. We may well believe that he was really dead, since they made him suffer no more.

34. But one of the soldiers with a spear pierced his side, and forth-

with came thereout blood and water. 35. And he that saw *it* bare record, and his record is true; and he knoweth that he saith true, that ye might believe.

The death of Christ, which is the salvation of the world, ought to be rendered certain and indubitable by all sorts of proofs and testimonies: by that of the soldiers, who were going to break his legs; of the centurion, who saw him expire; of the soldier, who with his spear pierced his side; of the guards, who stood round about him, and who, from the impression his death made upon them, believed in him; of the people, who smote their breasts as they returned; and lastly, of the disciple, who took particular notice of every thing, and saw the blood and water flow out of his side. This affords a new assistance and support to our faith, and is a new benefit conferred upon us by the goodness of God. Christ would not have one drop of his blood remain unshed for the salvation of mankind. It is all for us, he reserves not the least part of it for himself. The wound in our blessed Saviour's side ought to be most dear and amiable to us, since it is from this mysterious opening of his heart after he was dead, that the sacraments of life proceed. The death of Christ is so far from rendering him of no use to us, that it begins to form his church, and, by the water of baptism, to fix and establish therein a fountain of purity and holiness, which will never cease to flow after his death, but which receives all its virtue and efficacy from his meritorious blood. It is not sufficient that our blessed Saviour wash us; he must likewise feed and renew us. O wonderful transfusion of the blood of Christ, from the Head into the members, from his natural into his mystical body, from the side of Jesus Christ into the Christian's heart! Let faith and gratitude continually open mine to receive the quickening virtue of this blood, which conveys eternal life to us.

36. For these things were done, that the scripture should be fulfilled, A bone of him shall not be broken.

The truth of the prophecies and the power of God evidently appear from hence, that not only every thing which the Jews did against Christ was exactly foretold, but even their designs and attempts against him, which he rendered ineffectual, were so too. The Scripture fulfilled literally in the figurative lamb, was only a type of the literal accomplishment which it was to have in the true Lamb prefigured thereby. It is likewise still continually fulfilled, both in the church, which God will always preserve entire and in unity; and in the saints, whom he fills with his strength, and whenever he pleases secures so effectually as not to suffer a hair of their head to perish notwithstanding all the power of their enemies.

37. And again another scripture saith, They shall look on him whom they pierced.

Christ will come to judge the world in the very same flesh in which he was crucified, that he may put his enemies to shame and confusion. Let us with humility, faith, love, and gratitude, look upon him whom we ourselves have pierced. Let us enter into that heart which was opened by and for us. Let us not close it up by our ingratitude, after having pierced it ourselves by our blind rage and fury. Grant, O Jesus, that thy cross may, through thy grace, be now the object of my desires and my religion, to the end I may not be of the number of those to whom, at the last day, it will be only an object of horror and despair.

SECT. VI.—JOSEPH AND NICODEMUS.—CHRIST'S BURIAL.

38. ¶ And after this Joseph of Arimathea, being a disciple of Jesus, but secretly for fear of the Jews, besought Pilate that he might take away the body of Jesus: and Pilate gave *him* leave. He came therefore, and took the body of Jesus.

How wonderful is the power of Christ's death, which gives those the courage to confess him publicly under his greatest humiliation who confessed him only secretly while he wrought so many miracles! Let us reverence this power, that we may receive from it the strength and resolution to live in the spirit of his cross, and not to be ashamed either of him or his humiliations. God delays not the effect of his promises relating either to the saints or to their Head. Scarce have they sunk under the power of the world, but he begins to raise them again, and to defeat the designs of their enemies. The Jews have Jesus Christ no longer in their power: God raises up holy persons to intrust them with these precious remains.

39. And there came also Nicodemus, (which at the first came to Jesus by night,) and brought a mixture of myrrh and aloes, about a hundred pounds *weight*. 40. Then took they the body of Jesus, and wound it in linen clothes with the spices, as the manner of the Jews is to bury.

John mentions with so much care the timorousness of these two disciples, on purpose to make us admire this great change wrought in them by the right hand of the Most High, and to cause us to give glory to his grace. God sometimes defers healing the infirmities of his servants, that their cure and the power of his grace may shine forth more illustriously on some singular and important occasion which is to happen. This reason ought to restrain us from censuring such persons too severely, or in an insulting manner, in hopes that God will strengthen them in his appointed time. In this costly burial of his Son, God authorizes the last respects which we pay to the bodies of the deceased. He causes that poverty, which Christ retained even to his grave, to be honoured by the liberality of his servants. If we have any thing extraordinary to spend on such occasions as this, we ought to lay it out in honour of such holy persons as have been ill treated and oppressed by the power of the world: this is to contribute to the vindication of providence, and to the performance of the promises of God.

41. Now in the place where he was crucified there was a garden; and in the garden a new sepulchre, wherein was never man yet laid.
42. There laid they Jesus therefore because of the Jews' preparation *day;* for the sepulchre was nigh at hand.

This new sepulchre, in which Jesus is laid after his death, is an emblem of the virgin's womb in which he was conceived, and of the heart of a Christian who is desirous to receive him worthily. It is not sufficient only to die to sin by baptism or repentance, we must likewise bury the body of sin, and hide ourselves from the world by silence and retirement, every one according to his state and condition. Every thing here is subservient to the mysteries of Christ. The Jewish Sabbath serves to represent and to accomplish the Sabbath or rest of his body in the sepulchre, which is only the preparation for that great Sabbath or rest which he will quickly enjoy in glory. Happy those pious souls who have suffered themselves to be laid, as it were, in the sepulchre of a holy retirement, there to keep the Sabbath in abstaining from sin and from all worldly vanities, and to wait for the eternal Sabbath of God which is reserved for all faithful souls!

CHAPTER XX.

SECT. I.—MARY MAGDALENE GOES FROM THE SEPULCHRE TO THE APOSTLES.—PETER AND JOHN RUN THITHER.

1. THE first *day* of the week cometh Mary Magdalene early, when it was yet dark, unto the sepulchre, and seeth the stone taken away from the sepulchre.

Christ's death does not cool or slacken the ardent zeal of Mary Magdalene. She knows that she must surmount all obstacles in order to seek and find Jesus Christ. Let us learn of her also now, not to lose any time when we have any good work to accomplish. A faithful soul stops therein for a while, when it meets with natural or religious impediments, such as were the night and the Sabbath to Mary Magdalene; but as soon as ever they are removed, it returns to its work without the least delay. The diligence of this eminent soul receives an immediate reward. Nothing is given to God gratis. God himself takes away the hinderances which obstruct our endeavours in doing good, when we have been so faithful as to overcome our own sloth, and have been stopped by nothing but the invincible difficulty of other obstacles.

2. Then she runneth, and cometh to Simon Peter, and to the other disciples whom Jesus loved, and saith unto them, They have taken away the Lord out of the sepulchre, and we know not where they have laid him.

A faithful soul which thinks it has lost Christ, is deeply sensible of its loss—it sighs, it weeps, and leaves no means untried to find him again. The first thing it has to do is to go to Peter and John, that is, to a holy pastor who has both authority and charity. It sometimes happens that Christ goes in some manner out of a heart which is his living sepulchre, by depriving it of his sensible presence only to try it; and a timorous soul is afraid that its own faults have driven or taken him away. Solicitude and grief are a plain indication of our love for that which we have lost; and when we have a love for it, we entreat everybody to assist us in recovering it. That humility which inspires us with a sense of our own weakness, and causes us to seek for assistance, is a very proper means to qualify us to find Jesus Christ. It is in the church, and to the ministers thereof, that Christ has left his authority and his love. It is thither that souls must have recourse in their troubles and their wants.

3. Peter therefore went forth, and that other disciple, and came to the sepulchre.

A pastor, when called to the assistance of souls, ought to be very ready to go to them. When to assist a soul in seeking Christ requires his presence, he must lay every thing aside. Authority ought never to go without charity: these two must be inseparable companions in a pastor. Authority goes foremost, and begins the outward action; but charity goes along with it. Mission is the first external qualification of a pastor; but pastoral charity is the very life and soul of his mission. Grant, O Lord, that in thy church we may never see authority without charity; and that the most eminent in authority may be the most eminent in charity!

4. So they ran both together: and the other disciple did outrun Peter, and came first to the sepulchre.

We must love like Peter, and be loved like John, in order to run to seek Jesus Christ; but before we can either love or run, we ourselves must be loved. It is neither to him who willeth, nor to him who runneth, that the glory of the good-will and of the race is due; but to him who showeth mercy in preventing both with his love. Charity, by the fervency of its desires, always gets the start, and runs before authority, to prepare the way for it, and to keep it from depressing those with all its weight who are as yet but weak. The tenderness and compassion of the pastoral charity must make the first approach to a heart which is become a sepulchre void of Jesus Christ.

5. And he stooping down, *and looking in,* saw the linen clothes lying; yet went he not in.

The illuminated and respectful love of John represents to

us the contemplative life which is chiefly employed in devotion and in the study of truth. It is this love which discovers truth; but before it pretends to penetrate into it, and to adhere thereto, it waits till the authority of the church examines it, and the pastors approve of it. John sees the linen clothes by stooping down. It is by humility that prayer and contemplative love discover the truth. The linen clothes in which the body of Christ was wrapped, are an emblem of the word and of the Scripture in which the divine truths are as it were closely wrapped up. How mean and humble soever this word may appear, which, as well as Christ himself, came down from heaven to earth, let us love it, and meditate upon it with that care and reverence which are due to the word of God.

6. Then cometh Simon Peter following him, and went into the sepulchre, and seeth the linen clothes lie, 7. And the napkin that was about his head, not lying with the linen clothes, but wrapped together in a place by itself. 8. Then went in also that other disciple which came first to the sepulchre, and he saw, and believed.

The ardent and faithful love of Peter represents to us the active life, and the exercise of authority in the pastors. It belongs chiefly to them to enter into the sanctuary of the truths of faith, by searching into the Scripture, and to publish those truths to the flock. Faith may be compared to a veil for the head, which is folded up. It is a part of the pastoral authority to judge of it, and to unfold the mysteries thereof to the charity of the faithful. It belongs to the pastors to initiate them in the mysteries of faith, and to discover the secrets of religion to them with authority. Grant, Lord, that authority may always guide charity into the adorable recesses of the Scripture and of truth; and that charity may follow authority thither, and in this respect obediently submit to its direction.

9. For as yet they knew not the scripture, that he must rise again from the dead. 10. Then the disciples went away again unto their own home.

Why did Jesus Christ leave his apostles so long in ignorance, if it were not to teach both them and us that it is only by means of his light and grace that the knowledge of the truth is to be attained?

SECT. II.—THE APPEARANCE OF TWO ANGELS AND OF CHRIST TO MARY MAGDALENE.

11. ¶ But Mary stood without at the sepulchre weeping: and as she wept, she stooped down, *and looked* into the sepulchre,

The love of pious Mary Magdalene is constant and persevering in the search after her Saviour: let ours be so too, in imitation of her example. Happy is that person who weeps for the death of Christ! He shall be comforted, as she was, with the joy of his new life. Christ suffers those whom he loves, and by whom he is loved, to weep; because there is nothing better in this life than a heart afflicted for the sake of Christ. Nothing prepares us better for the visitations and graces of our blessed Saviour than the tears of repentance, or those which flow from our grief for the heavenly Bridegroom's absence, and from our ardent desire to possess him. These tears ought to be accompanied with humility and lowliness of mind, and with a diligent inquiry and search after the desired good.

12. And seeth two angels in white, sitting, the one at the head, and the other at the feet, where the body of Jesus had lain.

Christ comforts those by degrees who are his. First, he here gives them consolation by his angels and his servants. God never fails to send comforters to those souls who expect them only from him. To look for visits from angels would be dangerous; but the ministers of our blessed Lord are visible angels, who ought to be to us instead, not only of angels, but of Jesus Christ himself. It is probable that these two angels, sitting at these places, were before employed there in worshipping Christ, and in paying their homage to this adorable dead person. They had served him and ministered unto him during his mortal life, and they did not abandon him in the grave. Mary Magdalene joins with them in their duties, and imitates their piety; and they take part in her grief, and come to comfort her.

13. And they said unto her, Woman, why weepest thou? She saith unto them, Because they have taken away my Lord, and I know not where they have laid him.

Jesus Christ is, in a peculiar manner, the Lord of those who seek him with tears of repentance. It is one part of Christian consolation, to engage a soul, afflicted at the absence of its Lord, in discourse concerning him, and to give it occasion to speak of the chief object of its desires. It is the method of God's conduct toward us, to prepare us for the favours he designs us, by renewing our application, our fervency, and our desires in relation to him or to his graces. Mary Magdalene is so taken up with the thoughts of her Saviour, that she supposes that everybody thinks of him as well as she; and that any one must read in her heart the name of him whom she seeks. Would to God our hearts might always be found full of such ardent zeal, and thus eagerly desirous to enjoy our God and our Saviour.

14. And when she had thus said, she turned herself back, and saw Jesus standing, and knew not that it was Jesus.

The second consolation which God gives his servants in this life, is by the presence of Jesus Christ himself, but unknown. The impatience of Mary Magdalene, inflamed with a holy passion for Christ, causes her to cast her eyes on every side to see if she can discover the object of her love. There is no rest here on earth for one who loves God; and much less for one who does not love him. None for the latter, because he seeks his happiness where he can never find it; none for the former, because he has not yet found him for whom he seeks. Grant, O Lord, that I may never have any concern or inquietude but only with regard to thee; and that I may have a lively sense of thy absence and of my own banishment!

15. Jesus saith unto her, Woman, why weepest thou? whom seekest thou? She, supposing him to be the gardener, saith unto him, Sir, if thou have borne him hence, tell me where thou hast laid him, and I will take him away.

The third consolation which Christ gives his servants, is by his word. He expresses in two words—*weepest* and *seekest*—the whole employment of Mary Magdalene's love: and this is all which a penitent has to do. To weep without seeking, is a slothful and inactive repentance: to seek without weeping, is a rash and presumptuous one. Give me, Lord, I beseech thee, both these motions of penitential love, that I may weep on the account of my sins, and that I may seek thy grace! A firm and steadfast love, like that of Mary Magdalene, is neither frightened nor perplexed with any thing—nothing being impossible to one who loves. The difficulty of undertaking that which is good is generally great, for no other reason but only because the love we have for it is but small. The love of Mary Magdalene looks upon dangers and difficulties as nothing; forasmuch as she counts it her gain to lose every thing in seeking him who alone is the true, and therefore her only good. Let us be ashamed of our lukewarmness. The only cause why we are so remiss and unconcerned about the interests of God, is because we love some other thing which we do not love for his sake.

16. Jesus saith unto her, Mary. She turned herself, and saith unto him, Rabboni; which is to say, Master.

The fourth consolation which Christ, risen from the dead, bestows upon his servants, is the making of himself known to them. The word of Jesus Christ is full of light, and illuminates the eyes and the mind of those who love him. How great is the power of one single word in the mouth of Christ! How deeply does it penetrate and effect a heart which has been acquainted therewith by means of a long familiarity with him in prayer and meditation upon his word! The word of Christ works no further upon the heart than he intends it should work. It draws from the mouth of Mary Magdalene a compendious confession of faith. Christ is really become, after a new manner, the Master of Mary Magdalene, of all men whom he has redeemed with his blood, and of the whole world which he has purchased by his cross. Let us remember, and frequently say to ourselves, that he is our Master; that we ought to serve and please none but him; and ultimately to refer every thing to him alone.

17. Jesus saith unto her, Touch me not: for I am not yet ascended to my Father: but go to my brethren, and say unto them, I ascend unto my Father, and your Father; and *to* my God, and your God.

The fifth consolation which Christ gives his servants, is in discovering to them the secret and the spirit of all his mysteries. The sixth and last is, the giving them the grace to make those mysteries known to others. The sanctity of the mystery of the resurrection requires a worship which is more spiritual and disengaged from sense. Earth is not the place where we are to enjoy the chaste embraces of the Bridegroom. Now is the time only to hear his voice, and to obey it; to behold him, as it were, disguised under the appearance of a stranger, but not to touch him by having the advantage of a clear and open sight. What comfort and consolation is it to us to have the same God and Father with Jesus Christ, as being his brethren! This is an instance of the most exceeding goodness, and such as is altogether divine, that Christ, in the state of his power, should vouchsafe to call those by his name who had either denied or forsaken him in the days of his humiliation and sufferings. Men are very far from forgetting so soon the occasions of their resentment. Thus to call them his brethren and the children of God, is to give them assurance of making them partakers with himself of the heavenly inheritance. And nothing can be more comfortable or more suitable to this mystery.

18. Mary Magdalene came and told the disciples that she had seen the Lord, and *that* he had spoken these things unto her.

Is it thus, O Lord, that thou so quickly sendest away a pious soul which has sought thee so long and with so many tears? She does not make the least complaint on this account: it is sufficient for her to know that thou, her Lord and Saviour, art alive, victorious over death and over all thy enemies. She sought thee out of the love she bore toward thee, and not out of love to herself. Mary Magdalene is a new apostle, and the first who preaches Jesus Christ risen from the dead. It is her whole joy to do the will of her Master, and to make him known to men by executing his commission. Whoever is honoured with the mission of Christ, ought to quit the complacency and satisfaction which he finds at his feet, in contemplating and meditating upon his mysteries by himself, that he may publish and impart the knowledge of him to others.

SECT. III.—JESUS APPEARS TO THE APOSTLES, AND GIVES THEM THE HOLY GHOST.

19. ¶ Then the same day at evening, being the first *day* of the week, when the doors were shut where the disciples were assembled for fear of the Jews, came Jesus, and stood in the midst, and saith unto them, Peace *be* unto you.

The wishes of Christ have always their effect. He conveys peace into the bottom of hearts whenever he desires it for them. The reconciliation between God and man is finished and completed by the resurrection of Christ; and it is the grace of this mystery which he here makes known to them. He comes on purpose, by his peace, to fortify the minds of his disciples against the fear of the world, which he has so lately overcome upon the cross, by sinking under the efforts of its malice. None but Christ raised from the dead could possibly dispel that fear which had seized them from the time of their entrance into the garden of olives. It is good to have recourse to this mystery against the terrors of the world, and against inward troubles; and to beseech Jesus Christ to pronounce over us these words, "Peace be unto you." He will not pronounce them in vain.

20. And when he had so said, he showed unto them *his* hands and his side. Then were the disciples glad, when they saw the Lord.

Jesus retains the scars of his wounds on purpose to show that he triumphed only by sufferings; to confirm the truth of his incarnation, death, and resurrection; to excite in us a constant sense of gratitude; and to offer continually to his Father the price of our redemption. The glorious wounds of Christ have nothing now in them but what affords consolation and strength to his true disciples. He teaches us never to separate in this life these two mysteries, Jesus crucified, and Jesus risen again; since he unites them in his person and his glory, and proves the one by the other to his apostles. We may justly say that the great devotion of the church, in relation to these two mysteries, began here: a devotion which Christ himself inspired into the apostles, and which the apostles settled in the church. Let us receive it from her, and show ourselves faithful in the observance of it.

21. Then said Jesus to them again, Peace *be* unto you: as *my* Father hath sent me, even so send I you.

The mission of Jesus Christ, in order to his bringing peace to men, is the source and the pattern of the mission of his ministers as to the principle, the power, the end, the manner, and the love thereof, etc. The gifts of God, and especially the evangelical mission, ought to be received in the peace of heart. To qualify a man to receive a commission to preach Jesus Christ to the world, it is necessary that he should have this peace: not a human peace, which arises from presumption, but the peace of Christ, which proceeds from a just confidence alone in his grace and his protection. This "as" affords a large field of meditation. Some men take great delight when any occasion is offered to extol the dignity of the apostolical mission, and to compare that of bishops and pastors with that of Jesus Christ. But with what shame and fear ought they to be filled, if they do but compare the life, the conduct, and the deportment of Christ, with the lives and conversations of those who glory in being partakers of his mission! They ought to depend upon it as certain, that they are sent only upon the same conditions and for the same end—namely, to preach the truth and to establish the kingdom of God, by opposing the corruption of the world, and by suffering and acting to the end for the advancement of his glory.

22. And when he had said this, he breathed on *them*, and saith unto them, Receive ye the Holy Ghost:

Jesus Christ, who, together with the Father, is the principle from whence the Holy Ghost proceeds, by the very same power whereby he bestowed on man in creating him a reasonable soul, which is an emanation from, and a participation of, the supreme and sovereign reason, does now breathe into the Christian the Holy Ghost as a second soul, as the new principle of the new life. That which Jesus Christ is hereafter to do invisibly from heaven in his church, he now does visibly on earth, to show us that he himself in his human nature is the true principle from which it is all derived. The laity receive the Holy Ghost only for themselves; priests and bishops receive it for the good of others. That person is no other than a monster in the church, who by his sacred office is a dispenser of the Holy Spirit, and who by the corruption of his own heart, and by a disorderly, worldly, voluptuous, and scandalous life, is at the same time a member and instrument of the devil.

23. Whosesoever sins ye remit, they are remitted unto them; *and* whosesoever *sins* ye retain, they are retained.

The Holy Ghost is given to the apostles, and to priests, that they may remit or retain sins according as they shall judge that he himself remits or retains them. That such a judgment may be pronounced upon sinners as is fit to be approved of God, and to be confirmed in heaven, it must be such as is according to the Spirit of God, who is given for that purpose, and to the rules prescribed by Christ to sinners, of which the priest is only the minister. To see the conduct of abundance of priests, one would imagine that they had received only the power of remitting sin, and that the power of retaining it was forbid them. This is to divide and separate words which are inseparable.

SECT. VI.—THOMAS SEES AND BELIEVES.—MANY MIRACLES NOT WRITTEN.

24. ¶ But Thomas, one of the twelve, called Didymus, was not with them when Jesus came.

There is no salvation for any person, unless he keep himself inseparably united to the society of Christ's disciples, and to the body of the pastors of his Church. This absence of Thomas had other reasons in the purposes and designs of God than what appear to the eyes of men. We always lose very considerably when we forsake the assemblies of the faithful. It is to unity that Christ manifests himself, and not to singularity. It is to the apostolic church that God reveals his truth, and not to any number of persons separated from the church, and cut off from its unity. Thomas is not at all concerned at his misfortune and loss, because he is insensible of it, and even thinks that he has lost nothing. Thus it is with respect to those who return to the unity of the church:

they often return but imperfectly at first, and are not thoroughly sensible how much they have lost during their separation, until they have continued for some time in the church, and until Christ has likewise there manifested himself to them.

25. The other disciples therefore said unto him, We have seen the Lord. But he said unto them, Except I shall see in his hands the print of the nails, and put my finger into the print of the nails, and thrust my hand into his side, I will not believe.

Christ permits the incredulity of one apostle in order to strengthen the faith of the whole church, by showing that his most intimate friends did not believe his resurrection until they were forced, as it were, by the evidence of the clearest proofs and most indisputable testimonies. Observe here the delusion of the mind of man, to imagine that his senses will be more faithful witnesses to him of the truth, than the word of truth itself. With what resolutions soever a man arms his heart against faith, God knows very well in what part to assault it, so as to subdue it thereto. He would not have left Thomas so long in this state of infidelity and rebellion, had he not designed to make it subservient to promote the humility of this disciple, the glory of his own grace, the conversion of unbelievers, etc.

26. ¶ And after eight days again his disciples were within, and Thomas with them: *then* came Jesus, the doors being shut, and stood in the midst, and said, Peace *be* unto you.

God frequently does as much for one particular soul as for many others. Observe here the surprising and wonderful goodness of our blessed Saviour, who does not at all lessen the value of the favour done the rest of his disciples, by doing it for the sake of this one, but takes occasion from his absence to honour and comfort them all a second time. A holy and happy octave this for these disciples, begun and ended with the same grace and favour! This affords matter of consolation to such souls as are sometimes hindered from solemnizing the great mysteries on the proper days: the octave supplies that defect. But to our greater comfort and consolation it is likewise a figure of that grand octave of the resurrection which we shall celebrate in heaven, where Jesus will consummate our faith, where he will be present with his disciples, where he will manifest himself unto them, where he will shed abroad in their hearts an inconceivable peace, and settle them in the possession of it forever, exclusively of the world, against which the gate of heaven shall be shut to all eternity.

27. Then saith he to Thomas, Reach hither thy finger, and behold my hands; and reach hither thy hand, and thrust *it* into my side; and be not faithless, but believing.

Let us admire the charity, the mildness, and the application of the good Shepherd, in healing those who are not yet strong enough in the faith. If the faith of Thomas did not precede this experiment made with his hands, it is an extraordinary instance of condescension in Christ to permit him to take this freedom. And if he did believe before he touched our blessed Saviour's body, Christ thereby shows that he has more command over the heart of man than man himself, and that whenever he pleases he is able to make him change his resolutions. Christ here suffers the mind of man to satisfy itself by experience; but the reprehension which he immediately subjoins, is a sufficient token that he does not approve of the imperfection which caused this sort of evidence to be desired. This charitable reprehension, accompanied with the internal operation of Christ, contributed more than any thing besides to the opening of Thomas's eyes.

28. And Thomas answered and said unto him, My Lord and my God.

The elevation of the heart, and this short, ready, fervent, and perfect confession of faith, afford us a pattern of that confession which we ought to make every moment, if possible, and which nothing hinders us from renewing on all occasions. Thomas was the last in believing, but he is the first of the apostles who distinctly confesses the divinity of Christ since his death. It is in this effect of the resurrection that Christ makes his divinity evidently appear under this humanity itself. Thomas beholds him in his human nature, and he therein discovers his Lord; he opens his eyes to miracles, and in them he finds the proofs of his divine nature. Thou, O Jesus, art truly the Lord of my soul, since thou hast redeemed it by the sacrifice of thy human nature. Thou art its God, because thou art its sanctification by thy grace and thy Spirit, and its chief good and eternal happiness by thy glory!

29. Jesus saith unto him, Thomas, because thou hast seen me, thou hast believed: blessed *are* they that have not seen, and *yet* have believed.

Blessed is that heart which is endued with docility in respect of the divine word. Faith and charity have no manner of dependence upon sight, which on the contrary is apt to lessen the value of them. This sentence is full of comfort to those who have not seen Jesus Christ in the flesh, and have known him only by means of the gospel. How perfect soever the faith of Thomas might possibly be, yet it had always these two defects—namely, that it was too slow, and that he would have it depend upon sight. We must endeavour to find the exact medium between a precipitate and rash faith, and one which is too backward and timorous. To be able to do this is undoubtedly an effect of thy grace, O Lord, and a gift of thy Spirit, the glory whereof is entirely due to thee alone.

30. ¶ And many other signs truly did Jesus in the presence of his disciples, which are not written in this book:

What a multitude of unprofitable books are there in the world, while we are left in ignorance concerning so many wonders done by the Son of God! It was only for the instruction of the disciples that many signs and miracles were wrought. A pastor ought not to neglect any soul; but there are some souls which are given to him in a peculiar manner, and of which he ought to take a peculiar care. The having good things to write, is not a sufficient reason to engage men in writing books; since John leaves so many miracles of Christ buried in silence: they must likewise have some token of the will of God, or some engagement from his providence, and must take care that they be not influenced to undertake that work by self-love rather than by the love of truth, or by a desire either to make it known or to defend it.

31. But these are written, that ye might believe that Jesus is the Christ, the Son of God; and that believing ye might have life through his name.

That person does by no means answer the designs of God who neglects to read the gospel, which was written on purpose to establish a lively belief of the divinity and incarnation of Christ in souls, and to guide them to eternal life. It is neither his own satisfaction, nor the love of the world's esteem, nor a desire to entertain the curiosity of the public, which induces a man of God to write concerning the things of God; but it is a desire to make God known, and to promote the salvation of his brethren, by explaining the truths of Christianity and the mysteries of our blessed Saviour: it is, particularly, his love of God and of the church militant here on earth, and the perfecting of the body of Jesus Christ in heaven.

CHAPTER XXI.

SECT. I.—CHRIST'S APPEARANCE AT THE SEA OF TIBERIAS.—THE MIRACULOUS FISHING.

1. After these things Jesus shewed himself again to his disciples at
the sea of Tiberias; and on this wise shewed he *himself*. 2. There were
together Simon Peter, and Thomas called Didymus, and Nathanael of
Cana in Galilee, and the *sons* of Zebedee, and two other of his disciples.
3. Simon Peter saith unto them, I go a fishing. They say unto him, We
also go with thee. They went forth, and entered into a ship immediately; and that night they caught nothing.

This fishing of the apostles exhibits to us a representation of that which relates to souls, wherein a man must labour in the spirit of charity and unity to draw them out of the abyss of sin. But without Jesus Christ they labour only in the dark and to no purpose. Peter, the first in the list of the apostles, is the first also in labour: it is his part to invite others thereto, and to encourage them in it by his own example. A zealous and apostolical pastor willingly sacrifices the repose of the night to the exercise of his ministry and to the salvation of souls. It frequently happens that a good pastor takes abundance of pains in relation to souls, and yet is not able to gain even one. But God will place all his labour to account, as much as if he had converted multitudes. This fishing, which figuratively represents to us the preaching of the gospel, does even literally denote that which the apostles did afterwards, who led constantly a laborious life, and were very far from taking advantage of their dignity to draw from the hands of the faithful such contributions as might enable them to live at their ease. They are not ashamed to live by their own labour; and all along their humility, their poverty, and their laborious life, instruct and encourage their successors to imitate their example.

4. But when the morning was now come, Jesus stood on the shore; but the disciples knew not that it was Jesus. 5. Then Jesus saith unto them, Children, have ye any meat? They answered him, No.

The condescension of Jesus Christ, after he was risen from the dead, is a figure of that which the most eminent and perfect pastors owe to the most weak. This extreme poverty of the apostles, of persons who are just going to subdue the world to Christ, plainly shows how much he despises wealth: since he does not think fit to make any use at all of the power of his new state to free them from poverty. He frequently permits those whom he loves best to labour for a long time, and in the night of affliction, before he comes to their assistance; because affliction and labour endured in his Spirit, are much more for their advantage than any temporal relief. However, he is never wanting to them in time of pressing need. The kindness and goodness with which he prevents their application to him, instructs the rich how to anticipate and prevent the requests of the poor. We may here behold a rough draught of this present life. It is no more than one night, during which we labour continually in the midst of the sea of this world. Happy that morning when we shall find Jesus Christ on the shore, in the port of eternal salvation, where he will feed us with food altogether divine.

6. And he said unto them, Cast the net on the right side of the ship, and ye shall find. They cast therefore, and now they were not able to draw it for the multitude of fishes.

Jesus could have saved them this labour, in giving them something to eat; but he chooses rather to bless, in his apostles, labour which he sanctified in his own person, than to manifest his power in a more evident and remarkable manner. He teaches them, and us at the same time, to avoid idleness ourselves, and to make the poor avoid it also by our giving them alms in order to assist and enable them to work, not to support and encourage them in laziness. O what fruit do men produce by their labours in the ecclesiastical ministry, when they are employed therein by the appointment of God, and follow the truth of his word! The right side is the side of the elect: when the net is cast on that side, it is always filled without breaking. The blessing which God gives to his word in the mouth of a preacher, is the cause of all the fruit which it brings forth; and this blessing is no other than his will itself. When God has touched a soul, and caused it to enter into the apostolical net, all is not yet effected: it must be drawn out of the water, and disengaged from the habits of sin in which it was deeply plunged. This is the work which requires the chief labour of pastors: in bringing this to effect, no cares, no endeavours must be spared.

7. Therefore that disciple whom Jesus loved saith unto Peter, It is the Lord. Now when Simon Peter heard that it was the Lord, he girt *his* fisher's coat *unto him*, (for he was naked,) and did cast himself into the sea.

The love of John is clear-sighted and full of light; that of Peter active and zealous. Let us pray for the light and understanding of the former, and imitate the zeal and activity of the latter. The mutual dependence which God has established in his church, not only among the people, but even among the pastors, shows itself plainly on this occasion. There are some who, being intent on the discovery of truth, are instrumental in making Christ known to others; and these, as it were in return, making use of their light, edify them by their good works, and encourage them by their example. John does not proudly take advantage of his light and knowledge to prevent Peter, because he is humble, and not at all puffed up therewith; and Peter, as soon as ever he is informed, leaves not one moment unemployed, because he is faithful and fervent in using his utmost endeavours.

8. And the other disciples came in a little ship, (for they were not far from land, but as it were two hundred cubits,) dragging the net with fishes.

All such in the church as piously lend their assistance to guide souls to the haven of salvation, must labour only in conjunction with the ordinary pastors, and act under their authority. The ways of going to God are different: some are ordinary, as in those who came in this little ship; others are extraordinary, as in Peter, whose zeal prompted him to cast himself into the sea. He is an emblem of pastors who are obliged to go to Christ through the rough sea of this world, through the waters of persecution, through the bitterness of affliction, and with the labour and pains of one who swims to gain the shore.

9. As soon then as they were come to land, they saw a fire of coals there, and fish laid thereon, and bread.

Here are miracles upon miracles. The same power which filled the net with fishes in the midst of the sea, creates others upon the land, to show these disciples that it was not from any want of power to give them fish that Christ asked them for some, and ordered them to fish for them. He makes his providence manifest to them to the end that they may put their whole trust and confidence therein, and that they may never lay aside labour through fear of not obtaining what is necessary. At the same time he teaches them to be content with necessaries, by preparing nothing sumptuous or superfluous for them, as he could have done.

10. Jesus saith unto them, Bring of the fish which ye have now caught.

Every circumstance of this fishing is mysterious and full of instruction. It seems as if our blessed Saviour designed here to intimate to his apostles both the obligation they were under to live by their labour, and the right they had to support and maintenance as long as they should employ themselves in the fishing which relates to souls. It is by means of this kind of fishing that Jesus Christ feeds, as it were, deliciously on those souls which his ministers draw out of the depths of sin and error, and bring to him. Of these his mystical body is formed, and is daily growing to perfection.

11. Simon Peter went up, and drew the net to land full of great fishes, an hundred and fifty and three: and for all there were so many, yet was not the net broken.

How lawful soever our employments may be, we meet with success only in proportion as Jesus Christ engages us in them. It is the hand of Peter, it is the pastoral hand, which must draw the net to land, and present to Jesus Christ the fruit of the spiritual fishing. In the church of heaven, where there will be none but saints, how great soever the number of them be, yet will not the net be broken. There will be no longer any division or schism to be feared in the bosom of unity, in the centre of peace, in the kingdom of perfect charity. Vouchsafe, Lord, to give us a foretaste of these fruits of peace, and to shed abroad in our hearts the love of unity and the spirit of charity.

12. Jesus saith unto them, Come *and* dine. And none of the disciples durst ask him, Who art thou? knowing that it was the Lord.
13. Jesus then cometh, and taketh bread, and giveth them, and fish likewise.

Jesus shows plainly that he is the master of the family in his church: it belongs to him to feed and to assist it. No person has any share in the heavenly banquet of Christ risen from the dead, unless he be invited thereto by his word, and drawn by his grace. The apostles do not of themselves take their food: it is Jesus Christ who gives it, and distributes it among them in what proportion he thinks fit, as the sole master of his own gifts.

14. This is now the third time that Jesus showed himself to his disciples, after that he was risen from the dead.

These three appearances of Jesus Christ are so many evidences of his resurrection. He seems to design to make his apostles amends for the three days wherein they were deprived of the comfort of his presence. He obviates all suspicions of mistake and delusion; it being impossible that so many persons could be deceived all at once, and at so many different times.

SECT. II.—PETER'S LOVE.—CHRIST COMMITS HIS SHEEP TO HIM, AND FORETELLS HIS MARTYRDOM.

15. ¶ So when they had dined, Jesus saith to Simon Peter, Simon, *son* of Jonas, lovest thou me more than these? He saith unto him, Yea, Lord; thou knowest that I love thee. He saith unto him, Feed my lambs.

Jesus, by his wisdom, gives Peter, in these few words, an opportunity of making some reparation for his infidelity, while he himself inspires into the secret recesses of his heart the will and purpose of doing it. This profession of love is fervent and undaunted, but it is likewise humble and modest. Peter is very far from preferring himself before any one, remembering that it was his advancing himself above all the rest of the apostles which was the occasion of his fall. Christ here teaches his church that she ought to have great regard to charity and zeal in those whom she chooses for the sacred ministry; and, above all, that a pastor's love toward Jesus Christ ought to be eminent and remarkable. Whoever does not feed the sheep of Christ at all, or feeds them as being his own, is not properly a pastor, but either a hireling or a thief.

16. He saith to him again a second time, Simon, *son* of Jonas, lovest thou me? He saith unto him, Yea, Lord; thou knowest that I love thee. He saith unto him, Feed my sheep."

Peter depends now only upon the knowledge which Jesus Christ has of his heart, and not, as formerly, upon his own opinion. His answer, which is so full of Christian confidence, courage, and humility, makes it evident that he has profited by his fall in all respects. He is very sensible what degree of love and strength the grace of Christ has given him, without being unmindful of the weakness of his own nature. Christ knows Peter's heart even better than he himself does; but he repeats the same question to him several times, to teach those to whom the ordaining of pastors belongs, not to content themselves with a slight inquiry into the qualifications of those who are to undertake the care of souls.

17. He saith unto him the third time, Simon, *son* of Jonas, lovest thou me? Peter was grieved because he said unto him the third time, Lovest thou me? And he said unto him, Lord, thou knowest all things; thou knowest that I love thee. Jesus saith unto him, Feed my sheep.

Our blessed Saviour requires of Peter three protestations of love, to the expiation of his three denials; to teach us that the tongue ought to be made at least as instrumental to charity as it has been to concupiscence. Christ here requires of pastors nothing but love, and recommends nothing to them but the care of his sheep; because their love of Christ, and their love of labour, are the two things concerning which they ought chiefly to examine themselves: it belongs to those who confer upon them their mission to examine into the rest. It is therefore an instance of extreme rashness for a person to take upon himself the pastoral office, without having either a love for Jesus Christ, or a will and inclination to feed and serve his flock. Far from being any ground at all for proud and lofty thoughts, it is a just cause of fear and trembling, for a man to have a more extensive service to perform, and a greater account to give to God, not only of the lambs, which are the laity, but likewise of the sheep, which represent the clergy.

18. Verily, verily, I say unto thee, When thou wast young, thou girdedst thyself, and walkedst whither thou wouldest: but when thou shalt be old, thou shalt stretch forth thy hands, and another shall gird thee, and carry *thee* whither thou wouldest not.

The cross is, in this life, part of the reward of such pastors as are faithful in the discharge of their duty. The greater share we have in the authority of Jesus Christ, the greater must we expect to have in his sufferings. God does not require of us that we should not feel within ourselves any repugnance or aversion to the evils of this life; but only that we should oppose that aversion, and overcome it by his grace; that we should subdue the carnal will by the spiritual, and the love of temporal life by the love of that which is eternal. It is the pastor himself who is to feed his Master's sheep; but it is another who is to crucify the pastor, when his death is to glorify God. This is the last consecration of the hands of an apostle, which have been already consecrated by the Christian sacrifice and the ministry of salvation, to have them nailed to the cross of Christ, as part of his victim and sacrifice.

19. This spake he, signifying by what death he should glorify God. And when he had spoken this, he saith unto him, Follow me.

A Christian, and more especially a pastor, ought to make it his study how to imitate his Master. To glorify God, and to follow Jesus Christ,—this is the whole work which he has to do. The prediction of so cruel a death is dreadful news to the flesh; but it is matter of great comfort and consolation to faith, for a man to be assured that by his death he shall glorify God. Nothing is more for the glory of Christ, than to have disciples who choose rather to lay down their lives than to renounce his doctrine: this is what the philosophers could never find in their schools. There is seldom any danger now of being exposed to death for the sake of Christ; but there is still enough to try the fidelity of a true Christian and of a faithful pastor, who is desirous to follow Jesus Christ even to the cross.

20. Then Peter, turning about, seeth the disciple whom Jesus loved following; which also leaned on his breast at supper, and said, Lord, which is he that betrayeth thee? 21. Peter seeing him saith to Jesus, Lord, and what *shall* this man *do?*

How great is the difference between Peter before the death of Christ, and Peter after his resurrection! The cross of Christ terrified him then, and now even his own does not in the least dismay him. It rejoices him to be assured that he shall recover an opportunity of being crucified with Christ, which his infidelity caused him to lose. He then pretended to distinguish himself from all the rest of the apostles, by dying alone with his Master; but now he is very desirous to share that honour with his friends and brethren. This is no instance of human friendship. This solicitous care of Peter for John, is an evident token of the union between these two apostles, and of a friendship which Christ in nowise blames. We may even justly say that Peter did no more than follow the example and inclination of our blessed Saviour, in loving with a particular affection "the disciple whom Jesus loved." How wonderful, O Jesus, are the effects of thy grace! and how proper to inspire trust and confidence, not only into thy disciples, but even into the greatest sinners!

22. Jesus saith unto him, If I will that he tarry till I come, what *is that* to thee? follow thou me. 23. Then went this saying abroad among the brethren, that that disciple should not die: yet Jesus said unto him, He shall not die; but, if I will that he tarry till I come, what *is that* to thee?

Jesus here teaches pastors that their solicitous care should never carry them so far as to pry into the designs of God concerning others in relation to the future, but only to assist them to continue faithful to him. Let us use our utmost endeavours to follow Christ in discharging our own duty, and to render ourselves worthy of his cross: this is our proper business; it belongs to God to dispose of others according to the good pleasure of his will. Peter, being as yet imperfect in his friendship, is drawn aside to curiosity, to teach us to avoid it. This was a very unseasonable curiosity: for that which Christ had just told him concerning his martyrdom, ought to have engaged him to employ his whole mind in paying him the great duties of thanksgiving, humiliation, acceptance of his cross, etc. Let us take great care that we do not receive the graces of God negligently. Instead of seriously reflecting upon them within ourselves, we often suffer our minds to wander abroad in vain and impertinent curiosity.

24. This is the disciple which testifieth of these things, and wrote these things: and we know that his testimony is true.

Great saint! we receive thy testimony, we believe every thing which thou hast written, we reverence the truths which thou hast taught us, and which thou learnedst in the bosom of truth itself. Grant us, Lord, the grace to love, to relish, and to practise them, and to make all the use of them which we ought; that we may be counted worthy to behold them openly one day in that very fountain from whence thy beloved disciple drew them!

25. And there are also many other things which Jesus did, the which, if they should be written every one, I suppose that even the world itself could not contain the books that should be written. Amen.

We know only the least part of those things which Jesus did and taught upon earth. If we do not make use of that which is written, to what end would that which is not have served, but only to our greater condemnation? Let us be content to adore that of which we know nothing. Let us put in practice every part of his law which we do know; let us beg the grace that we may be willing to perform what we are able, and that we may be able to perform what we are willing; and let us labour without intermission, desiring earnestly that happiness which we expect. Yes, Lord Jesus, come quickly; for it is thou whom we expect, and we look not for another. Amen.

END OF "REFLECTIONS."

APPENDIX.

THE CONSTITUTION UNIGENITUS;

OR,

THE DECREE OF POPE CLEMENT XI. CONDEMNING QUESNEL'S "MORAL REFLECTIONS ON THE NEW TESTAMENT."

Clement, Bishop, Servant of the Servants of God, to all the Faithful of Christ, Greeting and Apostolical Benediction:—

THE only-begotten Son of God, who became the Son of man for our salvation and that of the whole world, while he instructed his disciples in the doctrine of truth, and in the persons of the apostles taught his whole church, ordering things present, and foreseeing those which were to come, did, by a most excellent and wholesome admonition, advise us to "beware of false prophets, who come to us in sheep's clothing;" by which name are chiefly pointed out to us those lying teachers, and deceitful seducers, who, by means of a specious show of piety instilling secretly corrupt tenets, introduce damnable sects under the fair appearance of sanctity and holiness; and who, in order the more easily to surprise the unwary, laying by as it were the wolf's skin, and covering themselves with sentences of the divine law as with a kind of sheep's clothing, wickedly abuse the words of the Holy Scriptures, and even those of the New Testament, which they many ways falsify to the perdition of themselves and of others; being taught, it seems, by the example and instructions of the first father of lies, from whom they are descended. That the most proper and expeditious way to deceive, is to pretend the authority of the divine word, whenever the imposture of wicked and abominable error is designed to be introduced.

Being forewarned by this truly divine admonition, when we first heard, to the great grief of our heart, that a certain book, printed formerly in French, in several volumes, (under the title of "The New Testament in French, with Moral Reflections upon every verse," &c., Paris, 1699. And otherwise, "An Abridgment of the Morality of the Gospel, of the Acts of the Apostles, of the Epistles of St. Paul, of the Canonical Epistles, and of the Revelations; or, Christian Thoughts upon the Text of those Sacred Books," &c., Paris, 1693, and 1694,) though already condemned by us, and really containing the falsehood of corrupt doctrine in many places intermixed with catholic truths, was notwithstanding still looked upon by many as free from all error, was frequently put into the hands of the faithful, and, by the advice and endeavours of some restless spirits, always attempting something new, was too industriously dispersed everywhere, and even translated into Latin, that the contagion of pernicious doctrine might, if possible, be conveyed from one nation to another, and from one kingdom to another people; we were extremely afflicted to see the flock of Christ intrusted to our care, thus gradually led aside by these crafty seducements, into the way of perdition. And therefore being excited thereto, as well by the motions of our own pastoral care, as by the frequent complaints of those who are zealous for the orthodox faith, but most of all by the letters and petitions of very many of our venerable brethren, especially of the bishops of France, we have resolved to make use of some more effectual remedy, in order to put a stop to this spreading disease, which might otherwise in time break out into all manner of bad consequences.

And having seriously applied our mind to consider the real cause of this growing evil, we have clearly discovered, that the chief mischief of this book owes its progress and increase to its lying concealed within, and because, like corrupted matter, it cannot come forth unless the sore be lanced. For the book itself, at the first sight, allures the reader by a certain show of piety; its "words are softer than oil," yet are they really darts, and which, from a bow ready bent, are prepared to do mischief, and are "privily shot at those who are upright in heart." We therefore judged, that we could not possibly do any thing either more seasonable or safe, than to lay open the fallacious doctrine of the book, not in general only, as we have hitherto done, but more distinctly and plainly, by extracting out of it many particular propositions; that so the noxious seeds of the tares, being separated from the midst of the wheat which covered them, might be openly exposed to the sight of all the faithful in Christ. And thus having detected, and as it were placed in open view, not one or two, but many and most grievous errors, as well those formerly condemned, as those lately discovered, we trust that, by the blessing of God, all will at length find themselves obliged to yield to the truth, now so clearly discovered and made manifest to them.

That this method will be of the greatest advantage to the Catholic cause; that it will contribute very much to the healing of those divisions which have risen, more especially in the flourishing kingdom of France, from the various opinions entertained by the minds of men, which seem to be still widening into more grievous ruptures; and that, lastly, it will be very useful, and in a manner necessary to the quieting of consciences: not only the above-mentioned bishops have signified to us, but more particularly our most dear son in Christ, his Most Christian Majesty himself, Louis King of France, whose extraordinary zeal, in maintaining the purity of the Catholic faith and extirpating error, we can never sufficiently commend, has more than once assured us; for those reasons requesting of us, with repeated instances truly pious, worthy of the Most Christian King, and with earnest entreaties, that we would provide for the urgent necessity of souls, by passing the censure of our apostolical judgment without delay.

Wherefore, by the blessing of God, and trusting in his heavenly assistance, we set about this beneficial work with great diligence and application, as the weightiness of the affair required; and ordered a great many propositions, faithfully extracted out of the fore-mentioned book, according to the above-cited editions, and expressed both in French and Latin, to be accurately discussed by several professors in divinity, first in the presence of two of our venerable brethren, cardinals of the holy Roman Church, and then afterward to be weighed and examined with the utmost diligence and mature deliberation, in our own presence, and that of several other cardinals, in many repeated congregations, in which each proposition was most exactly compared with the text of the book. The propositions are such as follow, namely:—

1. What else remains to a soul which has lost God and his grace, but sin, and the consequences of sin, a proud poverty, and a slothful indigence, that is, a general inability as to labour, prayer, and every good work? Luke xvi. 3.

2. The grace of Jesus Christ, the efficacious principle of every kind of good, is necessary to every good action: without it, not only nothing is done, but likewise nothing can be done. John xv. 5.

3. In vain, O Lord, thou commandest, if thou thyself dost not give that which thou commandest. Acts xvi. 10.

4. Yes, Lord, all things are possible to him to whom thou makest all things possible, by working the same in him. Mark ix. 23.

5. When God does not soften the heart by the internal unction of his grace, exhortations and external graces serve for nothing but to harden it the more. Rom. ix. 18.

6. The difference between the Jewish and the Christian covenant consists in this, that in the former God requires the sinner to avoid sin and to fulfil the law, leaving him at the same time in his state of inability; whereas, in the latter, he gives the sinner that which he commands, by purifying him with his grace. Rom. xi. 27.

7. What advantage was there for a man under the old covenant, wherein God left him to his own weakness, at the same time imposing upon him the yoke of his law? But how great is the happiness to be admitted into a covenant, wherein God confers that upon us which he requires of us? Heb. viii. 7

8. We belong not to the new covenant, but only so far as we are partakers of that new grace, which works in us that which God commands us to do. Heb. viii. 10.

9. The grace of Christ is a sovereign grace, without which we can never confess Christ, and with which we never deny him. 1 Cor. xii. 3.

10. Grace is an operation of the almighty hand of God, which nothing can hinder or retard. Matt. xx. 34.

11. Grace is nothing else but the will of Almighty God, commanding and doing that which he commands. Mark ii. 11.

12. When God willeth to save a soul, the undoubled effect, always and everywhere, follows the will of God. Mark. ii. 11.

13. When God willeth to save a soul, and touches it with the internal hand of his grace, no human will resists him. Luke v. 13.

14. At how great a distance soever from salvation an obstinate sinner may be, yet when Jesus shows himself to him by the salutary light of his grace, he must of necessity submit, he must run to him, he must humble himself, and adore his Saviour. Mark v. 6, 7.

15. When God accompanies his command, and external word with the unction of his Spirit, and the internal power of his grace, it then works in the heart that obedience which it requires. Luke ix. 60.

16. There are no charms but what yield to those of grace; because nothing resists the Almighty. Acts viii. 12.

17. Grace is that voice of the Father which teaches men inwardly, and makes them come unto Jesus Christ: whoever comes not unto him, after having heard the outward voice of the Son, is in nowise taught by the Father. John vi. 45.

18. The seed of the word, which the hand of God waters, does always bring forth its fruit. Acts xi. 21.

19. The grace of God is nothing else but his all-powerful will: this is the idea which God himself gives us of it in all his Scriptures. Rom. xiv. 4.

20. The true idea of grace is this: God willeth our obedience, and he is obeyed; he commands, and every thing is done; he speaks as Lord, and all things are subject to him. Mark iv. 39.

21. The grace of Jesus Christ is a strong, powerful, sovereign, and invincible grace, as being the operation of the almighty will, and a consequence and imitation of the operation of God in making his Son man, and raising him from the dead. 2 Cor. v. 21.

22. The agreement of the almighty operation of God in the heart of man with the free consent of his will, is immediately showed us in the incarnation, as in the source and first pattern of all the other operations of mercy and grace, which are all of them as free, and as much depending on God, as that original operation. Luke i. 38.

23. God himself has given us an idea of the almighty operation of his grace, representing it to us by that power, whereby he produces the creatures out of nothing, and restores life to the dead. Rom. iv. 17.

24. The just idea which the centurion has of the almighty power of God, and of Jesus Christ, in healing bodies by the sole motion of his will, is the emblem of that idea which we ought to frame, concerning the almighty power of his grace in healing souls of concupiscence. Luke vii. 7.

25. God enlightens and heals the soul as well as the body, by the sole motion of his will; he commands, and is immediately obeyed. Luke xviii. 42.

26. No graces are given except by faith. Luke viii. 48.

27. Faith is the first grace, and the fountain of all others. 2 Pet. i. 3.

28. The first grace which God grants to the sinner, is the remission of his sins. Mark xi. 25.

29. No grace is granted out of the church. Luke x. 35, 36.

30. All those whom God willeth to save through Jesus Christ are infallibly saved. John vi. 40.

31. The desires of Christ have always their effect: he conveys peace into the bottom of hearts, when he wishes it to them. John xx. 19.

32. Jesus Christ gave himself up to death, that he might by his blood forever deliver the first-begotten, or the elect, out of the hand of the destroying angel. Gal. iv. 4–7.

33. O how much must a man have renounced earthly things and himself, in order to have a well-grounded confidence to appropriate to himself as one may say, Jesus Christ, his love, death, and mysteries, as Paul does, when he says, "Who loved me, and gave himself for me!" Gal. ii. 19, 20.

34. The grace of Adam produced nothing but human merits. John i. 16.

35. The grace of Adam is a consequence of the creation, and was due to nature when sound and entire. 2 Cor. v. 21.

36. The essential difference between the grace of Adam and of the state of innocency, and the Christian grace, consists in this—that every one would have received the former in his own person; whereas the latter is received only in the person of Jesus Christ risen again, to whom we are united. Rom. vii. 4.

37. The grace of Adam, by sanctifying him in himself, was propor-

tioned to him: the Christian grace, by sanctifying us in Jesus Christ, is all-powerful, and worthy of the Son of God. Ephes. i. 6.

38. The sinner is free only as to evil, without the grace of the deliverer. Luke viii. 29.

39. The will which is not prevented by grace, has no light but to go astray, no warmth of desire but to precipitate itself, and no strength but to wound itself: it is capable of all evil, and incapable of all good. Matt. xx. 3, 4.

40. Without grace we can love nothing but to our condemnation. 2 Thess. iii. 18.

41. All knowledge of God, even that which is natural, even that in the heathen philosophers, can come only from God; and without grace, it produces nothing but presumption, vanity, and opposition to God himself, instead of affections, of adoration, of gratitude, and of love. Rom. i. 19.

42. Nothing but the grace of Christ renders man fit for the sacrifice of faith: without this sacrifice, there is nothing but impurity, nothing but unworthiness. Acts xi. 9.

43. The first effect of baptismal grace is, to make us die to sin; insomuch that the spirit, the heart, and the senses have no more life for sin, than a dead man has for the things of the world. Rom. vi. 2.

44. There are but two sorts of love, from whence the motions of the will and all our actions proceed: the love of God, which does all things for God's sake, and which is rewarded by him; and the love of ourselves and of the world, which does not ultimately refer that to God which ought to be referred to him, and which for this very reason becomes bad. John v. 29.

45. When the love of God reigns no longer in the heart of sinners, carnal love or concupiscence must necessarily reign therein, and corrupt all its actions. Luke xv. 13.

46. Concupiscence or charity renders the use of the senses good or evil. Matt. v. 28.

47. Obedience to the law must flow from some source, and this source is charity. When the love of God is its inward principle, and the glory of God its end, then that which appears outwardly is clean; otherwise, it is nothing but hypocrisy or false righteousness. Matt. xxiii. 26.

48. What else can we possibly be but darkness, wandering, and sin, without the light of faith, without Christ, and without charity? Ephes. v. 8.

49. As there is no sin without the love of ourselves, so there is no good work without the love of God. Mark vii. 21–23.

50. In vain do we cry to God, "My Father," if it be not the spirit of charity which cries. Rom. viii. 15.

51. Faith justifies when it works; but it does not work at all, except by charity or love. Acts xiii. 39.

52. All other means of salvation are contained in faith, as in their seed and bud; but this faith is not without love and confidence. Acts x. 43.

53. Charity alone does Christian actions in a Christian manner, with relation to God and Jesus Christ. Col. iii. 14.

54. It is charity alone which speaks to God, it is this alone which God hears. 1 Cor. xiii. 1.

55. God crowns nothing but charity: he who runs by any other impulse, and from any other motive, runs in vain. 1 Cor. ix. 24.

56. God rewards nothing but charity; because charity alone honours God. Matt. xxv. 36.

57. Every thing is wanting to a sinner, when hope is wanting; and there is no hope in God, where there is no love of God. Matt. xxvii. 5.

58. There is neither God nor religion, where there is no charity. 1 John iv. 8.

59. The prayer of the wicked is a new sin, and that which God grants to them is a new judgment upon them. John x. 25.

60. If nothing but the fear of punishment excite to repentance, the more vehement this is, the more it leads to despair. Matt. xxvii. 5.

61. Fear restrains only the hand, but the heart is addicted to sin, so long as it is not guided by the love of righteousness. Luke xx. 19.

62. He who abstains from evil, only through fear of punishment, commits it in his heart, and is already guilty before God. Matt. xxi. 46.

63. A baptized person is still under the law, as a Jew, if he fulfil not the law, or fulfil it only out of fear. Rom. vi. 14.

64. Under the curse of the law no good is ever done, because a man sins either by doing evil, or by avoiding it only through fear. Gal. v. 18.

65. Moses, the prophets, the priests, and the doctors of the law, died without raising up any child to God, since they made only slaves by fear. Mark xii. 19.

66. He who would draw near to God, must neither come to him with brutal passions, nor be led, as beasts are, by natural instinct, or by fear; but by faith and by love, as children. Heb. xii. 20.

67. Servile fear represents God to itself no otherwise than as a hard, imperious, unjust, and untractable Master. Luke xix. 21.

68. The goodness of God has abridged or shortened the way of salvation, by including it all in faith and prayer. Acts ii. 21.

69. Faith, the use, the increase, and the reward of faith, are all a gift of the pure bounty of God. Mark ix. 23.

70. God never afflicts the innocent; and afflictions always serve either to punish sin, or to purify the sinner. John ix. 3.

71. Man, on the account of self-preservation, may dispense with him-

self from observing a law which God made for his benefit and advantage. Mark ii. 28.

72. One mark of the Christian church is, that it is catholic, comprehending all the angels of heaven, all the elect and just of the earth, and of all ages. Heb. xii. 22–24.

73. What is the church but the congregation of the children of God, continuing in his bosom, adopted in Christ, subsisting in his person, redeemed with his blood, living by his Spirit, acting by his grace, and expecting the grace of the world to come. 2 Thess. i. 1, 2.

74. The church, or Christ entire, has the incarnate Word for its head, and all the saints for members. 1 Tim. iii. 16.

75. The church is one sole man composed of many members; of which Christ is the Head, the Life, the Subsistence, and the Person; it is one single Christ, consisting of many saints, of whom he is the Sanctifier. Eph. ii. 14–16.

76. There is nothing more spacious than the church of God, because it is composed of all the elect and just of all ages. Eph. ii. 20–22.

77. He who does not lead a life becoming a child of God, and a member of Christ, ceases to have inwardly God for his Father, and Christ for his Head. 1 John ii. 22.

78. A person is cut off from the elect or chosen people, of whom the Jewish people were a figure, and of whom Christ is the Head, as well by not living according to the gospel, as by not believing the gospel. Acts iii. 23.

79. It is useful and necessary at all times, in all places, and for all sorts of persons, to study and know the spirit, piety, and mysteries of the holy Scripture. 1 Cor. xiv. 5.

80. The reading of the holy Scripture is for everybody. Acts viii. 28.

81. The sacred obscurity of the word of God is no reason for the laity to excuse themselves from reading it. Acts viii. 31.

82. The Lord's day ought to be sanctified by Christians in reading pious books, and above all, the holy Scriptures. It is very prejudicial to endeavour to withdraw a Christian from reading them. Acts xv. 21.

83. It is a great mistake to imagine that the knowledge of the mysteries of religion ought not to be imparted to women by the reading of the sacred books. The abuse of the Scriptures, and the rise of heresies, have not proceeded from the simplicity of women, but from the conceited learning of men. John iv. 26.

84. To wrest the New Testament out of the hands of Christians, or to keep it closed up, by taking from them the means of understanding it, is no other than to shut or close up the mouth of Christ in respect of them. Matt. v. 2.

85. To forbid Christians the reading of the holy Scripture, especially

of the Gospel, is to forbid the use of light to the children of light, and to make them suffer a sort of excommunication. Luke xi. 33.

86. To deprive the unlearned people of this comfort of joining their voice with the voice of the whole church, is a custom contrary to apostolical practice, and to the design of God. 1 Cor. xiv. 16.

87. It is a method full of wisdom, light, and charity, to allow souls some time humbly to bear the state of sin, to be thoroughly sensible of that state, and to begin at least to make satisfaction to the justice of God before they be reconciled. Acts ix. 9.

88. We are ignorant of the nature of sin, and of true repentance, when we would fain be reinstated immediately in the possession of those good things of which sin has stripped us, and refuse to bear the shame of that separation. Luke xvii. 11, 12.

89. The fourteenth degree of the conversion of a sinner is, That being now reconciled, he has a right to be present at the sacrifice of the church. Luke xv. 23.

90. The church has authority to excommunicate, so as that she exercise her power by the chief pastors, with the presumed consent at least of the whole body. Matt. xviii. 17.

91. The fear of an unjust excommunication ought never to hinder us from performing our duty. We never go without the pale of the church, even when we seem to be driven out of it by the wickedness of men, so long as we continue united to God, to Jesus Christ, and to the church itself by charity. John ix. 22, 23.

92. To suffer peaceably an unjust excommunication and anathema, rather than betray the truth, is to imitate St. Paul; so far is it from rising up against authority, or breaking unity. Rom. ix. 3.

93. Jesus sometimes heals the wounds which the precipitate conduct of the chief pastors makes without his order. He restores to its former state what they cut off by an inconsiderate zeal. John xviii. 11.

94. Nothing gives the enemies of the church a worse opinion concerning the church, than to see therein an absolute dominion exercised over the faith of believers, and divisions fomented on the account of such things as are prejudicial neither to the faith nor to manners. Rom. xiv. 16.

95. Truths are come to that pass as to be a sort of foreign language to the generality of Christians; and the manner of preaching them is like an unknown tongue: so remote is it from the plain method of the apostles, and so much above the common capacity of the faithful. Nor is it sufficiently observed, that this defect is one of the most evident signs of the old age of the church, and of the wrath of God against his children. 1 Cor. xiv. 21.

96. God permits all the powers of the earth to oppose the preachers

of the truth, that the victory it gains may not be attributed to any thing but to divine grace. Acts xvii. 8.

97. It happens but too often, that those members which are united to the church in a more holy and strict manner, are looked upon and treated as unworthy to continue in the church, or as already separated from it. But the just person lives by faith, and not by the opinion of men. Acts iv. 11.

98. A state of persecution and penalties which a man endures, as a heretic, as a wicked and impious person, is generally the last trial, and the most meritorious, as being that which gives a man a greater conformity to Jesus Christ. Luke xxii. 37.

99. Stiffness in opinion, prepossession, and obstinacy in refusing either to examine things, or to own that we have been mistaken, do continually, in respect of abundance of persons, change that into a savour of death which God has placed in his church, that it might be therein a savour of life; namely, good books, instructions, holy examples, etc. 2 Cor. ii. 15,16.

100. That is a deplorable time, when God is thought to be honoured by persecuting the truth and the disciples thereof. This time is come. To be accounted and treated by the ministers of religion as an impious wretch, unworthy of all commerce with God, as a rotten member, capable of spreading a general corruption in the society of the saints, is to pious persons a death more terrible than that of the body. In vain does any man flatter himself with the purity of his intentions, and with a certain zeal for religion, in persecuting good men with fire and sword, if he is either blinded with his own passion, or hurried on by that of others, because he will examine nothing. We often think we sacrifice to God a wicked person, and we sacrifice to the devil a servant of God. John xvi. 2.

101. Nothing is more opposite to the Spirit of God, and to the doctrine of Jesus Christ, than to make oaths common in the church; because to do this is to multiply the occasions of perjury, to lay snares for the weak and the ignorant, and to make the name and the truth of God subservient sometimes to the designs of the wicked. Matt. v. 37.

Wherefore, having heard the judgment of the aforesaid cardinals and other divines, exhibited to us both by word and in writing, and having, in the first place, implored the assistance of the Divine light, by appointing public as well as private prayers to that end; we do, by this our constitution, which shall be of perpetual force and obligation, declare, condemn, and reject, respectively, all and every one of the propositions before recited, as false, captious, shocking, offensive to pious ears, scandalous, pernicious, rash, injurious to the church and her practice, contumelious not only against the church, but likewise against the secular powers, seditious, impious, blasphemous, suspected of heresy, and plainly savouring thereof, and likewise favouring heretics, heresies, and schism, erroneous, bordering very near upon heresy, often condemned, and, in fine, even heretical, and manifestly reviving several heresies, and chiefly those which are contained in the infamous propositions of Jansenius, even in the very sense in which those propositions were condemned.

Commanding all the faithful in Christ of both sexes not to presume to hold, teach, or preach otherwise concerning the propositions aforesaid, than is contained in this our constitution: insomuch that whosoever shall teach, defend, or publish them, or any of them, jointly or separately, or shall treat of them by way of dispute, either publicly or privately, unless it be to impugn them, shall, *ipso facto*, without any other declaration, incur the censures of the church, and all the other penalties appointed by the law against such delinquents.

However, by our condemning in express terms the aforesaid propositions, it is by no means our intention in any manner to approve of other things contained in the same book; especially, since in the course of our examination thereof, we found in it many other propositions very like those which have been condemned as above mentioned, nearly related to them, and tainted with the same errors; and likewise not a few which, under a certain imaginary pretence of a persecution carried on at this time, do foment disobedience and contumacy, and recommend them under the false name of Christian patience, which therefore we thought it too tedious, and not in the least necessary particularly to recite; and finally, which is yet more intolerable, because we found even the sacred text of the New Testament corrupted with damnable errors, and in many things conformable to another French translation done at Mons, long since condemned, but disagreeing very much with, and differing from the vulgar edition, (which has been approved in the church by the use of so many ages, and ought to be looked upon as authentic by all the orthodox,) and besides all this, frequently wrested with the greatest perverseness to strange, foreign, and often hurtful senses.

For which causes, we, by our apostolical authority, made known by the tenor of these presents, do again forbid, and in like manner condemn the said book, as being very artfully contrived on purpose by good words and fair speeches, as the apostle expresses it, that is, under a false appearance of godly instruction, to deceive the hearts of the simple; whether it bear the forementioned title or any other, wherever, and in whatever other language, edition, or version hitherto printed, or hereafter to be printed, (which God forbid;) as we also in like manner do prohibit and forbid all and singular books or pamphlets in defence thereof, as well written as printed and already published, or which may perhaps be published, (which God forbid;) enjoining all and every one of the faithful not to read, transcribe, keep, or use any of the said books, under the pain of excommunication to be incurred, *ipso facto*, by those who act contrary hereto.

We require, moreover, our venerable brethren, the patriarchs, archbishops, bishops, and other ordinaries of places, and also the inquisitors of heresy, that they restrain and coerce all those who shall contradict and rebel against this constitution, by the censures and penalties aforesaid, and the other remedies of law and fact, and even by calling to their assistance, if there be occasion, the secular power.

Our will also is, that the same credit be in all respects given even to the printed copies of these presents, subscribed by any notary public, and bearing the seal of any person placed in ecclesiastical dignity, which would be given to the original letters themselves, were they produced or shown.

Let no one therefore infringe or audaciously oppose this our declaration, condemnation, mandate, prohibition, and interdict. And if any one presume to attempt this, let him know, that he will incur the indignation of almighty God, and of his blessed apostles Peter and Paul. Given at Rome at St. Mary Major's, in the year of our Lord one thousand seven hundred and thirteen, on the sixth of the Ides of September, and in the thirteenth year of our pontificate.

J. CARD, Datary.
F. OLIVERIO.

Seen by the Court. L. SERGARDO.

Registered in the office of the Secretary of Briefs.
L. MARTINETTO.

In the year of our Lord Jesus Christ, one thousand seven hundred and thirteen, Indiction the sixth, the tenth day of September, and in the thirteenth year of the pontificate of the most holy father in Christ, and our Lord Clement XI. by divine providence Pope, the apostolical Letters aforesaid were published by affixing them to the doors of the church of St. John Lateran, of the Basilica of the Prince of the Apostles, of the apostolical Chancery, and of the Court general in Monte Citorio, in the Campo di Fiori, and in the other usual and customary places, by me, Pietro Romulatio, apostolical Cursitor.

ANTONIO PLACENTIO,
Master of the Cursitors.

RECOMMENDATIONS OF QUESNEL'S MORAL REFLECTIONS.

THE MANDATE OF MONSEIGNEUR LOUIS ANTHONY DE NOAILLES,

Bishop and Count of Chalons, now Archbishop of Paris, Duke and Peer of France.

Louis Anthony, by the divine permission, bishop and count of Chalons, and peer of France, to all priests, pastors, vicars, and other ecclesiastical persons of our diocese, greeting and benediction.

If priests ought continually to read the divine Scriptures, if those sacred books ought never to be out of their hands, according to St. Jerome's advice to his dear Nepotian, they are then, no doubt, under a particular obligation to study the Gospels, and all the books of the New Testament. This is the end, and the most precious and sacred part of all the Scriptures, because it contains whatever it has pleased God to conserve to men of the words and actions of the Word incarnate, and of the instructions which his apostles, formed by himself, and filled with his divine Spirit, left to the church. The pastors who succeed them in their functions, and are appointed, as they were, to form Jesus Christ in souls, ought to begin this work by causing him first to live in their own hearts. And how shall they be able to effect this, if they do not carefully feed upon those gracious words which proceeded out of his mouth, if they do not attentively meditate upon the great mysteries which he wrought for our redemption, and the divine virtues which he practised for our edification, and if, consequently, they have not always before their eyes these sacred books, which inform us of all the wonderful things relating to him? It was on this account that we always exhorted you to make these books your chief study and your chaste delight, after the example of St. Augustine. But now we importune you anew to do it, because we have a new assistance to offer you, in order to your profiting by this holy reading, in this work which we now impart to you. Our predecessor thought he made you a great present in giving you it, at a time when it was yet but imperfect. What advantage, therefore, may we not justly hope you will reap from it, now that the author has enlarged and enriched it with many pious and learned reflections; that he has gathered together all the finest and most affecting things which the holy fathers have written upon the New Testament, and made an extract out of them, full of spiritual unction and light! The difficulties which occur are here explained with clearness, and the sublime truths of religion treated of with such force, and yet such gentleness of the Holy Spirit, as make them relished by the most hard and insensible hearts. Here you will find enough to instruct and edify yourselves. Here you will learn how to instruct the people committed to your charge. Here you will see the bread of the word, with which you are to feed them, broken to your hand, and ready to be distributed to them, and so exactly proportioned to their dispositions, that it will be no less the milk of weak and feeble souls, than substantial food for the most strong. So that this one book will serve instead of a whole library to you. It will fill you with that excellent knowledge of Jesus Christ, for which St. Paul counted all things but loss, and will put you into a capacity of communicating it to others, provided you bring along with you, to this holy study, a sincere humility, a pure heart, a good conscience, and a faith unfeigned, as the same apostle expresses it. This is what we earnestly exhort and conjure you to do, assuring you, upon the word of this apostle, that in doing this, you will both save yourselves and them that hear you. Given at Chalons, in our episcopal palace, the 23d day of June, 1695.

(Signed) LOUIS ANT,
Bishop and Count of Chalons.
By Monseigneur LEMAIRE.

THE MANDATE OF MONSEIGNEUR FELIX,

The most illustrious Bishop and Count of Chalons, Peer of France.

FELIX, by the divine permission, bishop and count of Chalons, peer of France, to all pastors and vicars of our diocese, greeting and benediction. If it be true, as St. Augustine expresses it, that the gospel is to us in respect of Jesus Christ, what his sacred humanity was in respect of the eternal Word; and that it is as impossible for us to know him without the assistance of this precious depositum, as it would have been for men, after the fall, to know the eternal Word, if he had not vouchsafed to take upon him human nature; there is then no doubt but that one of the principal obligations of the Christian life consists in having this holy book continually before our eyes, that we may take from thence the food of our souls, and the rules of our life and conversation. But this necessity, which regards all the faithful in general, who are capable of informing themselves of the truths of salvation, according to the spirit of the church, does much more peculiarly oblige those who are appointed and settled in the church, as you are, on purpose to make known the law of God, and to teach the people all the maxims of Christianity contained in the gospel. This is what has induced us to exhort you earnestly, on all occasions to be constant and diligent in this holy study, which is so suitable to your ministry; and to tell you, in the language of the holy fathers, that the New Testament being the book of priests, and the very substance of the priesthood, you ought to spend as much time in reading and meditating upon it, as the exercise of your office will permit; and that it is in the word of Christ that you will find that light, strength, and consolation, of which you stand in need; and that you will draw from this fountain that learning and knowledge belonging to the saints, which is so necessary to all those who are called to the guidance and direction of souls. But we thought we could not possibly engage you more effectually in this so holy and useful an employment, than by imparting to you this excellent work, which the providence of God has put into your hands, and which we have examined with great care and application. The author must needs have been inspired with that charity which is full of light, of which St. Augustine speaks; and must have been a long time a disciple in the school of the Holy Ghost, who dictated this divine book, otherwise he could not have penetrated with so much perspicuity and illumination into the knowledge of the mysteries and doctrines of the incarnate Word. And we hope that God will pour his blessing upon your diligent reading of it, which we recommend to you with so much earnestness. It will not only be useful to you for your own edification, but it will likewise enable you to prepare with the greater ease those Christian instructions which you owe to your people; this author having illustrated the text of the Gospel with most pious reflections, which, though they be short, do notwithstanding generally convey abundance of light into the understanding, and of spiritual unction into the heart. But in order to find therein all these advantages, it is necessary that you bring along with you to the reading of them great purity of mind, without which, says one of the fathers, a man meets with nothing but darkness and precipices in this fountain of light and life. You must likewise enter into the knowledge of the divine truths with a plain and lively faith, an humble piety, and above all, a sincere desire of learning to know and to love our Lord Jesus Christ, and to make your life and actions conformable to his divine example. You will likewise do well to recommend to those under your care a reading so useful as this, in proportion to their capacity, and to the disposition in which they are to profit thereby. Given at Chalons, the 9th day of November, 1671.

FELIX,
Bishop and Count of Chalons.
By Monseigneur HERBUNOT.

THE APPROBATION OF THE DOCTORS IN DIVINITY OF THE FACULTY OF PARIS.

As the public could not better testify the esteem it had for the book entitled, "An Abridgment of the Morality of the Gospel," than by wishing that the person to whom it was indebted for that present, would be pleased further to enrich it with his Reflections upon the other books of the New Testament: so that author could not better manifest his zeal for the advantage of the public, than by taking himself off from his other employments, to satisfy an impatience which seemed to contribute equally to the glory of God and to the salvation of souls. This is what he has done in this work; in which, without keeping too close to the letter, of which notwithstanding he never loses sight, he improves all occasions to insinuate a thousand important truths, capable of instructing and edifying at one and the same time; he removes the difficulties which might otherwise stop those who are not of themselves in a capacity to add to their faith knowledge; he teaches the happy art of making both those truths which we are able to understand, and those mysteries which we ought to adore without desiring to comprehend them, subservient to piety; and he establishes the principles, and fixes the rules of a life which is so much the more truly Christian, as it is entirely built upon the oracles of the Holy Ghost, and the interpretation of the fathers. Were there no other proof that there is no part of ecclesiastical learning which escapes the penetration of this author's genius, the extent of his knowledge, and the delicacy of his judgment; these Reflections alone would be sufficient to oblige everybody to look upon him as a great master in the morality of Jesus Christ. The warmth and fervour with which they are filled, is never separated from light; the heart does not therein drag the understanding after it, nor the understanding impose upon the heart, but they act in concert throughout the whole, and mutually assist each other: and in whatever state and condition Providence has thought fit to place those who read this work, there is ground to hope that while they learn the means of discharging their obligations, of which they cannot but be sensible, they will regulate their conduct by their duties, and their duties by the law of Jesus Christ. Signed this 21st day of February, 1687.

BLAMPIGNON, Parish priest of St Mederic.
L. HIDEUX, Parish priest of the Holy Innocents.
L. ELLIE DU PIN.

STEREOTYPED BY L. JOHNSON AND CO.
PHILADELPHIA.

www.ingramcontent.com/pod-product-compliance
Lightning Source LLC
LaVergne TN
LVHW021057110826
845150LV00001B/97

* 9 7 8 1 4 2 5 5 6 6 8 4 5 *